We are shaped and fashioned by what w[...]
Johann Wolfgang von G[...]

D1359504

TO KNOW HISTORY
IS TO
LOVE HISTORY

Welcome to Prentice Hall's **T.L.C. Edition**.
That's **T**eaching and **L**earning **C**lassroom Edition.

Dear Student,

Your instructor already knows—and loves—history. *Do you?* **Welcome to the new and exciting T.L.C. Edition—** this is the book that will change the way you feel about history. Prentice Hall developed this text to bring history to you with more visual appeal than ever. This is the book that you will want to read because it is interesting. You will think about what you're reading because it has relevance to your life. With this book and the multimedia tools we crafted to accompany it, you will truly experience history's dramatic trials and passionate triumphs in a way that adds meaning to your own life.

And you will score better on tests because preparation will be easier and less time consuming than you ever dreamed possible.

Read on and find out why this book is just the T.L.C. you need to say "I DO" know—and love—history.

TO KNOW HISTORY IS TO LOVE HISTORY

Imagine if you could make sense of all the names, dates, events, and people who made history?
Imagine putting it all into a context that made you rethink your world, your life, yourself—
with the fascinating perspective that only history provides? All it takes is the T.L.C. you are now

holding in your hand.
Here's what makes
this T.L.C. Edition
different...

■ You will be compelled
to READ this
dramatically different,
vividly illustrated,
less dense textbook
because it is not at
all overwhelming.

■ You will be inspired to
THINK about *what* you
are reading *as* you
are reading.

■ You will come to class
READY to take notes
with your automatically
bundled, portable, and
easy-to-use *HistoryNotes*.

OVERVIEW
MAJOR INDIAN TREATIES AND LEGISLATION OF THE LATE NINETEENTH CENTURY

1863	Nez Percé Treaty	Signed illegally on behalf of the entire tribe in which the Nez Percé abandoned 6 million acres of land in return for a small reservation in northeastern Oregon. Led to Nez Percé wars, which ended in 1877 with the surrender of Chief Joseph.
1867	Medicine Lodge Treaty	Assigned reservations in existing Indian Territory to Comanches, Plains (Kiowa), Appaches, Kiowas, Cheyennes, and Arapahoes, bringing these tribes together with Sioux, Shoshones, Bannocks, and Navajos.
1868	Treaty of Fort Laramie	Successfully ended Red Cloud's war by evacuating federal troops from Sioux Territory along the Bozeman Trail; additionally granted Sioux ownership of the

AMERICAN COMMUNITIES
Communities Struggle with Diversity in Seventeenth-Century Santa Fé

IT WAS A HOT AUGUST DAY IN 1680 WHEN THE FRANTIC MESSEN-
GERS rode into the small mission outpost of El Paso with the news
that the Pueblo Indians to the north had risen in revolt. The
corpses of more than 400 colonists lay bleeding in the dust. Two
thousand Spanish survivors huddled inside the Palace of Governors in Santa Fé, surrounded by 3,000 angry warriors. The
Pueblo leaders had sent two crosses into the palace—white for
surrender, red for death. Which would the Spaniards choose?

    Spanish colonists had been in New Mexico for nearly a
century. Franciscan priests came first, followed by a military
expedition from Mexico in search of precious metals. In 1609,
high in the picturesque foothills of the Sangre de Cristo Mountains, the colonial authorities founded La Villa Real de la Santa
Fé de San Francisco—"the royal town of the holy faith of St.
Francis"—soon known simply as Santa Fé. Colonization efforts
included the conversion of the Pueblo Indians
to Christianity, making them subjects of
the king of Spain, and forcing them
to work for the colonial elite who
lived in the town.
    In the face of overwhelm-
ing Spanish power, the Pueblos
adopted a flexible attitude. Twenty
thousand of them converted to Christianity, but most of these thought of the new

eral years before, the Spanish governor had executed three Pueblo
religious leaders and publicly whipped dozens more for secretly
practicing their religion. One of those leaders, Popé of San Juan
Pueblo, vowed to overthrow the regime. During the next several
years he carefully organized a conspiracy among more than
twenty Indian towns.
    Popé's job was not difficult, for there were plenty of local
grievances. The Hopis of northern Arizona, for example, still
tell of a missionary who capped his ever-escalating demands on
them with the order that all the young women of the village be
brought to live with him. When the revolt began, the Hopis surrounded the missionary's house. "I have come to kill you," the
chief announced. "You can't kill me," the priest cried from
behind his locked door. "I will come [back] to life and wipe out
your whole tribe." But the chief shouted back, "my gods have
more power than you have." He and his men
broke down the door, hung the missionary from the beams, and lit a fire
beneath his feet.
    When the Indians
demanded the surrender of the
Spanish inside Santa Fé's Palace
of Governors, the besieged colonists
sent back the red cross, signaling defiance. But after a siege lasting five days, the

Under 10 percent black population
10 to 29 percent
30 to 49 percent
50 percent and over

To be able to be caught up into the world of thought—that is to be educated.

Edith Hamilton

QUICK REVIEW

Jim Crow

◆ Neither major party addressed problem of racism and nativism in campaign of 1896.

◆ Local and state governments in the South codified racism in Jim Crow laws.

◆ The Supreme Court upheld the new discriminatory legislation.

18–9
Booker T. Washington, Atlanta Exposition Address (1895)

Nativism Favoring the interests and culture of native-born inhabitants over those of immigrants.

Jim Crow laws Segregation laws that became widespread in the South during the 1890s.

Segregation A system of racial control that separated the races, initially by custom but increasingly by law during and after Reconstruction.

African-American Representation in Congress, 1867–1900
Black men served in the U.S. Congress from 1870 until 1900. All were Republicans.

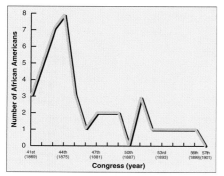

McKinley's triumph ended the popular challenge to the nation's governing system. With prosperity returning by 1898 and nationalism rising swiftly, McKinley encouraged Americans to go for "a full dinner pail," the winning Republican slogan of the 1900 presidential election.

NATIVISM AND JIM CROW

Campaign rhetoric aside, McKinley and Bryan differed only slightly on the major problems facing the nation in 1896. Neither Bryan the reformer nor McKinley the prophet of prosperity addressed the escalation of racism and **nativism** (anti-immigrant feeling) throughout the nation.

Toward the end of the century, many political observers noted, the nation's patriotic fervor took on a strongly nationalistic and antiforeign tone. Striking workers and their employers alike tended to blame "foreigners" for the hard times. Semisecret organizations such as the American Protective Association sprang up to defend American institutions. Fourth of July orators continued to celebrate freedom and liberty but more often boasted about the might and power of their nation.

In the South, local and state governments codified racist ideology by passing discriminatory and segregationist legislation, which became known as **Jim Crow laws**. The phrase, dating from the early decades of the nineteenth century, was made popular by a white minstrel in black face who used the name "Jim Crow" to characterize all African Americans. Before the Civil War, abolitionists described segregated railroad cars as "Jim Crow." By the end of the century, "Jim Crow" referred to the customs of **segregation** that were becoming codified by law and practice throughout the South. With nine of every ten black Americans living in this region, the significance of this development was sweeping.

"The supremacy of the white race of the South," New South promoter Henry W. Grady declared in 1887, "must be maintained forever . . . because the white race is the superior race." To secure their privileges, Grady and other white Southerners acted directly to impose firm standards of segregation and domination and to forestall any appearance of social equality. State after state in the South enacted new legislation to cover facilities such as restaurants, public transportation, and even drinking fountains. Signs "White Only" and "Colored" appeared over theaters, parks, rooming houses, and toilets. In banks, post offices, and stores, blacks were required to wait until all whites had been served, and special rules prohibited such common practices as trying on shoes or hats before purchasing them.

The United States Supreme Court upheld the new discriminatory legislation. Its decisions in the *Civil Rights Cases* (1883) overturned the Civil Rights Act of 1875, and in *Plessy v. Ferguson* (1896) the Court upheld a Louisiana state law formally segregating railroad cars on the basis of the "separate but equal" doctrine. In *Cumming v. Richmond County Board of Education* (1899), the Court allowed separate schools for blacks and whites, even where facilities for African American children did not exist.

Southern states enacted new literacy tests and property qualifications for voting, demanding proof of $300 to $500 in property and the ability to read and write. Loopholes permitted poor whites to vote even under these conditions, except where they threatened the Democratic Party's rule. "**Grandfather clauses**," invented in Louisiana, exempted from all restrictions those who had been entitled to vote on January 1, 1867, together with their sons and grandsons, a measure that effectively enfranchised whites while

■ You will **EXPERIENCE** history in class—with your instructor's lectures, enhanced by totally dramatic, multimedia representation of significant historical events.

■ You will make sense of it all by tying together everything you learned by **DOING** review and assessment activities in the text and with One Key.

...and finally, you will begin to realize that *to know history is to love history.*

With T.L.C. comes all the **FREE** resources you need to succeed in History.

Q: Wondering why *HistoryNotes* was bound free with your text?

A: BETTER TEST SCORES!

This new tool replaces your traditional study guide, and offers you an incredible, portable system for taking and organizing notes, and for doing practice activities. *HistoryNotes* provides for every chapter of this T.L.C. text:

■ Map exercises

■ Review/study activities

■ Practice tests

■ Space on each page for note taking.

Map Exercise 15-B

Outline and label the following areas or places:

1. independent republic of Texas, 1836
2. Gadsden Purchase, 1853
3. Mexico after 1853
4. ceded to Texas 1845
5. ceded by Treaty of Guadelupe Hidalgo 1848

Everything you need to succeed
—all in one place.

Everything you need to succeed—*all in one place.*

With OneKey, you can get a better grade!

You will study smarter using the interactive E-book version of this text, which allows you to take pre-tests and quizzes by chapter, and then incorrect answers are linked directly to the portion of the text where you need further review/study. Interactive flashcards and crossword puzzles also offer a fun way to master concepts.

You will see the text come to life.

All maps from this text become interactive to illustrate the important relationship between what happened—and where it happened. Audio and video clips animate dramatic speeches and events from the text, and biographies introduce you to people who made an impression on history.

AND INCLUDED IN EVERY NEW COPY OF THIS TEXT:
United States History Documents CD-ROM

Organized chronologically according to main periods within U.S. history, this tool offers access to more than 300 authentic primary source documents in an easily navigable .pdf file.

Out of Many

A HISTORY OF THE AMERICAN PEOPLE

TEACHING AND LEARNING CLASSROOM EDITION

BRIEF FOURTH EDITION

VOLUME ONE

John Mack Faragher

YALE UNIVERSITY

Mary Jo Buhle

BROWN UNIVERSITY

Daniel Czitrom

MOUNT HOLYOKE COLLEGE

Susan H. Armitrage

WASHINGTON STATE UNIVERSITY

PEARSON

Prentice
Hall

Upper Saddle River, New Jersey 07458

Library of Congress Cataloging-in-Publication Data

Out of many: a history of the American People / John Mack Faragher . . . — [et al.], Brief
  4th TLC ed.
    p. cm.
  Includes bibliographical references and index.
  ISBN 0-13-193339-6 (v. 1) — ISBN 0-13-193338-8 (v2) — ISBN 0-13-193337-X (combined v.)
  1. United States—History.   I. Faragher, John Mack, 1945–
  E178.1.0935 2005b
  973—dc22   2004060756

VP, Editorial Director: Charlyce Jones Owen
Associate Editor: Emsal Hasan
Editorial Assistant: Maureen Diana
Editor-in-Chief, Development: Rochelle Diogenes
Senior Development Editor: Roberta Meyer
Senior Media Editor: Deborah O'Connell
AVP, Director of Production
  and Manufacturing: Barbara Kittle
Managing Editor: Joanne Riker
Production Editor: Randy Pettit
Prepress and Manufacturing Manager: Nick Sklitsis
Prepress and Manufacturing Buyer: Benjamin Smith
Director of Marketing: Heather Shelstad
Marketing Assistant: Cherron Gardner
Creative Design Director: Leslie Osher
Cover Design: Kathy Mrozek

Interior Designer: Anne DeMarinis
Director, Image Resource Center: Melinda Reo
Manager Visual Research: Beth Brenzel
Manager, Rights and Permissions: Zina Arabia
Manager, Cover Visual Research and
  Permissions: Karen Sanatar
Color Scanning Services: Joe Conti, Cory Skidds,
  Greg Harrison, Rob Uibelhoer, Ron Walko
Image Permission Coordinator: Michelina Viscusi
Compositor: Preparé, Inc.
Printer/Binder: Courier Companies, Inc.
Cover Printer: The Lehigh Press, Inc.
Cover Art: (top) Library of Congress, (bottom) Library of
  Congress, (rear) Howard Chandler Christy, Library of
  Congress

Credits and acknowledgments borrowed from other sources and reproduced, with permission, in this textbook appear on appropiate page within text or on page C-1.

Copyright © 2006, 2003, 2000, 1997, 1994 by Pearson Education, Inc., Upper Saddle River, New Jersey, 07458

Pearson Prentice Hall. All rights reserved. Printed in the United States of America. This publication is protected by Copyright and permission should be obtained from the publisher prior to any prohibited reproduction, storage in a retrieval system, or transmission in any form or by any means, electronic, mechanical, photocopying, recording, or likewise. For information regarding permission(s), write to: Rights and Permissions Department.

Pearson Prentice Hall™ is a trademark of Pearson Education, Inc.
Pearson® is a registered trademark of Pearson plc.
Prentice Hall® is a registered trademark of Pearson Education, Inc.

Pearson Education Ltd., London
Pearson Education Australia Pty., Limited, Sydney
Pearson Education Singapore, Pte., Ltd.
Pearson Education North Asia Ltd., Hong Kong

Pearson Education Canada, Ltd., Toronto
Pearson Educación de Mexico, S.A. de C.V.
Pearson Education — Japan, Tokyo
Pearson Education Malaysia, Pte., Ltd.

10 9 8 7 6 5 4 3

ISBN 0-13-193339-6
Revised Printing: ISBN 0-13-195129-7

To our students,
our sisters,
and our brothers

BRIEF CONTENTS

CONTENTS

1

A Continent of Villages, to 1500   2

2

When Worlds Collide, 1492–1590   26

3

Planting Colonies in North America, 1588–1701   48

4

SLAVERY AND EMPIRE, 1441–1770   70

5

THE CULTURES OF COLONIAL NORTH AMERICA, 1700–1780   100

6

FROM EMPIRE TO INDEPENDENCE, 1750–1776   130

VISUALIZING THE PAST
The Rattlesnake as a National Symbol   160

7

THE CREATION OF THE
UNITED STATES,
1776–1786   162

AMERICAN COMMUNITIES: *A National Community Evolves
   at Valley Forge   164*

8

THE UNITED STATES
OF NORTH AMERICA,
1786–1800   188

AMERICAN COMMUNITIES: *Mingo Creek Settlers Refuse to
   Pay the Whiskey Tax   190*

9

AN AGRARIAN REPUBLIC, 1790–1824   214

10

THE GROWTH OF DEMOCRACY, 1824–1840   242

11

THE SOUTH AND SLAVERY, 1790S–1830 272

12

INDUSTRY AND THE NORTH, 1790S–1840S 302

13

COMING TO TERMS WITH THE NEW AGE, 1820S–1850S 322

14

THE TERRITORIAL EXPANSION OF THE UNITED STATES, 1830S–1850S 346

15

THE COMING CRISIS, THE 1850S 372

16

THE CIVIL WAR, 1861–1865   400

VISUALIZING THE PAST
The Civil War   430

17

RECONSTRUCTION, 1863–1877   432

21

URBAN AMERICA AND THE PROGRESSIVE ERA, 1900–1917   560

22

WORLD WAR I, 1914–1920   586

23

THE TWENTIES, 1920–1929 614

VISUALIZING THE PAST
Advertising and the Modern Woman 640

24

THE GREAT DEPRESSION AND THE NEW DEAL, 1929–1940 642

25

WORLD WAR II, 1941–1945   670

26

THE COLD WAR, 1945–1952   704

27

AMERICA AT MIDCENTURY, 1952–1963   736

28
THE CIVIL RIGHTS MOVEMENT, 1945–1966   760

29

WAR ABROAD, WAR AT HOME, 1965–1974   790

MAPS

OVERVIEW TABLES

PREFACE

Out of Many: A History of the American People, offers a distinctive and timely approach to American history, highlighting the experiences of diverse communities of Americans in the unfolding story of our country. The stories of these communities offer a way of examining the complex historical forces shaping people's lives at various moments in our past. The debates and conflicts surrounding the most momentous issues in our national life—independence, emerging democracy, slavery, westward settlement, imperial expansion, economic depression, war, technological change—were largely worked out in the context of local communities. Through communities we focus on the persistent tensions between everyday life and those larger decisions and events that continually reshape the circumstances of local life. Each chapter opens with a description of a representative community. Some of these portraits feature American communities struggling with one another: African slaves and English masters on the rice plantations of colonial Georgia, or *Tejanos* and Americans during the Texas war of independence. Other chapters feature portraits of communities facing social change: the feminists of Seneca Falls, New York, in 1848, or the African Americans of Montgomery, Alabama, in 1955. As the story unfolds we find communities growing to include ever larger groups of Americans: the soldiers from every colony who forged the Continental Army into a patriotic national force at Valley Forge during the American Revolution, or the moviegoers who aspired to a collective dream of material prosperity and upward mobility during the 1920s.

Out of Many is also the only American history text with a truly continental perspective. With community vignettes from New England to the South, the Midwest to the far West, we encourage students to appreciate the great expanse of our nation. For example, a vignette of seventeenth-century Sante Fé , New Mexico, illustrates the founding of the first European settlements in the New World. We present territorial expansion into the American West from the viewpoint of the Mandan villagers of the upper Missouri River of North Dakota. We introduce the policies of the Reconstruction era through the experience of African Americans in Hale County, Alabama. A continental perspective drives home to students that American history has never been the preserve of any particular region.

In these ways *Out of Many* breaks new ground, but without compromising its coverage of the traditional turning points that we believe are critically important to an understanding of the American past. Among these watershed events are the Revolution and the struggle over the Constitution, the Civil War and Reconstruction, and the Great Depression and World War II. In *Out of Many*, however, we seek to integrate the narrative of national history with the story of the nation's many diverse communities. The Revolutionary and Constitutional period tested the ability of local communities to forge a new unity, and success depended on their ability to build a nation without compromising local identity. The Civil War and Reconstruction formed a second great test of the balance between the national ideas of the Revolution and the power of local and sectional communities. The Depression and the New Deal demonstrated the importance of local communities and the growing power of national institutions during the greatest economic challenge in our history. *Out of Many* also looks back in a new and comprehensive way—from the vantage point of the beginning of a new century and the end of the cold war—at the salient events of the last fifty years and their impact on American communities. The community focus of *Out of Many* weaves the stories of the people and the nation into a single compelling narrative.

Out of Many includes expanded coverage of our diverse heritage. Our country is appropriately known as "a nation of immigrants," and the history of immigration to America, from the seventeenth to the twenty-first centuries, is fully integrated into the text. There is sustained and close attention to our place in the world, with special emphasis on our relations with the nations of the Western Hemisphere, especially our near neighbors, Canada and Mexico. In a completely new final chapter we consider the promises and the risks of American diversity in the new century. The statistical data has been completely updated with the results of the 2000 census. We have also incorporated new scholarship on the South, popular culture, science and technology, and the Cold War.

THE TEACHING AND LEARNING CLASSROOM EDITION

With each edition of *Out of Many* we have sought to strengthen its unique integration of the best of traditional American history with its innovative community-based focus and strong continental perspective. This new version is no exception. A wealth of special features and pedagogical aids reinforces our narrative and helps students grasp key issues.

NEW Single Column Design. The new **Teaching and Learning Classroom Edition** of *Out of Many* offers a new inviting look and format designed to provide an easy-to-read visual and textual learning experience.

NEW Pedagogical Support. The **Teaching and Learning Classroom Edition** introduces students to new pedagogical tools to help reinforce chapter content and provide easy access to important concepts for review.

- **Chapter-opening Questions.** These inquiry-based preview questions correspond to the major sections of the chapter and are repeated within the chapter with these sections to provide a roadmap for study and review.

- **Quick Reviews.** Found at key places within the margins of each chapter, these brief summaries of events and concepts provide an at-a-glance list of the important topics discussed in the text.

- **Marginal Glossary and Key Terms.** Within each chapter key terms are boldfaced in the text and repeated in the margin with a definition or description. A list of the key terms identified in the chapter is also provided at the end of the chapter.

- **Map Questions.** To stress the importance of map literacy and exploration, each map includes a question suitable for assignment that encourages students to fully review and analyze its content.

Community and Diversity. *Out of Many* opens with an introduction, titled "Community and Diversity," that acquaints students with the major themes of the book, providing them with a framework for understanding American history.

Map Explorations. Several maps in each chapter are highlighted and provided in an interactive format on the new *ONEKEY* website available with the text. They provide interactive exploration of key geographical, chronological, and thematic concepts to reinforce the content contained in the maps and the text. Students can access each map individually using the url provided with the map or find them within chapters when exploring the website.

Overview tables. Overview tables provide students with a summary of complex issues.

Graphs, charts, and tables. Every chapter includes one or more graphs, charts, or tables that help students understand important events and trends.

Photos and Illustrations. The abundant illustrations in *Out of Many*, include many that have never before been used in an American history text. None of the images is anachronistic—each one dates from the historical period under discussion. Extensive captions treat the images as visual primary source documents from the American past, describing their source and explaining their significance. In addition, each chapter opens with a stunning visual collage of images that relate to the chapter content and introduce students to the importance of visual documents in the study of history. An image key is included to place each image in its historical context.

Chronologies. A chronology at the end of each chapter helps students build a framework of key events.

Review Questions. Review questions at the end of chapters help students review, reinforce, and retain the material in each chapter and encourage them to relate the material to broader issues in American history.

Recommended Readings. The works in the short, annotated Recommended Reading list at the end of each chapter have been selected with the interested introductory student in mind.

TEACHING AND LEARNING CLASSROOM RESOURCES

In classrooms across the country, many instructors encounter students who perceive history as merely a jumble of names, dates, and events. *Out of Many* brings our dynamic past alive for these students with a text and accompanying print and multimedia classroom resources that combine sound scholarship, engaging narrative, and a rich array of cutting-edge pedagogical tools.

PRINT SUPPLEMENTS

INSTRUCTOR'S RESOURCE BINDER

New to this edition, this resource is a true time-saver in developing and preparing lecture presentation. The binder contains the full array of resources available for use in and out of the classroom, all organized by chapter. In addition, a copy of the *Instructor's Resource Center on CD-ROM* is included which provides electronic access to the print resources in the binder as well as all the maps, graphs, and illustrations from the text that can be easily downloaded for use in the classroom. Contents of the binder include:

- *Instructor's Resource Manual:* Contains chapter outlines, detailed chapter overviews, lecture topics, discussion questions, readings, and information about audio-visual resources.

- *Test Item File:* Offers more than 1,500 multiple-choice, identification, matching, true-false, and essay test questions and 10–15 questions per chapter on the maps found in each chapter. The guide includes a collection of blank maps that can be photocopied and used for map testing purposes or for other class exercises. In addition, there is a special file of questions on the interactive maps, primary source documents offered with the text, and *Exploring America* activities from the accompanying website.

- *Prentice Hall TestGenerator:* This commercial-quality computerized test management program, available for Windows and Macintosh environments, allows instructors to select items from the *Test Item File* and design their own exams.

- *Transparency Package:* Includes full-color transparency acetates of all the maps, charts, and graphs in the text for use in the classroom. Each transparency is accompanied by a page of descriptive material and discussion questions.

HISTORY NOTES, VOLUMES I AND II

History Notes is a new type of study aid that tests for each chapter that students can use to assess their level of understanding of chapter material. It includes identification terms, multiple-choice questions, short essay questions, and map questions. *History Notes* is available free when packaged with *Out of Many.*

DOCUMENTS SET, VOLUMES I AND II

This collection of more than 300 primary source documents directly relates to the themes and content of the text. Each document is approximately two pages long and includes a brief introduction and study questions intended to encourage students to analyze the document critically and relate it to the content of the text. The *Documents Set* is available at a substantial discount when packaged with *Out of Many.*

RETRIEVING THE AMERICAN PAST

Written and developed by leading historians and educators, this reader is an on-demand history database that offers 300 primary source documents on key topics in American History. Each module includes an introduction, several primary documents and secondary sources, follow-up questions, and recommendations for further reading. By deciding which modules to include and the order in which they will appear, instructors can compile a custom reader to fit their needs. Contact your local Prentice Hall representative for more information about this exciting custom publishing option.

MANY LIVES, MANY STORIES: BIOGRAPHIES IN AMERICAN HISTORY

This two-volume collection of sixty-two biographies in American history was written specifically to match the chapter sequence and themes of *Out of Many.* Introductions, pre-reading questions, suggested readings, and a special prologue about the role of biography in the study of American history enrich this important new supplement. Available free when packaged with *Out of Many.*

PRENTICE HALL'S *OneSearch* WITH *Research Navigator*™

This brief guide introduces students to tools for finding, evaluating and using resourcese on the internet. It includes a section of avoiding plagiarism and using sources effectively, tips for finding information related to history on the internet and for documenting electronic sources, and an access code to the *Research Navigator*™ website. *OneSearch* is available for free when packaged with *Out of Many.* Contact your local Prentice Hall representative for details.

PRENTICE HALL AND PENGUIN BUNDLE PROGRAM

Prentice Hall and Penguin are pleased to provide adopters of *Out of Many* with an opportunity to receive significant discounts when orders for *Out of Many* are bundled together with Penguin titles in American history. Please contact your local Prentice Hall representative for details.

MULTIMEDIA SUPPLEMENTS

U.S. HISTORY DOCUMENTS CD-ROM

Bound into every copy of *Out of Many* and organized according to the main periods in American History, this document CD-ROM contains over 300 primary source documents in an easily-navigated PDF file. Each document is accompanied by essay questions that can be answered via the CD-ROM or via a dedicated website.

OneKey

A unique online resource, *OneKey* lets you and your students access the many teaching and learning resources for *Out of Many* all in one place. For students, it means access to documents, quizzes, map explorations, interactive learning activities, video, audio, e-book portions of the text, and other pedagogical material organized by major sections within chapters to reinforce and apply what they are learning in class and from the text. For instructors, it means access to the student's resources, *and* all of the instructional material available to use in teaching with the text, including instructor's manual material, test questions from the test item file, additional documents for assignment, images, maps, charts, and graphs from the text, video and audio clips, and Powerpoint™ presentations and questions for use with *Personal Response* technology in the classroom. Access to this unique website is free to students when packaged with the text. For more information about this exciting new resource, contact your local Prentice Hall representative for a tour.

COMPANION WEBSITE™

www.prenhall.com/faragher

With the *Out of Many Companion Website*™ students can take full advantage of the Web in tandem with the text to enrich their study of American history. The *Companion Website*™ features chapter review tests, learning objectives, and study questions that students can use to assess their comprehension of chapter content.

INSTRUCTOR'S RESOURCE CENTER ON CD-ROM

This CDROM, like the OneKey website, includes all of the print supplements, multimedia resources, and images and art from *Out of Many*. It is provided in the *Instructor's Resource Binder*.

RESEARCH NAVIGATOR™

This unique resource helps your students make the most of their research time. From finding the right articles and journals, to citing sources, drafting and writing effective papers, and completing research assignments, **Research Navigator**™ simplifies and streamlines the entire process. Access to **Research Navigator**™ is available with every copy of the *OneSearch* guide and with the *OneKey* website. For more information, contact your local Prentice Hall representative.

ACKNOWLEDGMENTS

In the years it has taken to bring *Out of Many* from idea to reality and to improve it in successive editions, we have often been reminded that although writing history sometimes feels like isolated work, it actually involves a collective effort. We want to thank the dozens of people whose efforts have made the publication of this book possible.

We wish to thank our many friends at Prentice Hall for their efforts in creating this new Teaching and Learning Edition of *Out of Many*: Yolanda de Rooy, President; Charlyce Jones Owen, Editorial Director; Heather Shelstad, Director of Marketing; Leslie Osher, Creative Design Director; Randy Pettit, Production Editor; Anne DeMarinis and Kathy Mzorek, Interior and Cover Designers, and Martha Williams, Copy Editor.

Historians around the country greatly assisted us by reading and commenting on chapters for this and previous editions. We want to thank each of them for the commitment of their valuable time.

Each of us depended on a great deal of support and assistance with the research and writing that went into this book. We want to thank: Kathryn Abbott, Nan Boyd, Krista Comer, Jennifer Cote, Crista DeLuzio, Keith Edgerton, Carol Frost, Jesse Hoffnung Garskof, Pailin Gaither, Jane Gerhard, Todd Gernes, Mark Krasovic, Melani McAlister, Cristiane Mitchell, J. C. Mutchler, Keith Peterson, Alan Pinkham, Tricia Rose, Gina Rourke, Jessica Shubow, Gordon P. Utz, Jr., and Maura Young.

Our families and close friends have been supportive and ever so patient over the many years we have devoted to this project. But we want especially to thank Paul Buhle, Meryl Fingrutd, Bob Greene, and Michele Hoffnung.

ABOUT THE AUTHORS

Chris Freitag

John Mack Faragher

John Mack Faragher is Arthur Unobskey Professor of American History and Director of the Howard R. Lamar Center for the Study of Frontiers and Borders at Yale University. Born in Arizona and raised in southern California, he received his B.A. at the University of California, Riverside, and his Ph.D. at Yale University. He is the author of *Women and Men on the Overland Trail* (1979), which won the Frederick Jackson Turner Award of the Organization of American Historians, *Sugar Creek: Life on the Illinois Prairie* (1986), *Daniel Boone: The Life and Legend of an American Pioneer* (1992), and (with Robert V. Hine) *The American West: A New Interpretive History* (2000).

Mari Jo Buhle

Mari Jo Buhle is William R. Kenan Jr. University Professor and Professor of American Civilization and History at Brown University, specializing in American women's history. She received her B.A. from the University of Illinois, Urbana–Champaign, and her Ph.D. from the University of Wisconsin, Madison. She is the author of *Women and American Socialism, 1870–1920* (1981) and *Feminism and Its Discontents: A Century of Struggle with Psychoanalysis* (1998). She is also coeditor of *Encyclopedia of the American Left*, second edition (1998). Professor Buhle held a fellowship (1991–1996) from the John D. and Catherine T. MacArthur Foundation.

Daniel Czitrom

Daniel Czitrom is Professor of History at Mount Holyoke College. Born and raised in New York City, he received his B.A. from the State University of New York at Binghamton and his M.A. and Ph.D. from the University of Wisconsin, Madison. He is the author of *Media and the American Mind: From Morse to McLuhan* (1982), which won the First Books Award of the American Historical Association and has been translated into Spanish and Chinese. He has served as a historical consultant and a featured on-camera commentator for several documentary film projects, including two recent PBS series, *New York: A Documentary Film* and *American Photography: A Century of Images.*

Susan H. Armitage

Susan H. Armitage is Claudius O. and Mary R. Johnson Distinguished Professor of History at Washington State University. She earned her Ph.D. from the London School of Economics and Political Science. Among her many publications on western women's history are three coedited books, *The Women's West* (1987), *So Much To Be Done: Women on the Mining and Ranching Frontier* (1991), and *Writing the Range: Race, Class, and Culture in the Women's West* (1997). She currently serves as an editor of a series of books on women and American history for the University of Illinois Press. She is the editor of *Frontiers: A Journal of Women's Studies.*

COMMUNITY & DIVERSITY

One of the most characteristic features of our country has always been its astounding variety. The American people include the descendants of native Indians, colonial Europeans, Africans, and migrants from virtually every country and continent. Indeed, as we enter a new century the United States is absorbing a flood of immigrants from Latin America and Asia that rivals the great tide of people from eastern and southern Europe one hundred years ago. What's more, our country is one of the world's most spacious, incorporating more than 3.6 million square miles of territory. The struggle to meld a single nation out of our many far-flung communities is what much of American history is all about. That is the story told in this book.

Every human society is made up of communities. A community is a set of relationships linking men, women, and their families to a coherent social whole that is more than the sum of its parts. In a community people develop the capacity for unified action. In a community people learn, often through trial and error, how to transform and adapt to their environment. The sentiment that binds the members of a community together is the mother of group identity and ethnic pride. In the making of history, communities are far more important than even the greatest of leaders, for the community is the institution most capable of passing a distinctive historical tradition to future generations.

Communities bind people together in multiple ways. They can be as small as local neighborhoods, in which people maintain face-to-face relations, or as large as the nation itself. This book examines American history from the perspective of community life—an ever-widening frame that has included larger and larger groups of Americans.

Networks of kinship and friendship, and connections across generations and among families, establish the bonds essential to community life. Shared feelings about values and history establish the basis for common identity. In communities, people find the power to act collectively in their own interest. But American communities frequently took shape as a result of serious conflicts among groups, and within communities there has often been significant fighting among competing groups or classes. Thus the term community, as we use it here, includes tension and discord as well as harmony and agreement.

For years there have been persistent laments about the "loss of community" in modern America. But community has not disappeared—it is continually being reinvented. Until the late eighteenth century, community was defined primarily by space and local geography. But in the nineteenth century communities began to be reshaped by new and powerful historical forces such as the marketplace, industrialization, the corporation, mass immigration, mass media, and the growth of the nation-state. In the twentieth century, Americans have struggled to balance commitments to several communities simultaneously. These were defined not simply by local spatial arrangements, but by categories as varied as racial and ethnic groups, occupations, political affiliations, and consumer preferences.

The "American Communities" vignettes that open each chapter reflect this shift. Most of the vignettes in the pre–Civil War chapters focus on geographically defined communities, such as the ancient Indian city at Cahokia, or the experiment in industrial urban planning in early nineteenth-century Lowell, Massachusetts. In the post–Civil War chapters different and more modern kinds of communities make their appearance. In the 1920s, movies and radio offered a new kind of community—a community of identification with dreams of freedom, material success, upward mobility, youth and beauty. In the 1950s, rock'n'roll music helped germinate a new national community of teenagers, with profound effects on the culture of the entire country in the second half of the twentieth century. In the late 1970s, fear of nuclear accidents like the one at Three Mile Island brought concerned citizens together in communities around the country and produced a national movement opposing nuclear power.

William Sidney Mount (1807–1868) *California News* 1850. Oil on canvas. The Long Island Museum of American Art, History and Carriages. Gift of Mr. and Mrs. Ward Melville, 1955.

The title for our book was suggested by the Latin phrase selected by John Adams, Benjamin Franklin, and Thomas Jefferson for the Great Seal of the United States: E *Pluribus Unum*—"Out of Many Comes Unity." These men understood that unity could not be imposed by a powerful central authority but had to develop out of mutual respect among Americans of different backgrounds. The revolutionary leadership expressed the hope that such respect could grow on the basis of a remarkable proposition: "We hold these truths to be self-evident, that all men are created equal; that they are endowed by their Creator with certain unalienable rights; that among these are life, liberty, and the pursuit of happiness." The national government of the United States would preserve local and state authority but would guarantee individual rights. The nation would be strengthened by guarantees of difference.

"Out of Many"—that is the promise of America, and the premise of this book. The underlying dialectic of American history, we believe, is that as a people we need to locate our national unity in the celebration of the differences that exist among us; these differences can be our strength, as long as we affirm the promise of the Declaration. Protecting the "right to be different," in other words, is absolutely fundamental to the continued existence of democracy, and that right is best protected by the existence of strong and vital communities. We are bound together as a nation by the ideal of local and cultural differences protected by our common commitment to the values of our Revolution.

Today those values are endangered by terrorists using the tactics of mass terror. In the wake of the September 11, 2001, attack on the United States, and with the continuing threat of biological, chemical, or even nuclear assaults, Americans can not afford to lose faith in our historic vision. The United States is a multicultural and transnational society. The thousands of victims buried in the smoking ruins of the World Trade Center included people from dozens of different ethnic and national groups. We must fight to protect and defend the promise of our diverse nation.

Our history shows that the promise of American unity has always been problematic. Centrifugal forces have been powerful in the American past, and at times the country has seemed about to fracture into its component parts. Our transformation from a collection of groups and regions into a nation has been marked by painful and often violent struggles. Our past is filled with conflicts between Indians and colonists, masters and slaves, Patriots and Loyalists, Northerners and

Harvey Dinnerstein, *Underground, Together* 1996, oil on canvas, 90" x 107". Photograph courtesy of Gerold Wunderlich & Co., New York, NY.

Southerners, Easterners and Westerners, capitalists and workers, and sometimes the government and the people. War can bring out our best, but it can also bring out our worst. During World War II thousands of Japanese American citizens were deprived of their rights and locked up in isolated detention centers simply because of their ethnic background. Americans often appear to be little more than a contentious collection of peoples with conflicting interests, divided by region and background, race and class.

Our most influential leaders have also sometimes suffered a crisis of faith in the American project of "liberty and justice for all." Thomas Jefferson not only believed in the inferiority of African Americans, but he feared that immigrants from outside the Anglo-American tradition might "warp and bias" the development of the nation "and render it a heterogeneous, incoherent, distracted mass." We have not always lived up to the American promise, and there is a dark side to our history. It took the bloodiest war in American history to secure the human rights of African Americans, and the struggle for full equality for all our citizens has yet to be won. During the great influx of immigrants in the early twentieth century, fears much like Jefferson—s led to movements to Americanize the foreign born by forcing them, in the words of one leader, "to give up the languages, customs, and methods of life which they have brought with them across the ocean, and adopt instead the language, habits, and customs of this country, and the general standards and ways of American living." Similar thinking motivated Congress at various times to bar the immigration of Africans, Asians, and other ethnic groups and people of color into the country, and to force assimilation on American Indians by denying them the freedom to practice their religion or even to speak their own language. Such calls for restrictive unity still resound in our own day.

But other Americans have argued for a more fulsome version of Americanization. "What is the American, this new man?" asked the French immigrant Michel Crèvecoeur in 1782. "A strange mixture of blood which you will find in no other country." In America, he wrote, "individuals of all nations are melted into a new race of men." A century later Crèvecoeur was echoed by historian Frederick Jackson Turner, who believed that "in the crucible of the frontier, the immigrants were Americanized, liberated, and fused into a mixed race, English in neither nationality nor characteristics. The process has gone on from the early days to our own."

The process by which diverse communities have come to share a set of common American values is one of the most fundamental aspects of our history. It did not occur, however, because of compulsory Americanization programs, but because of free public education, popular participation in democratic politics, and the impact of popular culture. Contemporary America does have a common culture: We share a commitment to freedom of thought and expression, we join in the aspirations to own our own homes and send our children to college, we laugh at the same television programs.

To a degree that too few Americans appreciate, this common culture resulted from a complicated process of mutual discovery that took place when different ethnic and regional groups encountered one another. Consider just one small and unique aspect of our culture: the barbecue. Americans have been barbecuing since before the beginning of written history. Early settlers adopted this technique of cooking from the Indians—the word itself comes from a native term for a framework of sticks over a fire on which meat was slowly cooked. Colonists typically barbecued pork, fed on Indian corn. African slaves lent their own touch by introducing the use of hot sauces. The ritual that is a part of nearly every American family's Fourth of July silently celebrates the heritage of diversity that went into making our common culture.

The American educator John Dewey recognized this diversity early in the last century. "The genuine American, the typical American, is himself a hyphenated character," he declared, "international and interracial in his make-up." The point about our "hyphenated character," Dewey believed, "is to see to it that the hyphen connects instead of separates." We, the authors of *Out of Many*, share Dewey's perspective on American history. "Creation comes from the impact of diversity," wrote the American philosopher Horace Kallen. We also endorse Kallen's vision of the American promise: "A democracy of nationalities, cooperating voluntarily and autonomously through common institutions, . . . a multiplicity in a unity, an orchestration of mankind." And now, let the music begin.

Thomas Satterwhite Noble, *Last Sale of Slaves on the Courthouse Steps*, 1860, oil on canvas, Missouri Historical Society.

Out of Many

A HISTORY OF THE AMERICAN PEOPLE

Painting by Michael Hampshire, "Community Life of Cahokia". Mounds State Historic Site

10

A CONTINENT OF VILLAGES

TO 1500

WHAT EVENTS led to the migration of Asian peoples into North America?

WHAT WERE the consequences of the global warming that began around 13,000 B.C.E.?

HOW DID the development of settled agriculture change Indian societies?

WHAT IMPORTANT differences were there among Indian societies in the Southwest, South, and Northeast on the eve of colonization?

AMERICAN COMMUNITIES

Cahokia: Thirteenth-Century Life on the Mississippi

AS THE SUN ROSE OVER THE RICH FLOODPLAIN, THE PEOPLE OF THE riverbank city set about their daily tasks. Some went to shops where they manufactured tools, crafted pottery, worked metal, or fashioned ornamental jewelry—goods destined to be exchanged in the far corners of the continent. Others left their densely populated neighborhoods for the outlying countryside, where in the summer heat they worked the seemingly endless fields that fed the city. From almost any point people could see the great temple that rose from the center of their city—the temple where priests in splendid costumes acted out public rituals of death and renewal.

This thirteenth-century city was not in preindustrial Europe but in North America. Its residents lived and worked on the banks of the Mississippi River, across from present-day St. Louis, at a place archaeologists have named **Cahokia***. In the mid-1200s, Cahokia was an urban cluster of perhaps 30,000 people. Its farm fields were abundant with corn, beans, and pumpkins. The temple, a huge earthwork pyramid, covered fifteen acres at its base and rose as high as a ten-story building. On top were the sacred residences of chiefs and priests, who dressed in elaborate headdresses made from the plumage of American birds.*

By the fourteenth century, Cahokia had been abandoned, but its great central temple mound and dozens of smaller ones in the surrounding area, as well as hundreds more throughout the Mississippi Valley, remained to puzzle the European immigrants who resettled the valley in the eighteenth and nineteenth centuries. Treasure seekers plundered the mounds, most of which were eventually dynamited and plowed under for farmland. Only a few were saved, inside parks and estates. Cahokia's central mound survived because in the nineteenth century its summit became the site of a monastery, now long gone.

The Europeans who first explored and excavated these mounds were convinced that they were the ruins of a vanished civilization but could not believe they were the work of Indians. The first comprehensive study of Cahokia, published in 1848 under the sponsorship of the Smithsonian Institution, noted that "the moundbuilders were an agricultural people, considerably advanced in arts, manners, habits, and religion." But because "Indians were hunters averse to labor, and not known to have constructed any works approaching [the] skillfulness of design or [the] magnitude" of Cahokia, surely those wonders were constructed by a "lost race."

The Smithsonian scientists were wrong. Historians now know that the ancestors of contemporary Native Americans constructed massive earthworks in the Mississippi Valley. The vast

urban complex of Cahokia flourished from the tenth to the fourteenth century, and at its height stretched six miles along the Mississippi River. Its residents were not nomadic hunters but farmers, members of an agricultural society—which archaeologists call the Mississippian—with highly productive techniques of cultivation. Hundreds of acres of crops fed the people of Cahokia, the most populated urban community north of the complex civilization of the Aztecs in Mexico. Mississippian farmers constructed ingenious raised plots of land on which they heaped compost in wide ridges for improved drainage and protection against unseasonable frosts. To their square houses of wood and mud they attached pens in which they kept flocks of domesticated turkeys and, perhaps, small herds of young deer, which they slaughtered for meat and hides. Cahokia was at the center of a long-distance trading system that linked it to other Indian communities over a vast area. Copper came from Lake Superior, mica from the southern Appalachians, conch shells from the Atlantic coast, and Cahokia's specialized artisans were renowned for the manufacture of high-quality flint hoes, exported throughout the Mississippi Valley.

The archaeological evidence suggests that Cahokia was a city-state supported by tribute and taxation. Like the awe-inspiring public works of early urban societies in other parts of the world—the pyramids of ancient Egypt, the acropolis of Athens—the great temple mound of Cahokia was intended to reflect the city's wealth and power. The mounds and other colossal public works at Cahokia were the monuments of a society ruled by an elite. From their residences atop the mound, priests and governors looked down upon their subjects.

The 1848 Smithsonian report on Cahokia reflected the stereotypical American view that all Indian people lived in hunting bands. But the history of North America before European colonization demonstrates that the native inhabitants of the continent lived in strong, vibrant communities that ranged from small hunting bands to large agricultural cities like Cahokia and splendid imperial capitals like those of the Aztecs of Mexico or the Mayans of Central America. North America before colonization was, as one historian phrases it, "a continent of villages," a land with thousands of local communities. Over many centuries the Indian peoples of North America developed a variety of community types, each with its own system of family and social organization, each integrated with its natural surroundings. The wonders of Cahokia are but one aspect of the little-understood history of the Indians of the Americas.

Cahokia

SETTLING THE CONTINENT

"Why do you call us Indians?" a Massachusetts native complained to Puritan missionary John Eliot in 1646. Christopher Columbus, who mistook the Taino people of the Caribbean for the people of the East Indies, called them *Indios*. By the middle of the sixteenth century this Spanish word had passed into English as "Indians" and was commonly used to refer to all the native peoples of the Americas. Today anthropologists often use the term "Amerindians," and many people prefer "Native Americans," but most indigenous Americans call themselves "Indian people."

WHO ARE THE INDIAN PEOPLE?

At the time of their first contacts with Europeans at the beginning of the sixteenth century, the native inhabitants of the Western Hemisphere represented over 2,000 cultures, spoke hundreds of different languages, and made their livings in scores of fundamentally different environments. Just as the term "European" includes the English, French, and Spanish, so "Indian" covers an enormous diversity among the peoples of the Americas.

No single physical type characterized all the native peoples of the Americas. Although most had straight, black hair and dark, almond-shaped eyes, their skin color ranged from mahogany to light brown and few fit the "redskin" descriptions used by North American colonists of the eighteenth and nineteenth centuries. Indeed, it was only when Europeans had compared Indian peoples with natives of other continents, such as Africans, that they seemed similar enough to be classified as a group.

Once Europeans realized that the Americas were in fact a "New World," rather than part of the Asian continent, a debate began over how people might have moved there from Europe and Asia, where the Judeo-Christian Bible indicated God had created the first man and woman. Writers proposed elaborate theories of **transoceanic migrations**. Common to all these theories was a belief that the Americas had been populated for a few thousand years at most, and that native societies were the degenerate offspring of a far superior Old World culture. A number of Spanish scholars thought more deeply about the question of Indian origins. In 1590, Joseph de Acosta reasoned that because Old World animals were present in the Americas, they must have crossed by a land bridge that could have been used by humans as well.

MIGRATION FROM ASIA

Acosta was the first to propose the Asian migration hypothesis that is today supported by most of the scientific evidence. The first "hard" data linking American Indians with Asians appeared in the 1980s with the finding that Indians and northeast Asians share a common and distinctive pattern in the arrangement of the teeth. But perhaps the most compelling support for the hypothesis comes from genetic research. Studies comparing the DNA variation of populations around the world consistently demonstrate the close genetic relationship of the two populations, and recently geneticists studying a virus sequestered in the kidneys of all humans found that the strain of virus carried by Navajos and Japanese is nearly identical, while that carried by Europeans and Africans is quite different.

The migration could have begun over a land bridge connecting the continents. During the last Ice Age (the Wisconsinan Glaciation, from 70,000 to 10,000 years ago, the final act in the geologic epoch known as the Pleistocene), huge glaciers locked up massive volumes of water, and sea levels were as much as 300

WHAT EVENTS led to the migration of Asian peoples into North America?

IMAGE KEY

for pages 2–3

a. Native Americans build thatch houses beside a massive pyramid in "Community Life at Cahokia" by Michael Hampshire.

b. A hut from the coastal Algonquian village of Secoton.

c. In July 1585 John White visited the coastal Algonquian village of Secoton where he painted this composite scene.

d. Projectile point embedded in the rib bones of a long-extinct North American species of bison.

e. The ruins of the Anasazis' Pueblo Bonito in Chaco Canyon, northern New Mexico.

f. "The New Queen Being Taken to the King," engraved from a drawing by an early French colonist of a hierarchical community of Florida.

Cahokia   One of the largest urban centers created by Mississippian peoples, containing 30,000 residents in 1250.

Transoceanic migrations A population migration across oceans.

Beringia A subcontinent bridging Asia and North America, named after the Bering Straits.

feet lower than today. Asia and North America were joined by a huge subcontinent of ice-free, treeless grassland, 750 miles wide from north to south. Geologists have named this area **Beringia**, from the Bering Straits. Summers there were warm, winters were cold, dry, and almost snow-free. This was a perfect environment for large mammals—mammoth and mastodon, bison, horse, reindeer, camel, and saiga (a goatlike antelope). Small bands of Stone Age hunter-gatherers were attracted by these animal populations. Accompanied by a huskylike species of dog, hunting bands gradually moved as far east as the Yukon River basin of northern Canada, where field excavations have uncovered the fossilized jawbones of several dogs and bone tools estimated to be about 27,000 years old.

Other evidence suggests that the migration from Asia began about 30,000 years ago—around the same time that Japan and Scandinavia were being settled. This evidence is based on blood type. The vast majority of modern Native Americans have type O blood and a few have type A, but almost none have type B. Because modern Asian populations include all three blood types, however, the migrations

MAP EXPLORATION

To explore an interactive version of this map, go to **http://www.prenhall.com/faraghertlc/map1.1**

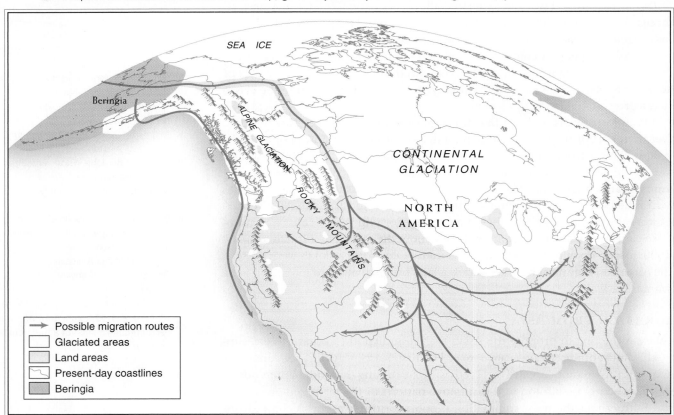

MAP 1-1

Migration Routes from Asia to America During the Ice Age, Asia and North America were joined where the Bering Straits are today, forming a migration route for hunting peoples. Either by boat along the coast, or through a narrow corridor between the huge northern glaciers, these migrants began making their way to the heartland of the continent as much as 30,000 years ago.

WHAT GEOGRAPHICAL features shaped the dispersal of Asian migrants throughout the Americas?

must have begun before the evolution of type B, which geneticists believe occurred about 30,000 years ago. The study of the evolution of language offers another kind of evidence. Linguists argue that it would require at least 35,000 years to develop, from a single common base, the nearly 500 distinct languages of the Americas.

By 25,000 years ago human communities were established in western Beringia, which is present-day Alaska. But access to the south was blocked by a huge glacial sheet covering much of what is today Canada. How did the hunters get over those 2,000 miles of deep ice? The argument is that the climate began to warm with the passing of the Ice Age, and about 13,000 B.C.E. (before the common era, which began 2,000 years ago) glacial melting created an ice-free corridor—the original "Pan-American Highway"—along the eastern front range of the Rocky Mountains. Soon hunters of big game had reached the Great Plains.

In the past several years, however, new archaeological finds along the Pacific coast of North and South America have thrown this theory into question. Newly excavated early human sites in Washington State, California, and Peru have been radiocarbon dated to be 11,000 to 12,000 years old. The most spectacular find, at Monte Verde in southern Chile, produced striking evidence of tool making, house building, rock painting, and human footprints conservatively dated at 12,500 years ago, long before the highway had been cleared of ice. Many archaeologists now believe that migrants moved south in boats along a coastal route rather than over land—an ancient "Pacific Coast Highway." These people were probably gatherers and fishers rather than hunters of big game.

There were two later migrations into North America. About 5000 B.C.E. the **Athapascan** or Na-Dene people began to settle the forests in the northwestern area of the continent. Although they eventually adopted a technology similar to that of neighboring peoples, the Na-Dene maintained a separate cultural and linguistic identity. Eventually Athapascan speakers, the ancestors of the Navajos and Apaches, migrated across the Great Plains to the Southwest. The final migration began about 3000 B.C.E., after Beringia had been submerged, when a maritime hunting people crossed the Bering Straits in small boats. The Inuits (also known as the Eskimos) colonized the polar coasts of the Arctic, the Yupiks the coast of southwestern Alaska, and the Aleuts the Aleutian Islands (which are named for them).

While scientists debate the timing and mapping of these migrations, many Indian people hold to their oral traditions that say they have always lived in North America. Every culture has its origin stories, offering explanations of the customs and beliefs of the group. Yet a number of anthropologists argue that these origin stories may shed light on ancient history. The Haida people of the Northwest Pacific Coast tell of a time, long ago, when the islands were much larger; but then the oceans rose, they say, and "flood tide woman" forced them to move to higher ground. Could these stories preserve a memory of the changes at the end of the Ice Age? It is notable that many Indian traditions include a long journey from a distant place of origin to a new homeland.

CLOVIS: THE FIRST AMERICAN TECHNOLOGY

The earliest tools found at North American archaeological sites, crude stone or bone choppers and scrapers, are similar to artifacts from the same period found in Europe or Asia. About 10,000 B.C.E., however, ancient Americans developed a much more sophisticated style of tool making, named after the site of its first discovery near Clovis, New Mexico. The **Clovis tradition** was a powerful new and sophisticated technology, unlike anything found in the Old World. In the years since the initial discovery, archaeologists have unearthed Clovis artifacts at sites ranging from Montana to Mexico, Nova Scotia to Arizona, all of them dating back to within

QUICK REVIEW

The Earliest Americans

◆ No single physical type characterized the peoples of the Americas.

◆ Migration from Asia began about 30,000 years ago.

◆ Stone Age hunters brought tools and animals with them on their journey.

Athapascan A people that began to settle the forests in the northwestern area of North America around 5000 B.C.E.

Clovis tradition A powerful new and sophisticated style of tool making, unlike anything found in the Old World.

These Clovis points are typical of thousands that archaeologists have found at sites all over the continent, dating from a period about 12,000 years ago. When inserted in a spear shaft, these three- to six-inch fluted points made effective weapons for hunting mammoth and other big game. The ancient craftsmen who made these points often took advantage of the unique qualities of the stone they were working to enhance their aesthetic beauty.

© Warren Morgan/CORBIS

QUICK REVIEW

The Clovis Tradition

◆ Emerged around 10,000 B.C.E.

◆ A new and powerful style of tool making.

◆ Clovis artifacts found throughout North and Central America.

WHAT WERE the consequences of the global warming that began around 13,000 B.C.E.?

1,000 or 2,000 years of one another, suggesting that the Clovis technology spread quickly throughout the continent.

The evidence suggests that Clovis bands were mobile communities of foragers numbering perhaps thirty to fifty individuals from several interrelated families. They returned to the same hunting camps year after year, migrating seasonally within territories of several hundred square miles. Near Delbert, Nova Scotia, archaeologists discovered the floors of ten tents arranged in a semicircle, their doors opening south to avoid the prevailing northerly winds. Both this camp and others found throughout the continent overlooked watering places that would attract game. Clovis blades have been excavated amid the remains of mammoth, camel, horse, giant armadillo, and sloth.

New Ways of Living on the Land

About 13,000 B.C.E., a global warming trend began to alter the North American climate. As the giant continental glaciers began to melt, the northern latitudes were colonized by plants, animals, and humans. Meltwater created the lake and river systems of today and raised the level of the surrounding seas, flooding Beringia as well as vast stretches of the Atlantic and Gulf coasts and creating fertile tidal pools and offshore fishing banks. These huge transformations produced new patterns of wind, rainfall, and temperature, reshaping the ecology of the entire continent and gradually producing the distinct North American regions of today. The great integrating force of a single continental climate faded, and with its passing the continental Clovis culture fragmented into many different regional patterns.

HUNTING TRADITIONS

One of the most important effects of this massive climatic shift was the stress it placed on the big game animals best suited to an Ice Age environment. The archaeological record shows the extinction of thirty-two classes of large New World animals, including not only the mammoth and mastodon but also, in North America, of the horse and camel, both of which evolved in America and then migrated to Asia across Beringia. Lowered reproduction and survival rates of large animals may have forced hunting bands to intensify their efforts, leading to what some archaeologists have called the "**Pleistocene Overkill**."

As the other large-mammal populations declined, hunters on the Great Plains concentrated on the herds of American bison, or buffalo. To hunt these animals people needed a weapon they could throw quickly with great accuracy and speed at fast-moving targets over distances of as much as a hundred yards. In archaeological sites dating from about 8000 B.C.E., a new style of tool is found mingled with animal remains. This technology, named "Folsom" after the site of the first major excavation in New Mexico, was a refinement of the Clovis tradition, featuring more delicate but deadlier spear points. Hunters probably hurled the lances to which these points were attached with wooden spear-throwers, with far greater speed than they could achieve with their arms alone. By 7000 B.C.E., Folsom evolved into a tradition that archaeologists call "Plano"; the points are found with grinding tools for vegetable foods, demonstrating the development of a varied diet on the Great Plains.

These archaeological finds suggest the growing complexity of early Indian communities. Hunters frequently stampeded herds of bison into canyon traps or over cliffs. At one such kill site in southeastern Colorado, dated at about 6500 B.C.E., archaeologists uncovered the remains of nearly 200 bison that had been slaughtered and then systematically butchered on a single occasion. Such tasks required a sophisticated division of labor among dozens of men and women and the cooperation of a number of communities. Taking food in such great quantities also suggests a knowledge of basic preservation techniques. These people must have been among the first to make jerky (dried strips of meat) and pemmican (a mixture of dried meat, animal fat, and berries that can keep into the winter when stored in hide containers).

DESERT CULTURE

The retreat of the glaciers led to new ways of finding food in other regions: hunting in the arctic, foraging in the arid deserts, fishing along the coasts, hunting and gathering in the forests. These developments took place roughly 10,000 to 2,500 years ago, during what archaeologists call the **Archaic period** (corresponding to the late phases of the Stone Age in Eurasia and Africa).

In the Great Basin of present-day Utah and Nevada the warming trend associated with the end of the Ice Age created a desert where once there had been enormous inland seas. Here Indian people developed Desert culture, a way of life based on the pursuit of small game and the intensified foraging of plant foods. Small communities or bands of desert foragers migrated seasonally within a small range. They collected seeds, fiber, and prickly pear from the yucca one season, then moved to highland mesas or plateaus to gather grass seed, acorns, juniper berries, and piñon nuts, and next to mountain streams to spear and net fish.

Archaeologists today find the artifacts of desert foragers in the caves and rock shelters in which they lived. In addition to stone tools, there are objects of wood, hide, and fiber, wonderfully preserved for thousands of years in the dry climate. Desert culture persisted into the nineteenth century among modern Shoshone and Ute communities.

Descriptions of the culture of the modern Shoshones suggest that their emphasis on sharing and gift giving, their condemnation of hoarding, and their limitations on the accumulation of material goods, fostered by a nomadic lifestyle, prevented individuals or families from acquiring excessive wealth and forged a strong sense of

Pleistocene Overkill   Intensified hunting efforts brought on in response to lowered reproduction and survival rates of large animals.

Archaic period   The period roughly 10,000 to 2,500 years ago marked by the retreat of glaciers.

MAP EXPLORATION

To explore an interactive version of this map, go to **http://www.prenhall.com/faraghertlc/map1.2**

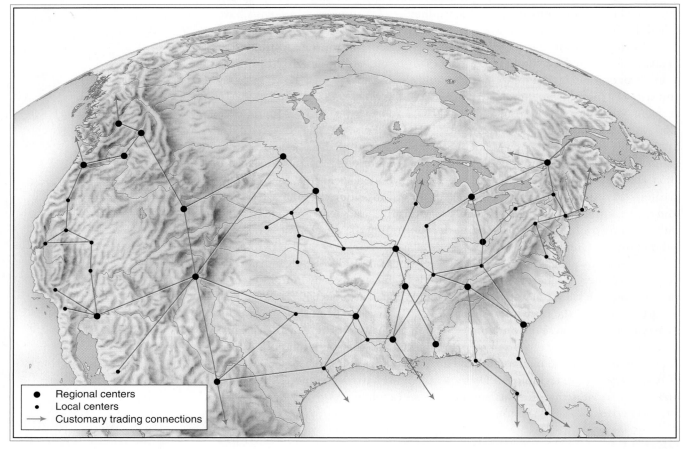

Regional centers
Local centers
Customary trading connections

MAP 1-2

Native North American Trade Networks, ca. c.e. 1400 By determining the origin of artifacts found at ancient sites, historians have devised a conjectural map of Indian trade networks. Among large regional centers and smaller local ones, trade connected Indian peoples of many different communities and regions.

HOW DID the environment influence the relationship between trade and culture?

community among these people of the desert. Desert communities were characterized by a kind of social equality in which decisions were made by consensus among the adults and leadership tended to be informal, based on achievement and reputation. Men of one band generally married women from another, and wives came to live with the people of their husband's families, creating important linkages between groups that contributed to the sense of shared ethnic identity.

The innovative practices of the Desert culture gradually spread from the Great Basin to the Great Plains and the Southwest, where foraging for plant foods began to supplement hunting. Archaeologists estimate that about 6,000 years ago, Indians carried Desert culture to California, where, in the natural abundance of the valleys and coasts, they developed an economy capable of supporting some of the densest populations and the first permanently settled communities in North America. Another dynamic center in the West developed along the Northwest Pacific Coast, where Indian communities developed a way of life based on the use of abundant fish and sea mammals. Here, densely populated, permanently settled communities were also possible.

FOREST EFFICIENCY

There were similar trends east of the Mississippi. Before European settlers destroyed countless acres of woodland in the eighteenth and nineteenth centuries, the whole of eastern North America was a vast forest.

During the Archaic period, forest communities achieved a comfortable and secure life based on their sophisticated knowledge of the rich and diverse available resources, a principle that archaeologists call "forest efficiency." Indian communities of the forest hunted small game and gathered seeds, nuts, roots, and other wild plant foods. They also developed the practice of burning the woodlands and prairies to stimulate the growth of berries, fruits, and edible roots. These burns created meadows and edge environments that provided harvestable food and attracted grazing animals, which were hunted for their meat and hides. Another important resource was the abundant fish of the rivers.

Archaeological sites in the East suggest that during the late Archaic period community populations grew and settlements became increasingly permanent, providing convincing evidence of the viability of forest efficiency. The artifacts these people buried with their dead—axes, fishhooks, and animal bones with males, nut-cracking stones, beads, and pestles with females—reflect the different roles of men and women in their society.

QUICK REVIEW

Forest Living

◆ Eastern North America a vast forest.

◆ Indian communities took advantage of rich forest resources.

◆ Indians developed settled forest communities.

THE DEVELOPMENT OF FARMING

The use of a wide variety of food sources during the Archaic period eventually led many Indian people to develop and adopt the practice of farming. The dynamic center of this development in North America was in the highlands of Mexico, from which the new technology spread north and east.

HOW DID the development of settled agriculture change Indian societies?

MEXICO

At the end of the Stone Age ("Stone Age" is generic for all the world, while "Archaic" is specific to the New World and is the equivalent of "Mesolithic" for Europe), people in four different parts of the world developed farming systems, each based on a different crop: rice in Southeast Asia, wheat in West Asia, maize (or Indian corn) in Mexico, and potatoes in the Andean highlands of South America. In Mexico a great variety of other crops—most importantly beans and squash, but also tomatoes, peppers, avocados, cocoa (chocolate), and vanilla—supplemented maize. Today, maize and potatoes, the two American crops, contribute more to the world's food supply than do wheat and rice. These "miracle crops" fueled the expansion of European human and livestock populations in the three centuries after 1650.

Archaeological evidence suggests that plant cultivation in the highlands of central Mexico began about 5,000 years ago. Ancient Mexicans developed crops that responded well to human care and produced larger quantities of food in a limited space than did plants growing in the wild. Maize was particularly productive; over time it was adapted to a wide range of American climates, and farming spread throughout the temperate regions of North America, those characterized by relatively mild climates.

As farming became increasingly important, it radically reshaped social life. Where a foraging society might require 100 square miles to support 100 people, a farming society required only 1 square mile. Population growth and the need for people to remain near their fields throughout the year led to the appearance of villages and permanent architecture and eventually to the emergence of large, densely settled communities like Cahokia. Autumn harvests had to be stored during winter months, and the storage and distribution of food had to be managed. The division of labor increased with the appearance of specialists like toolmakers, crafts workers, administrators, priests, and rulers as well as farmers and food processors.

By 1000 B.C.E. urban communities governed by permanent bureaucracies had begun to form in **Mesoamerica**, the region stretching from central Mexico to Central America. By the beginning of the first millennium C.E. (common era), highly productive farming was supporting complex urban civilizations in the Valley of Mexico (the location of present-day Mexico City), the Yucatan Peninsula, and other parts of Mesoamerica. Like many of the ancient civilizations of Asia and the Mediterranean, these Mesoamerican civilizations were characterized by the concentration of wealth and power in the hands of an elite class of priests and rulers, the construction of impressive temples and other public structures, and the development of systems of mathematics and astronomy and several forms of hieroglyphic writing. These civilizations also engaged in warfare between states and held terrifying public rituals of human sacrifice.

The great city of Teotihuacan in the Valley of Mexico, which emerged about 100 B.C.E., had a population of as many as 200,000 at the height of its power around 500 C.E. Teotihuacan's elite class of religious and political leaders controlled an elaborate state-sponsored trading system that stretched from present-day Arizona to Central America and may have included coastal shipping connections with the civilizations of Peru. The city had a highly specialized division of labor. Artisans manufactured tools and produced textiles, stoneware, pottery, and obsidian blades. The bureaucratic elite collected taxes and tribute. Farmers worked the fields, and armies of workers constructed such monumental edifices as the Pyramids of the Sun and Moon, which still dominate the site's ruins.

Teotihuacan began to decline in the sixth century, and by the eighth century it was mostly abandoned. A new empire, that of the Toltecs, dominated central Mexico from the tenth to the twelfth century. By the fourteenth century a people known as the **Aztecs**, migrants from the north, had settled in the Valley of Mexico and begun a dramatic expansion into a formidable imperial power (see Chapter 2).

The Mayan peoples of the Yucatan peninsula developed a group of competing city-states that flourished from about 300 B.C.E. until 900 C.E. Their achievements included advanced writing and calendar systems and a sophisticated knowledge of mathematics.

THE RESISTED REVOLUTION

Historians once described the development of farming as a revolution. They believed that agricultural communities offered such obvious advantages that their neighbors must have rushed to adopt this way of life. Societies that remained without a farming tradition must simply have been too "primitive" to achieve this breakthrough; vulnerability to fickle nature was the penalty for their ignorance.

But there is very little evidence to support this notion of a "revolution" occurring during a short, critical period. The adoption of farming was a gradual process, one that required hundreds, even thousands of years. Moreover, ignorance of cultivation was never the reason that cultures failed to take up farming, for all hunter-gatherer peoples understand a great deal about plant reproduction. The Menominee Indians of the northern forests of Wisconsin, for example, when gathering wild rice, purposely allowed some of it to fall back into the water to ensure a crop for the next season, and Paiutes of the Great Basin systematically irrigated stands of their favorite wild food sources.

As this new farming technology became available, cultures in different regions assessed its advantages and limitations. In California and the Pacific Northwest, acorn gathering or salmon fishing made the cultivation of food crops seem a waste

QUICK REVIEW

Mesoamerica

◆ Mesoamerica was the birthplace of agriculture in North America.

◆ Olmecs: first literate urban culture in region.

◆ Mayan civilization flourished between about 300 B.C.E. and 900 C.E.

Mesoamerica   The region stretching from central Mexico to Central America.

Aztecs   A warrior people who dominated the Valley of Mexico from 1100–1521.

of time. In the Great Basin, several peoples attempted to farm but without success. Before the invention of modern irrigation systems, which require sophisticated engineering, only the Archaic Desert culture could prevail in this harsh environment. In the neighboring Southwest, however, farming resolved certain ecological dilemmas and transformed the way of life. Like the development of more sophisticated traditions of tool manufacture, farming represented another stage in economic intensifications (like the advance in tool making represented by Clovis technology) that kept populations and available resources in balance. It seems that where the climate favored it, people tended to adopt farming as a way of increasing the production of food, thus continuing the Archaic tradition of squeezing as much productivity as they could from their environment. In a few areas, however, farming truly did result in a revolutionary transformation, creating urban civilizations like the one in central Mexico or at Cahokia, on the banks of the Mississippi.

INCREASING SOCIAL COMPLEXITY

Farming created the basis for much greater social complexity within Indian communities. There were significantly more elaborate systems of kinship. Greater population density prompted families to group themselves into **clans**. Often different clans became responsible for different social, political, or ritual functions. Clans became an important mechanism for binding together the people of several communities into a tribe. Tribes, based on ethnic, linguistic, and territorial unity, were led by leaders or chiefs from honored clans, who were often advised by councils of elders. These councils sometimes arbitrated disputes between individuals or families, but most crimes—theft, adultery, rape, murder—were avenged by the aggrieved kinship group itself. In all likelihood, the city of Cahokia was governed by such a system.

The primary functions of chiefs were the supervision of the economy, the collection and storage of the harvest, and the distribution of food to the clans. Differences in wealth, though small by the standards of modern societies, might develop between the families of a farming tribe. These inequalities were kept in check by redistribution according to principles of sharing similar to those operating in foraging communities. Nowhere in North America did Indian cultures develop a concept of the private ownership of land or other resources, which were usually considered the common resource of the people and were worked collectively.

Indian communities practiced a rather strict division of labor according to gender, which in its details varied tremendously from culture to culture. Among foraging peoples, hunting was generally assigned to men, and the gathering of food and the maintenance of home-base camps were the responsibility of women. This pattern probably originated during the Archaic period. But the development of farming called these patterns into question. In Mexico, where communities became almost totally dependent on crops, both men and women worked in the fields. Where hunting remained important, the older division of labor remained, with women responsible for fieldwork.

In most North American Indian farming communities, women and men belonged to separate social groupings, each with its own rituals and lore. Membership in these societies was one of the most important elements of a person's identity. Marriage ties, on the other hand, were relatively weak, and in most Indian communities divorce was usually simple. The couple separated without a great deal of ceremony, the children almost always remaining with the mother. All Indian women controlled their own bodies, were free to determine the timing of reproduction, and were free to use secret herbs to prevent pregnancy, induce abortion, or ease the pains of childbirth.

Farming communities were far more complex than foraging communities, but they were also less stable. Growing populations demanded increasingly large

Clans   Groups of allied families.

surpluses of food, and this need often led to social conflict and warfare. Moreover, farming systems were especially vulnerable to changes in climate, such as drought, as well as to crises of their own making, such as soil depletion or erosion.

FARMERS OF THE SOUTHWEST

Farming communities began to emerge in the arid Southwest during the first millennium B.C.E. Among the first to develop a settled farming way of life were the Mogollon people, who lived from around 250 B.C.E. to 1450 C.E. along what is today the southern Arizona–New Mexico border. Living along mountain ridges and near streams in permanent villages of ingenious pit houses well suited to the region's temperature extremes, these people used digging sticks to cultivate maize, beans, and squash. Some of the Mogollon pit structures may have been what Southwestern peoples today call *kivas,* which are used for community religious rituals.

From about 300 C.E. to 1500 the people of the Hohokam ("those who are gone," in the language of the modern tribes of the area) culture flourished in the region along the floodplain of the Salt and Gila rivers in southern Arizona. The Hohokams, who lived in agricultural villages, built and maintained the first irrigation system in America north of Mexico, channeling river water many miles to desert fields of maize, beans, squash, tobacco, and cotton. They made jewelry from shells and developed a process for etching shells with animal designs. They shared many traits with Mesoamerican civilization to the south, including platform mounds for religious ceremonies and large courts for ball playing.

THE ANASAZIS

The best-known farming culture of the Southwest is that of the Anasazis, which

In Chaco Canyon, in northern New Mexico, lie the ruins of Pueblo Bonito, built in the twelfth century C.E. during the golden age of the Anasazis, an agricultural people who created a complex urban civilization amid the arid landscape of the Colorado Plateau. Until the invention of the modern construction techniques, Pueblo Bonito held the record as the world's largest apartment house.
Photo by David Hiser.

developed around the first century C.E. several hundred miles to the north of the Hohokam communities in the Four Corners area, where today Arizona, New Mexico, Utah, and Colorado meet on the great plateau of the Colorado River. Around 750, possibly in response to population pressure and an increasingly dry climate, the Anasazis began a shift from pit-house villages to densely populated, multistoried apartment complexes that the Spanish invaders called *pueblos.* These clustered around central complexes with circular underground *kivas.* The Anasazis grew high-yield varieties of maize in terraced fields irrigated by canals flowing from mountain catchment basins. To supplement this vegetable diet, they hunted animals for their meat, using the bow and arrow that first appeared in the region about 500 C.E.

Anasazi culture extended over an area larger than California. The sites of more than 25,000 Anasazi communities are known in New Mexico alone. Only a few have been excavated, so there is much that archaeologists do not yet understand. The most prominent of the Anasazi centers was Pueblo Bonito in Chaco Canyon. Completed in the twelfth century, this complex of 650 interconnected rooms is a monument to the golden age of the Anasazis.

The Anasazis faced a major crisis in the thirteenth century. The arid climate became even dryer, and growing Anasazi populations had to redouble their efforts to improve food production, building increasingly complex irrigation canals, dams, and terraced fields. A devastating drought from 1276 to 1293 (precisely dated with the aid of tree-ring analysis) resulted in repeated crop failures and eventual famine. This was accompanied by the arrival of Athapascan migrants who for a thousand years or more had been moving south from subarctic regions. These people were the immediate ancestors of the Navajos and the Apaches, and judging by their descendants, they must have been fierce fighters. By the fourteenth and fifteenth centuries, the Athapascans were raiding Anasazi farming communities, taking food, goods, and possibly slaves. (Indeed, the name *Anasazi* means "the place where they fought us" in Athapascan.) Gradually the Anasazis abandoned the Four Corners area altogether. Their movements have not yet been fully traced, but most seem to have resettled in communities along the Rio Grande, joining with local residents to form the Pueblo people of modern times.

FARMERS OF THE EASTERN WOODLANDS

Archaeologists date the beginning of the farming culture of eastern North America, known as Woodland culture, from the first appearances of pottery in the region about 3,000 years ago. The Woodland culture was based on a sophisticated way of life that combined gathering and hunting with the cultivation of a few crops. Sunflowers provided seeds and cooking oil. The presence of pipes in archaeological digs indicates that these farmers grew tobacco, which had spread north from the Caribbean, where it was first domesticated.

Woodland people began cultivating maize during the first millennium C.E. but even before had begun to adopt an increasingly settled existence and a more complex social organization. Between 1700 and 700 B.C.E., the people of the Poverty Point culture in the lower Mississippi Valley erected a remarkable site consisting of a series of concentric semicircular earthen mounds, covering an area about a mile square. The people of the Adena culture occupied the Ohio River basin from present-day Indiana to Pennsylvania from before 1000 B.C.E. to about 250 C.E. They lived in permanent or semipermanent villages and built large burial mounds.

Between about 200 B.C.E and the fifth century C.E, the Hopewell people settled in the Mississippi-Ohio Valley. Hopewell communities were devoted to mortuary cults, in which the dead were honored through ceremony, display, and the construction of enormous and elaborate burial mounds. Hopewell chiefs mobilized an elaborate trade network that acquired obsidian from the Rocky Mountains, copper from the Great Lakes, mica from the Appalachians, and shells from the Gulf coast. Hopewell artisans converted these materials into goods that played an important role in Hopewell trade and were buried with their dead in Hopewell graves.

MISSISSIPPIAN SOCIETY

The Hopewell culture collapsed in the fifth century, perhaps as a result of shifting climate patterns. Local communities continued to practice their late Archaic subsistence strategies but abandoned the expensive cultural displays demanded by the Hopewell mortuary cult. Following the collapse of Hopewell, however, several important innovations were introduced in the East. The bow and arrow, developed on the Great Plains, appeared east of the Mississippi about the seventh century, greatly increasing the efficiency of hunting. Also between 450 and 800, maize farming spread widely in the East. Indian farmers had developed a new variety of maize called Northern Flint, with large cobs and plentiful kernels that matured in a short enough time to make it suitable for cultivation in temperate northern latitudes. A shift from digging sticks to flint hoes also took place about this time, further increasing the productive potential of maize farming.

It was on the basis of these innovations that the powerful new Mississippian culture arose in the seventh or eighth century. The Mississippians were master maize farmers who lived in permanent villages along the floodplain of the Mississippi River.

The creation of man and woman depicted on a pot (dated about C.E. 1000) from the ancient villages of the Mimbres River of southwestern New Mexico, the area of Mogollon culture. Mimbres pottery is renowned for its spirited artistry. Such artifacts were usually intended as grave goods, to honor the dead.

National Museum of the American Indian/Smithsonian Institution.

Human figures dance on this characteristic piece of red-on-buff pottery of the Hohokams (dated about 1000 C.E.). The Hohokams, located on the floodplain of the Gila River near present-day Phoenix, Arizona, were the first irrigation farmers of North America. The Pima and Tohono O'Odham people of Arizona may be descended from them.

Arizona State Museum, University of Arizona. Photo by Helga Teiwes.

Cahokia, the most important of these, was the urban heart of Mississippian America. Cahokia's dense urban center, with its monumental temple, its residential neighborhoods, and its surrounding farmlands was mirrored in many other regional centers, each with thousands of residents. There were cities on the Arkansas River near Spiro, Oklahoma; on the Black Warrior River at Moundville, Alabama; at Hiawassee Island on the Tennessee River; and along the Etowah and Okmulgee Rivers in Georgia. The Great Serpent Mound, the largest effigy earthwork in the world, was constructed by Mississippian peoples in southern Ohio.

These centers, linked by the vast river transportation system of the Mississippi and its many tributaries, became the earliest city-states north of Mexico, hierarchical chiefdoms that extended political control over the farmers of the surrounding countryside. With continued population growth, these cities engaged in vigorous and probably violent competition for the limited space along the rivers. It may have been the need for more orderly ways of allocating territories that stimulated the evolution of political hierarchies. The tasks of preventing local conflict, storing large food surpluses, and redistributing foodstuffs from farmers to artisans and elites required a leadership class with the power to command. Mound building and the use of tribute labor in the construction of other public works testified to the power of chiefs, who lived in sumptuous quarters atop the mounds.

Mississippian culture reached its height between the eleventh and thirteenth centuries C.E., the same period in which the Anasazis constructed their desert cities. Both groups adapted to their own environment the technology that was spreading northward from Mexico. Both developed impressive artistic traditions, and their feats of engineering reflect the beginnings of science and technology. They were complex societies characterized by urbanism, social stratification, craft specialization, and regional trade—except for the absence of a writing system, all the traits of European civilization.

THE POLITICS OF WARFARE AND VIOLENCE

Warfare among Indian peoples certainly predated the colonial era. Organized violence was probably rare among hunting bands, who could seldom manage more than a small raid against an enemy. Certain hunting peoples, though, such as the southward-moving Athapascans, must have engaged in systematic raiding of settled farming communities. Warfare was also common among farming confederacies fighting to gain additional lands for cultivation. The first Europeans to arrive in the southeastern part of the continent described highly organized combat among large tribal armies. The bow and arrow was a deadly weapon of war, and the practice of scalping seems to have originated among warring tribes, who believed one could capture a warrior's spirit by taking his scalp lock.

The archaeological remains of Cahokia reveal that during the thirteenth and fourteenth centuries the residents surrounded the central sections of their city with a heavy log stockade. There must have been a great deal of violent warfare with other nearby communities. Also during this period, numerous towns were formed throughout the river valleys of the Mississippi, each based on the domination of farming countrysides by metropolitan centers. Eventually conditions in the upper Mississippi Valley deteriorated so badly that Cahokia and many other sites were abandoned altogether, and as the cities collapsed, people relocated in smaller, decentralized communities. Among the peoples of the South, however, Mississippian patterns continued into the period of colonization.

CULTURAL REGIONS OF NORTH AMERICA ON THE EVE OF COLONIZATION

An appreciation of the ways human cultures adapted to geography and climate is fundamental to an understanding of American history, for just as regions shaped the development of Indian cultures in the centuries before the arrival of Europeans, so they continued to influence the character of American life in the centuries thereafter.

In order to understand the impact of regions on Indian cultures, anthropologists divide North America into several distinct "culture areas" within which groups shared a significant number of cultural traits: Arctic, Subarctic, Great Basin, Great Plains, California, Northwest, Plateau, Southwest, South, and Northeast.

THE POPULATION OF INDIAN AMERICA

In determining the precolonial population of the Americas, historical demographers consider a number of factors—the population densities that different technological and economic systems could support, the archaeological evidence, the very earliest European accounts, and the estimated impact of epidemic diseases. (For a discussion of epidemics among Indian peoples, see Chapter 2.) Although estimates vary, there is general agreement among historians that in the fifteenth century the population of America north of Mexico was between 7 and 10 million. Perhaps as many as 25 million people lived in the complex societies of Mesoamerica. Thus, at the time of their first contact with European explorers and settlers, the peoples of the Western Hemisphere numbered 60 to 70 million, about the same as Europe's population at the time.

The largest populations of the continent were in the Southwest, South, and Northeast. Since it was in these culture areas that European explorers, conquerors, and colonists first concentrated their efforts, they deserve more detailed examination.

THE SOUTHWEST

The single overwhelming fact of life in the Southwest is aridity. Summer rains average only ten to twenty inches annually, and on much of the dry desert cultivation is impossible. A number of rivers, however, flow out of the pine-covered

WHAT IMPORTANT differences were there between Indian societies in the Southwest, South, and Northeast on the eve of colonization?

The Great Serpent Mound in southern Ohio, the shape of an uncoiling snake more than 1,300 feet long, is the largest effigy earthwork in the world. Monumental public works like these suggest the high degree of social organization of the Mississippian people.

George Gerster/Comstock Images.

⭠ MAP EXPLORATION

To explore an interactive version of this map, go to **http://www.prenhall.com/faraghertlc/map1.3**

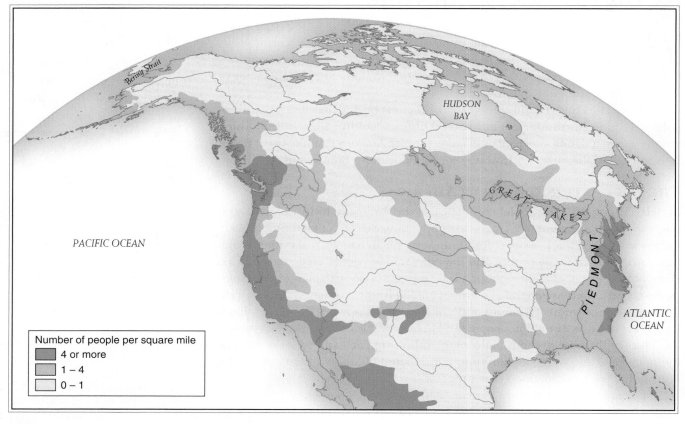

Number of people per square mile

▓	4 or more
▒	1 – 4
░	0 – 1

MAP 1-3

Indian Settlement Before European Colonization   Based on what is called the "carrying capacity" of different subsistence strategies—the population density they could support—historical demographers have mapped the hypothetical population density of Indian societies in the fifteenth century, before the era of European colonization. Populations were most dense in farming societies or in coastal areas with marine resources and least dense in extreme environments like the Great Basin.

WHY WERE some regions more populated than others?

mountain plateaus. Flowing south to the Gulf of Mexico or the Gulf of California, these narrow bands of green winding through parched browns and reds have made possible irrigation farming along their courses.

On the eve of European colonization, Indian farmers had been cultivating their Southwest fields for nearly 3,000 years. In the floodplain of the Gila and Salt rivers lived the Pimas and Tohono O'Odhams, descendants of the ancient Hohokams. Working small irrigated fields along the Colorado River, even on the floor of the Grand Canyon, were the Yuman peoples. In their oasis communities, desert farmers cultivated corn, beans, squash, sunflowers, and cotton, which they traded throughout the Southwest. Often described as individualists, desert farmers lived in dispersed settlements that the Spanish called *rancherias*, their dwellings separated by as much as a mile. That way, say the Pimas, people avoid getting on each other's nerves. Rancherias were governed by councils of adult men whose decisions required unanimous consent, although a headman was chosen to manage the irrigation works.

Rancherias   Dispersed settlements of Indian farmers in the Southwest.

East of the Grand Canyon lived the Pueblo peoples, named by the Spanish for their unique dwellings of stacked, interconnected apartments. Although speaking several languages, the Pueblos had a great deal in common, most notably their commitment to communal village life. A strict communal code of behavior that regulated personal conduct was enforced by a maze of matrilineal clans and secret religious societies; unique combinations of these clans and societies formed the governing systems of different Pueblo villages. Seasonal public ceremonies in the village squares included singing and chanting, dancing, colorful impersonations of the ancestral spirits called *kachinas*, and the comic antics of clowns who mocked in slapstick style those who did not conform to the communal ideal (pretending to drink urine or eat dirt, for example, in front of the home of a person who kept an unclean house).

The Pueblos inhabit the oldest continuously occupied towns in the United States. The village of Oraibi, Arizona, dates from the twelfth century, when the Hopis ("peaceful ones") founded it in the isolated central mesas of the Colorado Plateau. Using dry-farming methods and drought-resistant plants, these western Pueblo Indians produced rich harvests of corn and squash amid shifting sand dunes. On a mesa top about fifty miles southwest of present-day Albuquerque, New Mexico, Anasazi immigrants from Mesa Verde built Acoma, the "sky city," in the late thirteenth century. The Pueblo people established approximately seventy other villages during the next 200 years; fifty of these were still in existence in the seventeenth century when the Spanish founded Santa Fé, and two dozen survive today, including the large Indian towns of Laguna, Isleta, Santo Domingo, Jémez, San Felipe, and Taos.

The Athapascans, more recent immigrants, also lived in the arid deserts and mountains. They hunted and foraged, traded meat and medicinal herbs with farmers, and often raided and plundered these same villages and rancherias. Gradually, some of the Athapascan people adopted the farming and handicraft skills of their Pueblo neighbors; they became known as the Navajos. Others, more heavily influenced by the hunting and gathering traditions of the Great Basin and Great Plains, remained nomadic and became known as the Apaches.

THE SOUTH

The South enjoys a mild, moist climate with short winters and long summers, ideal for farming. From the Atlantic and Gulf coasts, a broad fertile plain extends inland to the Piedmont, a plateau separating the coastal plains from the Appalachian Mountains. The upper courses of the waterways originating in the Appalachian highlands offered ample rich bottom land for farming. The extensive forests, mostly of yellow pine, offered abundant animal resources. In the sixteenth century, large populations of Indian peoples farmed this rich land, fishing or hunting local fauna to supplement their diets. They lived in communities ranging from villages of twenty or so dwellings to large towns of a thousand or more inhabitants.

Mississippian cultural patterns continued among many of the peoples of the South. Along the waterways many farming towns were organized into chiefdoms. Because most of these groups were decimated by disease in the first years

 MAP EXPLORATION
To explore an interactive version of this map, go to
http://www.prenhall.com/faraghertlc/map1.4

MAP 1-4
Southwestern Indian Groups on the Eve of Colonization   The Southwest was populated by desert farmers like the Pimas, Tohono O'Odhams, Yumans, and Pueblos, as well as by nomadic hunters and raiders like the Apaches.

HOW DID the lack of rain shape the lives of the Indians of the Southwest?

Mesoamerican maize cultivation, as illustrated by an Aztec artist for the *Florentine Codex*, a book prepared a few years after the Spanish conquest. The peoples of Mesoamerica developed a greater variety of cultivated crops than those found in any other region in the world, and their agricultural productivity helped sustain one of the world's great civilizations.
American Museum of Natural History.

Kachinas   Impersonations of the ancestral spirits by Southwest Indians.

MAP EXPLORATION

To explore an interactive version of this map,
go to **http://www.prenhall.com/faraghertlc/map1.5**

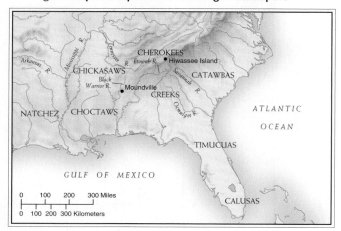

MAP 1-5

Southern Indian Groups on the Eve of Colonization   On the eve of colonization the Indian societies of the South shared many traits of the complex Mississippian farming culture.

WHAT FACTORS contributed to the growth of large Indian populations in the South?

QUICK REVIEW

The South

◆ Mild, moist climate.

◆ Indian peoples of the South farmed, fished, and hunted.

◆ Peoples of the South shared agricultural festivals.

of colonization, they are poorly documented. We know most about the Natchez, farmers of the rich floodplains of the lower Mississippi Delta, who survived into the eighteenth century before being destroyed in a war with the French. Overseeing the Natchez was a ruler known as the Great Sun, who lived in royal splendor on a ceremonial mound in the capital. Natchez was a class society. Noble families ruled the majority, whom they called the "stinkards." Persistent territorial conflict with other confederacies elevated warriors to an honored status among the Natchez. Public torture and human sacrifice of enemies were common.

These chiefdoms were rather unstable. Under the pressure of climate change, population growth, and warfare many were weakened and others collapsed. As a result thousands of people left behind the grand mounds and earthworks to migrate to the woodlands and hill country where they took up hunting and foraging, returning to the tried and true methods of forest efficiency. They formed communities and ethnic confederacies that were less centralized and more egalitarian than the Mississippian chiefdoms and would prove considerably more resilient to conquest.

Among the most prominent of these new ethnic groups were a people in present-day Mississippi and Alabama who came to be known as the Choctaws. Another group in western Tennessee became known as the Chickasaws, and another people in Georgia were known as the Creeks. On the mountain plateaus lived the Cherokees, the single largest confederacy, which included more than sixty towns. For these groups farming was somewhat less important, hunting somewhat more so. There were no ruling classes or kings, and leaders included women as well as men. Most peoples reckoned their descent matrilineally (back through generations of mothers), and after marriage husbands left the homes of their mothers to reside with the families of their wives. Women controlled household and village life and were influential in the matrilineal clans that linked communities together. Councils of elderly men governed the confederacies but were joined by clan matrons for annual meetings at the central council house.

The peoples of the South celebrated a common round of agricultural festivals that brought clans together from surrounding communities. At the harvest festival, for example, people thoroughly cleaned their homes and villages. They fasted and purified themselves by consuming the "black drink," which induced visions. They extinguished the old fires and lit new ones, then celebrated the new crop of sweet corn with dancing and other festivities. During the days that followed, villages, clans, and groups of men and women competed against one another in the ancient stick-and-ball game that the French named lacrosse; in the evenings men and women played chunkey, a gambling game.

THE NORTHEAST

The Northeast, the colder sector of the eastern woodlands, has a varied geography of coastal plains and mountain highlands, great rivers, lakes, and valleys. After 500 C.E. cultivation became the main support of the Indian economy in those places where the growing season was long enough to bring a crop of corn to maturity. In such areas of the Northeast, along the coasts and in the river valleys, Indian populations were large and dense.

The Iroquois of present-day Ontario and upstate New York have lived in the region for at least 4,500 years. They were among the first northeastern peoples to adopt cultivation. Iroquois women produced crops of corn, beans, squash, and sunflowers sufficient to support up to fifty longhouses, each occupied by a large matrilineal extended family. Some of those houses were truly long; archaeologists have excavated the foundations of some that extended 400 feet and would have housed dozens of families. Typically, these villages were surrounded by substantial wooden walls or palisades, clear evidence of intergroup conflict and warfare.

Population growth and the resulting intensification of farming in Iroquoia stimulated the development of chiefdoms there as elsewhere. By the fifteenth century several centers of population, each in a separate watershed, had coalesced from east to west across upstate New York. These were the five Iroquois chiefdoms or nations: the Mohawks, Oneidas, Onondagas, Cayugas, and Senecas. Iroquois oral histories collected during the nineteenth century recall this as a period of persistent violence, possibly the consequence of conflicts over territory.

Historians believe that the Iroquois founded a confederacy to control this violence. The confederacy outlawed warfare among the member nations and established regulated forms of gift exchange and payment to replace revenge. Iroquois oral history refers to the founder of the confederacy, Chief Deganawida the Lawgiver, as "blocking out the sun" as a demonstration of his powers, suggesting that these events might have taken place during a full solar eclipse, such as the one in the Northeast in 1451. Deganawida's message was proclaimed by his supporter, Hiawatha, a great orator, who convinced all the five Iroquois nations to join in confederacy. As a model of their government, the confederacy used the metaphor of the longhouse; each nation, it was said, occupied a separate hearth but acknowledged a common mother. The confederacy suppressed violence among its members but did not hesitate to encourage war against neighboring Iroquoian speakers, such as the Hurons or the Eries, who constructed defensive confederacies of their own at about the same time.

The other major language group of the Northeast was Algonquian, whose speakers belonged to at least fifty distinct cultures. The Algonquian peoples north of the Great Lakes and in northern New England were hunters and foragers, organized into bands with loose ethnic affiliations. Several of these peoples, including the Micmacs, Crees, Montagnais, and Ojibwas (also known as the Chippewas), were the first to become involved in the fur trade with European newcomers. Among the Algonquians of the Atlantic coast from present-day Massachusetts south to Virginia, as well as among those in the Ohio Valley, farming led to the development of settlements as densely populated as those of the Iroquois.

In contrast to the Iroquois, most Algonquian peoples were patrilineal. In general, they lived in less extensive dwellings and in smaller villages, often without palisade fortifications. Although Algonquian communities were relatively autonomous, they began to form confederacies during the fifteenth and sixteenth centuries. Among these groupings were those of the Massachusetts, Narragansetts, and Pequots of New England; the Delawares and the peoples of Powhatan's confederacy on the mid-Atlantic coast; and the Shawnees, Miamis, Kickapoos, and Potawatomis of the Ohio Valley.

MAP EXPLORATION

To explore an interactive version of this map, go to
http://www.prenhall.com/faraghertlc/map1.6

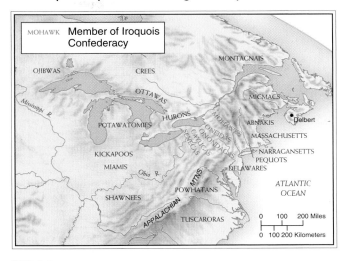

MAP 1-6

Northeastern Indian Groups on the Eve of Colonization   The Indians of the Northeast were mostly village peoples. In the fifteenth century five Iroquois groups—the Mohawks, Oneidas, Onondagas, Cayugas, and Senecas—joined together to form the Iroquois Five Nation Confederacy.

WHERE WERE the largest and most dense concentrations of Indians in the Northeast?

QUICK REVIEW

The Northeast

◆ Varied geography of plains, mountains, rivers, lakes, and valleys.

◆ The Iroquois have lived in the region for 4,500 years.

◆ Population growth and intensification of farming led to the development of chiefdoms.

CHRONOLOGY

30,000–15,000 B.C.E.	First humans in the Americas.	200 B.C.E.–400 C.E.	Hopewell culture flourishes.
13,000 B.C.E.	Global warming trend begins.	650	Bow and arrow, flint hoes, and Northern Flint corn in the Northeast.
10,000 B.C.E.	Clovis technology.		
9000 B.C.E.	Extinction of big-game animals.	775–1150	Hohokam site of Snaketown reaches its greatest extent.
8000 B.C.E.	Beginning of the Archaic period.		
7000 B.C.E.	First cultivation of plants in the Mexican highlands.	1000	Tobacco in use throughout North America.
5000 B.C.E.	Athapascan migrations to America begin.	1150	Founding of Hopi village of Oraibi, oldest continuously occupied town in the United States.
4000 B.C.E.	First settled communities along the Pacific coast.		
3000 B.C.E.	Inupiat and Aleut migrations begin.	1200	High point of Mississippian and Anasazi cultures.
1500–1000 B.C.E.	Maize and other Mexican crops introduced into the Southwest.	1276	Severe drought begins in the Southwest.
1000 B.C.E.	Beginning of Adena culture; First urban communities in Mexico.	1300	Arrival of Athapascans in the Southwest.
250 B.C.E.	Beginning of Mogollon culture in the Southwest.	1451	Founding of Iroquois Confederacy.

CONCLUSION

Over the thousands of years that elapsed between the settlement of North America and the invasion of Europeans at the end of the fifteenth century, Indian peoples developed hundreds of distinctive cultures that were fine-tuned to the geographic and climatic possibilities and limitations of their homelands. In the northern forests, they hunted game and perfected the art of processing furs and hides. Along the coasts and rivers they harvested the abundant runs of fish and learned to navigate the waters with sleek and graceful boats. In the arid Southwest, they mastered irrigation farming and made the deserts bloom, while in the humid Southeast, they mastered the large-scale production of crops that could sustain large cities with sophisticated political systems. North America was not a "virgin" continent, as so many of the Europeans believed. Indians had transformed the natural world, making it over into a human landscape.

"Columbus did not discover a new world," wrote historian J. H. Perry. "He established contact between two worlds, both already old." North America had a rich history, one that Europeans did not understand and later generations of Americans have too frequently ignored. The European colonists who came to settle encountered thousands of Indian communities with deep roots and vibrant traditions. In the confrontation that followed, Indian communities viewed the colonists as invaders and called upon their traditions and their gods to help them defend their homelands.

SUMMARY

Settling the Continent The origins of the American Indians, their migration to the Americas, and early cultural development are covered. Scientific research indicates that first Americans migrated from Asia over a land bridge to North America during the last ice age beginning approximately 30,000 years ago. Over time, new technology and methods of hunting were developed that spread throughout the continent.

New Ways of Living on the Land The warming of the climate contributed to the transformation of plant and animal life causing regional climate and cultural regions to develop in the Great Plains, the southwest, and east of the Mississippi River.

The Development of Farming The development of farming helped transform many Indian cultures, though some hunting groups resisted farming. Farming of maize originated in Mexico about 5,000 years ago and led to the development of large, complex urban communities. Farming stimulated increasing social complexity in terms of political organization, economic systems of production and distribution, and gender-related division of labor. Religious traditions arose to reflect means of securing food. In different regions, farming led to the creation of large, urban, socially stratified societies. Competition for land fostered conflict among Indian peoples.

Cultural Regions of North America on the Eve of Colonization Regional cultures influenced by regional environments had developed in North America on the eve of European colonization. The Indian population numbered in the millions by 1500.

REVIEW QUESTIONS

1. List the evidence for the hypothesis that the Americas were settled by migrants from Asia.

2. Discuss the impact of environmental change and human hunting on the big-game populations of North America.

3. Review the principal regions of the North American continent and the human adaptations that made social life possible in each of them.

4. Define the concept of "forest efficiency." How does it help to illuminate the major developments of the Archaic period?

5. Why did the development of farming lead to increasing social complexity? Discuss the reasons why organized political activity began in farming societies.

6. What were the hunting and agrarian traditions? In what ways did the religious beliefs of Indian peoples reflect their environmental adaptations?

7. What factors led to the organization of the Iroquois Confederacy?

KEY TERMS

Archaic period (p. 9)
Athapascan (p. 7)
Aztecs (p. 12)
Beringia (p. 6)
Cahokia (p. 4)
Clans (p. 13)

Clovis tradition (p. 7)
Kachinas (p. 19)
Mesoamerica (p. 12)
Pleistocene overkill (p. 9)
Rancherias (p. 18)
Transoceanic migrations (p. 5)

RECOMMENDED READING

Tom D. Dillehay, *The Settling of the Americas: A New Prehistory* (2000). A summary of the most recent archaeological findings, suggesting a much earlier migration to the Americas. For the newest discoveries, see the recent issues and websites of *National Geographic* and *Scientific American.*

Roger C. Echo-Hawk and Walter R. Echo-Hawk, *Battlefields and Burial Grounds: The Indian Struggle to Protect Ancestral Graves in the United States* (1994). A passionate discussion by a Pawnee lawyer and historian of the double standard that allows Indian graves to be ransacked while white graves are held sacred.

Thomas E. Emerson, *Cahokia and the Archaeology of Power* (1997). The fascinating story of North America's first metropolis.

Patricia Galloway, *Choctaw Genesis, 1500–1700* (1995). A path-breaking work that uses both archaeological and written evidence to tie together the precolonial and colonial periods of a tribal people of the South.

Alvin M. Josephy Jr., ed., *America in 1492* (1992). Important essays by leading scholars of the North American Indian experience. Includes beautiful illustrations and maps as well as an excellent bibliography.

Alice B. Kehoe, *North American Indians: A Comprehensive Account* (1992). The best general anthropological survey of the history and culture of the Indians of North America. Organized by culture areas, it covers all the peoples of the continent.

Stephen Plog, *Ancient Peoples of the American Southwest* (1998). Covers the shift to agriculture with a focus on both the costs and the benefits. An accessible text with wonderful photographs.

Robert Silverberg, *Mound Builders of Ancient America: The Archaeology of a Myth* (1968). A history of opinion and theory about the mound builders.

William C. Sturtevant, general ed., *Handbook of North American Indians,* 20 vols. proposed (1978–). The most comprehensive collection of the best current scholarship. The completed series will include a volume for each of the culture regions of North America; volumes on origins, Indian–white relations, languages, and art; a biographical dictionary; and a general index.

David Hurst Thomas, *Skull Wars: Kennewick Man, Archaeology, and the Battle for Native American Identity* (2000). A readable account of the controversy over Kennewick Man and the changing ideas about ancient North American history. When scholars, bureaucrats, and Indians go to court over these issues, he argues, everyone loses.

Russell Thornton, *American Indian Holocaust and Survival: A Population History since 1492* (1987). The best introduction to the historical demography of North America. Provides a judicious review of all the evidence in a field of considerable controversy.

Our lord and king it is true that the strange people have come to the shores of the great sea . . .
—Miguel Leon-Portilla

The meeting of Cortes and Montezuma at Tenochtitlan, 8 November 1519.

The Granger collection, New York.

2

WHEN WORLDS COLLIDE

1492–1590

HOW DID social change in Europe contribute to European expansion overseas?

WHAT FACTORS contributed to the defeat of the Aztecs and Incas by European forces?

WHAT IMPORTANT differences were there among Spanish, English, and French patterns of colonization?

AMERICAN COMMUNITIES

The English and the Algonquians at Roanoke

It was late August 1590 when English ships sailed through Hatteras Inlet into Pamlico Sound, off the coast of present-day North Carolina, and made their way north through rough seas to Roanoke Island, where Governor John White had left the first English community in North America three years before. Anxiously, White went ashore in search of the 115 colonists—mostly single men, but also twenty families, including his own daughter, son-in-law, and granddaughter Virginia Dare, the first English baby born in America. Finding the houses "taken down" and possessions "spoiled and scattered about," White suddenly noticed some writing on a tree trunk: "in fair capital letters was graven CROATOAN." Because this was the name of a friendly Indian village fifty miles south and because White found no sign of a cross, which he had instructed the colonists to leave if they were in trouble, he felt sure that his people awaited him at Croatoan, and he returned to his ship, anxious to speed to their rescue.

The Roanoke settlement had been sponsored by Walter Raleigh, a wealthy adventurer who sought profit and prestige by organizing an English colony to compete with the Spanish. When his men returned from a reconnoitering expedition to the area in 1584, they reported that the coastal region was densely populated by a "very handsome and goodly people." At an island the Indians called Roanoke, the English had been "entertained with all love and kindness" by a chief named Wingina. The leader of several surrounding villages, Wingina welcomed the English as potential allies in his struggle to extend his authority over still others. So when Raleigh's adventurers asked the chief's permission to establish a settlement on the island, he readily granted it, even sending two of his men back to England to assist in preparations for the enterprise. Manteo and Wanchese, the Indian emissaries, worked with Thomas Harriot, an Oxford scholar, and John White, an artist. The four men learned one another's language, and there seems to have been a good deal of mutual respect among them.

But when an all-male force of Englishmen returned in 1585 to establish the colony of Virginia (christened in honor of England's virgin queen, Elizabeth I), the two Indian emissaries offered Chief Wingina conflicting reports. Although Manteo, from the village of Croatoan, argued that their technology would make the English powerful allies, Wanchese described the disturbing inequalities of English society and warned of potential brutality. Wanchese was right to suspect English intentions, for Raleigh's plans were based not on respect for the Indians but on the expectation of exploiting them. He warned of their treachery. Indeed, Raleigh had directed the mission's commander to "proceed with extremity" should the Indians prove difficult and "bring them all in subjection to civility," meaning that they

should be made serfs to English colonial masters. Raleigh anticipated that his colony would return profits through the lucrative trade in furs, a flourishing plantation agriculture, or gold and silver mines. In any case, the Indians would supply the labor.

The English colony was incapable of supporting itself. After building a rough fort on the island, the colonists turned to Wingina for supplies. With the harvest in the storage pits, with fish running in the streams, and fat game in the woods, Wingina did the hospitable thing. But as fall turned to winter and the stores declined, constant English demands threatened the Indians' resources. Wingina's people were also stunned by the new diseases that came with the intruders. "The people began to die very fast, and many in [a] short space," Harriot wrote. The "disease was so strange that they neither knew what it was, nor how to cure it." In the spring Wingina and his people ran out of patience. But before the Indians could act, the English caught wind of the rising hostility, and in May 1586 they surprised the villagers, killing several of the leading men and beheading Wingina. With the plan of using Indian labor now clearly impossible, the colonists returned to England.

John White and Thomas Harriot, who had spent their time exploring the physical and human world of the coast and recording their findings in notes and sketches, were appalled by this turn of events. Back in England, Harriot insisted to Raleigh that the attack on the villagers came "upon causes that on our part might easily enough have been borne" and argued that "through discreet dealing" the Indians might "honor, obey, fear and love us." White proposed a new plan for a colony of real settlers, who might live in harmony with the Indians. Harriot and White clearly considered English civilization superior to Indian society, but their vision of colonization was considerably different from that of the plunderers.

In 1587, Raleigh arranged for John White to return to America as governor of a new civilian colony. The party was supposed to land on Chesapeake Bay, but their captain dumped them instead at Roanoke so he could get on with the profitable activity of plundering the Spanish. Thus, the colonists found themselves amid natives who were alienated by the bad treatment of the previous expedition. Within a month one of White's colonists had been shot full of arrows by attackers under the leadership of Wanchese, who after Wingina's death became the most millitant opponent of the English among the Roanoke Indians. White retaliated with a counterattack that increased the hostility of the Indians. The colonists begged White to return home in their only seaworthy ship and to press Raleigh for support. Reluctantly, White set sail but arrived just as a war began between England and Spain. Three anxious years passed before White was able to return to Roanoke, only to find the settlement destroyed and the colonists gone.

Roanoke

As White and his crew set their sights for Croatoan that August morning in 1590, a great storm blew up. White and the ship's captain agreed that they would have to leave the sound for deeper waters. It proved White's last glimpse of America. Tossed home on a stormy sea, he never returned. The English settlers of Roanoke became known as the Lost Colony, their disappearance and ultimate fate one of the enduring mysteries of colonial history.

The Roanoke experience is a reminder of the underlying assumptions of New World colonization. The English, writes the historian and geographer Carl Sauer, had "naked imperial objectives." It also suggests the wasted opportunity of the Indians' initial welcome. But in an unexpected way, the Roanoke story also

emphasizes the importance of community. There is evidence that the lost colonists lived out the rest of their lives with the Algonquians. In 1609 the English at Jamestown learned from local Indians that "some of our nation planted by Sir Walter Raleigh [are] yet alive," and many years later an English surveyor at Croatoan Island was greeted by natives who told him that "several of their Ancestors were white People," that "the English were forced to cohabit with them for Relief and Conversation, and that in the process of Time, they conformed themselves to the Manners of their Indian Relations." It may be that Virginia Dare and the other children married into Indian families, creating the first mixed community of English and Indians in North America.

The Expansion of Europe

Roanoke and other European colonial settlements of the sixteenth century came in the wake of Christopher Columbus's voyage of 1492. There may have been many unrecorded contacts between the peoples of America and the Old World before Columbus. Archaeological excavations at L'Anse aux Meadows on the fogbound Newfoundland coast provide evidence for a Norse landing in North America in the tenth or eleventh century. Norse sagas recounted the exploits of their pioneer heroes, yet they were forgotten within a century. But the contact with the Americas established by Columbus had earthshaking consequences. Within a generation of his voyage, continental exchanges of peoples, crops, animals, and germs had reshaped the Atlantic world. The key to understanding these remarkable events is the transformation of Europe during the several centuries preceding the world of Columbus.

EUROPEAN COMMUNITIES

Western Europe was an agricultural society, the majority of its people peasant farmers. Farming and livestock raising had been practiced in Europe for thousands of years, but great advances in farming technology took place during the late Middle Ages. Water mills, iron plows, improved devices for harnessing ox and horse power, and systems of crop rotation greatly increased productivity. Over several centuries farmers more than doubled the quantity of European land in cultivation.

Most Europeans were village people, living in family households. Men performed the basic field work; women were responsible for child care, livestock, and food preparation. In the European pattern, daughters usually left the home and village of their families to live among their husband's people. Women were furnished with dowries but generally excluded from inheritance. Divorce was almost unknown.

Europe was a world of social contrasts. Europe was characterized by a social system historians have called **feudalism**. The land was divided into hundreds of small territories, each ruled by a family of lords who claimed a disproportionate share of wealth and power. Feudal lords commanded labor service from peasants and tribute in the form of crops. They were the main beneficiaries of medieval economic expansion, accumulating great estates and building castles.

Most Europeans were Christians, united under the authority of the Roman Catholic Church, whose complex organization spanned thousands of local communities with a hierarchy that extended from parish priests all the way to the pope

HOW DID social change in Europe contribute to European expansion overseas?

IMAGE KEY
for pages 26–27

a. An illustration of a banana blossom.

b. The meeting of Cortex and Montexuma at Tenochitlan, 8 November 1519.

c. Pyramid of Kukulcan at Chichen Itza.

d. Peter Minuet purchases Manhattan island from the local Native Americans.

e. Aztec Indians, with smallpox contracted from the Spaniards, ministered to by a medicine man.

f. John White finding no trace of the colony of Roanoke on his return to Virginia in 1590.

Feudalism   A medieval European social system in which land was divided into hundreds of small holdings.

A French peasant labors in the field before a spectacular castle in a page taken from the illuminated manuscript *Tres Riches Heures*, made in the fifteenth century for the duc de Berry. In 1580 the essayist Montaigne talked with several American Indians at the French court who "noticed among us some men gorged to the full with things of every sort while their other halves were beggars at their doors, emaciated with hunger and poverty" and "found it strange that these poverty-striken halves should suffer such injustice, and that they did not take the others by the throat or set fire to their houses."

Art Resource, Musee Conde, Chantilly/Giraudon, Art Resource, NY

QUICK REVIEW

European Society

◆ European states were hierarchical.

◆ Most Europeans were peasant farmers.

◆ Most Europeans were Christians united under the authority of the Roman Catholic Church.

in Rome. At the core of Christian belief was a set of communal values: love of God the father, loving treatment of neighbors, and the fellowship of all believers. Yet the Catholic Church insisted on its dogmas and actively persecuted heretics, nonbelievers, and believers in older "pagan" religions, who were branded "witches." The church legitimized the power relationships of Europe and counseled the poor and downtrodden to place their hopes in heavenly rewards.

Europe was also home to numerous communities of Jews, who had fled from their homeland in Palestine after a series of unsuccessful revolts against Roman rule in the first century C.E. Both church and civic authorities subjected the Jews to discriminatory treatment. Restricted to ghettos and forbidden from owning land, many Jews turned adversity to advantage, becoming merchants who specialized in long-distance trade. But Jewish success only seemed to stimulate Christian hostility. Thus, in the thirteenth and fourteenth centuries the Jews were forced out of England, France, and Spain.

For the great majority of Europeans, living conditions were harsh. Most rural people survived on bread and porridge, supplemented with seasonal vegetables and an occasional piece of meat or fish. Infectious diseases abounded; perhaps a third of all children died before their fifth birthday, and only half the population reached adulthood. Famines periodically ravaged the countryside. A widespread epidemic of bubonic plague, known as the "Black Death," swept in from Asia and wiped out a third of Europe's population between 1347 and 1353. Disease led to famine and violence, as groups fought for shares of a shrinking economy.

THE MERCHANT CLASS AND THE NEW MONARCHIES

Strengthened by the technological breakthroughs of the late Middle Ages, the European economy proved it had a great capacity for recovery. During the fourteenth century disease and famine did not reappear in the same calamatous pattern, and there was an expansion of commerce, especially trade in basic goods, such as cereals and timber, minerals and salt, wine, fish, and wool. Commercial expansion stimulated the growth of markets and towns.

During this revival the monarchs of Western Europe emerged as the new centers of power, building legitimacy by promising internal order as they unified their realms. In the fifteenth century they began the construction of royal bureaucracies and standing armies and navies. In many cases, these new monarchs found support among the rising merchant class, which in return sought lucrative royal contracts and trading monopolies. The alliance between commercial interests and the new states was an important development that prepared the way for European expansion.

THE RENAISSANCE

The heart of this dynamic European commercialism lay in the city-states of Italy. During the late Middle Ages, the cities of Venice, Genoa, and Pisa launched armed commercial fleets that seized control of trade in the Mediterranean. Their merchants became the principal outfitters of the Crusades, a series of great military expeditions promoted by the Catholic Church to recover Palestine from the Muslims. The conquest of the Holy Land by Crusaders at the end of the eleventh century delivered the silk and spice trades of Asia into the hands of the Italian merchants. Asian civilization also supplied a number of technical innovations that further propelled European economic growth, including the compass, gunpowder, and the art of printing with movable type—"the three greatest inventions known to man," according to English philosopher Francis Bacon.

Contact with Muslim civilization provided Western scholars with access to important ancient Greek and Roman texts that had been lost to them during the Middle Ages but preserved in the great Muslim libraries. The revival of interest in classical antiquity sparked the period of intellectual and artistic flowering in Europe during the fourteenth, fifteenth, and sixteenth centuries known as the **Renaissance**. The revolution in publishing (made possible by the perfection of the printing press and movable type), the beginning of regular postal service, and the growth of universities helped spread this revival throughout the elite circles of Europe.

The Renaissance celebrated human possibility. This human-centered perspective was evident in many endeavors. The Gothic style of medieval cathedrals, whose soaring forms were intended to take human thoughts heavenward,

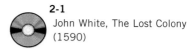

2-1
John White, The Lost Colony (1590)

1-10
Thomas Harriot, The Algonquian People of the Atlantic Coast (1588)

 MAP EXPLORATION
To explore an interactive version of this map,
go to **http://www.prenhall.com/faraghertlc/map2.1**

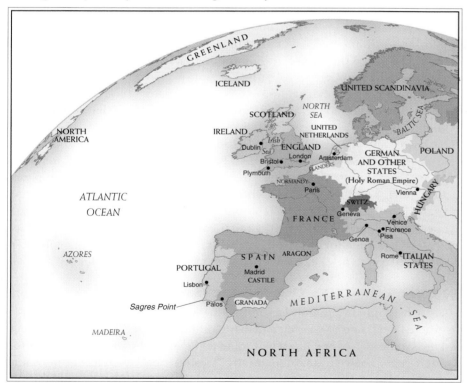

MAP 2-1
Western Europe in the Fifteenth Century   By the middle of the century, the monarchs of western Europe had unified their realms and begun to build royal bureaucracies and standing armies and navies. These states, all with extensive Atlantic coastlines, sponsored the voyages that inaugurated the era of European colonization.

WHY WERE some European states better positioned for colonizing than others?

Renaissance   The intellectual and artistic flowering in Europe during the fourteenth, fifteenth, and sixteenth centuries sparked by a revival of interest in classical antiquity.

gradually gave way to the use of measured classical styles, thought to encourage rational reflection. In painting and sculpture there was a new focus on the human body. Artists modeled muscles with light and shadow to produce heroic images of men and women. These were aspects of a movement that became known as "humanism," a revolt against religious authority in which the secular took precedence over the purely religious. This Renaissance outlook was a critical component of the spirit that motivated the exploration of the Americas.

PORTUGUESE EXPLORATIONS

Portugal, a narrow land along the western coast of the Iberian Peninsula with a long tradition of seafaring, became the first of the new Renaissance kingdoms to explore distant lands. Lisbon, the principal port on the sea route between the Mediterranean and northwestern Europe, was a bustling cosmopolitan city with large enclaves of Italian merchants. By 1385 local merchants had grown powerful enough to place their own favorite, João I, on the throne, and he had ambitious plans to establish a Portuguese trading empire.

A central figure in this development was the son of the king, Prince Henry, known to later generations as "the Navigator." In the spirit of Renaissance learning, Henry established an academy of eminent geographers, instrument makers, shipbuilders, and seamen at his institute on the southwestern tip of Portugal at Sagres Point. By the mid-fifteenth century, as a result of their efforts, all educated Europeans knew the world was a spherical globe. The idea that fifteenth-century Europeans believed the world to be "flat" is one of the many myths about Columbus's voyage. Studying the seafaring traditions of Asia and the Muslim world, the men of Sagres Point incorporated them into the design of a new ship called the caravel, faster and better handling than any ship previously known in Europe.

Using caravels, the Portuguese explored the Atlantic coast of northwestern Africa for direct access to the lucrative gold and slave trades of that continent. By the time of Prince Henry's death in 1460, they had colonized the Atlantic islands of the Azores and the Madeiras and founded bases along the western African "Gold Coast." In 1488 Portuguese captain Bartholomew Días rounded the southern tip of Africa, and ten years later Vasco da Gama, with the aid of Arab pilots, reached India. The Portuguese eventually erected strategic trading forts along the coasts of Africa, India, and China, the first and longest lasting outposts of European world colonization, and gained control of much of the Asian spice trade. Most important for the history of the Americas, the Portuguese established the Atlantic slave trade. (For a full discussion of slavery, see Chapter 4.)

COLUMBUS REACHES THE AMERICAS

In 1476, Christopher Columbus, a young Genoan sailor, joined his brother in Lisbon, where he became a seafaring merchant for Italian traders. Gradually he developed the simple idea of opening a new route to the Indies by sailing west across the Atlantic Ocean, known at that time as the "Western Sea." Such a venture would require royal backing, but when he approached the various monarchs of Europe with his idea, their advisers laughed at his geographic ignorance, pointing out that his calculation of the distance to Asia was much too short. They were right, Columbus was wrong. But it turned out to be an error of monumental good fortune.

Columbus finally sold the plan to the monarchs of Castile and Aragon, Isabel and Ferdinand. These two had just completed the ***Reconquista***, a centuries-long struggle between Catholics and Muslims that finally ended Muslim rule in Spain. Through these many generations of warfare, the Spanish had developed a military

---

QUICK REVIEW

Portuguese Explorations

◆ Prince Henry the Navigator played a key role in sponsoring exploration.

◆ Technological innovations made longer sea voyages possible.

◆ The Portuguese explored the Atlantic coast of Africa seeking direct access to gold and slaves.

1-2
Christopher Columbus, Letter to Ferdinand and Isabella of Spain (1494)

Reconquista   The long struggle (ending in 1492) during which Spanish Christians reconquered the Iberian peninsula from Muslim occupiers.

tradition that thrived on conquest and plunder. The Catholic monarchs of Spain were eager for new lands to conquer, and observing the successful Portuguese push to the south along the west coast of Africa, they became interested in opening lucrative trade routes of their own to the Indies. Columbus called his undertaking "the Enterprise of the Indies," suggesting his commercial intentions. But his mission was more than commercial. His expedition included men and supplies for founding a settlement, for one of his prime goals was to "occupy" the islands he found, establishing title for Spain by the right of occupancy. Like the adventurers who later established the first English colony at Roanoke, Columbus's objectives were starkly imperial.

Columbus's ships left the port of Palos, Spain, in August 1492, pushed west across the Atlantic by the prevailing trade winds. By October, flocks of birds and bits of driftwood announced the ships' approach to land. The first men to sight land were Luis Torres and Rodrigo de Triana. It turned out to be a small, flat island somewhere in the Bahamas, now thought by many to be Samana Cay. But Columbus believed he was in the Indies, somewhere near the Asian mainland.

He explored the northern island coasts of Cuba and Hispaniola before heading home, fortuitously catching the westerly winds that blow from the American coast toward Europe north of the tropics. One of Columbus's most important contributions was the discovery of the clockwise circulation of the Atlantic winds and currents that would carry thousands of European ships back and forth to the Americas.

Leading Columbus's triumphal procession to the royal court were half a dozen kidnapped Taino Indians from the Bahamas, dressed in bright feathers with ornaments of gold. The natives, Columbus noted, were "of a very acute intelligence," but had "no iron or steel weapons." A conflict between the Tainos and several armed Spaniards had ended quickly with the deaths of two natives. "Should your majesties command it," Columbus announced to Ferdinand and Isabel, "all the inhabitants could be made slaves." Moreover, he reported that "there are many spices and great mines of gold and of other metals." In fact, none of the spices

Christopher Columbus by Italian artist Sebastiano del Piombo. The explorer is dressed in the finery of a prosperous Italian Renaissance gentleman including a tricorn hat and sumptuous mantle. 1519, oil on canvas.

Ewing Galloway, Index Stock Imagery, Inc

This ship, thought to be similar to Columbus's *Niña*, is a caravel, a type of vessel developed by the naval experts at Henry the Navigator's institute at Sagres Point in Portugal. To the traditional square-rigged Mediterranean ship, they added the "lateen" sail of the Arabs, which permitted much greater maneuverability. Other Asian improvements, such as the stern-post rudder and multiple masting, allowed caravels to travel farther and faster than any earlier ships and made possible the invasion of America.

From *Illustrated History of Ships & Boats* by Lionel Casson, © 1964 by Lionel Casson. Used by permission of Doubleday, a division of Random House, Inc

This image accompanied Columbus's account of his voyage, which was published in Latin and reissued in many other languages and editions that circulated throughout Europe before 1500. The Spanish King Ferdinand is shown directing the voyage to a tropical island, where the natives flee in terror. Columbus's impression of Native Americans as a people vulnerable to conquest shows clearly in this image.

The Granger Collection

familiar to Europeans grew in the Caribbean and there were only small quantities of precious metal in the riverbeds of the islands. But the sight of the little gold ornaments worn by the Indians infected Columbus with gold fever. He left a small force behind in a rough fort on Hispaniola—the first European foothold in the Americas.

The monarchs, enthusiastic about Columbus's report, financed a convoy of seventeen ships and 1,500 men that left in late 1493 to begin the colonization of the islands. Like the later English colonists at Roanoke, Columbus expected that Indians would provide the labor. But at Hispaniola Columbus found his fort in ruins and his men killed by Indians who, like the Algonquians at Roanoke, had lost patience with continuing European demands. The Spanish destroyed the nearby native villages, enslaving the Tainos and demanding tribute in gold. Columbus sent boatloads of slaves back to Spain, but most soon sickened and died, and the supply of gold quickly ran out.

Columbus made two additional trips to the Caribbean, both characterized by the same violent raiding for slaves and obsessive searching for gold. He died in Spain in 1506, still convinced that he had opened the way to the Indies. This belief persisted among many Europeans well into the sixteenth century. But others had already begun to see the discoveries from a different perspective. Amerigo Vespucci of Florence, who voyaged to the Caribbean in 1499, was the first to describe Columbus's Indies as *Mundus Novus*, a "New World." When European geographers finally named this continent in the sixteenth century, they honored Vespucci's insight by calling it America.

THE SPANISH IN THE AMERICAS

Acentury after Columbus's death, before the English had planted a single successful New World colony of their own, the Spanish had created a huge and wealthy empire in the Americas. In theory, all law and policy for the empire came from Spain; in practice, the isolation of the settlements led to a good deal of local autonomy. The Spanish created a caste system, in which a small minority of settlers and their offspring controlled the lives and labor of millions of Indian and African workers. But it was also a society in which colonists, Indians, and Africans mixed to form a new people.

WHAT FACTORS contributed to the defeat of the Aztecs and Incas by European forces?

THE INVASION OF AMERICA

The first stages of the Spanish invasion of America included frightful violence. Armies marched across the Caribbean islands, plundering villages, slaughtering men, and capturing women. Columbus and his successors established an institution known as

 # MAP EXPLORATION

To explore an interactive version of this map, go to
http://www.prenhall.com/faraghertlc/map2.2

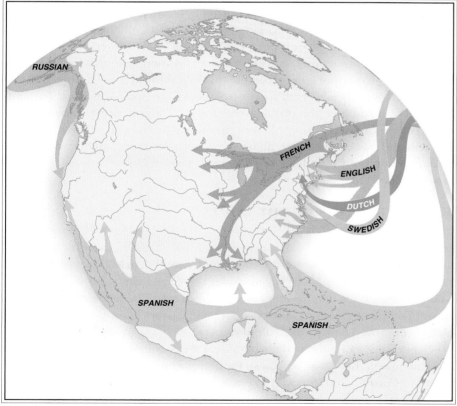

MAP 2-2

The Invasion of America   In the sixteenth century the Spanish first invaded the Caribbean and used it to stage their successive wars of conquest in North and South America. In the seventeenth century, the French, English, and Dutch invaded the Atlantic coast. The Russians, sailing across the northern Pacific, mounted the last of the colonial invasions in the eighteenth century.

WHAT IMPORTANT differences were there among the Spanish, French, and English approaches to conquest and settlement of the Americas?

the *encomienda*, in which Indians were compelled to labor in the service of Spanish lords. The relationship was supposed to be reciprocal, with lords protecting Indians in exchange for service, but in practice it amounted to slavery. Faced with labor shortages, slavers raided the Bahamas and soon had entirely depopulated them. The depletion of gold on Hispaniola led to the invasion of the islands of Puerto Rico and Jamaica in 1508, then Cuba in 1511. Meanwhile, rumors of wealthy societies to the west led to scores of probing expeditions. The Spanish invasion of Central America began in 1511, and two years later Vasco Núñez de Balboa crossed the Isthmus of Panama to the Pacific Ocean. In 1517 Spaniards landed on the coast of Mexico, and within a year they made contact with the Aztec empire.

The Aztecs had migrated to the highland valley of Mexico from the deserts of the American Southwest in the thirteenth century, in the wake of the collapse of the Toltec empire (see Chapter 1). The warlike Aztecs settled a marshy lake district and built the city of Tenochtitlán. By the early fifteenth century they dominated the peoples of the highlands, in the process building a powerful state. By 1519, the population of the Aztec capital numbered approximately 300,000, five times the size of the largest city in Spain.

Hernán Cortés, a veteran of the conquest of Cuba, landed on the Mexican coast with armed troops in 1519. Within two years he overthrew the Aztec empire, a spectacular military accomplishment that has no parallel in the annals of conquest. Cortés skillfully exploited the resentment of the many native peoples who lived under Aztec domination, forging Spanish–Indian alliances that became a model for the subsequent European colonization of the Americas. Here, as at Roanoke and dozens of other sites of European invasion, colonists found Indians eager for allies to support them in their conflicts with their neighbors. Still, the Aztecs were militarily powerful, successfully drove the Spaniards from Tenochtitlán, and put up a bitter and prolonged defense of their besieged capital. But in the meantime the Aztecs suffered a devastating smallpox epidemic that killed thousands and undermined their ability to resist. In the aftermath of conquest, the Spanish unmercifully plundered Aztec society, providing the Catholic monarchs with wealth beyond their wildest imagining.

THE DESTRUCTION OF THE INDIES

The Indian peoples of the Americas resisted Spanish conquest, but most proved a poor match for mounted warriors with steel swords and man-eating dogs. The record of the conquest, however, includes many brave Indian leaders and thousands of martyrs. The Carib people (from whom the Caribbean takes its name) successfully defended the outermost islands until the end of the sixteenth century, and in the arid lands of northern Mexico the nomadic tribes known collectively as the Chichimecs proved equally difficult to subdue.

Some Europeans protested the horrors of the conquest. Principal among them was Bartolomé de Las Casas, a Spanish Catholic priest who had participated in the plunder of Cuba in 1511, but who several years later suffered a crisis of conscience and began to denounce the Spanish conquerors. The Christian mission in the New World was to convert the Indians to Christianity, he argued, and "the means to effect this end are not to rob, to scandalize, to capture or destroy them, or to lay waste their lands." Long before the world recognized the concept of universal human rights, Las Casas was proclaiming that "the entire human race is one," which earned him a reputation as one of the towering moral figures in the early history of the Americas.

In his brilliant history of the conquest, *The Destruction of the Indies* (1552), Las Casas blamed the Spanish for cruelties that resulted in millions of Indian deaths—in effect, genocide. Translated into several languages and widely circulated through-

QUICK REVIEW

Cortés and the Aztecs

◆ Hernán Cortés arrived in Mexico in 1519.

◆ Cortés exploited resentment towards the Aztecs to overthrow their empire.

◆ Small pox outbreaks undermined the Aztecs' ability to resist the Spanish.

1-5
Bartolomé de Las Casas, "Of the Island of Hispaniola" (1542)

The Cruelties Used *by the Spaniards on the Indians*, from a 1699 English edition of *The Destruction of the Indies* by Bartolomé de Las Casas. These scenes were copied from a series of engravings produced by Theodore de Bry that accompanied an earlier edition.

British Library

out Europe, Las Casas's book was used by other European powers to condemn Spain, thereby covering up their own dismal colonial records—creating a "Black Legend" of Spanish colonization. Although later scholars disputed Las Casas's estimates of huge population losses, recent demographic studies suggest that the native people of Hispaniola numbered in the hundreds of thousands when Columbus arrived, and fifty years later they had been reduced to a few hundred. In Mexico, the 1519 population of 25 million plummeted to only a million a century later.

Las Casas was incorrect, however, in attributing most of these losses to warfare. To be sure, thousands of lives were lost in battle, but these deaths accounted for but a small proportion of the overall population decline. Thousands more starved because their economies were destroyed or their food stores taken by conquering armies. Even more important, native birthrates fell drastically after the conquest. Indian women were so "worn out with work," one Spaniard wrote, that they avoided conception, induced abortion, and even "killed their children with their own hands so that they shall not have to endure the same hardships."

Epidemic diseases—influenza, plague, smallpox, measles, typhus—were the primary cause of the drastic reduction of native populations. Indian peoples lacked the antibodies necessary to protect them from European germs and viruses. Smallpox first came from Spain in 1518, exploding in an epidemic so virulent that, in the words of an early Spanish historian, "it left Hispaniola, Puerto Rico, Jamaica, and Cuba desolated of Indians." The epidemic crossed into Mexico in 1520, destroying the Aztecs, then spread along the existing Indian trade network, in 1524 strategically weakening the Inca empire eight years before it was conquered by Spanish conquistador Francisco Pizarro. Spanish chroniclers wrote that this single epidemic killed half the Native Americans it touched. Disease was the secret weapon of the Spanish, and it helps explain their extraordinary success in the conquest.

Warfare, famine, lower birthrates, and epidemic disease knocked the population of Indian America into a downward spiral that did not swing upward until the beginning of the twentieth century. By that time the native population had fallen by 90 percent. It was the greatest demographic disaster in world history. The outstanding difference between the European colonial experience in the Americas and Africa or Asia was this radical reduction in the native population.

This drawing of victims of the smallpox epidemic that struck the Aztec capital of Tenochtitlán in 1520 is taken from the *Florentine Codex*, a postconquest history written and illustrated by Aztec scribes. "There came amongst us a great sickness, a general plague," reads the account, "killing vast numbers of people. It covered many all over with sores: on the face, on the head, on the chest, everywhere…. The sores were so terrible that the victims could not lie face down, nor on their backs, nor move from one side to the other. And when they tried to move even a little, they cried out in agony."

The Granger Collection

It is possible that the New World sent one disease, venereal syphilis, back across the Atlantic. The first recorded epidemic of syphilis in Europe took place in Spain in 1493, and many historians think it may have been carried home by the sailors on Columbus's ships. By 1495 the disease was spreading rapidly among Europe's armies, and by the sixteenth century it had found its way to Asia and Africa.

INTERCONTINENTAL EXCHANGE

The passage of diseases between the Old and New Worlds was one part of the large-scale continental exchange that marks the beginning of the modern era of world history. The most obvious exchange was the vast influx into Europe of the precious metals plundered from the Aztec and Incan empires of the New World. Most of the golden booty was melted down, destroying forever thousands of priceless Indian artifacts. Silver from mines the Spanish discovered and operated in Mexico and Peru tripled the amount of silver coin circulating in Europe between 1500 and 1550, then tripled it again before 1600. The result was runaway inflation, which stimulated commerce and raised profits but lowered the standard of living for most people.

But of even greater long-term importance were the New World crops brought to Europe. Maize (Indian corn) from Mexico, the staff of life for most North Americans, became a staple crop in Mediterranean countries, the dominant feed for livestock elsewhere in Europe, and the primary provision for the slave ships of Africa. Over the next few centuries, potatoes from Peru provided the margin between famine and subsistence for the peasant peoples of northern Europe and Ireland.

Although the Spanish failed to locate valuable spices such as black pepper or cloves in the New World, new tropical crops more than compensated. Tobacco was first introduced to Europe about 1550 as an antidote against disease but was soon in wide use as a stimulant. American vanilla and chocolate both became highly valued. American cotton proved superior to Asian varieties for the production of cheap textiles. Each of these native plants, along with tropical transplants from the Old World to the New—sugar, rice, and coffee were among the most important—supplied the basis for important new industries and markets that altered the course of world history.

Columbus introduced domesticated animals into Hispaniola and Cuba, and livestock were later transported to Mexico. The movement of Spanish settlement into northern Mexico was greatly aided by an advancing wave of livestock, for grazing animals seriously disrupted native fields and forests. Horses, used by Spanish stockmen to tend their cattle, also spread northward. In the seventeenth century they reached the Great Plains of North America, where they eventually transformed the lives of the nomadic hunting Indians (see Chapter 5).

THE FIRST EUROPEANS IN NORTH AMERICA

Ponce de León, governor of Puerto Rico, was the first conquistador to attempt to extend the Spanish conquest to North America. In 1513 he landed on the southern Atlantic coast, which he named in honor of the Easter season—*pascua florida*. Warriors from the powerful Indian chiefdoms there beat back Ponce de León's attempts to take slaves and finally suceeded in killing him in 1521. Seven years later another Spanish attempt to colonize Florida, under the command of Pánfilo de Narváez, also ended in disaster. Most of Narváez's men were lost in a shipwreck, but a small group of them survived, living and wandering for several years among the Indian peoples of the Gulf coast and the Southwest until they were finally rescued in 1536 by Spanish slave hunters in northern Mexico. One of these castaways, Alvar Núñez Cabeza de Vaca, published an account of his adventures in which he told of a North American empire known as Cíbola, with golden cities "larger than the city of Mexico."

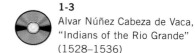

1-3
Alvar Núñez Cabeza de Vaca, "Indians of the Rio Grande" (1528–1536)

Cabeza de Vaca's report inspired two Spanish expeditions. The first attempt to penetrate the mystery of North America was mounted by Hernán de Soto, a veteran of the conquest of Peru. After landing in Florida in 1539 with a Cuban army of over 700 men, he pushed hundreds of miles through the heavily populated South, commandeering food and slaves from the Mississippian Indian towns in his path. But de Soto failed to locate another Aztec empire. In present-day Alabama, thousands of warriors besieged his army, and a few months later the ancestors of the modern Chickasaws chewed the Spaniards apart. His army depleted by half, de Soto desperately drove his men westward, crossing the Mississippi and marching deep into present-day Arkansas before returning to the banks of the great river, where he died in 1542. The native peoples of the South had successfully turned back Spanish invasion. But de Soto also introduced epidemic diseases that drastically depopulated and undermined the Mississippian chiefdoms of the South.

In the year of the de Soto expedition, 1539, Spanish officials in Mexico launched a second attempt to conquer North America, this one aimed at the Southwest. Francisco Vásquez de Coronado led 300 mounted men and infantry and 800 Indian porters north along well-marked Indian trading paths, passing through the settlements of Piman Indians near the present border of the United States and Mexico and finally reaching the Pueblo villages along the Rio Grande. The initial resistance of the Pueblo people was quickly quashed. But Coronado was deeply disappointed by these towns "of stone and mud, rudely fashioned" and sent out expeditions in all directions in search of the legendary golden cities of Cíbola. He led his army as far north as the Great Plains, where they observed great herds of "shaggy cows" (buffalo) and made contact with nomadic hunting peoples but returned without gold. For the next fifty years Spain lost all interest in the Southwest.

THE SPANISH NEW WORLD EMPIRE

By the late sixteenth century the Spanish had control of a powerful empire in the Americas. A century after Columbus, some 200,000 European immigrants, most of them Spaniards, had settled in the Americas. Another 125,000 Africans had been forcibly resettled as slaves on the Spanish plantations of the Caribbean, as well as on the Portuguese plantations of Brazil. (The Portuguese colonized Brazil under the terms of the **Treaty of Tordesillas**, a 1494 agreement dividing the Americas between Spain and Portugal. See Chapter 4.) Most of the Spanish settlers lived in the more than 200 urban communities founded during the conquest, including cities such as Santo Domingo in Hispaniola; Havana in Cuba; Mexico City, built atop the ruins of Tenochtitlán; and Quito and Lima in the conquered empire of the Incas.

Spanish women came to America as early as Columbus's second expedition, but over the course of the sixteenth century they made up only about 10 percent of the immigrants. Thus, from the beginning male colonists married or cohabited with Indian or African women. The result was the growth of large mixed-ancestry groups known respectively as *mestizos* and *mulattoes*. The Spanish established a frontier of inclusion, their communities characterized by a great deal of marriage and sexual mixing between male colonists and native women. Hundreds of thousands of Indians died, but Indian genes were passed on to generations of mixed ancestry people, who became the majority population in the mainland Spanish American empire.

Treaty of Tordesillas   Treaty negotiated by the pope in 1494 to resolve the territorial claims of Spain and Portugal.

MAP EXPLORATION

To explore an interactive version of this map, go to **http://www.prenhall.com/faraghertlc/map2.3**

MAP 2-3

European Exploration, 1492–1591 By the mid-sixteenth century Europeans had explored most of the Atlantic coast of North America and penetrated into the interior in the disastrous expeditions of de Soto and Coronado.

WHAT WERE the reasons behind the different experiences of the French, Spanish, and English explorations?

Populated by Indians, Africans, Spanish colonists, and their mixed offspring, the New World colonies of Spain made up one of the largest empires in the history of the world. The empire operated, in theory, as a highly centralized and bureaucratic system. But the Council of the Indies, composed of advisers of the Spanish king who made all the laws and regulations for the empire, was located in Spain. Thus, what looked in the abstract like a centrally administered empire tolerated a great deal of local decision making.

NORTHERN EXPLORATIONS AND ENCOUNTERS

1-4
Jacques Cartier: First Contact with the Indians (1534)

WHAT IMPORTANT differences were there among Spanish, English, and French patterns of colonization?

When the Spanish empire was at the height of its power in the sixteenth century, the merchants and monarchs of other European seafaring states looked across the Atlantic for opportunities of their own. France was first to sponsor expeditions to the New World in the early sixteenth century. At first the French attempted to plant settlements on the coasts of Brazil and Florida, but Spanish opposition ultimately persuaded them to concentrate on the North Atlantic. England did not develop its own plans to colonize North America until the second half of the sixteenth century.

FISH AND FURS

Long before France and England made attempts to found colonies, however, European fishermen were exploring the coastal North American waters of the North Atlantic. The Grand Banks, off the coast of Newfoundland, had abundant cod. It is possible that European fishermen were working those waters before Columbus's voyages. Certainly by 1500 hundreds of ships and thousands of sailors were sailing annually to the Grand Banks.

The first official voyages of exploration in the North Atlantic used the talents of experienced European sailors and fishermen. With a crew from Bristol, England, Genovese captain John Cabot reached Labrador in 1497, but the English did little to follow up on his voyage. In 1524, Tuscan captain Giovanni da Verrazano, sailing for the French, explored the North American coast from Cape Fear (North Carolina) to the Penobscot River (Maine). Encouraged by his report, the French king commissioned experienced captain Jacques Cartier to locate a "Northwest Passage" to the Indies. Although in his voyages of 1534, 1535, and 1541 Cartier failed to find a Northwest Passage, he reconnoitered the St. Lawrence River, which led deep into the continental interior to the Great Lakes, with easy access to the Ohio and Mississippi Rivers, giving France an incomparable geographic edge over other colonial powers. Cartier's attempts to plant settlements on the St. Lawrence failed, but he established France's imperial claim to the lands of Canada.

The French and other northern Europeans thus discovered the Indian people of the northern woodlands, and the Indians in turn discovered them. The contacts between Europeans and natives here took a different form than in the tropics, based on commerce rather than conquest. The Indians immediately appreciated the usefulness of textiles, glass, copper, and ironware. For his part, Cartier was interested in the fur coats of the Indians.

In his sketch of this "Capitaine" of the Illinois nation (drawn about 1700), the French artist Charles Becard de Granville carefully tinted the tattooing of the warrior's face and body, his distinctive costume and feather headdress, his spear and tobacco pipe.

Louis Nicolas, *Capitaine de La Nation*, from the "Codex Canadienses." From the collection of Gilcrease Museum, Tulsa, Oklahoma

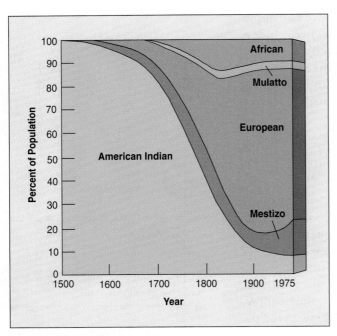

The African, Indian, and European Population of the Americas

In the 500 years since the European invasion of the Americas, the population has included varying proportions of Native American, European, and African peoples, as well as large numbers of persons of mixed ancestry.

Colin McEvedy and Richard Jones, *Atlas of the World Population History* (New York: Penguin, 1978), 280.

QUICK REVIEW

The Fur Trade

◆ Fur traders were critical to New France's success.

◆ Indians were active participants in the trade.

◆ In the early seventeenth century, the French made an effort to monopolize the trade.

Protestant Reformation   Martin Luther's challenge to the Catholic Church, initiated in 1517, calling for a return to what he understood to be the purer practices and beliefs of the early church.

Predestination   The belief that God decided at the moment of Creation which humans would achieve salvation.

Protestants   All European supporters of religious reform under Charles V's Holy Roman Empire.

Europeans, like Indians, used furs for winter clothing. But the growing population of the late Middle Ages had so depleted the wild game of Europe that the price of furs had risen beyond the reach of most people. The North American fur trade, thus, filled an important demand and produced high profits.

Beginning in the sixteenth century, the fur trade would continue to play an important role in the Atlantic economy for three centuries. By no means were Indians simply the victims of European traders. They had a sharp eye for quality, and cutthroat competition among traders provided them with the opportunity to hold out for what they considered good prices. But the fur trade was essentially an unequal exchange, with furs selling in Europe for ten or twenty times what Indians received for them. The trade also had negative consequences. European epidemic disease followed in the wake of the traders, and violent warfare broke out between tribes over access to hunting grounds. Moreover, as European manufactured goods, such as metal knives, kettles, and firearms, became essential to their way of life, Indians became dependent upon European suppliers. Ultimately, the fur trade was stacked in favor of Europeans.

By 1600, over a thousand European ships were trading for furs each year along the northern coast. The village of Tadoussac on the St. Lawrence, where a wide bay offered Europeans safe anchorage, became the customary place for several weeks of trading each summer, a forerunner of the western fur-trade rendezvous of the nineteenth century. Early in the seventeenth century the French would move to monopolize the trade there by planting colonies along the coast and on the St. Lawrence.

THE PROTESTANT REFORMATION AND THE FIRST FRENCH COLONIES

The first French colonies in North America, however, were planted farther south by a group of religious dissenters known as the Huguenots. The **Protestant Reformation**—the religious revolt against the Roman Catholic Church—had begun in 1517 when German priest Martin Luther publicized his differences with Rome. Luther declared that eternal salvation was a gift from God and not related to works or service to the Catholic Church. His protests—Protestantism—fit into a climate of widespread dissatisfaction with the power and prosperity of the Catholic Church. Luther attracted followers all over northwestern Europe, including France, where they were persecuted by Catholic authorities. Converted to Luther's teachings in 1533, Frenchman John Calvin fled to Switzerland, where he developed a radical theology. His doctrine of **predestination** declared that God had chosen a small number of men and women for "election," or salvation, while condemning the vast majority to eternal damnation. Calvinists were instructed to cultivate the virtues of thrift, industry, sobriety, and personal responsibility, which Calvin argued were signs of election and essential to the Christian life.

Calvin's followers in France—the Huguenots—were concentrated among merchants and the middle class but also included a portion of the nobility opposed to the central authority of the Catholic monarch. In 1560 the French monarchy defeated the attempt of a group of Huguenot nobles to seize power, which inaugurated nearly forty years of violent religious struggle. In an attempt to establish a religious refuge in the New World, Huguenot leaders were behind the first French attempts to establish colonies in North America. In 1562, Jean Ribault and 150 **Protestants** from Normandy landed on Parris Island, near present-day Beaufort, South Carolina, and began the construction of a fort and crude mud huts. Ribault soon returned to France for supplies, where he was caught up in the religious wars. The colonists nearly starved and were finally forced to resort to cannibalism before being rescued by a passing British ship. In 1564, Ribault established another Huguenot colony, Fort Caroline on the St. Johns River of Florida, south of present-day Jacksonville.

The Spanish were alarmed by these moves. They had shown no interest in colonizing Florida but worried about protecting their ships, riding home to Spain loaded with gold and silver on the offshore Gulf Stream. Not only was Fort Caroline manned by Frenchmen but also by Protestants—deadly enemies of the Catholic monarchs of Spain. "We are compelled to pass in front of their port," wrote one official, "and with the greatest ease they can sally out with their armadas to seek us." In 1565 the Spanish crown sent Don Pedro Menéndez de Avilés, captain general of the Indies, to crush the Huguenots. After establishing a settlement south of the French at a place called St. Augustine, he marched his men overland through the swamps to surprise the Huguenots from the rear. "I put Jean Ribault and all the rest of them to the knife," Menéndez wrote triumphantly to the king, "judging it to be necessary to the service of the Lord Our God and of Your Majesty." The Spanish built a fort and established a garrison at St. Augustine, which thus became the oldest continuously occupied European city in North America.

SIXTEENTH-CENTURY ENGLAND

 The Founding of St. Augustine, Florida, 1565

The English movement across the Atlantic, like the French, was tied to social change at home. Perhaps most important were changes in the economy. As the prices of goods rose steeply—the result of New World inflation—English landlords, their rents fixed by custom, sought ways to increase their incomes. Seeking profits in the woolen trade, many converted the common pasturage used by tenants into grazing land for sheep, dislocating large numbers of farmers. Between 1500 and 1650 a third of all the common lands in England were "enclosed" in this way. Deprived of their livelihoods, thousands of families left their traditional rural homes and sought employment in English cities, crowding the roads with homeless people.

Sixteenth-century England also became deeply involved in the struggles of the Reformation. At first, King Henry VIII of England (reigned 1509–1547) supported the Catholic Church and opposed the Protestants. But there was great public resentment in England over the vast properties owned by the Church and the loss of revenue to Rome. When the pope refused to grant Henry an annulment of his marriage to Catherine of Aragon, daughter of Ferdinand and Isabel of Spain, the king exploited this popular mood. Taking up the cause of reform in 1534, he declared himself head of a separate Church of England. He later took over the English estates of the Catholic Church—about a quarter of the country's land—and used their revenues to begin constructing a powerful English state system, including a standing army and navy. Working through Parliament, Henry carefully enlisted the support of the merchants and landed gentry for his program, parceling out a measure of royal prosperity in the form of titles, offices, lands, and commercial favors. By 1547, when Henry died, he had forged a solid alliance with the wealthy merchant class.

Henry was succeeded by his young and sickly son Edward VI, who soon died. Next in succession was Edward's half-sister Mary, who attempted to reverse her father's Reformation from the top by martyring hundreds of English Protestants, gaining herself the title of "Bloody Mary." But upon her death in 1558, her half-sister Elizabeth I (reigned 1558–1603) came to the throne. Elizabeth sought to end the religious turmoil by tolerating a variety of views within the English church. The Spanish monarch, head of the most powerful empire in the world, declared himself the defender of the Catholic faith and vowed to overthrow her.

Fearing Spanish subversion on the neighboring Catholic island of Ireland, Elizabeth urged enterprising supporters such as Walter Raleigh and his half-brother Humphrey Gilbert to subdue the Irish Catholics and settle homeless English families on their land. During the 1560s, Raleigh, Humphrey, and many other commanders invaded the island and viciously attacked the Irish, forcing them to retreat beyond a frontier line of English settlement along the coast. So ferociously did the Irish resist the conquest that an image of the "wild Irish" became fixed in the English mind. Gilbert retaliated with even greater brutality, decapitating captured Irish men and women and using their heads as paving stones, "so that none should come into his tent for any cause but commonly he must pass through a lane of heads." Such barbarism did not prevent the English from considering the Irish an inferior race, and the notion that civilized people could not mix with such "savages" was an assumption English colonists would carry with them to the Americas.

EARLY ENGLISH EFFORTS IN THE AMERICAS

England's first ventures in the New World were made against the backdrop of its conflict with Spain. In 1562 John Hawkins violated Spanish regulations by transporting a load of African slaves to the Caribbean, bringing back valuable tropical goods. Thus, the English began their participation in the slave trade. (For a full discussion see Chapter 4.) The Spanish attacked Hawkins on another of his voyages in 1567, an event English privateers such as Francis Drake used as an excuse for launching a series of devastating and lucrative raids against Spanish New World ports and fleets. The voyages of these English "Sea Dogs" greatly enriched their investors, including Elizabeth herself. The English, thus, began their American adventures by slaving and plundering.

A consensus soon developed among Elizabeth's closest advisers that the time had come to enter the competition for America. In a state paper written for the queen, Richard Hakluyt summarized the advantages that would come from colonies: They could provide bases from which to raid the Spanish in the Caribbean, outposts for an Indian market for English goods, and plantations for growing tropical products, freeing the nation from a reliance on the long-distance trade with Asia. Moreover, by populating them with the "multitudes of loiterers and idle vagabonds" of England, colonies offered a solution to the problem of social dislocation and homelessness. He urged Elizabeth to establish such colonies "upon the mouths of the great navigable rivers" from Florida to the St. Lawrence.

Although Elizabeth declined to commit the state to Hakluyt's plan, she authorized and invested in several private attempts at exploration and colonization. In the late 1570s, Martin Frobisher conducted three voyages of exploration in the North Atlantic. Fresh from the Irish wars, Raleigh and Gilbert planned the first true colonizing ventures. In 1583 Gilbert sailed with a flotilla of ships from Plymouth and landed at St. John's Bay, Newfoundland. He encountered fishermen from several other nations but nevertheless claimed the territory for his queen. But Gilbert's ship was lost on the return voyage.

Following his brother's death, Raleigh decided to establish a colony southward, in the more hospitable climate of the mid-Atlantic coast. Although the Roanoke enterprise of 1584–87 seemed far more promising than Gilbert's, it too eventually failed (as described in the opening of the chapter). The greatest legacy of the expedition was the work of Thomas Harriot and John White, who mapped the area, surveyed its

The care that John White brought to his painting is evident in this watercolor of an Algonquian mother and daughter (1585). The woman's fringed deerskin skirt is edged with white beads, and the decoration on her face and upper arms seems to be tattooed. The little wooden doll in this girl's hand was a gift from White. All the Indian girls, wrote Thomas Harriot, "are greatly delighted with puppets and babes which were brought out of England."

John White (1570–1593), "Woman and Child of Pomeiooc." Watercolor. British Museum, London. The Bridgeman Art Library International Ltd

---

CHRONOLOGY

1000	Norse settlement at L'Anse aux Meadows.
1347–1353	Black Death in Europe.
1381	English Peasants' Revolt.
1488	Bartolomeu Días sails around the African continent.
1492	Christopher Columbus first arrives in the Caribbean.
1494	Treaty of Tordesillas.
1497	John Cabot explores Newfoundland.
1500	High point of the Renaissance.
1508	Spanish invade Puerto Rico.
1513	Juan Ponce de León lands in Florida.
1514	Bartolomé de Las Casas begins preaching against the conquest.
1516	Smallpox introduced to the New World.
1517	Martin Luther breaks with the Roman Catholic Church.
1519	Hernán Cortés lands in Mexico.
1534	Jacques Cartier first explores the St. Lawrence River.
1539–1540	Hernán de Soto and Francisco Vásquez de Coronado expeditions.
1550	Tobacco introduced to Europe.
1552	Bartolomé de Las Casas's *Destruction of the Indies* published.
1558	Elizabeth I of England begins her reign.
1562	Huguenot colony planted along the mid-Atlantic coast.
1565	St. Augustine founded.
1572	St. Bartholomew's Day Massacre in France.
1583	Humphrey Gilbert attempts to plant a colony in Newfoundland.
1584–1587	Walter Raleigh's colony on Roanoke Island.
1588	English defeat the Spanish Armada.
1590	John White returns to find Roanoke colony abandoned.

---

commercial potential, and studied the Indian residents. Harriot's *A Briefe and True Report of the Newfound Land of Virginia* (1588), illustrated by engravings of White's watercolors, provided the single most accurate description of North American Indians at the moment of their contact with Europeans.

King Philip II of Spain was outraged at the English incursions into territory reserved by the pope for Catholics. He had authorized the destruction of the French colony in Florida, and now he committed himself to smashing England. In 1588 he sent a fleet of 130 ships carrying 30,000 men to invade the British Isles. Countered by captains such as Drake and Hawkins, who commanded smaller and more maneuverable ships, and frustrated by an ill-timed storm that the English chose to interpret as an act of divine intervention, the Spanish Armada foundered. The Spanish monopoly of the New World had been broken in the English Channel.

CONCLUSION

The Spanish opened the era of European colonization in the Americas with Columbus's voyage in 1492. The consequences for the Indian peoples of the Americas were disastrous. The Spanish succeeded in constructing the world's most powerful empire on the backs of Indian and African labor. Inspired by the Spanish success, the French and the English attempted to colonize the coast of North America. By the end of the sixteenth century, however, they had not succeeded in establishing any lasting colonial communities. Instead, a very different kind of colonial encounter, based on commerce rather than conquest, was taking place in northeastern North America. In the next century the French would turn this development to their advantage. Along the mid-Atlantic coast in Virginia, however, the English would put their Irish experience to use, pioneering an altogether new kind of American colonialism.

SUMMARY

The Expansion of Europe The political, economic, social, and cultural transformation of Europe, including technological advances, paved the way for European expansion overseas. Voyages of exploration aimed at reaching Asia first by moving south and east and later going west across the Atlantic. The European mastery of the seas set the stage for American colonization.

The Spanish in the Americas In the sixteenth century, the Spanish constructed an empire in the Americas that stretched from Florida and the Southwest of present-day United States down through most of Central and South America. Their success was aided by a variety of political, military, technological, and natural factors. A consequence of this meeting of two worlds was the intercontinental exchange of people, animals, plants, disease, and cultures.

Northern Explorations and Encounters Following the Spanish success in the Americas, other European nations launched exploration and colonization efforts with mixed results. Religious turmoil in Europe as well as social and political changes influenced these early efforts that soon afterwards generated more substantial and successful colonization endeavors.

REVIEW QUESTIONS

1. Discuss the roles played by the rising merchant class, the new monarchies, Renaissance humanism, and the Reformation in the development of European colonialism.

2. Define a "frontier of inclusion." In what ways does this description apply to the Spanish empire in the Americas?

3. Make a list of the major exchanges that took place between the Old World and the New World in the centuries following the European invasion of America. Discuss some of the effects these exchanges had on the course of modern history.

4. In what ways did colonial contact in the Northeast differ from contacts in the Caribbean and Mexico?

5. In what ways might the English experience in Ireland have shaped expectations about American colonization?

KEY TERMS

Feudalism (p. 29)
Predestination (p. 42)
Protestant Reformation (p. 42)
Protestants (p. 42)

Reconquista (p. 32)
Renaissance (p. 31)
Treaty of Tordesillas (p. 39)

RECOMMENDED READING

David Noble Cook, *Born to Die: Disease and New World Conquest, 1492–1650* (1998). A synthetic history of the impact of disease, including Indian and European views.

Cyclone Covey, trans. and ed., *Cabeza de Vaca's Adventures in the Unknown Interior of America* (1983). The captivity narrative that lured the Spanish into North America. An eye-opening story of the peoples and places of the pre-conquest Southwest.

Alfred W. Crosby Jr., *The Columbian Exchange: Biological and Cultural Consequences of 1492* (1972). Pathbreaking account of the intersection of the biospheres of the Old and New Worlds.

Richard Flint, *Great Cruelties Have Been Reported: The 1544 Investigation of the Coronado Expedition* (2001). Testimony regarding the treatment of Indians and subsequent human rights debates in Spain.

Charles Gibson, *Spain in America* (1966). Still the best introductory history of Spain's American empire.

Lewis Hanke, *The Spanish Struggle for Justice in the Conquest of America* (1949; reprint, 1965). The classic account of Las Casas's attempts to rectify the wrongs committed by the Spanish against the Indians.

Charles M. Hudson, *Knights of Spain, Warriors of the Sun: Hernando de Soto and the South's Ancient Chiefdoms* (1997). A very readable history of the de Soto expedition, told from the viewpoint of the Indians.

Miguel Leon-Portilla, *The Broken Spears: The Aztec Account of the Conquest of Mexico* (1962; expanded ed., 1992). The history of the Spanish conquest as told by the Aztecs, drawn from manuscripts dating as early as 1528, only seven years after the fall of Tenochtitlán.

Samuel Eliot Morison, *The European Discovery of America: The Northern Voyages,* A.D. *500–1600* (1971) and *The Southern Voyages,* A.D. *1492–1616* (1974). The most detailed treatment of all the important European explorations of the Americas.

David Beers Quinn, *Set Fair for Roanoke: Voyages and Colonies, 1584–1606* (1985). The story of Roanoke—the Indian village, the English settlement, and the Lost Colony.

Kirkpatrick Sale, *The Conquest of Paradise: Christopher Columbus and the Columbian Legacy* (1990). A harsh view of Columbus, but important information on the world of the Caribbean and the disastrous effects of the encounter with Europeans.

Carl Ortwin Sauer, *Sixteenth Century North America: The Land and the People as Seen by the Europeans* (1971). An excellent source for the explorations of the continent, providing abundant descriptions of the Indians.

Hugh Thomas, *Conquest: Montezuma, Cortés, and the Fall of Old Mexico* (1993). A fascinating account, written by a master of historical style that incorporates the Aztec view as well as the words of the conquerors.

Gustavo Verdesio, *Forgotten Conquests: Rereading New World History from the Margins* (2001). An argument that the old master historical narrative represents only one of many possible histories, and a suggestion for finding the colonial subjects who did not produce documents.

These seventeen ships . . . made a long, a troublesome, and costly voyage . . . with contrary winds after they set sail, and so scattered with mist and tempests that few of them arrived together . . .

—Thomas Dudley, March 28, 1631

New Amsterdam, 17th century. City Hall and Great Dock in the late 17th century.

Matoaks als Rebecka daughter to the mighty Prince Powhatan Emperour of Attanoughkomouck als Virginia converted and baptized in the Christian faith and Wife to the Wor.ll Mr Tho. Rolff.

3

PLANTING COLONIES IN NORTH AMERICA
1588–1701

HOW DID conditions in New Spain and New France differ from Virginia and New England?

HOW DID tobacco change the nature of English colonization in Virginia?

WHAT WERE the social and political values of Puritanism?

WHAT ROLE did the crown play in the founding of English colonies after 1660?

WHAT LED to violent conflict between Indians and colonists?

AMERICAN COMMUNITIES

Communities Struggle with Diversity in Seventeenth-Century Santa Fé

IT WAS A HOT AUGUST DAY IN 1680 WHEN THE FRANTIC MESSENGERS rode into the small mission outpost of El Paso with the news that the Pueblo Indians to the north had risen in revolt. The corpses of more than 400 colonists lay bleeding in the dust. Two thousand Spanish survivors huddled inside the Palace of Governors in Santa Fé, surrounded by 3,000 angry warriors. The Pueblo leaders had sent two crosses into the palace—white for surrender, red for death. Which would the Spaniards choose?

Spanish colonists had been in New Mexico for nearly a century. Franciscan priests came first, followed by a military expedition from Mexico in search of precious metals. In 1609, high in the picturesque foothills of the Sangre de Cristo Mountains, the colonial authorities founded La Villa Real de la Santa Fé de San Francisco—"the royal town of the holy faith of St. Francis"—soon known simply as Santa Fé. Colonization efforts included the conversion of the Pueblo Indians to Christianity, making them subjects of the king of Spain, and forcing them to work for the colonial elite who lived in the town.

In the face of overwhelming Spanish power, the Pueblos adopted a flexible attitude. Twenty thousand of them converted to Christianity, but most of these thought of the new religion as simply an appendage to their complex culture. The Christian God was but a minor addition to their numerous deities; church holidays were included in their own religious calendar and celebrated with native dances and rituals.

Most anthropologists agree that the Pueblos were a spirited people. Many of their public dances included erotic displays and sometimes ended in spectacles of mock public intercourse, symbolizing the powerful force that brought the separate worlds of men and women together, and also created community. The celibacy of the Franciscan priests not only astounded the Pueblos but horrified them, for it marked the priests as only half-persons. The Pueblos also found the Franciscan practice of subjecting themselves to prolonged fasts and tortures, such as self-flagellation, inexplicable. "You Christians are crazy," one Pueblo chief told a priest. "You go through the streets in groups, flagellating yourselves, and it is not well that the people of this pueblo should be encouraged to commit such madness."

The missionaries, outraged by what they considered Pueblo sacrileges, invaded underground kivas, destroyed sacred Indian artifacts, publicly humiliated holy men, and compelled whole villages to perform penance by working in irrigation ditches and fields. Such violations of the deepest traditions of Pueblo community life eventually led to the revolt of 1680. In New Mexico, sev-

Santa Fé

eral years before, the Spanish governor had executed three Pueblo religious leaders and publicly whipped dozens more for secretly practicing their religion. One of those leaders, Popé of San Juan Pueblo, vowed to overthrow the regime. During the next several years he carefully organized a conspiracy among more than twenty Indian towns.

Popé's job was not difficult, for there were plenty of local grievances. The Hopis of northern Arizona, for example, still tell of a missionary who capped his ever-escalating demands on them with the order that all the young women of the village be brought to live with him. When the revolt began, the Hopis surrounded the missionary's house. "I have come to kill you," the chief announced. "You can't kill me," the priest cried from behind his locked door. "I will come [back] to life and wipe out your whole tribe." But the chief shouted back, "my gods have more power than you have." He and his men broke down the door, hung the missionary from the beams, and lit a fire beneath his feet.

When the Indians demanded the surrender of the Spanish inside Santa Fé's Palace of Governors, the besieged colonists sent back the red cross, signaling defiance. But after a siege lasting five days, the Pueblos agreed to allow most of them to flee south to El Paso, "the poor women and children on foot and unshod," in the words of one Spaniard's account, and "of such a hue that they looked like dead people." The Indians then ransacked the missions and churches, desecrating the holy furnishings with human excrement and leaving the mutilated bodies of priests lying on their altars. They transformed the governor's chapel into a traditional kiva, his palace into a communal dwelling. On the elegant inlaid stone floors where the governor had held court, Pueblo women now ground their corn.

Santa Fé became the capital of a Pueblo confederacy led by Popé. He forced Christian Indians to the river to scrub away the taint of baptism. Then he ordered the destruction of everything Spanish. But this the Pueblos could not do. The colonists had introduced horses and sheep, fruit trees and wheat, new tools and new crafts, all of which the Indians found useful. Moreover, the Pueblos sorely missed the support of the Spanish in their struggle against their traditional enemies, the nomadic Navajos and Apaches. Equipped with stolen horses and weapons, these nomadic peoples had become considerably more dangerous, and their raids on the unprotected Pueblo villages became much more destructive after the colonists fled. With chaos mounting, Popé was deposed in 1690, and many of the

Indians found themselves thinking the unthinkable: if only the Spanish would come back!

Come back they did, beginning in 1692, and after six years of fighting they succeeded in reestablishing Spanish authority. But both sides had learned a lesson, and over the next generation the colonists and the Indians reached an implicit understanding. Pueblos dutifully observed Catholicism in the missionary chapels, while missionaries tolerated the practice of traditional religion in the Indians' underground kivas. Royal officials guaranteed the inviolability of Indian lands, and Pueblos pledged loyalty to the Spanish monarch. Pueblos turned out for service on colonial lands, and colonists abandoned the system of forced labor. Together the Spanish and the Pueblos held off the nomadic tribes for the next 150 years. Colonist and Indian communities remained autonomous, but they learned to live with one another.

SPAIN AND ITS COMPETITORS IN NORTH AMERICA

At the beginning of the seventeenth century the Spanish controlled the only colonial outposts on the mainland, a series of forts along the Florida coast to protect the Gulf Stream sea lanes used by the convoys carrying wealth from their New World colonies to Spain. During the first two decades of the new century, however, the Spanish, French, Dutch, and English were all drawn into planting far more substantial colonies in North America.

In New Spain and New France there was a good deal of cultural and sexual mixing between colonists and natives. These areas became frontiers of inclusion, where native peoples were part of colonial society. The Dutch at first followed the French model when they established their colony on the Hudson River. But soon they changed course, fearing the great success of the English, who from the beginning adopted a different model of colonization, in which settlers and Indians lived in separate societies. The "frontiers of exclusion" in Virginia, New England, and New Netherlands offered a dramatic contrast to the situation in New Spain and New France.

NEW MEXICO

After the 1539 expedition of Francisco Vásquez de Coronado failed to turn up vast Indian empires to conquer in the northern Mexican deserts, the Spanish interest in the Southwest faded. The densely settled farming communities of the Pueblos did offer a harvest of converts for Christianity, however, and by the 1580s Franciscan missionaries were at work in the Southwest. Soon rumors drifted back to Mexico City of rich mines along the Rio Grande, raising the hopes of Spanish officials that they might find another Aztec empire. In 1598, Juan de Oñate, the son of a wealthy mining family of New Spain, financed a colonizing expedition made up of Indian and mestizo soldiers with the purpose of mining both gold and souls.

Moving north into the upper Rio Grande Valley, Oñate encountered varying degrees of resistance. He lay siege at Acoma, set high atop a great outcropping of desert rock. Indian warriors killed dozens of Spaniards with their arrows, and women and children bombarded them with stones. But in the end, the attackers succeeded in climbing the rock walls and laying waste to the town, killing 800 men, women, and children. All surviving warriors had one of their feet severed, and more than 500 people were enslaved. In 1606 Spanish authorities in Mexico recalled Oñate, not for his violence, but for his failure to locate the fabled gold mines.

HOW DID conditions in New Spain and New France differ from Virginia and New England?

IMAGE KEY

for pages 48–49

a. Several sugarcane stems. Sugar was an important New World crop.

b. A map of New Netherland showing a view of New Amsterdam (New York).

c. Beavers were a plentiful source of clothing and income for their pelts.

d. Matoaka, or Pocahontas (c. 1595–1617), the daughter of Native American Chief Powhatan, after her conversion to Christianity and marriage to settler John Rolfe under the new name Rebecca.

e. A tattered historical beaver hat from 1620.

f. New Amsterdam traders bargaining with each other.

g. An illustration of a tobacco plant.

h. John Winthrop (1588–1649), governor of the Massachusetts Bay Colony.

i. Ships sail into the port of New Amsterdam (New York).

j. Colonists square off against Indians in a detail of a 17th century map of new England.

MAP EXPLORATION

To explore an interactive version of this map, go to
http://www.prenhall.com/faraghertlc/map3.1

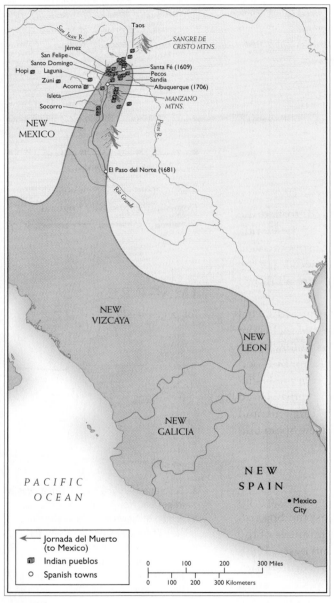

MAP 3-1

New Mexico in the Seventeenth Century   By the end of the seventeenth century, New Mexico contained 3,000 colonial settlers in several towns, surrounded by an estimated 50,000 Pueblo Indians living in some fifty farming villages. The isolation and sense of danger among the Hispanic settlers are evident in their name for the road linking the colony with New Spain, *Jornada del Muerto*, "the Road of Death."

WHAT ROLE did church officials play in the government of New Mexico?

2-2

Samuel de Champlain's Battle
With the Iroquois, July 1609

The Spanish empire was based on the use of Indian labor to produce valuable commodities—precious metals, tobacco, or sugar. Without mines to exploit, interest in New Mexico waned. But the Church convinced the Spanish monarchy to subsidize New Mexico as a special missionary colony. In 1609, a new governor founded the capital of Santa Fé, and from this base the Franciscan missionaries penetrated all the surrounding Indian villages. The Pueblos who most resisted Christianity—the Acomas, the Zunis, and the isolated Hopis—retained their old customs, including their way of tracing kinship through the maternal line. But many other communities were dramatically affected by contact with Spanish culture and adopted the Spanish pattern of reckoning descent through both the father's and mother's ancestors.

The colonial economy of New Mexico, based on small-scale agriculture and sheep raising, was never very prosperous. Indians labored for both colonists and priests. Population growth was almost entirely the result of marriages between colonial men and Indian women. By the late seventeenth century this northernmost outpost of the far-flung Spanish empire in America contained some 3,000 mestizos (of mixed Indian and European ancestry) in a few towns along the Rio Grande, surrounded by an estimated 50,000 Pueblos in some fifty villages. New Mexico was a "frontier of inclusion."

NEW FRANCE

In the early seventeenth century the French devised a strategy to monopolize the northern fur trade. In 1605 Samuel de Champlain, acting as the agent of a royal monopoly, helped establish the outpost of Port Royal on the Bay of Fundy. It proved impossible, however, to control the coastal trade from that location. In 1608 he founded the settlement of Quebec on the St. Lawrence River at a site where he could intercept the traffic in furs to the Atlantic. He forged an alliance with the Huron Indians, who controlled access to the rich fur grounds of the Great Lakes, and in 1609 and 1610 joined them in making war on their traditional enemies, the Five Nation Iroquois Confederacy. Champlain sent agents and traders to live among native peoples, where they learned native languages and customs, and directed the flow of furs to Quebec.

The St. Lawrence was like a great roadway leading directly into the heart of the continent, and it provided the French with enormous geographic and political advantage. But the river froze during the winter, isolating the colonists, and the short growing season limited agricultural productivity in the region. Many Frenchmen went to Canada and Acadia as *engagés* ("hired men") in the fur trade or the fishery, as craftsmen or as farmers, but nine out of ten of them returned to France. Huguenot dissenters would have been willing colonists, but French authorities refused to let them emigrate, declaring that New France would be an exclusively Catholic colony. It was the most serious mistake France made, for by closing Canada to Huguenot refugees they

MAP EXPLORATION

To explore an interactive version of this map, go to
http://www.prenhall.com/faraghertlc/map3.2

MAP 3-2

New France in the Seventeenth Century   By the late seventeenth century, French settlements were spread from the town of Port Royal in Acadia to the post and mission at Sault Ste. Marie on the Great Lakes. But the heart of New France comprised the communities stretching along the St. Lawrence River between the towns of Quebec and Montreal.

HOW DID French settlements differ from their English counterparts?

destroyed their only hope for mass emigration. As a result the population of Acadia on the Bay of Fundy and Canada on the St. Lawrence grew slowly in the seventeenth century, reaching a total of only about 15,000 by 1700. Quebec City, the administrative capital, was small by Spanish colonial standards, and Montreal, founded in 1642 as a missionary and trading center, remained little more than a frontier outpost. Small clusters of riverbank farmers known as *habitants* lived on the lands of *seigneurs,* or landlords. By using Indian farming techniques, habitants were able to produce subsistence crops, and eventually they developed a modest export economy.

The communities of Canada looked west toward the continental interior rather than toward the Atlantic. It was typical for the sons of habitants to take to the woods in their youth, working as independent traders or as ***coureurs de bois***, paid agents of the fur companies. Most eventually returned to take up farming, but others remained in Indian villages, where they married Indian women and raised families. Such French traders were living on the Great Lakes as early as the 1620s, and from the late 1660s to the 1680s the French established outposts at each of the strategic points on the lakes. By the 1670s, French fur traders and missionaries were exploring the reaches of the upper Mississippi River. In 1681–82, fur-trade commandant Robert Sieur de La Salle navigated the mighty river to its mouth on the Gulf of Mexico and claimed its entire watershed for France.

 3-3
Early French Explorations of the Mississippi River (1673)

Coureurs de bois   French for "woods runner," an independent fur trader in New France.

This illustration, taken from Samuel de Champlain's 1613 account of the founding of New France, depicts him joining the Huron attack on the Iroquois in 1609. The French and their Huron allies controlled access to the great fur grounds of the West. The Iroquois then formed an alliance of their own with the Dutch, who had founded a trading colony on the Hudson River. The palm trees in the background of this drawing suggest that it was not executed by an eyewitness but rather but an illustrator more familiar with South American scenes.

Samuel de Champlain, Les Voyages . . ., Paris, 1613. Illus. opp. p. 322. Early battle wih the Iroquois. Rare Books Div., the N.Y. Public Library, Astor, Lenox, and Tilden Foundations.

2-8
A Jesuit Priest Describes
New Amsterdam (1642)

QUICK REVIEW

New Netherlands

◆ United Province of the Netherlands played a key role in sixteenth-century Europe's economy.

◆ The Dutch established trading outposts throughout the Americas.

◆ Dutch expansion led by the Dutch East India Company and the Dutch West India Company.

Beaver Wars   Series of bloody conflicts, occurring between 1640s and 1680s, during which the Iroquois fought the French for control of the fur trade in the east and the Great Lakes region.

NEW NETHERLAND

The United Provinces of the Netherlands, commonly known as Holland, was only a fraction of the size of France, but it was the center of Europe's economic transformation in the sixteenth century. On land reclaimed from the sea by an elaborate system of dikes, Dutch farmers used new methods of crop rotation and deep tilling that dramatically increased their yields, producing large surpluses that supported the growth of the world's most urban and commercial nation. After a century of rule by the Hapsburgs, the prosperous Dutch rose up against their Spanish masters and in 1581 suceeded in establishing their political independence. Amsterdam became the site of the world's first stock exchange and investment banks. Dutch investors built the largest commercial fleet in Europe and captured the lucrative Baltic and North Sea trade in fish, lumber, iron, and grain. It was said that the North Sea was Holland's "America."

Soon the Dutch were establishing trading outposts in America itself. Early in the seventeenth century the United Netherlands organized two great monopolies, the Dutch East India Company and the Dutch West India Company, combining naval military might and commercial strength in campaigns to seize the maritime trade of Asia and the Atlantic. Backed by powerfully armed men-of-war ships, during the first half of the seventeenth century Dutch traders built a series of trading posts in China, Indonesia, India, Africa, Brazil, the Caribbean, and North America, and Holland became the greatest commercial power in the world. The Dutch first appeared in North America in 1609 with the explorations of Henry Hudson, and within a few years they had founded settlements on the Hudson River at Fort Orange (today's Albany) and at New Amsterdam, on Manhattan Island, at the river's mouth. Seeking to match French success, they negotiated a commercial alliance with the Iroquois Confederacy to obtain furs. Access to superior Dutch products, including metal tools and firearms, greatly increased the power of the Iroquois, who embarked on a series of military expeditions against their neighbors, known as the **Beaver Wars**, which made them the strategic middlemen of the Dutch. In the late 1640s, the Iroquois attacked and dispersed the Hurons, who had long controlled the flow of furs from the Great Lakes to their allies the French. The Dutch also succeeded in overwhelming a small colony of Swedes on the lower Delaware River, incorporating that region into their sphere of influence in the 1640s.

ENGLAND IN THE CHESAPEAKE

England first attempted to plant colonies in North America during the 1580s, in Newfoundland and at Roanoke Island in present-day North Carolina (see Chapter 2). Both attempts were failures. England's war with Spain (1588 to 1604) suspended further efforts, but thereafter the English once again turned to the Americas.

HOW DID tobacco change the nature of English colonization in Virginia?

JAMESTOWN AND THE POWHATAN CONFEDERACY

Early in his reign, King James I (reigned 1603–25) issued royal charters for the colonization of the mid-Atlantic region, known as Virginia, to English joint-stock companies, which raised capital by selling shares. In 1607, a London group of investors known as the **Virginia Company** sent ships to Chesapeake Bay, where a hundred men built a fort they named Jamestown in honor of the king. It was destined to become the first permanent English settlement in North America.

Virginia Company A group of London investors who sent ships to Chesapeake Bay in 1607.

The Chesapeake was already home to an estimated 24,000 Algonquian people. The English colonists were immediately confronted by Powhatan, the powerful *werowance* (leader) of a confederacy of Algonquian tribes. Powhatan had mixed feelings about the English. The Spanish had already attempted to plant a base nearby, bringing conflict and disease to the region. But he looked forward to valuable trade with the English, as well as their support for his struggle to extend his confederacy over outlying tribes.

The English saw themselves as conquistadors, and like the first Roanoke colonists, they proved unable to support themselves. Hating the idea of physical labor, they survived the first year only with Powhatan's material assistance. Jamestown grew so dependent on Algonquian stores that Captain John Smith and his men plundered food from surrounding tribes. In retaliation, Powhatan decided to starve the colonists out. He now realized that the English had come "not for trade, but to invade my people and possess my country." During the terrible winter of 1609–10 hundreds of colonists starved and a number resorted to cannibalism. Of the 500 colonists at Jamestown in the fall, only 60 remained alive by the spring.

Determined to prevail, the Virginia Company sent out a large additional force of men, women, and livestock, committing themselves to a protracted war against the Indians. The grim fighting persisted until 1613, when the English captured Powhatan's favorite daughter, teenaged Pocahontas. Worn down by war and disease, and eager to see his child again, Powhatan accepted a treaty of peace in 1614. Pocahontas adopted English ways and married John Rolfe, one of the leading settlers. But she fell sick and died on a visit to England in 1617. Crushed by the news, Powhatan abdicated in favor of his brother Opechancanough before dying of despair.

TOBACCO, EXPANSION, AND WARFARE

Tobacco provided the Virginia colonists with the "merchantable commodity" for which Thomas Harriot, the scientist who accompanied the Roanoke expedition, had searched (see Chapter 2).

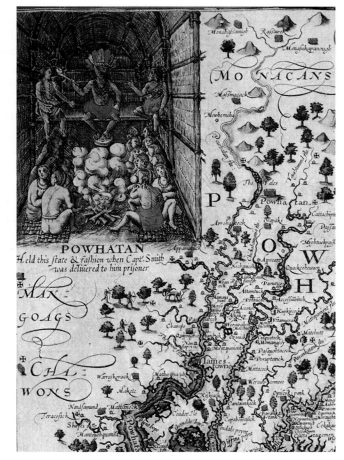

This illustration is a detail of John Smith's map of Virginia. It includes the names of many Indian villages, suggesting how densely settled the Indian population was on the coast of Chesapeake Bay. For the inset of Powhatan and his court in the upper left, the engraver borrowed images from John White's drawings of the Indians of the Roanoke area.

Princeton University Library. Manuscripts Division. Department of Rare Books and Special Collections. Princeton University Library

This illustration from John Smith's memoirs (1624), was engraved by the artist Robert Vaughn. Seizing Chief Opechancanough, Powhatan's brother, by the scalplock, Smith attempts to obtain needed supplies from the Indians. Opechancanough later succeeded Powhatan and ruled the Chesapeake Algonquian Confederacy for a quarter century.

Library of Congress

QUICK REVIEW

Powhatan, Indian Leader

- Leader of a confederacy of Algonquian tribes.
- Besieged Jamestown when colonists began stealing corn.
- Instructed in English manners and religion by John Rolf.
- Father of Pocahontas.

2-9
George Alsop, The Importance of Tobacco (1660)

House of Burgesses The legislature of colonial Virginia. First organized in 1619, it was the first institution of representative government in the English colonies.

Indentured Servants Individuals who contracted to serve a master for a period of four to seven years in return for payment of the servant's passage to America.

Tobacco had been introduced to the English by Francis Drake in the 1580s, and by the 1610s the smoking craze created strong demand for the product. Pocahontas's husband John Rolfe developed a mild hybrid variety with considerable appeal, and soon the first commercial shipments of cured Virginia leaf reached England. Tobacco provided the Virginia Company with the first returns on its investment. Its cultivation quickly exhausted the soil, however, creating pressures for further expansion into Indian territory.

The settlers pressed the Indians for additional lands. Outraged, Opechancanough prepared the Chesapeake Algonquians for a final assault. He encouraged a cultural revival under the guidance of the shaman Nemattanew, who instructed his followers to reject the English and their ways but to learn the use of firearms. This was the first of many Indian resistance movements led jointly by strong political and religious figures. The uprising, which began on Good Friday, March 22, 1622, completely surprised the English. Nearly a third of the settlers, 347 people, were killed, yet the colony managed to hang on. The attack stretched into a ten-year war of attrition in which both sides committed horrors.

The Indians finally sued for peace in 1632, but in the meantime the war had bankrupted the Virginia Company. In 1624 the king converted Virginia into a royal colony with civil authorities appointed by the crown, although the colony's **House of Burgesses**, created in 1619, continued to include representatives of Virginia's boroughs. Although disease, famine, and warfare took a heavy toll, continual emigration from England allowed the colonial population to double every five years from 1625 to 1640, by which time it numbered approximately 10,000. Meanwhile, decimated by violence and disease, the Algonquians shrank to about the same number.

Numerical strength soon shifted in favor of the English. In 1644 Opechancanough organized a final desperate revolt in which more than 500 colonists were killed. But the next year the Virginians crushed the Algonquians, capturing and executing their leader. A formal treaty granted the Indians a number of small reserved territories. By 1670 the Indian population had fallen to just 2,000, overwhelmed by the 40,000 English colonists.

INDENTURED SERVANTS

At least three-quarters of the English migrants to the Chesapeake came as **indentured servants**. In exchange for the cost of their transportation to the New World, men and women contracted to labor for a master for a fixed term. Most indentured servants were young, unskilled males, who served for two to seven years; but some were skilled craftsmen, women, or even children (the latter were expected to serve a master until they reached the age of twenty-one).

African slaves were first introduced to the Chesapeake in 1619, but slaves were more expensive than servants, and as late as 1680 they made up less than 7 percent of the Chesapeake population. In the hard-driving economy of the Chesapeake, however, masters treated servants as cruelly as they treated slaves. After arriving, bound laborers were inspected by planters who poked muscles, peered into open mouths, and pinched women. Approximately two out of five servants died during indenture. Those who survived were eligible for "freedom dues"—clothing, tools, a gun, or a spinning wheel, help getting started on their own—and many former servants headed west in the hope of cutting a farm from the wilderness. But most former servants who were able to raise the price of passage returned home to England.

COMMUNITY LIFE IN THE CHESAPEAKE

Because most emigrants were men, whether free or indentured, free unmarried women often married as soon as they arrived in the Chesapeake. Moreover, in the disease-ridden environment of the early Chesapeake, English men seemed to suffer a higher rate of mortality than women, and widows remarried quickly, sometimes within days. Their scarcity provided women with certain advantages. Shrewd widows bargained for a remarriage agreement that gave them a larger share of the estate than those set by common law upon the death of their husband. So notable was the concentration of wealth in the hands of these widows that one historian has suggested that early Virginia was a "matriarchy." But because of high mortality rates, family size was smaller and kinship bonds—one of the most important components of community—were weaker than in England.

Visitors from England often remarked on the crude conditions of community life. Prosperous planters, investing everything in tobacco production, lived in rough wooden dwellings. On the western edge of the settlements, freed servants lived with their families in shacks, huts, or even caves. Colonists spread across the countryside in search of new tobacco lands, creating dispersed settlements and few towns. Before 1650 there were few community institutions such as schools and churches. Meanwhile, the Spanish in the Caribbean and Mexico were building communities that would grow into great cities with permanent institutions.

In contrast to the colonists of New France, who were developing a distinctive American identity because of their commercial connections with Native Americans, the population of the Chesapeake maintained close emotional ties to England. Colonial politics were shaped less by local developments than by a continuing relationship with the mother country.

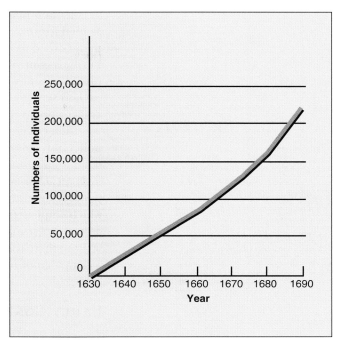

Population Growth of the British Colonies in the Seventeenth Century
The British colonial population grew steadily through the century, then increased sharply in the closing decade as a result of the new settlements of the Restoration colonies.

THE NEW ENGLAND COLONIES

Both in climate and in geography, the northern coast of North America was far different from the Chesapeake. "Merchantable commodities" such as tobacco could not be produced there, and thus it was far less favored for investment and settlement. Instead, the region became a haven for Protestant dissenters from England, who gave the colonies of the north a distinctive character.

THE SOCIAL AND POLITICAL VALUES OF PURITANISM

Most English men and women continued to practice a Christianity little different from traditional Catholicism. But the English followers of John Calvin, known as **Puritans** because they wished to purify and reform the English church from within, grew increasingly influential during the last years of Elizabeth's reign at the end of the sixteenth century. The Calvinist emphasis on enterprise meant that Puritanism appealed to merchants, entrepreneurs, and commercial farmers, those most responsible for the rapid economic and social transformation of England. But the Puritans were also the most vocal critics of the disruptive effects of that change, condemning the decline of the traditional rural community and the growing number

WHAT WERE the social and political values of Puritanism?

Puritans Individuals who believed that Queen Elizabeth's reforms of the Church of England had not gone far enough in improving the church. Puritans led the settlement of Massachusetts Bay Colony.

QUICK REVIEW

The Pilgrims

◆ Puritanism appealed to merchants, entrepreneurs, and commerical farmers.

◆ Puritans wanted reform of the Church of England.

◆ Pilgrims were separatists who believed the Church of England could not be reformed.

of "idle and masterlessmen" produced by the enclosure of common lands. They argued for reviving communities by placing reformed Christian congregations at their core to monitor the behavior of individuals. By the early seventeenth century Puritans controlled many congregations and had become an influential force at the universities in Oxford and Cambridge, training centers for the future political and religious leaders of England. (For a review of the Protestant Reformation and the enclosure movement in England, see Chapter 2.)

King James I, who assumed the throne after Elizabeth's death, abandoned her policy of religious tolerance. His persecution of the Puritans, however, merely stiffened their resolve and turned them toward open political opposition. An increasingly vocal Puritan minority in Parliament criticized King Charles I (reigned 1625–49), James's son and successor, for supporting "High Church" (of England) policies—which emphasized the authority of the church and its traditional forms of worship—as well as for marrying a Roman Catholic princess. In 1629, determined to rule without these troublesome opponents, Charles dismissed Parliament and launched a campaign of repression against the Puritans. This political turmoil provided the context for the migration of thousands of English Protestants to New England.

EARLY CONTACTS IN NEW ENGLAND

The northern Atlantic coast seemed an unlikely spot for English colonies, for the region was dominated by French and Dutch traders. In 1613, desperate to keep their colonial options open, the English had dispatched a fleet from Jamestown that destroyed the French post on the Bay of Fundy and harassed the Dutch on the Hudson. The following year Captain John Smith of Virginia explored the northern coastline and christened the region "New England." The land was "so planted with Gardens and Corne fields," he wrote, that "I would rather live here than any where." But Smith's plans for a New England colony were aborted when he was captured by the French.

Then a twist of fate transformed English fortunes. From 1616 to 1618 an epidemic ravaged the native peoples of the northern Atlantic coast. Modern estimates confirm the testimony of a surviving Indian that his people were "melted down by this disease, whereof nine-tenths of them have died." The native population of New England as a whole dropped from an estimated 120,000 to less than 70,000. So crippled were the surviving coastal societies that they could not provide effective resistance to the planting of English colonies.

PLYMOUTH COLONY AND THE MAYFLOWER COMPACT

The first English colony in New England was founded by a group of religious dissenters known to later generations as the **Pilgrims**. They were called **Separatists** because rather than reform the English church from within they believed it to be so corrupt that they had to establish their own independent congregations. One group moved to Holland in 1609, but fearful that tolerant Dutch society was seducing their children, they decided on emigration to North America. Backed by the Virginia Company of London and led by tradesman William Bradford, 102 people sailed from Plymouth, England, on the *Mayflower* in September 1620.

The little group, mostly families but including a substantial number of single men hired by the investors, arrived in Massachusetts Bay at the site of the former Indian village of Patuxet, which the English then named Plymouth. Soon the hired men began to grumble about Pilgrim authority, and to reassure them Bradford drafted an agreement by which the male members of the expedition did "covenant and combine [themselves] together into a civil body politic." The **Mayflower Compact** was the first document of self-government in North America.

Pilgrims   Settlers of Plymouth Colony, who viewed themselves as spiritual wanderers.

Separatists   Members of an offshoot branch of Puritanism. Separatists believed that the Church of England was too corrupt to be reformed and hence were convinced they must "separate" from it to save their souls.

Mayflower Compact   The first document of self-government in North America.

Weakened by scurvy and malnutrition, nearly half the Pilgrims perished over the first winter. Like the earlier settlers of Roanoke and Jamestown, however, they were rescued by Indians. Massasoit, the sachem (leader) of the Pokanokets (also known as the Wampanoags), offered the newcomers food and advice in return for an alliance against his enemies, the Narragansets. It was the familiar pattern of Indians attempting to incorporate European colonists into their world.

The Pilgrims succeeded during the first two or three decades in establishing the self-sufficient community they desired. So strong was their communal agreement that the annual meeting of property-owning men reelected William Bradford to thirty consecutive terms as governor. By midcentury, however, the Plymouth population had dispersed into eleven separate communities, and the growth of diverse local interests had begun to disrupt this Separatist retreat.

THE MASSACHUSETTS BAY COLONY

In England, the political climate of the late 1620s convinced a number of influential Puritans that the only way to protect their congregations was by emigration. In 1629 a royal charter was granted to a group of wealthy Puritans who called their enterprise the **Massachusetts Bay Company**, and an advance force of 200 settlers left for the fishing settlement of Naumkeag on Massachusetts Bay, which they renamed Salem. They hoped to establish what John Winthrop, their leader and first governor, called "a city on a hill," a New England model of reform for old England. The Puritan emigration became known as the **Great Migration**, a phrase that would be repeated many times in American history. Between 1629 and 1643 some 20,000 people relocated to Massachusetts. They built the town of Boston in 1630 and within five years ringed it with towns as far as thirty miles inland.

INDIANS AND PURITANS

The Algonquian Indians of southern New England found the English very different from the French and Dutch traders who had preceded them. The principal concern of the English was not commerce, although the fur trade remained an important part of their economy, but the acquisition of Indian land for their growing settlements.

Ravaged by disease, the Pokanokets' northern neighbors, the Massachusetts, were ill-prepared for the Puritan landings that took place after 1629. The English believed they had the right to take what they thought of as "unused" lands—lands not being used, that is, in the "English way"—and depopulated Massachusetts villages became prime targets for expansion. As one colonist wrote, "Their land is spacious and void, and there are few and [they] do but run over the grass, as do also the foxes and wild beasts." The Indians did not consider that land could be privately owned, but understood it as a community resource. Conflicts between settlers over title, however, made it necessary to obtain original deeds from Indians, and the English used a variety of tactics to pressure them into signing "quitclaims," or documents in which the signers relinquished all claim to specified properties.

By the late 1630s the most powerful tribes in the vicinity of the Puritans were the Narragansets of present-day Rhode Island and their traditional enemies the Pequots, principal trading partners of the Dutch. The Pequots lived on Long Island Sound near the mouth of the Connecticut River, where they controlled the production of

QUICK REVIEW

Mayflower Compact

◆ Mayflower Compact signed in 1620.

◆ Established self-government in North America.

◆ Pilgrim leaders urged all adult males to sign the compact.

2-4
Reasons for the Plantation in New England (1629)

2-5
John Winthrop, "A Model of Christian Charity" (1630)

Massachusetts Bay Company   A group of wealthy Puritans who were granted a royal charter in 1629 to settle in Massachusetts Bay.

Great Migration   Puritan emigration to North America between 1629 and 1643.

Governor John Winthrop, c. 1640, a portrait by an unknown artist. American Antiquarian Society

wampum, woven belts of sea shells used as a medium of exchange in the Indian trade. In 1637 the Narragansets, in alliance with the English, who were looking for an excuse to smash the Dutch, went to war against the Pequots. Narraganset warriors and English troops attacked the main Pequot village, killing most of its slumbering residents, including women and children. Unaccustomed to such tactics, the shocked Narragansets cried out to the English: "It is too furious, it slays too many."

THE NEW ENGLAND MERCHANTS

In England, the conflict between King Charles I and the Puritans in Parliament broke into armed conflict in 1642. Several years of violent confrontation led to the execution of the king in 1649 and the proclamation of an English Commonwealth, headed by the Puritan leader Oliver Cromwell. Because the Puritans were on the victorious side in the English Civil War, they no longer had the same incentive to migrate to New England. A number of settlers even returned to England.

New England's economy had depended on the sale of supplies and land to arriving immigrants, but as the Great Migration ended the importance of this "newcomer market" declined. Lacking a single exportable commodity, New England traders developed a diversified trade with a variety of commodities, including oak barrel staves, pine ship's masts, salted cod fish, and farm products. By the 1660s the New England merchants had a commercial fleet that was the envy of other colonies: 300 trading and fishing vessels that voyaged throughout the Atlantic—to the fishing grounds of the North Atlantic, to the sugar-producing colonies of the West Indies, to the wine-producing islands of the Atlantic, and to Africa and England.

COMMUNITY AND FAMILY IN MASSACHUSETTS

The Puritans stressed the importance of well-ordered communities. The Massachusetts General Court, the governing body of the colony, granted townships to a group of proprietors, the leaders of a congregation wishing to settle new lands. These men then distributed fields, pasture, and woodlands in quantities proportional to the social status of the recipient, with wealthy families receiving more than others. The Puritans believed that social hierarchy was ordained by God and made for well-ordered communities. Settlers typically clustered their dwellings in a central village, near the meetinghouse that served as both church and civic center. Some towns, particularly those along the coast such as Boston, soon became centers of shipping. These clustered settlements and strong, vital communities made seventeenth-century New England quite different from Chesapeake society.

The ideal Puritan family was also well ordered. Parents often participated in the choice of mates for their offspring, and children typically married in the order of their births, younger siblings waiting until arrangements had been made for their elders. But well-disciplined children also needed education. Another source of New England's strength was the impressive system the Puritans built to educate their young. In 1647 Massachusetts required that towns with 50 families or more support a public school; those with 100 families were to establish a grammar school that taught Latin, knowledge of which was required for admission to Harvard College, founded in 1636. The colony of Connecticut enacted similar requirements. Literacy was higher in New England than elsewhere in North America, and even in most of Europe.

The Mason Children, by an unknown Boston artist, c. 1670. These Puritan children—David, Joanna, and Abigail Mason—are dressed in finery, an indication of the wealth and prominence of their family. The cane in young David's hand indicates his position as the male heir, while the rose held by Abigail is a symbol of childhood innocence.

Attributed to the Freake-Gibbs Painter, American, active Boston, MA, ca. 1670. *The Mason Children: David, Joanna, and Abigail*, ca. 1670. Oil on canvas, 39" x 421" ¹/₂ in. the fine Arts Museum of San Francisco, Gift of Mr. And Mrs. John D. Rockefeller 3ʳᵈ, 1979, 7.3

But because girls were excluded from grammar schools, far fewer New England women than men could read and write. By 1639 the first printing press in the English colonies was in operation in Boston, and the following year it brought out the first American English publication, *The Bay Psalm Book.*

DISSENT AND NEW COMMUNITIES

The Puritans emigrated in order to practice their variety of Christianity, but they had little tolerance for other religious points of view. Religious disagreement among the colonists soon provoked the founding of new colonies. Thomas Hooker, minister of the congregation at Cambridge, disagreed with the policy of restricting suffrage to male church members. In 1636 he led his followers west to the Connecticut River, where they founded the town of Hartford near the site of the trading post abandoned by the Dutch after epidemic disease had destroyed nearby Indian communities in 1634.

Another dissenter was the minister Roger Williams, who came to New England in 1631 to take up duties for the congregation in Salem. Williams believed in religious tolerance and the separation of church and state (discussed in Chapter 5). He also preached that the colonists had no absolute right to Indian land but must bargain for it in good faith. These were dangerous ideas, and Williams was banished from the colony in 1636. With a group of his followers, he emigrated to the Narraganset country, where he purchased land from the Indians and founded the town of Providence.

In 1644 Roger Williams received a royal charter creating the colony of Rhode Island, named for the principal island in Narraganset Bay, as a protection for these dissenting communities. A new royal charter of 1663 guaranteed self-government and complete religious liberty.

THE RESTORATION COLONIES

The Puritan Commonwealth established in England after the execution of King Charles attempted to provide a measure of central control over the colonies with the passage in 1651 of an Act of Trade and Navigation, which was intended to keep Dutch ships out of England's overseas possessions. But the regime was preoccupied with English domestic affairs and left the colonies largely to their own devices. Cromwell ruled as Lord Protector of the Commonwealth, but the new order failed to survive his death in 1658. While wishing to reserve for itself certain significant powers of state, Parliament was desperate for political stability after nearly two decades of civil war. In 1660 it restored the Stuart monarchy, placing Charles II, son of the former king, on the throne. One of Charles's most important acts was the establishment of several new proprietary colonies, known as the Restoration Colonies.

WHAT ROLE did the crown play in the founding of English colonies after 1660?

EARLY CAROLINA

In 1663 the king issued his first charters, calling for the establishment of a new colony called Carolina, which stretched from Virginia south to Spanish Florida. Virginians had already begun moving into the northern parts of this territory, and in 1664 the Carolina proprietors appointed a governor for the settlements in the area of Albermarle Sound and created a popularly elected assembly. By 1675 North Carolina, as it became known, was home to 5,000 small farmers and large tobacco planters.

Settlement farther south began in 1670 with the founding of coastal Charles Town (Charleston today). Most South Carolina settlers came from Barbados, a Caribbean colony the English had founded in 1627, which had grown rich from

MAP EXPLORATION

To explore an interactive version of this map, go to
http://www.prenhall.com/faraghertlc/map3.3

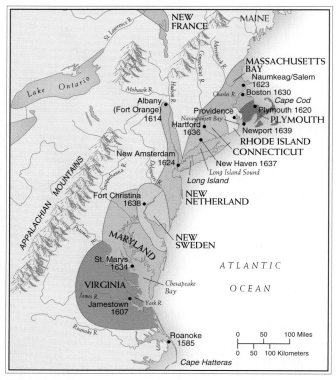

MAP 3-3

European Colonies of the Atlantic Coast, 1607–1639 Virginia on Chesapeake Bay was the first English colony in North America, but by the mid-seventeenth century Virginia was joined by settlements of Scandinavians on the Delaware River, and Dutch on the Hudson River, as well as English religious dissenters in New England. The territories indicated here reflect the vague boundaries of the early colonies.

HOW MANY European nations had established colonies on the Atlantic coast by the middle of the seventeenth century?

MAP EXPLORATION

To explore an interactive version of this map, go to
http://www.prenhall.com/faraghertlc/map3.4

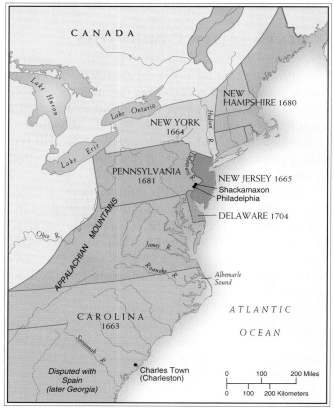

MAP 3-4

The Restoration Colonies After the restoration of the Stuart monarchy in 1660, King Charles II of England created the new proprietary colonies of Carolina, New York, Pennsylvania, and New Jersey. New Hampshire was set off as a royal colony in 1680, and in 1704 the lower counties of Pennsylvania became the colony of Delaware.

EXAMINE THE processes underlying the founding of the Restoration Colonies. How has the political landscape changed since 1639?

the production of sugar. By the 1670s the island had become overpopulated with English settlers and Africans. The latter, imported as slaves to work the plantations, made up a majority of the population. Hundreds of Barbadians, both masters and their slaves, relocated to South Carolina, lending a distinctly West Indian character to the colony.

FROM NEW NETHERLAND TO NEW YORK

King Charles II also coveted the lucrative Dutch colony of New Netherland. In response to the growth of New England's population and its merchant economy, in the 1640s the Dutch West India Company began to sponsor the emigration of European settlers to its colony in the Hudson River valley, seeking to convert New Netherland from a specialized fur-trade economy to a diversified supply center for the West Indies. The result was rising conflict with local Indian communities, pressed by the Dutch to cede their lands for agriculture. The British Navigation Act of 1651 was in part a response to what the English viewed as the Dutch threat to the English trade monopoly they sought to establish along the Atlantic coast. England's attempt to control Dutch shipping led to an inconclusive naval war with Holland from 1652 to 1654, and a decade later the two powers clashed again along the West African coast. Finally, in 1664, an English fleet sailed into Manhattan harbor and forced the surrender of New Amsterdam without firing a shot, inaugurating a second full-fledged Anglo-Dutch war, which ended with an inconclusive peace in 1667. A third and final conflict from 1672 to 1674 resulted in the bankruptcy of the Dutch West India Company and marked the ascension of the English to dominance in the Atlantic. Holland remained supreme in the Baltic and the East Indies.

Charles II granted the newly acquired Dutch colony to his brother James, the Duke of York, renaming it New York in his honor. Otherwise the English government did little to disturb the existing order, preferring simply to reap the benefits of acquiring this profitable and dynamic colony. Ethnically and linguistically diversified, accommodating a wide range of religious sects, New York boasted the most heterogeneous society in North America. In 1665, the communities of the Delaware Valley were split off as the **proprietary colony** of New Jersey, although it continued to be governed by New York until the 1680s.

THE FOUNDING OF PENNSYLVANIA

In 1676 proprietary rights to the western portion of New Jersey were sold to a group of English **Quakers** that included William Penn, who intended to make the area a religious haven for members of the Society of Friends, or Quakers. A dissenting sect, the Quakers were committed to religious toleration and pacifism. Penn himself had been imprisoned four times for publicly expressing these views. But he was the son of the wealthy and influential English admiral Sir William Penn, a close adviser to the king. In 1681, to settle a large debt owed to Sir William, King Charles granted the younger Penn a huge territory west of the Delaware River. The next year Penn supervised the laying out of his capital of Philadelphia on the Delaware.

Penn wanted this colony to be a "holy experiment." In his first **Frame of Government**, drafted in 1682, he included guarantees of religious freedom, civil liberties, and elected representation. He also attempted to deal fairly with the Algonquian Indians, not permitting colonization until settlement rights were negotiated and lands purchased. In 1682 and 1683, he made an agreement with the sachem Tammany of the Delaware tribe. Although Pennsylvania's relations with the Indians later soured, during Penn's lifetime his reputation for fair dealing led a number of Indian groups to resettle in the Quaker colony.

During the first decade of Pennsylvania's settlement, over 10,000 colonists arrived from England, and agricultural communities were soon spreading from the Delaware into the fertile interior valleys. In 1704 Penn approved the creation of a separate government for the area formerly controlled by the Scandinavians and Dutch. This area became the colony of Delaware.

CONFLICT AND WAR

Pennsylvania's ability to maintain peaceful relations with the Indians proved the great exception, for the last quarter of the seventeenth century was a time of great violence throughout the colonial regions of the continent. Much of this warfare was between colonists and Indians, but intertribal warfare and intercolonial rivalry greatly contributed to the violence.

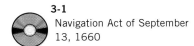
3-1
Navigation Act of September 13, 1660

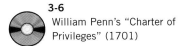
3-6
William Penn's "Charter of Privileges" (1701)

QUICK REVIEW

Pennsylvania

◆ Territory west of the Delaware River granted to William Penn in 1681.

◆ Penn supervised the establishment of Philadelphia in 1682.

◆ Penn, a Quaker, saw the colony as a "holy experiment."

Proprietary colony   A colony created when the English monarch granted a huge tract of land to an individual or group of individuals, who became "lords proprietor."

Quakers   Members of the Society of Friends, a radical religious group that arose in the mid-seventeenth century. Quakers rejected formal theology, focusing instead on the Holy Spirit that dwelt within them.

Frame of Government   William Penn's constitution for Pennsylvania which included a provision allowing for religious freedom.

WHAT LED to violent conflict between Indians and colonists?

2-6

The Taking of the Fort at Mystic: A Brief History of the Pequot War

Pequot War   Conflict between English settlers and Pequot Indians over control of land and trade in eastern Connecticut.

King Philip's War   Conflict in New England (1675–1676) between Wampanoags, Narragansetts, and other Indian peoples against English settlers; sparked by English encroachments on native lands.

Indians and New Englanders skirmish during King Philip's War in a detail from John Seller's "A Mapp of New England," published immediately after the war in 1675.

Courtesy of the John Carter Brown Library at Brown University

KING PHILIP'S WAR

During the nearly forty years of peace that followed the **Pequot War** of 1637, the Algonquian and English peoples of New England lived in close, if tense, contact. Several Puritan ministers, including John Eliot and Thomas Mayhew, began to preach to the Indians, and several hundred Algonquian converts eventually relocated in Christian Indian communities called "praying towns." Outside the colonial boundaries, however, there remained a number of independent Indian tribes, including the Pokanokets and the Narragansets of Rhode Island and the Abenakis of northern New England. The extraordinary expansion of the Puritan population, and their hunger for land, created pressures for further expansion into those territories.

In 1671 the colonial authorities at Plymouth forced the Pokanokets to concede authority over their home territory. This humiliation convinced the sachem Metacomet (called King Philip by the English), son of Massasoit, that his people must break their half-century alliance with Plymouth and take up armed resistance. Meanwhile, the Puritan colonies prepared for a war of conquest.

In the spring of 1675 Plymouth magistrates arrested and executed three Pokanoket men for the murder of a Christian Indian. Fearing that the moment of confrontation had arrived, Metacomet appealed to the Narragansets for a defensive alliance. The United Colonies (the New England colonies led by Massachusetts Bay) and New York, hoping for territorial gain, took this as the moment to send armed forces into Narraganset country, attacking and burning a number of villages. What became known as **King Philip's War** soon engulfed all of New England.

At first things went well for the Indians. They forced the abandonment of English settlements on the Connecticut River and torched several towns less than twenty miles from Boston. By the beginning of 1676, however, their campaign was collapsing. A combined colonial army invaded Narraganset country, burning villages, killing women and children, and defeating a large Indian force in a battle known as the Great Swamp Fight. In western New England, Metacomet appealed to the Iroquois for supplies and support, but instead they attacked and defeated his forces. Metacomet retreated back to his homeland, where the colonists annihilated his army in August 1676.

In their attack on Metacomet's army, the Iroquois were motivated by interests of their own. Continuing the role they had played in the Dutch trading system, they now cast themselves in the role of powerful intermediaries between other tribes and the English. By attacking Metacomet they demonstrated where they stood. In a series of negotiations conducted at Albany in 1677, the Iroquois Confederacy and the colony of New York created an alliance known as the **Covenant Chain**, which sought to establish Iroquois dominance over all other tribes and thus put New York in an economically and politically dominant position among the other colonies.

At the end of King Philip's War, some 4,000 Algonquians and 2,000 English colonists were dead, and dozens of native and colonial towns lay in ruins. Fearing attack from Indians close at hand, colonists destroyed most of the Christian Indian praying towns, killing many of the residents.

BACON'S REBELLION

At the same time as King Philip's War, another English-Indian confrontation took place in the Chesapeake. In the 1670s the Susquehannock people of the upper Potomac River came into conflict with the tobacco planters expanding northward from Virginia. Violent raids in 1675, led by wealthy backcountry settler Nathaniel Bacon, included the indiscriminate murder of Indians. The efforts of Virginia governor William Berkeley to suppress these unauthorized military expeditions so infuriated Bacon and his followers—many of them former indentured servants—that in the spring of 1676 they turned their fury against the colonial capital of Jamestown itself. Berkeley fled across the Chesapeake while Bacon pillaged and burned the capital. Soon thereafter Bacon died of dysentery, a common fate of the day, and his rebellion collapsed.

This brief but violent clash marked an important change of direction for Virginia. Bacon had issued a manifesto demanding not only the death or removal of all Indians from the colony, but also an end to the rule of aristocratic "grandees" and "parasites." The rebellion thus signaled a developing conflict between frontier districts such as Bacon's and the more established coastal region where the "Indian problem" had long since been settled. In 1677, in a replay of Virginia events known as **Culpeper's Rebellion**, backcountry men in the Albermarle region of North Carolina suceeded in overthrowing the established government, before being suppressed by English authorities. In the aftermath of these rebellions, colonial authorities in Virginia and North Carolina began to favor armed expansion into Indian territory, hoping to gain the support of backcountry men by enlarging the stock of available colonial land.

WARS IN THE SOUTH

There was also massive violence in South Carolina during the 1670s, as colonists there began the operation of a large-scale Indian slave trade. Charleston merchants encouraged Yamasees, Creeks, Cherokees, and Chickasaws to wage war on Indian tribes allied to rival

QUICK REVIEW

King Philip's War

- King Philip's War broke out in 1675.
- Conflict between Wampanoags and settlers led to war.
- Thousands of settlers and Indians died in the fighting.

3-4
Edward Randolph Describes King Philip's War (1685)

3-2
Nathaniel Bacon's Challenge to William Berkeley and the Governor's Response (1676)

Covenant Chain An alliance between the Iroquois Confederacy and the colony of New York which sought to establish Iroquois dominance over all other tribes and thus put New York in an economically and politically dominant position among the other colonies.

Bacon's Rebellion Violent conflict in Virginia (1675–1676), beginning with settler attacks on Indians but culminating in a rebellion led by Nathaniel Bacon against Virginia's government.

Culpeper's Rebellion The overthrow of the established government in the Albermarle region of North Carolina by backcountry men in 1677.

The Delawares presented William Penn with this wampum belt after the Shackamaxon Treaty of 1682. In friendship, a Quaker in distinctive hat clasps the hand of an Indian. The diagonal stripes on either side of the figures convey information about the territorial terms of the agreement. Wampum belts like this one, made from strings of white and purple shells, were used to commemorate treaties throughout the colonial period and were the most widely accepted form of money in the northeastern colonies during the seventeenth century.

Photograph by Gavin Ashworth. The Historical Society of Pennsylvania

OVERVIEW

CONFLICT AND WAR

The Beaver Wars 1640s–1680s	The Iroquois extend their authority as middlemen in the Dutch and English trade system by attacking neighbors as far west as Illinois.
King Philip's War 1675–1676	The Indian peoples of southern New England and the Puritan colonies fight for control of land.
Bacon's Rebellion 1675–1676	Backcountry settlers attack Indians, and colonial authorities try to suppress these attacks.
Wars in the South 1670s–1720s	British colonists in the Carolinas incite Creeks, Cherokees, and other Indian tribes to attack and enslave the mission Indians of Spanish Florida.
King William's War 1689–1697	The first of a series of colonial struggles between England and France, these conflicts occur principally on the frontiers of northern New England and New York.

MAP EXPLORATION

To explore an interactive version of this map, go to
http://www.prenhall.com/faraghertlc/3.5

MAP 3-5
Spread of Settlement: British Colonies, 1650–1700 The spread of settlement in the English colonies in the late seventeenth century created the conditions for a number of violent conflicts, including King Philip's War, Bacon's Rebellion, the Wars in the South, and King William's War.

WHAT FACTORS were behind the spread of British settlement in the second half of the seventeenth century?

colonial powers: the mission Indians of Spanish Florida, the Choctaw allies of the French, and the Tuscaroras, trading partners of the Virginians. The mission Indians of Florida were hit so hard that by 1710 more than 12,000 of them had been captured and sold, thousands of others had been killed or dispersed, and the Spanish mission system, in operation for more than a century, lay in ruins.

KING WILLIAM'S WAR

The year 1689 marked the beginning of nearly seventy-five years of armed conflict between English and French forces for control of the North American interior. The Iroquois-English Covenant Chain challenged New France's fur-trade empire, and in response the French pressed farther west in search of commercial opportunities. In the far north, the English countered French dominance with the establishment of Hudson's Bay Company, a royal fur-trade monopoly that sought to exploit the watershed of the great northern bay.

Hostilities began with English-Iroquois attacks on Montreal and violence between rival French and English traders on Hudson's Bay. These skirmishes were part of a larger conflict between England and France called the War of the League of Augsburg in Europe. In the North American colonies the conflict was known as **King William's War**. In 1690, the French and their Algonquian allies counterattacked, burning frontier settlements in New York, New Hampshire, and Maine, and pressing their attacks against the towns of the Iroquois. The same year, a Massachusetts fleet captured and briefly held the strategic French harbor at Port Royal, on the Bay of Fundy in Acadia, but a combined English and colonial force failed in its attempt to conquer the French settlements along the St. Lawrence. This inconclusive war was ended by the Treaty of Ryswick of 1697, which established an equally inconclusive peace. War between England and France resumed only five years later.

The persistent violence of the last quarter of the seventeenth century greatly concerned English authorities, who began to fear the loss of their North American possessions either from outside attack or from internal disorder. To shore up central control, in 1701 the English Board of Trade recommended making all charter and proprietary governments into royal colonies. After a brief period under royal rule, William Penn regained private control of his domain, but Pennsylvania was the only remaining proprietary colony. Among the royal charter colonies, only Rhode Island and Connecticut retained their original governments.

CONCLUSION

At the beginning of the seventeenth century the European presence north of Mexico was extremely limited: Spanish bases in Florida, a few Franciscan missionaries among the Pueblos, and fishermen along the North Atlantic coast. By 1700 the human landscape of the Southwest, the South, and the Northeast had been transformed. More than a quarter million migrants from the Old World had moved into these regions, the vast majority to the British colonies. Indian societies had been disrupted, depopulated, and in some cases destroyed. The Spanish and French colonies were characterized by the inclusion of Indians in the social and economic life of the community, but along the Atlantic coast, the English and eventually the Dutch established communities of exclusion, with resulting implications for the future of relations between colonists and Indians that were ominous.

During the long civil war at home the English colonies had been left to run their own affairs. But with the Restoration in 1660 and the establishment of the constitutional monarchy in 1689, the English state began to supervise its troublesome colonists more closely, beginning a long struggle over the limits of self-government. The violence and warfare of the last decades of the century suggested that conflict would continue to play a significant role in the future of colonial America.

QUICK REVIEW

France, Britain, and the Iroquois

- France attacked the Iroquois to prevent them from extending their influence.
- France and England went to war in 1689.
- War spilled over into North America devastating Iroquois.

King William's War The first of a series of colonial struggles between England and France; these conflicts occurred principally on the frontiers of northern New England and New York between 1689 and 1697.

CHRONOLOGY

1598	Juan de Oñate leads Spanish into New Mexico.
1607	English found Jamestown.
1608	French found Quebec.
1609	Spanish found Santa Fé.
1620	Pilgrim emigration.
1622	Indian uprising in Virginia.
1625	Jesuit missionaries arrive in New France.
1629	Puritans begin settlement of Massachusetts Bay.
1637	Pequot War.
1649	Charles I executed.
1660	Stuart monarchy restored, Charles II becomes king.
1675	King Philip's War.
1676	Bacon's Rebellion.
1680	Pueblo Revolt.
1681–1682	Robert Sieur de La Salle explores the Mississippi.
1689	King William's War.
1698	Spanish reconquest of the Pueblos completed.
1701	English impose royal governments on all colonies but Massachusetts, Connecticut, and Pennsylvania.

SUMMARY

Spain and its Competitors in North America The initial planting of colonies in North America outside of Mexico set up competition among European nations for land and trade with the Indians cultures. Several different nations were involved in such diverse areas as Canada and the present-day southwestern United States. Unlike earlier efforts, these colonies proved more substantial and long-term.

England in the Chesapeake The planting of English colonies in the Chesapeake demonstrated how difficult and expensive it was to maintain such settlements. The influence of regional conditions on colonial development was also illustrated.

The New England Colonies A combination of human and natural factors placed the New England colonies on a path distinct from those in the Chesapeake. In addition to the geography and climate, the New England colonists had different backgrounds, motivations, and aims from the Chesapeake colonists.

The Restoration Colonies Following the restoration of the English monarchy, several new colonies were established that cemented the English presence down much of the Atlantic Coast and stretching west over the Appalachian Mountains. These new colonies were all founded under the same type of charter but followed different paths of development.

Conflict and War The last quarter of the seventeenth century experienced much violence as warfare raged from Santa Fe in New Mexico to the Atlantic coast. It involved conflicts between Indians and colonists, between Indian tribes, and between different colonists.

REVIEW QUESTIONS

1. Using examples drawn from this chapter, discuss the differences between colonizing "frontiers of inclusion" and "exclusion."

2. What factors turned England's Chesapeake colony of Virginia from stark failure to brilliant success?

3. Discuss the role of religious dissent in the founding of the first New England colonies and in stimulating the creation of others.

4. Compare and contrast William Penn's policy with respect to Indian tribes with the policies of other English settlers, in the Chesapeake and New England, and with the policies of the Spanish, the French, and the Dutch.

5. What were the principal causes of colonial violence and warfare of the late seventeenth century?

KEY TERMS

Bacon's Rebellion (p. 65)
Beaver Wars (p. 54)
Coureurs de bois (p. 53)
Covenant Chain (p. 65)
Culpeper's Rebellion (p. 65)

Frame of Government (p. 63)
Great Migration (p. 59)
House of Burgesses (p. 56)
Indentured Servants (p. 56)
King Philip's War (p. 64)

RECOMMENDED READING

James Axtell, *The European and the Indian: Essays in the Ethnohistory of Colonial America* (1981). A readable introduction to the dynamics of mutual discovery between natives and colonizers.

Leslie Choquette, *Frenchmen into Peasants: Modernity and Tradition in the Peopling of French Canada* (1997). A history of French immigrants to Canada and Acadia, based on a comprehensive database of hundreds of individuals. The most detailed study of French mobility to date.

Frederic W. Gleach, *Powhatan's World and Colonial Virginia: A Conflict of Cultures* (1997). Reconstructing the worldview of the Chesapeake Algonquians as they attempted to maintain control of their homeland.

Harold Adams Innis, *The Fur Trade in Canada: An Introduction to Canadian Economic History* (1999). A new edition of a classic that remains the definitive history of the fur trade.

Andrew L. Knaut, *The Pueblo Revolt of 1680* (1995). The most complete and sophisticated account of the revolt.

Edmund S. Morgan, *American Slavery, American Freedom* (1975). A classic interpretation of early Virginia. Morgan argues that early American ideas of freedom for some were based on the reality of slavery for others.

Diana Newton, *Papists, Protestants, and Puritans, 1559–1714* (1998). The best survey of religious change during the Protestant Reformation, with a focus on the turmoil in England.

Neal Salisbury, *Manitou and Providence: Indians, Europeans, and the Making of New England* (1982). One of the best examples of the new ethnohistory of Indians; a provocative intercultural approach to the history of the Northeast.

Susan Sleeper-Smith, *Native Women and French Men: Rethinking Cultural Encounter in the Western Great Lakes* (2001). A study of Indian women who married French traders and became cultural brokers and creators of a middle ground.

David J. Weber, *The Spanish Frontier in North America* (1992). A powerful overview that includes the history of New Mexico and Florida.

The first object that saluted my eyes when I arrived on the coast was the sea, and a slave ship, which was then riding at anchor, and waiting for its cargo.

—*from* The Interesting Life of Olaudah Equiano

Fourteen men and six women from Guinea arriving on a Dutch ship at Jamestown, Virginia, in August 1619, the beginning of Negro slavery in the American colonies.

4

SLAVERY AND EMPIRE
1441–1770

WHAT WAS the relationship between the sugar industry and African slavery?

WHAT ROLE did African traders play in the slave trade?

HOW DID slavery in the North differ from slavery in the South?

HOW DID African slaves attempt to preserve African culture in America?

HOW DID slavery fuel the economic development of Europe in the seventeenth and eighteenth centuries?

HOW DID slavery shape southern colonial society?

AMERICAN COMMUNITIES

African Slaves Build Their Own Community in Coastal Georgia

AFRICANS LABORED IN THE STEAMY HEAT OF THE COASTAL GEORGIA *Rice fields, the breeches of the men rolled up over their knees, the sack skirts of the women gathered and tied about their hips, leaving them, in the words of one shocked observer, "two thirds naked." Standing on the banks of canals that channeled water to the fields, African slave drivers, whips at the ready, supervised the work. Upriver, groups cut away cypress and gum trees and cleared the swampland's jungle maze of undergrowth; others constructed levees, preparing to bring more land under cultivation. An English overseer or plantation master could be seen here and there, but overwhelmingly it was a country populated by Africans.*

These plantations were southern extensions of the South Carolina rice belt. Although slavery had been prohibited by Georgia's original charter of 1732, the restriction was lifted when Georgia became a royal colony two decades later. By 1770, 15,000 African Americans (80 percent of the region's population) lived on several hundred coastal rice plantations owned by a small elite of white people.

Rice was one of the most valuable commodities produced in mainland North America, surpassed in value only by tobacco and wheat. The growth of rice production in the lower South was matched by an enormous expansion in the Atlantic slave trade, and during the eighteenth century rice planters engaged in what one historian calls a "veritable orgy" of slave trading. Although the number of North American black people who were "country born" (native to America and, thus, born into slavery) grew steadily over the century, before the American Revolution the majority of black people on the rice plantations were what were known as "saltwater" Africans. These people had endured the shock of enslavement. Ripped from their homeland communities in West Africa by slave raiders, they were brutally marched to coastal forts. There, they were imprisoned, subjected to humiliating inspections of their bodies, and branded on the buttocks like animals. Packed into the stinking holds of ships, they were forced into a nightmarish passage across the Atlantic Ocean. When finally unloaded on a strange continent, they were sold at dockside auctions, then once again marched overland to their destinations on New World plantations. On the rice plantations of isolated coastal Georgia, enslaved Africans suffered from overwork and numerous physical ailments, the results of poor diet, minimal and inappropriate clothing, and inadequate housing. Mortality rates were exceptionally high, especially for infants. Colonial laws permitted masters to discipline and punish slaves indiscriminately. They were whipped, confined in irons, castrated, or sold away, with little regard for their relations with family or friends.

Africans struggled to make a place for themselves in this inhospitable world. They had little power but bargained with their masters to win acceptance of the familiar work routines of West Africa. Thus, low-country plantations operated according to the task system: once slaves finished their specific jobs, they could use their remaining time to hunt, fish, or cultivate family gardens. Masters often complained that "tasking" did not produce the same level of profit as the gang labor system of the sugar plantations, but African rice hands refused to work any other way. "Although it is not fixed by law," one planter wrote in 1767, the tasking system was "so well settled by long usage," that any master who tried to increase the workload was faced with "such discontent amongst his slaves as to make them of but little use to him."

Still, many slaves ran away, like slaves everywhere in the Americas. Readers of Savannah newspapers were urged to look out for fugitives: Statira, a woman of the "Gold Coast Country" with tribal markings on her temples, or "a negro fellow named Mingo, about 40 years old, and his wife Quante, a sensible wench about 20 with her child, a boy about 3 years old, all this country born." Some fled in groups, heading for the Creek Indian settlements in northern Florida, or toward St. Augustine, where the Spanish, in an attempt to undermine the English colonies of the Lower South, promised them safe haven. Some struck out violently at their masters: a group of nine Africans from a Savannah plantation killed their master and stole a boat, planning to head upriver, but were apprehended as they lay in wait to murder their hated overseers.

Georgia Sea Islands

So slaves resisted. But like slaves throughout the New World, the majority of Africans and African Americans of the Georgia coast remained and built communities of their own within the heartless world of slavery. Plantation slaves married, raised children, and over time constructed kinship networks. They passed on African names and traditions and created new ones. These links between individuals and families formed the basis for reestablished communities. Slave communities combined elements of African languages and English to form dialects that allowed newly arrived people from many different African ethnic groups as well as American-born slaves to communicate with one another. Neither individuals nor families alone can make a language; that is something only a community can do. Common African heritage and common slave status were the foundations of the African American community.

African Americans reworked traditional African dance, song, and story to fit New World circumstances, just as they reestablished traditional arts, such as woodworking, iron making, and weaving. Through their culture, the slaves shared a powerful awareness of their common oppression. They told or sang dialect tales of mistreatment, as in this song of Quow, the punished slave:

Was matter Buddy Quow?

I ble Obesha bang you. . . .

Dah Backrow Man go wrong you, Buddy Quow,

Dah Backrow Man go wrong you, Buddy Quow.

[What's the matter Brother Quow?

I believe the overseer's beat you. . . .

The white man's wronged you, Brother Quow,

The white man's wronged you, Brother Quow.]

Just as European settlers planted colonial communities, so Africans, who made up the largest ethnic group to come to North America during the colonial era, constructed distinctive communities of their own. The history of African Americans includes the story of the Atlantic slave trade, the plunder of Africa, and the profits of empire. But it is also a story of achievement under the most difficult circumstances, and of the making of families, kin networks, and communities. They "labor together and converse almost wholly among themselves," a minister wrote of low-country slaves. "They are, as 'twere, a nation within a nation."

THE BEGINNINGS OF AFRICAN SLAVERY

Household slaves had long been a part of the world of Mediterranean Europe. Many Europeans were disturbed, however, by the moral implications of enslaving Christians, and in the early fifteenth century the pope excommunicated a number of merchants engaged in selling such captives. Africans and Muslims, however, were sufficiently different in religion to quiet those concerns.

One of the goals of Portuguese expansion in the fifteenth century was access to the lucrative West African trade in gold, wrought iron, ivory, tortoiseshell, textiles, and slaves that had previously been dominated by the Moors of northern Africa. The first African slaves to arrive in Lisbon were kidnapped by a Portuguese captain in 1441. But European traders found it more efficient to leave the capture of men and women for slavery to Africans, who were willing to exchange the captured slaves for European commodities. By the mid-fifteenth century, the Portuguese were shipping a thousand or more slaves per year from Africa.

SUGAR AND SLAVERY

Sugar and slaves had gone together since Italian merchants of the fourteenth century had imported the first cane sugar from the Middle East and set up the first modern sugar plantations on the islands of the Mediterranean. Thus, the use of Africans as slaves came to the Americas along with the spread of sugar production. One of the first products Columbus introduced to the New World was sugar cane. Sugar plantations were soon operating on the island of Hispaniola. At first the Spanish tried to use the native Indian people as a slave labor force, but because disease and warfare had so reduced the indigenous population, colonists soon turned to African slaves who were already working in Spain. Meanwhile, the Portuguese, aided by Dutch financiers, created a center of sugar production in northeast Brazil that became a model of the efficient and brutal exploitation of African labor. By 1600, some 25,000 enslaved Africans labored on the plantations of Hispaniola and Brazil.

The Dutch, using their experience in Brazil, became responsible for the next extension of slavery in the Americas. In 1630 they seized Brazil and for over twenty years they controlled this lucrative colony. Skilled at finance and commerce, they greatly expanded the European market for sugar, converting it from a luxury item for the rich to a staple for European workers. It was the Dutch who introduced sugar cultivation in the tropics. As a result, Barbados became the most valuable of England's colonies. Once the profitability of sugar had been demonstrated, the English sought to expand their Caribbean holdings by seizing the island

WHAT WAS the relationship between the sugar industry and African slavery?

IMAGE KEY

for pages 70–71

a. White Hills map by John Foster, 1677, woodcut. America's first map.

b. Fourteen men and six women from Guinea arriving on a Dutch ship at Jamestown, Virginia in August 1619, the beginning of slavery in the American colonies.

c. Model of the slave ship *Brookes*, showing plan view of slave positions.

d. William Clark's *Ten Views Found in the Island of Antigua* shows slaves working on a plantation.

e. "To be sold, a cargo of ninety-four prime, healthy Negroes."

f. The London Coffee House near the docks of Philadelphia was the site of many slave auctions in the mid-eighteenth century.

g. The Old Plantation, showing slaves at work.

h. Goods from the American colonies being unloaded from eighteenth-century ships on London's Old Custom House Quay.

of Jamaica from the Spanish in 1655 and making it over in the image of Barbados. Jamaica became the crown jewel of Britain's eighteenth-century empire.

The French repeated the process. They first developed sugar plantations on the small island of Martinique, then seized the eastern half of Hispaniola from the Spanish and created a sugar colony called St. Domingue (present-day Haiti). Caribbean sugar and slaves had become the centerpiece of the European colonial system.

WEST AFRICANS

The men and women whose labor made these tropical colonies so profitable came from the long-established societies and local communities of West Africa. In the sixteenth century more than a hundred different peoples lived along the coast of West Africa, from Cape Verde south to Angola. In the north were the Wolofs, Mandingos, Hausas, Ashantis, and Yorubas; to the south the Ibos, Sekes, Bakongos, and Mbundus.

In all these societies the most important institution was the local community, which was organized by kinship. Decisions about production, storage, and distribution of goods were generally made by clan leaders and village chiefs; local courts arbitrated disputes. Men often took a second or third wife. This marriage system, known as polygyny, produced very large composite families with complex internal relationships.

West African societies were based on sophisticated farming systems many thousands of years old. Africans practiced shifting cultivation: they cleared land by burning, used hoes or digging sticks to cultivate fields, and after several years moved on to other plots while the cleared land lay fallow. Men worked at clearing the land, women at cultivation and the sale of surpluses in the lively West African markets. The West African familiarity with regular agricultural labor was important in the history of slavery, because it proved to be practically impossible to convert large numbers of foraging or nomadic peoples into efficient plantation workers.

Farming sustained large populations and thriving networks of commerce, and in some areas kingdoms and states developed. Along the upper Niger River, where the grassland gradually turns to desert, towns such as Timbuktu developed into trading centers. There were a number of lesser states and kingdoms along the coast, and it was with these that the Portuguese first bargained for Africans who could be sold as slaves.

Varieties of household slavery were common in West African societies, although slaves there were often treated more as members of the family than as mere possessions. The West African familiarity with "unfree" labor made it possible for African and European traders to begin the trade in human merchandise.

THE AFRICAN SLAVE TRADE

The movement of Africans across the Atlantic to the Americas was the largest forced migration in world history. The Atlantic slave trade, which began with the Portuguese in the fifteenth century and did not end in the United States until 1807 (and continued elsewhere in the Americas until the 1870s), is a brutal chapter in the making of America.

THE DEMOGRAPHY OF THE SLAVE TRADE

Scholars today estimate that slave ships transported 10 to 11 million Africans to the Americas during the four-century history of the trade. Seventy-six percent arrived from 1701 to 1810—the peak period of colonial demand for labor, when tens of thousands of people were shipped from Africa each year. Of this vast multitude, about half were delivered to Dutch, French, or British sugar planta-

---

QUICK REVIEW

West African Society

◆ Hundreds of different peoples lived on the coast of West Africa.

◆ West Africans were sophisticated farmers.

◆ Local communities were organized by kinship.

WHAT ROLE did African traders play in the slave trade?

QUICK REVIEW

The Demand for Labor

◆ Indians first forced into slavery in the Americas.

◆ By 1700 Indian slave trade replaced by slaves from Africa.

◆ Sugar played a key role in the expansion of slavery.

tions in the Caribbean, a third to Portuguese Brazil, and 10 percent to Spanish America. A much smaller proportion—about one in twenty, or an estimated 600,000 men, women, and children—were transported to the British colonies of North America. With the exception of the 1750s, when the British colonies were engulfed by the **Seven Years' War**, the slave trade continued to rise in importance in the decades before the Revolution.

Among the Africans brought to the Americas, men generally outnumbered women two to one. Because most Africans were destined for fieldwork, this ratio probably reflected the preferences of plantation owners. The majority of captured and transported Africans were young people, between the ages of fifteen and thirty. Nearly every ethnic group in West Africa was represented among them.

SLAVERS OF ALL NATIONS

All the nations of Western Europe participated in the slave trade. Dutch slavers began challenging Portuguese control of the trade at the end of the sixteenth century, and Holland became the most prominent slave-trading nation during the sugar boom of the seventeenth century. The English also entered the trade in the sixteenth century.

Although the Portugese established a colony in Angola, for the most part the European presence in Africa was confined to coastal outposts. By the early eighteenth century, more than two dozen trading forts dotted the 220 miles of the Gold Coast alone. As the slave trade peaked in the middle of the eighteenth century, however, the forts of trading companies gave way to independent European and American traders who set up operations with the cooperation of local headmen or chiefs. This informal manner of trading offered opportunities for small operators, such as the New England slavers who entered the trade in the early eighteenth century. Many great New England fortunes were built from profits in the slave trade.

THE SHOCK OF ENSLAVEMENT

The slave trade was a collaboration between European or American and African traders. Dependent on the favor of local rulers, many colonial slave traders lived permanently in coastal forts and married African women, reinforcing their commercial ties with family relations. In many areas a mixed-ancestry group became prominent in the coastal slave trade. Continuing the practice of the Portuguese, the grim business of slave raiding was left to the Africans themselves. Slaves were not at all reticent about condemning the participation of their fellow Africans. "I must own to the shame of my own countrymen," wrote Ottobah Cugoano, who was sold into slavery in the mid-eighteenth century, "that I was first kidnapped and betrayed by those of my own complexion."

Most Africans were enslaved through warfare. Sometimes large armies launched massive attacks, burning whole towns and taking hundreds of prisoners. More common were smaller raids in which a group of armed men attacked at nightfall, seized everyone within reach, then escaped with their captives. Kidnapping, called "panyaring" in the jargon of the slave trade, was also common.

MAP EXPLORATION

To explore an interactive version of this map, go to **http://www.prenhall.com/faraghertlc/map4.1**

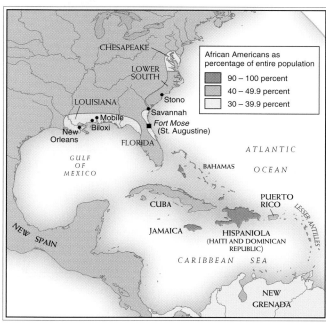

MAP 4-1

Slave Colonies of the Seventeenth and Eighteenth Centuries   By the eighteenth century the system of slavery had created societies with large African populations throughout the Caribbean and along the southern coast of North America.

HOW DID the sugar boom contribute to the importation of large numbers of Africans to the Americas?

QUICK REVIEW

Demography of Slavery

◆ 10 to 11 million Africans brought to the Americas over the course of four hundred years.

◆ Almost twice as many men as women were enslaved.

◆ Most Africans captured and transported to the Americas were between the ages of fifteen and thirty.

Seven Years' War   War fought in Europe, North America, and India between 1756 and 1763, pitting France and its allies against Great Britain and its allies.

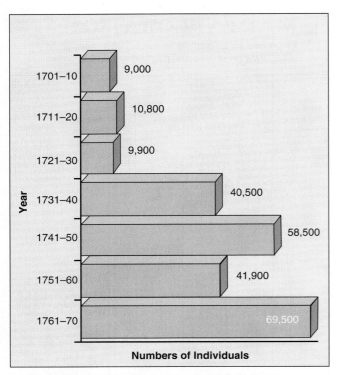

Estimated Number of Africans Imported to British North America, 1701–1775

These official British statistics include only slaves imported legally and consequently undercount the total number who arrived on American shores. But the trend over time is clear. With the exception of the 1750s, when the British colonies were engulfed by the Seven Years' War, the slave trade continued to rise in importance in the decades before the Revolution.

R.S. Simmons, *The American Colonies: From Settlement to Independence* (London, Longman, 1976), 186.

A slave coffle in an eighteenth-century print. As the demand for slaves increased, raids extended deeper and deeper into the African interior. Tied together with forked logs or bark rope, men, women, and children were marched hundreds of miles toward the coast, where their African captors traded them to Europeans.

North Wind Picture Archives

As the demand for slaves increased in the eighteenth century with the expansion of the plantation system in the Americas, these raids extended deeper and deeper into the African interior. The march to the coast was filled with terrors. One account describes a two-month trip in which many captives died of hunger, thirst, or exhaustion, several attempted suicide, and the whole party was forced to hide to avoid being seized by a rival band of raiders. The captives finally arrived on the coast, where they were sold to an American vessel bound for South Carolina.

Enslavement was an unparalleled shock. Venture Smith, an African born in Guinea in 1729, was eight years old when he was captured. After many years in North American slavery, he still vividly recalled the attack on his village, the torture and murder of his father, and the long march of his people to the coast. "The shocking scene is to this day fresh in my mind," he wrote, "and I have often been overcome while thinking on it."

On the coast, European traders and African raiders assembled their captives. Prisoners waited in dark dungeons or in open pens called "barracoons." To lessen the possibility of collective resistance, traders split up families and ethnic groups. Captains carefully inspected each man and woman, and those selected for transport were branded on the back or buttocks with the mark of the buyer. Olaudah Equiano remembered that "those white men with horrible looks, red faces, and long hair, looked and acted . . . in so savage a manner; . . . I had never seen among any people such instances of brutal cruelty." Equiano's narrative, written during the 1780s, after he had secured his freedom, is one of the few that provide an African account of enslavement. He and his fellow captives became convinced that they "had got into a world of bad spirits" and were about to be eaten by cannibals. A French trader wrote that many prisoners were "positively prepossessed with the opinion that we transport them into our country in order to kill and eat them."

THE MIDDLE PASSAGE

In the eighteenth century, English sailors christened the voyage of slave ships as the "**Middle Passage**," the middle part of a trading triangle from England to Africa to America and back to England. From coastal forts and barracoons, crews rowed small groups of slaves out to the waiting ships and packed them into shelves below deck only six feet long by two and a half feet high. "Rammed like herring in a barrel," wrote one observer, slaves were "chained to each other hand and foot, and stowed so close, that they were not allowed above a foot and a half for each in breadth." People were forced to sleep "spoon fashion," and the tossing of the ship knocked them about so violently that the skin over their elbows sometimes was worn to the bone from scraping on the planks. "It was more than a week after I left the ship before I could straighten my limbs," one former slave later remembered. One ship designed to carry 450 slaves regularly crossed the Atlantic tightly packed with more than 600.

MAP EXPLORATION

To explore an interactive version of this map, go to **http://www.prenhall.com/faraghertlc/map4.2**

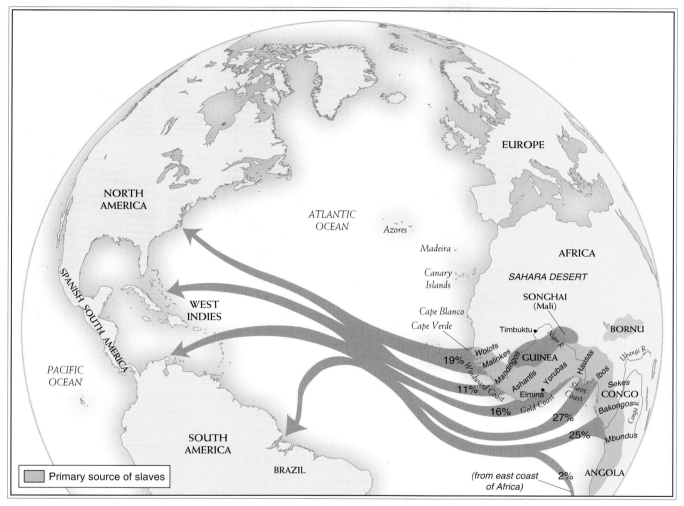

MAP 4-2
The African Slave Trade   The enslaved men, women, and children transported to the Americas came from West Africa, the majority from the lower Niger River (called the Slave Coast) and the region of the Congo and Angola.

HOW AND why were the people of Africa enslaved and brought to America?

Their holds filled with human cargo, the ships headed toward Cape Verde to catch the trade winds blowing toward America. A favorable voyage from Senegambia to Barbados might be accomplished in as little as three weeks, but a ship from Guinea or Angola becalmed in the doldrums or driven back by storms might take as much as three months.

The voyage was marked by a daily routine. In the morning the crew opened the hatch and brought the captives on deck, attaching their leg irons to a great chain running the length of the bulwarks. After a breakfast of beans came a ritual known as "dancing the slave." While an African thumped an upturned kettle or plucked a banjo, the crew commanded men and women to jump up and down in a bizarre session of exercise. A day spent chained on deck was concluded by a second bland meal and then the stowing away. During the night, according to one

Middle Passage   The voyage between West Africa and the New World slave colonies.

Slaves below deck on a Spanish slaver, a sketch made when the vessel was captured by a British warship in the early nineteenth century. Slaves were "stowed so close, that they were not allowed above a foot and a half for each in breadth," wrote one observer. The close quarters and unsanitary conditions created a stench so bad that Atlantic sailors said you could "smell a slaver five miles down wind."

The Granger Collection

seaman, there issued from below "a howling melancholy noise, expressive of extreme anguish." Down in the hold, the groans of the dying, the shrieks of women and children, and the suffocating heat and stench were, in the words of Olaudah Equiano, "a scene of horror almost inconceivable."

Among the worst of the horrors was the absence of adequate sanitation. There were "necessary tubs" set below deck, but Africans, "endeavoring to get to them, tumble over their companions," as one eighteenth-century ship's surgeon wrote. "And as the necessities of nature are not to be resisted, they ease themselves as they lie." Efficient captains ordered crews to scrape and swab the holds daily, but so sickening was the task that on many ships it was rarely performed and Africans were left to wallow in their urine and feces. When first taken below deck, the boy Equiano remembered, "I received such a salutation in my nostrils as I had never experienced in my life," and "became so sick and low that I was not able to eat." Atlantic sailors said you could "smell a slaver five miles down wind." Many captives sickened and died in these conditions. Many others contracted dysentery, known as the "flux." Frequent shipboard epidemics of smallpox, measles, and yellow fever added to the misery. The dying continued even as the ships anchored at their destinations. Historians estimate that during the Middle Passage of the eighteenth century one in every six Africans perished.

The unwilling voyagers offered plenty of resistance. As long as ships were still within sight of the African coast, hope remained alive and the danger of revolt was great. One historian has found references to fifty-five slave revolts on British and American ships from 1699 to 1845. Once on the open sea, however, the captives' resistance took more desperate form. The sight of the disappearing coast of Africa "left me abandoned to despair," wrote Equiano. "I now saw myself deprived of all chance of returning to my native country, or even the least glimpse of hope of gaining the shore." He witnessed several Africans jump overboard and drown, "and I believe many more would very soon have done the same if they had not been prevented by the ship's crew." Captains took the precaution of spreading netting along the sides of their ships. "Could I have got over the nettings," Equiano declared, "I would have jumped over the side."

ARRIVAL IN THE NEW WORLD

As the ship approached its destination the crew prepared the human cargo for market. All but the most rebellious were freed from their chains and allowed to wash themselves and move about the deck. Captains did what they could to get their Africans into presentable condition. To impress buyers, slavers might parade Africans off the ship to the tune of an accordion or the beat of a drum. But the toll of the Middle Passage was difficult to disguise. One observer described a disembarking group as "walking skeletons covered over with a piece of tanned leather."

Some cargoes were destined for a single wealthy planter, or consigned to a merchant who sold the captives in return for a commission; in other cases the captain himself was responsible. Buyers painstakingly examined the Africans, who once again suffered the indignity of probing eyes and poking fingers. This caused "much dread and trembling among us," wrote Equiano, and "bitter cries." In ports such as Charleston, sales were generally made by auction, or by a cruel method known as the scramble—fixed prices set in advance, the Africans driven into a corral, and on cue the buyers rushing among them, grabbing their pick. The noise, clamor, and eagerness of the buyers, Equiano remembered, renewed all the terrible apprehensions of the Africans. "In this manner, without scruple, are relations and friends separated, most of them never to see each other again." Bought by a Virginian, Equiano was taken to an isolated tobacco plantation where he found himself unable to communicate with any of his fellow slaves, who came from other ethnic groups.

POLITICAL AND ECONOMIC EFFECTS ON AFRICA

Africa began the sixteenth century with genuine independence. But as surely as Europe and America grew stronger as a result of the trade and the labor of slaves, so Africa grew weaker by their loss. In the short term, slave-trading kingdoms on the coast increased their power at the expense of interior states. But these coastal states found that the slave trade was a viper that could easily strike back at them. "Merchants daily seize our own subjects, sons of the land and sons of our noblemen, they grab them and cause them to be sold," King Dom Affonso of the Kongo wrote to the Portuguese monarch in the sixteenth century. "And so great, Sir, is their corruption and licentiousness that our country is being utterly depopulated."

More serious still, however, than the loss of millions of men and women over the centuries was the long-term stagnation of the West African economy. Labor was drawn away from farming and other productive activities, and imported consumer goods such as textiles and metal wares stifled local manufacturing. African traders were expert at driving a hard bargain for slaves, but even when they appeared to get the best of the exchange, the ultimate advantage lay with the Europeans, who received wealth-producing workers in return for mere consumer goods.

For every man or woman taken captive, at least another died in the chronic slave raiding. Many of the new West African states became little more than machines for supplying captives to European traders, and a "gun-slave cycle" pushed neighboring kingdoms into a destructive arms race. The resulting political and cultural demoralization prepared the way for the European conquest of Africa in the nineteenth century.

Africans as a Percentage of Total Population of the British Colonies, 1650–1770
Although the proportion of Africans and African Americans was never as high in the south as in the Caribbean, the ethnic structure of the south diverged radically from that of the north during the eighteenth century.

Robert w. Fogel and Stanley L. Engerman, *Time on the Cross* (Boston: Little, Brown, 1974), 21.

THE DEVELOPMENT OF NORTH AMERICAN SLAVE SOCIETIES

New World slavery was nearly two centuries old before it became an important system of labor in North America. There were slaves in each of the British colonies during the seventeenth century, but in 1700 slaves accounted for only 11 percent of the colonial population. During the eighteenth century slavery greatly expanded, and by 1770 Africans and African Americans in British North America numbered 460,000, or more than 20 percent of the colonial population.

SLAVERY COMES TO NORTH AMERICA

The first Africans in Virginia arrived in 1619. But because slaves generally cost twice as much as indentured servants, yet had the same appallingly short life expectancy, they offered planters little economic benefit. Consequently, over the next several decades planters in the Chesapeake region employed far more indentured servants than slaves. Until the 1670s the Chesapeake was what historians term a *society with slaves*, a society in which slavery was one form of labor among several.

In the last quarter of the seventeenth century, however, a number of developments encouraged the transformation of the Chesapeake from a society with slaves into a *slave society*, a society in which slavery was the dominant form of labor. In the aftermath of Bacon's Rebellion, planters consolidated their control of the Virginia colony. Because people were living longer, possibly the result of being better fed and more resistant to disease, more servants were surviving their indentures, and such a population could be troublesome. But these improvements in living conditions also affected Africans, increasing their rates of survival and allowing planters to amortize the purchase price of slaves over a considerably longer span. Also contributing to the transition was the development of better opportunities for European immigrants in colonies such as Pennsylvania, and the beginning of direct shipments of slaves from West Africa to the North American mainland by the English Royal African Company. Thus, the work force of indentured servants was replaced by a work force of slaves.

As the proportions of slaves in the colonial population rose, colonists wrote slavery into law, a process best observed in the case of Virginia. In 1662 colonial officials declared that children inherited the status of their slave mothers; five years later they added that baptism as a Christian could no longer alter conditions of servitude. Two important avenues to freedom were thus closed. The colony then placed life-threatening violence in the hands of masters, declaring in 1669 that the death of a slave during punishment "shall not be accounted felony." Such regulations accumulated piecemeal until 1705, when Virginia gathered them into a comprehensive slave code that became a model for other colonies.

Thus, the institution of slavery was strengthened just as the Atlantic slave trade reached flood tide in the eighteenth century. During that century's first decade, more Africans were imported into North America than the total number for the previous century. The English colonies were primed for an unprecedented growth of plantation slavery.

THE TOBACCO COLONIES

During the eighteenth century the European demand for tobacco increased more than tenfold, and it was supplied largely by increased production in the Chesapeake. Tobacco was far and away the single most

Portrait of Olaudah Equiano, by an unknown English artist, ca. 1780. Captured in Nigeria in 1756 when he was eleven years old, Equiano was transported to America and was eventually purchased by an English sea captain. After ten years as a slave, he succeeded in buying his own freedom and dedicated himself to the antislavery cause. His book *The Interesting Narrative of the Life of Olaudah Equiano* (1789) was published in numerous editions, translated into several languages, and became the prototype for dozens of other slave narratives in the nineteenth century.

Portrait of a Negro Man, Olaudah Equiano, ca. 1780, (previously attributed to Joshua Reynolds) by English School. Royal Albert Memorial Museum, Exeter, Devon, UK/Bridgeman Art Library, London/New York important commodity produced in eighteenth-century North America, accounting for more than a quarter of the value of all colonial exports.

The expansion of tobacco production could not have taken place without a corresponding growth in the size of the slave labor force. Unlike sugar, tobacco did not require large plantations and could be produced successfully on small farms. But it was a crop that demanded a great deal of hand labor and close attention. As tobacco farming grew, slaveholding became widespread. By 1770 more than a quarter million slaves labored in the colonies of the Upper South (Maryland, Virginia, and North Carolina), and because of the exploding market for tobacco, their numbers were expanding at about double the rate of the general population.

Shipments from Africa accounted for part of the growth of the slave population. In the Caribbean and Brazil, where profits from sugar were high, many sugar planters chose to work their slaves to death, replenishing them with a constant stream of new arrivals, mostly men, from Africa. In Virginia, however, lower rates of profit caused tobacco planters to pay more attention to the health of their labor force, establishing work routines that were not quite so deadly. Moreover, food supplies were more plentiful in North America, which made the Chesapeake populations of Africans more resistant to disease. By the 1730s the slave population of the Chesapeake had become the first in the Western Hemisphere to achieve self-sustained population growth. By the 1750s, about 80 percent of Chesapeake slaves were "country-born."

THE LOWER SOUTH

The Chesapeake did not become a slave society until almost a century after its founding. But in South Carolina settlement and slavery went hand in hand, and the colony was a slave society from the beginning. The most valuable part of the early Carolina economy was the Indian slave trade. Practicing a strategy of divide and conquer, using Indian tribes to fight one another, Carolinians enslaved tens of thousands of Indians before the 1730s, shipping many to slave markets in the Caribbean, employing others to raise cattle or to fell timber.

By 1715, however, planter preference had turned toward African rather than Indian slaves. Rice production was rapidly becoming the most dynamic sector of the South Carolina economy, and with their experience in agriculture West Africans made much better rice workers than Indians. Another important crop was added in the 1740s, when a young South Carolina woman named Elizabeth Lucas Pinckney successfully adapted West Indian indigo to the low-country climate. The indigo plant, native to India, produced a deep blue dye important in textile manufacture. Rice grew in the lowlands, but indigo could be cultivated on high ground, and with different seasonal growing patterns, planters were able to harmonize their production. Rice and indigo were two of the most valuable commodities exported from the mainland colonies of North America.

The boom in these two crops depended on the growth of African slavery. Before the international slave trade to the United States was ended in 1808, at least 100,000 had arrived in South Carolina. It is estimated that one of every five ancestors of today's African Americans passed through Charleston on the way to the rice fields.

By the 1740s, many of the arriving Africans were being taken to Georgia, a colony created by an act of the English Parliament in 1732. Its leader, James Edward Oglethorpe, hoped to establish a buffer against Spanish invasion from Florida and make it a haven for poor British farmers who could then sell their products in the markets of South Carolina. Under Oglethorpe's influence, Parliament agreed to prohibit slavery in Georgia. Soon, however, Georgia's coastal regions were being colonized by South Carolina planters with their slaves. In 1752,

QUICK REVIEW

Growth of Slavery

◆ Slavery grew rapidly in the South.

◆ The use of slaves made economic sense on tobacco and rice plantations.

◆ Northern slaves worked as servants, craftsmen, and day laborers.

 2–3
An Act Concerning Servants and Slaves

 2–13
Gottlieb Mittelberger, The Passage of Indentured Servants (1750)

Oglethorpe and Georgia's trustees abandoned their experiment, and the colony was opened to slavery under royal authority. The Georgia coast had already become an extension of the Carolina low-country slave system.

By 1770 there were nearly 90,000 African Americans in the Lower South, about 80 percent of the coastal population of South Carolina and Georgia. In the words of one eighteenth-century observer, "Carolina looks more like a negro country than like a country settled by white people." The African American communities of the Lower South achieved self-sustained growth in the middle of the eighteenth century, a generation later than those in the Chesapeake.

SLAVERY IN THE SPANISH COLONIES

Slavery was basic to the Spanish colonial labor system, yet doubts about the enslavement of Africans were raised by both church and crown. The papacy denounced slavery many times as a violation of Christian principles. But the institution of slavery remained intact, and later in the eighteenth century, when sugar production expanded in Cuba, the slave system there was as brutal as any in the history of the Americas.

The character of slavery varied with local conditions. One of the most benign forms operated in Florida. In 1699 the Spanish declared Florida a refuge for escaped slaves from the British colonies, offering free land to fugitives who would help defend their colony. Over the next half-century, refugee Indians and fugitive Africans established many communities in the countryside surrounding St. Augustine.

In New Mexico, the Spanish depended on Indian slavery. In the sixteenth century the colonial governor sent Indian slaves to the mines of Mexico. The enslavement of Indians was one of the causes of the **Pueblo Revolt** (see Chapter 3). During the eighteenth century, the Spanish were much more cautious in their treatment of the Pueblos, who were officially considered Catholics. But they captured and enslaved "infidel Indians" such as the Apaches or nomads from the Great Plains, using them as house servants and fieldworkers.

FRENCH LOUISIANA

Slavery was also important in Louisiana, the colony founded by the French in the lower Mississippi Valley in the early eighteenth century. The French Company of the Indies imported some 6,000 African slaves, and planters invested in tobacco and indigo plantations on the Mississippi River in the country of the Natchez Indians. But in 1629, the Natchez and the slaves together rose in an armed uprising, the Natchez Rebellion, that took the lives of more than 200 French settlers, 10 percent of the population. Although colonial authorities were able to put down the rebellion, the Louisiana French pulled back from a total commitment to slavery.

After the Natchez Rebellion, Louisiana's economy grew more diversified. Several thousand French colonists established farms and plantations on the Gulf Coast and in a narrow strip of settlement along the Mississippi River. African slaves amounted to no more than a third of the colonial population of 10,000. It was not until the end of the eighteenth century that the colony of Louisiana became an important North American slave society.

SLAVERY IN THE NORTH

Although none of the northern colonies could be characterized as a slave society, slavery was an important form of labor in many areas. Over the course of the eighteenth century it grew increasingly significant in the commercial farming regions of southeast Pennsylvania, central New Jersey, and Long Island, where slaves made up about 10 percent of the rural residents. In the vicinity of Newport,

Pueblo Revolt Rebellion in 1680 of Pueblo Indians in New Mexico against their Spanish overlords, sparked by religious conflict and excessive Spanish demands for tribute.

London Coffee House.

The London Coffee House, near the docks of Philadelphia, was the center of the city's business and political life in the mid-eighteenth century. Sea captains and merchants congregated here to do business, and as this contemporary print illustrates, it was the site of many slave auctions. Slavery was a vital part of the economy of northern cities.

The Library Company of Philadelphia.

Rhode Island, the proportion of slaves in the population reached nearly 25 percent. Elsewhere in the New England countryside slavery was relatively uncommon.

It was widespread in all the port cities, however, including Boston. Slave ownership was nearly universal among the wealthy and ordinary among craftsmen and professionals. By 1750 slaves and small free black populations made up 15 to 20 percent of the residents of Boston, New York City, and Philadelphia.

The Quakers of Pennsylvania and New Jersey, many of whom kept slaves, were the first colonists to voice antislavery sentiment. In *Considerations on the Keeping of Negroes* (1754), John Woolman urged his readers to imagine themselves in the place of the African people. Suppose, he wrote,

> that our ancestors and we had been exposed to constant servitude in the more servile and inferior employments of life; that we had been destitute of the help of reading and good company; that amongst ourselves we had had few wise and pious instructors; that the religious amongst our superiors seldom took notice of us; that while others in ease had plentifully heaped up the fruit of our labour, we had received barely enough to relieve nature, and being wholly at the command of others had generally been treated as a contemptible, ignorant part of mankind. Should we, in that case, be less abject than they now are?

In 1758 the Philadelphia Friends Meeting voted to condemn slavery and urged masters to voluntarily free their slaves. It was not until the Revolution, however, that antislavery attitudes became more widespread in the colonies.

African to African American

The majority of Africans transported to North America arrived during the eighteenth century. They were met by a rapidly growing population of country-born slaves, or "creoles" (from the French *créole* and Spanish *criollo*, meaning "born" or "raised"), a term first used by slaves in Brazil to distinguish their children, born in the New World, from newly arrived Africans. The perspective of

HOW DID African slaves attempt to preserve African culture in America?

The slave deck of the bark "Wildfire," brought into Key West on April 30, 1860.

The Granger Collection

creoles was shaped by their having grown up under slavery, and that perspective helped them to determine which elements of African culture they would incorporate into the emerging culture of the African American community. That community was formed out of the relationship between creoles and Africans, and between slaves and their European masters.

QUICK REVIEW

Slave Society

◆ Traces of African culture remained in slave society.

◆ Labor consumed most of slave's time.

◆ Kinship played a key role in solidifying African American communities.

THE DAILY LIFE OF SLAVES

Because slaves formed the overwhelming majority of the labor force that made the plantation colonies so profitable, it is fair to say that Africans built the South. As an agricultural people, Africans, both women and men, were accustomed to the routines of rural labor, and this was put to use on the plantations. Most Africans were field hands, and even domestic servants labored in the fields when necessary.

Masters provided their workers with rude clothing, sufficient in the summer but nearly always inadequate in the winter. Increasingly the plantations were supplied by cheap goods from the new industrial looms of England. Stiff shoes were a necessity in the cold months, but they so cramped the feet that everyone looked forward to shedding them in the spring and going barefoot all summer and fall. Hand-me-down clothes from the master's family offered slaves an opportunity to brighten their costumes, and many of them dressed in a variety of styles and colors. Similarly, they relieved the monotony of their rations of corn and pork with vegetables from their small gardens, game and fish from field and stream, and wild plant foods from the forests.

On small plantations and farms, which were typical in the tobacco country of the Chesapeake, Africans might work side by side with their owners and, depending on the character of the master, might enjoy a standard of living not too different from that of other family members. The work was more demanding and living conditions less sustaining on the great rice and indigo plantations of the Lower South, where slaves usually lived separately from the master in their own quarters. But large plantations, with large numbers of slaves, created the concentration of population necessary for the emergence of African American communities and African American culture.

FAMILIES AND COMMUNITIES

The family was the most important institution for the development of African American community and culture, but **slave codes** did not provide for legal slave marriages, for that would have contradicted the master's freedom to dispose of his property as he saw fit. "The endearing ties of husband and wife are strangers to us," declared the Massachusetts slaves who petitioned for their freedom in 1774, "for we are no longer man and wife than our masters or mistresses think proper." Despite the barriers, however, during the eighteenth century slaves in both the Chesapeake and the Lower South created the families that were essential for the development of African American culture.

On large plantations throughout the southern colonies, travelers found Africans living in family households. In the Lower South, where there were greater concentrations of slaves on the great rice plantations, husbands and wives often lived together in the slave quarters, and this was clearly the ideal. On the smaller plantations of the Upper South, men often married women from neighboring farms, and with the permission of both owners visited their families in the evenings or on Sundays.

Emotional ties to particular places, connections between the generations, and relations of kinship and friendship linking neighboring plantations and farms were the foundation stones of African American community life. Kinship was especially important. African American parents encouraged their children to use family terms in addressing unrelated persons: "auntie" or "uncle" became a respectful way

Slave Codes   A series of laws passed mainly in the Southern colonies in the late seventeenth and early eighteenth centuries to defend the status of slaves and codify the denial of basic civil rights to them.

of addressing older men and women, "brother" and "sister" affectionate terms for agemates. Fictive kinship may have been one of the first devices enslaved Africans used to humanize the world of slavery. During the Middle Passage, it was common for children to call their elders "aunt" and "uncle," for adults to address all children as "son" or "daughter."

AFRICAN AMERICAN CULTURE

The eighteenth century was the formative period in the development of the African American community, for it was then that the high birthrate and the growing numbers of country-born provided the necessary stability for the evolution of culture. During this period, men and women from dozens of African ethnic groups molded themselves into a new people. Distinctive patterns in music and dance, religion, and oral tradition illustrate the resilience of the human spirit under bondage as well as the successful struggle of African Americans to create a spiritually sustaining culture of their own.

Eighteenth-century masters were reluctant to allow their slaves to become Christians, fearing that baptism would open the way to claims of freedom or give Africans dangerous notions of universal brotherhood and equality with masters. One frustrated missionary was told by a planter that a slave was "ten times worse when a Christian than in his state of paganism." The majority of black southerners before the American Revolution practiced some form of African religion. Large numbers of African Americans were not converted to Christianity until the **Great Awakening**, which swept across the South after the 1760s (see Chapter 5).

One of the most crucial areas of religious practice concerned the rituals of death and burial. In their separate graveyards, African Americans often decorated graves with shells and pottery, an old African custom. African Americans generally believed that the spirits of their dead would return to Africa. The burial ceremony was often held at night to keep it secret from masters, who objected to the continuation of African traditions. The deceased was laid out, and around the body men and women would move counterclockwise in a slow dance step while singing ancestral songs. The pace gradually increased, finally reaching a frenzied but joyful conclusion. As slaves from different backgrounds joined together in the circle, they were beginning the process of cultural unification.

Great Awakening Tremendous religious revival in colonial America striking first in the Middle Colonies and New England in the 1740s and then spreading to the Southern colonies.

An Overseer Doing *His Duty*, a watercolor sketch made by Benjamin Henry Latrobe during a trip to Virginia in 1798. The majority of masters in the tobacco region owned only one or two slaves and worked with them in the fields. In his portrayal of this overseer, relaxing as he supervises his workers, Latrobe clearly expressed his disgust for slavery.

Benjamin Harry Latrobe, *An Overseer Doing His Duty.* Watercolor on paper. Collection of the Maryland Historical Society, Baltimore

Music and dance may have formed the foundation of African American culture, coming even before a common language. Many eighteenth-century observers commented on the musical and rhythmic gifts of Africans. Olaudah Equiano remembered his people, the Ibos, as "a nation of dancers, musicians, and poets." Thomas Jefferson, raised on a Virginia plantation, wrote that blacks "are more generally gifted than the whites, with accurate ears for tune and time." Many Africans were accomplished players of stringed instruments and drums, and their style featured improvisation and rhythmic complexity, elements that would become prominent in African American music. In America, slaves re-created African instruments, as in the case of the banjo, and mastered the art of the European violin and guitar. Fearing that slaves might communicate by code, authorities often outlawed drums. But using bones, spoons, or sticks, or simply "patting juba" (slapping their thighs), slaves produced elaborate multirhythmic patterns.

One of the most important developments of the eighteenth century was the invention of an African American language. An English traveler during the 1770s complained he could not understand Virginia slaves, who spoke "a mixed dialect between the Guinea and English." But such a language made it possible for country-born and "saltwater" Africans to communicate. The two most important dialects were Gullah and Geechee, named after two of the African peoples most prominent in the Carolina and Georgia low country, the Golas and Gizzis of the Windward Coast. These creole languages were a transitional phenomenon, gradually giving way to distinctive forms of black English, although in certain isolated areas, such as the sea islands of the Carolinas and Georgia, they persisted into the twentieth century.

THE AFRICANIZATION OF THE SOUTH

The African American community often looked to recently arrived Africans for religious leadership and medical magic. Throughout the South, many whites had as much faith in slave conjurers and herb doctors as the slaves themselves did, and slaves won fame for their healing powers. This was one of many ways in which white and black Southerners came to share a common culture. Acculturation was by no means a one-way street; English men and women in the South were also being Africanized.

Slaves worked in the kitchens of their masters, and thus introduced an African style of cooking into colonial diets already transformed by the addition of Indian

This eighteenth-century painting by an anonymous artist depicts a celebration in the slave quarters on a South Carolina plantation. One planter's description of a slave dance seems to fit this scene: the men leading the women in "a slow, shuffling gait, edging along by some unseen exertion of the feet, from one side to the other–sometimes curtseying down and remaining in that posture while the edging motioning from one side to the other continued." The woman, he wrote, "always carried a handkerchief held at arm's length, which was waved in a graceful motion to and fro as she moved."

Abby Aldrich Rockefeller Folk Art Museum, Williamsburg, VA

crops. African American culinary arts are responsible for such southern culinary specialty perennials as barbecue, fried chicken, black-eyed peas, and collard greens. And the liberal African use of red pepper, sesame seeds, and other sharp flavors established the southern preference for highly spiced foods. In Louisiana a combination of African, French, and Indian elements produced a distinguished American regional cuisine, exemplified by gumbos (soups) and jambalayas (stews).

Mutual acculturation is also evident in many aspects of material culture. Southern basket weaving used Indian techniques and African designs. Woodcarving often featured African motifs. African architectural designs featuring high, peaked roofs (to drain off the heat) and broad, shady porches gradually became part of a distinctive southern style. The West African iron-working tradition was evident throughout the South, especially in the ornamentation of the homes of Charleston and New Orleans.

Even more important were less tangible aspects of culture. Slave mothers nursed white children as well as their own. As one English observer wrote, "each child has its [black] Momma, whose gestures and accent it will necessarily copy, for children, we all know, are imitative beings." In this way many Africanisms passed into the English language of the South: goober (peanut), yam, banjo, okay, tote, buddy. Some linguists have argued that the southern "drawl," evident among both black and white speakers, derived from the incorporation of African intonations of words and syllables.

VIOLENCE AND RESISTANCE

Slavery was a system based on the use of force and violence. Fear underlay the daily life of both masters and slaves. Owners could be humane, but slaves had no guarantees of benevolent treatment, and the kindest master could turn cruel. Even the most cultured plantation owners of the eighteenth century thought nothing about floggings of fifty or seventy-five lashes. "Der prayer was answered," sang the Africans of South Carolina, "wid de song of a whip." Although the typical planter punished slaves with extra work, public humiliation, or solitary confinement, the threat of the lash was omnipresent. There were sadistic masters who stabbed, burned, maimed, mutilated, raped, or castrated their slaves.

Fugitive slaves flee through the swamps in Thomas Moran's *The Slave Hunt* (1862). Many slaves ran away from their masters, and colonial newspapers included notices urging readers to be on the lookout for them. Some fled in groups or collected together in isolated communities called "maroon" colonies, located in inaccessible swamps and woods.

Thomas Moran, *The Slave Hunt*, 1862, oil on canvas, 86.4 × 111.8 cm. Gift of Laura A. Clubb, The Philbrook Museum of Art, Tulsa, Oklahoma

Yet African Americans demonstrated a resisting spirit. In their day-to-day existence they often refused to cooperate: they malingered, they mistreated tools and animals, they destroyed the master's property. Flight was also an option, and judging from the advertisements placed by masters in colonial newspapers, even the most trusted Africans ran away.

Runaways sometimes collected together in communities called "maroons," from the Spanish *cimarron*, meaning "wild and untamed." The African communities in Spanish Florida were often called maroons. Indeed, as a whole these mixed African and Creek Indian peoples in Florida called themselves Seminoles, a name deriving from their pronunciation of cimarron. Maroons were also found in the backcountry of the Lower South, and although they were less common in the Upper South, a number of fugitive communities existed in the Great Dismal Swamp between Virginia and North Carolina. In the 1730s, a group of escaped Africans built a community of grass houses and set up a tribal government there, but they were soon dispersed by the authorities.

The most direct form of resistance was revolt. The first notable slave uprising of the colonial era occurred in New York City in 1712. Taking an oath of secrecy, twenty-three Africans vowed revenge for what they called the "hard usage" of their masters. They armed themselves with guns, swords, daggers, and hatchets, killed nine colonists, and burned several buildings before being surrounded by the militia. Six of the conspirators committed suicide rather than surrender. Those captured were hanged, burned at the stake, or broken on the wheel. In 1741 New York authorities uncovered what they thought was another conspiracy. Thirteen black leaders were burned alive, eighteen hanged, and eighty sold and shipped off to the West Indies. A family of colonists and a Catholic priest, accused of providing weapons, were also executed.

There were also isolated but violent uprisings in the Lower South, where slaves were a majority of the population, in 1704, 1720, and 1730. In 1738 a series of violent revolts broke out throughout South Carolina and Georgia. Then in 1739, the largest slave rebellion of the colonial period took place when a group of twenty recently arrived Angolans sacked the armory in Stono, South Carolina. They armed themselves and began a march toward Florida and freedom. Beating drums to attract other slaves to their cause, they grew to nearly one hundred. They plundered a number of planters' homes along the way and killed some thirty colonists. Pausing in a field to celebrate their victory with dance and song, they were overtaken by the militia and destroyed in a pitched battle. That same year there was an uprising in Georgia. Another took place in South Carolina the following year. Attributing these revolts to the influence of newly arrived Africans, colonial officials shut off the slave trade through Charleston for the next ten years.

Wherever masters held slaves, fears of uprisings persisted. But compared with such slave colonies as Jamaica, Guiana, or Brazil, there were few slave revolts in North America. The conditions favoring revolt—large African majorities, brutal exploitation with correspondingly low survival rates, little acculturation, and geographic isolation—prevailed only in some areas of the Lower South. Indeed, the very success of African Americans in British North America at establishing families, communities, and a culture of their own inevitably made them less likely to take the risks that rebellions required.

SLAVERY AND THE ECONOMICS OF EMPIRE

Slavery contributed enormously to the economic growth and development of Europe during the colonial era, and it was an important factor in Great Britain, just before the Industrial Revolution of the eighteenth century. Slavery was the most dynamic force in the Atlantic economy during that century,

QUICK REVIEW

Resistance to Slavery

- Refusal to cooperate or destruction of property.
- Running away and establishing fugitive communities.
- Revolting.

2–12
James Oglethorpe: The Stono Rebellion (1739)

HOW DID slavery fuel the economic development of Europe in the seventeenth and eighteenth centuries?

MAP EXPLORATION
To explore an interactive version of this map, go to
http://www.prenhall.com/faraghertlc/map4.3

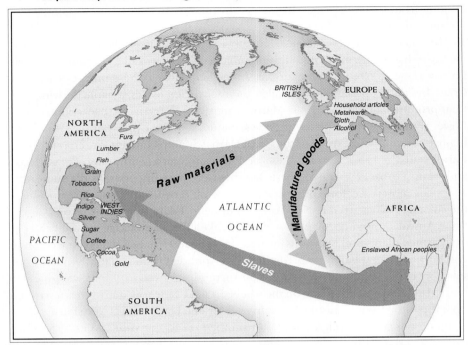

MAP 4-3

Triangular Trade Across the Atlantic   The pattern of commerce among Europe, Africa, and the Americas became known as the "Triangular Trade." Sailors called the voyage of slave ships from Africa to America the "Middle Passage" because it formed the crucial middle section of this trading triangle.

HOW WERE Europe, Africa, and America linked together by commerce?

creating the conditions for industrialization. But because slave-owning colonists single-mindedly committed their resources to the expansion and extension of the plantation system, they derived very little benefit from the economic diversification that characterized industrialization.

SLAVERY THE MAINSPRING

The slave colonies—the sugar islands of the West Indies and the colonies of the South—accounted for 95 percent of exports from the Americas to Great Britain from 1714 to 1773. Although approximately half of all Great Britain's American colonists lived in New England and the mid-Atlantic, the colonies in those regions contributed less than 5 percent of total exports during this period. Moreover, there was the prime economic importance of the slave trade itself, which one economist of the day described as the "foundation" of the British economy, "the mainspring of the machine which sets every wheel in motion." The labor of African slaves was largely responsible for the economic success of the British Empire in the Americas.

Slavery greatly contributed to the economic development of Great Britain in three principal ways. First, slavery provided an enormous stimulus to the growth of manufacturing by creating a huge colonial market for exports. Second, slavery generated enormous profits that became a source of investment in the economy. Economic historians estimate that annual profits during the eighteenth century averaged 15 percent of invested capital in the slave trade, 10 percent in plantation agriculture.

QUICK REVIEW

British Trade Policy

◆ All trade in empire to be conducted in English or colonial ships.

◆ Channeling of colonial trade through England or another English colony.

◆ Subsidization of English goods offered for sale in the colonies.

◆ Colonists prohibited from large-scale manufacture of certain products.

OVERVIEW
THE COLONIAL WARS

King William's War 1689–1697		France and England battle on the northern frontiers of New England and New York.
Queen Anne's War 1702–1713		England fights France and Spain in the Caribbean and on the northern frontier of New France. Part of the European conflict known as the War of the Spanish Succession.
War of Jenkins's Ear 1739–1743		Great Britain versus Spain in the Caribbean and Georgia. Part of the European conflict known as the War of the Austrian Succession.
King George's War 1744–1748		Great Britain and France fight in Acadia and Nova Scotia; the second American round of the War of the Austrian Succession.
French and Indian War 1754–1763		Last of the great colonial wars pitting Great Britain against France and Spain. Known in Europe as the Seven Years' War.

The profits of the slave trade and slave production contributed greatly to the accumulation of capital. This capital funded the first modern banks and insurance companies and eventually found its way into a wide range of economic activities. Merchant capitalists were prominent investors in the expansion of the merchant marine, the improvement of harbors, the construction of canals.

The multiplier effects of these activities are best seen in the growth of English ports such as Liverpool and Bristol. There the African and American trades provided employment for ships' crews, dockmen, construction workers, traders, shopkeepers, lawyers, clerks, factory workers, and officials of all ranks down to the humblest employees of the custom house. It was said of Bristol that "there is not a brick in the city but what is cemented with the blood of a slave."

Third, and finally, slavery contributed to the economic development of Great Britain by supplying the raw cotton essential to the Industrial Revolution. In 1787 slave plantations in the Caribbean supplied 69 percent of the raw cotton for British mills. The insatiable demand for cotton led to the development of the cotton gin and the rise of cotton plantations in the United States (see Chapter 11).

THE POLITICS OF MERCANTILISM

When imperial officials argued that colonies existed solely for the benefit of the mother country, they had in mind principally the great wealth produced by slavery. To ensure that this wealth benefited their states, European imperial powers created a system of regulations that became known as "**mercantilism**." The essence of mercantilist policy was the political control of the economy by the state. First advanced in France in the seventeenth century under the empire of Louis XIV, in the eighteenth century mercantilist politics were most successfully applied by Great Britain. The monarchy and Parliament established a uniform national monetary system, regulated wages, encouraged agriculture and manufacturing, and erected tariff barriers to protect themselves from foreign competition. England also sought to organize and control colonial trade to the maximum advantage of its own shippers, merchants, manufacturers, and bureaucrats.

The mercantilists viewed the economy as a "zero-sum" game, in which total economic gains were equal to total losses. Profits were thought to result from successful speculation, crafty dealing, or simple plunder—all forms of stealing wealth.

Mercantilism Economic system whereby the government intervenes in the economy for the purpose of increasing national wealth.

1-6
Thomas Mun, from England's Treasure by Foreign Trade (1664)

The institution of slavery confirmed the theory, for slavery was nothing more than a highly developed system by which some people stole the labor of others. The essence of the competition between states, the mercantilists argued, was the struggle to acquire and hoard the fixed amount of wealth that existed in the world. The nation that accumulated the largest treasure of gold and silver specie would be the most powerful.

WARS FOR EMPIRE

The mercantilist era was, thus, a period of intense and violent competition among European states. Wars usually arose out of Old World issues, spilling over into the New World, but they also originated in conflicts over the colonies themselves.

Colonial wars in the southern region had everything to do with slavery. The first fighting of the eighteenth century took place during **Queen Anne's War** (known in Europe as the War of the Spanish Succession), a conflict that pitted Great Britain and its allies against France and Spain. In 1702 troops from South Carolina invaded Florida, plundering and burning St. Augustine in an attempt to destroy the refuge for fugitive slaves there. A combined French and Spanish fleet took revenge in 1706 by bombarding Charleston. The British finally prevailed, and in 1713, as part of the Peace of Utrecht, Spain ceded to the English the exclusive lucrative right to supply slaves to its American colonies.

The entrance of British slavers into Spanish ports also provided an opportunity for illicit trade, and sporadic fighting between the two empires broke out over this issue a number of times during the next two decades.

In the northern region, the principal focus of this imperial struggle was control of the Indian trade. In 1704, during Queen Anne's War, the French and their Algonquian Indian allies raided New England frontier towns, such as Deerfield, Massachusetts, dragging men, women, and children into captivity in Canada. In turn, the English mounted a series of expeditions against the strategic French fortress of Port Royal in Acadia, which they captured in 1710. At the war's conclusion in 1713, France was forced to cede Acadia, Newfoundland, and Hudson's Bay to Great Britain in exchange for guarantees of security for the French-speaking residents of those provinces. Nearly thirty years of peace followed, but from 1744 to 1748 England again battled France in **King George's War** (known in Europe as the War of the Austrian Succession). The French attacked the British in Nova Scotia. Indian and Canadian raids again devastated the border towns of New England and New York, and hundreds of British subjects were killed or captured.

BRITISH COLONIAL REGULATION

Mercantilists used means other than war to win the wealth of the world. The British monarchy, for example, chartered the East India Company, the Hudson's Bay Company, and the Royal African Company as trading monopolies in their respective regions.

English manufacturers complained that merchant-dominated trading monopolies too frequently carried foreign (particularly Dutch) products to colonial markets, ignoring English domestic industry. Reacting to these charges, between 1651 and 1696 Parliament passed the Navigation Acts, which created the legal and institutional structure of Britain's eighteenth-century colonial system. The acts defined the colonies as both suppliers of raw materials and as markets for English manufactured goods. Merchants from other nations were expressly forbidden to trade in the colonies, and all trade had to be conducted in ships built in England or the British colonies themselves.

The regulations specified a list of colonial products that could be shipped only to England. These included the products of the southern slave colonies

Queen Anne's War American phase (1702–1713) of Europe's War of the Spanish Succession.

King George's War The third Anglo-French war in North America (1744–1748), part of the European conflict known as the War of the Austrian Succession.

The New England artist John Greenwood painted this amusing view of New England sea captains in Surinam in 1757. By the early eighteenth century, New England merchant traders like these had become important participants in the traffic in slaves and sugar to and from the West Indies. Northern ports thus became important pivots in the expanding commercial network linking plantations with Atlantic markets.

John Greenwood, *Sea Captains Carousing in Surinam*, 1757. Oil on bed ticking, 95.9 × 191.2 cm. The Saint Louis Art Museum, Museum Purchase.

(sugar, molasses, rum, tobacco, rice, and indigo), those of the northern Indian trade (furs and skins), and those essential for supplying the shipping industry (pine masts, tar, pitch, resin, and turpentine). The bulk of these products were not destined for English consumption; at great profit they were reexported elsewhere.

England also placed limitations on colonial enterprises that might compete with those at home. A series of enactments—including the Wool Act of 1699, the Hat Act of 1732, and the Iron Act of 1750—forbade the manufacture of those products. Moreover, colonial assemblies were forbidden to impose tariffs on English imports as a way to protect colonial industries. Banking was disallowed, local coinage prohibited, and the export of coin from England forbidden. Badly in need of a circulating monetary medium, Massachusetts illegally minted copper coin, and several colonies issued paper currency, forcing Parliament to explicitly legislate against the practice. The colonists depended mostly on "commodity money" (furs, skins, or hogsheads of tobacco) and the circulation of foreign currency. Official rates of exchange between commodity money, colonial paper, foreign currency, and English pounds allowed this chaotic system to operate without too much difficulty.

As the trade in colonial products increased, the British came to agree that it made little sense to tamper with such a prosperous system. Prime Minister Robert Walpole pursued a policy later characterized as one of "salutory neglect." Any colonial rules and regulations deemed contrary to good business practice were simply ignored and not enforced. Between 1700 and 1760 the quantity of goods exported from the colonies to the mother country rose 165 percent, while imports from Britain to North America increased by more than 400 percent. In part because of the lax enforcement, but mostly because the system operated to the profit of colonial merchants, colonists complained very little about the operation of the mercantilist system before the 1760s.

The Colonial Economy

Despite the seemingly harsh mercantilist regulations, the economic system operated to the benefit of planters, merchants, and white colonists in general. Southern slave owners made healthy profits on the sale of their commodities. They enjoyed a protected market in which competing goods from outside the empire were heavily taxed. Planters found themselves with steadily increasing purchasing power. Pennsylvania, New York, and New England, and increasingly the Chesapeake as well, produced grain, flour, meat, and dairy products. None of these was included in the list of **enumerated goods** and, thus, they could be sold freely abroad. They found their most ready market in the British West Indies and the Lower South, where food production was slighted in favor of sugar and rice. Most of this trade was carried in New England ships. Indeed, the New England shipbuilding industry was greatly stimulated by the allowance under the Navigation Acts for ships built and manned in the colonies. So many ships were built for English buyers that by midcentury nearly a third of all British tonnage was American made.

The greatest benefits for the port cities of the North came from their commercial relationship to the slave colonies. New England merchants had become important players in the slave trade by the early eighteenth century, and soon thereafter they began to make inroads into the export trade of the West Indian colonies. It was in the Caribbean that northern merchants most blatantly ignored mercantilist regulations. In violation of Spanish, French, and Dutch regulations prohibiting foreign trade, New Englanders traded foodstuffs for sugar in foreign colonies. They illegally sent the sugar to New England. By 1750 more than sixty distilleries in Massachusetts Bay were exporting more than 2 million gallons of rum, most of it produced from sugar obtained illegally. Because the restrictive rules and regulations enacted by Britain for its colonies were not enforced, such growth and prosperity among the merchants and manufacturers of the port cities of the North prospered.

By the mid-eighteenth century, the Chesapeake and Lower South regions were major exporters of tobacco, rice, and indigo, and the Middle colonies major exporters of grain to Europe. The carrying trade in the products of slave labor made it possible for the Northern and Middle colonies to earn the income necessary to purchase British imports despite the lack of valuable products from their own regions. Gradually, the commercial economies of the Northeast and the South were becoming integrated. From the 1730s to the 1770s, for example, while the volume of trade between Great Britain and Charleston doubled, the trade between Charleston and northern ports grew sevenfold. The same relationship was developing between the Chesapeake and the North. Merchants in Boston, Newport, New York, and Philadelphia increasingly provided Southern planters not only with shipping services, but also with credit and insurance. Like London, Liverpool, and Bristol—though on a smaller scale—the port cities of the North became pivots in the expanding trade network linking slave plantations with Atlantic markets. This trade provided Northern merchants with the capital that financed commercial growth and development in their cities and the surrounding countryside. Slavery thus contributed to the growth of a score of Northern port cities, forming an indirect but essential part of their economies.

Slavery and Freedom

The prosperity of the eighteenth-century plantation economy thus improved the living conditions for the residents of Northern cities as well as for a large segment of the population of the South, providing them with the opportunity for a kind of freedom unknown in the previous century. The price

QUICK REVIEW

Colonial Exports

- Chesapeake colonies: tobacco.
- South Carolina: rice and indigo.
- Middle colonies: wheat.

Enumerated goods Items produced in the colonies and enumerated in acts of Parliament that could be legally shipped from the colony of origin only to specified locations.

HOW DID slavery shape southern colonial society?

of prosperity and freedom was the oppression and exploitation of millions of Africans and African Americans. Freedom for white men based on the slavery of African Americans is the most important contradiction of American history.

THE SOCIAL STRUCTURE OF THE SLAVE COLONIES

At the summit of Southern colonial society stood a small elite of wealthy planters, in contrast with the mass of slave men and women who formed the working population. Slavery had produced a society in which property was concentrated in the hands of a wealthy few. The richest 10 percent of colonists owned more than half the cultivated land and over 60 percent of the wealth. Although there was no colonial aristocracy— no nobility or royal appointments—the landed elite of the slave colonies came very close to constituting one.

The typical wealthy Virginia planter lived in a Tidewater county; owned several thousand acres of prime farmland and more than a hundred slaves; resided in a luxurious plantation mansion, built perhaps in the fashionable Georgian style; and had an estate valued at more than £10,000. Elected to the House of Burgesses and forming the group from which the magistrates and counselors of the colony were chosen, these "first families of Virginia"—the Carters, Harrisons, Lees, Fitzhughs, Washingtons, Randolphs, and others—were a self-perpetuating governing class.

A similar elite ruled the Lower South, although wealthy landowners spent little time on their plantations. They lived instead in fashionable Charleston, where they made up a close-knit group who controlled the colonial government. "They live in as high a style here, I believe, as any part of the world," a visitor wrote.

A considerable distance separated this slave-owning elite from typical Southern landowners. About half the adult white males were small planters and farmers. But while the gap between rich and middling colonists grew larger during the eighteenth century, the prosperity of the plantation economy created generally favorable conditions for the landowning class as a whole. Slave ownership, for example, became widespread among this group during the eighteenth century. In Virginia at midcentury, 45 percent of heads of household held one to four slaves and even poorer farmers kept one or two.

Despite the prosperity that accompanied slavery in the eighteenth century, however, a substantial portion of colonists owned no land or slaves at all. Some rented land or worked as tenant farmers, some hired out as overseers or farm workers, and still others were indentured servants. Throughout the plantation region, landless men constituted about 40 percent of the population. A New England visitor found a "much greater disparity between the rich and poor in Virginia" than at home.

WHITE SKIN PRIVILEGE

But all the white colonists of eighteenth-century North America shared the privileged status of their skin color. As slavery became increasingly important, however, Virginia officials took considerable care to create legal distinctions between the status of colonists and that of Africans. Beginning in 1670, free Africans were prohibited from owning Christian servants. Ten years later, another law declared that any African, free or slave, who struck a Christian would receive thirty lashes on his bare back. One of the most important measures was designed to suppress intimate interracial

QUICK REVIEW

Southern Social Structure

◆ Topped by small elite of wealthy planters.

◆ About half of all white adult males were small planters and farmers.

◆ A substantial portion of colonists owned no land or slaves.

RUN away from the subscriber in *Albemarle*, a Mulatto slave called *Sandy*, about 35 years of age, his stature is rather low, inclining to corpulence, and his complexion light; he is a shoemaker by trade, in which he uses his left hand principally, can do coarse carpenters work, and is something of a horse jockey; he is greatly addicted to drink, and when drunk is insolent and disorderly, in his conversation he swears much, and in his behaviour is artful and knavish. He took with him a white horse, much scarred with traces, of which it is expected he will endeavour to dispose; he also carried his shoemakers tools, and will probably endeavour to get employment that way. Whoever conveys the said slave to me, in *Albemarle*, shall have 40 s. reward, if taken up within the county, 4 l. if elsewhere within the colony, and 10 l. if in any other colony. from

THOMAS   JEFFERSON.

Thomas Jefferson placed this advertisement in the *Virginia Gazette* on September 14, 1769. Americans need to seriously consider the historical relationship between the prosperity and freedom of white people and the oppression and exploitation of Africans and African Americans.

Virginia Historical Society

CHRONOLOGY

1441	African slaves first brought to Portugal.
1518	Spain grants official license to Portuguese slavers.
1535	Africans constitute a majority on Hispaniola.
1619	First Africans brought to Virginia.
1655	English seize Jamaica.
1662	Virginia law makes slavery hereditary.
1670	South Carolina founded.
1672	Royal African Company organized.
1691	Virginia prohibits interracial sexual contact.
1698	Britain opens the slave trade to all its merchants.
1699	Spanish declare Florida a refuge for escaped slaves.
1702	South Carolinians burn St. Augustine.
1705	Virginia Slave Code established.
1706	French and Spanish navies bombard Charleston.
1710	English capture Port Royal in Acadia.
1712	Slave uprising in New York City.
1713	Peace of Utrecht.
1721–1748	Robert Walpole leads British cabinet.
1729	Natchez Rebellion in French Louisiana.
1733	Molasses Act.
1739	Stono Rebellion in South Carolina.
1739–1743	War of Jenkins's Ear.
1740–1748	King George's War.
1741	Africans executed in New York for conspiracy.
1752	Georgia officially opened to slavery.
1770s	Peak period of the English colonies' slave trade.
1808	Importation of slaves into the United States ends.

contacts between white servants and enslaved Africans. A 1691 act "for prevention of that abominable mixture and spurious issue which hereafter may encrease in this dominion" established severe penalties for interracial sexual relationships.

Such penalties were rarely applied to masters, who frequently forced themselves on African women. But some slave women may have willingly established intimate relations with masters to better their condition or the opportunities for their children. After the death of his wife, Thomas Jefferson's father-in-law took a slave woman as his concubine. They had six children. After Jefferson's wife died, it was rumored that he established a sexual relationship with Sally Hemings, the youngest of those children, and his late wife's half-sister. Recent scientific tests have confirmed that Jefferson was likely the father of Sally's children, who enjoyed a privileged position in the household and were freed in Jefferson's will.

Relationships between white masters or indentured servants and African slaves produced a rather large group of mulattoes. Because by law children inherited the bondage or free status of their mothers, the majority of those of mixed ancestry were slaves; a minority, the children of European women and African men, were free. According to a Maryland census of 1755, more than 60 percent of mulattoes were slaves. But Maryland mulattoes also made up three-quarters of a small free African American population. This group, numbering about 4,000 in the 1770s, was denied the right to vote, to hold office, or to testify in court— all on the basis of racial background. Denied the status of citizenship enjoyed by even the poorest white men, free blacks were an outcast group who raised the status of white colonials by contrast.

Racism set up a wall of contempt between colonists and African Americans. Despite their close association, said Thomas Jefferson, the two peoples were divided by "deep rooted prejudices entertained by the whites" and "ten thousand recollections, by the blacks, of the injuries they have sustained." Perhaps he knew of these feelings from his long relationship with Sally Hemings. "I tremble for my country when I reflect that God is just," Jefferson concluded in a deservedly famous passage, and remember "that his justice cannot sleep forever."

CONCLUSION

During the eighteenth century nearly half a million Africans were kidnapped from their homes, marched to the African coast, and packed into ships for up to three months before arriving in British North America. They provided the labor that made colonialism pay. Southern planters, northern merchants, and especially British traders and capitalists benefited greatly from the commerce in slave-produced crops, and that prosperity filtered down to affect many of the colonists of British North America. Slavery was fundamental to the operation of the British empire in North America. Mercantilism was a system designed to channel colonial wealth produced by slaves to the nation-state, but as long as profits were high, the British tended to wink at colonists' violations of mercantilist regulations.

Although African Americans received little in return, their labor helped build the greatest accumulation of capital that Europe had ever seen. But despite enormous hardship and suffering, African Americans survived by forming new communities in the colonies, rebuilding families, restructuring language, and reforming culture. African American culture added important components of African knowledge and experience to colonial agriculture, art, music, and cuisine. The African Americans of the English colonies lived better lives than the slaves worked to death on Caribbean sugar plantations, but lives of misery compared with the men they were forced to serve. As the slaves sang on the Georgia coast, "Dah Backrow Man go wrong you, Buddy Quow."

SUMMARY

The Beginnings of African Slavery African slavery evolved out of an existing Mediterranean tradition. It was adapted to the rise of changing modes of agricultural production. The slave trade focused on African societies familiar with slavery and farming.

The African Slave Trade Various European nations participated in the African slave trade. The trade was an exercise in brutality that profoundly affected African societies.

The Development of North American Slave Societies Slavery was an acceptable labor system throughout colonial America. Slave societies developed in different regions in different European settlements and so were quite diverse. The presence of slavery did not necessarily mean a slave society developed.

African to African American Building upon their African heritage, the people wrenched from their homelands across the Atlantic Ocean constructed a community that was adapted to their situations. Family life, culture, methods of accommodation and resistance, and acculturation created the African Americans and their communities. In the process, African influences became integrated into the life, culture, and society of the South.

Slavery and the Economics of Empire Slavery was the mainspring of colonial economic development and a major force behind the rise of European empires in the

Americas. The competition for wealth among European nations stimulated wars and attempts by England to regulate the economy of its colonies.

Slavery and Freedom Slavery created a stratified society with a small planter elite that controlled most of the wealth and power. In most cases, wealth was connected to owning land. But wealth was not the only determinant of status. Skin color played as large a role.

REVIEW QUESTIONS

1. Trace the development of the system of slavery, and discuss the way it became entrenched in the Americas.

2. Describe the effects of the slave trade both on enslaved Africans and on the economic and political life of Africa.

3. Describe the process of acculturation involved in becoming an African American. In what ways did slaves "Africanize" the South?

4. Explain the connection between the institution of slavery and the building of a commercial empire.

5. In what ways did colonial policy encourage the growth of racism?

KEY TERMS

Enumerated goods (p. 94)   **Pueblo Revolt** (p. 82)
Great Awakening (p. 86)   **Queen Anne's War** (p. 92)
King George's War (p. 92)   **Seven Years' War** (p. 75)
Mercantilism (p. 91)   **Slave codes** (p. 85)
Middle Passage (p. 76)

RECOMMENDED READING

Ira Berlin, *Many Thousands Gone: The First Two Centuries of Slavery in North America* (1998). A history of colonial slavery with attention to the differences between the regions of the Chesapeake, the Lower South, Louisiana, and the North. Emphasizes the distinction between slave societies and societies with slaves.

Michael Craton, *Sinews of Empire: A Short History of British Slavery* (1974). An introduction to the British mercantilist system that emphasizes the importance of slavery. Includes a comparison of the mainland colonies with the Caribbean.

Philip D. Curtin, *The African Slave Trade: A Census* (1969). The pioneer work in the quantitative history of the slave trade. All subsequent histories of the slave trade are indebted to Curtin.

Winthrop D. Jordan, *White over Black: American Attitudes Toward the Negro, 1550–1812* (1968). Remains the best and most comprehensive history of racial attitudes. A searching examination of British and American literature, folklore, and history.

Herbert S. Klein, *The Atlantic Slave Trade* (1999). A new and important synthesis of the most recent studies of the slave trade, covering the social and cultural effects of the trade, especially for Africans.

Peter Kolchin, *American Slavery, 1619–1877* (1993). This survey features comparisons with slavery in Brazil and the Caribbean and serfdom in Russia. Includes a comprehensive bibliographic essay.

Philip D. Morgan, *Slave Counterpoint: Black Culture in the Eighteenth-Century Chesapeake and Low-Country* (1998). A comprehensive and detailed examination of cultural forms and ways of life in the two regions that leaves hardly a stone unturned.

Walter Rodney, *How Europe Underdeveloped Africa* (1974). This highly influential book traces the relationship between Europe and Africa from the fifteenth to the twentieth century and demonstrates how Europe's industrialization became Africa's impoverishment.

Mechal Sobel, *The World They Made Together: Black and White Values in Eighteenth-Century Virginia* (1987). Demonstrates the ways in which both Africans and Europeans shaped the formation of American values, perceptions, and identities.

Ian K. Steele, *Warpaths: Invasions of North America* (1994). A new synthesis of the colonial wars from the sixteenth to the eighteenth century that places Indians as well as empires at the center of the action.

*Mr. Lawrence, Be pleased to send me
a geenteel sute of Cloaths made of superfine
broad Cloth handsomely chosen...*
—George Washington, April, 26, 1763

CITY HALL AND GREAT DOCK.

New Amsterdam, in 17th century. City Hall and Great Dock
in the late 17th century.

5

THE CULTURES OF COLONIAL NORTH AMERICA

1700–1780

HOW DID Indians adapt to the new conditions created by colonization?

HOW DID the structure of colonial society differ from European social structure?

TO WHAT extent did North America participate in the Enlightenment?

1780

1700

AMERICAN COMMUNITIES

From Deerfield to Kahnawake: Crossing Cultural Boundaries

TWO HOURS BEFORE DAYLIGHT ON FEBRUARY 29, 1704, THE REVEREND John Williams and his wife, Eunice, of Deerfield, Massachusetts, awoke to "horrid shouting and yelling" and the crash of axes and hatchets breaking open the doors and windows of their house. Leaping out of bed they knew immediately that the town was under attack by Indians and their French allies; this frontier settlement on the northwestern fringe of New England had already been attacked six times in the perennial fighting with New France. Never before, however, had the enemy penetrated the town's stockade. Suddenly the door burst open and "with painted faces and hideous exclamations" Indians began pushing inside. "I reached up my hands for my pistol," Williams remembered, "cocked it, and put it to the breast of the first Indian that came up." It misfired, and as the couple stood trembling in their nightclothes, they were bound and dragged into the central hall with their seven children. In horror they were forced to watch the invaders club and kill their resisting six-year-old son, their screaming newborn infant daughter, and their black nursemaid. The family was hustled out into the frigid dawn and, with more than a hundred other captives, marched north through snow and ice toward Canada, leaving the frightful sight of the burning town behind.

This raid was one of the most infamous events in a long series of attacks and counterattacks between English and French colonists. At Deerfield, one hundred and forty residents of the town managed to hold off the invasion and survive, but fifty others died in the attack. Among the captives, twenty-one were murdered along the way, in most cases because they were too weak to travel; those murdered included Mrs. Williams, who had not yet recovered from a difficult childbirth just six weeks before. The governor of Massachusetts ordered a day of fasting and prayed that "the Designs of the barbarous Savages against us be defeated; our exposed Plantations preserved; and the poor Christian Captives in their hands returned." Authorities raised the bounty on Indian scalps from £10 to £100 and organized bloody raids of their own on the French and Indian settlements to the north.

Most of the Deerfield captives were delivered to the French authorities in Montreal. Within two years, fifty-nine of them had been ransomed and returned home to Deerfield, the Reverend Williams and four of his surviving children among them. Williams soon published an account of his captivity, The Redeemed Captive Returning to Zion. *In colonial America, with its many peoples and cultures, readers were fascinated by the problems and dilemmas of crossing the frontiers between colonial and Indian societies, as well as the borders between the English, French, and Spanish empires. What was life like for you, people wanted to know, on the other side of the frontier? How were you changed by your experience? Did you remain loyal to your community? Can you still be trusted?*

Questions of this sort were vitally important to the colonists, for over the years hundreds of Europeans who had been captured by Indians had chosen to remain with their captors rather than return home. Among the Deerfield captives, thirty-one—including ten-year-old Eunice Williams, her mother's namesake—remained in Canada. Eunice and many of the other Deerfield captives lived at Kahnawake, a community of Catholic Indians near Montreal. Like Deerfield, Kahnawake was a farming town of fifty or sixty homes clustered around a central church and surrounded by a stockade to protect it from enemy raiders. The differences between the two communities, however, were more striking than the similarities.

Founded in the seventeenth century by Jesuit missionaries as a refuge for Iroquois converts, Kahnawake not only became home to a great variety of Native American Catholics but also welcomed people of mixed Indian and European ancestry. The "great mixture of the blood of whites with that of aborigines is observable in the persons of the inhabitants," wrote one visitor, struck by the appearance of people who seemed to be Indians in all respects except their blue eyes. Such mixing was also evident in the community's culture, the exotic combination of European and Indian clothing, the use of both Indian and French names, and the special ways the community bent Catholic ritual to fit traditional Iroquois practices. Community members crossed boundaries in other ways, too: many residents were smugglers who engaged in the illegal trade of furs and other Indian products across the frontier into New York. According to the frustrated authorities in Montreal, Kahnawake operated as "a sort of republic," insisting on its freedom and independence.

As the historian John Demos writes, Kahnawake was "a unique experiment in bicultural living." Its residents were skilled at offering sympathetic sanctuary to traumatized captive children, and by the time Eunice Williams's father and siblings were ransomed, she told the man who had come to fetch her that she was "unwilling to return." Soon she converted to Catholicism. Over the years the father sent several emissaries to retrieve her, but all she would say were two words of Iroquois: jaghte oghte, *meaning "maybe not." She refused to acknowledge her English name, having taken another:* A'ongonte, *which in Iroquois means "she has been planted as a person." In 1713, at the age of sixteen, she married a Kahnawake Mohawk. Father and daughter would meet only once more, the following year, when he went to Kahnawake a final time to beg her to return. But she would "not so much as give me one pleasant look," Williams wrote mournfully. "She is yet obstinately resolved to live and dye here."*

And that is what happened. A'ongonte and her husband remained good Catholics, raising a family and working as traders. John Williams died in 1729, surrounded by his children

Deerfield

and grandchildren but longing for his "unredeemed" daughter. It was not until 1739 that A'ongonte found the courage to bring her family south for a visit, for she feared being held in New England against her will. Her brother Stephen wrote in his diary that at long last "we had ye joyfull, Sorrowfull meeting of our poor Sister that we had been Sepratd from fer above 36 years." After that A'ongonte visited only rarely because of the continuing

warfare. "We have a great desire of going down to see you," she wrote to her brother through an interpreter near the end of their lives in the 1770s, "but do not know when an oppertunity may offer. . . . I pray the Lord that he may give us grace so to Live in this as to be prepared for a happey meeting in the world to Come." And, perhaps as a sign of reconciliation, she signed the letter, "Loving Sister until death, Eunice Williams."

NORTH AMERICAN REGIONS

American colonial history is too often written as if only the British colonists along the Atlantic coast really mattered. But as the experience of the Deerfield community and the Williams family suggests, this is a mistake eighteenth-century colonists could not afford to make. In the first place, Indian America was a critically important part of the eighteenth-century world. From the fringes of colonial societies into the native heart of the continent, from the eastern foothills of the Appalachians to the western flank of the Sierra Nevada in California, hundreds of Indian cultures—despite being deeply affected by the spread of colonial culture—remained firmly in control of their homelands. And in addition to the British provinces stretching along the Atlantic coast, there were Hispanic colonists who defended the northern borderlands of the Spanish Caribbean and Mexican empire in isolated communities from Florida to California, and French communities that occupied the valley of the St. Lawrence River and scattered down the Mississippi Valley from the Great Lakes to the Gulf of Mexico. There were impressive similarities among these colonial societies, representing a continuation in the New World of traditional Old World beliefs, customs, and institutions, as well as a general pattern of European adaptation to American conditions.

INDIAN AMERICA

As the native peoples of the Atlantic coastal plain lost their lands to colonists through battles or treaties and moved into or beyond the Appalachian Mountains, they became active in the fur trade. Indians demonstrated a remarkable capacity for change and adaptation. They began participating in a commercial economy, using metal tools, building their homes of logs as frontier settlers did, but in the process they also became dependent on firearms, metal tools, and other manufactured goods they had no capacity to produce themselves. Yet, until the American Revolution, they continued to assert a proud independence and gained considerable skill at playing colonial powers off against one another.

In general, the French had significantly better relations with native peoples than the English, but inevitably as they pursued their expansionist plans they came into conflict with Indian groups, and when opposed they could be just as cruel and violent as any other European power. In the early eighteenth century the Fox Indians blocked French passage between the Great Lakes and the upper Mississippi, attempting to make themselves into middlemen in the fur trade. Sporadic fighting continued until the French defeated the tribe in 1716. But Fox warriors rose again in 1726, and it took massive violence before the French were able to force the tribe into signing a treaty in 1738. On the lower Mississippi, the Natchez and Chickasaw tribes opposed the arrival of the French, engaging them in a series of bloody conflicts during the 1720s, which concluded only when the French decimated the Natchez in 1731.

HOW DID Indians adapt to the new conditions created by colonization?

IMAGE KEY

for pages 100-101

a. A brown patterned neckcloth.
b. New Amsterdam City Hall and Great Dock in the late 17th century.
c. A small pile of muscovado sugar.
d. A mounted moth.
e. A half-loom width of oyster silk damask of the 18th century.
f. Dried tobacco leaves.
g. A merchant ship.
h. A Jesuit missionary baptizing an Indian in New France.
i. A hand-colored woodcut of a settler's log cabin in the Blue Ridge Mountains (Appalachians).
j. George Whitefield extends his hands over kneeling worshippers while wearing black ministerial robes in a 1770 painting by John Wallaston.

A portrait of the Delaware chief Tishcohan by Gustavus Hesselius, painted in 1732. In his purse of chipmunk hide is a clay pipe, a common item of the Indian trade. Tishcohan was one of the Delaware leaders forced by Pennsylvania authorities into signing a fraudulent land deal that reversed that colony's history of fair dealing with Indians over land. He moved west to the Ohio River as settlers poured into his former homeland.

The Historical Society of Pennsylvania

The preeminent concern of the Indians of the eastern half of the continent was the tremendous growth of colonial population in the British Atlantic coastal colonies, especially the movement of settlers westward. In the 1730s and 1740s Pennsylvania perpetrated a series of fraudulent seizures of western lands from the Delawares. Particularly in the light of Pennsylvania's previous history of fair dealing with Indian peoples, these acts were another disturbing sign of things to come. Thus, Indian alliances with the French resulted not from any great affection but from their great fear of British expansion.

Meanwhile, a long-term population decline continued among the Indian peoples of North America. Indian America continued to take a terrific beating from epidemics of European disease. There was no systematic census of North American Indians before the nineteenth century, but historians estimate that from a high of 7 to 10 million Native Americans north of Mexico in 1500, the population had probably fallen to around a million by 1800. Thus, during the eighteenth century colonial population overtook and began to overwhelm the native population of the continent. Population loss did not affect all Indian tribes equally, however. Native peoples with a century or more of colonial contact and interaction had lost 50 percent or more of their numbers, but most Indian societies in the interior had yet to be struck by the horrible epidemics.

Colonization introduced other less distressing changes in Indian cultures. By the early eighteenth century, Indians on the southern fringe of the Great Plains were using horses stolen from the Spanish in New Mexico. Horses enabled Indian hunters to exploit the buffalo herds much more efficiently, and on the base of this more productive economy a number of groups built a distinctive and elaborate nomadic culture. Great numbers of Indian peoples moved onto the plains during the eighteenth century, pulled by this new way of life, pushed by colonial invasions and disruptions radiating southwest from Canada and north from the Spanish borderlands. The invention of nomadic Plains Indian culture was another of the dramatic cultural innovations of the eighteenth century. The mounted Plains Indian, so often used as a symbol of native America, was actually a product of the colonial era.

THE SPANISH BORDERLANDS

Mexico City, the administrative capital of New Spain, was the most sophisticated urban area in the Western Hemisphere, the site of one of the world's great universities, with broad avenues and spectacular architecture. New Spain's northern borderland provinces of Florida, Texas, New Mexico, and California, however, were far removed from this sophistication. Officials of the viceroyalty of New Spain, who oversaw these colonies, thought of them as buffer zones, protecting New Spain from the expanding colonial empires of Spain's New World rivals.

In Florida, the oldest of European colonies in North America, fierce fighting among the Spanish, the British, and the Indians had by the early eighteenth century reduced the colonial presence to little more than the forts of St. Augustine on the Atlantic and Pensacola on the Gulf of Mexico, each surrounded by small colonized territories populated with the families of Spanish troops. In their weakened condition, the Spanish had no choice but to establish cooperative relations with the Creek and Seminole Indians who dominated the region, as well as the hundreds of African American runaways who considered St. Augustine a refuge from the cruel slave

MAP EXPLORATION

To explore an interactive version of this map, go to **http://www.prenhall.com/faraghertlc/map5.1**

Legend:
- New France
- New England
- New York
- Pennsylvania
- Chesapeake
- Lower South
- Backcountry
- Northern New Spain
- Indian America

MAP 5-1

Regions in Eighteenth-Century North America   By the middle of the eighteenth century, European colonists had established a number of distinctive colonial regions in North America. The northern periphery of New Spain, the oldest and most prosperous European colony, stretched from Baja California to eastern Texas, then jumped to the settlements on the northern end of the Florida peninsula; cattle ranching was the dominant way of life in this thinly populated region. New France was like a great crescent, extending from the plantation communities along the Mississippi near New Orleans to the French colonial communities along the St. Lawrence; in between were isolated settlements and forts, connected only by the extensive French trading network.

WHAT STEPS did Spain take to reinforce and expand its holdings in North America in the eighteenth century?

regimes in Georgia and Carolina. Like the community of Kahnawake, eighteenth-century Florida included a growing mestizo population and a considerable number of free African Americans and Hispanicized Indians from the old missions.

Nearly 2,000 miles to the west, New Mexico was similarly isolated from the mainstream of New Spain. At midcentury New Mexico included some 20,000 Pueblo Indians (their numbers greatly reduced by disease since their first contact with Europeans) and perhaps 10,000 mestizo colonists. The prosperity of these colonists, who supported themselves with subsistence agriculture, was severely limited by a restrictive colonial economic policy that forced them to exchange their wool, pottery, buffalo hides, and buckskin for imported goods at unfavorable rates. Unlike the colonial population of Florida, however, the settlements of New Mexicans were gradually expanding, following the valleys and streams that led east and north from the original colonial outposts scattered along the upper Rio Grande.

The Spanish also founded new northern outposts during the eighteenth century. Concerned about French colonization of the Mississippi Valley, they established a number of military posts or *presidios* on the fringes of the colony of Louisiana and in 1716 began the construction of a string of Franciscan missions among the Indian peoples of Texas. By 1750 the settlement of San Antonio had become the center of a developing frontier province. The Spanish also established new colonial outposts west of New Mexico, in what is today southern Arizona. In the 1690s, Jesuit missionaries, led by Father Eusebio Kino, founded missions among the desert Indians of the lower Colorado River and Gila River valleys. Mission San Xavier del Bac near Tucson is acclaimed the most striking example of Spanish colonial architecture in the United States. Cattle ranching, introduced by the Jesuits, and farming spread along the lower Rio Grande Valley; in fact, ranching continued to define the region's economy for the next 200 years.

Midcentury also found the Spanish considering new settlements along the California coast. Juan Cabrillo, an associate of Hernán Cortés, had first explored the coastal waters in 1542 and was the first European to sail into the fine harbor at San Diego. In 1603 explorer Sebastián Vizcaíno had come upon Monterey Bay. The Spanish did little to follow up on these finds, but in 1769, acting on rumors of Russian expansion along the northern Pacific coast (for a discussion of Russian America, see Chapter 9), officials in Mexico City ordered Gaspar de Portolá, governor of what is now Baja California, to establish a Spanish presence in the north. With him were Franciscan missionaries led by Junípero Serra, president of the missions in Baja. At the harbor of San Diego, Portolá and Serra founded the first mission and pueblo complex in present-day California. Portolá then proceeded overland, becoming the first European to explore the interior valleys and mountains, and in 1770 he and Serra established their headquarters at Monterey Bay on the central coast. Two years later Juan Bautista de Anza established an overland route across the blistering deserts connecting Arizona and California, and in 1776 he led a colonizing expedition that founded the pueblo of San Francisco. Over the next fifty years the number of California settlements grew to include twenty-one missions and a half-dozen presidios and pueblos, including the town

The Church of San Xavier del Bac, constructed in the late eighteenth century, is located a few miles south of the city of Tucson, where Jesuit Father Eusebio Kino founded a mission among the Pima Indians in 1700. Known as the White Dove of the Desert, it is acclaimed as the most striking example of Spanish colonial architecture in the United States.

Photograph by Jack W. Dyckinga

of Los Angeles. Founded in 1781 by a group of mestizo settlers from Sinaloa, Mexico, by the end of the century Los Angeles, with a population of only 300, was California's largest town.

Region	Population
New France	70,000
New England	400,000
New York	100,000
Pennsylvania	230,000
Chesapeake	390,000
Lower South	100,000
Backcountry	100,000
Northern New Spain	20,000
Indian America	1,500,000

For the Spanish, conquest demanded conversion to Catholicism, which, according to theory, would lead Indians toward "civilization." Like the efforts of the Jesuits at Kahnawake and elsewhere in New France, the Spanish experiment in cultural transformation was designed to make Indians into Catholics and loyal Spanish subjects by educating them and putting them to work raising cattle and crops. The most extensive mission project took place in California, where under the direction of priests thousands of Indian laborers produced a flourishing local economy based on irrigated farming as well as horse, cattle, and sheep ranching. Indian people also constructed the adobe and stone churches, built on Spanish and Moorish patterns, whose ruins symbolize California's colonial society.

To keep the system functioning, the Franciscan missionaries resorted to cruel and sometimes violent means of controlling their Indian subjects: shackles, solitary confinement, and whipping posts. Indians resisted from the very beginning, but the arms and organization of Spanish soldiers were usually sufficient to suppress the uprisings. Another form of protest was flight: whole villages sometimes fled.

Overwork, inadequate nutrition, overcrowding, poor sanitation, and epidemic disease contributed to death rates that exceeded birthrates. During the period of the mission system the native population of California fell by at least 25 percent.

THE FRENCH CRESCENT

In France, as in Spain, church and state were closely interwoven. During the seventeenth century the French prime ministers, Cardinal Richelieu and Cardinal Mazarin, laid out a fundamentally Catholic imperial policy, and under their guidance colonists constructed a second Catholic empire in North America. In 1674 church and state collaborated in establishing the bishopric of Quebec, which founded local seminaries, oversaw the appointment and review of priests, and laid the foundation of the resolutely Catholic culture of New France. Meanwhile, Jesuit missionaries continued to carry Catholicism deep into the continent.

The number of French colonists rose from fewer than 15,000 in 1700 to more than 70,000 at midcentury. During the eighteenth century the French used their trade network and alliances with the Indians to establish a great crescent of colonies, military posts, and settlements that extended from the mouth of the St. Lawrence River southwest through the Great Lakes, then down the Mississippi River to the Gulf of Mexico. Although the maritime colony of Acadia was ceded to the British in 1713 (see Chapter 4), the French anchored the crescent on the northeast by founding the fortress of Louisbourg on Ile Royale (Cape Breton Island), which soon became the most important

QUICK REVIEW

Spanish Colonies

◆ Mexico City was the capital of New Spain.

◆ Conflict with Indians and the British reduced the Spanish presence in Florida.

◆ New Mexico was isolated from the mainstream of New Spain.

☆ MAP EXPLORATION

To explore an interactive version of this map, go to
http://www.prenhall.com/faraghertlc/map5.2

MAP 5-2

The French Crescent The French empire in North America was based on a series of alliances and trade relations with Indian nations linking a great crescent of colonies, settlements, and outposts that extended from the mouth of the St. Lawrence River, through the Great Lakes, and down the Mississippi River to the Gulf of Mexico. In 1713 Acadia was ceded to the British, but the French established the fortress of Louisbourg to anchor the eastern end of the crescent.

WHAT WAS the relationship between church and state in New France?

French port in the North Atlantic. The colony of Louisiana formed the other end of the crescent at the mouth of the Mississippi. Over this vast territory the French laid a thin colonial veneer, the beginning of what they planned as a great continental empire that would limit the Protestant British to a narrow strip of Atlantic coastline.

At the heart of the French empire in North America were the farming communities of the colony of Canada along the banks of the St. Lawrence, including the towns of Montreal and Quebec. There were also farming communities in the Illinois country, which shipped wheat down the Mississippi to supply the booming sugar plantations of Louisiana. By the mid-eighteenth century, those plantations, extending along the river from Natchez and Baton Rouge to New Orleans, had become the most profitable French enterprise in North America.

One of the most distinctive French stamps on the North American landscape were the "long lots" stretching back from the rivers that provided each settler family a share of good bottomland to farm as well as frontage on the waterways, the "interstate highway system" of the French Crescent. Long lots were laid out along the lower Mississippi River in Louisiana and at sites on the upper Mississippi such as Kaskaskia and Prairie du Chien, as well as at the strategic passages of the Great Lakes, the communities of Mackinac, Sault Ste. Marie, and Detroit. In 1750, Detroit was a stockaded town with a military garrison, a small administrative center, several stores, a Catholic church, and 100 households of *métis* (French for mestizo) families. French and métis farmers worked the land along the Detroit River, not far from communities inhabited by more than 6,000 Ottawa, Potawatomi, and Huron Indians.

Communities of this sort that combined both French and Indian elements were in the tradition of the inclusive frontier. Detroit looked like "an old French village," said one observer, except that its houses were "mostly covered with bark," in Indian style. Detroit had much of the character of the mixed community of Kahnawake on the St. Lawrence.

Family and kinship in these interior communities were also cast in the Indian pattern. Households often consisted of several related families, but wives limited their births, having on average only two or three children. There were arranged marriages and occasional polygamy, but women had easy access to divorce and enjoyed property rights. Yet the people focused their activities on commerce and identified themselves overwhelmingly as Catholic.

The persistence of French colonial long lots in the pattern of modern landholding is clear in this enhanced satellite photograph of the Mississippi River near New Orleans. Long lots, the characteristic form of property holding in New France, were designed to offer as many settlers as possible a share of good bottomland as well as a frontage on the waterways, which served as the basic transportation network.

EROS Data Center, U.S. Geological Survey

NEW ENGLAND

Just as New Spain and New France had their official church, so did the people of New England: local communities in all the New England colonies but Rhode Island were governed by Puritan congregations. Under the plan established in Massachusetts, the local church of a community was free to run its own affairs under the guidance of the General Court (the governor and the representatives selected by the towns). The Puritan colonies allotted each congregation a tract of communal land. Church members divided this land among themselves on the basis of status and seniority, laying out central villages such as Deerfield and building churches (called meetinghouses) that were maintained through taxation. Adult male church members constituted the freemen of the town, and thus there was very little distinction between religious and secular authority. At the town meeting the freemen chose their minister, voted on his salary and support, and elected local men to offices ranging from town clerk to fence viewer.

The Puritan tradition was a curious mix of freedom and repression. Although local communities had considerable autonomy, they were tightly bound by the restrictions of the Puritan faith and the General Court. Contrary to widespread beliefs, the Puritans did not come to America to create a society where religion could be freely practiced. Rather, they sought to establish their own version of the "right and perfect way," which placed severe restraints on individuals. Not only did the Puritans exile dissidents such as Roger Williams and Anne Hutchinson who threatened the religious orthodoxy of Massachusetts (see Chapter 3), but

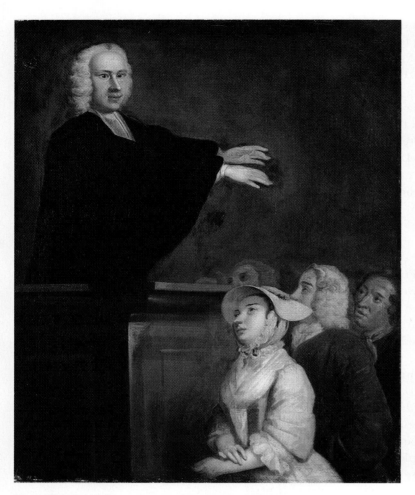

George Whitefield (who, contemporaries noted, was cross-eyed) enjoyed a remarkable career as a powerful preacher on both sides of the Atlantic. This portrait shows him preaching indoors to a rapt audience. During his tour of the colonies, Whitefield reportedly had a similar effect on crowds of thousands who gathered outdoors to hear his sermons.

John Wollaston, "George Whitefield" ca. 1770. By courtesy of the National Portrait Gallery, London

The Toleration Act Act passed in 1661 by King Charles II ordering a stop to religious persecution in Massachusetts.

they also banned Anglicans and Baptists and exiled, jailed, whipped, and even executed members of the Society of Friends, who came repeatedly among them to preach the tenets of the Quaker faith.

One of the first formal arguments for religious toleration was made by New Englander Roger Williams, leader of dissenting Rhode Island. "Forced worship," he wrote, "stinks in God's nostrils." After the religious excesses of the English civil war, this argument began to have an appeal. In 1661, King Charles II ordered a stop to religious persecution in Massachusetts. **The Toleration Act**, passed by Parliament in 1689, was at first resisted by the Puritans. Under pressure from English authorities, however, Massachusetts and Connecticut reluctantly allowed other Protestant denominations to begin practicing their religions openly in 1700, although Congregationalism (as the Puritan Church had become known because the congregations governed themselves) continued to be supported officially through taxation. By the 1730s there were Anglican, Baptist, and Presbyterian congregations in many New England towns.

As towns grew too large for the available land, groups of residents left together, "hiving off" to form new churches and towns elsewhere. The region was knit together by an intricate network of roads and rivers. Seventy-five years after the Indians of southern New England suffered their final defeat in King Philip's War (see Chapter 3), Puritan farm communities had taken up most of the available land of Massachusetts, Connecticut, and Rhode Island, leaving only a few communities of Pequots, Narragansets, and Wampanoags on restricted reservations. Northern Algonquians and Catholic Iroquois allied with the French in Quebec, however, and maintained a defensive barrier that prevented New Englanders from expanding northward into Maine, New Hampshire, and the region later called Vermont. Deerfield represented the far northern limit of safe settlement. By midcentury, then, as the result of growing population, New England was reaching the limit of its land supply.

THE MIDDLE COLONIES

The colony of New York had one of the most ethnically diverse populations on the continent, in striking contrast to the ethnically homogeneous neighboring New England colonies of Connecticut and Massachusetts. At midcentury, society along the lower Hudson River, including the counties in northern New Jersey, was a veritable mosaic of ethnic communities: the Dutch of Flatbush, the Huguenots of New Rochelle, the Flemish of Bergen County, and the Scots of Perth Amboy were but a few. African Americans, both slave and free, made up more than 15 percent of the lower Hudson population. Congregations of Puritans, Baptists, Quakers, and Catholics worshiped without legal hindrance. New York City was also home to the first Jewish community in the country, established in 1654. Several hundred Jewish families attended services in North America's first synagogue, built in 1730. There was a great deal of intermingling (as there was at places such as Kahnawake), but these different communities would long retain their ethnic and religious distinctions, which made New York something of a cultural "salad bowl" rather than a "melting pot."

New York City grew by leaps and bounds in the eighteenth century, but because the elite who had inherited the rich lands and great manors along the upper Hudson chose to rent to tenants rather than to sell, this region was much less attractive to immigrants. By contrast, Pennsylvania was what one German immigrant called "heaven for farmers." The colony's Quaker proprietors were willing to sell land to anyone who could pay the modest prices. Thus, as the region around New York City filled up, immigrants by the thousands made the decision to land at Philadelphia, Pennsylvania's growing port on the Delaware River. During the eighteenth century the population of this region and an extended area that encompassed portions of New Jersey, Delaware, and Maryland grew more dramatically than any other in North America. Boasting some of the best farmland in North America, the region was soon exporting abundant produce through Philadelphia.

The Quakers who had founded Pennsylvania quickly became a minority, but, unlike the Puritans, they were generally comfortable with religious and ethnic pluralism. Many of the founders of the Society of Friends had been imprisoned for their beliefs in pre-Restoration England, and they were determined to prevent a repetition of this injustice in their own province. Indeed, the Quakers were opposed to all signs of rank, and among American Friends, women preached equally with men.

These Quaker attitudes were well suited to the ethnically and religiously diverse population of Pennsylvania. Although the Society of Friends remained the affiliation of the governing elite, it never became an established church. Most German immigrants were Lutherans or Calvinists, most North Britons were Presbyterians, and there were plenty of Anglicans and Baptists as well.

The institutions of government were another pillar of community organization. Colonial officials appointed justices of the peace from among the leading local men, and these justices provided judicial authority for the countryside. Property-owning farmers chose their own local officials. Country communities were tied together by kinship bonds and by bartering and trading among neighbors. The substantial stone houses and great barns of the Pennsylvania countryside testified to the social stability and prosperity of this system. The communities of the middle colonies, however, were more loosely bound than those of New England. Rates of mobility were considerably higher, with about half the population moving in any given decade. Because land was sold in individual lots rather than in communal parcels, farmers tended to disperse themselves at will over the open countryside. Villages gradually developed at crossroads and ferries but with little forethought or planning. It was Pennsylvania, which emphasized individual settlement, that provided the basic model for American expansion.

THE BACKCOUNTRY

By 1750 Pennsylvania's exploding population had pushed beyond the first range of the Appalachian highlands. Settlers occupied the northern reaches of the Great Valley, which extended southwest from Pennsylvania into Virginia. Although they hoped to become commercial farmers, these settlers began

The two-story log house, built in Pennsylvania in the early eighteenth century, is one of the oldest surviving examples of the method and style of log construction introduced in America by the Scandinavian colonists on the lower Delaware River. Learning New World farming and woodland hunting techniques from the Indians, these settlers forged a tradition of settlement that proved enormously successful for pioneers.

Courtesy Henry Glassie

MAP EXPLORATION

To explore an interactive version of this map, go to
http://www.prenhall.com/faraghertlc/map5.3

	Areas settled by 1720
	Areas settled by 1740
	Areas settled by 1760

MAP 5-3
Spread of Settlement: Movement into the Backcountry, 1720–1760
The spread of settlement from 1720 to 1760 shows the movement
of population into the backcountry during the midcentury.

HOW DID the movement into the backcountry affect
the relations among colonists, Indians, and English
authorities?

more modestly, planting Indian corn and raising hogs, hunting in the woods for meat and furs, and building log cabins. This strategy had originated with the settlers of the New Sweden colony on the lower Delaware River.

The movement into the Pennsylvania and Virginia backcountry that began during the 1720s was the first of the great pioneer treks that would take Americans into the continental interior. Many, perhaps most, of these pioneers held no legal title to the lands they occupied; they simply hacked out and defended their squatters' claims from Indian tribes and all other comers. Many of these settlers came from the northern borders of England and Ireland, where there was considerable clan and ethnic violence, so they adapted well to the violence of the backcountry. To the Delawares and Shawnees, who had been pushed into the interior, or the Cherokees, who occupied the Appalachian highlands to the south, these pioneers presented a new and deadly threat. Rising fears and resentments over this expanding population triggered much eighteenth-century warfare.

One of the distinctive characteristics of the backcountry was the settlers' disdain for rank. But the myth of frontier equality was simply that. Most pioneers owned little or no land, whereas "big men" held great tracts and dominated local communities with their bombastic style of personal leadership. Here the men were warriors, the women workers.

THE SOUTH

The Chesapeake and the Lower South were triracial societies, with intermingled communities of white colonists and black slaves, along with substantial Indian communities living on the fringes of colonial settlement. Much of the population growth of the region resulted from the forced migration of enslaved Africans, who by 1750 made up 40 percent of the population. Colonial settlement had filled not only the Tidewater area of the southern Atlantic coast, but a good deal of the Piedmont as well. Specializing in rice, tobacco, and other commercial crops, these colonies were overwhelmingly rural. Farms and plantations were dispersed across the countryside, and villages or towns were few.

English authorities made the Church of England the state religion in the Chesapeake colonies. Residents paid taxes to support the Church and were required to attend services. No other churches were allowed into Virginia and Maryland (despite being founded by Catholics) and dissenters were excluded or exiled. Before the 1750s, the Toleration Act was little enforced in the South; at the same time, the Anglican establishment was internally weak. It maintained neither a colonial bishop nor local institutions for training clergy.

Along the rice coast, the dominant institution of social life was the large plantation. Transforming the tangle of woods and swamps along the region's rivers into an ordered pattern of dams, dikes, and flooded fields required a heavy capital investment. Consequently, only men of means could undertake rice cultivation. By midcentury, established rice plantations were typically dominated by a large main house, generally located on a spot of high ground overlooking the fields. Nearby, but a world apart, were the slave quarters, rough wooden cabins lining two sides of a muddy pathway near the out-buildings and barns.

Because tobacco, unlike rice, could be grown profitably in small plots, the Chesapeake included a greater variety of farmers and a correspondingly diverse landscape. Tobacco quickly drained the soil of its nutrients, and plantings had to be shifted to fresh ground every few years. Former tobacco land could be planted with corn for several years but then required twenty years or more of rest before reuse. The landscape was, thus, a patchwork of fields, many in various stages of ragged second growth. The poorest farmers lived in wooden cabins little better than the shacks of the slaves. More prosperous farm families lived with two or three slaves in houses that nevertheless were considerably smaller than the substantial homes of New England.

In the Lower South, where the plantations were little worlds unto them-selves, there was little community life outside the plantation. But by midcentury the Chesapeake had given rise to well-developed neighborhoods based on kin-ship networks and economic connections. Encouraging the developing sense of community more than any other institution was the county court, which held both executive and judicial power. On court day, white people of all ranks held a great gathering that included public business, horse racing, and perhaps a barbecue. The gentleman justices of the county, appointed by the governor, included the heads of the leading planter families. These men in turn selected the grand jury, com-posed of substantial freeholders. One of the most significant bonding forces in this free white population was a growing sense of racial solidarity in response to the increasing proportion of African slaves dispersed throughout the neighborhoods.

TRADITIONAL CULTURE IN THE NEW WORLD

In each of these North American colonial societies the family and kin-ship, the church, and the local community were the most significant fac-tors in everyday life. Throughout the continent, colonists tended to live much as they had in their European homelands at the time their colonies were settled. Thus, the residents of New Mexico, Quebec, and New Eng-land continued to be attached to the religious passions of the seventeenth century long after their mother countries had put those religious con-troversies aside in favor of imperial geopolitics. Nostalgia for Europe helped to fix a conservative colonial attitude toward culture.

These were oral cultures, depending on the transmission of infor-mation by the spoken word rather than through print, on the passage of traditions through storytelling, song, music, and crafts. North American colonial folk cultures, traditional and suspicious of change, preserved an essentially medieval worldview. The rhythms of life were regulated by the hours of sunlight and the seasons of the year. People rose with the sun and went to bed soon after it went down. The demands of the season deter-mined their working routines. They farmed with simple tools and were sub-ject to the whims of nature, for drought, flood, or pestilence might quickly sweep away their efforts. Experience told them that the natural world imposed limitations within which men and women had to learn to live. Even patterns of reproduction conformed to nature's cycle: in nearly every European colonial community of North America the number of births peaked in late winter, then fell to a low point during the summer. For African Americans, by contrast, births peaked in early summer. Historians have not yet accounted for this intriguing pattern or provided an expla-nation for the differences between white and black families, but apparently

During the eighteenth century, quantities of imported English manufactures began to appear in many colonial houses. This elegant mahogany clothespress, made in England in the 1740s, may have graced the Boston home of Charles Apthorp, once called "the greatest and most noble merchant" in America.

Clothespress, 1730–1740. England, London, Mahogany, glass. H 98 in. (249 cm); W 45-34 in. (116 cm). Gift of Albert Sack. Courtesy, Museum of Fine Arts, Boston there was some "inner" seasonal clock tied to old European and African patterns. Human sexual activity itself seemed to fluctuate with the rural working demands created by the seasons.

These were also communal cultures. In Quebec, villagers worked side by side to repair the roads; in New Mexico they collectively maintained the irrigation canals; and in New England they gathered in town meetings to decide the dates when common fields were to be plowed, sowed, and harvested. Houses offered little privacy, with families often sleeping together in the same chamber, sitting together on benches rather than in chairs, and taking their supper from a common bowl or trencher.

Throughout North America, most colonists continued the traditional European occupation of working the land. Plantation agriculture was designed to be a commercial system, in which crops were commodities for sale. Commercial farming also developed in some particularly fertile areas, notably southeastern Pennsylvania, which became known as the breadbasket of North America, as well as in the country surrounding colonial cities such as New York, Boston, and Quebec. The majority of the farmers of eighteenth-century North America, however, grew crops and raised livestock for their own needs or for local barter, and communities were largely self-sufficient. Most farmers attempted to produce small surpluses as well, which they sold to pay their taxes and buy some manufactured goods. But rather than specializing in the production of one or two crops for sale, they attempted to remain as independent of the market as possible, diversifying their activities. The primary goal was ownership of land and the assurance that children and descendants would be able to settle within the community on lands nearby.

Rural households often practiced crafts or trades as a sideline. Farm men were also blacksmiths, coopers, weavers, or carpenters. Some farm women were independent traders in dairy products or eggs. Others served the community as midwives and medicinal experts.

In colonial cities, artisans and craftsmen worked at their trades full time, organizing themselves according to the European craft system. In the colonial cities of the Atlantic coast, carpenters, ironmakers, blacksmiths, shipwrights, and scores of other tradesmen had their own self-governing associations. Young men who wished to pursue a trade served several years as apprentices, working in exchange for learning the skills and secrets of the craft. After completing their apprenticeships they sought employment in a shop. Their search often required them to migrate to some other area, thus becoming "journeymen." As in farming, the ultimate goal was independence.

With the exception of midwifery, there were few opportunities for women outside the household. By law, husbands held managerial rights over family property, but widows received support in the form of a one-third lifetime interest, known as "dower," in a deceased husband's real estate (the rest of the estate being divided among the heirs). And in certain occupations, such as printing (which had a tradition of employing women), widows succeeded their husbands in business.

THE FRONTIER HERITAGE

The colonial societies of eighteenth-century North America also shared perspectives unique to their common frontier heritage. European colonists came from Old World societies in which land was scarce and monopolized by property-owning elites. They settled in a continent where, for the most part, land was abundant and cheap. This was probably the most important distinction between North America and Europe. American historians once tied the existence of this "free land"

A spinner and carpenter from *The Book of Trades*, an eighteenth-century British survey of the crafts practiced in colonial America. In colonial cities artisans organized themselves into the traditional European craft system, with apprentices, journeymen, and masters. There were few opportunities for the employment of women outside the household, but women sometimes earned income by establishing sidelines as midwives or spinners.

The Granger Collection

directly to the development of democracy. But the colonial experience encouraged assumptions that were anything but democratic.

One of the most important of those colonial assumptions was the popular acceptance of forced labor. A woman of eighteenth-century South Carolina once offered advice on how to achieve a good living. "Get a few slaves," she declared, and "beat them well to make them work hard." There was a labor shortage throughout all the colonies. In a land where free men and women could work for themselves on their own plot of ground, there was little incentive to work for wages. Thus, the use of forced labor was one of the few ways a landowner could secure an agricultural work force. In the Spanish borderlands, captured Apache children were made lifetime servants, and an Indian slave trade flourished through the eighteenth century. In Quebec one could see African American slaves from the French Caribbean working side-by-side with enslaved Indians captured by other tribes in the West and sold to French traders. In Philadelphia, according to Benjamin Franklin, wages for free workers were so high that most of the unskilled labor was "performed chiefly by indentured servants." All the colonists came from European cultures that believed in social hierarchy and subordination, and involuntary servitude was easily incorporated into their worldview.

At least half the immigrants to eighteenth-century British America arrived as indentured servants. This system allowed poor immigrants to arrange passage across the Atlantic in exchange for four or five years of service in America. Usually indentured servants were single men, often skilled artisans. Sometimes families without means emigrated as **redemptioners**. Under this system, they arranged with the ship's owner to pay their passage upon arrival in North America. If no one in the colonies stepped forth to pay, they sold themselves into service for the payment. Family members were sometimes separated. In addition, during the eighteenth century the British sent over, mostly to the Chesapeake, some 50,000 convicts sentenced to seven or fourteen years at hard labor. One historian, accounting for the cost of passage and upkeep, estimates that indentured servants earned their masters, on average, about £50 sterling over their terms of service, the equivalent of something like $4,000 or $5,000 in today's values. But at the conclusion of their terms of service, eighteenth-century servants enjoyed more opportunity than their seventeenth-century counterparts, probably because of the rise in overall prosperity in the British colonies. Over the course of the century the chance of former servants achieving positions of moderate comfort rose from one in five in 1700 to better than fifty-fifty by 1750. The majority of redemptioners, for example, appear to have become small farmers.

The expectation of property ownership was a second important assumption that flowed from the frontier heritage and abundance of land in colonial America. This expectation led to rising popular demands in all regions that more and more land be taken from the Indian inhabitants and opened to white settlement. Some colonists justified such wars of dispossession by arguing, as Puritans did, that Indians deserved to lose their lands because they had failed to use their lands to the utmost capacity. Others simply maintained that Indians should be dispossessed because they were "savages." But whatever their specific justifications, the majority of colonists, whether British, Spanish, or French, accepted the violence and brutality directed against Indian tribes as an essential aspect of colonial life. This attitude was as true of inclusive as exclusive societies—with the difference that in the former, native peoples were incorporated into colonial society, while in the latter, tribes were pushed from the frontier. Thus did the Puritan minister Cotton Mather praise Hannah Dustin, a New England woman who escaped her captors during **King William's War** by killing and scalping nine sleeping Indians, including two women and six children. With this as the prevailing attitude, one can understand why Eunice Williams was hesitant to return to Deerfield after she had married an Indian.

DIVERGING SOCIAL AND POLITICAL PATTERNS

Despite these important similarities among the colonial regions of North America, in the eighteenth century the experience of the British colonies began to diverge sharply from that of the French and Spanish. Immigration, economic growth, and provincial political struggles all pushed British colonists in a radically new direction.

POPULATION GROWTH AND IMMIGRATION

All the colonial regions of North America experienced unprecedented growth in the eighteenth century. "Our people must at least be doubled every twenty years," wrote Benjamin Franklin in a remarkable 1751 essay on population, and he was

---

Redemptioner Similar to an indentured servant, except that a redemptioner signed a labor contract in America rather than in Europe.

King William's War The first Anglo-French conflict in North America (1689–1697), the American phase of Europe's War of the League of Augsburg.

HOW DID the structure of colonial society differ from European social structure?

5–1
Benjamin Franklin, "Observations Concerning the Increase of Mankind, Peopling of Countries, &c." (1751)

nearly right. In 1700 there were 290,000 colonists north of Mexico; fifty years later they had grown to approximately 1.3 million, an average annual growth rate of about 3 percent. Typical preindustrial societies grow at rates of less than 1 percent per year, approximately the pace of Europe's expansion in the eighteenth century.

High fertility played an important role in this extraordinary growth. It was common for women in the British colonies to bear seven or more children during their childbearing years, and colonial women in the French villages along the St. Lawrence or the towns of New Mexico were equally fertile. In addition, mortality rates were low: in most colonial areas there were fewer than 30 deaths for every 1,000 persons, a death rate 15 or 20 percent lower than rates in Europe. Moreover, levels of infant mortality were low. Blessed with fertile lands and the effectiveness of Indian agricultural techniques, North America had no famines. For the colonists, North America was a remarkably healthy environment.

Yet, although all North American colonial societies had high fertility rates, the British colonies grew far more rapidly than did those of other nations. The difference is explained by immigration. The Spanish, fearful of depleting their population at home, severely limited the migration of their own subjects to their colonies, and absolutely forbade the immigration of foreigners. The French, dedicated to keeping their North American colonies exclusively Catholic, ignored the desire of Protestant Huguenots to emigrate. Instead they sent thousands of Catholic *engagés* to Canada, but most returned, discouraged by the climate and the lack of commercial opportunity. The English, however, sent an estimated 400,000 of their own countrymen to populate their North American colonies during the seventeenth and eighteenth centuries. Moreover, the British were the only colonial power to encourage the immigration of foreign nationals.

SOCIAL CLASS

Although traditional working roles were transferred to North America, attempts to transplant the European class system by creating land monopolies were far less successful. In New France the landowning seigneurs claimed privileges similar to those enjoyed by their aristocratic counterparts at home; the Spanish system of **encomienda** and the great manors created by the Dutch and continued by the English along the Hudson River also represented attempts to bring the essence of European feudalism to North America. But in most areas, because settlers had free access to land, these monopolies proved difficult or impossible to maintain. There was a system of economic rank and an unequal distribution of wealth, prestige, and power. North American society was not aristocratic, but neither was it without social hierarchy.

In New Spain the official criterion for status was racial purity. *Españoles* (Spaniards) or *gente de razon* (literally, "people of reason") occupied the top rung of the social ladder, with mestizos, mulattoes, and others on descending levels.

 MAP EXPLORATION

To explore an interactive version of this map, go to
http://www.prenhall.com/faraghertlc/map5.4

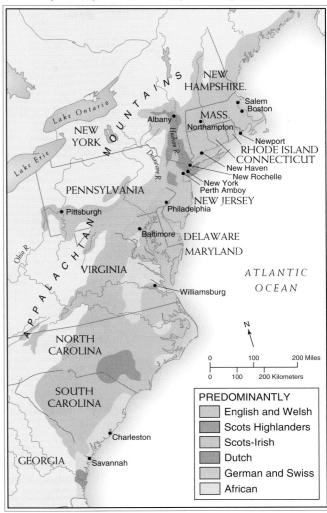

MAP 5-4

Ethnic Groups in Eighteenth-Century British North America   The first federal census, taken in 1790, revealed remarkable ethnic diversity. New England was filled with people from the British Isles, but the rest of the colonies were a patchwork. Most states had at least three different ethnic groups within their borders, and although the English and Scots-Irish were heavily represented in all colonies, in some they had strong competition from Germans (eastern and southern Pennsylvania) and from African peoples (Virginia and South Carolina).

IN WHAT areas were Scots and Scots-Irish most heavily concentrated?

Engagés   Catholic immigrants to New France.

Encomienda   In the Spanish colonies, the grant to a Spanish settler of a certain number of Indian subjects, who would pay him tribute in goods and labor.

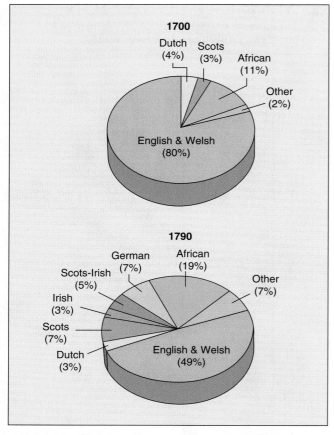

The Ancestry of the British Colonial Population
The legacy of eighteenth-century immigration to the British colonies was a population of unprecedented ethnic diversity.

5–2
James Otis, The Rights of the British Colonies Asserted and Proved (1763)

QUICK REVIEW

Population Growth

◆ 1700: 290,000 colonists north of Mexico.
◆ 1750: 1.3 million colonists north of Mexico.
◆ High fertility rates fueled population growth.

African slaves and Indians were at the bottom. In the isolated northern borderlands, however, these distinctions tended to disappear, with *castas* (persons of mixed background) enjoying considerably more opportunity. Mestizos who acquired land might suddenly be reclassified as *españoles*. The landlords of New France and the Spanish borderlands may have lacked the means to accumulate real wealth, but they lived lives of elegance compared to the hard toil of the people who owed them labor service or rent.

Despite their lack of titles, the wealthy planters and merchants in the British colonies lived far more extravagantly than the seigneurs of New France or the dons of the Spanish borderlands. What separated the culture of class in the British colonies from that of New France or New Mexico was not so much the material conditions of life as the prevailing attitude toward social rank. In the Catholic cultures, the upper class attempted to obscure its origins, claiming descent from European nobility. But in British North America people celebrated social mobility. The class system was remarkably open, and the entrance of newly successful planters, commercial farmers, and merchants into the upper ranks was not only possible but also common, although by mid-century most upper-class families had inherited, not earned, their wealth.

To be sure, there was a large lower class in the British colonies. Slaves, bound servants, and poor laboring families made up at least 40 percent of the population. For them, the standard of living did not rise above bare subsistence. Most lived from hand to mouth, often suffering through seasons of severe privation. A small proportion of poor whites could expect their condition to improve during their lifetimes, but slaves were a permanently servile population. Enslaved African Americans stood apart from the gains in the standard of living enjoyed by immigrants from Europe. Their lives had been degraded beyond measure from the conditions prevailing in their native lands.

The feature of the class system most often commented on by eighteenth-century observers was not the character or composition of the lower ranks but rather the size and strength of the middle class, a rank entirely absent in the colonies of France and Spain. As one Pennsylvanian wrote at midcentury, "The people of this province are generally of the middling sort." More than half the population of the British colonies, and nearly 70 percent of all white settlers, might be so classified. Most were families of landowning farmers of small to moderate means, but the group also included artisans, craftsmen, and small shopkeepers.

Households solidly in the center of this broad ranking owned land or other property worth approximately £500 and earned the equivalent of about £100 per year. They enjoyed a standard of living higher than that of the great majority of people in England and Europe. The low mortality of British Americans was important testimony to generally better living conditions. Touring the British Isles at midcentury, Benjamin Franklin was shocked at the squalid conditions of farmers and workers.

ECONOMIC GROWTH AND INCREASING INEQUALITY

One of the most important differences among North American colonial regions in the eighteenth century was the economic stagnation in New France and New Spain compared with the impressive economic growth of the British colonies. Weighed down by royal bureaucracies and overbearing regulations, neither the French Crescent nor New Spain evidenced much prosperity. In British North America, however, per capita production grew at an annual rate of 0.5 percent. Granted, this was considerably less than the average annual growth rate of 1.5 percent that prevailed during the era of industrialization, from the early nineteenth through the mid-twentieth century. But as economic growth steadily increased the size of the economic pie, most middle- and upper-class British Americans began to enjoy improved living conditions, better than those of any people in Europe. Improving standards of living and open access to land encouraged British colonists to see theirs as a society where hard work and savings could translate into prosperity, thus producing an upward spiral of economic growth.

At the same time, this growth produced increasing social inequality. In the commercial cities, for example, prosperity was accompanied by a concentration of assets in the hands of wealthy families. In Boston and Philadelphia at the beginning of the century, the wealthiest 10 percent of households owned about half of the taxable property; by about midcentury this small group owned 65 percent or more. In the commercial farming region of Chester County in southeastern Pennsylvania, the holdings of the wealthiest 10 percent of households increased more modestly, from 24 to 30 percent of taxable property during the first half of the century. But at the same time the share of taxable property owned by the poorest third fell from 17 to 6 percent. The general standard of living may have been rising, but the rich were getting richer and the poor poorer. The greatest concentrations of wealth occurred in the cities and in regions dominated by commercial farming, whether slave or free, while the greatest economic equality continued to be found in areas of self-sufficient farming such as the backcountry.

Another eighteenth-century trend worked against the hope of social mobility in the countryside. As population grew and as generations succeeded one another in older settlements, all the available land in the towns was taken up. Under the pressure of increased demand, land prices rose almost beyond the reach of families of modest means. As a family's land was divided among the heirs of the second and third generations, parcels became ever smaller and, thus, more intensively farmed. Eventually the soil was exhausted.

By the eighteenth century, many farm communities did not have sufficient land to provide those of the emerging generation with farms of their own. There were notable increases in the number of landless poor in the towns of New England as well as the disturbing appearance of the "strolling poor," homeless people who traveled from town to town looking for work or a handout. Destitute families crowded into Boston, which by midcentury was spending more than £5,000 annually on relief for the poor, who were required to wear a large red P on their clothing. In other regions, land shortages in the older settlements almost inevitably prompted people to leave in search of cheap or free land.

In New England, young men unable to obtain land in hometowns often moved to the towns and cities of the seaboard, for New England enjoyed a strong seafaring tradition. Fishing and shipping had first become important during the late seventeenth century, as merchants struggled to find a successful method of earning foreign exchange. The expanding slave market in the South opened new opportunities, prompting the growth of thriving coastal ports such as New Haven, Newport,

QUICK REVIEW

Poverty in the Colonies

◆ Gap between rich and poor widened in the eighteenth century.

◆ Most cities had workhouses or shelters.

◆ Young men in New England who could not obtain land often moved to coastal cities and towns.

Salem, and Boston. By midcentury New England had become the most urban of all North America's regions. Boston, the largest city in the British colonies, was the metropolis of a region that included not only New England but also the maritime settlements of Nova Scotia and Newfoundland, where New England merchants dominated commerce and recruited seamen for their fishing and shipping fleets.

CONTRASTS IN COLONIAL POLITICS

The administration of the Spanish and French colonies was highly centralized. French Canada was ruled by a superior council including the royal governor (in charge of military affairs), the intendant (responsible for civil administration), and the bishop of Quebec. New Spain was governed by the Council of the Indies, which sat in Spain, and direct executive authority over all political affairs was exercised by the viceroy in Mexico City. Although local communities had informal independence, the highly bureaucratized and centralized governments of the French Crescent and the Spanish borderlands left little room for the development of vigorous traditions of self-government.

The situation in the British colonies was quite different. During the early eighteenth century the British government of Prime Minister Robert Walpole assumed that a decentralized administration would best accomplish the nation's economic goals. Contented colonies, Walpole argued, would present far fewer problems. Each of the colonies was administered by royally appointed governors, its taxes and finances set by constituent assemblies. Those who owned property could vote for representatives to the assembly. Because many people—mostly white males—owned property, the proportion of adult white men able to vote was 50 percent or higher in all the British colonies. Proportionally, the electorate of the British colonies was the largest in the world.

That did not mean, however, that the British colonies were democratic. The basic principle of order in eighteenth-century British culture was the ideal of deference to natural hierarchies. The well-ordered family, in which children were to be strictly governed by their parents, and wives by their husbands, was the common metaphor for civil order. Members of subordinate groups, such as women, the non-English, African American slaves, servants, and Indians—who in some colonies constituted nine of every ten adults in the population—could not vote or hold public office. Moreover, for the most part the men who did vote chose wealthy landowners, planters, or merchants to serve as their leaders. Thus, provincial assemblies were controlled by colonial elites.

To educated British colonists, the word "democracy" implied rule by the mob, the normal order of things turned upside-down. Over the century there was, however, an important trend toward stronger institutions of representative government. By midcentury most colonial assemblies in British North America had achieved considerable power over provincial affairs and shared authority with governors and other imperial officials. They collected local revenues and allocated funds for government programs, asserted the right to audit the accounts of public officers, and in some cases even acquired the power to approve the appointment of provincial officials. Because the assemblies controlled the finances of government—the "purse strings"—most royal governors were unable to resist this trend.

The royal governors who were most successful at realizing their agendas were those who became adept at playing one provincial faction off against another. All this conflict had the important effect of schooling the colonial elite in the art of politics. It was not democratic politics, but schooling in the ways of patronage, coalition building, and behind-the-scenes intrigue that would have important implications for the development of American institutions.

THE CULTURAL TRANSFORMATION OF BRITISH NORTH AMERICA

Despite broad similarities, the colonial regions of North America developed along divergent lines during the eighteenth century. The British colonies were marked by increasing ethnic diversity, economic growth, social tensions, and conflictual politics that proved to be training for self-government. In the middle decades of the eighteenth century, significant cultural transformation began to take place. New ideas and writings associated with the Enlightenment made their way across the Atlantic on the same ships that transported European immigrants and European goods. In New Spain and New France, by contrast, colonial officials worked diligently to suppress these challenging new ideas and writings. The Catholic Church effectively banned the works of hundreds of authors. In Mexico, officials of the Inquisition conducted house-to-house searches in pursuit of prohibited texts that they feared had been smuggled into the country.

THE ENLIGHTENMENT CHALLENGE

Drawing from the discoveries of Galileo, Copernicus, and the seventeenth-century scientists René Descartes and Sir Isaac Newton, **Enlightenment** thinkers in Britain and on the Continent argued that the universe was governed by natural laws that people could understand and apply to their own advantage. John Locke, for example, articulated a philosophy of reason in proposing that the state existed to provide for the happiness and security of individuals, who were endowed with inalienable rights to life, liberty, and property. Enlightenment writers emphasized rationality, harmony, and order, themes that stood in stark contrast to folk culture's traditional emphasis on the unfathomable mysteries of God and nature and the inevitability of human failure and disorder.

Enlightenment thinking undoubtedly appealed most to those whose ordered lives had improved their lot. The colonial elite had good reason to believe in progress. They sent their sons to college, where the texts of the new

TO WHAT extent did North America participate in the Enlightenment?

Enlightenment   Intellectual movement stressing the importance of reason and the existence of discoverable natural laws.

The first page of the *New England Primer* (1689), published in Boston, which in its various editions sold more than 5 million copies. In addition to the letters of the alphabet, illustrated by crude but charming woodcuts and couplets, the book contained simple moral texts based on Biblical history and wisdom.

Courtesy American Antiquarian Society

thinkers were promoted. Harvard, established in 1636, remained the only institution of higher education in British America until 1693, when Anglicans established the College of William and Mary at Williamsburg, soon to become the new capital of Virginia. Puritans in Connecticut, believing that Harvard was too liberal, founded Yale College in 1701. The curricula of these colleges, modeled on those of Oxford and Cambridge in England, were designed to train ministers, but gradually each institution introduced courses and professors influenced by the Enlightenment.

A mixture of traditional and Enlightenment views characterized the colonial colleges, as it did the thought of men like Cotton Mather. A conservative defender of the old order, Mather wrote a book supporting the existence of witches. On the other hand, he was also a member of the Royal Society, an early supporter of inoculation against smallpox, and a defender of the Copernican sun-centered model of the universe.

About half the adult men and a quarter of the adult women of the British colonies could read, a literacy rate that was comparable to those of England and Scandinavia. In striking contrast, in the French and Spanish colonies reading was a skill confined to a tiny minority of upper-class men. In New England, where the Puritans were committed to Bible reading and developed a system of public education, literacy rates were 85 percent among men and approximately 50 percent among women—the highest in the entire Atlantic world. But the tastes of ordinary readers ran to traditional rather than Enlightenment fare. Not surprisingly, the bestselling book of the colonial era was the Bible. In second place was that unique American literary form, the captivity narrative, (including the Reverend John Williams's *The Redeemed Captive Returning to Zion*, cited in the beginning of this chapter), most with a lot less religion and a great deal more gore.

Another popular literary form was the **almanac**, a combination calendar, astrological guide, and sourcebook of medical advice and farming tips reflecting the concerns of traditional folk culture. The best remembered is *Poor Richard's Almanac* (1732–57), published by Philadelphia newspaper publisher Benjamin Franklin, although it was preceded and outlived by a great many others. What was so innovative about Franklin's almanac, and what made it so important, was the manner in which the author used this traditional literary form to promote the new Enlightenment emphasis on useful and practical knowledge. Posing as the simple bumpkin Poor Richard, the highly sophisticated Franklin was one of the first Americans to bring Enlightenment thought to ordinary folk.

The growth of the economy in the British colonies and the development of a colonial upper class stimulated the emergence of a more cosmopolitan Anglican culture, particularly in the cities of the Atlantic coast. A rising demand for drama, poetry, essays, novels, and history was met by urban booksellers who imported British publications.

A DECLINE IN RELIGIOUS DEVOTION

At the same time that these new ideas were flourishing, religion seemed in decline. South of New England, the Anglican Church was weak, its ministers uninspiring, and many families remained "unchurched." A historian of religion has estimated that only one adult in fifteen was a member of a congregation. Although this figure may understate the impact of religion on community life, it helps keep things in perspective.

The Puritan churches of New England also suffered declining membership and falling attendance at services, and many ministers began to warn

Almanac A combination calendar, astrological guide, and sourcebook of medical advice and farming tips.

of Puritanism's "declension," pointing to the "dangerous" trend toward the "evil of toleration." By the second decade of the eighteenth century only one in five New Englanders belonged to an established congregation. When Puritanism had been a sect, membership in the church was voluntary and leaders could demand that followers testify to their religious conversion. But when Puritanism became an established church, attendance was expected of all townspeople, and conflicts inevitably arose over the requirement of a conversion experience. An agreement of 1662, known as the **Half-Way Covenant**, offered a practical solution: members' children who had not experienced conversion themselves could join as "half-way" members, restricted only from participation in communion. Thus, the Puritans chose to manage rather than to resolve the conflicts involved in becoming an established religion. Tensions also developed between congregational autonomy and the central control that traditionally accompanied the establishment of a state church. In 1708 the churches of Connecticut agreed to the Saybrook Platform, which enacted a system of governance by councils of ministers and elders rather than by congregations. This reform also had the effect of weakening the passion and commitment of church members.

In addition, an increasing number of **Congregationalists** began to question the strict **Calvinist theology of predestination**—the belief that God had predetermined the few men and women who would be saved in the Second Coming. In the eighteenth century many Puritans turned to the much more comforting idea that God had given people the freedom to choose salvation by developing their faith and by doing good works. This belief, known as Arminianism, was in harmony with the Enlightenment view that men and women were not helpless pawns but rational beings who could actively shape their own destinies. Also implicit in these new views was an image of God as a loving rather than a punishing father. Arminianism became a force at Harvard in the early eighteenth century, and soon a new generation of Arminian ministers began to assume leadership in New England's churches. These liberal ideas appealed to groups experiencing economic and social improvement, especially commercial farmers, merchants, and the comfortable middle class with its rising expectations. But among ordinary people, especially those in the countryside where traditional patterns lingered, there was a good deal of opposition to these unorthodox new ideas.

THE GREAT AWAKENING

The first stirrings of a movement challenging this rationalist approach to religion occurred during the 1730s, most notably in the movement sparked by Reverend Jonathan Edwards in the community of Northampton, in western Massachusetts. As the leaders of the community increasingly devoted their energies to the pursuit of wealth, the enthusiasm seemed to go out of religion. The congregation adopted rules allowing church membership without evidence of a conversion experience and adopted a seating plan for the church that placed wealthy families in the prominent pews, front and center. But the same economic forces that made the "River Gods"—as the wealthy landowners of the Connecticut Valley were known—also impoverished others. Young people from the community's poorer families grew disaffected as they were forced to postpone marriage because of the scarcity and expense of the land needed to set up a farm household. Increasingly they refused to attend church meetings, instead gathering together at night for "frolics" that only seemed to increase their discontent.

Half-Way Covenant Plan adopted in 1662 by New England clergy to deal with the problem of declining church membership, allowing children of baptized parents to be baptized whether or not their parents had experienced conversion.

Congregationalists Members of Puritan churches governed by congregations.

Calvinist theology of predestination Belief that God has predestined certain individuals to be saved and others to be damned.

Reverend Edwards made this group of young people his special concern. Believing that they needed to "have their hearts touched," he preached to them in a style that appealed to their emotions. For the first time in a generation, the meetinghouse shook with the fire and passion of Puritan religion. "Before the sermon was done," one Northampton parishioner remembered about one notable occasion, "there was a great moaning and crying through the whole house—What shall I do to be saved?—Oh I am going to Hell!—Oh what shall I do for Christ?" Religious fervor swept through the community, and church membership began to grow. There was more to this than the power of one preacher, for similar revivals were soon breaking out in other New England communities, as well as among German pietists and Scots–Irish Presbyterians in Pennsylvania. Complaining of "spiritual coldness," people abandoned ministers whose sermons read like rational dissertations for those whose preaching was more emotional.

These local revivals became an intercolonial phenomenon thanks to the preaching of George Whitefield, an evangelical Anglican minister from England, who in 1738 made the first of several tours of the colonies. By all accounts, his preaching had a powerful effect. Even Benjamin Franklin, a religious skeptic, wrote of the "extraordinary influence of [Whitefield's] oratory" after attending an outdoor service in Philadelphia where 30,000 people crowded the streets to hear him. Whitefield began as Edwards did, chastising his listeners as "half animals and half devils," but he left them with the hope that God would be responsive to their desire for salvation. Whitefield avoided sectarian differences. "God help us to forget party names and become Christians in deed and truth," he declared.

Historians of religion consider this widespread colonial revival of religion, which later generations called the **Great Awakening**, to be an American version of the second phase of the Protestant Reformation (see Chapter 2). Religious leaders condemned the laxity, decadence, and officialism of established Protestantism and reinvigorated it with calls for piety and purity. People undergoing the economic and social stresses of the age, unsure about their ability to find land, marry, and participate in the promise of a growing economy, found relief in religious enthusiasm.

In Pennsylvania, two important leaders were William Tennent and his son Gilbert. An Irish-born Presbyterian, the elder Tennent was an evangelical preacher who established a school in Pennsylvania to train like-minded men for the ministry. His lampooned "Log College," as it was called, ultimately evolved into the College of New Jersey—later Princeton University— founded in 1746. In the early 1740s, disturbed by what he called the "presumptuous security" of the colonial church, Tennent toured with Whitefield and delivered the famous sermon "The Dangers of an Unconverted Ministry," in which he called upon Protestants to examine the religious convictions of their own ministers.

Among Presbyterians, open conflict broke out between the revivalists and the old guard, and in some regions the church hierarchy divided into separate organizations. In New England, similar factions, known as the **New Lights** and the **Old Lights**, accused each other of heresy. The New Lights railed against Arminianism as a rationalist heresy and called for a revival of Calvinism. The Old Lights condemned emotional enthusiasm as part of the heresy of believing in a personal and direct relationship with God outside the order of the church. Itinerant preachers appeared in the countryside, stirring up trouble. Many congregations split into feuding factions, and ministers found themselves challenged by their newly awakened parishioners. Never had there been such turmoil in New England churches.

Great Awakening   North American religious revival in the middle of the eighteenth century.

New Lights   People who experienced conversion during the revivals of the Great Awakening.

Old Lights   Religious faction that condemned emotional enthusiasm as part of the heresy of believing in a personal and direct relationship with God outside the order of the church.

Although some historians have raised questions about how cohesive these revivals were, they were so widespread and were typical of so many communities that they might be seen as one of the first national events in American history. They began somewhat later in the South, developing first in the mid-1740s among Scots–Irish Presbyterians, and then achieved full impact with the organizational work of Methodists and particularly Baptists in the 1760s and early 1770s. These revivals not only affected white Southerners but also introduced many slaves to Christianity for the first time. Local awakenings were often a phenomenon shared by both white and black people. The Baptist churches of the South in the era of the American Revolution included members of both races and featured spontaneous preaching by slaves as well as masters. In the nineteenth century white and black Christians would go their separate ways, but the joint experience of the eighteenth-century Awakening shaped the religious cultures of both groups.

Many other "unchurched" colonists were brought back to Protestantism by eighteenth-century revivalism. But a careful examination of statistics suggests that the proportion of church members in the general population probably did not increase during the middle decades of the century. While the number of churches more than doubled from 1740 to 1780, the colonial population grew even faster, increasing threefold. The greatest impact was on families already associated with the churches. Before the Awakening, attendance at church had been mostly an adult affair, but throughout the colonies the revival of religion had its deepest effects on young people, who flocked to church in greater numbers than ever before. For years the number of people experiencing conversion had been steadily falling, but now full membership surged. Church membership previously had been concentrated among women, leading Cotton Mather, for one, to speculate that perhaps women were indeed more godly. But men were particularly affected by the revival of religion, and their attendance and membership rose.

THE POLITICS OF REVIVALISM

Revivalism appealed most of all to groups who felt bypassed by the economic and cultural development of the British colonies during the first half of the eighteenth century. The New Lights tended to draw their greatest strength from small farmers and less prosperous craftsmen. Many members of the upper class and the comfortable "middling sort" viewed the excesses of revivalism as indications of anarchy, and they became even more committed to rational religion.

Some historians have argued for important political implications of revivalism. In Connecticut, for example, Old Lights politicized the religious dispute by passing a series of laws in the General Assembly designed to suppress revivalism. In one town, separatists refused to pay taxes that supported the established church and were jailed. New Light judges were thrown off the bench, and others were denied their elected seats in the assembly. The arrogance of these actions was met with popular outrage: by the 1760s the Connecticut New Lights had organized themselves politically and, in what amounted to a political rebellion, succeeded in turning the Old Lights out of office. These New Light politicians would provide the leadership for the American Revolution in Connecticut.

Such direct connections between religion and politics were rare. There can be little doubt, however, that for many people revivalism offered the first opportunity to participate actively in public debate and public action that affected the direction of their lives. Choices about religious styles, ministers, and doctrine were thrown open for public discourse, and ordinary people began to believe

QUICK REVIEW

The Great Awakening

- Opposition to rationalist approach to religion grew in the 1730s.
- Jonathan Edwards focused his attention on inspiring young people.
- Movement spread throughout the colonies.

CHRONOLOGY

1636	Harvard College founded.	**1716**	Spanish begin construction of Texas missions.
1644	Roger Williams's *Bloudy Tenent of Persecution.*	**1730s**	French decimate the Natchez and defeat the Fox Indians.
1662	Half-Way Covenant in New England.	**1732**	Franklin begins publishing *Poor Richard's Almanac.*
1674	Bishopric of Quebec established.	**1738**	George Whitefield first tours the colonies.
1680s	William Penn begins recruiting settlers from the European Continent.	**1740s**	Great Awakening gets under way in the Northeast.
1682	Mary Rowlandson's *Sovereignty and Goodness of God.*	**1740**	Parliament passes a naturalization law for the colonies.
1689	Toleration Act passed by Parliament.	**1746**	College of New Jersey (Princeton) founded.
1690s	Beginnings of Jesuit missions in Arizona.	**1760s**	Great Awakening achieves full impact in the South.
1693	College of William and Mary founded.		
1700s	Plains Indians begin adoption of the horse.	**1769**	Spanish colonization of California begins.
1701	Yale College founded. Iroquois sign treaty of neutrality with France.	**1775**	Indian revolt at San Diego.
1704	Deerfield raid.	**1776**	San Francisco founded.
1708	Saybrook Platform in Connecticut.	**1781**	Los Angeles founded.

that their opinions actually counted for something. Underlying the debate over these issues were insecurities about warfare, economic growth, and the development of colonial society. Revivalism empowered ordinary people to question their leaders, an experience that would prove critical in the political struggles to come.

CONCLUSION

By the middle of the eighteenth century a number of distinct colonial regions had emerged in North America, all of them with rising populations who demanded that more land be seized from the Indians. Some colonies attempted to ensure homogeneity, whereas others embraced diversity. Within the British colonies, New England in particular seemed bound to the past, whereas the Middle Colonies and the backcountry pointed the way toward pluralism and expansion. These developments placed them in direct competition with the expansionist plans of the French and at odds with Indian peoples committed to the defense of their homelands.

The economic development of the British colonies introduced new social and cultural tensions that led to the Great Awakening, a massive revival of religion that was the first transcolonial event in American history. Thousands of people experienced a renewal of religious passions, but rather than resuscitating old traditions, the Awakening pointed people toward a more active role in their own political futures. These transformations added to the differences between the British colonies, on the one hand, and New Spain and the French Crescent, on the other.

SUMMARY

North American Regions The development of regional cultures was a multicultural enterprise. Relations between Indian peoples and European colonists followed differing patterns. The same was true of colonial development. The resulting colonial societies reflected the meeting of peoples and cultures.

Diverging Social and Political Patterns Immigration fueled population growth in the British colonies. Both in terms of status and mobility, the development of classes in the colonies differed from the social structure in England, and it also varied by region. British policy influenced colonial development.

The Cultural Transformation of British North America New ideas from Europe combined with trends in development helped transform the British colonies in the eighteenth century. The interplay between the traditional and the new stimulated strong movements in response to the ongoing changes.

REVIEW QUESTIONS

1. What were the principal colonial regions of North America? Discuss their similarities and their differences. Contrast the development of their political systems.

2. Why did the Spanish and the French close their colonies to immigration? Why did the British open theirs? How do you explain the ethnic homogeneity of New England and the ethnic pluralism of New York and Pennsylvania?

3. What were the principal trends in the history of Indian America in the eighteenth century?

4. Discuss the development of class differences in the Spanish, French, and British colonies in the eighteenth century.

5. Discuss the effects of the Great Awakening on the subsequent history of the British colonies.

KEY TERMS

Almanac (p. 122)

Calvinist theology of predestination (p. 123)

Congregationalists (p. 123)

Encomienda (p. 117)

Engagés (p. 117)

Enlightenment (p. 121)

Great Awakening (p. 124)

Half-Way Covenant (p. 123)

King William's War (p. 116)

New Lights (p. 124)

Old Lights (p. 124)

Redemptioner (p. 116)

The Toleration Act (p. 110)

RECOMMENDED READING

Jon Butler, *Becoming America: The Revolution Before 1776* (2000). A history that emphasizes the diversity, economic prosperity, participatory politics, and religious pluralism of the eighteenth-century British colonies.

Edward Countryman, *Americans: A Collision of Histories* (1996). An important new synthesis that includes the many peoples and cultures of North America.

John Demos, *The Unredeemed Captive: A Family Story from Early America* (1994). A moving history of the Deerfield captives, focusing on the experience of Eunice Williams, the unredeemed captive.

W. J. Eccles, *The Canadian Frontier, 1534–1760* (1983). An introduction to the history of French America by a leading scholar on colonial Canada.

David Hackett Fischer, *Albion's Seed: Four British Folkways in America* (1990). An engaging history with fascinating details on the regions of New England, Pennsylvania, Virginia, and the backcountry.

Jack P. Greene, *Pursuits of Happiness: The Social Development of Early Modern British Colonies and the Formation of American Culture* (1986). A distillation of a tremendous amount of historical material on community life in British North America.

Frank Lambert, *Inventing the "Great Awakening"* (1999). Argues that the revivialists themselves created the idea of the Great Awakening to further their evangelical work.

Jackson Turner Main, *The Social Structure of Revolutionary America* (1965). A detailed treatment of colonial social structure, with statistics, tables, and enlightening interpretations.

D. W. Meinig, *The Shaping of America: Atlantic America, 1492–1800* (1986). A geographer's overview of the historical development of the North American continent in the era of European colonialism. Provides a survey of the British and French colonies.

Lucy Eldersveld Murphy, *A Gathering of Rivers: Indians, Métis, and Mining in the Western Great Lakes, 1737–1832* (2000). Demonstrates the success of Indian communities in adapting to colonialism through the diversification of their economies, intermarriage, and constructing multiethnic communities.

David J. Weber, *The Spanish Frontier in North America* (1992). A magnificent treatment of the entire Spanish borderlands, from Florida to California. Includes important chapters on colonial government and social life.

Marianne S. Wokeck, *Trade in Strangers: The Beginning of Mass Migration to North America* (1999). The first important study of immigration in the eighteenth century, arguing that these migrations served as models for European mass migration in the next century.

My dear Jack, All the Provinces [are] arming and Training in the same Manner, for they are all determined to die or be Free . . .
—Eliza Farmer, June 28, 1775

A NEW METHOD OF MACARONY MAKING AS PRACTISED AT BOSTON

Tarring and Featherimg, 1773.
A New Method of Macarony Making, as Practiced at Boston. American edition of an English mezzotint satire, 1774, on the treatment given to John Malcom, an unpopular Commisioner of Customs at Boston

6

FROM EMPIRE TO INDEPENDENCE
1750–1776

WHAT WERE the most important weaknesses of the British Empire in North America at the outset of the Seven Years' War?

WHAT FACTORS led to the growth of American nationalism in the 1760s?

HOW DID political and economic problems in Britain contribute to unrest in the colonies?

WHAT STEPS did Britain take to punish Massachusets for the colonists' acts of resistance?

WHO MADE up the second Continental Congress and why was it formed?

AMERICAN COMMUNITIES

The First Continental Congress Shapes a National Political Community

BRITAIN'S NORTH AMERICAN COLONIES HAD ENJOYED CONSIDERABLE prosperity during the late seventeenth and early eighteenth centuries. Beginning with the Stamp Act in 1765, however, the British government began to apply pressure, largely in the form of taxes and new trade restrictions, that drew increasing resistance from the colonies. In convening the First Continental Congress in September 1774, the colonies made clear their displeasure with the government's actions. Fifty-six elected delegates from twelve of the colonies met at Philadelphia to draft a common response to what they called the **Intolerable Acts**—*the closing of the port of Boston, the suspension of Massachusetts government, and several other measures of British repression—that were the latest attempt to force the colonies to accept the power of Parliament to make laws binding them "in all cases whatsoever." This was the first meeting of the colonies since the* **Stamp Act Congress** *of 1765 (discussed later in this chapter). If the colonies now failed to act together, they would be "attacked and destroyed by piecemeal," declared Arthur Lee of Virginia. "Every part will in its turn feel the vengeance which it would not unite to repel." Abigail Adams, the politically astute wife of John Adams of Massachusetts, agreed. "You have before you," she wrote to her husband, "the greatest national concerns that ever came before any people."*

The opening minutes of the first session on September 5 did not bode well. One delegate moved that they begin with prayer; another responded that they were "so divided in religious sentiments, some Episcopalians, some Quakers, some Anabaptists, some Presbyterians and some Congregationalists, so that we could not join in the same act of worship." Were the delegates to be stymied from the very beginning by things that separated rather than united them? John Adams's cousin, fellow Massachusetts delegate Samuel Adams, jumped to his feet. He was no bigot, he said, "and could hear a prayer from any gentleman of piety and virtue who was at the same time a friend to his country." The delegates finally agreed to ask a local clergyman, a supporter of the American cause, to officiate. The minister took for his text the Thirty-fifth Psalm: "Plead my cause, O Lord, with them that strive with me; fight against them that fight against me." John Adams was delighted. The minister "prayed with such fervor, such Ardor, such Earnestness and Pathos, and in Language so elegant and sublime," he wrote home, that "it has had an excellent Effect upon every Body here."

This incident highlighted the most important task confronting the Continental Congress: they had to develop trust in one another, for what they were doing was considered treason by *the British authorities. They had to find a way to support the common cause without compromising their local identities. At first it was as if the delegates were "ambassadors from a dozen belligerent powers of Europe," wrote John Adams. The delegates represented different colonies, whose traditions and histories were as different as those of separate countries. Moreover, these lawyers, merchants, and planters, who were leaders in their respective colonies, were strangers to one another. Their political opinions ranged from loyalty to the British crown and empire to a belief in the necessity of violent revolution. "Every man," Adams wrote, "is a great man, an orator, a critic, a statesman, and therefore every man, upon every question, must show his oratory, his criticism, and his political abilities." As a result, he continued, "business is drawn and spun out to an immeasurable length. I believe that if it was moved and seconded that we should come to a resolution that three and two make five, we should be entertained with logic and rhetorick, law, history, politicks and mathematics concerning the subject for two whole days."*

During seven weeks of deliberations, the men of the Continental Congress succeeded in forging an agreement on the principles and policies they would have to follow in addressing the most serious crisis in the history of Britain's North American colonies. Equally important, the delegates found ways to work together and harmonize their interests. They immediately resolved that each colony would have one vote, thereby committing themselves to preserving provincial autonomy. They sent their most vexing problems to committees, whose members could sound each other out on the issues without speaking for the public record, and they added to their daily routine a round of dinners, parties, and late-night drinking. The greatest single accomplishment of the Continental Congress was the creation of a community of leadership for the united colonies. "It has taken us much time to get acquainted," John Adams wrote to Abigail, but he left Philadelphia thinking of his fellow representatives as "a collection of the greatest men upon this continent."

The First Continental Congress, thus, took the first steps toward the creation of a national political community. The bonds of community can be local, regional, national, or international. In a town or village the feeling of association comes from daily, face-to-face contact, but for larger groups these feelings must be created, or "imagined," as the historian Benedict Anderson puts it. The delegates took some of the first steps in this direction. In their final declaration they pledged to "firmly agree and associate, under the sacred ties of virtue, honor and love of our country." They urged

Philadelphia

their fellow Americans to "encourage frugality, economy, and industry, and promote agriculture, arts and the manufactures of this country," to "discountenance and discourage every species of extravagance and dissipation, especially all horse-racing, and all kinds of gaming, cock fighting, exhibitions of shows, plays, and other expensive diversions and entertainments." In other words, they called upon the common religious and cultural traditions of British Americans. They asked their countrymen to remember "the poorer sort" among them during the coming economic troubles. And in demanding that their fellow Americans "break off all dealings" and treat with contempt anyone violating the compact, the delegates were declaring who was "inside" and who was "outside" their community. Drawing boundaries is the essential first act in the construction of a new community.

Patrick Henry of Virginia, one of the delegates already committed to independence, was exuberant when the First Continental Congress adjourned in late October. "The distinctions between Virginians, Pennsylvanians, New Yorkers, and New Englanders, are no more. I am not a Virginian, but an American," he declared. Henry voiced an important truth. Great Britain had forced the colonists to recognize that they shared a community of interest distinct from that of the mother country. Theirs was a first attempt to overcome local diversity and difference in pursuit of a common national goal. In the months and years to come the strength of local community would sometimes threaten to pull them apart, and the "imagined community" of America would be sorely tested as the colonies cautiously moved toward independence.

THE SEVEN YEARS' WAR IN AMERICA

The first attempt at cooperation among the leaders of the British colonies occurred in 1754, when representatives from New England, New York, Pennsylvania, and Maryland met to consider a joint approach to the French and Indian challenge. Even as the delegates met, fighting between French Canadians and Virginians began on the Ohio River, the first shots in a great global war for empire, known in Europe as the Seven Years' War, that pitted Britain (allied with Prussia) against the combined might of France, Austria, and Spain. In North America this would be the final and most destructive armed conflict between the British and the French before the French Revolution. Ultimately it decided the future of the vast region between the Appalachian Mountains and the Mississippi River and lay the ground for the conflict between the British and the colonists that led to the American Revolution.

WHAT WERE the most important weaknesses of the British Empire in North America at the outset of the Seven Years' War?

THE ALBANY CONFERENCE OF 1754

The 1754 meeting, which included an official delegation from the Iroquois Confederacy, took place in the New York town of Albany on the Hudson River, convened by the British Board of Trade. British officials wanted the colonies to consider a collective response to the continuing conflict with New France and the Indians of the interior. High on the agenda was the negotiation of a settlement with the leaders of the Iroquois Confederacy, who had grown impatient with colonial land grabbing. Because the powerful Iroquois Confederacy, with its Covenant Chain of alliances with other Indian tribes, occupied such a strategic location between New France and the British colonies, the British could ill afford Iroquois discontent. But the official Iroquois delegation walked out of the conference, refusing all offers to join a British alliance.

The Albany Conference did adopt **Benjamin Franklin's Plan of Union**, which proposed that Indian affairs, western settlement, and other items of mutual interest be placed under the authority of a grand council made up of representatives elected by the colonial assemblies and led by a royally appointed president. But the colonial assemblies rejected the Albany Plan of Union.

Intolerable Acts   American term for the Coercive Acts and the Quebec Act.

Stamp Act Congress   October 1765 meeting of delegates sent by nine colonies, held in New York City, that adopted the Declaration of Rights and Grievances and petitioned against the Stamp Act.

Benjamin Franklin's Plan of Union   Plan put forward in 1754 calling for an intercolonial union to manage defense and Indian affairs. The plan was rejected by participants at the Albany Congress.

IMAGE KEY

for pages 130–131

a. Green tea and dried tea leaves.

b. Flank and breast feathers.

c. Tarring & Feathering, 1773. "A New Method of Macarony Making, as Practiced at Boston." American edition of an English mezzotint satire, 1774, on the treatment given to John Malcolm, an unpopular commissioner of customs at Boston.

d. A "No Stamp Act" teapot.

e. Three Imrie/Risley by Wilson 1750s 77mm diorama figures, Roger Ranger with two soldiers, French and Indian War, on a diorama base.

f. Propaganda of 1765 against the Stamp Act that was emblazoned on teapots.

g. American colonists force feed hot tea to an English tax collector after tar and feathering the agent under a Liberty Tree in colonial Boston.

h. Colored engraving, published by Paul Revere, shows British troops disembarking from a ship in Boston in 1768.

i. The Declaration of Independence.

 MAP EXPLORATION

To explore an interactive version of this map, go to
http://www.prenhall.com/faraghertlc/map6.1

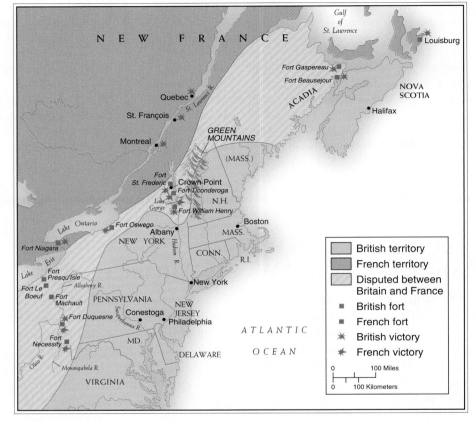

MAP 6-1

The War for Empire in North America, 1754–1763 The Seven Years' War in America (also known as the French and Indian War) was fought in three principal areas: Nova Scotia and what was then Acadia, the frontier between New France and New York, and the upper Ohio River—gateway to the Old Northwest.

HOW DID the Indian trade affect the war? Which military defeats dealt the worst blows to the French?

COLONIAL AIMS AND INDIAN INTERESTS

The absence of cooperation among the colonies in North America would prove to be one of the greatest weaknesses of the British Empire, because the ensuing war would be fought at a number of widespread locations and required the coordination of command. There were three principal flash points of conflict in North America. The first was along the northern Atlantic coast. In 1713 France had ceded to Britain its colony of Acadia (which the British renamed Nova Scotia), but France then built the fortress of Louisburg, from which it guarded its fishing grounds and the St. Lawrence approach to New France. The French subsequently reinforced Louisburg to such an extent that it became known as the Gibraltar of the New World.

A second zone of conflict was the border region between New France and New York, from Niagara Falls to Lake Champlain, where Canadians and New Yorkers were in furious competition for the Indian trade. Unable to compete effectively against superior English goods, the French resorted to armed might, constructing fortifications on Lake George and reinforcing their base at Niagara. In this zone the strategic advantage was held by the Iroquois Confederacy.

It was the Ohio country—the trans-Appalachian region along the Ohio River—that became the primary focus of British and French attention. This rich land was a prime target of British backcountry settlers and frontier land speculators. The French worried that their isolated settlements would be overrun by the expanding British population and that the loss of the Ohio River would threaten their entire Mississippi trading empire. To reinforce their claims, in 1749 the French sent a heavily armed force down the Ohio River to ward off the British, and in 1752, supported by their northern Indian allies, they expelled a large number of British traders from the region. To prevent the British from returning to the west, they began the next year to construct a series of forts running south from Lake Erie to the junction of the Allegheny and Monongahela rivers, the site known as the Forks of the Ohio River.

The French "have stripped us of more than nine parts in ten of North America," one British official cried, "and left us only a skirt of coast along the Atlantic shore." In preparation for a general war, the British established the port of Halifax in Nova Scotia as a counter to Louisburg. In northern New York, they strengthened existing forts and constructed new ones. Finally, the British king decided to directly challenge the French claim to the upper Ohio Valley. He conferred an enormous grant of land on the Ohio Company, organized by Virginia and London capitalists, and the company made plans to build a fort at the Forks of the Ohio River.

The impending conflict did not involve only the competing colonial powers, however, for the Indian peoples of the interior had interests of their own. In addition to its native inhabitants, the Ohio country had become a refuge for Indian peoples who had fled the Northeast—Delawares, Shawnees, Hurons, and Iroquois among them. Most of the Ohio Indians opposed the British and were anxious to preserve the Appalachians as a barrier to westward expansion. They were also disturbed by the French movement into their country. The French outposts, however, unlike those of the British, did not become centers of expanding agricultural settlements.

The Iroquois Confederacy as a whole sought to play off one European power against the other, to its own advantage. In the South the Creeks carved out a similar role for themselves among the British, the French in Louisiana, and the Spanish in Florida. The Cherokees and Choctaws attempted, less successfully, to do the same. It was in the interests of these Indian tribes, in other words, to perpetuate the existing colonial stalemate. Their position would be greatly undermined by an overwhelming victory for either side.

FRONTIER WARFARE

At the Albany Congress the delegates received news that Colonel George Washington, a young militia officer sent by the governor of Virginia to expel the French from the region granted to the Ohio Company, had been forced to surrender his troops to a French force near the headwaters of the Monongahela River. The Canadians now commanded the interior country from their base at Fort Duquesne.

3–9
"The Storm Arising in the West," George Washington Delivers a Warning to the French (1753)

Taking up the challenge, the British government dispatched two Irish regiments under General Edward Braddock across the Atlantic in 1755 to attack and destroy Fort Duquesne. Meanwhile, colonial militias (the equivalent of today's National Guard) commanded by colonial officers were to strike at the New York frontier and the North Atlantic coast. An army of New England militiamen succeeded in capturing two important French forts on the border of Nova Scotia, but the other two prongs of the campaign were failures. The offensive in New York was repulsed. And in the worst defeat of a British army during the eighteenth

3–10
The Closing of the Frontier
(1763)

French and Indian War   The last
of the Anglo-French colonial wars
(1754–1763) and the first in which
fighting began in North America.
The war ended with France's defeat.

century, Braddock's force was destroyed by a smaller number of French and Indians on the upper Ohio, and Braddock himself was killed.

Braddock's defeat was followed by the outbreak of full-scale warfare between Britain and France in 1756. Known as the Seven Years' War in Europe, in North America it came to be called the **French and Indian War**. The fighting of 1756 and 1757 was a near catastrophe for Great Britain. Canadians captured the British forts in northern New York. Indians pounded backcountry settlements, killed thousands of settlers, and raided deep into the coastal colonies, throwing British colonists into panic. The absence of colonial cooperation greatly hampered the British attempt to mount a counterattack. When British commanders tried to exert direct control over provincial troops, in order to coordinate their strategy, they succeeded only in angering local authorities.

THE CONQUEST OF CANADA

In the darkest days of 1757, William Pitt, an enthusiastic advocate of British expansion, became prime minister of Great Britain. "I know that I can save this country," Pitt declared, "and that no one else can." Deciding that the global war could be won in North America, he subsidized the Prussians to fight the war in Europe and reserved his own forces and resources for naval and colonial operations. Pitt committed the British to the conquest of Canada and the elimination of all French competition in North America. Such a goal could be achieved only with a tremendous outpouring

The death of General James Wolfe, at the conclusion of the battle in which the British captured Quebec in 1759, became the subject of American artist Benjamin West's most famous painting, which was exhibited to tremendous acclaim in London in 1770.

Benjamin West (1738–1820), The Death of General Wolfe, 1770. Oil on canvas, 152.6 x 214.5 cm. Transfer from the Canadian War Memorials, 1921. (Gift of the 2nd Duke of Westminster, Eaton Hall, Cheshire, 1918). National Gallery of Canada, Ottawa, Ontario of men and money. By promising that the war would be fought "at His Majesty's expense," Pitt was able to buy colonial cooperation. A massive infusion of British currency and credit greatly stimulated the North American economy. Pitt dispatched over 20,000 regular British troops across the Atlantic. Combining them with colonial forces, he massed over 50,000 armed men against Canada.

The British attracted Indian support for their plans by "redressing the grievances complained of by the Indians, with respect to the lands which have been fraudulently taken from them," in the words of a British official. In 1758 officials promised the Iroquois Confederacy and the Ohio Indians that the crown would "agree upon clear and fixed boundaries between our settlements and their hunting grounds, so that each party may know their own and be a mutual protection to each other of their respective possessions."

Thus did Pitt succeed in reversing the course of the war. Regular and provincial forces captured Louisburg in July 1758, setting the stage for the penetration of the St. Lawrence Valley. A month later a force of New Englanders captured the strategic French fort of Oswego on Lake Ontario, thereby preventing the Canadians from resupplying their western posts. Encouraged by British promises, many Indian tribes abandoned the French alliance. The French were forced to give up Fort Duquesne, and a large British force soon took control of this French fort at the Forks of the Ohio, renaming the post Fort Pitt (Pittsburgh today) in honor of the prime minister. "Blessed be God," wrote a Boston editor. "The long looked for day is arrived that has now fixed us on the banks of the Ohio." The last of the French forts on the New York frontier fell in 1759. In the South, regular and provincial British troops invaded the homeland of the Cherokees and crushed them.

British forces now converged on Quebec, the heart of French Canada. In the summer of 1759 British troops, responding to General James Wolfe's order to "burn and lay waste the country," plundered farms and shelled the city of Quebec. Finally, in an epic battle fought on the Plains of Abraham before the city walls, more than 2,000 British, French, American, and Canadian men lost their lives, including both Wolfe and the French commander, the Marquis de Montcalm. The British army prevailed, and Quebec fell. Finally, the conquest of Montreal in 1760 marked the destruction of the French empire in America.

In the final two years of the war the British swept French ships from the seas, invaded Havana and conquered Cuba, took possession of several other important Spanish and French colonies in the Caribbean, achieved dominance in India, and even captured the Spanish Philippines. In the **Treaty of Paris**, signed in 1763, France lost all its possessions on the North American mainland. It ceded its claims east of the Mississippi to Great Britain, with the exception of New Orleans. That town, along with the other French trans-Mississippi claims, passed to Spain. For its part, in exchange for the return of all its Caribbean and Pacific colonies, Spain ceded Florida to Britain. The imperial rivalry in eastern North America that had begun in the sixteenth century now came to an end with complete victory for the British Empire.

THE STRUGGLE FOR THE WEST

Both the French and the British had long used gift-giving as a way of gaining favor with Indians. The Spanish officials who replaced the French in Louisiana made an effort to continue the old policy. But the British military governor of the western region, General Jeffery Amherst, in one of his first official actions, banned presents to Indian chiefs and tribes, demanding that they learn to live without "charity." Not only were Indians angered by Amherst's reversal of custom, but they were also frustrated by his refusal to supply them with the ammunition they required for hunting. Many were left starving.

> ### QUICK REVIEW
> **European Territories, 1763**
> - Britain: territories in North America from Hudson's Bay to the Caribbean, from the Atlantic to the Mississippi.
> - France: territory on the mainland reduced to two small islands.
> - Spain: Cuba, the Philippines, Louisiana, and California.

Treaty of Paris   The formal end to British hostilities against France and Spain in February 1763.

In this climate, hundreds of Ohio Indians became disciples of an Indian visionary named Neolin ("The Enlightened One" in Algonquian), known to the English as the Delaware Prophet. The core of Neolin's teaching was that Indians had been corrupted by European ways and needed to purify themselves by returning to their traditions and preparing for a holy war.

In May 1763, the Indian confederacy simultaneously attacked all the British forts in the West. Although they sacked and burned eight British posts, the Indians failed to take the key forts of Niagara, Detroit, and Pitt. The Indians fought on for another year, but most of the Indians sued for peace, fearing the destruction of their villages. The British came to terms because they knew they could not overwhelm the Indian peoples. The war thus ended in stalemate.

Even before the uprising, the British had been at work on a policy they hoped would help to resolve frontier tensions. In the **Royal Proclamation of 1763**, the British government set aside the region west of the crest of the Appalachian Mountains as "Indian Country," and required the specific authorization of the crown for any purchase of these protected Indian lands.

Colonists had expected that the removal of the French threat would allow them to move unencumbered into the West, regardless of the wishes of the Indian inhabitants. They could not understand why the British would award territory to Indian enemies who had slaughtered more than 4,000 settlers during the previous war. In fact, the British proved unable and ultimately unwilling to prevent the westward migration that was to be a dynamic part of the colonization of British North America. Within a few years of the war, New Englanders by the thousands were moving into the northern Green Mountain district, known as Vermont. In the middle colonies, New York settlers pushed ever closer to the homeland of the Iroquois, while others settled within the protective radius of Fort Pitt in western Pennsylvania. Hunters, stock herders, and farmers crossed over the first range of the Appalachians in Virginia and North Carolina, planting pioneer communities in what are now West Virginia and eastern Tennessee.

Moreover, the press of population growth and economic development turned the attention of investors and land speculators to the area west of the Appalachians. In response to demands by settlers and speculators, British authorities were soon pressing the Iroquois and Cherokees for cessions of land in Indian Country. No longer able to play off rival colonial powers, Indians were reduced to a choice between compliance and resistance. Weakened by the recent war, they chose to sign away lands.

The individual colonies were even more aggressive. Locked in a dispute with Pennsylvania about jurisdiction in the Ohio country, in 1773 Virginia governor John Murray, Earl of Dunmore, sent a force to occupy Fort Pitt. In 1774, in an attempt to gain legitimacy for his dispute with Pennsylvania, Dunmore provoked a frontier war with the Shawnees. After defeating them, he forced their cession of the upper Ohio River Valley to Virginia.

Royal Proclamation of 1763 Royal proclamation setting the boundary known as the Proclamation Line.

THE IMPERIAL CRISIS IN BRITISH NORTH AMERICA

■ ■ ■ ■ ■ ■ ■ ■ ■ ■ ■ ■
WHAT FACTORS led

to the growth of American

nationalism in the 1760s?
■ ■ ■ ■ ■ ■ ■ ■ ■ ■ ■ ■

No colonial power of the mid-eighteenth century could match Britain in projecting imperial power over the face of the globe. During the years following its victory in the Seven Years' War, Britain turned confidently to the reorganization of its North American empire. This new colonial policy plunged British authorities into a new and ultimately more threatening conflict with the colonists, who had begun to develop a sense of a separate identity.

MAP EXPLORATION

To explore an interactive version of this map, go to **http://www.prenhall.com/faraghertlc/map6.2**

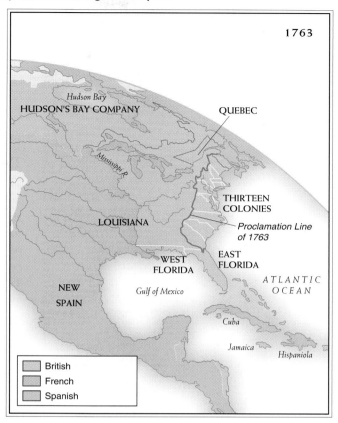

MAP 6-2

European Claims in North America, 1750 and 1763   As a result of the British victory in the Seven Years' War, the map of colonial claims in North America was fundamentally transformed.

HOW DID the balance of power in North America change between 1750 and 1763?

THE EMERGENCE OF AMERICAN NATIONALISM

Despite the anger of frontier settlers over the Proclamation of 1763, the conclusion of the Seven Years' War had left most colonists proud of their place in the British empire. But during the war many had begun to note important contrasts between themselves and the mother country. The soldiers of the British army, for example, shocked Americans with their profane, lewd, and violent behavior. But the colonists were equally shocked by the swift and terrible punishment that aristocratic officers used to keep these soldiers in line. Those who had witnessed such savage punishments found it easy to believe in the threat of Britain enslaving American colonists.

Colonial forces, by contrast, were composed of volunteer companies. Officers tempered their administration of punishment, knowing they had to maintain the enthusiasm of their troops. Discipline thus fell considerably below the standards to which British officers were accustomed. "Riff-raff," one British general said of the colonials, "the lowest dregs of the people, both officers and men." For their part, many colonial officers believed that the British ignored the important role the Americans had played in the Seven Years' War. During that war many colonists began to see themselves as distinct from the British.

THE New-England Courant.

[Nº 35]

From MONDAY March 26. to MONDAY April 2. 1722.

[masthead article text in period typography, largely illegible]

James Franklin began publishing the *New-England Courant* in Boston 1721. When Franklin criticized the government, he was jailed, and the paper continued under the editorship of his brother Benjamin. The *Courant* ceased publication in 1726, and the Franklin brothers went on to other papers – James to the *Rhode Island State Gazette*, Benjamin to the *Pennsylvania Gazette* in Philadelphia. Before the *Zenger* case in 1735, few editors dared to challenge the government.

Massachusetts Historical Society

Whigs The name used by advocates of colonial resistance to British measures during the 1760s and 1770s.

Republicanism A complex, changing body of ideas, values, and assumptions, closely related to country ideology, that influenced American political behavior during the eighteenth and nineteenth centuries.

The Seven Years' War also strengthened a sense of identity among the colonies. Farmers who never before had ventured outside the communities of their birth fought in distant regions with men like themselves from other colonies. Such experiences reinforced a developing nationalist perspective. From 1735 to 1775, while trade with Britain doubled, commerce among the colonies increased by a factor of four. People and ideas moved along with goods. The first stage lines linking seaboard cities began operation in the 1750s. Spurred by Postmaster Benjamin Franklin, many colonies built or improved post roads for transporting the mails.

THE PRESS, POLITICS, AND REPUBLICANISM

The pages of the colonial press reveal the political assumptions held by informed colonists. For decades governors had struggled with colonial assemblies over their respective powers. As commentary on the meaning of these struggles, colonial editors often reprinted the writings of the radical **Whigs** of eighteenth-century England, pamphleteers such as John Trenchard and Thomas Gordon, political theorists such as John Locke, and essayists such as Alexander Pope and Jonathan Swift. They warned of the growing threat to liberty posed by the unchecked exercise of power. In their more emotional writings they argued that a conspiracy existed among the powerful—kings, aristocrats, and Catholics—to quash liberty and institute tyranny. Outside the mainstream of British political opinion, these ideas came to define the political consensus in the British colonies, a point of view called "**republicanism.**"

THE SUGAR AND STAMP ACTS

The emerging sense of American political identity was soon tested by British measures designed to raise revenues in the colonies. To quell Indian uprisings and stifle discontent among the French and Spanish populations of Quebec and Florida, 10,000 British troops remained stationed in North America at the conclusion of the Seven Years' War. The cost of maintaining this force added to the enormous debt Britain had run up during the fighting and created a desperate need for additional revenues. In 1764, the Chancellor of the Exchequer, George Grenville, deciding to obtain the needed revenue from America, pushed through Parliament a measure known as the Sugar Act.

The **Sugar Act** placed a duty on sugar imported into the colonies and revitalized the customs service, introducing stricter registration procedures for ships and adding more officers. In fact, the duty was significantly less than the one that had been on the books and ignored for years, but the difference was that the British now intended to enforce it. In anticipation of American resistance, the legislation increased the jurisdiction of the vice-admiralty court at Halifax, where customs cases were heard. These courts were hated because there was no presumption of innocence and the accused had no right to a jury trial. These new regulations promised not only to squeeze the incomes of American merchants but also to cut off their lucrative smuggling operations. Moreover, colonial taxes, which had been raised during the war, remained at an all-time high. In many cities, merchants as well as artisans protested loudly. Boston was especially vocal: in response to the sugar tax, the town meeting proposed a boycott of certain English imports. This movement for nonimportation soon spread to other port towns.

James Otis Jr., a Massachusetts lawyer fond of grand oratory, was one of the first Americans to strike a number of themes that would become familiar over the next fifteen years. A man's "right to his life, his liberty, his property" was "written on the heart, and revealed to him by his maker," he argued in language echoing the rhetoric of the Great Awakening. It was "inherent, inalienable, and indefeasible by any laws, pacts, contracts, covenants, or stipulations which man could devise." He declared that "an act against the Constitution is void." There could be "no taxation without representation."

But it was only fair, Grenville argued in return, that the colonists help pay the costs of the empire, and what better way to do so than by a tax? Taxes in the colonies were much lower than taxes at home. In early 1765, unswayed by American protests, he followed the Sugar Act with a second and considerably more sweeping revenue measure, the Stamp Act. This tax required the purchase of specially embossed paper for all newspapers, legal documents, licenses, insurance policies, ship's papers, and even dice and playing cards.

THE STAMP ACT CRISIS

During the summer and autumn of 1765 the American reaction to the **Stamp Act** created a crisis of unprecedented proportions. The stamp tax had to be paid in hard money, and it came during a period of economic stagnation. Many colonists complained of being "miserably burdened and oppressed with taxes."

Of more importance for the longer term, however, were the constitutional implications. Although colonial male property owners elected their own assemblies, they could not vote in British elections. But the British argued that Americans were subject to the acts of Parliament because of **virtual representation**. That is, members of Parliament were thought to represent not just their districts, but all citizens of the empire. As one British writer put it, the colonists were "represented in Parliament in the same manner as those inhabitants of Britain are who have not voices in elections." But in an influential pamphlet of 1765, *Considerations on the Propriety of Imposing Taxes*, Maryland lawyer Daniel Dulany rejected this theory. Because Americans were members of a separate political community, he insisted, Parliament could impose no tax on them. Instead, he argued for "**actual representation**," emphasizing the direct relationship that must exist between the people and their political representatives.

It was just such constitutional issues that were emphasized in the Virginia Stamp Act Resolutions, pushed through the Virginia assembly by the passionate young lawyer Patrick Henry in May 1765. Although the Virginia House of Burgesses rejected the most radical of Henry's resolutions, they were all reprinted throughout the colonies. By the end of 1765 the assemblies of eight other colonies had approved similar measures denouncing the Stamp Act and proclaiming their support of "no taxation without representation."

In Massachusetts the leaders of the opposition to the Stamp Act came from a group of upper- and middle-class men who had long opposed the conservative leaders of the colony. These men had worked years to establish a political alliance with Boston craftsmen and workers who met at taverns, in volunteer fire companies, or at social clubs. One of these clubs, known as the Loyall Nine, included a member named Samuel Adams, an associate and friend of James Otis, who had made his career in local politics. Using his contacts with professionals, craftsmen,

Sugar Act Law passed in 1764 to raise revenue in the American colonies. It lowered the duty from 6 pence to 3 pence per gallon on foreign molasses imported into the colonies and increased the restrictions on colonial commerce.

Stamp Act Law passed by Parliament in 1765 to raise revenue in America by requiring taxed, stamped paper for legal documents, publications, and playing cards.

Virtual representation The notion that parliamentary members represented the interests of the nation as a whole, not those of the particular district that elected them.

Actual representation The practice whereby elected representatives normally reside in their districts and are directly responsive to local interests.

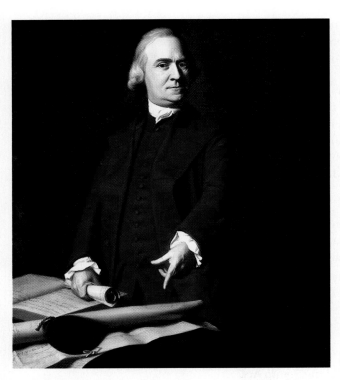

Samuel Adams, a second cousin of John Adams, was a leader of the Boston radicals and an organizer of the Sons of Liberty. The artist of this portrait, John Singleton Copley, was known for setting his subjects in the midst of everyday objects; here he portrays Adams in a middle-class suit with the charter guaranteeing the liberties of Boston's freemen.

John Singleton Copley (1738–1815), Samuel Adams, ca. 1772. Oil on canvas, 49 1/2 × 39 1/2 in (124.7 × 100.3 cm). Deposited by the City of Boston, 30.76c. Courtesy, Museum of Fine Arts, Boston. Reproduced with permission. © 2000 Museum of Fine Art

QUICK REVIEW

British Taxation

- Cost of troops in North America pushed Britain to seek new revenue.
- 1764: passage of the Sugar Act.
- Opponents of the tax linked it to larger issues of political rights.

4–4
"Letters From a Farmer in Pennsylvania" (1767)

Nonimportation movement A tactical means of putting economic pressure on Britain by refusing to buy its exports to the colonies.

Declaratory Act Law passed in 1776 to accompany repeal of the Stamp Act that stated that Parliament had the authority to legislate for the colonies "in all cases whatsoever."

and laboring men, Adams helped put together an anti-British alliance that spanned Boston's social classes. In August 1765 Adams and the Loyall Nine were instrumental in organizing a protest of Boston workingmen against the Stamp Act.

Whereas Boston's elite had prospered during the eighteenth century, the conditions for workers and the poor had worsened. Unemployment, inflation, and high taxes had greatly increased the level of poverty during the depression that followed the Seven Years' War, and many were resentful. A large Boston crowd assembled on August 14, 1765, in the shade of an old elm tree and strung up effigies of several British officials, including Boston's stamp distributor, Andrew Oliver. The restless crowd then vandalized Oliver's office and home. At the order of Oliver's brother-in-law, Lieutenant Governor Thomas Hutchinson, leader of the Massachusetts conservatives, the town sheriff tried to break up the crowd, but he was pelted with paving stones and bricks. Soon thereafter, Oliver resigned his commission. The unified action of Boston's social groups had had its intended effect.

Twelve days later, however, a similar crowd gathered at the aristocratic home of Hutchinson himself. As the family fled through the back door, the crowd smashed through the front with axes. Inside they demolished furniture, chopped down the interior walls, consumed the contents of the wine cellar, and looted everything of value, leaving the house a mere shell. As these events demonstrated, it was not always possible to keep popular protests within bounds. During the fall and winter, urban crowds in commercial towns from Halifax in the North to Savannah in the South forced the resignation of many British tax officials.

In many colonial cities and towns, groups of merchants, lawyers, and craftsmen sought to moderate the resistance movement by seizing control of it. Calling themselves the Sons of Liberty, these groups encouraged moderate forms of protest. They circulated petitions, published pamphlets, and encouraged crowd actions only as a last resort; always they emphasized limited political goals. There were few repetitions of mob attacks, but by the end of 1765 almost all the stamp distributors had resigned or fled, making it impossible for Britain to enforce the Stamp Act.

REPEAL OF THE STAMP ACT

In the fall of 1765, British merchants, worried about the effects of the growing **nonimportation movement** among the colonists, began petitioning Parliament to repeal the Stamp Act. However, it was not until March 1766 that a bill for repeal passed the House of Commons. This news was greeted with celebrations throughout the American colonies, and the nonimportation associations were disbanded. Overlooked in the mood of optimism was Parliament's assertion in this **Declaratory Act** of its full authority to make laws binding the colonies "in all cases whatsoever." The notion of absolute parliamentary supremacy over colonial matters was basic to the British theory of empire. Even Pitt, friend of America that he was, asserted "the authority of this kingdom over the colonies to be sovereign and supreme, in every circumstance of government and legislation whatsoever." The Declaratory Act signaled that the conflict had not been resolved but merely postponed.

"SAVE YOUR MONEY AND SAVE YOUR COUNTRY"

Colonial resistance to the Stamp Act was stronger in urban than in rural communities, stronger among merchants, craftsmen, and planters than among farmers and frontiersmen. When Parliament next moved to impose its will, as it had promised to do in the Declaratory Act, imposing new duties on imported goods, the American opposition again adopted the tactic of nonimportation. But this time resistance spread from the cities and towns into the countryside. As the editor of the *Boston Gazette* phrased the issue, "Save your money and you save your country." It became the slogan of the movement.

THE TOWNSHEND REVENUE ACTS

During the 1760s there was a rapid turnover of government leaders that made it difficult for Britain to form a consistent and even-handed policy toward the colonies. In 1767, after several failed governments, King George III asked William Pitt to again become prime minister. Pitt enjoyed enormous goodwill in America, and a government under his leadership stood a good chance of reclaiming colonial credibility. But, suffering from a prolonged illness, he was soon forced to retire, and his place as head of the cabinet was assumed by Charles Townshend, Chancellor of the Exchequer.

One of the first problems facing the new government was the national debt. At home there were massive unemployment, riots over high prices, and tax protests. The large landowners forced a bill through Parliament slashing their taxes by 25 percent. The government feared continued opposition at home far more than opposition in America. So as part of his plan to close the budget gap, Townshend proposed a new revenue measure for the colonies that placed import duties on commodities such as lead, glass, paint, paper, and tea. By means of these **Townshend Revenue Acts**, enacted in 1767, Townshend hoped to redress colonial grievances against internal taxes such as those imposed by the Stamp Act. For most colonists, however, it proved to be a distinction without a difference.

The most influential response to the Townshend Revenue Acts came in a series of articles by John Dickinson, *Letters from a Farmer in Pennsylvania*, that were reprinted in nearly every colonial newspaper. Dickinson was a wealthy Philadelphia lawyer, but in this work he posed as a humble farmer. Parliament had the right to regulate trade through the use of duties, he conceded. It could place prohibitive tariffs, for example, on foreign products. But it had no constitutional authority to tax goods in order to raise revenues in America. As the preface to the Revenue Acts made clear, the income they produced would be used to pay the salaries of royal officials in America. Thus, Dickinson pointed out, since colonial assemblies were no longer paying their salaries, colonial administrators would not be subject to the financial oversight of elected representatives.

HOW DID political and economic problems in Britain contribute to unrest in the colonies?

4–5
John Dickinson, from "Letters from a Farmer in Pennsylvania" (1768)

MAP EXPLORATION

To explore an interactive version of this map, go to
http://www.prenhall.com/faraghertlc/map6.3

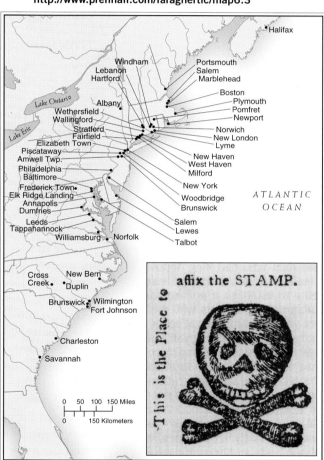

MAP 6-3
Demonstrations Against the Stamp Act, 1765   From Halifax in the North to Savannah in the South, popular demonstrations against the Stamp Act forced the resignation of British tax officials. The propaganda of 1765 even reached the breakfast table, emblazoned on teapots.
Source: *No Stamp Act* teapot, Colonial Williamsburg Foundation.

WHAT GROUPS in British North America were most opposed to the Stamp Act?

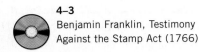

4–3
Benjamin Franklin, Testimony
Against the Stamp Act (1766)

Other Americans warned that this was part of the British conspiracy to suppress American liberties. Their fears were reinforced by Townshend's stringent enforcement of the Revenue Acts. He created a new and strengthened Board of Commissioners of the Customs and established a series of vice-admiralty courts at Boston, Philadelphia, and Charleston to prosecute violators of the duties—the first time these hated institutions had appeared in the most important American port cities. To demonstrate his power, he also suspended New York's assembly. That body had refused to vote public funds to support the British troops garrisoned in the colony. Until the citizens of New York relented, Townshend declared, they would no longer be represented.

In response to these measures, some men argued for violent resistance. But it was Dickinson's essays that had the greatest effect on the public debate, not only because of their convincing arguments but also because of their mild and reasonable tone. "Let us behave like dutiful children," Dickinson urged, "who have received unmerited blows from a beloved parent." As yet, no sentiment for independence existed in America.

NONIMPORTATION: AN EARLY POLITICAL BOYCOTT

Associations of nonimportation and nonconsumption, revived in October 1767 when the Boston town meeting drew up a long list of British products to boycott, became the main weapon of the resistance movement. Over the next few months other port cities, including Providence, Newport, and New York, set up nonimportation associations of their own. Artisans took to the streets in towns and cities throughout the colonies to force merchants to stop importing British goods. The associations published the names of uncooperative importers and retailers. These people then became the object of protesters, who sometimes resorted to violence. Coercion was very much a part of the movement.

Adopting the language of Protestant ethics, nonimportation associations pledged to curtail luxuries and stimulate local industry. These aims had great appeal in small towns and rural districts, which previously had been uninvolved in the anti-British struggle. In 1768 and 1769 colonial newspapers paid a great deal of attention to women's support for the boycott. Groups of women, some calling themselves Daughters of Liberty, organized spinning and weaving bees to produce homespun for local consumption. The actual work performed at these bees was less important than the symbolic message. "The industry and frugality of American ladies," wrote the editor of the *Boston Evening Post*, "are contributing to bring about the political salvation of a whole continent." Other women renounced silks and satins and pledged to stop serving tea to their husbands.

Nonimportation was greatly strengthened in May 1769 when the Virginia House of Burgesses enacted the first provincial legislation banning the importation of goods enumerated in the Townshend Acts, and slaves and luxury commodities as well. Over the next few months all the colonies but New Hampshire enacted similar associations. Because of these efforts, the value of colonial imports from Britain declined by 41 percent.

THE MASSACHUSETTS CIRCULAR LETTER

Boston and Massachusetts were at the center of the agitation over the Townshend Revenue Acts. In February 1768, the Massachusetts House of Representatives approved a letter, drawn up by Samuel Adams, addressed to the speakers of the other provincial assemblies. Designed largely as a propaganda device and having little practical significance, the letter denounced the Townshend Revenue Acts, attacked the British plan to make royal officials independent of colonial assemblies

QUICK REVIEW

Resistance

◆ New York and Boston merchants launch nonimportation movement in response to Sugar Act.

◆ Sugar Act followed by more sweeping revenue measure, the Stamp Act.

◆ Response to Stamp Act overwhelming and intense.

Townshend Revenue Acts Acts of Parliament, passed in 1767, imposing duties on colonial tea, lead, paint, paper, and glass.

and urged the colonies to find a way to "harmonize with each other." Massachusetts governor Francis Bernard condemned the document for stirring up rebellion and dissolved the legislature. In Britain, Lord Hillsborough, secretary of state for the colonies, ordered each royal governor in America to likewise dissolve his colony's assembly if it should endorse the letter. Before this demand reached America, the assemblies of New Hampshire, New Jersey, and Connecticut had commended Massachusetts. Virginia, moreover, had issued a circular letter encouraging a "hearty union" among the colonies and urging common action against the British measures that "have an immediate tendency to enslave us."

Throughout this crisis there were rumors and threats of mob rule in Boston. Because customs agents enforced the law against smugglers and honest traders alike, they enraged merchants, seamen, and dockworkers. In June 1768, a crowd assaulted customs officials who had seized John Hancock's sloop *Liberty* for nonpayment of duties. So frightened were the officials that they fled the city. Hancock, reportedly the wealthiest merchant in the colonies and a vocal opponent of the British measures, had become a principal target of the customs officers. In September the Boston town meeting called on the people to arm themselves, and in the absence of an elected assembly it invited all the other towns to send delegates to a provincial convention. There were threats of armed resistance, but little support for it in the convention, which broke up in chaos. Nevertheless the British, fearing insurrection, occupied Boston with infantry and artillery regiments on October 1, 1768. With this action, they sacrificed a great deal of goodwill and respect and added greatly to the growing tensions.

In Paul Revere's version of the Boston Massacre, issued three weeks after the incident, the British fire an organized volley into a defenseless crowd. Revere's print may have been inaccurate, but it was enormously effective propaganda. It hung in so many Patriot homes that the judge hearing the murder trial of these British soldiers warned the jury not to be swayed by "the prints exhibited in our houses."

The Library of Congress

THE POLITICS OF REVOLT AND THE BOSTON MASSACRE

The British troops stationed in the colonies were the object of scorn and hostility over the next two years. There were regular conflicts between soldiers and radicals in New York City, often focusing on the **Sons of Liberty**. These men would erect "liberty poles" festooned with banners and flags proclaiming their cause, and the British troops would promptly destroy them. When the New York assembly finally bowed to Townshend in December 1769 and voted an appropriation to support the troops, the New York City Sons of Liberty organized a demonstration and erected a large liberty pole. The soldiers chopped it down, sawed it into pieces, and left the wood on the steps of a tavern frequented by the Sons. This led to a riot in which British troops used their bayonets against several thousand New Yorkers armed with cutlasses and clubs. Several men were wounded.

Confrontations also took place in Boston. Sam Adams played up reports and rumors of soldiers harassing women, picking fights, or simply taunting residents with versions of "Yankee Doodle." Soldiers were often hauled into Boston's courts, and local judges adopted a completely unfriendly attitude toward these members of the occupying army.

On the evening of March 5, 1770, a crowd gathered at the Customs House and began taunting a guard, calling him a "damned rascally scoundrel lobster" and worse. A captain and seven soldiers went to his rescue, only to be pelted with snowballs and stones. Suddenly, without orders, the frightened soldiers began to fire.

Sons of Liberty Secret organizations in the colonies formed to oppose the Stamp Act.

4–6
The Boston "Massacre" or Victims of Circumstance? (1770)

Boston Massacre After months of increasing friction between townspeople and the British troops stationed in the city, on March 5, 1770, British troops fired on American civilians in Boston.

WHAT STEPS did Britain take to punish Massachusetts for the colonists' acts of resistance?

Tea Act of 1773 Act of Parliament that permitted the East India Company to sell through agents in America without paying the duty customarily collected in Britain, thus reducing the retail price.

Five of the crowd fell dead, and six more were wounded, two of these dying later. The soldiers escaped to their barracks, but a mob numbering in the hundreds rampaged through the streets demanding vengeance. Fearing for the safety of his men and the security of the state, Thomas Hutchinson, now governor of Massachusetts, ordered British troops out of Boston. The **Boston Massacre** became infamous throughout the colonies, in part because of the circulation of an inflammatory print produced by the Boston engraver Paul Revere, which depicted the British as firing on a crowd of unresisting civilians. But for many colonists, the incident was a disturbing reminder of the extent to which relations with the mother country had deteriorated. During the next two years, many people found themselves pulling back from the brink. "There seems," one Bostonian wrote, "to be a pause in politics."

The growth of American resistance was slowed as well by the news that Parliament had repealed most of the Townshend Revenue Acts on March 5, 1770—the same day as the Boston Massacre. In the climate of apprehension and confusion, there were few celebrations of the repeal, and the nonimportation associations almost immediately collapsed. Over the next three years, the value of British imports rose by 80 percent. The parliamentary retreat on the question of duties, like the earlier repeal of the Stamp Act, was accompanied by a face-saving measure—retention of the tax on tea "as a mark of the supremacy of Parliament," in the words of Frederick Lord North, the new prime minister.

FROM RESISTANCE TO REBELLION

There was a lull in the American controversy during the early 1770s, but the situation turned violent in 1773, when Parliament again infuriated the Americans. This time it was the ill-advised **Tea Act of 1773**, and it propelled the colonists onto a swift track from resistance to outright rebellion.

INTERCOLONIAL COOPERATION

In June 1772, Governor Hutchinson inaugurated another controversy by announcing that henceforth his salary and those of other royally appointed Massachusetts officials would be paid by the crown. In effect, this made the executive and judiciary branches of the colony's government independent of elected representatives. In October, the Boston town meeting appointed a Committee of Correspondence to communicate with other towns regarding this challenge. The next month the meeting issued what became known as the Boston Pamphlet, a series of declarations written by Samuel Adams and other radicals, concluding that British encroachments on colonial rights pointed to a plot to enslave Americans.

In March 1773, the Virginia House of Burgesses appointed a standing committee for correspondence among the colonies "to obtain the most early and authentic intelligence" of British actions affecting America, "and to keep up and maintain a correspondence and communication with our sister colonies." The Virginia committee, including Patrick Henry, Richard Henry Lee, and young Thomas Jefferson, served as a model, and within a year all the colonies except Pennsylvania, where conservatives controlled the legislature, had created committees of their own. These committees became the principal channel for sharing information, shaping public opinion, and building cooperation among the colonies before the Continental Congress of 1774.

The information most damaging to British influence came from the radicals in Boston. In June 1773, the Boston committee circulated a set of confidential letters from Governor Hutchinson to the ministry in Britain, obtained in London by Benjamin Franklin from friends within the British government. Because Franklin had pledged to keep the letters to himself, he became the center of a scandal in London and was dismissed from his position as postmaster general. But the British cause in the colonies suffered much more than Franklin's reputation. The letters revealed Hutchinson's call for "an abridgement of what are called English liberties" in the colonies. "I wish to see some further restraint of liberty," he had written, "rather than the connection with the parent state should be broken." This statement seemed to be the "smoking gun" of the conspiracy theory, and it created a torrent of anger against the British and their officials in the colonies.

THE BOSTON TEA PARTY

It was in this context that the colonists received the news that Parliament had passed a Tea Act. Colonists were major consumers of tea, but because of the tax on it that remained from the Townshend duties, the market for colonial tea had collapsed, bringing the East India Company to the brink of bankruptcy. This company was the sole agent of British power in India, and Parliament could not allow it to fail. The British, therefore, devised a scheme in which they offered tea to Americans at prices that would tempt the most patriotic tea drinker. The radicals argued that this was merely a device to make palatable the payment of unconstitutional taxes—further evidence of the British effort to corrupt the colonists.

In October a mass meeting in Philadelphia denounced anyone importing the tea as "an enemy of his country." The town meeting in Boston passed resolutions patterned on those of Philadelphia, but the tea agents there, including two of Governor Hutchinson's sons, resisted the call to refuse the shipments.

The first of the tea ships arrived in Boston Harbor late in November. Mass meetings in Old South Church, which included many country people drawn to the scene of the crisis, resolved to keep the tea from being unloaded. Governor Hutchinson was equally firm in refusing to allow the ship to leave the harbor. Five thousand people on December 16, 1773, crowded into the church to hear the captain of the tea ship report to Samuel Adams that he could not move his ship. "This meeting can do nothing more to save the country," Adams declared. This was the signal for a disciplined group of fifty or sixty men, including farmers, artisans, merchants, professionals, and apprentices, to march to the wharf disguised as Indians. There they boarded the ship and dumped into the harbor 45 tons of tea, valued at £18,000, all the while cheered on by Boston's citizens. "Boston Harbor's a tea-pot tonight," the crowd chanted.

The Boston Tea Party was only the first of such protests. Other incidents of property destruction soon followed. When the Sons of Liberty learned that a cargo of tea had landed secretly in New York, they dressed themselves as Indians and dumped the tea chests into the harbor. At Annapolis a ship loaded with tea was destroyed by fire, and arson also consumed a shipment stored at a warehouse in New Jersey. But it was the action in Boston at which the British railed. The government became convinced that something had to be done about the rebellious colony of Massachusetts.

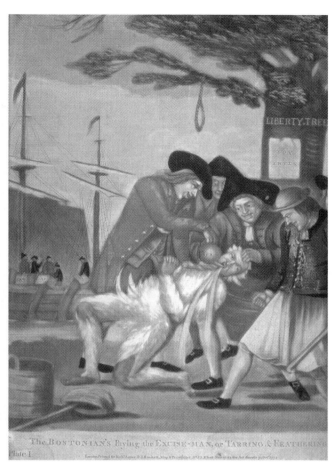

A British tax man is tarred and feathered and forced to drink tea, while the Boston Tea Party takes place in the background, in this image from 1774.

Christie's Images, Inc.

4–7
John Andres to William Barrell, Letter Regarding the Boston Tea Party (1773)

Boston Tea Party   Incident that occurred on December 16, 1773, in which Bostonians, disguised as Indians, destroyed £18,000 worth of tea belonging to the British East India Company in order to prevent payment of the duty on it.

THE INTOLERABLE ACTS

During the spring of 1774 an angry Parliament passed a series of acts—called the **Coercive Acts**, but known by Americans as the Intolerable Acts—that were calculated to punish Massachusetts and strengthen the British hand. The Boston Port Bill prohibited the loading or unloading of ships in any part of Boston Harbor until the town fully compensated the East India Company and the customs service for the destroyed tea. The Massachusetts Government Act annulled the colonial charter: delegates to the upper house would no longer be elected by the assembly but henceforth were to be appointed by the king. Civil officers throughout the province were placed under the authority of the royal governor, and the selection of juries was given over to governor-appointed sheriffs. Town meetings, an important institution of the resistance movement, were prohibited from convening more than once a year except with the approval of the governor, who was to control their agendas. With these acts the British terminated the long history of self-rule by communities in the colony of Massachusetts. The Administration of Justice Act protected British officials from colonial courts, thereby encouraging them to vigorously pursue the work of suppression. Those accused of committing capital crimes while putting down riots or collecting revenue, such as the soldiers involved in the Boston Massacre, were now to be sent to England for trial.

5–3
The Crisis Comes to a Head:
April 19, 1775

Coercive Acts   Legislation passed by Parliament in 1774; included the Boston Port Act, the Massachusetts Government Act, the Administration of Justice Act, and the Quartering Act of 1774.

OVERVIEW

ELEVEN BRITISH MEASURES THAT LED TO REVOLUTION

Legislation	Year	
Sugar Act	1764	Placed prohibitive duty on imported sugar; provided for greater regulation of American shipping to suppress smuggling.
Stamp Act	1765	Required the purchase of specially embossed paper for newspapers, legal documents, licenses, insurance policies, ships' papers, and playing cards; struck at printers, lawyers, tavern owners, and other influential colonists. Repealed in 1766.
Declaratory Act	1766	Asserted the authority of Parliament to make laws binding the colonies "in all cases whatsoever."
Townshend Revenue Acts	1767	Placed import duties, collectible before goods entered colonial markets, on many commodities including lead, glass, paper, and tea. Repealed in 1770.
Tea Act	1773	Gave the British East India Company a monopoly on all tea imports to America, hitting at American merchants.
Coercive or Intolerable Acts	1774	
Boston Port Bill		Closed Boston harbor.
Massachusetts Government Act		Annulled the Massachusetts colonial charter.
Administration of Justice Act		Protected British officials from colonial courts by sending them home for trial if arrested.
Quartering Act		Legalized the housing of British troops in private homes.
Quebec Act		Created a highly centralized government for Canada.

Additional measures affected the other colonies and encouraged them to see themselves in league with suffering Massachusetts. The **Quartering Act** legalized the housing of troops at public expense, not only in taverns and abandoned buildings but also in occupied dwellings and private homes.

Finally, in the Quebec Act, the British authorized a permanent government for the territory taken from France during the Seven Years' War. This government was both authoritarian and antirepublican, with a royal government and an appointed council. Furthermore, the act confirmed the feudal system of land tenure along the St. Lawrence. It also granted religious toleration to the Roman Catholic Church and upheld the church's traditional right to collect tithes, thus, in effect, establishing Catholicism as the state religion in Quebec.

To the American colonists, the **Quebec Act** was a frightening preview of what imperial authorities might have in store for them, and it confirmed the prediction of the **Committees of Correspondence** that there was a British plot to destroy American liberty.

In May, General Thomas Gage arrived in Boston to replace Hutchinson as governor. The same day, the Boston town meeting called for a revival of nonimportation measures against Britain. In Virginia the Burgesses declared that Boston was enduring a "hostile invasion" and made provision for a "day of fasting, humiliation, and prayer, devoutly to implore the divine interposition for averting the heavy calamity, which threatens destruction to our civil rights and the evils of civil war." For this expression of sympathy, Governor Dunmore suspended the legislature. Nevertheless, throughout the colony on the first of June, funeral bells tolled, flags flew at half mast, and people flocked to the churches.

THE FIRST CONTINENTAL CONGRESS

It was amid this crisis that town meetings and colonial assemblies alike chose representatives for the **First Continental Congress**. The delegates who arrived in Philadelphia in September 1774 included the most important leaders of the American cause. Cousins Samuel and John Adams, the radicals from Massachusetts, were joined by Patrick Henry and George Washington from Virginia and Christopher Gadsden of South Carolina. Many of the delegates were conservatives: John Dickinson and Joseph Galloway of Philadelphia and John Jay and James Duane from New York. With the exception of Gadsden, a hothead who proposed an attack on British forces in Boston, the delegates wished to avoid war and favored a policy of economic coercion.

After one of their first debates, the delegates passed a Declaration and Resolves, in which they asserted that all the colonists sprang from a common tradition and enjoyed rights guaranteed "by the immutable laws of nature, the principles of the English constitution, and the several charters or compacts" of their provinces. Thirteen acts of Parliament, passed since 1763, were declared in violation of these rights. Until these acts were repealed, the delegates pledged, they would impose a set of sanctions against the British. These would include not only the nonimportation

MAP EXPLORATION
To explore an interactive version of this map, go to
http://www.prenhall.com/faraghertlc/map6.4

MAP 6-4

The Quebec Act of 1774 With the Quebec Act, Britain created a centralized colonial government for Canada and extended that colony's administrative control southwest to the Ohio River, invalidating the sea-to-sea boundaries of many colonial charters.

HOW DID the boundaries set by the Quebec Act of 1774 contribute to rising tensions between the colonists and imperial authorities?

Quartering Act Acts of Parliament requiring colonial legislatures to provide supplies and quarters for the troops starioned in America.

Quebec Act Law passed by Parliament in 1774 that provided an appointed government for Canada, enlarged the boundaries of Quebec, and confirmed the privileges of the Catholic Church.

Committees of Correspondence Committees formed in Massachusetts and other colonies in the pre-Revolutionary period to keep Americans informed about British measures that would affect the colonies.

and nonconsumption of British goods, but also a prohibition on the export of colonial commodities to Britain or its other colonies.

To enforce these sanctions, the Continental Congress urged that "a committee be chosen in every county, city, and town, by those who are qualified to vote for representatives in the legislature, whose business it shall be attentively to observe the conduct of all persons." This call for democratically elected local committees in each community had important political ramifications. The following year, these groups, known as Committees of Observation and Safety, took over the functions of local government throughout the colonies. They organized militia companies, called extralegal courts, and combined to form colonywide congresses or conventions. By dissolving the colonial legislatures, royal governors unwittingly aided the work of these committees. The committees also scrutinized the activities of fellow citizens, suppressed the expression of Loyalist opinion from pulpit or press, and practiced other forms of coercion. Throughout most of the colonies the committees formed a bridge between the old colonial administrations and the revolutionary governments organized over the next few years. Committees began to link localities together in the cause of a wider American community. It was at this point that people began to refer to the colonies as the American "states."

LEXINGTON AND CONCORD

On September 1, 1774, General Gage sent troops from Boston to seize the stores of cannon and ammunition the Massachusetts militia had stored at armories in Charlestown and Cambridge. In response, the Massachusetts House of Representatives, calling itself the Provincial Congress, created a **Committee of Safety** empowered to call up the militia. On October 15 the committee authorized the creation of special units, to be known as "**minutemen**," who stood ready to be called at a moment's notice. The armed militia of the towns and communities surrounding Boston faced the British army, quartered in the city.

In Virginia, at almost the same moment, Patrick Henry predicted that hostilities would soon begin in New England. "Gentlemen may cry peace, peace!—but there is no peace," he thundered in prose later memorized by millions of American schoolchildren. "Is life so dear, or peace so sweet, as to be purchased at the price of chains and slavery? Forbid it, Almighty God! I know not what course others may take, but as for me, give me liberty or give me death!" Later, on April 14, 1775, General Gage received orders to strike at once against the Massachusetts militia.

On the evening of April 18, 1775, Gage ordered 700 men to capture the store of American ammunition at the town of Concord. Learning of the operation, the Boston committee dispatched two men, Paul Revere and William Dawes, to alert the militia of the countryside. By the time the British forces had reached Lexington, midway to their destination, some seventy armed minutemen had assembled on the green in the center of town, but they were disorganized and confused. "Lay down your arms, you damned rebels, and disperse!" cried one of the British officers. The Americans began to withdraw in the face of overwhelming opposition, but they took their arms with them. "Damn you, why don't you lay down your arms!" someone shouted from the British lines. "Damn them! We will have them!" No order to fire was given, but shots rang out, killing eight Americans and wounding ten others.

PREMIERE ASSEMBLÉE DU CONGRÈS

The engraving of the first session of the Continental Congress, published in France in 1782, is the only contemporary illustration of the meeting. Peyton Randolph of Virginia presides from the elevated chair, but otherwise there are no recognizable individuals. The Congress had to find a way to form a community among the leaders from each of the colonies without compromising their local identities.

Library of Congress

First Continental Congress Meeting of delegates from most of the colonies held in 1774 in response to the Coercive Acts. The Congress endorsed the Suffolk Resolves, adopted the Declaration of Rights and Grievances, and agreed to establish the Continental Association.

Committee of Safety Any of the extralegal committees that directed the revolutionary movement and carried on the functions of government at the local level in the period between the breakdown of royal authority and the establishment of regular governments.

Minutemen Special companies of militia formed in Massachusetts and elsewhere beginning in late 1744.

MAP EXPLORATION
To explore an interactive version of this map, go to **http://www.prenhall.com/faraghertlc/map6.5**

MAP 6-5
The First Engagements of the Revolution   The first military engagements of the American Revolution took place in the spring of 1775 in the countryside surrounding Boston.

WHAT SPARKED the clashes at Lexington and Concord?

QUICK REVIEW

Congressional Response to the Intolerable Acts

- All agreed that Acts were unconstitutional.
- Sought to impose a set of sanctions against Britain.
- Urged the creation of Committees of Observation and Safety.

The British marched on to Concord, where they burned a small quantity of supplies and cut down a liberty pole. Meanwhile, news of the skirmish at Lexington had spread through the country, and the militia companies of communities from miles around converged on the town. Seeing smoke, they mistakenly concluded that the troops were burning homes. "Will you let them burn the town!" one man cried, and the Americans moved to the Concord bridge. There they attacked a British company, killing three soldiers—the first British casualties of the Revolution. The British immediately turned back for Boston but were attacked by Americans at many points along the way. Reinforcements met them at Lexington, preventing a complete disaster, but by the time they finally marched into Boston, 73 were dead and 202 wounded or missing. The British troops were vastly outnumbered by the approximately 4,000 Massachusetts militiamen, who suffered 95 casualties. The engagement forecast what would be a central problem for the British: they would be forced to fight an armed population defending their own communities against outsiders.

 5–7
Joseph Warre, "Account of the Battle of Lexington" (1775)

DECIDING FOR INDEPENDENCE

"We send you momentous intelligence," read the letter received by the Charleston, South Carolina, Committee of Correspondence on May 8, reporting the violence in Massachusetts. Community militia companies mobilized throughout the colonies. At Boston, thousands of militiamen from Massachusetts and the surrounding provinces besieged the city, leaving the British no escape but by sea; their siege would last for nearly a year. Meanwhile, delegates from twelve colonies reconverged on Philadelphia.

WHO MADE up the first Continental Congress and why was it formed?

THE SECOND CONTINENTAL CONGRESS
The members of the Second Continental Congress, which opened on May 10, 1775, represented twelve of the British colonies on the mainland of North America. From New Hampshire to South Carolina, Committees of Observation and Safety had

Soon after the fighting at Lexington and Concord, the artist Ralph Earl and the engraver Amos Doolittle visited the location and interviewed participants. They produced a series of four engravings of the incident, the first popular prints of the battles of the Revolutionary War. This view shows the British soldiers marching back to Boston through the hail of sniper fire from colonial militiamen.

Connecticut Historical Society

QUICK REVIEW

The Second Continental Congress

◆ Opened on May 10, 1775.
◆ May 15: Congress resolved to put the colonies in a state of defense.
◆ June 15: George Washington nominated to be commander-in-chief.

elected colonywide conventions, and these extralegal bodies in turn had chosen delegates. Consequently, few conservatives or Loyalists were among them. Georgia, unrepresented at the first session of the Continental Congress, remained absent at the opening of the second. The newest mainland colony, it depended heavily on British subsidies, and its leaders were cautious, fearing both slave and Indian uprisings. But in 1775 the political balance in Georgia shifted in favor of the radicals, and by the end of the summer the colony had delegates in Philadelphia.

Among the delegates at the Continental Congress were many familiar faces and a few new ones, including Thomas Jefferson, a plantation owner and lawyer from Virginia, gifted with one of the most imaginative and analytical minds of his time. All the delegates carried news of the enthusiasm for war that raged in their home provinces. "A frenzy of revenge seems to have seized all ranks of people," said Jefferson. George Washington attended all the sessions in uniform. "Oh that I was a soldier," an envious John Adams wrote to his wife, Abigail. The delegates agreed that defense was the first issue on their agenda.

On May 15, the Second Continental Congress resolved to put the colonies in a state of defense, but the delegates were divided on how best to do it. They lacked the power and the funds to immediately raise and supply an army. After debate and deliberation, John Adams made the practical proposal that the delegates simply designate as a Continental Army the militia forces besieging Boston. On June 14, the Congress resolved to supplement the New England militiamen with six companies of expert riflemen raised in Pennsylvania, Maryland, and Virginia. The delegates agreed that in order to emphasize their national aspirations, they had to select a man from the South to command these New England forces. All eyes turned to George Washington. Although Washington had suffered defeat at the beginning of the Seven Years' War, he had subsequently compiled a distinguished record. On June 15, Jefferson and Adams nominated Washington to be commander-in-chief of all Continental forces, and he was elected by a unanimous vote. He served without salary. The Continental Congress soon appointed a staff of major generals to support him. On June 22, in a highly significant move, the

Congress voted to finance the army with an issue of $2 million in bills of credit, backed by the good faith of the Confederated Colonies. Thus began the long and complicated process of financing the Revolution.

CANADA, THE SPANISH BORDERLANDS, AND THE REVOLUTION

How did the rest of North America react to the coming conflict? The Continental Congress contacted many of the other British colonies. In one of their first acts, delegates called on "the oppressed inhabitants of Canada" to join in the struggle for "common liberty." After the Seven Years' War, the British treated Quebec as a conquered province, and French Canadians felt little sympathy for the empire. On the other hand, the Americans were traditional enemies, much feared because of their aggressive expansionism. Indeed, when the Canadians failed to respond positively and immediately, the Congress reversed itself and voted to authorize a military expedition against Quebec to eliminate any possibility of a British invasion from that quarter, thus killing any chance of the Canadians' joining the anti-British cause. This set a course toward the development of the separate nations of the United States and Canada.

There was some sympathy at first for the American struggle in the British island colonies. The legislative assemblies of Jamaica, Grenada, and Barbados declared themselves in accord with the Continental Congress, but the British navy prevented them from sending representatives. A delegation from Bermuda succeeded in getting to Philadelphia, but the Americans were so preoccupied with more pressing matters they were unable to provide any assistance, and the spark of resistance on the island sputtered out. The island colonies would remain aloof from the imperial crisis, largely because the colonists there were dependent on a British military presence to guard against slave revolts. Things at first seemed more promising in Nova Scotia (not then a part of Canada), where many New Englanders had relocated after the expulsion of the Acadians. There had been Stamp Act demonstrations in Halifax, and when the British attempted to recruit among the Nova Scotians for soldiers to serve in Boston, one community responded that since "almost all of us [were] born in New England, [we are] divided betwixt natural affection to our nearest relations and good faith and friendship to our king and country." The British naval stronghold at Halifax, however, secured the province for the empire. Large contingents of British troops also kept Florida (which Britain had divided into the two colonies of East and West Florida) solidly in the empire.

In Cuba, some 3,000 exiled Spanish Floridians, who had fled rather than live under British rule in 1763, clamored for Spain to retake their homeland. Many of them were active supporters of American independence. (Two centuries later there would be thousands of Cuban exiles in Florida.) Spanish authorities in Cuba, who also administered the newly acquired colony of Louisiana, were somewhat torn in their sympathies. They certainly felt no solidarity with the cause of rebellion, which they understood posed a great danger to monarchy and empire. But with painful memories of the British invasion of Havana in 1763, they passionately looked forward to working revenge on their traditional enemy, as well as to regaining control of the Floridas and eliminating the British threat to their Mexican and Caribbean colonies. In 1775, Spain adopted the recommendation of the Havana authorities and declared a policy of neutrality in the looming independence struggle.

Secretly, however, Spain looked for an opportunity to support the Americans. That presented itself in the late spring of 1776, when a contingent of Americans arrived in Spanish New Orleans via the Mississippi River bearing a proposal from patriot forces in Virginia. British naval supremacy was making it impossible

QUICK REVIEW

Fighting in 1775 and 1776

◆ Americans forced back from Canada.

◆ British forced out of Boston to Halifax.

◆ Americans turns back British assault in Charleston.

to obtain supplies from overseas. Would the Spanish be willing to quietly sell guns, ammunition, and other provisions to the Americans in New Orleans and allow them to be shipped by way of the Mississippi and Ohio rivers? If they were cooperative, the Americans might be willing to see the Spanish retake possession of the Floridas and administer them as a "protectorate" for the duration of the independence struggle. Authorities forwarded the proposal to Spain, where a few months later the Spanish king and his ministers approved the plan. Havana and New Orleans became important supply centers for the patriots.

FIGHTING IN THE NORTH AND SOUTH

Both North and South saw fighting in 1775 and early 1776. In June the Continental Congress assembled an expeditionary force against Canada. One thousand Americans moved north up the Hudson River corridor, and in November General Richard Montgomery forced the capitulation of Montreal. Meanwhile, Benedict Arnold set out from Massachusetts with another American army, and after a torturous march through the forests and mountains of Maine, he joined Montgomery outside the walls of Quebec. Unlike the assault of British General Wolfe in 1759, however, the American assault failed to take the city. Montgomery and 100 Americans were killed, and another 300 were taken prisoner. Although Arnold held his position, the American siege was broken the following spring by British reinforcements who had come down the St. Lawrence. By the summer of 1776 the Americans had been forced back from Canada.

Elsewhere there were successes. Washington installed artillery on the heights south of Boston, placing the city and harbor within cannon range. General William Howe, who had replaced Gage, had little choice but to evacuate the city. In March the British sailed out of Boston harbor for the last time, heading north to Halifax with at least 1,000 American Loyalists. In the South, American militia rose against the Loyalist forces of Virginia's Governor Dunmore, who had alienated the planter class by promising freedom to any slave who would fight with the British. After a decisive defeat of his forces, Dunmore retreated to British naval vessels, from which he shelled and destroyed much of the city of Norfolk, Virginia, on January 1, 1776. In North Carolina, the rebel militia crushed a Loyalist force at the Battle of Moore's Creek Bridge near Wilmington in February, ending British plans for an invasion of that province. The British decided to attack Charleston, but at Fort Moultrie in Charleston harbor an American force turned back the assault. It would be more than two years before the British would try to invade the South again.

NO TURNING BACK

Hopes of reconciliation died with the mounting casualties. The Second Continental Congress, which was rapidly assuming the role of a new government for all the provinces, reconvened in September 1775 and received news of the king's proclamation that the colonies were in formal rebellion. Although the delegates disclaimed any intention of denying the sovereignty of the king, they now moved to organize an American navy. They declared British vessels open to capture and authorized privateering. The Congress took further steps toward de facto independence when it authorized contacts with foreign powers through its agents in Europe. In the spring of 1776, France, hoping that the creation of a new American nation might provide the opportunity of gaining a larger share of the colonial trade while also diminishing British power, joined Spain in approving the shipping of supplies to the rebellious provinces. The Continental Congress then declared colonial ports open to the trade of all nations but Britain.

The emotional ties to Britain proved difficult to break. But in 1776 help arrived in the form of a pamphlet written by Thomas Paine, a radical Englishman recently arrived in Philadelphia. In *Common Sense*, Paine proposed to offer "simple fact, plain argument, and common sense" on the crisis. For years Americans had defended their actions by wrapping themselves in the mantle of British traditions. But Paine argued that the British system rested on "the base remains of two ancient tyrannies," aristocracy and monarchy, neither of which was appropriate for America. Paine placed the blame for the oppression of the colonists on the shoulders of King George. *Common Sense* was the single most important piece of writing during the Revolutionary era, selling more than 100,000 copies within a few months of its publication in January 1776. It reshaped popular thinking and put independence squarely on the agenda.

In April, the North Carolina convention, which operated as the revolutionary replacement for the old colonial assembly, became the first to empower its delegates to vote for a **declaration of independence**. News that the British were recruiting a force of German mercenaries to use against the Americans provided an additional push toward what now began to seem inevitable. In May the Continental Congress voted to recommend that the individual states move as quickly as possible toward the adoption of state constitutions. When John Adams wrote, in the preamble to this statement, that "the exercise of every kind of authority under the said crown should be totally suppressed," he sent a strong signal that the delegates were on the verge of approving a momentous declaration.

THE DECLARATION OF INDEPENDENCE

On June 7, 1776, Richard Henry Lee of Virginia offered a motion to the Continental Congress: "That these united colonies are, and of right ought to be, free and independent states, that they are absolved from all allegiance to the British crown, and that all political connection between them and the state of Great Britain is, and ought to be, totally dissolved." After some debate, a vote was postponed until July, but a committee composed of John Adams, Thomas Jefferson, Benjamin Franklin, Roger Sherman of Connecticut, and Robert Livingston of New York was asked to prepare a draft declaration of American independence. The committee assigned the writing to Jefferson.

The intervening month allowed the delegates to sample the public discussion and debate and receive instructions from their state conventions. By the end of the month, all the states but New York had authorized a vote for independence. When the question came up for debate again on July 1, a large majority in the Continental Congress supported independence. The final vote, taken on July 2, was twelve in favor of independence, none against, with New York abstaining. The delegates then turned to the declaration itself and made a number of changes in Jefferson's draft, striking out, for example, a long passage condemning slavery. In this and a number of other ways the final version was somewhat more cautious than the draft, but it was still a stirring document.

Its central section reiterated the "long train of abuses and usurpations" on the part of King George that had led the Americans to their drastic course; there was no mention of Parliament,

5–4
A Freelance Writer Urges
His Readers to Use
Common Sense (1776)

Declaration of Independence The document by which the Second Continental Congress announced and justified its decision to renounce the colonies' allegiance to the British government.

"The Manner in which the American Colonies Declared themselves INDEPENDENT of the King of ENGLAND," a 1783 English print. Understanding that the coming struggle would require the steady support of ordinary people, in the Declaration of Independence the upper-class men of the Continental Congress asserted the right of popular revolution and the great principle of human equality.

The Granger Collection

CHRONOLOGY

1713	France cedes Acadia to Britain.	1764	Sugar Act.
1745	New Englanders capture Louisburg.	1765	Stamp Act and Stamp Act Congress.
1749	French send an expeditionary force down the Ohio River.	1766	Declaratory Act.
		1767	Townshend Revenue Acts.
1753	French begin building forts from Lake Erie to the Ohio.	1768	Treaties of Hard Labor and Fort Stanwix.
1754	Albany Congress.	1770	Boston Massacre.
1755	British General Edward Braddock defeated by a combined force of French and Indians. Britain expels Acadians from Nova Scotia.	1772	First Committee of Correspondence organized in Boston.
		1773	Tea Act.
1756	Seven Years' War begins in Europe.		Boston Tea Party.
1757	William Pitt becomes prime minister.	1774	Intolerable Acts.
1758	Louisburg captured by the British for the second time.		First Continental Congress.
			Dunmore's War.
1759	British capture Quebec.	1775	Fighting begins at Lexington and Concord.
1763	Treaty of Paris.		Second Continental Congress.
	Pontiac's uprising.	1776	Americans invade Canada.
	Proclamation of 1763 creates "Indian Country."		Thomas Paine's *Common Sense*.
	Paxton Boys massacre.		Declaration of Independence.

5–8
Thomas Jefferson, "Original Rough Draught" of the Declaration of Independence (1776)

the principal opponent since 1764. But it was the first section that expressed the highest ideals of the delegates:

> We hold these truths to be self-evident, that all men are created equal, that they are endowed by their creator with certain unalienable rights, that among these are life, liberty, and the pursuit of happiness. That to secure these rights, governments are instituted among men, deriving their just powers from the consent of the governed. That whenever any form of government becomes destructive of these ends, it is the right of the people to alter or to abolish it, and to institute a new government, laying its foundation on such principles, and organizing its powers in such form, as to them shall seem most likely to effect their safety and happiness.

There was very little debate in the Continental Congress about these principles. The delegates, mostly men of wealth and position, realized that the coming struggle for independence would require the steady support of ordinary people, so they asserted this great principle of equality and the right of revolution. There was little debate about the implications or potential consequences. Surely no statement would reverberate more through American history; the idea of equality inspired the poor as well as the wealthy, women as well as men, blacks as well as whites.

But it was the third and final section that may have contained the most meaning for the delegates: "For the support of this declaration, with a firm reliance on the protection of divine providence, we mutually pledge to each other our lives, our fortunes, and our sacred honor." In voting for independence, the delegates proclaimed their community, but they also committed treason against their king and empire. They could be condemned as traitors, hunted as criminals, and stand on the scaffold to pay for their sentiments. On July 4, 1776, these men approved the text of the Declaration of Independence without dissent.

CONCLUSION

Great Britain emerged from the Seven Years' War as the dominant power in North America. Yet despite its attempts at strict regulation and determination of the course of events in its colonies, it faced consistent resistance and often complete failure. Perhaps British leaders felt as John Adams had when he attended the first session of the Continental Congress in 1774: How could a motley collection of "ambassadors from a dozen belligerent powers" effectively organize as a single, independent, and defiant body? The British underestimated the political consensus that existed among the colonists about the importance of "republican" government. They also underestimated the ability of the colonists to inform one another, to work together, to build a sentiment of nationalism that cut across the boundaries of ethnicity, region, and economic status. Through newspapers, pamphlets, Committees of Correspondence, community organizations, and group protest, the colonists discovered the concerns they shared, and in so doing they fostered a new American identity. Without that identity it would have been difficult for them to consent to the treasonous act of declaring independence, especially when the independence they sought was from an international power that dominated much of the globe.

SUMMARY

The Seven Years' War in America Colonial expansion created tensions among European nations, colonists, and Indian peoples. Events in Europe combined with competition for land and resources in the Americas culminated in the Seven Years' War. The end of the war eliminated one source of conflict but stimulated several others.

The Imperial Crisis in British North America Attempts by the British government to tighten regulation and increase taxation of the colonies triggered a series of crises. American colonists began questioning their relationship with Great Britain as they resisted efforts at more rigorous regulation.

"Save Your Money and Save Your Country" British attempts to raise revenue from the colonies generated more widespread resistance. Greater colonial unity and violence characterized British colonial relations.

From Resistance to Rebellion Colonial resistance became more unified as Great Britain again tried to tighten its rule of the colonies and raise revenues. Violence became more regular. Eventually, the protest movement convened a national legislature. War broke out as resistance became rebellion.

Deciding for Independence The expanding conflict between Great Britain and the rebellious colonists created a unified front in the colonies that approximated a national congress. Other North American colonies, especially British, were affected by the coming war. The outbreak of fighting stimulated the creation of a colonial military and eventually led to the Declaration of Independence that established the United States.

REVIEW QUESTIONS

1. How did overwhelming British success in the Seven Years' War lead to an imperial crisis in British North America?

2. Outline the changes in British policy toward the colonies from 1750 to 1776.

3. Trace the developing sense of an American national community over this same period.

4. What were the principal events leading to the beginning of armed conflict at Lexington and Concord?

5. How were the ideals of American republicanism expressed in the Declaration of Independence?

KEY TERMS

Actual representation (p. 141)

Benjamin Franklin's Plan of Union (p. 133)

Boston Massacre (p. 146)

Boston Tea Party (p. 147)

Coercive Acts (p. 148)

Committees of Correspondence (p. 149)

Committee of Safety (p. 150)

Declaration of Independence (p. 155)

Declaratory Act (p. 142)

First Continental Congress (p. 149)

French and Indian War (p. 136)

Intolerable Acts (p. 132)

Minutemen (p. 150)

Nonimportation movement (p. 142)

Quartering Act (p. 149)

Quebec Act (p. 149)

Republicanism (p. 140)

Royal Proclamation of 1763 (p. 138)

Sons of Liberty (p. 145)

Stamp Act (p. 141)

Stamp Act Congress (p. 132)

Sugar Act (p. 140)

Tea Act of 1773 (p. 146)

Townshend Revenue Acts (p. 143)

Treaty of Paris (p. 137)

Virtual representation (p. 141)

Whigs (p. 140)

RECOMMENDED READING

Benedict Anderson, *Imagined Communities: Reflections on the Origin and Spread of Nationalism*, rev. ed. (1991). An argument that the essential first act of national consciousness is the effort to create a community that encompasses more than just local individuals and groups.

Fred Anderson, *The Crucible of War: The Seven Years' War and the Fate of Empire in British North America, 1754–1766* (2000). A new and powerful history of the war, arguing that it created a "hollow British empire."

Bernard Bailyn, *The Ideological Origins of the American Revolution* (1967). Whereas other accounts stress economic or social causes, this classic argument emphasizes the role of ideas in the advent of the Revolution. Includes an analysis of American views of the imperial crisis.

David A. Copeland, *Debating the Issues in Colonial Newspapers: Primary Documents on Events of the Period* (2000). A rich collection of eighteenth-century newspaper articles, with extensive coverage of the role of the press in the coming of the Revolution.

Eric Foner, *Tom Paine and Revolutionary America* (1976). Combines a biography of Paine with a community study of the Revolution in Philadelphia and Pennsylvania.

William H. Hallahan, *The Day the Revolution Began: 19 April 1775* (2000). How the news of Lexington and Concord spread across the world.

Francis Jennings, *Empire of Fortune: Crowns, Colonies, and Tribes in the Seven Years' War in America* (1988). The French and Indian War examined from the point of view of the Iroquois Confederacy. This is opinionated, but exciting history.

Pauline Maier, *American Scripture: Making the Declaration of Independence* (1997). The deep background of this foundation of American democracy.

Richard L. Merritt, *Symbols of American Community, 1735–1775* (1966). A study of colonial newspapers that provides evidence for a rising sense of national community. The French and Indian War emerges as the key period for the growth of nationalist sentiment.

William R. Nester, *"Haughty Conquerors": Amherst and the Great Indian Uprising of 1763* (2000). The underlying causes of Pontiac's rebellion, the fighting itself, and the consequences.

The Rattlesnake as a National Symbol

WHAT OTHER characteristics of snakes in general, and rattlesnakes in particular, might have appealed to Revolutionary Era Americans in choosing a national symbol?

One of the tasks facing the Revolutionary generation was to create symbols around which to rally. There was no official flag, no anthem, no Uncle Sam. Benjamin Franklin made perhaps the earliest attempt to create a visual symbol for the prospective nation when he drew "Join, Or Die" to accompany his 1754 Plan of Union. He pictured the colonies as a snake cut into pieces. Why a snake? In mythology, snakes can reattach themselves. Twenty years later, Paul Revere used the snake for the masthead of the revolutionary newspaper, the *Massachusetts Spy*. Once war began, military units adopted the snake as their battle flag. The most famous of these is the Gadsden flag. Christopher Gadsden was a delegate to the Second Continental Congress from South Carolina who played a leading role in creating the U.S. Navy and in appointing Esek Hopkins of Rhode Island as its first commander. He gave the Gadsden flag to Hopkins for his personal standard.

In 1775, pleased with the popular adoption of the snake as a national symbol, Benjamin Franklin noted, that:

> As if anxious to prevent all pretentions of quarrelling with her, the weapons with which nature has furnished her, she conceals in the roof of her mouth, so that, to those who are unacquainted with her, she appears to be a most defenceless animal; and even when those weapons are shewn and extended for her defence, they appear weak and contemptible; but their wounds however small, are decisive and fatal: — Conscious of this, she never wounds till she has generously given notice, even to her enemy, and cautioned him against the danger of treading on her.—Was I wrong, Sir, in thinking this a strong picture of the temper and conduct of America?

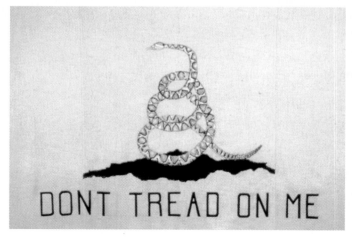

◄ The Gadsden flag, used initially by the U.S. Navy. By 1775 the lines indicating the divisions among the colonies have disappeared. The snake has become the rattlesnake, a reptile unique to North America, and one with a highly poisonous venom. "Don't Tread On Me" captured the revolutionaries' insistence that they fought only to defend their liberties.

Corbis / Bettmann

When rotated, Franklin's snake described the North American coastline: He omitted Georgia, only recently founded and inhabited largely by convicts freed from British prisons.

Revere's snake has reattached itself, although the lines where the divisions had been are still visible. Franklin only pictured twelve colonies, but Revere added "G" for Georgia. Further, Revere's snake confronts the British lion. The united serpent is far larger than the lion, something which anticipated Thomas Paine's argument in *Common Sense* that it made no sense for an island to rule a continent.

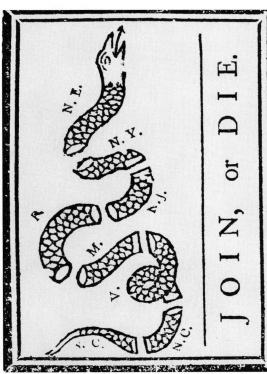

▲

When rotated, Franklin's snake imitated the North American coastline; he omitted Georgia, which was newly found and inhabited largely by convicts freed from British prisons.

North Wind Picture Archives

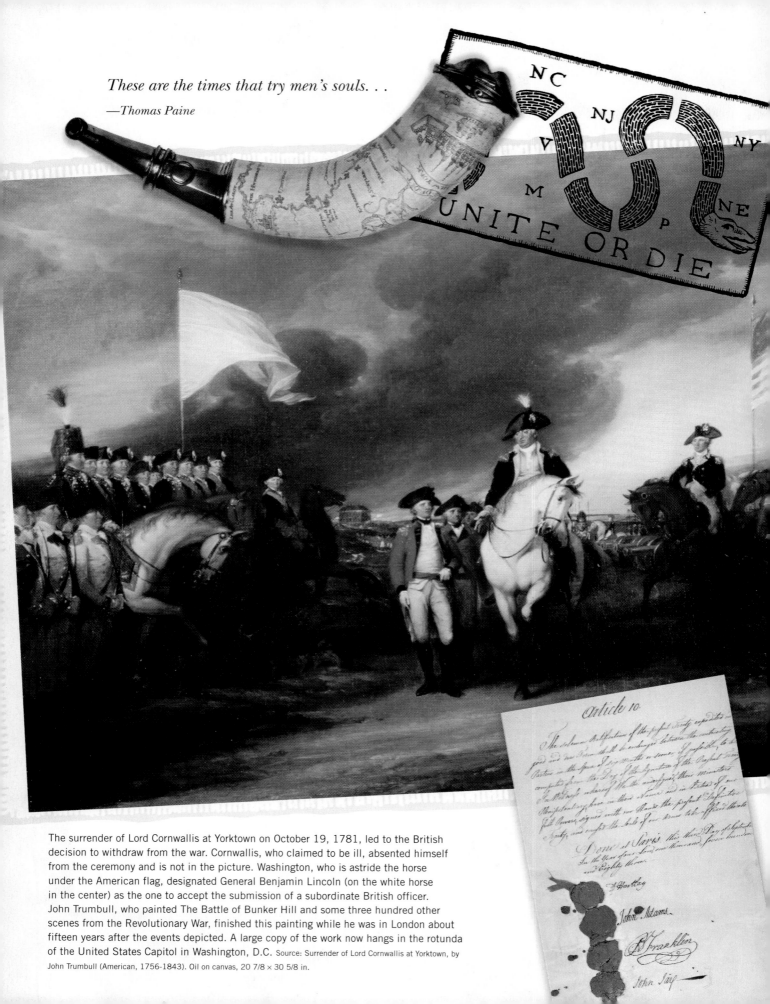

These are the times that try men's souls. . .
—Thomas Paine

The surrender of Lord Cornwallis at Yorktown on October 19, 1781, led to the British decision to withdraw from the war. Cornwallis, who claimed to be ill, absented himself from the ceremony and is not in the picture. Washington, who is astride the horse under the American flag, designated General Benjamin Lincoln (on the white horse in the center) as the one to accept the submission of a subordinate British officer. John Trumbull, who painted The Battle of Bunker Hill and some three hundred other scenes from the Revolutionary War, finished this painting while he was in London about fifteen years after the events depicted. A large copy of the work now hangs in the rotunda of the United States Capitol in Washington, D.C. Source: Surrender of Lord Cornwallis at Yorktown, by John Trumbull (American, 1756-1843). Oil on canvas, 20 7/8 × 30 5/8 in.

THE CREATION OF THE UNITED STATES
1776–1786

WHAT STRATEGIES and tactics did American forces employ in the war for independence?

WHAT CONCERNS were reflected in the terms of the Articles of Confederation?

HOW DID political debate in America change in the years after 1774?

AMERICAN COMMUNITIES

A National Community Evolves at Valley Forge

A DRUM ROLL USHERED IN A JANUARY MORNING IN 1778, SUMMON-ING the Continental Army to roll call. Along a two-mile line of log cabins, doors slowly opened and ragged men stepped out onto the frozen ground of **Valley Forge**. "There comes a soldier," wrote army surgeon Albigense Waldo. "His bare feet are seen through his worn-out shoes, his legs nearly naked from the tattered remains of an only pair of stockings, his breeches not sufficient to cover his nakedness, his shirt hanging in strings, his hair disheveled, his face meagre." The reek of foul straw and unwashed bodies filled the air. "No bread, no soldier!" The chant began as a barely audible mur-mur, then was picked up by men all along the line. "No bread, no soldier! No bread, no soldier!" At last the chanting grew so loud it could be heard at General Washington's headquarters, a mile away. The 11,000 men of the American army were surviving on little more than "firecake," a mixture of flour and water baked hard before the fire that, according to Waldo, turned "guts to paste-board." Two thousand men were without shoes; others were without blankets and had to sit up all night about the fires to keep from freezing. Addressing the Conti-nental Congress, Washington wrote, "Three or four days of bad weather would prove our destruction."

Valley Forge was to become a national symbol of endurance. After marching hundreds of weary miles and suffering a series of terrible defeats at the hands of a British force nearly twice their number, the sol-diers of the Continental Army had retreated to this winter head-quarters only to find themselves at the mercy of indifferent local suppliers. Contractors demanded exorbitant rates for food and clothing, rates the Congress had refused to pay, and as a result local farmers preferred to deal with the British, who paid in pounds sterling, not depreciated Continental currency.

The 11,000 men of the Continental Army, who had not been paid for nearly six months, were divided into sixteen brigades composed of regiments from nine states. An unsympathetic observer described them as "a vagabond army of ragamuffins," and indeed many of the men were drawn from the ranks of the poor and disadvantaged: indentured servants, landless farmers, and nearly a thousand African Americans, both slave and free. Most of the men came from thinly settled farm districts or small towns where precautions regarding sanitation had been unnecessary. Every thaw revealed ground covered with "much filth and nastiness," and officers ordered sentinels to fire on any man "easing himself elsewhere than at ye vaults." Typhoid fever and other infectious diseases spread quickly. Along with dysentery, malnutrition, and exposure,

these diseases claimed as many as 2,500 lives that winter. More than 700 women—wives, lovers, cooks, laundresses, and prostitutes—lived at Valley Forge that winter, and they were kept busy nursing the sick and burying the dead.

"What then is to become of this army?" Washington wor-ried during the depth of the winter. But six months later the force he marched out of Valley Forge was considerably stronger for its experience there. Most important were the strong relationships that formed among the men, twelve of whom bunked together in each cabin, grouped by state regiments and brigade. In these units they fashioned "a band of brotherhood" and "shared with each other their hardships, dangers, and sufferings," wrote com-mon soldier Joseph Plumb Martin. And they "sympathized with each other in trouble and sickness, assisted in bearing each other's burdens, [and] endeavored to conceal each other's faults." During the coming trials of battle, Washington, who referred to his staff as "family," would rely greatly on the bonds of affection his men had developed during that hard winter.

As psychologists know today, it is this sense of community that contributes most to success in warfare.

To some American Patriots—as the supporters of the Revolution called themselves— the European-style Continental Army betrayed the ideals of the citizen-soldier and the autonomy of local communities that were central tenets of the Revolution. Washington argued strongly, however, that the Revolution could not be won without a national army insulated from politics and able to withstand the shifting popular mood. Moreover, through the developing sense of community among these men—who came from hundreds of localities and a variety of ethnic backgrounds—the Continental soldiers became living examples of the egalitarian ideals of the Revolution. They were a popular democratic force that counterbalanced the conservatism of the new republic's elite leadership. The national spirit they built at Valley Forge would sustain them through four more years of war and provide momentum for the long process of forging a national political system out of the persistent localism of Ameri-can politics. "I admire them tremendously!" wrote one European officer serving with Washington. "It is incredible that soldiers composed of men of every age, even children of fifteen, of whites and blacks, almost naked, unpaid, and rather poorly fed, can march so well and withstand fire so steadfastly." Asked to explain why his men served, another officer declared: "Nothing but virtue and that great principle, the love of our country."

Valley Forge

THE WAR FOR INDEPENDENCE

At the beginning of the Revolution, the British had the world's best-equipped and most disciplined army, as well as a navy that was unopposed in American waters. But they greatly underestimated the American capacity to fight. They also misperceived the sources of the conflict. Seeing the rebellion as the work of a small group of disgruntled conspirators, initially they defined their objective as defeating this Patriot opposition. In the wake of a military victory, they believed, they could easily reassert political control. But the geography of eastern North America offered no single vital center whose conquest would end the war. The **Patriots** had the advantage of fighting on their own ground and among a population thinly spread over a territory stretching along 1,500 miles of coastline and extending 100 miles or more into the interior. When the British succeeded in defeating the Patriots in one area, resistance would spring up in another. The key factor in the outcome of the war for independence, then, was the popular support for the American cause.

THE PATRIOT FORCES

Most American men of fighting age had to face the call to arms. From a population of approximately 350,000 eligible men, more than 200,000 saw action, though no more than 25,000 were engaged at any one time. More than 100,000 served in the **Continental Army**, under Washington's command and the authority of the Continental Congress; the other soldiers served in Patriot militia companies.

These militias—armed bodies of men drawn from local communities—proved important in the defense of their own areas, for they had homes as well as local reputations to protect. Because men preferred to serve with their neighbors in local companies rather than subject themselves to the discipline of the regular service, the states failed to meet their quotas for regiments in the Continental Army. Serving short terms of enlistment, often with officers of their own choosing, militiamen resisted discipline. Indeed, in the face of battle, militia companies demonstrated appalling rates of desertion.

The failings of the militias in the early battles of the war sobered Congress, and it both greatly enlarged state quotas for the army and extended the term of service to three years or the war's duration. To spur enlistment Congress offered bounties, regular wages, and promises of free land after victory.

Discipline was essential in a conflict in which men fired at close range, charged each other with bayonets, and engaged in hand-to-hand combat. According to the best estimates, a total of 25,674 American men died in the Revolution, approximately 6,000 from wounds suffered in battle, 10,000 from the effects of disease, the rest as prisoners of war or missing in action. Regiments of the Continental Army experienced the highest casualty rates, sometimes 30 or 40 percent. Indeed, the casualty rate over all was higher than in any other American conflict except the Civil War. In most areas the war claimed few civilian lives, for it was confined largely to direct engagements between the armies. In the backcountry and in regions of the South, however, where Patriot and Loyalist militias waged vicious campaigns, noncombatant casualties were considerable.

Both the Continentals and the militias played important political roles as well. At a time when Americans identified most strongly with their local communities or their states, the Continental Army, through experiences like the Valley Forge winter, evolved into a powerful force for nationalist sentiment. But shortages of food and pay led to many army mutinies. In the most serious incident, along the Pennsylvania Line in January 1781, enlisted men killed one officer,

■ ■ ■ ■ ■ ■ ■ ■ ■ ■
WHAT STRATEGIES and tactics did American forces employ in the war for independence?
■ ■ ■ ■ ■ ■ ■ ■ ■ ■

IMAGE KEY
for pages 162–163

a. An 18th-century powder horn decorated with a map.

b. An engraving printed by Benjamin Franklin in 1754 urging the colonies to unite.

c. The 1783 Treaty of Paris that ended the American Revolution and recognized the independence of the United States.

d. A drum belonging to William Diamond (Lexington Historical Society) and a fife said to have been played at the Lexington fight early in the morning of April 19, 1775.

e. A painting by a French army officer showing the diversity of American soldiers.

f. Benjamin West's painting of the American commissioners who negotiated the Peace of Paris.

g. Mather Brown's sensitive portrait of Thomas Jefferson is the earliest known likeness of him.

h. The *Surrender of Lord Cornwallis at Yorktown* on October 19, 1781, a painting by John Trumbull.

Valley Forge   Area of Pennsylvania approximately twenty miles northwest of Philadelphia where General George Washington's Continental troops were quartered from December 1777 to June 1778 while British forces occupied Philadelphia during the Revolutionary War.

Patriots   British colonists who favored independence from Britain.

William Ranney, *The Battle of Cowpens.*
Oil on canvas.

Photo by Sam Holland. Courtesy South Carolina State House

Continental Army The regular or professional army authorized by the Second Continental Congress and commanded by General George Washington during the Revolutionary War.

5–5
Abigail Adams and John Adams Letters; Abigail Adams Letter to Mercy Otis Warren

wounded two others, and set off from their winter quarters in New Jersey for Philadelphia to ask Congress to uphold its commitments. As they marched they were joined by British agents who encouraged them to go over to the king. Enraged at this attempt at subversion, the mutineers hanged the agents and gave up their resistance. Angry as they were at Congress, they were Americans first and hated the British. Over 100,000 men from every state served in the Continental Army, contributing mightily to the unity of purpose—the formation of a national community—that was essential to the process of nation making.

In most communities Patriots had seized control of local government during the period of committee organizing in 1774 and 1775 (see Chapter 6), and with war imminent they pressed the obligation to serve in a Patriot militia upon most eligible men. Probably the most important role of the Patriot militias was to force even the most apathetic of Americans to think seriously about the Revolution and to choose sides under the scrutiny of their neighbors.

As men marched off to war, many women assumed the management of family farms and businesses. Abigail Adams, for example, ran the Adams family's farm at Quincy for years. The Boston home of Mercy Otis Warren, daughter of James Otis, was a center of Patriot political activity. When the fighting shifted to their locales, women volunteered as seamstresses, cooks, nurses, and even spies.

When the months of fighting lengthened into years, many women left their homes to join husbands and lovers, fathers and brothers, in army encampments. Some were officially employed, but most voluntarily took care of their own men, and many fought with them side by side. Best known among the women who stayed by their husbands' sides even in camp were Martha Washington and Catherine Greene, wives of the two most important American generals of the war. But less socially prominent women were remembered as well. Mary Ludwig Hays (later McCauley) earned the name "Molly Pitcher" for her courage in bringing water to the Patriots during the Battle of Monmouth in June 1778. When her husband was overcome by heat, Mary Hays took his place at the cannon. In another instance, when Margaret Corbin's husband died in battle she stepped into his position. Other women, such as Deborah Sampson of Massachusetts, disguised themselves as men and enlisted.

THE LOYALISTS

Not all Americans were Patriots. Many sat on the fence, confused by the conflict and waiting for a clear turn in the tide of the struggle before declaring their allegiance. About a fifth of the population, perhaps as many as half a million people, remained loyal to the British crown. They called themselves **Loyalists**, but were known to Patriots as **Tories**, the popular name for the conservative party in England, which traditionally supported the authority of the king over Parliament. Loyalism was strongest in the Lower South, weakest in New England. Loyalists included members of ethnic minorities who had been persecuted by the dominant majority, such as the Highland Scots of the Carolinas and western New York, and southern tenant farmers who had Patriot landlords. Moreover, many slaves and most Indians, the latter fearing aggressive expansion by independent American states, identified with the Loyalists.

Patriots passed state treason acts that prohibited speaking or writing against the Revolution. They also punished Loyalists by issuing bills of attainder, a legal process (later made illegal by the **United States Constitution**) by which Loyalists lost their civil rights and their property. In some areas, notably New York, South Carolina, Massachusetts, and Pennsylvania, Loyalists faced mob violence.

The most infamous American supporter of the British cause was Benedict Arnold. Arnold was a hero of the early battles of the Revolution on the American side. But in 1779, angry and resentful about what he perceived to be assignments and rank below his station, he became a paid informer of General Henry Clinton, head of the British army in New York City. In 1780 Patriots uncovered Arnold's plot to betray the strategic post of West Point, which he commanded. After fleeing to the British, who paid him a handsome stipend and pension, he became the most hated man in America. During the last two years of the war he led British raids against his home state as well as against Virginia, and after the Revolution he lived in England until his death in 1801.

The British strategy for suppressing the Revolution depended on mobilizing the Loyalists, but in most areas this proved impossible. As many as 50,000 Loyalists, however, fought for the king during the Revolution. As many as 80,000 Loyalists fled the country during and after the Revolution. Many went to England or the British West

A Patriot mob torments Loyalists in this print published during the Revolution. One favorite punishment was the "grand Tory ride," in which a crowd hauled the victim through the streets astride a fence rail. In another men were stripped to "buff and breeches" and their naked flesh coated liberally with heated tar and feathers.

The Granger Collection

Loyalists British colonists who opposed independence from Britain.

Tories A derisive term applied to Loyalists in America who supported the king and Parliament just before and during the American Revolution.

United States Constitution The written document providing for a new central government of the United States.

MAP EXPLORATION

To explore an interactive version of this map, go to
http://www.prenhall.com/faragherlc/map7.1

* American victories   ← American troop movements
* British victories   ← British troop movements

MAP 7-1
Campaign for New York and New Jersey, 1775–1777

HOW DID American victories at Trenton and Princeton help turn the tide of the war?

QUICK REVIEW

Victories at Trenton and Princeton

* 1776: a series of defeats devastated the Continental Army.
* Christmas night 1776: Washington crosses the Delaware and launches a surprise attack.
* Victories at Trenton and Princeton revive the American cause.

Indies, but the largest number settled in Canada; the Canadian provinces of Ontario, Nova Scotia, and New Brunswick honor the Loyalist refugees as founders. Loyalist property was confiscated by the states and sold at public auction. Although the British government compensated many for their losses, most Loyalists were unhappy exiles. Despite their disagreement with the Patriots on essential political questions, they remained Americans, and they mourned the loss of their country.

THE CAMPAIGN FOR NEW YORK AND NEW JERSEY

During the winter of 1775–1776 the British developed a strategic plan for the war. From his base at Halifax, Nova Scotia, Sir William Howe was to take his army to New York City, which the British navy would make impregnable. From there Howe was to drive north along the Hudson, while another British army marched south from Canada to Albany. The two armies would converge, cutting New England off from the rest of the colonies, then turn eastward to reduce the rebellious Yankees into submission. Washington, who had arrived at Boston to take command of the militia forces there in the summer of 1775, anticipated this strategy, and in the spring of 1776 he shifted his forces southward toward New York.

In early July, as Congress was taking its final vote on the Declaration of Independence, the British began their operation at New York City, landing 32,000 men, a third of them Hessian mercenaries (from the German state of Hesse), on Staten Island. The Americans, meanwhile, set up fortified positions across the harbor in Brooklyn. Attacking in late August, the British inflicted heavy casualties on the Americans, and the militia forces under Washington's command proved unreliable under fire. The Battle of Long Island ended in disaster for the Patriots, and they were forced to withdraw across the East River to Manhattan.

The British now offered Congress an opportunity to negotiate, and on September 6, Benjamin Franklin, John Adams, and Edward Rutledge sat down with General Howe and his brother, Admiral Richard Howe, on Staten Island. But the meeting broke up when the Howes demanded repeal of the Declaration of Independence. The stage was set for another round of fighting. Six days later the British invaded Manhattan island, and only an American stand at Harlem Heights prevented the destruction of a large portion of the Patriot army. Enjoying naval control of the harbor, the British quickly outflanked the American positions. In a series of battles over the next few months, they forced Washington back at White Plains and overran the American posts of Fort Washington and Fort Lee, on either side of the Hudson River. By November the Americans were fleeing south across New Jersey in a frantic attempt to avoid the British under General Charles Cornwallis.

With morale desperately low, whole militia companies deserted; others, announcing the end of their terms of enlistment, left for home. American resistance seemed to be collapsing all around Washington. But rather than fall back farther, which would surely have meant the dissolution of his entire force, he decided to risk a counterattack. On Christmas night 1776, he led 2,400 troops back across the Delaware, and the next morning defeated the Hessian forces in a surprise attack on their headquarters at Trenton, New Jersey. The Americans inflicted further heavy losses on the British at Princeton and then drove them all the way back to the environs of New York City.

Although these small victories had little strategic importance, they salvaged American morale. As Washington settled into winter headquarters at Morristown, he realized he had to pursue a defensive strategy, avoiding direct confrontations with the British while checking their advances and hurting them wherever possible.

THE NORTHERN CAMPAIGNS OF 1777

The fighting with the American forces had prevented Howe from moving north up the Hudson River, and the British Advance southward from Canada had been stalled by American resistance at Lake Champlain. In 1777, however, the British decided to replay their strategy. From Canada they dispatched General John Burgoyne with nearly 8,000 British and German troops. Howe was to move his force from New York, first taking the city of Philadelphia, the seat of the Continental Congress, and then moving north to meet Burgoyne.

Fort Ticonderoga fell to Burgoyne on July 6, but by August the general found himself bogged down and harassed by Patriot militias in the rough country south of Lake George. After several defeats in September at the hands of an American army commanded by General Horatio Gates, Burgoyne retreated to Saratoga. There his army was surrounded by a considerably larger force of Americans, and on October 19, lacking alternatives, he surrendered his nearly 6,000 men. It would be the biggest British defeat until Yorktown, decisive because it forced the nations of Europe to recognize that the Americans had a fighting chance to win their Revolution.

The Americans were less successful against Howe. A force of 15,000 British troops left New York in July, landing a month later, at the northern end of Chesapeake Bay. At Brandywine Creek the British outflanked the Americans, inflicting heavy casualties and forcing a retreat. Ten days later, the British routed the Americans a second time with a frightful bayonet charge at Paoli that left many Patriots dead. When British troops occupied Philadelphia on September 26, Congress had already fled. Washington attempted a valiant counterattack at Germantown on October 4, but initial success was followed by miscoordination that eventually doomed the operation.

After this campaign the Continentals headed for winter quarters at Valley Forge, a few dozen miles from Philadelphia, the bitterness of their defeats muted somewhat by news of the surrender at Saratoga. In taking Philadelphia, the British had gained the most important city in North America, but it proved to have little strategic value. Central government was virtually nonexistent, and so the unified effort suffered little disruption. At the end of two years of fighting, the British strategy for winning the war had to be judged a failure.

 MAP EXPLORATION
To explore an interactive version of this map, go to
http://www.prenhall.com/faraghertlc/map7.2

MAP 7–2
Northern Campaigns, 1777–1778

QUICK REVIEW

French Alliance

◆ Congress negotiates alliance with France against the British

◆ France guarantees northern parts of country to the U.S.

◆ Warfare between France and Britain breaks out.

This engraving, published in London in 1779, shows an apocryphal incident during the battle in which John Paul Jones's ship *Bon Homme Richard* defeated the British *Serapis*. During the fighting, Jones supposedly shot an American sailor who attempted to lower the ship's flag as a sign of surrender; actually Jones only knocked him down with a pistol. Legend (and the artist) may have confused this incident with another earlier one—while Jones was still a Scotsman (note the bonnet)—in which Jones did kill a mutineer.

"Paul Jones Shooting a Sailor." Color engraving from the Olds Collection #366, no negative number. Collection of the New York Historical Society

THE FRENCH ALLIANCE AND THE SPANISH BORDERLANDS

During these first two years of fighting, the Americans were sustained by loans from France and Spain, allies against Britain. Both saw an opportunity to win back North American territories lost to Great Britain in the Seven Years' War. The Continental Congress maintained a diplomatic delegation in Paris headed by Benjamin Franklin. Through 1777 Franklin was unable to convince France to commit to an alliance.

In England, meanwhile, the Whig opposition argued strongly against the war. When, in December 1777, British Prime Minister Lord North received the news of Burgoyne's surrender, he dispatched agents to begin peace discussions with Franklin in Paris. Fears of British conciliation with the revolutionaries, as well as the victory at Saratoga, finally persuaded French Foreign Minister Vergennes to tie France to the United States. In mid-December he informed Franklin that the king's council had decided to recognize American independence.

In February 1778, the American delegation submitted to Congress a treaty of commerce and alliance it had negotiated with the French. In the treaty, to take effect upon a declaration of war between France and Britain, the French pledged to "maintain effectually the liberty, sovereignty, and independence" of the United States. France agreed to guarantee to the United States all the "northern parts of America" as well as other "conquests" made in the war, while the United States promised to recognize French acquisitions of British islands in the West Indies. Warfare between France and Britain broke out in June.

A year later Spain also entered the war. But the Spanish pursued an independent strategy against the British, taking the weakly defended Mississippi River towns of Natchez and Baton Rouge from the British in 1779, and winning the important Gulf ports of Mobile and Pensacola in 1780 and 1781, respectively. The first French ambassador to the United States arrived with instructions to do everything he could to prevent the Americans from enlarging their territory at the expense of the Spanish borderland colonies. Like the Spanish, the French also feared the potential power of an independent United States. Many American leaders did indeed have expansionist aspirations and understood that the wartime alliance with France and tacit support of Spain were expedients.

Worried over the consequences of French involvement, in the spring of 1778 Lord North sent a peace commission to America with promises to repeal the parliamentary legislation that had provoked the crisis in the first place and pledging never again to impose revenue taxes on the colonies. But the Continental Congress declared that any person coming to terms with the peace commission would be labeled a traitor; the only possible topics of negotiation were the withdrawal of British forces and the recognition of American independence.

When France entered the war, the British were forced to rethink their military strategy. With the West Indies at risk, they shipped 5,000 troops from New York to the Caribbean and suceeded in beating back a French attack. Fearing the arrival of the French fleet along the North American coast, the new British commander in America, General Henry Clinton, evacuated Philadelphia in June 1778. In hot pursuit were Washington's Continentals, fresh out of Valley Forge. At the Battle of Monmouth on June 28, the British blunted the American drive and retreated to New York. The Americans, centered at West Point, took up defensive positions surrounding the lower Hudson. Confidence in an impending victory now spread through the Patriot forces. But after a failed American-French joint campaign against British forces at Newport, Rhode Island, General Washington settled for a defensive strategy.

Although the Americans enjoyed several small successes in the Northeast over the next two years, the war there went into a stall.

INDIAN PEOPLES AND THE REVOLUTION IN THE WEST

At the beginning of the conflict both sides solicited the support of the Indians. A committee of the Continental Congress reported that "securing and preserving the friendship of Indian nations appears to be a subject of the utmost moment to these colonies." Most concerned about the stance of the Iroquois Confederacy—long one of the most potent political forces in colonial North America—a delegation from Congress told the Iroquois that the conflict was a "family quarrel" and urged them to keep out of it. British agents, on the other hand, pressed the Iroquois to unite against the Americans. Many Indian people were reluctant to get involved: "We are unwilling to join on either side of such a contest," an Oneida chief responded. "Let us Indians be all of one mind, and live with one another, and you white people settle your own disputes between yourselves."

Ultimately, however, the British were more persuasive. It became clear to Indians that a Patriot victory would mean the extension of American settlements into their

 MAP EXPLORATION

To explore an interactive version of this map, go to **http://www.prenhall.com/faraghertlc/map7.3**

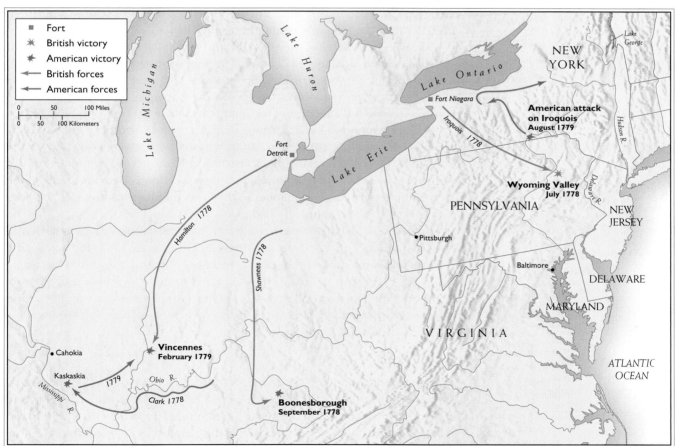

MAP 7-3
Fighting in the West, 1778–1779

WHAT ROLE did Indian peoples play in the fighting in the West?

Joseph Brant, the brilliant chief of the Mohawks who sided with Great Britain during the Revolution, in a 1786 painting by the American artist Gilbert Stuart. After the Treaty of Paris, Brant led a large faction of Iroquois people north into British Canada, where they established a separate Iroquois Confederacy.

Gilbert Stuart. *Joseph Brant*, 1786. Oil on canvas, 30" × 25". New York State Historical Association, Cooperstown

homelands. Native peoples fought in the Revolution for some of the same reasons Patriots did—for political independence, cultural integrity, and the protection of their land and property—but Indian fears of American expansion led them to oppose the Patriot rhetoric of natural rights and the equality of all men. Almost all the tribes that engaged in the fighting did so on the side of the British.

British officials marshaled the support of Cherokees, Creeks, Choctaws, and Chickasaws in the South, supplying them with arms from the British arsenal at Pensacola until it was taken by the Spanish in 1781. The consequence was a ferocious Indian war in the southern backcountry. In the summer of 1776, a large number of Cherokees, led by the warrior chief Dragging Canoe (*Tsiyu-Gunsini*), attacked dozens of American settlements. It took hard fighting before Patriot militia companies managed to drive the Cherokees into the mountains, destroying many of their towns. Although the Cherokees eventually made an official peace, sporadic violence between Patriots and Indians continued along the southern frontier.

Among the Iroquois of New York, the Mohawk leader Joseph Brant (*Thayendanegea*) succeeded in bringing most Iroquois warriors into the British camp, although he was opposed by the chiefs of the Oneidas and Tuscaroras, who supported the Patriots. In 1777 and 1778, Iroquois and Loyalist forces raided the northern frontiers of New York and Pennsylvania. In retaliation an American army invaded the Iroquois homelands in 1779. Supported by Oneida and Tuscarora warriors, the Americans destroyed dozens of western villages and thousands of acres of crops. For the first time since the birth of their confederacy in the fifteenth century, the Iroquois were fighting each other.

Across the mountains, the Ohio Indians formed an effective alliance under the British at Detroit, and in 1777 and 1778 they sent warriors south against pioneer communities in western Virginia and Kentucky that had been founded in defiance of the Proclamation of 1763. Boonesborough, Kentucky, was nearly destroyed by repeated attacks, and the Americans barely held out. Virginian George Rogers Clark countered by organizing an expedition of Kentucky militia against the old French settlements in the Illinois country, which were controlled by the British. They suceeded in taking the British post at Kaskaskia in the summer of 1778, and in early 1779, in a daring winter raid on Vincennes, they captured Colonel Henry Hamilton, British commander in the West, infamously known as "the Scalp Buyer" because of the bounty he had placed on Patriots' lives.

But Clark lacked the strength to attack the strategic British garrison at Detroit. Coordinating his Iroquois forces with those in Ohio, Brant mounted a new set of offensives that cast a shadow over Clark's successes. Raids back and forth across the Ohio River by Indians and Americans claimed hundreds of lives over the next three years. The war in the West would not end with the conclusion of hostilities in the East. With barely a pause, the fighting in the trans-Appalachian West between Americans and Indians would continue for another two decades.

THE WAR IN THE SOUTH

The most important fighting of the Revolution took place in the South. General Clinton regained the initiative for Britain in December 1778 by sending a force from New York against Georgia, the weakest of the colonies. The British crushed the Patriot militia at Savannah and began to organize the Loyalists in an effort to reclaim the colony. Several American counterattacks failed, including one in which the French fleet bombarded Savannah. Encouraged by their success in Georgia, the British decided to apply the lessons learned there throughout the South. This involved a fundamental change from a strategy of military conquest to one of pacification. Territory would be retaken step by step, then handed over to Loyalists who would reassert

MAP EXPLORATION

To explore an interactive version of this map, go to **http://www.prenhall.com/faraghertlc/map7.4**

MAP 7-4
Fighting in the South, 1778–1781

WHAT ROLE DID African American slaves play in the fighting in the South?

colonial authority loyal to the crown. In October 1779, Clinton evacuated Rhode Island, the last British stronghold in New England, and proceeded with 8,000 troops for a campaign against Charleston. Outflanking the American defenders, Clinton forced the surrender of more than 5,000 troops in May—the most significant American defeat of the war. Horatio Gates, the hero of Saratoga, led a detachment of Continentals southward, but in August they were defeated by General Cornwallis at Camden, South Carolina. Patriot resistance collapsed in the Lower South, and American fortunes were suddenly at their lowest ebb since the beginning of the war.

The southern campaign was marked by vicious violence between partisan militias of Patriots and Loyalists. The violence peaked in September 1780 with Cornwallis's invasion of North Carolina, where the Patriots were stronger and better organized. There the British found their southern strategy untenable: plundering towns and farms in order to feed the army in the interior had the effect of producing angry support for the Patriots.

Into 1781 the Continentals and Patriot militias waged what General Greene called a fugitive war of hit and run against the British. "I am quite tired of marching about the country in quest of adventures," Cornwallis wrote. Finally deciding he would not be able to hold the Carolinas as long as Virginia remained a base of support and supply for the Americans, he led his army north in the summer of 1781. After marauding through the Virginia countryside he reached the Chesapeake, where he expected reinforcements from New York. The British withdrawal from North Carolina allowed Greene to reestablish Patriot control of the Lower South.

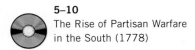

5–10
The Rise of Partisan Warfare
in the South (1778)

YORKTOWN

While the British raged through the South, the stalemate continued in the Northeast. In the summer of 1780, taking advantage of the British evacuation of Rhode Island, the French landed 5,000 troops at Newport under the command of General Rochambeau. But it was not until the spring of 1781 that the general risked joining his force to Washington's Continentals north of New York. They planned a campaign against the city, but in August Washington learned that the French Caribbean fleet was headed for the Chesapeake. Washington saw the opportunity for a decisive turn if only he and Rochambeau could move their troops south in coordination with the French naval operation, locking Cornwallis into his camp at Yorktown. Leaving a small force behind as a decoy, Washington and Rochambeau moved quickly down the coast to the Virginia shore.

More than 16,000 American and French troops had converged on the almost 8,000-man British garrison at Yorktown by mid-September. "If you cannot relieve me very soon," Cornwallis wrote to Clinton in New York, "you must expect to hear the worst." French and American heavy artillery hammered the British unmercifully until the middle of October. Cornwallis found it impossible to break the siege, and after the failure of a planned retreat across the York River, he opened negotiations for the surrender of his army. Two days later, on October 19, 1781, Cornwallis, pleading illness, sent his second-in-command, General Charles O'Hara, to surrender. O'Hara first approached General Rochambeau, but the Frenchman waved him toward Washington. It was almost incomprehensible to the British that they would be surrendering to former subordinates. Everyone knew this was an event of incalculable importance, but few guessed it was the end of the war, for the British still controlled New York.

In London, at the end of November, Lord North received the news "as he would have taken a ball in the breast," reported the colonial secretary. "Oh God!" he moaned, "it is all over!" British fortunes were at low ebb in India, the West Indies, Florida, and the Mediterranean; the cost of the war was enormous; and there was little support among the public and members of Parliament for it. King George III wished to press on, but North submitted his resignation, and in March 1782 the king was forced to accept the counsel of Lord Rockingham, who favored granting Americans their independence.

THE UNITED STATES IN CONGRESS ASSEMBLED

The motion for independence, offered to the Continental Congress by Richard Henry Lee on June 7, 1776, called for a confederation of the states. The **Articles of Confederation**, the first written constitution of the United States, created a national government of sharply limited powers. This arrangement reflected the concerns of people fighting to free themselves from a coercive central government.

WHAT CONCERNS
were reflected in the terms
of the Articles of Confederation?

THE ARTICLES OF CONFEDERATION

The debate over confederation that took place in the **Continental Congress** following the Declaration of Independence made it clear that the delegates favoring a loose union of autonomous states outnumbered those who wanted a strong central government. The following year a consensus finally emerged. In November 1777, the Articles of Confederation were formally adopted by the Continental Congress and sent to the states for ratification. The Articles created a national assembly, called the Congress, in which each state had a single vote. Delegates, selected annually in a manner determined by the individual state legislatures, could serve no more than three years out of six. A presiding president elected annually by Congress was eligible no more than one year out of three. Votes would be decided by a simple majority of the states, except for major questions, which would require the agreement of nine states.

Congress was granted national authority in the conduct of foreign affairs, matters of war and peace, and maintenance of the armed forces. It could raise loans, issue bills of credit, establish a coinage, and regulate trade with Indian peoples, and it was to be the final authority in jurisdictional disputes between states. It was charged with establishing a national postal system as well as a common standard of weights and measures. Lacking the power to tax citizens directly, however, the national government was to apportion its financial burdens among the states according to the extent of their surveyed land. The Articles explicitly guaranteed the sovereignty of the individual states, reserving to them all powers not expressly delegated to Congress. Ratification or amendment required the agreement of all thirteen states. This constitution thus created a national government of specific yet sharply circumscribed powers.

The legislatures of twelve states soon voted in favor of the Articles, but final ratification was held up for more than three years by the state of Maryland. Representing the interests of states without claims to lands west of the Appalachians, Maryland demanded that states cede to Congress their western claims, the new nation's most valuable resource, for "the good of the whole." It was 1781 before Virginia, the state with the largest western claims, broke the log-jam by promising to cede its lands. Maryland then agreed to ratification, and in March the Articles of Confederation took effect.

FINANCING THE WAR

Congress financed the Revolution through grants and loans from friendly foreign powers and by issuing paper currency. The total foreign subsidy by the end of the war approached $9 million, but this was insufficient to back the circulating Continental currency that Congress had authorized, the face value of which had risen to $200 million. Congress called on the states to raise taxes, payable in Continental dollars, so that this currency could be retired. But most of the states were unwilling to do this. In fact, the states resorted to printing currency of their own, which totaled another $200 million by the end of the war. The results of this growth in the money supply were the rapid depreciation of Continental currency and runaway inflation. People who received fixed incomes for services—Continental soldiers, for example, as well as merchants, landlords, and other creditors—were devastated. When Robert Morris, one of the wealthiest merchants in the country, became secretary of finance in May 1781, Continental currency had ceased to circulate; things of no value were said to be "not worth a Continental."

Morris persuaded Congress to charter the Bank of North America in Philadelphia, the first private commercial bank in the United States. There he deposited large quantities of gold and silver coin and bills of exchange obtained through loans from Holland and France. He then issued new paper currency backed by this

QUICK REVIEW

Powers of the Central Government Under the Articles of Confederation

- No national judiciary.
- No separate executive branch.
- Congress sole national authority.
- No Congressional authority to raise troops or impose taxes.

Articles of Confederation   Written document setting up the loose confederation of states that comprised the first national government of the United States.

Continental Congress   Convention of delegates from the colonies that first met to organize resistance to the Intolerable Acts.

The Continental Congress printed currency to finance the Revolution. Because of widespread counterfeiting, engravers attempted to incorporate complex designs, like the unique vein structure in the leaf on this 18-pence note. In case that wasn't enough, the engraver of this note also included the warning: "To counterfeit is Death."

Library of Congress

QUICK REVIEW

Treaty of Paris

◆ Peace talks began in July 1782.

◆ United States signed a preliminary treaty with Britain in November 1782.

◆ Final treaty signed September 3, 1783.

supply. Once confidence in the bank had developed, Morris was able to begin supplying the Continental Army through private contracts. He was also able to meet the interest payments on the debt, which in 1783 he estimated to be about $30 million.

NEGOTIATING INDEPENDENCE

Peace talks between the United States and Great Britain opened in July 1782, when Benjamin Franklin sat down with the British emissary in Paris. Congress had issued its first set of war aims in 1779. The fundamental demands were recognition of American independence and withdrawal of British forces. The American negotiators were to press for as much territory as possible, including Canada, and guarantees of the American right to fish the North Atlantic. As for its French ally, Congress instructed the commissioners to be guided by friendly advice, but also by "knowledge of our interests, and by your own discretion, in which we repose the fullest confidence." In June 1781, partly as a result of French pressure, Congress issued a new set of instructions: the commissioners were to settle merely for a grant of independence and withdrawal of troops, and to be subject to the guidance and control of the French in the negotiations.

Franklin, John Jay, and John Adams, the peace commissioners in Paris, were aware of French attempts to manipulate the outcome of negotiations and to limit potential American power. In violation of instructions and treaty obligations, and without consulting the French, they signed a preliminary treaty with Britain in November 1782. The British were delighted at the thought of separating the wartime allies. In the treaty, Britain acknowledged the United States as "free, sovereign & independent" and agreed to withdraw its troops from all forts within American territory "with all convenient speed." They guaranteed Americans "the right to take fish" in northern waters. The American commissioners pressed the British for Canada but settled for western territorial boundaries extending to the Mississippi. Britain received American promises to erect "no lawful impediments" to the recovery of debts, to cease confiscating Loyalist property, and to try to persuade the states to fairly compensate Loyalist exiles. Finally, the two nations agreed to unencumbered navigation of the Mississippi. The American commissioners had accomplished an astounding coup. The peace terms, they wrote to Congress, "appear to leave us little to complain of and not much to desire."

France was thus confronted with an accomplished fact. When the French criticized the commissioners, the Americans responded by hinting that resistance to the treaty provisions could result in a British–American alliance. France thereupon quickly made an agreement of its own with the British.

Though left out of the negotiations, Spain claimed sovereignty over much of the trans-Appalachian territory granted to the United States as a result of its successful campaign against the British on the Mississippi and the Gulf Coast. Spain also arranged a separate peace with Great Britain, in which it won the return of Florida. The final Treaty of Paris—actually a series of separate agreements among the United States, Great Britain, France, and Spain—was signed at Versailles on September 3, 1783.

MAP EXPLORATION

To explore an interactive version of this map, go to **http://www.prenhall.com/faraghertlc/map7.5**

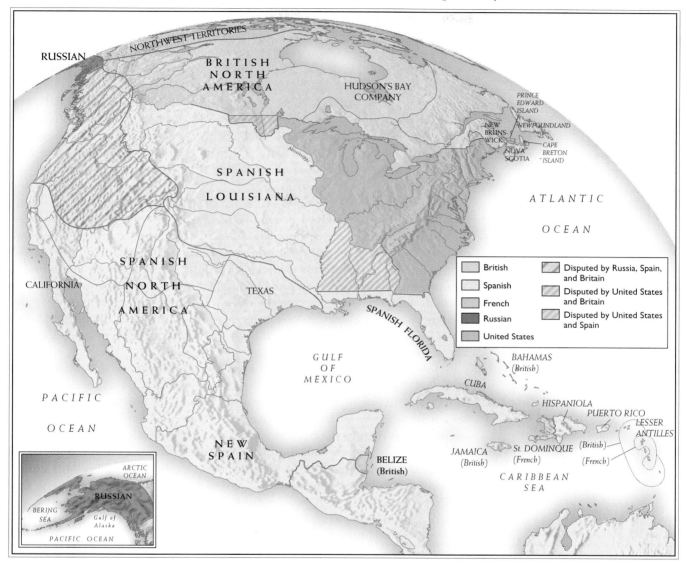

MAP 7-5

North America after the Treaty of Paris, 1783   The map of European and American claims to North America was radically altered by the results of the American Revolution.

HOW DID the Treaty of Paris alter the balance of power in North America?

THE CRISIS OF DEMOBILIZATION

During the two years between the surrender at Yorktown and the signing of the Treaty of Paris, the British continued to occupy New York City, Charleston, and a series of western posts. The Continental Army remained on wartime alert, with some 10,000 men and an estimated 1,000 women encamped at Newburgh, New York, north of West Point. The soldiers had long been awaiting their pay and were very concerned about the postwar bounties and land warrants promised them. The most serious problem, however, lay not among the enlisted men but in the officer corps.

Continental officers had extracted a promise from Congress of life pensions at half pay in exchange for enlistment for the duration of the war. By 1783, however, Congress had still not made specific provisions for veterans' pensions. With peace at hand, officers began to fear that the army would be disbanded before the problem was resolved, and they would lose whatever power they had to pressure Congress. In January 1783, a group of prominent senior officers petitioned Congress, demanding that pensions be converted to a bonus equal to five years of full pay. On Washington's urging, Congress agreed to do this.

As for the common soldiers, they wanted simply to be discharged. In May 1783, Congress voted the soldiers three months' pay as a bonus and instructed Washington to begin dismissing them. Some troops remained at Newburgh until the British had evacuated New York in November, but by the beginning of 1784 the Continental Army had shrunk to no more than a few hundred men.

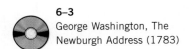

6–3
George Washington, The
Newburgh Address (1783)

THE PROBLEM OF THE WEST

Even during the Revolution thousands of Americans migrated west, and after the war settlers poured over the mountains and down the Ohio River. Thousands of Americans pressed against the Indian country north of the Ohio River, and destructive violence continued along the frontier. British troops continued to occupy posts in the Northwest and encouraged Indian attacks on vulnerable settlements. Spain refused to accept the territorial settlement of the Treaty of Paris, and they closed the port of New Orleans to Americans, effectively blockading the Mississippi River. Westerners who saw that route as their primary access to markets were outraged.

John Jay, appointed secretary for foreign affairs by the Confederation Congress in 1784, attempted to negotiate with the British for withdrawal from the Northwest but was told that was not possible until all outstanding debts from before the war were settled. Jay also negotiated with the Spanish for guarantees of territorial sovereignty and commercial relations, but they insisted that the Americans relinquish free navigation of the Mississippi. Congress would approve no treaty under those conditions, and under these frustrating circumstances, some Westerners considered leaving the Confederation. There were prominent Kentuckians who advocated rejoining the British, while others, including George Rogers Clark and General James Wilkinson, secretly worked for the Spanish as informants and spies. The people of the West "stand as it were upon a pivot," wrote Washington in 1784 after a trip down the Ohio. "The touch of a feather would turn them any way." In the West, local community interest continued to override the fragile development of national community sentiment.

In 1784, Congress took up the problem of extending national authority over the West. Legislation was drafted, principally by Thomas Jefferson, providing for "Government for the Western Territory." The legislation proposed a remarkably democratic colonial policy. The Western public domain would eventually be divided into states, fully the equal of the original thirteen, with guarantees of self-government and republican institutions. Once the population of a territory numbered 20,000, the residents could call a convention and establish a constitution and government of their own choosing. And once the population grew to equal that of the smallest of the original thirteen states, the territory could petition for statehood, provided it agreed to remain forever a member of the Confedera-

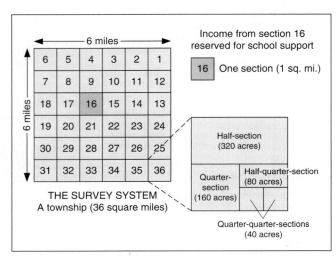

6 miles

6	5	4	3	2	1
7	8	9	10	11	12
18	17	16	15	14	13
19	20	21	22	23	24
30	29	28	27	26	25
31	32	33	34	35	36

6 miles

THE SURVEY SYSTEM
A township (36 square miles)

Income from section 16
reserved for school support

16 One section (1 sq. mi.)

Half-section
(320 acres)

Quarter-
section
(160 acres)

Half-quarter-section
(80 acres)

Quarter-quarter-sections
(40 acres)

The Land Ordinance of 1785 created an ordered system of survey (revised by the Northwest Ordinance of 1787), dividing the land into townships and sections.

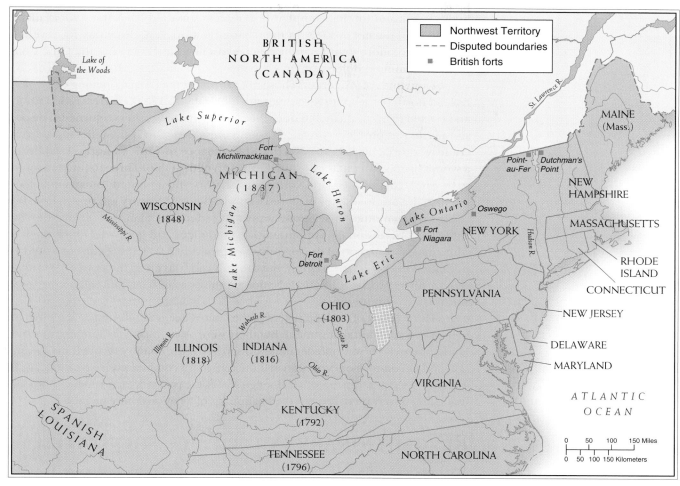

MAP EXPLORATION

To explore an interactive version of this map, go to **http://www.prenhall.com/faraghertlc/map7.6**

MAP 7-6
The Northwest Territory and the Land Survey System of the United States

IN WHAT ways did the Northwest Ordinance affect the admission of new states into the Union? What were the consequences for western lands?

tion. Congress accepted these proposals but rejected by a vote of seven to six Jefferson's clause forever prohibiting slavery in the West.

Passed the following year, the **Land Ordinance of 1785** provided for the survey and sale of Western lands. To avoid the chaos of overlapping surveys and land claims that had characterized Kentucky, the authors of the ordinance created an ordered system of survey, dividing the land into townships composed of thirty-six sections of one square mile (640 acres) each. This measure would have an enormous impact on the North American landscape, as can be seen by anyone who has flown over the United States and looked down at the patchwork pattern. Jefferson argued that land ought to be given away to actual settlers. But, eager to establish a revenue base for the government, Congress provided for the auction of public lands for not less than $1 per acre. In the treaties of Fort Stanwix in 1784 and Fort McIntosh in 1785, congressional commissioners forced the Iroquois and some of

Land Ordinance of 1785 Act passed by Congress under the Articles of Confederation that created the grid system of surveys by which all subsequent public land was made available for sale.

the Ohio Indians to cede a portion of their territory in what is now eastern Ohio, and surveyors were immediately sent there to divide up the land. These treaties were not the result of negotiation; the commissioners dictated the terms by seizing hostages and forcing compliance. The first surveyed lands were not available for sale until the fall of 1788. In the meantime, Congress, desperate for revenue, sold a tract of more than 1.5 million acres to a new land company, the Ohio Company, for a million dollars.

Thousands of Westerners chose not to wait for the official opening of the public land north of the Ohio River but settled illegally. In 1785 Congress raised troops and evicted many of them, but once the troops left the squatters returned. The persistence of this problem convinced many congressmen to revise Jefferson's democratic territorial plan. In the **Northwest Ordinance of 1787**, Congress established a system of government for the territory north of the Ohio. Three to five states were to be carved out of the giant Northwest Territory and admitted "on an equal footing with the original states in all respects whatsoever." Slavery was prohibited. But the initial guarantee of self-government in Jefferson's plan was replaced by the rule of a congressionally appointed court of judges and governor. Once the free white male population of the territory had grown to 5,000, these citizens would be permitted to choose an assembly, but the governor was given the power of absolute veto on all territorial legislation. National interest would be imposed on the localistic western communities.

The creation of the land system of the United States was the major achievement of the Confederation government. But there were other important accomplishments. Under the Articles of Confederation, Congress led the country through the Revolution and its commissioners negotiated the terms of a comprehensive peace treaty. In organizing the departments of war, foreign affairs, the post office, and finance, the Confederation government created the beginnings of a national bureaucracy.

Northwest Ordinance of 1787
Legislation that prohibited slavery in the Northwest Territories and provided the model for the incorporation of future territories into the union as co-equal states.

HOW DID political debate in America change in the years after 1774?

REVOLUTIONARY POLITICS IN THE STATES

Despite these accomplishments, most Americans focused not on the Confederation government in Philadelphia but on the governments of their own states. During the revolutionary era, most Americans identified politically and socially with their local communities and states rather than with the American nation. People spoke of "these United States," emphasizing the plural. The single national community feeling of the Revolution was overwhelmed by persistent localism. The states were the setting for the most important political struggles of the Confederation period and for long afterwards.

THE BROADENED BASE OF POLITICS

The political mobilization that took place in 1774 and 1775 greatly broadened political participation. Mass meetings in which ordinary people expressed their opinions, voted, and gained political experience were common, not only in the cities but in small towns and rural communities as well. During these years, a greater proportion of the population began to participate in elections. Compared with the colonial assemblies, the new state legislatures included more men from rural and western districts—farmers and artisans as well as lawyers, merchants, and large landowners. For example, many delegates to the Massachusetts provincial congress of 1774 were men from small farming communities who lacked formal education and owned little property.

This transformation was accompanied by a dramatic shift in the political debate. During the colonial period, when only the upper crust of society had been truly engaged in the political process, the principal argument took place between the Tory and Whig positions. The Tory position, argued by royal officials, was that colonial governments were simply convenient instruments of the king's prerogative, serving at his pleasure. Colonial elites, seeking to preserve and increase their own power, had argued for stronger assemblies. They used traditional Whig arguments about the need for a balanced government, represented by the governor, the upper house, and the assembly. This debate was ended by the Revolution. The Tory position lost all legitimacy. For the first time in American history, democracy became a term of approval. Patriots who took a Whig position on balanced government found themselves challenged by farmers, artisans, and other ordinary people armed with a new and radical democratic ideology.

One of the first post-Revolution debates focused on the appropriate governmental structure for the new states. The thinking of democrats was indicated by the title of a New England pamphlet of 1776: *The People the Best Governors.* Power, the anonymous author argued, should be vested in a single, popularly elected assembly. The people, the pamphlet said, "best know their wants and necessities, and therefore are best able to govern themselves." The ideal form of government, according to democrats, was the community or town meeting, in which the people set their own tax rates, created a militia, controlled their own schools and churches, and regulated the local economy. State government was necessary only for coordination among communities.

Conservative Americans took up the Whig argument on the need for a balanced government. The "unthinking many," wrote another pamphleteer, should be checked by a strong executive and an upper house. Both of these would be insulated from popular control by property qualifications and long terms in office, the latter designed to draw forth the wisdom and talent of the country's wealthiest and most accomplished men. The greatest danger, according to conservatives, was the possibility of majority tyranny, which might lead to the violation of property rights and to dictatorship. "We must take mankind as they are," one conservative wrote, "and not as we could wish them to be."

DECLARATIONS OF RIGHTS

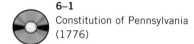

6–1
Constitution of Pennsylvania
(1776)

Fourteen states—the original thirteen plus Vermont—adopted constitutions between 1776 and 1780. Each of these documents was shaped by debate between radicals and conservatives, democrats and Whigs, and reflected a political balance of power. The constitutions of Pennsylvania, Maryland, and New York typified the political range of the times. Pennsylvania instituted a radical democracy, Maryland created a conservative set of institutions designed to keep citizens and rulers as far apart as possible, and New York adopted a system somewhere in the middle.

One of the most important innovations of the state constitutions was a guarantee of rights patterned on the Virginia Declaration of Rights of June 1776. Written by George Mason—a wealthy planter, democrat, and brilliant political philosopher—the Virginia declaration set a distinct tone in its very first article: "That all men are by nature equally free and independent, and have certain inherent rights, . . . namely, the enjoyment of life and liberty, with the means of acquiring and possessing property and pursuing and obtaining happiness and safety." The fifteen articles declared, among other things, that sovereignty resided in the people, that government was the servant of the people, and that the people had the "right to reform, alter, or abolish" that government. There were guarantees of due process and trial by jury in criminal prosecutions, and prohibitions of excessive bail and "cruel and unusual punishments." Freedom of the press was guaranteed as "one of the great bulwarks of liberty," and the people were assured of "the free exercise of religion, according to the dictates of conscience."

Eight state constitutions included a general declaration of rights similar to the first article of the Virginia declaration; others incorporated specific guarantees. A number of states proclaimed the right of the people to engage in free speech and free assembly, to instruct their representatives, and to petition for the redress of grievances—rights either inadvertently or deliberately omitted from Virginia's declaration. These declarations were important precedents for the **Bill of Rights**, the first ten amendments to the federal Constitution. Indeed, George Mason of Virginia was a leader of the democrats who insisted that the Constitution stipulate such rights.

A Spirit of Reform

The political upheaval of the Revolution raised the possibility of other reforms in American society. The 1776 Constitution of New Jersey, by granting the vote to "all free inhabitants" who met the property requirements, enfranchised women as well as men. The number of women voters eventually led to male protests and a new state law explicitly limiting the right to vote to "free white male citizens."

The New Jersey controversy may have been an anomaly, but women's participation in the Revolution wrought subtle but important changes. In 1776 Abigail Adams wrote to her husband John Adams, away at the Continental Congress, "In the new code of laws which I suppose it will be necessary for you to make I desire you would remember the ladies, and be more generous and favourable to them than your ancestors." In the aftermath of the Revolution, there was evidence of increasing sympathy in the courts for women's property rights and fairer treatment of women's petitions for divorce. And the postwar years witnessed an increase in opportunities for women seeking an education. From a strictly legal and political point of view, the Revolution may have done little to change women's role in society, but it did seem to help change expectations.

The most steadfast reformer of the day was Thomas Jefferson, who after completing work on the Declaration of Independence returned to Virginia to take a seat in its House of Delegates. In 1776 he introduced a bill that abolished the law of entails, which had confined inheritance to particular heirs in order that landed property remain undivided. Jefferson believed that "entail" and "primogeniture" (inheritance of all the family property by the firstborn son)—legal customs long in effect in aristocratic England—had no place in a republican society. The legislation had little practical effect because few estates were entailed, but the repeal was symbolically important, for it repudiated an ancient aristocratic custom. By 1790, every state but one had followed Virginia's lead (Rhode Island finally acted in 1798).

Jefferson's other notable success was his **Bill for Establishing Religious Freedom**. Indeed, he considered this document one of his greatest accomplishments. At the beginning of the Revolution, there were established churches—denominations officially supported and funded by the government—in nine of the thirteen colonies: the Congregationalists in Massachusetts, New Hampshire, and Connecticut and the Anglicans in New York and in the South. (See also Chapter 5 for a discussion of colonial religion.) Established religion was increasingly opposed in the eighteenth century, in part because of Enlightenment criticism of the power it had over free and open inquiry, but, more important, because of the growing sectarian diversity produced by the religious revival of the Great Awakening.

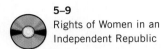

5–9
Rights of Women in an Independent Republic

Bill of Rights   A written summary of inalienable rights and liberties.

Bill for Establishing Religious Freedom A bill authored by Thomas Jefferson establishing religious freedom in Virginia.

AFRICAN AMERICANS AND THE REVOLUTION

For most African Americans there was little to celebrate in the American victory, for it perpetuated the institution of slavery. Few people were surprised when thousands of black fighters and their families departed with the Loyalists and the British at the end of the war, settling in the West Indies, Canada, and Africa. Most of these refugees were fugitive slaves rather than committed Loyalists. Virginia and South Carolina were said to have lost 30,000 and 25,000 slaves as a result of the war.

To many white Americans there was an obvious contradiction in waging a war for liberty while continuing to support the institution of slavery. Slavery was first abolished in the state constitution of Vermont in 1777, and in Massachusetts and New Hampshire in 1780 and 1784, respectively. Pennsylvania, Connecticut, and Rhode Island adopted systems of gradual emancipation during these years, freeing the children of slaves at birth. By 1804 every northern state had provided for abolition or gradual emancipation, although as late as 1810, 30,000 African Americans remained enslaved in the North.

In the Upper South, revolutionary idealism, the Christian egalitarianism of Methodists and Baptists, and a shift from tobacco farming to the cultivation of cereal grains such as wheat and corn combined to weaken the commitment of many planters to the slave system. There was a great increase in **manumissions**, grants of freedom to slaves by individual masters. In the Upper South there was a small but important movement to encourage gradual emancipation by convincing masters to free their slaves in their wills. George Washington not only freed several hundred of his slaves upon his death but also developed an elaborate plan for apprenticeship and tenancy for the able-bodied, and lodging and pensions for the aged. Planters in the Lower South, however, heavily dependent as they were on slave labor, resisted the growing calls for an end to slavery. Between 1776 and 1786 all the states but South Carolina and Georgia prohibited or heavily taxed the international slave trade, and this issue became an important point of conflict at the **Constitutional Convention** in 1787 (see Chapter 8).

Perhaps the most important result of these developments was the growth of the free African American population; from a few thousand in 1750, this population grew to more than 200,000 by the end of the century. Largely excluded from the institutions of white Americans, the African American community now had enough strength to establish schools, churches, and other institutions of its own. At first this development was opposed. In Williamsburg, Virginia, for instance, the leader of a black congregation was seized and whipped when he attempted to gain recognition from the Baptist Association. But by the 1790s, the Williamsburg African Church had grown to over 500 members, and the Baptist Association reluctantly recognized it. In Philadelphia, Reverend Absalom Jones established St. Thomas's African Episcopal Church. The incorporation of the word "African" in the names of churches, schools, and mutual benefit societies reflected the pride African Americans took in their heritage.

A small group of African American writers rose to prominence in the revolutionary era. Benjamin Banneker published a popular almanac that both white and black Americans consulted. The most famous African American writer, however, was Phyllis Wheatley, who came to public attention when her *Poems on Various Subjects, Religious and Moral* appeared in London in 1773, while she was still a domestic slave in Boston. Kidnapped in Africa as a young girl and converted to Christianity during the Great Awakening, Wheatley wrote poems that combined her piety and a concern for her people.

This portrait of the African American poet Phyllis Wheatley was included in the collection of her work published in London in 1773, when she was only twenty. Kidnapped in Africa when a girl, then purchased off the Boston docks, she was more like a daughter than a slave to the Wheatley family. She later married and lived as a free woman of color before her untimely death in 1784.

Library of Congress

QUICK REVIEW

African Americans and the Revolution

- Slavery abolished in North starting in the 1770s.
- A small group of African American writers gained prominence during the revolutionary era.
- By 1800 free black population reached 200,000.

Manumissions Grant of freedom to slaves by individual masters.

Constitutional Convention
Convention that met in Philadelphia in 1787 and drafted the Constitution of the United States.

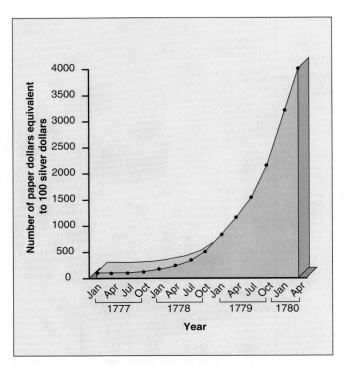

Postwar Inflation, 1777–1780: The Depreciation of Continental Currency
(Number of paper dollars equal to 100 silver dollars) The flood of Continental currency issued by Congress and the shortage of goods resulting from the British blockade combined to create the worst inflation Americans have ever experienced. Things of no value were said to be "not worth a Continental."

John McCusker, "How Much Is That in Real Money?" *Proceedings of the American Antiquarian Society*, N.S. 102 (1992): 297–359

QUICK REVIEW

Debt and the Balance of Trade

◆ Britain sought to keep America weak and dependent.

◆ Trade imbalance soared in the 1780s.

◆ Collapse of credit bubble in 1784 led to depression.

ECONOMIC PROBLEMS

During the Revolution, the shortage of goods resulting from the British blockade, the demand for supplies by the army and the militias, and the flood of paper currency issued by the Congress and the states combined to create the worst inflation that Americans have ever experienced. Continental dollars traded against Spanish dollars at the rate of 3 to 1 in 1777, 40 to 1 in 1779, and 146 to 1 in 1781, by which time Congress had issued more than $190 million in Continentals. Most of this paper money ended up in the hands of merchants, who paid only a fraction of its face value. There was a popular outcry at the incredible increase in prices, and communities and states in the North responded with laws regulating wages and prices.

The sponsors of wage and price schedules often blamed high prices on hoarding and profiteering. Although it is doubtful that such practices caused the inflation, many merchants did gouge their customers. Many communities experienced demonstrations and food riots; men and women demanded fair prices, and when they did not receive them, they broke into storehouses and took what they needed. People organized local committees to monitor economic activity and punish wrongdoers.

After the war, inflation was suddenly replaced by depression. Political revolution could not alter economic realities: the independent United States continued to be a supplier of raw materials and an importer of manufactured products, and Great Britain remained its most important trading partner.

With few exports to offset all the imports, the trade deficit with Britain for the period 1784–1786 rose to approximately £5 million. The deficit acted like a magnet, drawing hard currency from American accounts. Short of hard currency, the commercial banks in the United States insisted on immediate repayment of old loans and refused to issue new ones. The country was left with very little coin in circulation. It added up to a serious depression, lasting from 1784 to 1788. At their lowest level, in 1786, prices had fallen by 25 percent.

The depression struck while the country was burdened with the huge debt incurred during the Revolution. The total debt owed by the national and state governments amounted to more than $50 million in 1785. Not allowed to raise taxes on its own, the Confederation Congress requisitioned the states for the funds necessary for debt repayment. The states in turn taxed their residents. At a time when there was almost no money in circulation, people rightly feared being crushed by the burden of private debt and public taxes. Thus, the economic problem became a political problem.

STATE REMEDIES

Where there were manufacturing interests, as in the Northeast, states erected high tariffs to curb imports and protect infant industries. But shippers could avoid these duties simply by unloading their cargo in neighboring seaboard states that lacked tariffs; domestic merchants then distributed the products overland. To be effective, commercial regulation had to be national. Local sentiment had to give way to the unity of a national community.

The most controversial economic remedies were those designed to relieve the burden on debtors and ordinary taxpayers. In some areas, farmers called for laws permitting payment of taxes or debts in goods and commodities, a kind of institutionalized barter. More commonly, farmers and debtors pressed their state governments for legal tender laws, which would require creditors to accept at specified

CHRONOLOGY

1775   Lord Dunmore, royal governor of Virginia, appeals to slaves to support Britain.

1776   July: Declaration of Independence.

August: Battle of Long Island initiates retreat of Continental Army.

September: British land on Manhattan Island.

December: George Washington counterattacks at Trenton.

1777   Slavery abolished in Vermont.

September: British General William Howe captures Philadelphia.

October: British General John Burgoyne surrenders at Saratoga.

November: Continentals settle into winter quarters at Valley Forge.

December: France recognizes American independence.

1778   June: France enters the war.

June: Battle of Monmouth hastens British retreat to New York.

July: George Rogers Clark captures Kaskaskia.

December: British capture Savannah.

1779   Spain enters the war.

1780   February: British land at Charleston.

July: French land at Newport.

September: British General Charles Cornwallis invades North Carolina.

1781   February: Robert Morris appointed superintendent of finance.

March: Articles of Confederation ratified.

October: Cornwallis surrenders at Yorktown.

1782   Peace talks begin.

1783   March: Washington mediates issue of officer pensions.

September: Treaty of Paris signed.

November: British evacuate New York.

1784   Treaty of Fort Stanwix.

Postwar depression begins.

1785   Land Ordinance of 1785.

Treaty of Fort McIntosh.

1786   Jefferson's Bill for Establishing Religious Freedom.

Rhode Island currency law.

Shays's Rebellion.

---

rates of exchange a state's paper currency—regardless of its worth—for all debts public and private.

Understandably, creditors opposed such a plan. But farmers were strong enough to enact currency laws in seven states during the depression. For the most part, these were modest programs that worked rather well, caused little depreciation, and did not result in the problems feared by creditors. In most instances, the notes were loaned to farmers, who put up the value of their land as collateral.

SHAYS'S REBELLION

The combination of political uncertainty and economic instability developed into a crisis in a rural uprising of Massachusetts communities that shook the nation in 1786. Farmers in the western part of the state had been hit particularly hard during the depression, when country merchants pressed them to pay their debts in hard currency they didn't have. About a third of all male heads of household were sued for debt during the 1780s, and the county jails were filled with debtors who couldn't pay. Dozens of towns petitioned the state government for relief, but the legislature, dominated by urban and merchant interests, rejected legal tender and paper currency laws. During the spring and summer of 1786, farmers throughout the rural parts of the state mustered their community militia companies and closed the courts—precisely what they had done during the Revolution.

This uprising quickly became known as **Shays's Rebellion**, after Daniel Shays, one of the leaders of the "committee of the people" who had also been a leader in the

Shays's Rebellion An armed movement of debt-ridden farmers in western Massachusetts in the winter of 1786–1787. The rebellion created a crisis atmosphere.

6–6
Shays's Rebellion: Letters of Generals William Shepard and Benjamin Lincoln to Governor James Bodoin of Massachusetts (1787)

6–7
Divergent Reactions to Shays's Rebellion

Nationalists Group of leaders in the 1780s who spearheaded the drive to replace the Articles of Confederation with a stronger central government.

Revolution. Although the rebellion was most widespread in Massachusetts, similar disorders occurred in every other New England state except Rhode Island, where the farmers had already taken power. There were incidents outside New England as well.

The crisis ended in Massachusetts when a militia force raised in communities from the eastern part of the state marched west and crushed the Shaysites in January 1787 as they marched on the armory in Springfield. Fifteen of the leaders were subsequently sentenced to death; two were hanged before the remainder were pardoned, and several hundred farmers had to swear an oath of allegiance to the state. In fact, these men had wanted little more than temporary relief from their indebtedness, and rural discontent quickly disappeared once the depression began to lift in 1788.

The most important consequence of Shays's Rebellion was its effect on conservative **nationalists** unhappy with the distribution of power between the states and national government under the Articles of Confederation. The uprising "wrought prodigious changes in the minds of men respecting the powers of government," wrote the Secretary of War Henry Knox. "Everybody says they must be strengthened and that unless this shall be effected, there is no security for liberty and property." It was time, he declared, "to clip the wings of a mad democracy."

Conclusion

The Revolution was a tumultuous era, marked by violent conflict between Patriots and Loyalists, masters and slaves, settlers and Indian peoples. The advocates of independence emerged successful, largely because of their ability to pull together and to begin to define their national community. But fearful of the power of central authority, Americans created a relatively weak national government. By the mid-1780s, however, many nationalists were paraphrasing Washington's question of 1777: "What then is to become of this nation?" Most Americans would seek to answer that question by attempting to reform the national government and build a strong new national community.

Summary

The War for Independence The world's best-equipped and most disciplined army supported by a strong navy faced a newly formed, ill-trained, and poorly equipped American military. Still the war seesawed back and forth as fighting took place in the North, South, and West. A variety of military, geographic, diplomatic, and psychological factors contributed to the American victory.

The United States in Congress Assembled During and after the war for independence, the United States faced the task of creating a government while dealing with numerous crises. The Articles of Confederation created the first national government that successfully coped with paying for the war, diplomatic initiatives including the peace treaties with Britain and France, and issues over land.

Revolutionary Politics in the States Newly formed states established their own constitutions across a wide political spectrum. The broadened base of politics and concerns over the appropriate structure of government created a strong debate that led to important political and social reforms. Economic turmoil produced problems that led to political unrest, but also raised questions about the role of government.

REVIEW QUESTIONS

1. Assess the relative strengths of the Patriots and the Loyalists in the American Revolution.

2. What roles did Indian peoples and African Americans play in the Revolution?

3. Describe the structure of the Articles of Confederation. What were its strengths and weaknesses?

4. How did the Revolution affect politics within the states?

5. What were the issues in Shays's Rebellion? How do they help to illustrate the political conflict in the nation during the 1780s?

KEY TERMS

Articles of Confederation(p. 174)
Bill for Establishing Religious Freedom(p. 182)
Bill of Rights(p. 182)
Constitutional Convention(p. 183)
Continental Army(p. 165)
Continental Congress(p. 175)
Land Ordinance of 1785(p. 179)
Loyalists(p. 167)

Manumissions(p. 183)
Nationalists(p. 186)
Northwest Ordinance of 1787(p. 180)
Patriots(p. 165)
Shays's Rebellion(p. 185)
Tories(p. 167)
United States Constitution(p. 167)
Valley Forge(p. 164)

RECOMMENDED READING

Thomas Fleming, *Liberty! The American Revolution* (1997). This well-written account—derived from a public television series—includes wonderful contemporary images.

Merrill Jensen, *The New Nation: A History of the United States during the Confederation, 1781–1789* (1950). Still the standard work on the 1780s.

Max M. Mintz, *Seeds of Empire: The American Revolutionary Conquest of the Iroquois* (1999). The Revolution as a war for the control of Iroquois lands in upstate New York.

Charles Patrick Neimeyer, *America Goes to War: A Social History of the Continental Army* (1996). A detailed look at the men who fought and won the Revolution.

Mary Beth Norton, *Liberty's Daughters: The Revolutionary Experience of American Women, 1750–1800* (1980). A provocative and comprehensive history of women in the Revolutionary era.

John W. Pulis, *Moving On: Black Loyalists in the AfroAtlantic World* (1999). Essays on their military role, but especially on their communities in Canada, Great Britain, and Africa.

Ray Raphael, *A People's History of the American Revolution: How Common People Shaped the Fight for Independence* (2001). Demonstrates that the Revolution was much more fractious when viewed at the level of those who did the fighting and dying.

Charles Royster, *A Revolutionary People at War* (1979). A pathbreaking study of the Continental Army and popular attitudes toward it.

Here individuals of all nations are melted into a new race of men, whose labours and posterity will one day cause great changes in the world.

—Hector St. John Crevecour

Congress voting on the issue of independence.

8

THE UNITED STATES OF NORTH AMERICA
1786–1800

WHO WERE the Nationalists and what did they want?

GENERAL GEORGE WASHINGTON
Reviewing the Western army at Fort Cumberland, the 18th of October

WHAT WERE the most important accomplishments of Washington's presidency?

WHAT FACTORS led to the rise political parties in the 1790s?

WHAT ROLE did newspapers play in the political culture of post-Revolutionary America?

1786 | 1800

AMERICAN COMMUNITIES

Mingo Creek Settlers Refuse to Pay the Whiskey Tax

IT WAS A HOT JULY AFTERNOON IN 1794 WHEN THE FEDERAL MARSHAL and the tax collector arrived at the backcountry farm of William Miller in Mingo Creek, a community south of Pittsburgh. Like most of his neighbors, Miller had failed to pay the federal excise tax on his homemade whiskey still, and these authorities had come to serve him with a notice to appear in federal court in Philadelphia. "I felt myself mad with passion," said the farmer, knowing that the fine and the cost of the trip back east would ruin him. As the men argued, thirty or forty of Miller's neighbors suddenly appeared, armed with muskets and pitchforks. Members of the Mingo Creek Democratic Society, they had come to fight off this infringement on their liberty. There was an angry confrontation, and someone fired a gun into the air. No one was hit, and after a heated verbal confrontation, the two officials rode off. But the farmers were fuming and decided to make a "citizen's arrest" of the officials the next day.

At Mingo Creek, poverty was the outstanding fact of life. A third of the farm families owned no land but rented or simply squatted on the acres of others. The tax collector or "exciseman" was one of the great landlords of Mingo Creek, not only controlling most of the local wealth but monopolizing political office as well. Other landlords lived outside the community, the most powerful being President George Washington himself, who owned thousands of acres in the West, much of it in the vicinity of Mingo Creek. The president had evicted so many squatters from his land that local people considered him a grasping speculator. Washington returned the compliment by describing these frontier settlers as "a parcel of barbarians" who lived little better than "dogs or cats."

In the Ohio region farm families lived in miserable mud-floored log huts scattered along the creeks of the Monongahela Valley. But despite appearances, the farmers of Mingo Creek were bound together in networks of family and clan, work and barter, religion and politics. The militiamen had acted together in what they perceived to be the interests of their community.

As in all the other western territories, this was a violent place in a violent time. No-holds-barred fights at local taverns were common, and travelers remarked on the presence of one-eyed men, the victims of brutal gougings. Everyone knew of men or women lost in the continuing Indian wars. In 1782 militia companies from the area had taken their revenge by massacring ninety-six unresisting Christian Indians at Gnadenhutten, north of the Ohio River, hacking their bodies and bringing home their scalps as trophies. The new federal government had committed over 80 percent of its operating budget to defeating the Indians, but the failure of its campaigns had left backcountry families resentful.

It was to help pay the costs of these campaigns that Congress had placed the tax on whiskey in 1791. The tax applied to the owners of stills, whether they produced commercially or simply for family and neighbors. Corn was not worth the cost of shipping it East, but whiskey made from corn was another matter, and many a farm family depended on the income from their stills. Farmers throughout America protested that the excise ran counter to the principles of the Revolution. "Internal taxes upon consumption," declared the citizens of Mingo Creek, are "most dangerous to the civil rights of freemen, and must in the end destroy the liberties of every country in which they are introduced." Hugh Henry Brackenridge, editor of the Pittsburgh Gazette, argued for a tax on the "unsettled lands which all around us have been purchased by speculating men, who keep them up in large bodies and obstruct the population of the country." In other words, Congress should tax land speculators, like President Washington, instead of backcountry squatters.

Protest followed the course familiar from the Revolution. At first citizens gathered peacefully and petitioned their representatives, but when the tax collectors appeared, there was vigilante action. Faces blackened or covered with handkerchiefs, farmers tarred and feathered the tax men. Although the immediate issue was taxation, larger matters were at stake. The Mingo Creek Democratic Society was part of Thomas Jefferson's political movement that supported republicanism and the French Revolution, in opposition to the conservative principles of the Washington administration. The tax protesters made this linkage explicit when they raised banners proclaiming the French slogan of "Liberty, Equality, Fraternity" and then adding their own phrase, "and No Excise!" In North Carolina the rebels sang

Some chaps whom freedom's spirit warms
Are threatening hard to take up arms,
And headstrong in rebellion rise
'Fore they'll submit to that excise:
Their liberty they will maintain,
They fought for't, and they'll fight again.

But it was only in western Pennsylvania that the protests turned to riot. When the Mingo Creek militia went to arrest the tax collector, several of their number were killed in the confrontation. The tax collector and his family escaped from their house as it was consumed by a fire set by the farmers. In a community meeting afterward, the protesters resolved to attack and destroy Pittsburgh, where the wealthy and powerful local landlords resided. Terrified residents of the town saved the day by welcoming the rebels with free food and drink. "It cost me four barrels of whiskey that day," declared one man, but "I would rather spare that than a single quart of blood." Destruction was averted, but an angry farmer rode through the street waving a tomahawk and warning, "It is not the excise law only that must go down. A great deal more is to be done. I am but beginning yet."

Declaring the Whiskey Rebellion "the first ripe fruit" of the democratic sentiment sweeping the country, President George Washington organized a federal army of 13,000 men, larger than the one he had commanded during the Revolution, and ordered the occupation of western Pennsylvania. Federal soldiers dragged half-naked men from their beds and forced them into open pens, where they remained for days in the freezing rain. Authorities arrested twenty people, and a judge convicted two of

treason. The protest gradually died down. Washington pardoned the felons, sparing their lives.

Federal power had prevailed over the local community. In his Farewell Address to the nation the following year Washington warned of an excessive spirit of localism that "agitates the community with ill-founded jealousies and false alarms; kindles the animosity of one part against another; foments occasionally riot and insurrection." But resistance to the excise remained widespread, and no substantial revenue was ever collected from the tax on whiskey. More important, the whiskey rebels had raised some of the most important issues of the day: the power and authority of the new federal government, the relationship of the West to the rest of the nation, the nature of political dissent, and the meaning of the Revolution.

FORMING A NEW GOVERNMENT

Eight years before the **Whiskey Rebellion** a similar rural uprising, Shays's Rebellion (see Chapter 7), had solidified beliefs that the powers of the federal government must be increased lest the budding nation wither.

NATIONALIST SENTIMENT

Nationalists had long argued for a strengthened union of the states. In general, the nationalists were drawn from the elite circles of American life. "Although there are no nobles in America, there is a class of men denominated 'gentlemen,'" the French ambassador to America wrote home in 1786. "They are creditors, and therefore interested in strengthening the government, and watching over the execution of the law. The majority of them being merchants, it is for their interest to establish the credit of the United States in Europe on a solid foundation by the exact payment of debts, and to grant to Congress powers extensive enough to compel the people to contribute for this purpose." In addition to merchants, the ambassador identified others who leaned toward national government: former officers in the Continental Army whose experience with the Continental Congress had made them firm believers in a stronger central government, and conservatives who wanted to restrain what they considered the excessive democracy of the states.

The economic crisis that followed the Revolutionary War (see Chapter 7) provided the nationalists with their most important opportunity to organize. In March 1785, a group of men from Virginia and Maryland, including James Madison, George Mason, and George Washington, drafted an agreement to present to legislatures recommending uniform commercial regulations, duties, and currency laws. Early the next year, at Madison's urging, the Virginia legislature invited all the states to send representatives to a commercial conference to be held at Annapolis in the fall. Only five states sent strong nationalist delegates to the **Annapolis Convention** in September 1786. But this time, most Americans agreed that the Articles needed strengthening, especially in regard to commercial regulation and the generation of revenue. Early in 1787 the Confederation Congress cautiously endorsed the plan for a convention "for the sole and express purpose of revising the Articles of Confederation."

WHO WERE the Nationalists and what did they want?

Whiskey Rebellion Armed uprising in 1794 by farmers in western Pennsylvania who attempted to prevent the collection of the excise tax on whiskey.

Annapolis Convention Conference of state delegates at Annapolis, Maryland, that issued a call in September 1786 for a convention to meet at Philadelphia to consider fundamental changes.

George Washington presides over a session of the Constitutional Convention, meeting in Philadelphia's State House (now known as Independence Hall), in an engraving of 1799.

Free Library of Philadelphia

IMAGE KEY
for pages 188–189

a. The Articles of Confederation.
b. Congress voting on the issue of independence.
c. Phyllis Wheatley, an acclaimed African American poet.
d. The first Stars and Stripes, 1777.
e. The Bill of Rights–the first ten amendments to the U.S. Constitution.
f. A 1794 painting of President George Washington reviewing troops at Fort Cumberland.
g. John Adams in a framed painting by John Trumbull.
h. A 1792 cartoon from *Lady's Magazine* shows allegorical figure of "Columbia" receiving a petition for the "Rights of Woman."

THE CONSTITUTIONAL CONVENTION

Fifty-five men from twelve states assembled at the Pennsylvania State House in Philadelphia in late May 1787. Rhode Island, where radical localists held power (see Chapter 7), refused to send a delegation. A number of prominent men were missing. Thomas Jefferson and John Adams were serving as ambassadors in Europe, and crusty localist Patrick Henry declared that he "smelt a rat." But most of America's best-known leaders were present: George Washington, Benjamin Franklin, Alexander Hamilton, James Madison, George Mason, Robert Morris. Twenty-nine of them were college educated, thirty-four were lawyers, twenty-four had served in Congress, and twenty-one were veteran officers of the Revolution. At least nineteen owned slaves, and there were also land speculators and merchants. But there were no ordinary farmers or artisans present, and of course no women, African Americans, or Indians. The Constitution was framed by white men who represented America's social and economic elite.

On their first day of work, the delegates agreed to vote by states, as was the custom of Congress. They chose Washington to chair the meeting. James Madison, a young, conservative Virginian with a profound knowledge of history and political philosophy, took voluminous daily minutes of the entire convention. Madison and his fellow Virginians had arrived early and drafted what became known as the **Virginia Plan**. Presented by Governor Edmund Randolph of Virginia on May 29, it set the convention's agenda.

The authors of the Virginia Plan proposed scrapping the Articles of Confederation in favor of a "consolidated government" having the power to tax and to enforce its laws directly rather than through the states. "A spirit of locality," Madison declared, was destroying "the aggregate interests of the community," by which he meant the great community of the nation. The Virginia Plan would have reduced the states to little more than administrative districts. Representation in the bicameral national legislature was to be based on population districts, the members of the House of Representatives elected by popular vote, but senators chosen indirectly by state legislators so that they might be insulated from democratic pressure. The Senate would lead, controlling foreign affairs and the appointment of officials. An appointed chief executive and a national judiciary would together form a Council of Revision having the power to veto both national and state legislation.

The main opposition to these proposals came from the delegates from small states, who feared being swallowed up by the large ones. After two weeks of debate, William Paterson of New Jersey introduced an alternative, a set of "purely federal" principles known since as the **New Jersey Plan**. He proposed increasing the powers of the central government but retaining a single-house Congress in which the states were equally represented. After much debate, and a series of votes that split the convention down the middle, the delegates finally agreed to what has been called the **Great Compromise**: proportional representation in the House, representation by states in the Senate. The compromise allowed the creation of a strong national government while still providing an important role for the states.

Part of this agreement was a second, fundamental compromise that brought together the delegates from North and South. To boost their power in the new government, the Southern delegates wanted to include slaves in the population for the purpose of determining state proportional representation, but to exclude them when it came to apportioning taxes. Ultimately it was agreed that five slaves would be counted as equivalent to three freemen—the "three-fifths rule." Furthermore, the representatives of South Carolina and Georgia demanded protection for the slave trade, and after bitter debate the delegates included a provision preventing any federal restriction on the importation of slaves for twenty years. Another article legitimized the return of fugitive slaves from free states. The word "slave" was nowhere used in the text of the Constitution, but these provisions amounted to national guarantees for Southern slavery. Although many delegates were opposed to slavery, and regretted having to give in on this issue, they agreed with Madison, who wrote that "great as the evil is, a dismemberment of the union would be worse."

In the ensuing debate on the role of the branches of government the delegates favored a strong federal judiciary with the implicit power to declare acts of Congress unconstitutional. There was also considerable support for a president with veto power to check the legislature.

In early September, the delegates turned their rough draft of the Constitution over to a Committee of Style, which shaped it into an elegant and concise document providing the general principles and basic framework of government. The delegates voted their approval on September 17, 1787 and transmitted the document to Congress, agreeing that it would become operative after ratification by nine states. Despite some congressmen who were outraged that the convention had exceeded its charge of simply modifying the Articles of Confederation, Congress called for a special ratifying convention in each of the states.

6–9
Patrick Henry Speaks Against Ratification of the Constitution (1788)

7–2
William Maclay, "For the Independent Gazetteer" (1790)

6–8
The "Distracting Question" in Philadelphia (1787)

QUICK REVIEW

Central Government Under the Constitution

- More powerful than Congress under the Articles of Confederation.
- Establishment of strong single person executive.
- Establishment of the Supreme Court.
- Expanded economic powers for Congress.

Virginia Plan   Proposal calling for a national legislature in which the states would be represented according to population.

New Jersey Plan   Proposal of the New Jersey delegation for a strengthened national government in which all states would have an equal representation in a unicameral legislature.

Great Compromise   Plan proposed at the 1787 Constitutional Convention for creating a national bicameral legislature in which all states would be equally represented in the Senate and proportionally represented in the House.

MAP EXPLORATION

To explore an interactive version of this map, go to
http://www.prenhall.com/faraghertlc/map8.1

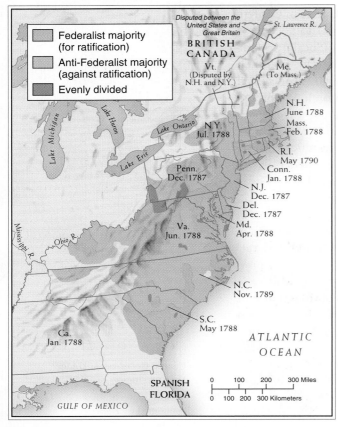

MAP 8-1

The Ratification of the Constitution, 1787–1790 The distribution of the vote for the ratification of the Constitution demonstrated its wide support in sections of the country linked to the commercial economy and its disapproval in more remote and backcountry sections. (Note that Maine remained a part of Massachusetts until admitted as a separate state in 1820.)

WHY DID some regions support the Constitution and others did not?

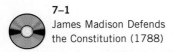

7–1
James Madison Defends the Constitution (1788)

Federalists Supporters of the Constitution who favored its ratification.

Anti-Federalists Opponents of the Constitution in the debate over its ratification.

RATIFYING THE NEW CONSTITUTION

The supporters of the new Constitution immediately adopted the name **Federalists** to describe themselves. In this, as in much of the subsequent process of ratification, the Federalists (or nationalists) grabbed the initiative, and their opponents had to content themselves with the label **Anti-Federalists**. The critics of the Constitution were by no means a unified group. Because most of them were localists, they represented a variety of social and regional interests. But most believed the Constitution granted far too much power to the central government, weakening the autonomy of communities and states. As local governments "will always possess a better representation of the feelings and interests of the people at large," one critic wrote, "it is obvious that these powers can be deposited with much greater safety with the state than the general government."

All the great political thinkers of the eighteenth century had argued that a republican form of government could work only for small countries. As French philosopher Montesquieu had observed, "In an extensive republic, the public good is sacrificed to a thousand private views." But in *The Federalist*, a brilliant series of essays in defense of the Constitution written in 1787 and 1788 by James Madison, Alexander Hamilton, and John Jay, Madison stood Montesquieu's assumption on its head. Rhode Island had demonstrated that the rights of property might not be protected in even the smallest of states. Asserting that "the most common and durable source of factions has been the various and unequal distribution of property," Madison concluded that the best way to control such factions was to "extend the sphere" of government. Rather than a disability, Madison argued, great size is an advantage: interests are so diverse that no single faction is able to gain control of the state, threatening the freedoms of others.

It is doubtful whether Madison's sophisticated argument, or the arguments of the Anti-Federalists for that matter, made much of a difference in the popular voting in the states to select delegates for the state ratification conventions. The alignment of forces generally followed the lines laid down during the fights over economic issues in the years since the Revolution. Agrarian-localist and commercial-cosmopolitan alignments characterized most of the states. The most critical convention took place in Massachusetts in early 1788. Five states—Delaware, Pennsylvania, New Jersey, Georgia, and Connecticut—had already voted to ratify, but the states with the strongest Anti-Federalist movements had yet to convene. If the Constitution lost in Massachusetts, its fate would be in great danger. At the convention, Massachusetts opponents of ratification enjoyed a small majority. But several important Anti-Federalist leaders, including Samuel Adams, were swayed by the enthusiastic support for the Constitution among Boston's townspeople, and on February 16 the convention voted narrowly in favor of ratification. To no one's surprise, Rhode Island rejected the Constitution in March, but Maryland and South Carolina approved it in April and May. On June 21 New Hampshire became the ninth state to ratify.

New York, Virginia, and North Carolina were left with the decision of whether to join the new Union. Anti-Federalist support was strong in each of these states. North Carolina voted to reject. (It did not join the Union until the next year, followed by a still reluctant Rhode Island in 1790.) In New York the delegates were moved to vote their support by a threat from New York City to secede from the state and join the Union separately if the state convention failed to ratify. The Virginia convention was almost evenly divided, but promises to amend the Constitution to protect the people from the potential abuses of the federal government persuaded enough delegates to produce a victory for the Constitution. The promise of a Bill of Rights was important in the ratification vote of five of the states.

THE BILL OF RIGHTS

Although the Bill of Rights—the first ten amendments to the Constitution—was adopted during the first session of the new federal Congress, it was first proposed during the debates over ratification. The various state ratification conventions had proposed a grab bag of over 200 potential amendments. Madison set about transforming these into a series of proposals that he introduced into the new Congress in June 1789. Congress passed twelve and sent them to the states, and ten survived the ratification process to become the Bill of Rights in 1791.

The First Amendment prohibits Congress from establishing an official religion and provides for the freedom of assembly. It also ensures freedom of speech, a free press, and the right of petition. The other amendments guarantee the right to bear arms, limit the government's power to quarter troops in private homes, and restrain the government from unreasonable searches or seizures; they assure the people their legal rights under the common law, including the prohibition of double jeopardy, the right not to be compelled to testify against oneself, and due process of law before life, liberty, or property can be taken away. Finally, the unenumerated rights of the people are protected, and the powers not delegated to the federal government are reserved to the states.

The first ten amendments to the Constitution have been a restraining influence on the growth of government power over American citizens. Their provisions have become an admired aspect of the American political tradition throughout the world. The Bill of Rights is the most important constitutional legacy of the Anti-Federalists.

QUICK REVIEW

Amendments to the Constitution

◆ First eight amendments concerned with individual rights.

◆ Guarantees of religious freedom, freedom of expression, protection against arbitrary legal proceedings.

◆ Powers not granted to the national government retained by the people and the states.

THE NEW NATION

Ratification of the Constitution was followed by the first federal elections— for the Congress and the presidency—and in the spring of 1789 the new federal government assumed power in the temporary capital of New York City. The inauguration of George Washington as the first president of the United States took place on April 30, 1789, on the balcony of Federal Hall, at the corner of Wall and Broad Streets. The first years under the new federal Constitution were especially important for the future, because they shaped the structure of the American nation-state in ways that would be enormously significant for later generations.

WHAT WERE the most important accomplishments of Washington's presidency?

THE WASHINGTON PRESIDENCY

Although he dressed in plain American broadcloth at his inauguration and claimed to be content with a plain republican title, Washington was counted among the nationalists. He was anything but a man of the people. By nature reserved and solemn, he chose to ride about town in a grand carriage drawn by six horses and

Two coins from the first decade of the federal republic illustrate political controversies of the period. The Washington cent was proposed by Treasury Secretary Alexander Hamilton in 1792 in the hope of enhancing popular respect for the new government by having the president's bust impressed on coins in the manner of European kings. But after long debate Congress defeated the plan, the opponents claiming it smacked of monarchy. The Liberty coin, issued by the Mint of the United States in 1795 when under the authority of Secretary of State Thomas Jefferson, features Liberty wearing a liberty cap and bearing a marked resemblance to the French Revolutionary icon Marianne.

Smithsonian Institution, NNC, Douglas Mudd

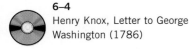
6–4
Henry Knox, Letter to George Washington (1786)

Judiciary Act of 1789   Act of Congress that implemented the judiciary clause of the Constitution by establishing the Supreme Court and a system of lower federal courts.

Judicial review   A power implied in the Constitution that gives federal courts the right to review and determine the constitutionality of acts passed by Congress and state legislatures.

escorted by uniformed liverymen. In the tradition of British royalty, he delivered his addresses personally to Congress and received from both houses an official reply. These customs were continued by John Adams, Washington's successor, but ended by Thomas Jefferson, who denounced them as "rags of royalty." On the other hand, Washington worked hard to adhere to the letter of the Constitution, refusing, for example, to use the veto power except where he thought the Congress had acted unconstitutionally, and personally seeking the "advice and consent" of the Senate.

Congress quickly moved to establish departments to run the executive affairs of state, and Washington soon appointed Thomas Jefferson his secretary of state, Alexander Hamilton to run the Treasury, Henry Knox the War Department, and Edmund Randolph the Justice Department, as attorney general. The president consulted each of these men regularly, and during his first term met with them as a group to discuss matters of policy. By the end of Washington's presidency the secretaries had coalesced in what came to be known as the cabinet, an institution that has survived to the present despite the absence of constitutional authority or enabling legislation. Washington was a powerful and commanding personality, but he understood the importance of national unity, and in his style of leadership, his consultations, and his appointments he sought to achieve a balance of conflicting political perspectives and sectional interests. These intentions would be sorely tested during the eight years of his administration.

AN ACTIVE FEDERAL JUDICIARY

The most important piece of legislation to emerge from the first session of Congress was the **Judiciary Act of 1789**, which implemented the judicial clause of the Constitution, which empowered Congress to determine the number of justices on the Supreme Court and create a system of federal courts. Congress established a high court of six justices (in 1869 this was increased to nine) and established three circuit and thirteen district courts. Strong nationalists argued for a powerful federal legal system that would provide a uniform code of civil and criminal justice throughout the country. But the localists in Congress fought successfully to retain the various bodies of law that had developed in the states. They wanted to preserve local community autonomy. The act gave federal courts limited original jurisdiction, restricting them mostly to appeals from state courts. But it thereby established the principle of federal **judicial review** of state legislation, despite the silence of the Constitution on this point.

Under the leadership of Chief Justice John Jay, the Supreme Court heard relatively few cases during its first decade. Still, it managed to raise considerable political controversy. In *Chisholm* v. *Georgia* (1793) it ruled in favor of two South Carolina residents who had sued the state of Georgia for the recovery of confiscated property. Thus did the Court overthrow the common law principle that a sovereignty could not be sued without its consent, and it supported the Constitution's grant of federal jurisdiction over disputes "between a state and citizens of another state." Many localists feared that this nationalist ruling threatened the integrity of the states. In response, they proposed the Eleventh Amendment to the Constitution, ratified in 1798, which declared that no state could be sued by citizens from another state.

HAMILTON'S CONTROVERSIAL FISCAL PROGRAM

Fiscal and economic affairs pressed upon the new government. Lacking revenues, and faced with the massive national debt contracted during the Revolution, the government took power in a condition of virtual bankruptcy. Congress passed the **Tariff of 1789**, a compromise between advocates of protective tariffs (with duties so high that they made foreign products prohibitively expensive, thus "protecting" American products) and those who wanted moderate tariffs that produced income for the federal government. Duties on imported goods, rather than direct taxes on property or incomes, would constitute the bulk of federal revenues until the twentieth century.

In 1790 Treasury Secretary Hamilton submitted a "Report on the Public Credit" in which he recommended that the federal government assume the obligations accumulated by the states during the previous fifteen years and redeem the national debt—owed to both domestic and foreign leaders—by agreeing to a new issue of interest-bearing bonds.

By this means, Hamilton sought to inspire the confidence of domestic and foreign investors in the public credit of the new nation. Congress endorsed his plan to pay off the $11 million owed to foreign creditors but balked at funding the domestic debt of $27 million and assuming the state debts of $25 million. Necessity had forced many individuals to sell off at deep discounts the notes, warrants, and securities the government had issued them during the Revolution. Yet Hamilton now advocated paying these obligations at face value, providing any speculator who held them with fabulous profits. An even greater debate took place over the assumption of the state debts, for some states, mostly those in the South, had already arranged to liquidate them, whereas others had left theirs unpaid. Congress remained deadlocked on these issues for six months, until congressmen from Pennsylvania and Virginia arranged a compromise.

Final agreement, however, was stalled by a sectional dispute over the location of the new national capital. Southerners supported Washington's desire to plant it on the Potomac River, but Northerners argued for Philadelphia. In return for Madison's pledge to obtain enough southern votes to pass Hamilton's debt assumption plan—which Madison had earlier opposed as a "radically immoral" windfall for speculators—Northern congressmen agreed to a location for the new federal district on the boundary of Virginia and Maryland. In July 1790, Congress passed legislation moving the temporary capital from New York to Philadelphia until the expected completion of the federal city in the District of Columbia in 1800. Two weeks later it adopted Hamilton's credit program. This was the first of many sectional compromises.

Hamilton now proposed the second component of his fiscal program, the establishment of a Bank of the United States. The bank, a public corporation funded by private capital, would serve as the depository of government funds and the fiscal agent of the Treasury. Congress narrowly approved it, but Madison's opposition

Tariff of 1789 Apart from a few selected industries, this first tariff passed by Congress was intended to raise revenue and not protect American manufacturers from foreign competition.

George Town and Federal City, or City of Washington, a colored aquatint of 1801 by T. Cartwright. When President John Adams first occupied the White House in 1800, Washington was still a small village, its streets merely muddy pathways.

Courtesy of The Library of Congress

7–3
Alexander Hamilton, Final Version of "An Opinion on the Constitutionality of an Act to Establish a Bank" (1791)

7–4
Questions Concerning the Constitutionality of the National Bank (1791)

raised doubts in the president's mind about the constitutionality of the measure, and Washington solicited the opinion of his cabinet. Here for the first time were articulated the classic interpretations of constitutional authority. Jefferson took a "strict constructionist" position, arguing that the powers of the federal government must be limited to those specifically enumerated in the Constitution. This position came closest to the basic agreement of the men who had drafted the document. Hamilton, on the other hand, reasoned that the Constitution "implied" the power to use whatever means were "necessary and proper" to carry out its enumerated powers—a loose constructionist position. Persuaded by Hamilton's opinion, Washington signed the bill, and the bank went into operation in 1791.

The final component of Hamilton's fiscal program, outlined in his famous "Report on Manufactures," was an ambitious plan, involving the use of government securities as investment capital for "infant industries," and high protective tariffs to encourage the development of an industrial economy. Many of Hamilton's specific proposals for increased tariff protection became part of a revision of duties that took place in 1792. Moreover, his fiscal program as a whole dramatically restored the financial health of the United States. Foreign investment in government securities increased and, along with domestic capital, provided the Bank of the United States with enormous reserves. Its bank notes became the most important circulating medium of the North American commercial economy, and their wide acceptance greatly stimulated business enterprise. "Our public credit," Washington declared toward the end of his first term, "stands on that ground which three years ago it would have been considered as a species of madness to have foretold."

THE BEGINNINGS OF FOREIGN POLICY

The Federalist political coalition, forged during the ratification of the Constitution, was sorely strained by these debates over fiscal policy. By the middle of 1792, Jefferson, representing the Southern agrarians, and Hamilton, speaking for Northern capitalists, were locked in a full-scale feud within the Washington administration. Hamilton conducted himself more like a prime minister than a cabinet secretary, greatly offending Jefferson, who considered himself the president's heir apparent. But the dispute went deeper than a mere conflict of personalities. Hamilton stated the difference clearly when he wrote that "one side appears to believe that there is a serious plot to overturn the State governments, and substitute a monarchy to the present republican system," while "the other side firmly believes that there is a serious plot to overturn the general government and elevate the separate powers of the States upon its ruins." The conflict between Hamilton and Jefferson was to grow even more bitter over the issue of American foreign policy.

The commanding event of the Atlantic world during the 1790s was the French Revolution, which had begun in 1789. Most Americans enthusiastically welcomed the fall of the French monarchy. After the people of Paris stormed the Bastille, Lafayette sent Washington the key to its doors as a symbol of the relationship between the two revolutions. But with the beginning of the Reign of Terror in 1793, which claimed upon the guillotine the lives of hundreds of aristocrats, American conservatives began to voice their opposition. The execution of King Louis XVI, and especially the onset of war between revolutionary France and monarchical Great Britain in 1793, firmly divided American opinion.

Most at issue was whether the Franco-American alliance of 1778 required the United States to support France in its war with Britain. All of Washington's cabinet agreed on the importance of American neutrality. With France and Britain prowling for each other's vessels on the high seas, the vast colonial trade of Europe was delivered up to neutral powers, the United States prominent among them. In other words, neutrality meant windfall profits. Jefferson believed it highly unlikely that the French would call upon the Americans to honor the 1778 treaty; the administration should simply wait and see. But Hamilton argued that so great was the danger of American involvement in the war that Washington should immediately declare the treaty "temporarily and provisionally suspended."

These disagreements revealed two contrasting perspectives on the course the United States should chart in international waters. Hamilton and the nationalists believed in the necessity of an accommodation with Great Britain, the most important trading partner of the United States and the world's greatest naval power. Jefferson, Madison, and the democrats,

QUICK REVIEW

Hamilton's Reports

◆ Plan to address Revolutionary War debt.

◆ Proposal to charter a national bank.

◆ Recommendation for government to promote industry.

7–5
Opposing Visions for the New Nation (1791)

MAP EXPLORATION

To explore an interactive version of this map, go to
http://www.prenhall.com/faraghertlc/map8.2

MAP 8-2
Spread of Settlement: The Backcountry Expands, 1770–1790   From 1770 to 1790 American settlement moved across the Appalachians for the first time. The Ohio Valley became the focus of bitter warfare between Indians and settlers.

WHY DID tensions between Indians and settlers increase during this period?

on the other hand, looked for more international independence, less connection with the British, and thus closer relations with Britain's traditional rival, France. They pinned their hopes on the future of American western expansion.

The debate in the United States grew hotter with the arrival in early 1793 of French ambassador Edmond Genêt. Large crowds of supporters greeted him throughout the nation, and among them he solicited contributions and distributed commissions authorizing American privateering raids against the British. Understandably, a majority of Americans still nursed a hatred of imperial Britain, and these people expressed a great deal of sympathy for republican France. Conservatives such as Hamilton, however, favored a continuation of traditional commercial relations with Britain and feared the antiaristocratic violence of the French. Washington sympathized with Hamilton's position, but most of all he wished to preserve American independence and neutrality. Knowing he must act before "Citizen" Genêt (as the ambassador was popularly known) compromised American sovereignty and involved the United States in a war with Britain, the president issued a proclamation of neutrality on April 22, 1793. In it he assured the world that the United States intended to pursue "a conduct friendly and impartial towards the belligerent powers," while continuing to do business with all sides.

Hamilton's supporters applauded the president, but Jefferson's friends were outraged. Throughout the country those sympathetic to France organized Democratic Societies, political clubs modeled after the Sons of Liberty. Society members corresponded with each other, campaigned on behalf of candidates, and lobbied with congressmen. People interpreted the international question in the light of issues of local importance. Thus, the members of the Mingo Creek Democratic Society used enthusiasm for the French Revolution as a way of organizing political opposition to the Washington administration. In a speech to Congress, President Washington denounced what he called these "self-created societies," declaring them "the most diabolical attempt to destroy the best fabric of human government and happiness."

Citizen Genêt miscalculated, however, alienating even his supporters, when he demanded that Washington call Congress into special session to debate neutrality. Jefferson, previously a confidant of the ambassador, now denounced Genêt as "hot-headed" and "indecent towards the President." But these words came too late to save his reputation in the eyes of Washington, and at the end of 1793 Jefferson left the administration. The continuing upheaval in France soon swept Genêt's party from power and he was recalled, but fearing the guillotine, he claimed sanctuary and remained in the United States. During his time in the limelight, however, he furthered the division of the Federalist coalition into a faction identifying with Washington, Hamilton, and conservative principles and a faction supporting Jefferson, Madison, democracy, and the French Revolution.

THE UNITED STATES AND THE INDIAN PEOPLES

Among the many problems of the Washington presidency, one of the most pressing concerned the West. The American attempt to treat the western tribes as conquered peoples after the Revolution had resulted only in further violence and warfare. In the Northwest Ordinance of 1787 (see Chapter 7), the Confederation Congress abandoned that premise for a new approach. "The utmost good faith shall always be observed towards the Indians," the Ordinance read. "Their lands and property shall never be taken from them without their consent." Yet the Ordinance was premised on the opening of Indian land north of the Ohio River to American settlement, its survey and sale, and the creation of new state governments. The Ordinance pointed in wildly contradictory directions.

Little Turtle, a war chief of the Miami tribe of the Ohio valley, led a large pan-Indian army to victory over the Americans in 1790 and 1791. After his forces were defeated at the Battle of Fallen Timbers in 1794, he became a friend of the United States. This lithograph is a copy of an oil portrait, which no longer survives, by the artist Gilbert Stuart.

Indiana Historical Society Library

    The Constitution was silent regarding Indian policy, but the new federal government continued to pursue this inconsistent policy. In 1790 Congress passed the **Intercourse Act**, the basic law by which the United States would "regulate trade and intercourse with the Indian tribes." To eliminate the abuses of unscrupulous traders, the act created a federal licensing system; subsequent legislation authorized the creation of subsidized trading houses, or "factories," where Indians could obtain goods at reasonable prices. Trade abuses continued unabated for lack of adequate policing power, but these provisions indicated the best intentions of the Washington administration.

    To clarify the question of Indian sovereignty, the act declared public treaties between the United States and the Indian nations to be the only legal means of obtaining Indian land. Treaty making, thus, became the procedure for establishing and maintaining relations. In the twentieth century, a number of Indian tribes have successfully appealed for the return of lands obtained by states or individuals in violation of this provision of the Intercourse Act.

    On the other hand, one of the federal government's highest priorities was the acquisition of western Indian land to supply a growing population of farmers. The federal government, in fact, was unable to control the flood of settlers coming down the Ohio River. An American expeditionary force was sent to evict the settlers, but inevitably they ended up fighting the Indians. In defense of their homelands, villages of Shawnees, Delawares, and other Indian peoples confederated with the Miamis under their war chief Little Turtle. In the fall of 1790 Little Turtle lured federal forces led by General

Intercourse Act Basic law passed by Congress in 1790 which stated that the United States would regulate trade and interaction with Indian tribes.

This portrait, sketched in about 1790 by John Trumbull, is the only known likeness of Alexander McGillivray, a Creek leader who effectively played off Spanish and American interests in the Southeast to gain a measure of independence for the Creeks in the 1780s.

Charles Allen Munn Collection, Fordham University Library, Bronx, N.Y.

Josiah Harmar into the confederacy's stronghold in Ohio and badly mauled them. In November 1791 the confederation inflicted an even more disastrous defeat on a large American force under General Arthur St. Clair, governor of the Northwest Territory. More than 900 Americans were killed or wounded, making this the worst defeat of an army by Indians in North American history.

In the aftermath of this defeat the House of Representatives launched the first formal investigation of the executive branch undertaken by the Congress. They found St. Clair's leadership "incompetent," and he soon resigned. Yet few Americans were willint to admit to the contradiction at the heart of American policy. "We acknowledge the Indians as brothers," yet we "seize their lands," Senator Benjamin Hawkins of North Carolina wrote to President Washington. "This doctrine it might be expected would be disliked by the independent Tribes. . . . It is the source of their hostility."

SPANISH FLORIDA AND BRITISH CANADA

The position of the United States in the West was made even more precarious by the hostility of Spain and Great Britain, who controlled the adjoining territories. Under the dynamic leadership of King Carlos III and his able ministers, Spain introduced liberal reforms to revitalize the rule-bound economy of its American empire; as a result the economy of New Spain grew rapidly in the 1780s. Moreover, Spain had reasserted itself in North America, acquiring the French claims to Louisiana before the end of the Seven Years' War, expanding into California, seizing the Gulf Coast during the American Revolution, and regaining Florida from Britain in the Treaty of Paris in 1783.

Spain's anti-American policy in the West had several facets. Controlling both sides of the lower Mississippi, they closed the river to American shipping, making it impossible for Western American farmers to market their crops through the port of New Orleans. They also sought to create a barrier to American settlement by promoting immigration to Louisiana and Florida. They succeeded in attracting several thousand of the Acadians whom the British had deported during the Seven Years' War. Reassembling their distinctive communities in the bayou country of Louisiana, these tough emigrants became known as the Cajuns. But otherwise the Spanish had little success with immigration and relied mostly on creating a barrier of pro-Spanish Indian nations in the lower Mississippi Valley. To consolidate these gains, in the early 1790s the Spanish constructed two new Mississippi River forts at sites that would later become the cities of Vicksburg and Memphis.

North of the Ohio River the situation was much the same. Thousands of Loyalists had fled the United States in the aftermath of the Revolution and settled in the country north of lakes Ontario and Erie. They were understandably hostile to the new republic. In 1791 the British Parliament passed the Canada Act, creating the province of Upper Canada (later renamed Ontario) and granting the Loyalists limited self-government. To protect this province, British troops remained at a number of posts within American territory at places such as Detroit, where they supplied the Indian nations with arms and ammunition, hoping to create a buffer to American expansion.

DOMESTIC AND INTERNATIONAL CRISES

Washington faced the gravest crisis of his presidency in 1794. In the West, the inability of the federal government to subdue the Indians, eliminate the British from the northern fur trade, or arrange with the Spanish for unencumbered use of the Mississippi River stirred frontiersmen to loud protests. There were rumblings of rebellion and secession from western communities. As the opening to this chapter illustrates, this discontent was strengthened by Hamilton's federal excise tax on whiskey, which hit backcountry farmers hardest. In the Old Northwest and Old Southwest, English and Spanish secret agents gave liberal bribes to entice American settlers to quit the Union and join themselves to Canada or Florida. In the Atlantic, Great Britain declared a blockade of France and seized vessels trading with the French West Indies. From 1793 to the beginning of 1794 the British confiscated the cargoes of more than 250 American ships, threatening hundreds of merchants with ruin. The United States was being "kicked, cuffed, and plundered all over the ocean," declared Madison, and in Congress he introduced legislation imposing retaliatory duties on British ships and merchandise.

The Whiskey Rebellion, which broke out in the summer of 1794, thus came at a time when President Washington considered the nation to be under siege. The combination of Indian attack, international intrigue, and domestic insurrection, he believed, created the greatest threat to the nation since the Revolution. In April the president had dispatched Chief Justice John Jay to London to arrange a settlement with the British. At the same time, war seemed increasingly likely, and Washington feared that any sign of federal weakness in the face of western rebellion would invite British or Spanish intervention. With Hamilton's urging he took the decisive course described in the opening of this chapter: he raised a large militia even as he pursued halfhearted negotiations with local authorities and made preparations to occupy the area around Pittsburgh, including Mingo Creek. It is clear now that the president overreacted, for although there were riots and violence in western Pennsylvania, there was no organized insurrection. Nevertheless, his mobilization of federal military power dramatically demonstrated the federal commitment to the preservation of the Union, the protection of the western boundary, and the supremacy of the national over the local community.

This action was reinforced by an impressive American victory against the Indian confederacy. Following the disastrous defeat of St. Clair by Little Turtle, Washington appointed General Anthony Wayne to lead a greatly strengthened American force to subdue the Indian confederacy and secure the Old Northwest. At the battle of Fallen Timbers, fought in the Maumee country of northern Ohio on August 20, 1794, Wayne crushed the Indians. Retreating, the warriors found the gates of Fort Miami closed and barred, the British inside unprepared to engage the powerful American force. The victory set the stage for the **Treaty of Greenville** in 1795, in which the representatives of twelve Indian nations ceded a huge territory encompassing most of present-day Ohio, much of Indiana, and other enclaves in the Northwest, including the town of Detroit and the tiny village of Chicago.

JAY'S AND PINCKNEY'S TREATIES

The strengthened American position in the West encouraged the British to settle their dispute with the United States so that they might concentrate on defeating republican France. In November 1794, Jay and the British signed an agreement providing for British withdrawal from American soil by 1796, limited American trade with the British East and West Indies, and "most-favored-nation" status for both countries (meaning that each nation would enjoy trade benefits equal to those the other accorded any other nation-state). The treaty represented a solid gain for the young republic. With only a small army and no navy to speak of, the United States was in no position to wage war.

Details of **Jay's Treaty** leaked out in a piecemeal fashion that inflamed public debate. The treaty represented a victory for Hamilton's conception of American neutrality. The Jeffersonians, on the other hand, were enraged over this accommodation with Great Britain at France's expense. The absence in the treaty of any mention of

7–7
Backcountry Turmoil Puts the New Government to the test (1794)

Treaty of Greenville Treaty of 1795 in which Native Americans in the Old Northwest were forced to cede most of the present state of Ohio to the United States.

Jay's Treaty Treaty with Britain negotiated in 1794 in which the United States made major concessions to avert a war over the British seizure of American ships.

MAP EXPLORATION

To explore an interactive version of this map, go to
http://www.prenhall.com/faraghertlc/map8.3

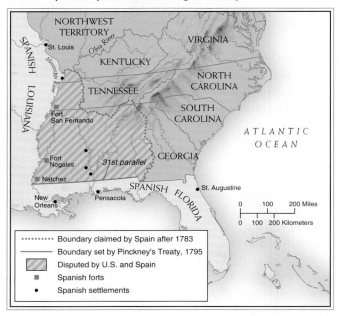

MAP 8-3

Spanish Claims to American Territory, 1783–1795 Before 1795 the Spanish claimed the American territory of the Old Southwest and barred Americans from access to the port of New Orleans, effectively closing the Mississippi River. This dispute was settled by Pinckney's Treaty in 1795.

WHAT WERE the terms of Pinckney's Treaty?

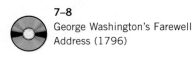

7–8
George Washington's Farewell Address (1796)

WHAT FACTORS led
to the rise of political parties in
the 1790s?

compensation for the slaves who had fled to the British side during the Revolution alienated Southerners. Throughout the country Democratic Societies and Jeffersonian partisans organized protests and demonstrations. Upon his return to the United States, Jay joked, he could find his way across the country by the light of his burning effigies. Despite these protests, the Senate, dominated by supporters of Hamilton, ratified the agreement in June 1795. In the House, a coalition of Southerners, Westerners, and friends of France attempted to stall the treaty by threatening to withhold the appropriations necessary for its implementation. They demanded that they be allowed to examine the diplomatic correspondence regarding the whole affair, but the president refused, establishing the precedent of "executive privilege" in matters of state.

The deadlock continued until late in the year, when word arrived in Philadelphia that the Spanish had abandoned their claims to the territory south of the Ohio River. Having declared war on revolutionary France, Spain had suffered a humiliating defeat. Fearing the loss of its American empire, the Spanish had suddenly found it expedient to mollify the quarrelsome Americans. In 1795 American envoy Thomas Pinckney negotiated a treaty in which Spain agreed to a boundary with the United States at the 31st parallel and opened the Mississippi to American shipping. This treaty fit the Jeffersonian conception of empire, and congressmen from the West and South were delighted with its terms. But administration supporters demanded their acquiescence in Jay's Treaty before the approval of Pinckney's Treaty.

These two important treaties finally established American sovereignty over the land west of the Appalachians and opened to American commerce a vast market extending from Atlantic ports to the Mississippi Valley. From a political standpoint, however, the events of 1794 and 1795 brought Washington down from his pedestal. Vilified by the opposition press, sick of politics, and longing to return to private life, Washington rejected the offer of a third term.

WASHINGTON'S FAREWELL ADDRESS

During the last months of his term, Washington published his Farewell Address to the nation. In it he argued not for American isolation, but rather for American disinterest in the affairs of Europe. "The great rule of conduct for us in regard to foreign nations is, in extending our commercial relations to have with them as little political connection as possible." Why, he asked "entangle our peace and prosperity in the toils of European ambition, rivalship, interest, humor, or caprice?" Thomas Jefferson, in his Inaugural Address of 1801, paraphrased this first principle of American foreign policy as "peace, commerce, and honest friendship with all nations, entangling alliances with none."

FEDERALISTS AND JEFFERSONIAN REPUBLICANS

The framers of the Constitution envisioned a one-party state in which partisan distinctions would be muted by patriotism and public virtue. "Among the numerous advantages promised by a well constructed Union," Madison had written in *The Federalist*, is "its tendency to break and control the violence of faction." Not only did he fail to anticipate the rise of political parties or factions, but he saw them as potentially harmful to the new nation. Despite the framers' intentions, in the twelve years between the ratification of the Constitution and the federal election of 1800 political parties became a fundamental part of the American system of government.

THE RISE OF POLITICAL PARTIES

Evident in the debates and votes of Congress from 1789 to 1795 was a series of shifting coalitions. These coalitions first began to polarize into political factions during the debate over Jay's Treaty in 1795, when agrarians, Westerners, Southerners, and supporters of France came together in opposition to the treaty. By the elections of 1796, people had begun to give names to the two factions. The supporters of Hamilton claimed the mantle of **Federalism**. Forced to find another term, the Jeffersonian opposition became known as the **Republicans**, meant to imply that the Federalists were really monarchists at heart. Hamilton insisted on labeling his opponents the Anti-Federalists, but historians often call this coalition the Jeffersonian Republicans.

These two political coalitions played a fitful role in the presidential election of 1796, which pitted John Adams, Washington's vice president, against Thomas Jefferson. Partisan organization was strongest in the Middle States, where there was a real contest of political forces, weakest in New England and the South, where sectional loyalty prevailed and organized opposition was weaker. The absence of party discipline was demonstrated when the ballots of the presidential electors, cast in their respective state capitals, were counted in the Senate. Adams was victorious, but the electors chose Jefferson rather than a Federalist for vice president. Thus, the new administration was born divided.

THE ADAMS PRESIDENCY

Adams was put in the difficult situation of facing a political opposition led by his own vice president. He nevertheless attempted to conduct his presidency along the lines laid down by Washington and retained most of the former president's appointees. This arrangement presented Adams with another problem. Although Hamilton had retired the year before, the cabinet remained committed to his advice, actively seeking his opinion and following it. As a result, Adams's authority was further undercut.

On the other hand, Adams benefited from the rising tensions between the United States and France. Angered by Jay's Treaty, the French suspended diplomatic relations at the end of 1796 and inaugurated a tough new policy toward American shipping. During the next two years they seized more than 300 American vessels and confiscated cargoes valued at an estimated $20 million. Hoping to resolve the crisis, Adams sent an American delegation to France. But in dispatches sent back to the United States the American envoys reported that agents of the French foreign ministry had demanded a bribe before any negotiations could be undertaken. Pressed for copies of these dispatches by suspicious Jeffersonian Republicans in Congress, in 1798 Adams released them after substituting the letters X, Y, and Z for the names of the French agents. The documents proved a major liability for the Jeffersonian Republicans, sparking powerful anti-French sentiment throughout the country. To the demand for a bribe, the American delegates had actually answered "Not a sixpence," but in the inflated rhetoric of the day the response became the infinitely more memorable: "Millions for defense, but not one cent for tribute!" The **XYZ Affair**, as it became known, sent Adams's popularity soaring.

QUICK REVIEW

Party Politics

◆ Washington's Farewell Address denounced partisanship.

◆ Candidates in presidential election of 1796: John Adams (Federalist), Thomas Jefferson (Republican).

◆ Adams won despite Hamilton's interference.

Federalism   The sharing of powers between the national government and the states.

Republicans   Party headed by Thomas Jefferson that formed in opposition to the financial and diplomatic policies of the Federalist party; favored limiting the powers of the national government and placing the interests of farmers over those of financial and commercial groups.

OVERVIEW

THE FIRST AMERICAN PARTY SYSTEM

Federalist Party	Organized by figures in the Washington administration who were in favor of a strong federal government, friendship with the British, and opposition to the French Revolution; its power base was among merchants, property owners, and urban workers tied to the commercial economy. A minority party after 1800, it was regionally strong only in New England.
Democratic Republican Party	Arose as the opposition to the Federalists; its adherents were in favor of limiting federal power; they were sympathetic to the French Revolution and hostile to Great Britain; the party drew strength from Southern planters and Northern farmers. The majority party after 1800.

Adams and the Federalists prepared the country for war during the spring of 1798. Congress authorized tripling the size of the army, and Washington came out of retirement to command the force. Fears of a French invasion declined after word arrived of the British naval victory over the French in August 1798 at Aboukir Bay in Egypt, but the "**Quasi-War**" between France and the United States continued.

THE ALIEN AND SEDITION ACTS

In the summer of 1798 the Federalist majority in Congress, with the acquiescence of President Adams, passed four acts severely limiting both freedom of speech and the freedom of the press and threatening the liberty of foreigners in the United States. Embodying the fear that immigrants, in the words of one Massachusetts Federalist, "contaminate the purity and simplicity of the American character" by introducing dangerous democratic and republican ideas, the Naturalization Act extended the period of residence required for citizenship from five to fourteen years. The Alien Act and the Alien Enemies Act authorized the president to order the imprisonment or deportation of suspected aliens during wartime. Finally, the Sedition Act provided heavy fines and imprisonment for anyone convicted of writing, publishing, or speaking anything of "a false, scandalous and malicious" nature against the government or any of its officers.

The Federalists intended these repressive laws as weapons to defeat the Jeffersonian Republicans. Led by Albert Gallatin, a Swiss immigrant and congressman from Pennsylvania (replacing Madison, who had retired from politics to devote his time to his plantation), the Jeffersonian Republicans contested all the Federalist war measures and acted as a genuine opposition party, complete with caucuses, floor leaders, and partisan discipline. For the first time, the two parties contested the election of Speaker of the House of Representatives, which became a partisan office. The more effective the Jeffersonian Republicans became, the more treasonous they appeared in the eyes of the Federalists. Disagreement with the administration was misconstrued by the Federalists as opposition to the state itself.

The Federalists thus pursued the prosecution of dissent, indicting leading Jeffersonian Republican newspaper editors and writers, fining and imprisoning at least twenty-five of them. The most vilified was Congressman Lyon, scorned by Federalists as "Ragged Matt the Democrat." Lyon was convicted in July 1798 of pub-

7–9
The Alien and Sedition Acts
(1798)

XYZ Affair   Diplomatic incident in 1798 in which Americans were outraged by the demand of the French for a bribe as a condition for negotiating with American diplomats.

Quasi-War   Undeclared naval war of 1797 to 1800 between the United States and France.

lishing libelous statements about President Adams and thrown into a Vermont prison. Later that year, however, he conducted a campaign from his cell and was reelected to Congress.

THE REVOLUTION OF 1800

The **Alien and Sedition Acts** were overthrown by the Jeffersonian Republican victory in the national elections of 1800. As the term of President Adams drew to a close, Federalists found themselves seriously divided. In 1799, by releasing seized American ships and requesting negotiations, the French convinced Adams that they were ready to settle their dispute with the United States. The president also sensed the public mood running toward peace. But the Hamiltonian wing of the party, always scornful of public sentiment, continued to beat the drums of war. When Federalists in Congress tried to block the president's attempt to negotiate, Adams threatened to resign and turn the government over to Vice President Jefferson. "The end of war is peace," Adams declared, "and peace was offered me." Adams considered the settlement of this conflict with France to be one of the greatest accomplishments of his career, but it earned him the scorn of conservative Federalists, including Hamilton.

The presidential campaign of 1800 was the first in which Jeffersonian Republicans and Federalists operated as two national political parties. Caucuses of congressmen nominated respective slates: Adams and Charles Cotesworth Pinckney of South Carolina for the Federalists, Jefferson and Aaron Burr of New York for the Jeffersonian Republicans. Both tickets thus represented attempts at sectional balance. The Jeffersonian Republicans presented themselves as the party of traditional agrarian purity, of liberty and **states' rights**, of "government rigorously frugal and simple," in the words of Jefferson. They were optimistic, convinced that they were riding the wave of the future. Divided and embittered, the Federalists waged a defensive struggle for strong central government and public order and often resorted to negative campaigning. They denounced Jefferson as an atheist, a Jacobin, and the father of mulatto children. (The first two charges were without foundation, but the last was apparently true, according to the results of recent DNA matching tests.)

The balloting for presidential electors took place between October and December 1800. Adams took all the New England states while Jefferson captured the South and West. Jefferson called it "the Revolution of 1800." Party discipline was so effective that one of the provisions of the Constitution was shown to be badly outmoded. By this clause, the candidate receiving a majority of electoral votes became president and the runner-up became vice president. But by casting all their ballots for Jefferson and Burr, Jeffersonian Republican electors unintentionally created a tie and forced the election into the House of Representatives. Because the new Jeffersonian Republican–controlled Congress would not convene until March 1801, the Federalist majority was given a last chance to decide the election. They attempted to make a deal with Burr, who refused but who also would not withdraw his name from consideration. Finally, on the thirty-fifth ballot the Federalists gave up and arranged with their opponents to elect Jefferson without any of them having to cast a single vote in his favor.

 7–10
Questions of Constitutionality and the Roots of Nullification (1798)

Alien and Sedition Acts Collective name given to four acts passed by Congress in 1798 that curtailed freedom of speech and the liberty of foreign residents in the United States.

States' rights Favoring the rights of individual states over rights claimed by the national government.

 MAP EXPLORATION
To explore an interactive version of this map, go to
http://www.prenhall.com/faraghertlc/map8.4

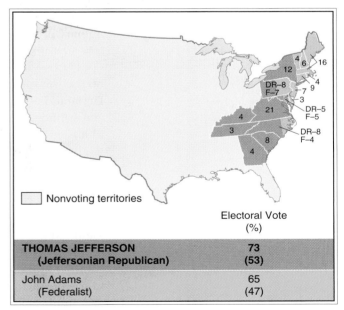

	Electoral Vote (%)
THOMAS JEFFERSON (Jeffersonian Republican)	**73** **(53)**
John Adams (Federalist)	65 (47)

MAP 8-4
The Election of 1800 In the presidential election of 1800, Democratic Republican victories in New York and the divided vote in Pennsylvania threw the election to Jefferson. The combination of the South and these crucial Middle States would keep the Democratic Republicans in control of the federal government for the next generation.

WHAT WERE the key issues in the election of 1800?

The presidential election of 1800 was the first to feature campaign advertising. "T. Jefferson, President of the United States of America; John Adams—no more," reads the streamer on this election banner, illustrated with an American eagle and a portrait of Jefferson. This was mild rhetoric in a campaign characterized by wild charges. The Republicans labeled Adams a warmonger and a monarchist, while the Federalists denounced Jefferson as an atheist, Jacobin, and sexual libertine.

The Granger Collection

QUICK REVIEW

Presidential Election of 1800

◆ Federalists could not overcome party disunity.

◆ First election in which Federalists and Republicans acted as national parties.

◆ Ticket of Jefferson and Burr an attempt at sectional balance.

8–6
A Matter of Honor or Vengeance? (1804)

Suffrage   The right to vote in a political election.

Congressman Matthew Lyon cast the symbolic final vote in a gesture of sweet revenge. The Twelfth Amendment, creating separate ballots for president and vice president, was ratified in time for the next presidential election.

DEMOCRATIC POLITICAL CULTURE

Accompanying the rise of partisan politics was a transformation in popular political participation. Consider the custom of celebrating Independence Day. At the beginning of the 1790s, in many communities, the day featured demonstrations of military prowess by veteran officers, followed by banquets for leaders. Relatively few Americans played a direct role. But during the political controversies of the decade a tradition of popular celebration developed. People took to the streets, set off fireworks, erected liberty poles, and listened to readings of the preamble of the Declaration of Independence, which more than any other document encapsulated and symbolized republican ideology. The first of these celebrations took place in Philadelphia, then other large cities, and eventually spread throughout the country. By 1800 the Fourth of July had become the nation's most important holiday.

There was a corresponding increase in the **suffrage**. In 1789 state regulations limited the franchise to a small percentage of the adult population. Women, African Americans, and Indians could not vote, but neither could a third to a half of all free adult males, who were excluded by tax-paying or property-owning requirements. Moreover, even among the eligible, the turnout was generally low. The traditional manner of voting was *viva voce*, by voice. At the polling place in each community individuals announced their selections aloud to the clerk of elections, who wrote them down. Not surprisingly, this system allowed wealthy men, landlords, and employers of the community to pressure poorer voters.

These practices changed with the increasing competition between Jeffersonian Republicans and Federalists. Popular pressure resulted in the introduction of universal white manhood suffrage in four states by 1800 and the reduction of property requirements in others. Thus was inaugurated a movement that would sweep the nation over the next quarter century. As a consequence voter turnout increased in all the states. The growth of popular interest in politics was a transformation as important as the peaceful transition from Federalists to Jeffersonian Republicans in national government.

"THE RISING GLORY OF AMERICA"

I n 1771, Philip Freneau and Hugh Henry Brackenridge addressed their graduating class at Princeton on "The Rising Glory of America." Thus far American contributions to learning and the arts had been slim, they admitted, but they were boundlessly optimistic about the potential of their country. Indeed, judged against the literary and artistic work of individuals in the colonial period, artists and others of the Revolutionary generation accomplished a great deal in their effort to build a national culture.

THE LIBERTY OF THE PRESS

At the beginning of the Revolution in 1775 there were thirty-seven weekly or semiweekly newspapers in the thirteen colonies, only seven of which were Loyalist in sentiment. By 1789 the number of papers in the United States had grown to ninety-two, including eight dailies; three papers were being published west of the Appalachians. Relative to population, there were more newspapers in the United States than in any other country in the world—a reflection of the remarkably high literacy rate of the American people (see Chapter 5). In New England almost 90 percent of the population could read, and even on the frontier, where Brackenridge edited the *Pittsburgh Gazette*, about two-thirds of the males were literate. During the political controversy of the 1790s, the press became the principal medium of Federalist and Jeffersonian Republican opinion, and papers came to be identified by their politics.

The prosecutions under the Sedition Act, however, threatened to curb the further development of the media, and in their opposition to these measures Jeffersonian Republicans played an important role in establishing the principle of a free press. In *An Essay on Liberty of the Press* (1799), the Virginia lawyer George Hay, later appointed to the federal bench by President Jefferson, wrote that "a man may say everything which his passions suggest." Were this not true, he argued, the First Amendment would have been "the grossest absurdity that was ever conceived by the human mind." In his first Inaugural Address, Jefferson echoed this early champion of the freedom of expression. "Error of opinion may be tolerated," he declared, "where reason is left free to combat it."

THE BIRTH OF AMERICAN LITERATURE

The literature of the Revolution understandably reflected the dominating political concerns of the times. The majority of "bestsellers" during the Revolutionary era were political. The most important were Thomas Paine's *Common Sense* (1776) and his series of stirring pamphlets, published under the running title *The American Crisis* (1776–1783), the first of which began with the memorable phrase "These are the times that try men's souls."

During the post-Revolutionary years there was an enormous outpouring of American publications. In the cities the number of bookstores grew in response to the demand for reading matter. Perhaps even more significant was the appearance in the countryside of numerous book peddlers who supplied farm households with Bibles, gazettes, almanacs, sermons, and political pamphlets.

WHAT ROLE did newspapers play in the political culture of post-Revolutionary America?

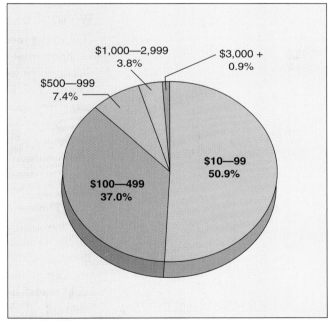

Housing Values, 1798

In 1798 Congress enacted a direct tax on buildings, resulting in an inventory of American housing that has never been equaled. The data revealed an enormous gap between rich and poor. The majority lived in squalid cabins valued at $99 or less, while the wealthiest 10 percent of Americans lived in dwellings that, taken together, were worth just over half the total value of all the nation's houses.

Lee Soltow, "Egalitarian America and Its Inegalitarian Housing in the Federal Period," *Social Science History* 9 (1985): 199–213.

Pages from Noah Webster's famous *American Spelling Book,* the largest seller of all American books during the nineteenth century. Believing that "the King's English" reflected aristocratic standards, Webster argued for spelling reform to create "the American language."

Courtesy of American Antiquarian Society

QUICK REVIEW

The Press

◆ By 1789 the United States had ninety-two newspapers.

◆ The press played a key role in the politics of the 1790s.

◆ Prosecutions under the Sedition Act threatened to curb further development of a free press.

Some of the most interesting American books of the postwar years examined the developing American character and proposed that the American, a product of many cultures, was a "new man" with ideas new to the world. John Filson, the author of the *Discovery, Settlement, and Present State of Kentucke* (1784), presented the narrative of one such new man, the Kentucky pioneer Daniel Boone. In doing so, he took an important step toward the creation of that most American of literary genres, the western.

Mason Locke Weems, a man trained as a doctor and ordained an Anglican minister, gave up both these careers in 1790 for bookselling and writing. Parson Weems, as he was known, wrote a short biography of the first president. "Washington, you know, is gone!" he wrote to his publisher. "Millions are gaping to read something about him. I am very nearly primed and cocked for 'em." His *Life of Washington* (1800, enlarged edition 1806) became the most popular history of the Revolution and introduced a series of popular and completely fabricated anecdotes, including the story of young George Washington and the cherry tree. The book was a pioneering effort in mass culture, and Weems, as one historian puts it, was "the father of the Father of his Country."

WOMEN ON THE INTELLECTUAL SCENE

One of the most interesting literary trends of the 1790s was the growing demand for books that appealed to women readers. Although women's literacy rates continued to be lower than men's, they rose steadily as girls joined boys in common schools. This increase was one of the most important social legacies of the democratic struggles of the Revolutionary era.

Some writers argued that the new republican order ought to provide new roles for women as well as for men. The first avowed feminist in American history was Judith Sargent Murray, who publicly stated her belief that women "should be taught to depend on their own efforts, for the procurement of an establishment in life." She was greatly influenced by the English feminist Mary Wollstonecraft.

There seemed to be general agreement among all parties, however, that the time had come for better educated and better informed women. Republican institutions of self-government were widely thought to depend on the wisdom and self-discipline of the American people. Civic virtue, so indispensable for the republic, must be taught at home. Thus were women provided the opportunity to be not simply "helpmates," but people "learned and wise." But they were also expected to be content with a narrow role, not to wish for fuller participation in American democracy.

CONCLUSION

In 1800, the population of Canada numbered about 500,000. Those of European background in New Mexico and the other Spanish North American colonies numbered approximately 25,000. And the Indian people of the continent numbered anywhere from 500,000 to a million. Overwhelming all these

CHRONOLOGY

1786	Annapolis Convention.
1787	Constitutional Convention.
1787–1788	*The Federalist* published.
1788	Constitution ratified. First federal elections.
1789	President George Washington inaugurated in New York City.
	Judiciary Act.
	French Revolution begins.
1790	Agreement on site on the Potomac River for the nation's capital.
	Indian Intercourse Act.
	Judith Sargent Murray publishes "On the Equality of the Sexes."
1791	Bill of Rights ratified.
	Bank of the United States chartered.
	Alexander Hamilton's "Report on Manufactures."
	Ohio Indians defeat General Arthur St. Clair's army.
1793	England and France at war; America reaps trade windfall.
	Citizen Genêt affair.
	President Washington proclaims American neutrality in Europe.
	British confiscate American vessels.
	Supreme Court asserts itself as final authority in *Chisholm* v. *Georgia*.
1794	Whiskey Rebellion.
	Battle of Fallen Timbers.
	Jay's Treaty with the British concluded.
1795	Pinckney's Treaty negotiated with the Spanish.
	Treaty of Greenville.
	Thomas Paine publishes *The Age of Reason.*
1796	President Washington's Farewell Address.
	John Adams elected president.
1797–1798	French seize American ships.
1798	XYZ Affair.
	"Quasi-war" with France.
	Alien and Sedition Acts.
	Kentucky and Virginia Resolves.
1799	Fries's Rebellion.
1800	Convention of 1800.
	Thomas Jefferson elected president.
	Mason Locke Weems publishes *Life of Washington.*

groups was the population of the United States, which stood at 5.3 million and was growing at the astounding annual rate of 3 percent.

During the last years of the eighteenth century the United States had adopted a new constitution and established a new national government. It had largely repaid the debt run up during the Revolution and made peace with adversaries abroad and Indian peoples at home. Americans had begun to learn how to channel their disagreements into political struggle. The nation had withstood a first decade of stress, but tensions continued to divide the people. As some of the rebel supporters had promised at the beginning of the Whiskey Rebellion, "their liberty they will maintain, / They fought for't, and they'll fight again." At the beginning of the new century it remained uncertain whether the new nation would find a way to control and channel the energies of an expanding people.

SUMMARY

Forming a New Government Rising nationalist sentiment fostered a movement for a new constitution. The resulting convention transformed the political structure of the nation. The strength of the new government was countered by constitutional guarantees of certain rights.

The New Nation The new government faced the task of establishing its role and organization under the leadership of George Washington. Legislation and plans set the course of the new nation. The government also instituted a policy on Indian relations and swiftly dealt with domestic and international crises.

Federalists and Jeffersonian Democrats Political differences stimulated the creation of political parties. A variety of issues and conflicting responses to the French Revolution led to questionable practices by the Federalists led by President John Adams. The election of 1800 was a revolution because it produced a peaceful transfer of power. During this period, a vibrant democratic political culture emerged.

"The Rising Glory of America" The 1790s witnessed the rise of an American culture. American artists achieved recognition while architecture reflected growing nationalism. High literacy rates contributed to the expansion of the press and a distinctive American literature in which women played a role.

REVIEW QUESTIONS

1. Discuss the conflicting ideals of local and national authority in the debate over the Constitution.

2. What were the major crises faced by the Washington and Adams administrations?

3. Describe the roles of Madison and Hamilton in the formation of the first American political parties.

4. What did Jefferson mean when he talked of "the Revolution of 1800"?

5. Discuss the contributions of the Revolutionary generation to the construction of a national culture.

KEY TERMS

Alien and Sedition Acts (p. 207)
Annapolis Convention (p. 191)
Anti-Federalists (p. 194)
Federalism (p. 205)
Federalists (p. 194)
Great Compromise (p. 193)
Intercourse Act (p. 201)
Jay's Treaty (p. 203)
Judicial review (p. 196)
Judiciary Act of 1789 (p. 196)

New Jersey Plan (p. 206)
Quasi-War (p. 193)
Republicans (p. 206)
States' rights (p. 205)
Suffrage (p. 207)
Tariff of 1789 (p. 208)
Treaty of Greenville (p. 197)
Virginia Plan (p. 203)
Whiskey Rebellion (p. 193)
XYZ Affair (p. 191)

RECOMMENDED READING

Akhil Reed Amar, *The Bill of Rights: Creation and Reconstruction* (1998). A legal analysis arguing that the first ten Amendments were meant to protect the majority from the potential tyranny of the federal government.

William N. Chambers, *Political Parties in a New Nation: The American Experience, 1776–1809* (1963). An introduction to the formation of the American party system. Though several decades old, it remains essential.

Stanley Elkins and Eric McKitrick, *The Age of Federalism* (1993). A massive and informative account of the politics of the 1790s, from the ratification of the Constitution to the election of Jefferson.

Joanne B. Freeman, *Affairs of Honor: National Politics in the New Republic* (2001). A major reassessment of political culture in the new republic, stressing the importance of the culture of honor.

Reginald Horsman, *The Frontier in the Formative Years, 1783–1815* (1970). A sensitive survey of developments in the West, emphasizing that the "western question" was one of the most important facing the young republic.

Jackson Turner Main, *The Antifederalists: Critics of the Constitution, 1781–1788* (1961). A detailed examination of the localist tradition in early American politics. Includes a discussion of the ratification of the Constitution from the point of view of its opponents.

Simon P. Newman, *Parades and the Politics of the Street: Festive Culture in the Early American Republic* (1997). The participation of ordinary Americans in the political culture of the new republic.

Willard Sterne Randall, *George Washington: A Life* (1997). The best one-volume biography of "the Father of his Country."

Thomas P. Slaughter, *The Whiskey Rebellion: Frontier Epilogue to the American Revolution* (1986). A detailed history of the rebellion in western Pennsylvania during the 1790s. Includes a thorough examination of the politics and culture of both the (Jeffersonian) backcountry and the federal government at a moment of crisis.

James M. Smith, *Freedom's Fetters: The Alien and Sedition Laws and American Civil Liberties* (1966). Remains the best overview of the Federalist threat to liberty, as well as the Democratic Republican (Jeffersonian) counterattack.

Bernard A. Weisberger, *American Afire: Jefferson, Adams, and the Revolutionary Election of 1800* (2000). Shows that the election and the transfer of power were victories for popular self-government and that they set a major precedent for all other elections.

Gordon Wood, *The Creation of the American Republic, 1776–1787* (1969). This general survey provides the best overview of the Constitutional Convention.

Since I started this letter we have been in a state of continual alarm, and now I have time to write only two or three lines to ask you to tell Papa that we are alive, in good health, and I hope safe from danger . . .

—Rosalie E. Calvert–August 30, 1814

"**Burning of the White House**" by Leslie Saalburg.

9

AN AGRARIAN REPUBLIC
1790–1824

WITH WHAT powers did the United States share North America in the decades after independence?

WHAT WERE the most important strengths of the American economy in the early 1800s?

WHAT VALUES were embodied in agrarian republicanism?

VENERATE THE PLOUGH

WHAT FACTORS led to conflict between the United States and Britain in North America?

WHAT WERE the consequences of the War of 1812?

WHAT WERE the principle provisions of the Missouri Compromise?

AMERICAN COMMUNITIES

Expansion Touches Mandan Villages on the Upper Missouri

IN MID-OCTOBER 1804, NEWS ARRIVED AT THE MANDAN VILLAGES, *prominently situated on bluffs overlooking the upper Missouri River, that an American expedition led by Meriwether Lewis and William Clark was coming up the river. The principal chiefs, hoping for expanded trade and support against their enemies the Sioux, welcomed these first American visitors. As the expedition's three boats and forty-three men approached the village, Clark wrote, "great numbers on both sides flocked down to the bank to view us." That evening the Mandans welcomed the Americans with an enthusiastic dance and gifts of food.*

Since the fourteenth century, when they had migrated from the East, the Mandans had lived along the Missouri, on the edge of the Great Plains in what is now North Dakota. They believed their homeland was "the very center of the world," and indeed it is in the heart of the North American continent. Mandan men hunted buffalo and Mandan women kept storage pits full with abundant crops of corn, beans, squash, sunflowers, and tobacco grown on the fertile soil of the river bottomlands. The Mandan villages were also the central marketplace of the northern Plains; at trading time in late summer they filled with Crows, Assiniboins, Cheyennes, Kiowas, and Arapahoes. Well before any of these people, or those of other tribes, had met a European, they were trading in kettles, knives, and guns acquired vicariously from the French and English to the east and leatherwork, glassware, and horses acquired from the Spanish in the Southwest.

Mandan Villages

The eighteenth century had been a golden age for the Mandan, who with their closely related Hidatsa neighbors numbered about 3,000 in 1804. In each of their five villages, earth lodges surrounded a central plaza. One large ceremonial lodge was used for community gatherings, and each of the other earth lodges was home to a senior woman, her husband, her sisters (perhaps married to the same man as she, for the Mandans practiced polygamy), their daughters and their unmarried sons, along with numerous grandchildren. Matrilineal clans, the principal institution of the community, distributed food to the sick, adopted orphans, cared for the dependent elderly, and punished wrongdoers. A village council of male clan leaders selected chiefs who led by consensus and lost power when people no longer accepted their opinions.

Lewis and Clark had been sent by President Thomas Jefferson to survey the Louisiana Purchase and to find an overland route to the Pacific Ocean. They were also instructed to inform the Indians that they now owed loyalty—and trade—to the American government, thereby challenging British economic control over the lucrative North American fur trade. Meeting with the village chiefs, the Americans offered the Mandans a military

and economic alliance. His people would like nothing better, responded Chief Black Cat, for the Mandans had fallen on hard times over the past decade. [Some twenty years earlier], "the smallpox destroyed the greater part of the nation," the chief said. "All the nations before this malady [were] afraid of them, [but] after they were reduced, the Sioux and other Indians waged war, and killed a great many." Black Cat was skeptical that the Americans would deter the Sioux, but Clark reassured him. "We were ready to protect them," Clark reported in his journal, "and kill those who would not listen to our good talk."

The Americans spent the winter with the Mandans, joining in their communal life and establishing firm and friendly relations with them. There were dances and joint hunting parties, frequent visits to the earth lodges, long talks around the fire, and, for many of the men, pleasant nights in the company of Mandan women. Lewis and Clark spent many hours acquiring important geographic information from the Mandans, who drew charts and maps showing the course of the Missouri, the ranges of the Rocky Mountains, and places where one could cross the Continental Divide. The information provided by the Mandans and other Indian peoples to the west was vital to the success of the expedition. Lewis and Clark's "voyage of discovery" depended largely on the willingness of Indian peoples to share their knowledge of the land with the Americans.

Also in need of interpreters who could help them communicate with other Indian communities on their way, the Americans hired several multilingual Frenchmen who lived with the Mandans. They also acquired the services of Sacajawea, the fifteen-year-old Lemhi wife of one of the Frenchmen, who became the only woman to join the westward journey. The presence of Sacajawea and her baby son was a signal, as Clark noted, to "all the Indians as to our friendly intentions"; everyone knew that women and children did not go on war parties.

When the party left the Mandan villages in March, Clark wrote, his men were "generally healthy, except venereal complaints which is very common amongst the natives and the men catch it from them." After an arduous journey across the Rockies, the party reached the Pacific Ocean at the mouth of the Columbia River, where they spent the winter. Overdue and feared lost, they returned in triumph to St. Louis in September 1806. Before long the Americans had established Fort Clark at the Mandan villages, giving American traders a base for challenging British dominance of the western fur trade. The permanent American presence brought increased contact, and with it much more disease. In 1837 a terrible smallpox epidemic carried away the vast majority of the Mandans, reducing the population to fewer than 150. Four Bears, a Mandan chief who had been a child at the time of the Lewis and Clark visit, spoke these last words to the remnants of his people:

"I have loved the whites," he declared. "I have lived with them ever since I was a boy." But in return for the kindness of the Mandans, the Americans had brought this plague. "I do not fear death, my friends," he said, "but to die with my face rotten, that even the wolves will shrink with horror at seeing me, and say to themselves, that is Four Bears, the friend of the whites." "They have deceived me," he pronounced with his last breath. "Those that I always considered as brothers turned out to be my worst enemies."

In sending Lewis and Clark on their "voyage of discovery" to claim the land and the loyalty of the Mandans and other western Indian communities, President Jefferson was motivated by his vision of an expanding American republic of self-sufficient farmers. During his and succeeding presidencies, expansion became a key element of national policy and pride. Yet, as the experience of the Mandans showed, what Jefferson viewed as enlargement of "the empire for liberty" had a dark side—the destruction, from disease and coerced displacement, of the communities created by America's first peoples. The effects—economic, political, and social—of continental expansion dominate the history of American communities in the first half of the nineteenth century.

North American Communities From Coast to Coast

At first glance, the United States of America in 1800 was little different from the scattered colonies of the pre-Revolution era. Two-thirds of the young nation's people still lived in a long thin line of settlement within fifty miles of the Atlantic coast. From New Hampshire to Georgia, most people lived on farms or in small towns. Because they rarely traveled far from home, people's horizons were limited and local. Nevertheless, the new nation was already transforming itself: between 1790 and 1800, according to the first and second federal censuses, the American population grew from 3.9 million to 5.3 million. Growth by migration was greatest in the trans-Appalachian West, a region that was already home to approximately 100,000 Indians. From 1800 to 1850, in an extraordinary burst of territorial expansion, Americans surged westward all the way to the Pacific. In 1800 few people would have predicted that within fifty years the nation would encompass the entire continent. Then the United States of America was a new and weak nation sharing a continent with many of the world's great powers.

SPANISH COLONIES

On paper, Spain possessed most of North America, but its control crumbled rapidly in the 1790s, affecting New Spain, the richest colony in Spanish America. Mexico City, with a population of 200,000, was by far the largest and most elegant city on the continent, but there were smoldering problems. Tensions mounted between the Spanish-born *peninsulares,* high officials and bureaucrats, and the native-born *criollos* of Spanish descent, who chafed at their subordination, especially after the success of the American Revolution. In the 1790s there were two abortive criollo conspiracies on behalf of independence in Mexico City alone. Furthermore, none of New Spain's northern provinces, created to protect the approaches to Mexico's fabulously wealthy silver mines, thrived. In all of the older settlements—San Antonio, Santa Fe, and Tucson—only a handful of persons of Spanish descent lived among a preponderantly native population. This was true even in the northern province, Alta (Upper) California, founded in 1769.

The exception was New Orleans, acquired from France at the end of the Seven Years' War in 1763. New Orleans was becoming a thriving international port. In 1801,

WITH WHAT powers did the United States share North America in the decades after independence?

IMAGE KEY
for pages 214–215

a. Thomas Jefferson (1743-1826), by Rembrandt Peale, c. 1805.
b. "Burning of the White House" by Leslie Saalburg.
c. A map of the Erie Canal.
d. An antique wooden compass used by Lewis and Clark.
e. The clipper ship *Flying Cloud*, which sailed in 1894 from New York to San Francisco in 89 days.
f. A symbol of the Philadelphia Society for Promoting Agriculture.
g. An 1833 portrait of two Sauk Indians by John Wesley Jarvis.
h. The Battle of Lake Erie in the War of 1812.
i. James Monroe and Robert R. Livingstone negotiations with Comte Talleyrand for the Louisiana Purchase.

MAP EXPLORATION

To explore an interactive version of this map, go to **http://www.prenhall.com/faraghertlc/map9.1**

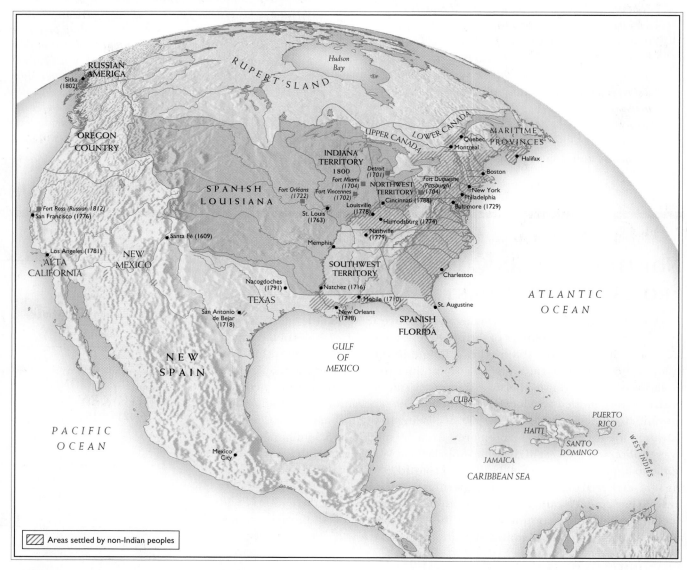

Areas settled by non-Indian peoples

MAP 9-1

America in 1800   In 1800, the new United States of America was surrounded by territories held by the European powers: British Canada, French Louisiana (secretly ceded that year to France by Spain), Spanish Florida, Spanish Mexico, and Russian Alaska expanding southward along the Pacific coast. Few people could have imagined that by 1850 the United States would span the continent. But the American settlers who had crossed the Appalachians to the Ohio River valley were already convinced that opportunity lay in the West.

WHAT MOTIVATED American settlers to move to the West?

IT shipped more than $3 million worth of tobacco, sugar, rice, cotton, fruits, and vegetables to Europe. Every year, a greater proportion of products for the New Orleans trade was supplied by Americans living some distance up the Mississippi River. Americans were uncomfortably aware that the city's crucial location at the mouth of the Mississippi meant that whatever foreign nation possessed New Orleans had the power to choke off the flourishing trade in the vast Mississippi Valley river system.

The Caribbean posed other challenges. The rich sugar-producing islands, variously colonies of Spain (Cuba, Puerto Rico, and Santo Domingo), France (Martinique, Guadaloupe, and Saint-Domingue), and Britian (Barbados, Jamaica, and a number of smaller islands), provided 80 to 90 percent of the European supply of sugar. They were all slave societies, with enslaved Africans as the labor force. Thus, they shared with the slaveholding American South a distinctive Afro–North American society that cut across national boundaries. This world was jolted by the 1791 revolt of black slaves in Saint-Domingue, France's richest colony. In 1804, under the leadership of Toussaint L'Ouverture, the former colony, renamed Haiti, became North America's first independent black nation. Its existence struck fear into the hearts of white slaveowners at the same time that it served as a beacon of hope to the enslaved.

BRITISH AND RUSSIAN COLONIES

British North America had been wrested from the French in the Seven Years' War (see Chapter 6). In 1800, its heart remained the former French colony of Quebec (at that time called the province of Lower Canada), with a predominantly French population of about 160,000. Most of the rest of the settlers elsewhere were American, either Loyalists driven out at the time of the Revolution or simply farmers in search of better land. British authorities discouraged American immigrants from settling among the French, directing them instead either to the Maritime Provinces or to Upper Canada, the first inland colony north of the Great Lakes, established in 1791. Farther west (and closed to settlement) lay Rupert's Land, the great stretch of the Canadian North and West that was administered by the Hudson's Bay Company. To allay popular demands stimulated by the American Revolution, Britain established legislative assemblies in Upper and Lower Canada and in the Maritimes in 1791, but, learning

This view shows Sitka, the center of Russian activities in Alaska, in 1827. Russian architectural styles and building techniques are apparent in the Church of St. Michael the Archangel in the right background, contrasting with the Asian and Indian origins of most of Sitka's inhabitants.

From an engraving by Freidrich H. von Kittlitz, 1827. Elmer E. Rosmusen Library Rare Books, University of Alaska, Fairbanks.

QUICK REVIEW

European Colonies in the Early Nineteenth Century

- Spain: challenged in its efforts to control New Spain and the Caribbean.
- Britain: government of Canada reflected lessons learned in the colonies.
- Russia: rapidly expanding presence centered on Alaska and the northwest.

WHAT WERE the most important strengths of the American economy in the early 1800s?

QUICK REVIEW

The American Economy in 1800

- Predominantly rural.
- 94 percent of Americans lived in communities of less than 2,500 people.
- Crops were grown for home use rather than for sale.

from its American fiasco, Britain kept the legislatures under strong executive control. British North America dominated the continental fur trade and was on friendly terms with many of the native peoples who were part of the trade. This economic grip was a challenge and frustration to many westward-moving Americans.

Finally, Russian settlement of what is now Alaska posed another threat. The Russian American Company, chartered by the tsar in 1799, set up headquarters in Sitka, in what is now the southeastern panhandle of Alaska, in 1802. This was the homeland of the Tlingits, a warrior society, who destroyed the Russians' first fortress in the Tlingit Revolt of 1802. The Russians reestablished Sitka by force in 1804 and over the next generation established Russian settlements along the Pacific coast as far south as Fort Ross, which was just north of San Francisco Bay and well within Spanish territory. The Russian presence in North America was rapidly expanding even as Spain's faltered. In 1800, however, this imperial duel was far from the consciousness of most Americans, who were more concerned about the continuing presence of the British to the north in Canada and the nearby racial powder keg in the Caribbean.

A NATIONAL ECONOMY

In 1800, the United States was a producer of raw materials. The new nation faced the same challenge that developing nations confront today. At the mercy of fluctuating world commodity prices they cannot control, such countries have great difficulty protecting themselves from economic dominance by stronger, more established nations.

THE ECONOMY OF THE YOUNG REPUBLIC

In 1800 the United States was predominantly rural and agricultural. In 1800, according to the census, 94 of 100 Americans lived in communities of fewer than 2,500 people, and four of five families farmed the land, either for themselves or for others. Farming families followed centuries-old traditions of working with hand tools and draft animals, producing most of their own food and fiber. Crops were grown for home use rather than for sale. Commodities such as whiskey and hogs (both easy to transport) provided small and irregular cash incomes or items for barter. As late as 1820, only 20 percent of the produce of American farms was consumed outside the local community.

In contrast to this pattern, the plantation agriculture of the South was wholly commercial and international. The demand for cotton was growing rapidly in response to the boom in the industrial production of textiles in England and Europe, but extracting the seeds from the fibers of the variety of cotton that grew best in the southern interior required an enormous investment of labor. The cotton gin, which mechanized this process, was invented in 1793, but not until the nineteenth century did cotton assume a commanding place in the foreign trade of the United States.

In 1790, increasing foreign demand for American goods and services hardly seemed likely. Trade with Britain, still the biggest customer for American raw materials, was considerably less than it had been before the Revolution. Britain and France both excluded Americans from their lucrative West Indian trade and taxed American ships with discriminatory duties. It was difficult to be independent in a world dominated by great powers.

SHIPPING AND THE ECONOMIC BOOM

Despite these restrictions on American commerce, the strong shipping trade begun during the colonial era and centered in the Atlantic ports became a major asset in the 1790s, when events in Europe provided America with extraordinary opportunities. The French Revolution, which began in 1789, soon initiated nearly twenty-five years of warfare between Britain and France. All along the Atlantic seaboard, urban centers thrived as American ships carried European goods that could no longer be transported on British ships without danger of French attack (and vice versa). Because America was neutral, its merchants had the legal right to import European goods and promptly reexport them to other European countries. In spite of British and French efforts to prevent the practice (see Chapter 8), reexports amounted to half of the profits in the booming shipping trade.

The vigorous international shipping trade had dramatic effects within the United States. The coastal cities all grew substantially from 1790 to1820. This rapid urbanization was a sign of vigorous economic growth (rather than a sign that poverty was pushing rural workers off the farms, as occurs in some developing countries today), for it reflected expanding opportunities in the cities. In fact, the rapid growth of cities stimulated farmers to produce the food to feed the new urban dwellers.

The long series of European wars also allowed enterprising Americans to seize such lucrative international opportunities as the China trade. In 1784 the *Empress of China* set sail from New York for Canton with forty tons of ginseng. When it returned in 1785 with a cargo of teas, silks, and chinaware, the sponsors of the voyage made a 30 percent profit. Other merchants were quick to follow.

The active American participation in international trade fostered a strong and diversified shipbuilding industry. All the major Atlantic ports boasted expanding shipbuilding enterprises. Demands for speed increased as well, resulting in what many people have regarded as the flower of American shipbuilding, the clipper ship. The narrow-hulled, many-sailed clipper ships of the 1840s and 1850s set records for ships of their size. In 1854, *Flying Cloud,* built in the Boston shipyards of Donald McKay, sailed from New York to San Francisco—a 16,000-mile trip that usually took 150 to 200 days—in a mere 89 days.

THE JEFFERSON PRESIDENCY

At noon on March 4, 1801, Thomas Jefferson walked from his modest boardinghouse through the swampy streets of the new federal city of Washington to the unfinished Capitol. George Washington and John Adams had ridden in elaborate carriages to their inaugurals. Jefferson, although accepting a military honor guard, demonstrated by his actions that he rejected the elaborate, quasi-monarchical style of the two Federalist presidents and their (to his mind) autocratic style of government as well.

For all its lack of pretension, Jefferson's inauguration as the third president of the United States was a momentous occasion in American history, for it marked the peaceful transition from one political party, the Federalists, to their hated rivals, the Jeffersonian Republicans. Beginning in an atmosphere of exceptional political bitterness, Jefferson's presidency was to demonstrate that a strongly led party system could shape national policy without leading either to dictatorship or to revolt. It was a great achievement.

REPUBLICAN AGRARIANISM

Jefferson brought to the presidency a clearly defined political philosophy. Behind all the events of his administration (1801–1809) and those of his successors in what became known as the Virginia Dynasty (James Madison, 1809–1817; James Monroe, 1817–1825) was a clear set of beliefs that embodied Jefferson's interpretation of the meaning of republicanism for Americans.

QUICK REVIEW

Growth of American Trade: 1793 – 1807

- French Revolution initiated renewed period of warfare between France and Britain.
- American merchants wanted to supply both sides.
- Expansion of trade led to development of shipbuilding industry and growth of coastal cities.

WHAT VALUES were embodied in agrarian republicanism?

8–2
Thomas Jefferson, "First Inaugural Address" (1801)

Tall, ungainly, and diffident in manner, Thomas Jefferson was nonetheless a man of genius, an architect, naturalist, political philosopher, and politician.

Courtesy of the Library of Congress

8–3
Margaret Bayard Smith Meets Thomas Jefferson (1801)

8–7
Fisher Ames, "The Republican No. II" (1804)

8–4
Constitutionality of the Louisiana Purchase (1803)

Jefferson's years as ambassador to France in the 1780s were particularly important in shaping his political thinking. Recoiling from the extremes of wealth and poverty he saw there, he came to believe that it was impossible for Europe to achieve a just society that could guarantee to most of its members the "life, liberty and . . . pursuit of happiness" of which he had written in the Declaration of Independence. Only America, he believed, provided fertile earth for the true citizenship necessary to a republican form of government. What America had, and Europe lacked, was room to grow.

Jefferson envisaged a nation of small family farms clustered together in rural communities—an agrarian republic. He believed that only a nation of roughly equal yeoman farmers, each secure in his own possessions and not dependent on someone else for his livelihood, would exhibit the concern for the community good that was essential in a republic. Indeed, Jefferson said that "those who labor in the earth are the chosen people of God," and so he viewed himself, though his "farm" was the large slave-owning plantation of Monticello.

Jefferson's vision of an expanding agrarian republic remains to this day one of our most compelling ideas about America's uniqueness and special destiny. But expansionism contained some negative aspects. The lure of the western lands fostered constant mobility and dissatisfaction rather than the stable, settled communities of yeoman farmers that Jefferson envisaged. Expansionism caused environmental damage, in particular soil exhaustion—a consequence of abandoning old lands, rather than conserving them, and moving on to new ones. Finally, expansionism bred a ruthlessness toward Indian peoples, who were pushed out of the way for white settlement or who, like the Mandans, were devastated by the diseases that accompanied European trade and contact. Jefferson's agrarianism thus bred some of the best and some of the worst traits of the developing nation.

JEFFERSON'S GOVERNMENT

Thomas Jefferson came to office determined to reverse the Federalist policies of the 1790s and to ensure an agrarian "republic of virtue." Accordingly, he proposed a program of "simplicity and frugality," promising to cut all internal taxes, to reduce the size of the army (from 4,000 to 2,500 men), the navy (from twenty-five ships to seven), and the government staff, and to eliminate the entire national debt inherited from the Federalists. He kept all of these promises, even the last, although the Louisiana Purchase of 1803 cost the Treasury $15 million. This diminishment of government was a key matter of republican principle to Jefferson. If his ideal yeoman farmer was to be a truly self-governing citizen, the federal government must not, Jefferson believed, be either large or powerful.

Perhaps one reason for Jefferson's success was that the federal government he headed was small and unimportant by today's standards. The national government's main service to ordinary people was mail delivery. Everything else—law and order, education, welfare, road maintenance, economic control—rested with state or local governments. Power and political loyalty were still local, not national.

This small national government also explains why for years the nation's capital was so unimpressive. Construction lagged on the President's House and the Capitol. Instead of the imposing dome we know so well today, the early Capitol consisted of two white marble boxes connected by a boardwalk. It is a telling indicator of the true location of national power that a people who had no trouble building new local communities across the continent should have had such difficulty establishing their federal city.

AN INDEPENDENT JUDICIARY

Although determined to reverse Federalist fiscal policies, Jefferson allowed 132 Federalist office holders to remain at their posts. Jefferson's restraint, however, did not extend to the most notorious Federalist appointees, the so-called midnight judges.

In the last days of the Adams administration, the Federalist-dominated Congress passed several acts that created new judgeships and other positions within the federal judiciary. In one of his last acts in office, President Adams appointed Federalists—quickly dubbed the "midnight judges"—to these new positions. William Marbury, whom President Adams had appointed Justice of the Peace for Washington, D.C., and three other appointees sued James Madison, Jefferson's secretary of state, to receive their commissions for their offices. Before the case came to trial, however, Congress, controlled by Jeffersonian Republicans who feared that the losing Federalist Party was trying to use the judiciary to increase the power of the federal government over the states, repealed the acts. This case, *Marbury* v. *Madison*, provoked a landmark decision from the Supreme Court, head of the federal judiciary.

At issue was a fundamental constitutional point: Was the judiciary independent of politics? In his celebrated 1803 decision in **Marbury v. Madison**, Chief Justice John Marshall, himself a strong Federalist and an Adams appointee, managed to find a way to please both parties. On the one hand, Marshall proclaimed that the courts had a duty "to say what the law is," thus unequivocally defending the independence of the judiciary and the principle of judicial review. On the other hand, Marshall conceded that the Supreme Court was not empowered by the Constitution to force the executive branch to give Marbury his commission. At first glance, Jefferson's government appeared to have won the battle over Adams's last-minute appointees. But in the long run, Marshall established the principle that only the federal judiciary could decide what was constitutional. This was a vital step in realizing the three-way balance of power among the branches of the federal government—executive (president), legislative (Congress), and judiciary (courts)—envisaged in the Constitution. Equally important, during his long tenure in office (1801–1835), Chief Justice Marshall consistently led the Supreme Court in a series of decisions that favored the federal government over state governments. Under Marshall's direction, the Supreme Court became a powerful nationalizing force, often to the dismay of defenders of states' rights.

OPPORTUNITY: THE LOUISIANA PURCHASE

In 1800 the United States was a new and fragile democracy in a world dominated by two contending great powers: Britain and France. If France sought to regain territory that it had once held in North America, this would pose a threat to both American commerce and national security. In 1799, the young general Napoleon Bonaparte seized control of France and began a career of military conquests. As had his predecessors, Napoleon looked at North America as a potential battleground on which to fight the British. In 1800, in a secret treaty, France reacquired the Louisiana Territory, the vast western drainage of the Mississippi and Missouri rivers, from Spain, which had held the region since 1763. From Louisiana, if he chose, Napoleon could launch an attack to regain Canada from the British. As a springboard to a new French North American empire, in 1802 Napoleon sent an

VENERATE THE PLOUGH

This symbol of the Philadelphia Society for Promoting Agriculture illustrates the principles of republican agrarianism. The yeoman farmer is ploughing his field under the approving gaze of the female figure of Columbia. His activity expresses the values of the American republic that she represents and in which Thomas Jefferson so strongly believed. As he said, "those who labor in the earth are the chosen people of God."

Library of Congress

QUICK REVIEW

Marbury v. *Madison* **(1803)**

◆ Case sparked by Jefferson's refusal to recognize Adam's "midnight judges."

◆ Justice Marshall ruled that the duty of the courts was "to say what the law is."

◆ Ruling made the Supreme Court a powerful nationalizing force.

7–12
Marbury v. *Madison* (1803)

Marbury v. *Madison* Supreme Court decision of 1803 that created the precedent of judicial review by ruling as unconstitutional part of the Judiciary Act of 1789.

MAP EXPLORATION

To explore an interactive version of this map, go to **http://www.prenhall.com/faraghertlc/map9.2**

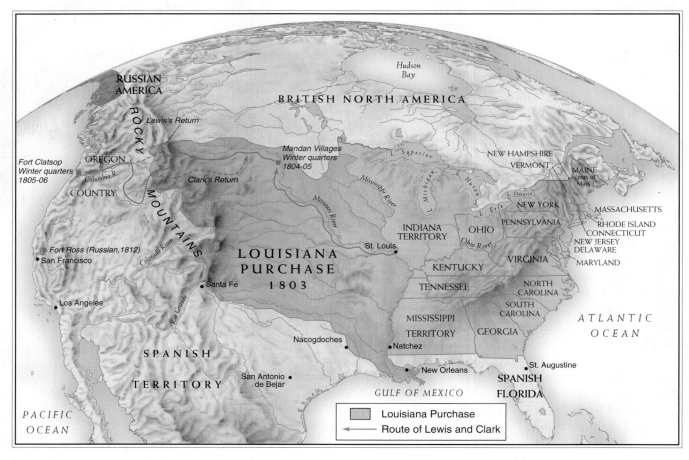

MAP 9-2

Louisiana Purchase   The Louisiana Purchase of 1803, the largest peaceful acquisition of territory in United States history, more than doubled the size of the nation. The Lewis and Clark expedition (1804–1806) was the first to survey and document the natural and human richness of the area. The American sense of expansiveness and continental destiny owes more to the extraordinary opportunity provided by the Louisiana Purchase than to anything else.

HOW DID the terrain of the Lewis and Clark expedition influence the routes of the journey?

army of 30,000 to reconquer Haiti (the former Saint-Domingue) and thereby crush Afro-Caribbean dreams of independence.

Initially, Jefferson offered to buy New Orleans and the surrounding area for $2 million (or up to $10 million, if necessary). As it happened, Napoleon was eager to sell. His army of 30,000 men had just withdrawn from Haiti, defeated by yellow fever as well as by an army of former slaves led by Toussaint L'Ouverture. In the wake of the French defeat, and in need of money for European military campaigns, Napoleon offered the entire Louisiana Territory, including the crucial port of New Orleans, to the Americans for $15 million. Exceeding his instructions, special American envoy James Monroe seized the opportunity and bought the entire Louisiana Territory from Napoleon in Paris in April 1803. Overnight, the size of the United States more than doubled. It was the largest peaceful acquisition of territory in United States history. Jefferson claimed that Louisiana was vital to the nation's republican future. "By enlarging the empire of liberty," Jefferson wrote, "we . . . provide new sources of renovation, should its principles, at any time, degenerate, in those portions of our country which gave them birth." In other words, expansion was essential to liberty.

INCORPORATING LOUISIANA

The immediate issue following the Louisiana Purchase was how to treat the French and Spanish inhabitants of the Louisiana Territory. Many people thought that the only way to deal with a population so "foreign" was to wipe out its customs and laws and to impose American ones as quickly as possible. But this did not happen. The incorporation of Louisiana into the American federal system was a remarkable story of adaptation between two different communities—American and French.

In 1803, when the region that is now the state of Louisiana became American property, it had a racially and ethnically diverse population of 43,000 people, of whom only 6,000 were American. French and French-speaking people were numerically and culturally dominant, especially in the city of New Orleans. There the French community effectively challenged the initial American plan of rapidly supplanting French culture and institutions with American ones. The U.S. representative in New Orleans and governor of Lower Louisiana Territory, William Claiborne, came to accept the value of French institutions to the region. As a result, with Claiborne's full support, Louisiana adopted a legal code in 1808 that was based on French civil law rather than English common law. This was not a small concession. French law differed from English law in many fundamental respects, such as in family property (communal versus male ownership), in inheritance (forced heirship versus free disposal), and even in contracts, which were much more strictly regulated in the French system. Remnants of the French legal system remain part of Louisiana state law to this day. In 1812, with the required 60,000 free inhabitants, Louisiana was admitted to the Union. New Orleans remained for years a distinctively French city, illustrating the flexibility possible under a federal system.

TEXAS AND THE STRUGGLE FOR MEXICAN INDEPENDENCE

Spain objected, in vain, to Napoleon's 1803 sale of Louisiana to America. For years Spain had attempted to seal off its rich colony of Mexico from commerce with other nations. Now, American Louisiana shared a vague and disputed boundary with Mexico's northern province of Texas (a parcel of land already coveted by some Americans).

Soon Napoleon brought turmoil to all of Mexico. In 1808, having invaded Spain, he installed his brother Joseph Bonaparte as king, forcing Spain's king, Charles IV, to renounce his throne. For the next six years, as warfare convulsed Spain, the country's long-prized New World empire slipped away. Mexico, divided between royalists loyal to Spain and populists seeking social and economic justice for mestizos and Indians, edged bloodily toward independence. Two populist revolts—one in 1810 led by Father Miguel Hidalgo and the other in 1813 led by Father José María Morelos—were suppressed by the royalists, who executed both revolutionary leaders. In 1812 a small force, led by Mexican republican Bernardo Gutiérrez but composed mostly of American adventurers, invaded Texas, captured San Antonio, assassinated the provincial governor Manuel Salcedo, and declared Texas independent. A year later, however, the Mexican republicans were defeated by a royalist army, which then killed suspected collaborators and pillaged the province so thoroughly that the local economy was devastated. The Mexican population declined to fewer than 2,000. Under these circumstances, Mexico's difficult path toward independence seemed, at least to some Americans, to offer yet another opportunity for expansion.

RENEWED IMPERIAL RIVALRY IN NORTH AMERICA

WHAT FACTORS led to conflict between the United States and Britain in North America?

F resh from the triumph of the Louisiana Purchase, Jefferson scored a major victory over the Federalist Charles Cotesworth Pinckney in the presidential election of 1804, garnering 162 electoral votes to Pinckney's 14. Jefferson's shrewd wooing of moderate Federalists had been so successful that the remaining Federalists dwindled to a highly principled but sectional group, unable to attract voters outside of its home base in New England. Jefferson's Louisiana success was not repeated, however, and few other consequences of the ongoing struggle between Britain and France were so easy to solve.

PROBLEMS WITH NEUTRAL RIGHTS

In his first inaugural address in 1801, Jefferson had announced a foreign policy of "peace, commerce, and honest friendship with all nations, entangling alliances with none." This was a difficult policy to pursue after 1803, when the Napoleonic Wars resumed. By 1805 Napoleon had conquered most of Europe, but Britain, the victor at the great naval battle of Trafalgar, controlled the seas. The United States, trying to profit from trade with both countries, was caught in the middle. The British did not look kindly as their former colonists tried to evade their blockade of the French by claiming neutrality. Beginning in 1805, the British targeted the American reexport trade between the French West Indies and France by seizing American ships that were bringing French West Indian goods to Europe. Angry Americans viewed these seizures as violations of their rights as shippers of a neutral nation.

An even more contentious issue arose from the substantial desertion rate of British sailors. Many deserters promptly signed up on American ships, where they drew better pay and sometimes obtained false naturalization papers as well. The numbers involved were large: as many as a quarter of the 100,000 seamen on American ships were British. Soon the British were stopping American merchant vessels and removing any man they believed to be British, regardless of his papers.

At least 6,000 innocent American citizens suffered forced impressment into the British navy from 1803 to 1812. In 1807 impressment turned bloody when the British ship *Leopard* stopped the American ship *Chesapeake* in American territorial waters and demanded to search for deserters. When the American captain refused, the *Leopard* opened fire, killing three men, wounding eighteen, and removing four deserters (three with American naturalization papers) from the damaged ship. An indignant public protested British interference and the death of innocent sailors.

THE EMBARGO ACT

QUICK REVIEW

Embargo Act (1807)

◆ Forbade American ships from sailing to foreign ports.

◆ Intended to force Britain and France to recognize neutral rights.

◆ The Act was an economic disaster for the United States.

Fully aware that commerce was essential to the new nation, Jefferson was determined to insist on America's right as a neutral nation to ship goods to Europe. He first tried diplomatic protests, then negotiations, and finally threats, all to no avail. In 1806 Congress passed the Non-Importation Act, hoping that a boycott of British goods, which had worked so well during the Revolutionary War, would be effective once again. It was not. Finally, in desperation, Jefferson imposed the **Embargo Act** in December 1807. This act forbade American ships from sailing to any foreign port, thereby cutting off all exports as well as imports. The intent of the act was to force both Britain and France to recognize neutral rights by depriving them of American-shipped raw materials.

But the results were a disaster for American trade. The commerce of the new nation, which Jefferson himself had done so much to promote, came to a standstill. Exports fell from $108 million in 1807 to $22 million in 1808, and the

Embargo Act Act passed by Congress in 1807 prohibiting American ships from leaving for any foreign port.

nation was driven into a deep depression. There was widespread evasion of the embargo. A remarkable number of ships in the coastal trade found themselves "blown off course" to the West Indies or Canada. Other ships simply left port illegally. Smuggling flourished. Pointing out that the American navy's weakness was due largely to the deep cuts Jefferson had inflicted on it, the Federalists sprang to life with a campaign of outspoken opposition to Jefferson's policy, and they found a ready audience in New England, the area hardest hit by the embargo.

MADISON AND THE FAILURE OF "PEACEABLE COERCION"

In this troubled atmosphere, Thomas Jefferson despondently ended his second term, acknowledging the failure of what he called "peaceable coercion." He was followed in office by his friend and colleague James Madison of Virginia. Although Madison defeated the Federalist candidate—again Charles Cotesworth Pinckney— by 122 electoral votes to 47, Pinckney's share of the votes was three times what it had been in 1804.

In March 1809, Congress admitted failure and the Embargo Act was repealed. But the struggle to remain neutral in the confrontation between the European giants continued. The next two years saw passage of several acts—among them the Non-Intercourse Act of 1809 and Macon's Bill Number 2 in 1810—that unsuccessfully attempted to prohibit trade with Britain and France unless they ceased their hostile treatment of U.S. shipping. Frustration with the ineffectiveness of government policy mounted.

A CONTRADICTORY INDIAN POLICY

The United States also faced other conflicts besides those with Britain and France over neutral shipping rights. In the West, the powerful Indian nations of the Ohio Valley were determined to resist the wave of expansion that had carried thousands of white settlers onto their lands. North of the Ohio River lived the Northwest Confederation of the Shawnees, Delawares, Miamis, Potawatomis, and several smaller tribes. To the south of the Ohio were the so-called "Five Civilized Tribes," the Cherokees, Chickasaws, Choctaws, Creeks, and (in Florida) the Seminoles.

According to the Indian Intercourse Act of 1790, the United States could not simply seize Indian land; it could only acquire it when the Indians ceded it by treaty. But this policy conflicted with the harsh reality of westward expansion. Commonly, settlers pushed ahead of treaty boundaries. When Indian peoples resisted the invasion of their lands, the pioneers fought back and called for military protection. Defeat of an Indian people led to further land cessions. The result for the Indians was a relentless cycle of invasion, resistance, and defeat.

Thomas Jefferson was deeply concerned with the fate of the western Indian peoples. Convinced that Indians had to give up hunting in favor of the yeoman-farmer lifestyle he so favored for all Americans, Jefferson directed the governors of the Northwest Territories to "promote energetically" his vision for civilizing the Indians, which included Christianizing them and teaching them to read. Many Indian peoples actively resisted these efforts at conversion. In addition, Jefferson's Indian civilization plan was never fully supported by territorial governors and settlers.

After the Louisiana Purchase, Jefferson offered traditionalist Indian groups new lands west of the Mississippi River, where they could live undisturbed by white settlers. But he failed to consider the pace of westward expansion. Less than twenty years later, Missouri, the first trans-Mississippi state, was admitted to the Union. Western Indians like the Mandans, who had seemed so remote, were now threatened by further westward expansion.

Tecumseh, a Shawnee military leader (top), and his brother Tenskwatawa, a religious leader called The Prophet, led a pan-Indian revitalization and resistance movement that posed a serious threat to American westward expansion. Tecumseh traveled widely, attempting to build a military alliance on his brother's spiritual message. He achieved considerable success in the Old Northwest, but less in the Old Southwest, where many Indian peoples put their faith in accommodation. Tecumseh's death at the Battle of the Thames (1813) and British abandonment of their Shawnee allies at the end of the War of 1812 brought an end to organized Indian resistance in the Old Northwest.

The Field Museum of Natural History; Library of Congress

INDIAN RESISTANCE

The Shawnees, a seminomadic hunting and farming tribe (the men hunted, the women farmed) of the Ohio Valley, had resisted white settlement in Kentucky and Ohio since the 1750s. The decisive defeat of the Indian Confederacy led by Little Turtle, a Miami Indian, at Fallen Timbers (1794) and the continuing pressure of American settlement, however, had left the Shawnees divided. One group, led by Black Hoof, accepted acculturation. The rest of the tribe tried to maintain traditional ways. Most broke into small bands and tried to eke out a living by hunting, but their numbers were reduced by disease and the survivors were further demoralized by the alcohol offered them illegally by private traders. One group of traditional Shawnees, however, led by the warrior Tecumseh, sought refuge farther west.

But there was no escape from white encroachment. Between 1801 and 1809, William Henry Harrison, governor of Indiana Territory, concluded fifteen treaties with the Delawares, Potawatomis, Miamis, and other tribes. These treaties opened eastern Michigan, southern Indiana, and most of Illinois to white settlement and forced the Indians into ever-smaller reservations. Many of these treaties were obtained by coercion, bribery, and outright trickery, and most Indians did not accept them.

In 1805 Tecumseh's brother, Tenskwatawa, known as The Prophet, began preaching a message of Indian revitalization: a rejection of all contact with the Americans, including the use of American alcohol, clothing, and trade goods, and a return to traditional practices of hunting and farming. He preached an end to quarreling, violence, and sexual promiscuity and to the accumulation of private property. Wealth was valuable only if it was given away, he said. If the Northwest Indians returned to traditional ways, Tenskwatawa promised, "the land will be overturned so that all the white people will be covered and you alone shall inhabit the land."

This was a powerful message, but it was not new. Just six years earlier, Handsome Lake had led the Seneca people of upstate New York in a similar revitalization movement. Tecumseh, however, succeeded in molding his brother's religious following into a powerful **pan-Indian military resistance movement**. With each new treaty that Harrison concluded, Tecumseh gained new followers among the Northwest Confederation tribes. Significantly, he also had the support of the British, who, after 1807, began sending food and guns to him from Canada.

The pan-Indian strategy was at first primarily defensive, aimed at preventing further westward expansion. But the Treaty of Fort Wayne in 1809, in which the United States gained 3 million acres of Delaware and Potawatomi land in Indiana, led to active resistance. Confronting Harrison directly, Tecumseh argued that the land belonged to the larger community of all the Indian peoples; no one tribe could give away the common property of all. He then warned that any surveyors or settlers who ventured into the 3 million acres would risk their lives.

Tecumseh took his message of common land ownership and military resistance to all the Indian peoples of the Northwest Confederacy. He was not uniformly successful, even among the Shawnees. Black Hoof, for example, refused to join. Tecumseh also recruited, with mixed success, among the tribes south of the Ohio River. In councils with Choctaws, Chickasaws, Creeks, and Cherokees, he promoted active resistance.

In November 1811, while Tecumseh was still recruiting among the southern tribes, Harrison marched to the pan-Indian village of Tippecanoe with 1,000 soldiers. The 600 to 700 Indian warriors at the town, urged on by Tenskwatawa, attacked Harrison's forces before dawn on November 7, hoping to surprise them. The attack failed, and in the battle that followed the Americans inflicted about 150 Indian casualties, while sustaining about as many themselves. Although Harrison

8–9
An "Uncommon Genius"
Advocates Indian Unity (1809)

Pan-Indian military resistance movement   Movement calling for the political and cultural unification of Indian tribes in the late eighteenth and early nineteenth centuries.

MAP EXPLORATION

To explore an interactive version of this map, go to **http://www.prenhall.com/faraghertlc/map9.3**

MAP 9-3

Indian Resistance, 1790–1816   American westward expansion put relentless pressure on the Indian nations in the Trans-Appalachian South and West. The Trans-Appalachian region was marked by constant warfare from the time of the earliest settlements in Kentucky in the 1780s to the War of 1812. Tecumseh's Alliance in the Old Northwest (1809–1811) and the Creek Rebellion in the Old Southwest (1813–1814) were the culminating struggles in Indian resistance to the American invasion of the Trans-Appalachian region.

WHAT HAPPENED to the Indians of the Trans-Appalachian region after 1814?

claimed victory, the truth was far different. Dispersed from Tippecanoe, Tecumseh's angry followers fell on American settlements in Indiana and southern Michigan, killing many pioneers and forcing the rest to flee to fortified towns. Tecumseh himself entered into a formal alliance with the British. For western settlers, the Indian threat was greater than ever.

THE WAR OF 1812

WHAT WERE the consequences of the War of 1812?

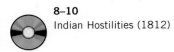
8–10
Indian Hostilities (1812)

Many westerners blamed the British for Tecumseh's attacks on pioneer settlements in the Northwest. British support of western Indians and the long-standing difficulties over neutral shipping rights were the two grievances cited by President Madison when he asked Congress for a declaration of war against Britain on June 1, 1812. Congress obliged him on June 18. But the war had other, more general causes as well.

A rising young generation of political leaders, first elected to Congress in 1810, strongly resented the continuing influence of Britain, the former mother country, on American affairs. These **War Hawks**, who included such future leaders as Henry Clay of Kentucky and John C. Calhoun of South Carolina, were young Jeffersonian Republicans from the West and South. They found all aspects of British interference, such as impressment of sailors and support for western Indians, intolerable. Eager to assert independence from England once and for all, these young men saw themselves finishing the job begun by the aging revolutionary generation. They also wanted to occupy Florida to prevent runaway slaves from seeking refuge with the Seminole Indians. Westerners wanted to invade Canada, hoping thereby to end threats from British-backed Indians in the Northwest, such as Tecumseh and his followers. As resentments against England and frustrations over border issues merged, the pressure for war—always a strong force for national unity—mounted.

Unaware that the British, seriously hurt by the American trade embargo, were about to adopt a more conciliatory policy, President James Madison yielded to the War Hawks' clamor for action in June 1812, and his declaration of war passed the U.S. Senate by the close vote of 19 to 13, the House by 79 to 49. All the Federalists voted against the war. (The division along party lines continued in the 1812 presidential election, in which Madison garnered 128 electoral votes to 89 for his Federalist opponent, DeWitt Clinton.) The vote was sectional, with New England and the Middle States in opposition and the West and South strongly prowar. Thus, the United States entered the **War of 1812** more deeply divided along sectional lines than during any other foreign war in American history.

The Americans had a few glorious moments, but on the whole the War of 1812 was an ignominious struggle that gained them little. As a result of Jefferson's economizing, the American army and navy were small and weak. In contrast, the British, fresh from almost ten years of Napoleonic Wars, were in fighting trim. The British navy quickly established a strong blockade, harassing coastal shipping along the Atlantic seaboard and attacking coastal settlements at will. In the most humiliating attack, the British burned Washington in the summer of 1814, forcing the president and Congress to flee. There were a few American military successes. Commodore Oliver Perry's ships defeated a British fleet on Lake Erie in 1813, whereupon Perry sent the famous message "We have met the enemy and they are ours." In early 1815 (after the peace treaty had been signed) Andrew Jackson improbably won a lopsided victory over veteran British troops in the **Battle of New Orleans**.

War Hawks   Members of Congress, predominantly from the South and West, who aggressively pushed for a war against Britain after their election in 1810.

War of 1812   War fought between the United States and Britain from June 1812 to January 1815 largely over British restrictions on American shipping.

Battle of New Orleans   Decisive American War of 1812 victory over British troops in January 1815 that ended any British hopes of gaining control of the lower Mississippi River Valley.

MAP EXPLORATION

To explore an interactive version of this map, go to **http://www.prenhall.com/faraghertlc/map9.4**

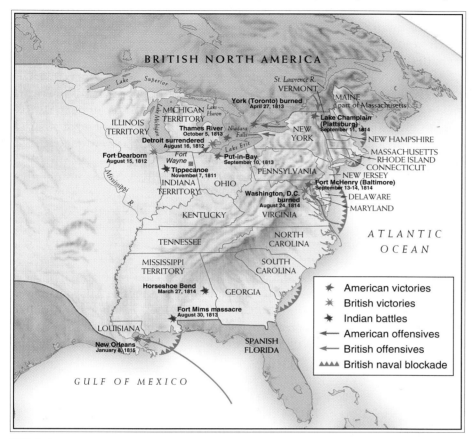

MAP 9-4
The War of 1812   On land, the War of 1812 was fought to define the nation's boundaries. In the North, American armies attacked British forts in the Great Lakes region with little success, and the invasion of Canada was a failure. In the South, the Battle of New Orleans made a national hero of Andrew Jackson, but it occurred after the peace treaty had been signed. On the sea, with the exception of Oliver Perry's victory in the Great Lakes, Britain's dominance was so complete and its blockade so effective that British troops were able to invade the Chesapeake and burn the capital of the United States.

WHAT EVENTS and ambitions led to the outbreak of war in 1812?

The New England states opposed the war. Massachusetts, Rhode Island, and Connecticut refused to provide militia or supplies, and other New England governors turned a blind eye to the flourishing illegal trade across the U.S.–Canadian border. Opposition to the war culminated in the Hartford Convention of 1814, where Federalist representatives from the five New England states met to discuss their grievances. At first the air was full of talk of secession from the Union, but soon cooler heads prevailed.

The convention did insist, however, that a state had the right "to interpose its authority" to protect its citizens against unconstitutional federal laws. This *nullification* threat from Hartford was ignored, for peace with Britain was announced as delegates from the convention made their way to Washington to deliver their message to Congress. There the convention's grievances were treated not as serious business but as an anticlimactic joke.

 8–12
Report and Resolutions of the Hartford Convention (1814)

Nullification   A constitutional doctrine holding that a state has a legal right to declare a national law null and void within its borders.

By 1814 the long Napoleonic Wars in Europe were slowly drawing to a close, and the British decided to end their war with the Americans. The peace treaty, after months of hard negotiation, was signed at Ghent, Belgium, on Christmas Eve in 1814. Like the war itself, the treaty was inconclusive. The major issues of impressment and neutral rights were not mentioned, but the British did agree to evacuate their western posts, and late in the negotiations they abandoned their insistence on a buffer state for neutral Indian peoples in the Northwest.

For all its international inconsequence, the war did have an important effect on national morale. Andrew Jackson's victory at New Orleans allowed Americans to believe that they had defeated the British. It would be more accurate to say that by not losing the war the Americans had ended their own feelings of colonial dependency. Equally important, they convinced the British government to stop thinking of America as its colony.

The War of 1812 was one of America's most divisive wars, arousing more intense opposition than any other American conflict, including Vietnam. Today most historians regard the war as both unnecessary and a dangerous risk to new and fragile ideas of national unity. Fortunately for its future, the United States as a whole came out unscathed, and the Battle of New Orleans had provided last-minute balm for its hurt pride.

The only clear losers of the war were the northwestern Indian nations and their southern allies. With the death of Tecumseh at the Battle of the Thames in 1813 and the defeat of the Southern Creeks in 1814, the last hope of a united Indian resistance to white expansion perished forever. Britain's abandonment of its Indian allies in the **Treaty of Ghent** sealed their fate. By 1815 American settlers were on their way west again.

DEFINING THE BOUNDARIES

With the War of 1812 behind them, Americans turned, more seriously than ever before, to the tasks of expansion and national development.

ANOTHER WESTWARD SURGE

The end of the War of 1812 was followed by a westward surge to the Mississippi River that populated the Old Northwest (Ohio, Indiana, Illinois, Michigan, and Wisconsin) and the Old Southwest (western Georgia, Alabama, Mississippi, and Louisiana). The extent of the population redistribution was dramatic: in 1790, about 95 percent of the nation's population had lived in states bordering the Atlantic Ocean; by 1820 fully 25 percent of the population lived west of the Appalachians.

What accounted for the westward surge? There were both push and pull factors. Between 1800 and 1820, the nation's population almost doubled, increasing from 5.3 million to 9.6 million. Overpopulated farmland in all of the seaboard states pushed farmers off the land, while new land pulled them westward. The defeat and removal of Indians in the War of 1812 was another important pull factor.

Geography facilitated lateral westward movement (Northerners tended to migrate to the Old Northwest, Southerners to the Old Southwest). Except in southern Ohio and parts of Kentucky and Tennessee, there was very little contact between regional cultures. New Englanders carried their values and lifestyles directly west and settled largely with their own communities; Southerners did the same.

One section of northern Ohio along Lake Erie, for example, had been Connecticut's western land claim since the days of its colonial charter. Rather than

---

QUICK REVIEW

Prelude to War

◆ Republican-controlled Congress balked at strengthening military.

◆ Divided Congress declared war.

◆ Support for war strongest in the South and West.

Treaty of Ghent   Treaty signed in December 1814 between the United States and Britain that ended the War of 1812.

WHAT WERE the principal provisions of the Missouri Compromise?

9–2
The Cherokee Treaty of 1817

MAP EXPLORATION

To explore an interactive version of this map, go to **http://www.prenhall.com/faraghertlc/map9.5**

MAP 9-5

Major Migration Routes, 1800–1820   The barrier of the Appalachian Mountains permitted only a few routes to the West. Settlers from the northern states took the Genesee Turnpike, Middle States migrants favored the Philadelphia–Pittsburgh Turnpike and the National Road, and Southerners used the Wilderness and Federal Roads. Because most westward movement was lateral, regional mixing among Western settlers was rare. New Englanders carried their attitudes West, and Southerners did the same.

Donald Meinig, *The Shaping of America*, vol. 2, Continental America (New Haven, CT: Yale University Press, 1994)

HOW DID westward movement vary by region between 1800 and 1820?

---

give up the land when the Northwest Territory was established in 1787, Connecticut held onto the Western Reserve (as it was known) and encouraged its citizens to move there. Group settlement was common. General Moses Cleaveland of the Revolutionary War led one of the first groups of Yankees, fifty-two in all. In 1795 they settled the community that bears his name (though not his spelling of it). Many other groups followed, naming towns such as Norwalk after those they had left in

QUICK REVIEW

Westward Surge, 1800–1820

◆ By 1820 25 percent of the population lived west of the Appalachians.

◆ Group settlement was common.

◆ Lure of new land pulled farmers west.

Settlement of the heavily forested Old Northwest and Old Southwest required much heavy labor to clear the land. One common laborsaving method settlers learned from Indians was to "girdle" the trees (cutting the bark all around), thereby killing them. Dead trees could be more easily chopped and burned.

Library of Congress

9–7
Henry Clay, "Defense of the American System" (1832)

Era of Good Feelings   The period from 1817 to 1823 in which the disappearance of the Federalists enabled the Republicans to govern in a spirit of seemingly nonpartisan harmony.

American System   The program of government subsidies favored by Henry Clay and his followers to promote American economic growth and protect domestic manufacturers from foreign competition.

Connecticut. These New Englanders brought to the Western Reserve their religion (Congregational), their love of learning (tiny Norwalk soon boasted a three-story academy), and their adamant opposition to slavery.

Western migration in the South was very different. On this frontier, the people clearing the land were doing it not for themselves but to create plantations for slave owners. More than half of the migrants to the Old Southwest after 1812 were involuntary—enslaved African Americans.

After the war, as cotton growing expanded, hopeful slave owners from older parts of the South (Virginia, North and South Carolina, Georgia) flooded into the region. Most of the settlers in the Old Southwest were small farm families living in forest clearings. Most did not own slaves, but they hoped to, for ownership of slaves was the means to wealth. The lifestyle and values of older Southern states were quickly replicated on this new frontier.

The western transplantation of distinctive regional cultures explains why, although by 1820 western states accounted for more than a third of all states (eight out of twenty-three), the West did not form a third, unified political region. Although there were common western issues—in particular, the demand for better roads and other transportation routes—communities in the Old Northwest, in general, shared New England political attitudes, whereas those in the Old Southwest shared southern attitudes.

THE ELECTION OF 1816 AND THE ERA OF GOOD FEELINGS

In 1816 James Monroe, the last of the Virginia Dynasty, was easily elected president over his Federalist opponent Rufus King (183 to 34 electoral votes). This was the last election in which Federalists ran a candidate. Monroe had no opponent in 1820 and was reelected nearly unanimously (231 to 1). The triumph of the Jeffersonian Republicans over the Federalists seemed complete.

Tall, dignified, dressed in the old-fashioned style of knee breeches and white-topped boots that Washington had worn, Monroe looked like a traditional figure. But his politics reflected changing times. When he visited Boston, as recently as 1815 the heart of a secession-minded Federalist region, he received an enthusiastic welcome, prompting the Federalist *Columbian Centinel* to proclaim an **"Era of Good Feelings."** The phrase has been applied to Monroe's presidency (1817–1825) ever since.

Monroe sought a government of national unity, and he chose men from North and South, Jeffersonian Republicans and Federalists, for his cabinet. He selected John Quincy Adams, a former Federalist, as his secretary of state, virtually assuring that Adams, like his father, would become president. To balance Adams, Monroe picked John C. Calhoun of South Carolina, a prominent War Hawk, as secretary of war. And Monroe supported the **American System**, a program of national economic development that became identified with Westerner Henry Clay, Speaker of the House of Representatives.

In supporting the American System, Monroe was following President Madison, who had proposed the program in his message to Congress in December 1815. Madison and Monroe broke with Jefferson's agrarianism to embrace much of the Federalist program for economic development, including the chartering of a national bank, a tax on imported goods to protect American manufacturers, and a national system of roads and canals. All three of these had first been proposed by Alexander Hamilton in the 1790s (see Chapter 8). At the time these proposals had met with bitter Jeffersonian Republican opposition. The support that Madison and Monroe gave to Hamilton's ideas following the War of 1812 was a crucial sign of the dynamism of the American commercial economy. Many Republicans now acknowledged that the federal government had a role to play in fostering the economic and commercial conditions in which both yeoman farmer and merchant could succeed.

In 1816 Congress chartered the **Second Bank of the United States** for twenty years. Located in Philadelphia, the bank had a capital of $35 million, of which the government contributed $7 million. The bank was to provide the large-scale financing that the smaller state banks could not handle and to create a strong national currency. Because they feared concentrated economic power, Jeffersonian Republicans had allowed the charter of the original Bank of the United States, founded in 1791, to expire in 1811. The Republican about-face in 1816 was a sign that the strength of commercial interests had grown to rival that of farmers, whose distrust for central banks persisted.

The Tariff of 1816 was the first substantial protective tariff in American history. In 1815, British manufacturers, who had been excluded for eight years (from the Embargo Act of 1807 to the end of the War of 1812), flooded the United States market with their products. American manufacturers complained that the British were dumping goods below cost in order to prevent the growth of American industries. Congress responded with a tariff on imported woolens and cottons, on iron, leather, hats, paper, and sugar. The measure had Southern as well as Northern support, although in later years differences over the passage of higher tariffs would become one of the most persistent sources of sectional conflict.

The third item in the American System, funding for roads and canals—internal improvements, as they came to be known—was more controversial. Monroe and Madison both supported genuinely national (that is, interstate) projects such as the National Road from Cumberland, Maryland, to Vandalia, Illinois. Congressmen, however, aware of the urgent need to improve transportation in general and sensing the political advantages that could accrue to them from directing funds to their districts, proposed spending federal money on local projects. Both Madison and Monroe vetoed such local proposals, believing them to be unconstitutional. Thus it was that some of the most famous projects of the day, such as the Erie Canal, which lay wholly within New York state, and the early railroads, were financed by state or private money.

The support of Madison and Monroe for measures initially identified with their political opposition was an indicator of their realism. The three aspects of the American System—bank, tariff, roads—were all parts of the basic infrastructure that the American economy needed in order to develop. Briefly, during the Era of Good Feelings, politicians agreed about the need for all three. Later, each would be a source of heated partisan argument.

THE DIPLOMACY OF JOHN QUINCY ADAMS

The diplomatic achievements of the Era of Good Feelings were due almost entirely to the efforts of one man, John Quincy Adams, Monroe's secretary of state. Adams set himself the task of tidying up the borders of the United States. Two accords with Britain—the **Rush-Bagot Treaty of 1817** and the Convention of 1818—fixed the border between the United States and Canada at the 49th parallel and resolved conflicting U.S. and British claims to Oregon with an agreement to occupy it jointly for ten (eventually twenty) years. The American claim to Oregon (present-day

Second Bank of the United States A national bank chartered by Congress in 1816 with extensive regulatory powers over currency and credit.

Rush-Bagot Treaty of 1817 Treaty between the United States and Britain that effectively demilitarized the Great Lakes by sharply limiting the number of ships each power could station on them.

8–8
Sacagawea Interprets for Lewis and Clark (1804)

British Columbia, Washington, Oregon, northern Idaho, and parts of Montana) was based on China trader Robert Gray's discovery of the Columbia River in 1792 and on the Lewis and Clark expedition of 1804–1806.

Adams's major diplomatic accomplishment was the Adams-Onís or **Transcontinental Treaty of 1819**, in which he skillfully wrested concessions from the faltering Spanish empire. Adams convinced Spain not only to cede Florida but also to drop all previous claims it had to the Louisiana Territory and Oregon. In return, the United States relinquished claims on Texas and assumed responsibility for the $5 million in claims that U.S. citizens had against Spain.

Finally, Adams picked his way through the remarkable changes occurring in Latin America, developing the policy that bears his president's name, the **Monroe Doctrine**. The United States was the first country outside Latin America to recognize the independence of Spain's former colonies. When the European powers (France, Austria, Russia, and Prussia) began talk of a plan to help Spain recover the lost colonies, what was the United States to do? The British, suspicious of the European powers, proposed a British-American declaration against European intervention in the hemisphere. Others might have been flattered by an approach from the British empire, but Adams would have none of it. Showing the national pride that was so characteristic of the era, Adams insisted on an independent American policy. He, therefore, drafted for the president the hemispheric policy that the United States has followed ever since.

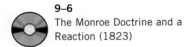

9–6
The Monroe Doctrine and a Reaction (1823)

On December 2, 1823, the president presented the Monroe Doctrine to Congress and the world. He called for the end of colonization of the Western Hemisphere by European nations (this was aimed as much at Russia and its Pacific coast settlements as at other European powers). Intervention by European powers in the affairs of the independent New World nations would be considered by the United States a danger to its own peace and safety. Finally, Monroe pledged that the United States would not interfere in the affairs of European countries or in the affairs of their remaining New World colonies.

All of this was a very loud bark from a very small dog. In 1823, the United States lacked the military and economic force to back up its grand statement. In fact, what kept the European powers out of Latin America was British opposition to European intervention, enforced by the Royal Navy. With this string of diplomatic achievements—the treaties with Britain and Spain and the Monroe Doctrine—the position of the United States on the North American continent was transformed. The Spanish presence was diminished, Russian expansion halted, and peace with Britain achieved. As a result, the United States was a much larger and stronger nation.

THE PANIC OF 1819

Across this impressive record of political and economic nation building fell the shadow of the Panic of 1819. A delayed reaction to the end of the War of 1812 and the Napoleonic Wars, the panic forced Americans to come to terms with their economic place in a peaceful world. As British merchant ships resumed trade on routes they had abandoned during the wars, the American shipping boom ended. And as European farm production recovered from the wars, the international demand for American foodstuffs declined and American farmers and shippers suffered.

Domestic economic conditions made matters worse. The western land boom that began in 1815 turned into a speculative frenzy that ended with a sharp contraction of credit by the Second Bank of the United States in 1819. State banks were forced to foreclose on many bad loans. Many small farmers were ruined, and they blamed the faraway Bank of the United States for their troubles. In the 1830s, Andrew Jackson would build a political movement on their resentment.

Transcontinental Treaty of 1819 Treaty between the United States and Spain in which Spain ceded Florida to the United States, surrendered all claims to the Pacific Northwest, and agreed to a boundary between the Louisiana Purchase territory and the Spanish Southwest.

Monroe Doctrine Declaration by President James Monroe in 1823 that the Western Hemisphere was to be closed off to further European colonization and that the United States would not interfere in the internal affairs of European nations.

Urban workers suffered both from the decline in international trade and from manufacturing failures caused by competition from British imports. As they lobbied for local relief, they found themselves deeply involved in urban politics, where they could express their resentment against the merchants and owners who had laid them off. Thus developed another component of Andrew Jackson's new political coalition.

Another confrontation arose over the tariff. Southern planters, hurt by a decline in the price of cotton, began to actively protest the protective tariff, which kept the price of imported goods high even when cotton prices were low. Manufacturers, hurt by British competition, lobbied for even higher rates, which they achieved in 1824 over Southern protests. Southerners then began to express doubts about the fairness of a political system in which they were always outvoted.

The Panic of 1819 was a symbol of this transitional time. It showed how far the country had moved since 1800, from Jefferson's republic of yeoman farmers toward a nation dominated by commerce. And the anger and resentment expressed by the groups harmed by the depression—farmers, urban workers, and southern planters—were portents of the politics of the upcoming Jackson era.

THE MISSOURI COMPROMISE

In the Missouri Crisis of 1819–1821, the nation confronted the momentous issue that had been buried in the general enthusiasm for expansion: as America moved west, would the largely Southern system of slavery expand as well? Until 1819, this question was decided regionally. The Northwest Ordinance of 1787 explicitly banned slavery in the northern section of trans-Appalachia but made no mention of it elsewhere. Because so much of the expansion into the Old Northwest and Southwest was lateral (Northerners stayed in the north, Southerners in the south), there was little conflict over sectional differences. In 1819, however, the sections collided in Missouri, which applied for admission to the Union as a slave state.

The Northern states, all of which had abolished slavery by 1819, looked askance at the extension of slavery. Southerners, on the other hand, did not believe Congress had the power to limit the expansion of slavery. They were alarmed that Northerners were considering national legislation on the matter. Slavery, in Southern eyes, was a question of property and, therefore, a matter for state rather than federal legislation. Thus, from the very beginning the expansion of slavery raised constitutional issues. Indeed, the aging politician of Monticello, Thomas Jefferson, immediately grasped the seriousness of the question of the expansion of slavery. As he prophetically wrote to a friend, "This momentous question like a fire bell in the night, awakened and filled me with terror. I considered it at once the [death] knell of the Union."

9–5
Thomas Jefferson Reacts to the "Missouri Question" (1820)

In 1819, Representative James Tallmadge Jr. of New York began more than a year of congressional controversy when he demanded that Missouri agree to the gradual end of slavery as the price of entering the Union. At first, the general public paid little attention, but religious reformers (Quakers prominent among them) organized a number of antislavery rallies in Northern cities that made politicians take notice. Former Federalists in the North who had seen their party destroyed by the achievements of Jefferson and his successors in the Virginia Dynasty eagerly seized on the Missouri issue. This was the first time that the growing Northern reform impulse had intersected with sectional politics. It was also the first time that Southern threats of secession were made openly in Congress.

9–12
The Trials of a Slave Girl

The Senate debate over the admission of Missouri, held in the early months of 1820, was the nation's first extended debate over slavery. Observers noted the high proportion of free African Americans among the listeners in

8–1
Memoirs of a Monticello Slave (1847)

MAP EXPLORATION

To explore an interactive version of this map, go to **http://www.prenhall.com/faraghertlc/map9.6**

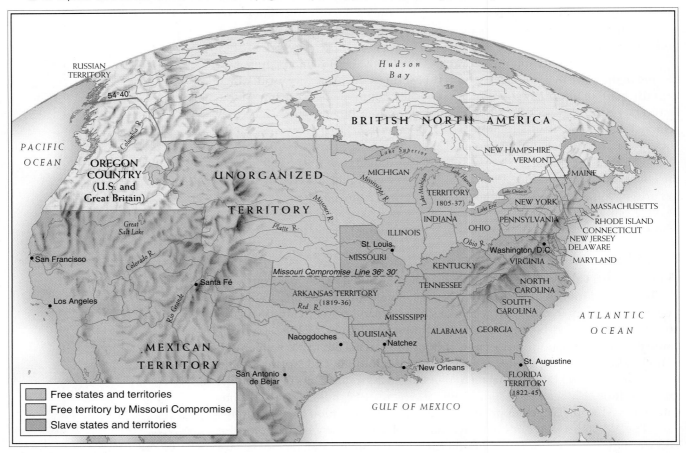

MAP 9-6
The Missouri Compromise   Before the Missouri Compromise of 1820, the Ohio River was the dividing line between the free states of the Old Northwest and the slaveholding states of the Old Southwest. The compromise stipulated that Missouri would enter the Union as a slave state (balanced by Maine, a free state), but slavery would be prohibited in the Louisiana Territory north of 36° 30′ (Missouri's southern boundary). This awkward compromise lasted until 1846 when the Mexican-American War reopened the issue of the expansion of slavery.

HOW DID westward expansion create added pressure to resolve the question of slavery?

Missouri Compromise   Sectional compromise in Congress in 1820 that admitted Missouri to the Union as a slave state and Maine as a free state and prohibited slavery in the northern Louisiana Purchase territory.

the Senate gallery. But the full realization that the future of slavery was central to the future of the nation would not become apparent to the general public until the 1850s.

In 1820, Congress achieved compromise over the sectional differences. Henry Clay forged the first of the many agreements that were to earn him the title of "the Great Pacificator" (peacemaker). The **Missouri Compromise** maintained the balance between free and slave states: Maine (which had been part of Massachusetts) was admitted as a free state in 1820 and Missouri as a slave state in the following year. A policy was also enacted with respect to slavery in the rest of the Louisiana Purchase: slavery was prohibited north of 36° 30′ north latitude—the southern boundary of Missouri—and permitted south of that line. This meant that the vast majority of the Louisiana Territory would be free. In reality, then, the Missouri Compromise could be only a temporary solution, because it left open the question of how the balance between slave and free states would be maintained.

CHRONOLOGY

1800	Thomas Jefferson elected president.		1814	Treaty of Ghent.
1802	Russian American Company headquarters established at Sitka, Alaska.		1815	Battle of New Orleans.
1803	Louisiana Purchase.		1816	James Monroe elected president.
	Marbury v. *Madison*.			Congress charters Second Bank of the United States.
	Ohio admitted to the Union.			Indiana admitted to the Union.
1804	Lewis and Clark expedition leaves St. Louis.		1817	Mississippi admitted to the Union.
	Thomas Jefferson reelected president.		1818	Illinois admitted to the Union.
1807	*Chesapeake-Leopard* incident.		1819	Panic of 1819.
	Embargo Act.			Adams-Onís Treaty.
1808	James Madison elected president.			Alabama admitted to the Union.
1809	Tecumseh forms military alliance among Northwest Confederacy peoples.		1819–1820	Missouri Crisis and Compromise.
1811	Battle of Tippecanoe.		1820	James Monroe reelected president.
1812	War of 1812 begins.			Maine admitted to the Union.
	James Madison reelected president.		1821	Missouri admitted to the Union as a slave state.
	Louisiana admitted to the Union.		1823	Monroe Doctrine.

CONCLUSION

In complex ways a developing economy, geographical expansion, and even a minor war helped shape American unity. Local, small, settled, face-to-face communities in both the North and the South began to send their more mobile, expectant members to new occupations in urban centers or west to form new settlements, displacing Indian communities in the process.

The westward movement was the novel element in the American national drama. Europeans believed that large size and a population in motion bred instability and political disintegration. Thomas Jefferson thought otherwise, and the Louisiana Purchase was the gamble that confirmed his guess. The westward population movement dramatically changed the political landscape and Americans' view of themselves.

Expansion would not create the settled communities of yeoman farmers Jefferson had hoped for. Rather, it would breed a nation of restless and acquisitive people and a new kind of national democratic politics that reflected their search for broader definitions of community.

QUICK REVIEW

The Missouri Compromise (1819 – 1821)

- Dealt with the issue of slavery in newly acquired territory.
- Henry Clay played a key role in reaching compromise.
- Maine entered union as a free state, Missouri as a slave state.
- Slavery was prohibited north of 36° 30' north latitude.

SUMMARY

North American Communities from Coast to Coast In 1800, European countries and the United States had established territorial claims and communities that spanned the North American continent. Each European colony developed along different paths and was subject to potential conflict arising from imperial rivalries. The United States experienced substantial growth, but political and economic dominance remained in traditional centers.

A National Economy In 1800, the United States was a producer of raw materials with an economy that was divided between self-sufficiency and market production. Events in Europe stimulated international trade that fueled development of other industries.

The Jefferson Presidency As president, Thomas Jefferson attempted to implement his philosophy of democratic government. Events overseas offered Jefferson the opportunity to expand the nation's territory dramatically.

Renewed Imperial Rivalry in North America The continuing conflict between England and France eventually created tensions and disputes with the United States. Jefferson's Indian policy and western expansion stimulated Indian revitalization and resistance movements.

The War of 1812 Grievances against the British led to the War of 1812. Military campaigns often involved British-Indian alliances against American forces allied with other Indian peoples and produced mixed results. Though the British captured Washington, D.C., they eventually sought peace. In New England, opposition to the war produced strong protests.

Defining the Boundaries Following the War of 1812, the United States turned its attention to national development and expansion. Migration surged into the trans-Appalachian West. Diplomacy secured and expanded American borders as well as signaling its stronger role as a diplomatic leader. An economic downturn and a crisis over the expansion of slavery signaled that the United States faced serious issues.

REVIEW QUESTIONS

1. What economic and political problems did the United States face as a new nation in a world dominated by war between Britain and France? How successful were the efforts by the Jefferson, Madison, and Monroe administrations to solve these problems?

2. The anti-European cast of Jefferson's republican agrarianism made it appealing to many Americans who wished to believe in their nation's uniqueness, but how realistic was it?

3. Some Federalists opposed the Louisiana Purchase, warning of the dangers of westward expansion. What are arguments for and against expansion?

4. What contradictions in American Indian policy did the confrontations between Tecumseh's alliance and soldiers and settlers in the Old Northwest reveal? Can you suggest solutions to them?

5. What did the War of 1812 accomplish?

6. What were the issues that made it impossible for the Era of Good Feelings to last?

KEY TERMS

American System (p. 234)
Battle of New Orleans (p. 230)
Embargo Act (p. 226)
Era of Good Feelings (p. 234)
Marbury v. *Madison* (p. 223)
Missouri Compromise (p. 238)
Monroe Doctrine (p. 236)
Nullification (p. 231)
Pan-Indian military resistance movement (p. 228)

Rush-Bagot Treaty of 1817 (p. 235)
Second Bank of the United States (p. 235)
Transcontinental Treaty of 1819 (p. 236)
Treaty of Ghent (p. 232)
War Hawks (p. 230)
War of 1812 (p. 230)

RECOMMENDED READING

Catharine Allgor, *Parlor Politics: In Which the Ladies of Washington Help Build a City and a Government* (2000). Argues that women played a vital role in the politics of the new capital city.

Stephen E. Ambrose, *Undaunted Courage: Meriweather Lewis, Thomas Jefferson, and the Opening of the American West* (1996). This very popular heroic version of the expedition is told by a master storyteller. It ought, however, to be supplemented by the Ronda version cited below that pays attention to the Indian side of the story.

Frank Bergon, ed., *The Journals of Lewis and Clark* (1989). A handy abridgment of the fascinating history of the expedition. (For more intensive study, Gary Moulton's six-volume unabridged edition of the expedition journals is unsurpassed.)

R. David Edmunds, *Tecumseh and the Quest for Indian Leadership* (1984). A sympathetic portrait.

Joseph J. Ellis, *American Sphinx: The Character of Thomas Jefferson* (1998). An engaging exploration of Jefferson's many contradictions.

John Mack Faragher, *Sugar Creek* (1987). The fullest examination of the lives of pioneers in the Old Northwest.

Donald Hickey, *The War of 1812: A Forgotten Conflict* (1989). Takes a fresh look at the events and historiography of the war.

Drew McCoy, *The Elusive Republic: Political Economy in Jeffersonian America* (1980). The most useful discussion of the ties between expansion and republican agrarianism.

Glover Moore, *The Missouri Controversy, 1819–1821* (1953). The standard account.

Peter S. Onuf, *Jefferson's Empire* (2000). A thoughtful study of Jefferson's ideas about republicanism, empire, and nationalism.

Merrill Peterson, *Thomas Jefferson and the New Nation* (1970). A good one-volume political biography of Jefferson. (The major biography, by Dumas Malone, is a multivolume work.)

James Ronda, *Lewis and Clark among the Indians* (1984). An innovative look at the famous explorers through the eyes of the Indian peoples they encountered.

I blush for my country when I see such things, and I often tremble with apprehension that our Constitution will not long withstand the current which threatens to overwhelm it . . .
—Benjamin B. French, September 1828

Andrew Jackson speaking to a crowd after his election. Politics in the olden time— General Jackson, President-elect, on his way to Washington.

10

THE GROWTH OF DEMOCRACY
1824–1840

1824   1840

AMERICAN COMMUNITIES

Martin Van Buren Forges a New Kind of Political Community

WHEN MARTIN VAN BUREN LEFT ALBANY FOR WASHINGTON IN THE fall of 1821 to take up his new position as junior senator from New York, he wrote complacently: "I left the service of the state [of New York] for that of the federal government with my friends in full and almost unquestioned possession of the state government in all its branches, at peace with each other and overflowing with kindly feelings towards myself." Thus did Van Buren sum up more than ten years of intense activity in New York State politics in which he and his allies, nicknamed the Bucktails (for the Indian-inspired insignia, the tail of a buck, that members wore on their hats), created one of the first modern democratic political parties. How could it be, Washington politicians asked, that this short, invariably pleasant but rather nondescript man had triumphed over the renowned DeWitt Clinton?

Tall, handsome, arrogant DeWitt Clinton, governor of New York from 1817 to 1823 (and again from 1825 until his death in 1828), had been swept into office on a tide of enthusiasm for his plan to build a canal the length of the state. Clinton soon gained legislative approval for the project—the Erie Canal—the most ambitious and most successful canal project in an era of canal building. An aristocrat in wealth, connections, and attitude, Clinton represented old-style politics. During his first terms as governor he ran the New York Jeffersonian Republican Party as though it were his personal property, dispensing patronage to relatives and friends (many of whom were Federalists) on the basis of their loyalty to him rather than their political principles.

Martin Van Buren was a new kind of politician. Born in the small, Dutch-dominated town of Kinderhook, New York, Van Buren was the son of a tavern keeper, not a member of the wealthy elite. He grew up with an enduring resentment of the aristocratic landowning families, such as the Van Schaacks and the Van Rensselaers (and, by extension, the Clintons), who disdained him when he was young. Masking his anger with charming manners, Van Buren took advantage of the growing strength of the Jeffersonian Republican Party in New York State to wrest control of the party from Clinton and forge it into a new kind of political organization. Clinton's use of patronage to reward friends at the expense of young party loyalists infuriated Van Buren and other rising politicians. Two years after Clinton became governor, Van Buren wrote bitterly to a friend: "A man to be a sound politician and in any degree useful to his country must be guided by higher and steadier considerations than those of personal sympathy and private regard. . . . In the name of all that is holy, where is the evidence of that towering mind and

those superior talents which it has been the business of puffers and toad eaters to attribute to [Clinton]?"

By 1819, Van Buren had gathered together enough other disgruntled Jeffersonian Republicans to form the Bucktail faction and openly challenge Clinton. Two years later, at the state constitutional convention of 1821 (where they made up three-fourths of the delegates), the Bucktails sealed their victory. Meeting in Albany to revise the out-of-date constitution of 1777, the convention voted to streamline the organization of state government and sharply curtail the patronage powers of the governor. To cement these changes, delegates enacted nearly total manhood suffrage: all adult male citizens who paid state or local taxes, served in the militia, or worked on state roads—more than four-fifths of the adult male population—were now eligible to vote directly for state legislators, governor, and members of Congress.

This dramatic democratization of politics reflected the state's changing population. Already the bustling port of New York was the nation's largest city, and the state's commercial opportunities were attracting shrewd Yankee traders from New England, "whose laws, customs and usages," conservative senator Rufus King complained, "differ from those of New York." The old ruling families, failing to recognize the new commercial and social values of the newcomers, were losing their grip on politics. Rising politicians like Van Buren and other Bucktails, in contrast, found opportunity in these changing conditions. Attuned to popular feeling, they responded to the state's growing and increasingly diverse population by creating a new kind of political community. A political party, they maintained, should be a democratic organization expressing the will of all its members, not an organization dominated by an elite group like Clinton's and bound together only by family ties and political favors. All party members, including leaders, would have to abide by majority rule. Party loyalty, rather than personal opinion or friendship, would be the bond that kept the party together and, rather than aristocratic background, the principal requirement for party leadership. "The first man we see step to the rear," wrote Bucktail Silas Wright Jr., still smarting from the factionalism and favoritism of the Clinton years, "we cut down." In the new party system, there would be no tolerance for politicans who followed their own self-interest rather than the larger good of the party.

By the time he departed for Washington in the fall of 1821, Van Buren had established in Albany a closely knit group of friends and allies who practiced these new political principles. Party decisions, reached by discussion in legislative caucus and *publicized by the party newspaper, the* Albany Argus, *were binding on all members and enforced by patronage decisions. The group, dubbed the "***Albany Regency***," ran New York State politics for twenty years. For all those years Martin Van Buren was in Washington, where he was a major architect of the new democratic politics of mass participation that has been called the Second American Party System. This new movement created, for the first time in American history, national communities of political partisans. Van Buren understood how to create these new communities. Van Buren believed that organization and discipline were essential not for their own sake but because they allowed democracy to flourish. He claimed that what made him different from DeWitt Clinton and earlier politicians was his "faith in the capacity of the masses of the people of our Country to govern themselves, and in their general integrity in the exercise of that function." This unprecedented confidence in popular opinion made American politics and politicians unique in the changing world of the early nineteenth century.*

THE NEW DEMOCRATIC POLITICS IN NORTH AMERICA

The early years of the nineteenth century were a time of extraordinary growth and change not only for the United States but also for all the countries of North America. Seen in continental perspective, the American embrace of popular democracy was unusual. Elsewhere crises over popular rights dominated.

HOW DID suffrage expand between 1800 and 1840?

CONTINENTAL STRUGGLES OVER POPULAR RIGHTS

In 1821, after eleven years of revolts (see Chapter 9), Mexico achieved its independence from Spain.

Briefly united under the leadership of Colonel Agustin de Iturbide, Mexico declared itself a constitutional monarchy that promised equality for everyone—peninsulares, criollos, mestizos, and Indians alike. But the initial unity was short-lived. Iturbide reigned as emperor of Mexico for little more than a year before he was overthrown by a military junta and later executed as a traitor. A series of weak presidents repeatedly invoked emergency powers and relied on the army as they attempted to revive a faltering economy and reconcile the differences between the centralists—the vested interests of clergy, large landowners, and the military—and the federalists, largely criollos and mestizos, who hoped to create a liberal republic modeled on the American one. The strongest of the early presidents was General Antonio Lopez de Santa Anna, elected to the presidency for the first time in 1833. He dominated Mexican politics for the next twenty years, during which he assumed dictatorial, centralized power, surviving the loss of Texas in 1836 and the other northern provinces in 1848 to the United States (see Chapter 15). The unresolved issue of elite versus popular rule continued to undermine the hope for unity, popular rights, and stable government in an independent Mexico.

The independence of Haiti in 1804 (see Chapter 9) set the pattern for events in many other Caribbean islands in subsequent years. Independence destroyed the sugar industry, for freed slaves refused to perform the killing labor demanded of them on sugar plantations. The British Caribbean islands were racked with revolts. In response, the British Parliament abolished slavery in all British colonies in 1834. As in Haiti, sugar production then plunged. The only island where sugar production increased was Spanish Cuba, where slavery remained legal until 1880. Elsewhere the economic collapse following emancipation destroyed the political authority of local white elites, forcing the British government to impose direct

Albany Regency   The tightly disciplined state political machine built by Martin Van Buren in New York.

IMAGE KEY
for pages 242–243

a. A \$5 note of the Second Bank of the United States.

b. Andrew Jackson speaking to a crowd after his election.

c. A Cherokee Indian newspaper, *Cherokee Phoenix*.

d. An old, antique Bible bound in leather with a gold cross on the cover.

e. A portrait of Andrew Jackson by Thomas Scully.

f. A 1829 painting of the Fairview Inn on the National Road, three miles west of Baltimore.

g. Americans endured poverty and unemployment by drinking, begging, and rioting in the streets of a city during the 1837 Specie Panic.

h. A banner for William Henry Harrison and John Tyler features political slogans of the Log Cabin campaign above the date of the rally.

i. An 1841 issue of the *Crockett Almanac*.

rule. Most of the British possessions in the Caribbean remained Crown Colonies until the 1920s. This sequence of events—revolt, emancipation, economic collapse, loss of local political autonomy—was closely observed by slaveowners in the American South and made them fear for their own futures.

Still a third crisis of popular rights occurred in British North America. In 1837 both Upper and Lower Canada rebelled against the limited representative government that the British government had imposed in the Constitutional Act of 1791. By far the most serious revolt was in predominantly French Lower Canada. Fearing that the true aim of the rebels was independence or, worse, becoming a part of the United States, the British government refused to recognize the French Canadian demand for their own political voice. In 1840, Britain abolished the local government of Lower Canada and joined it to Upper Canada in a union that most French Canadians opposed and in which they were a minority. In his report to the British government, Lord Durham announced that the purpose of union was to end the ethnic enmity between British and French by forcing the latter to assimilate and "abandon their vain hopes of nationality." Lord Durham suggested increased colonial self-government, but the British government, fearing further trouble, refused to grant it.

In comparison to these experiences, the rapid spread of suffrage in the United States and the growth of a vibrant, but stable, democratic political culture seemed extraordinary. But after a brilliant start, in the 1850s the United States, like its neighbors, foundered on sectional differences that not even political democracy could reconcile. (See Chapter 15.)

THE EXPANSION AND LIMITS OF SUFFRAGE

Before 1800 most of the original thirteen states had limited the vote to property owners or taxpayers amounting to less than half the white male population.

Westward expansion changed the nature of American politics. The new western states extended the right to vote to all white males over the age of twenty-one. Kentucky entered the Union with universal manhood suffrage in 1792, and Tennessee (1796) and Ohio (1803) entered with low taxpayer qualifications that approached universal suffrage. Soon older states such as New Jersey (1807) and Maryland (1810) dropped their property qualification for voting. By 1820, most of the older states had followed suit. There were laggards—Rhode Island, Virginia, and Louisiana did not liberalize their voting qualifications until later—but by 1840 more than 90 percent of adult white males in the nation could vote. And they could vote for more officials: governors and (most important) presidential electors were now elected by direct vote rather than chosen by small groups of state legislators.

Universal white manhood suffrage, of course, was far from true universal suffrage: the right to vote remained barred to most of the nation's free African American males and to women of any race. Only in five New England states (Maine, New Hampshire, Vermont, Massachusetts, and Rhode Island) could free African American men vote before 1865. In most of the other northern states, the right of free African American men to vote was limited, first by custom and later by law. In 1821 in New York, for example, the same Bucktail-dominated legislature that voted to extend the franchise to most white men also restricted it among African American men to those with property valued at \$250 or more, a very high amount at the time. As a result, only 68 of the nearly 13,000 African Americans in New York City qualified to vote in 1825.

Free African American men were denied the vote in all Southern states and, surprisingly, in the new Western states as well. The Ohio constitution of 1802 denied African Americans the right to vote, to hold public office, and to testify against

MAP EXPLORATION

To explore an interactive version of this map, go to **http://www.prenhall.com/faraghertlc/map10.1**

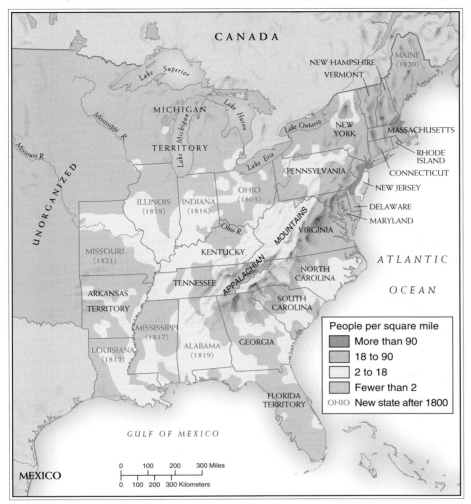

MAP 10-1

Population Trends: Westward Expansion, 1830   Westward population movement, a trickle in 1800, had become a flood by 1830. Between 1800 and 1830 the U.S. white and African American population more than doubled (from 5.3 million to 12.9 million), but the trans-Appalachian population grew tenfold (from 370,000 to 3.7 million). By 1830 more than a third of the nation's inhabitants lived west of the original thirteen states.

WHO WERE the western settlers and why did they leave the East?

white men in court cases. The constitutions of other Western states—Illinois, Indiana, Michigan, Iowa, Wisconsin, and (later) Oregon—attempted to solve the "problem" of free African Americans by simply denying them entry into the state at all.

The denial of suffrage to white women stemmed from the patriarchal belief that men headed households and represented the interests of all household members. Even wealthy single women who lived alone were considered subordinate to male relatives and denied the right to vote. (New Jersey had been an exception to this rule until it amended its constitution in 1807 to withdraw the franchise from propertied women.)

Although the extension of suffrage to all classes of white men seemed to indicate that women had no role in public affairs, in fact women's informal involvement

QUICK REVIEW

Suffrage

◆ By 1840 over 70 percent of adult white males could vote.

◆ African American men were allowed to vote in only five New England states.

◆ The right to vote was denied to women of any race.

MAP EXPLORATION

To explore an interactive version of this map, go to
http://www.prenhall.com/faraghertlc/map10.2

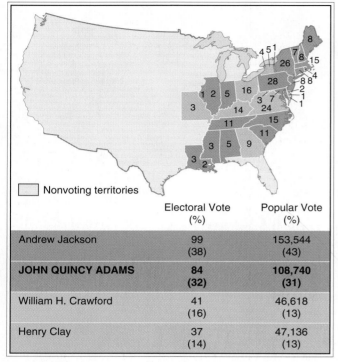

	Electoral Vote (%)	Popular Vote (%)
Andrew Jackson	99 (38)	153,544 (43)
JOHN QUINCY ADAMS	**84 (32)**	**108,740 (31)**
William H. Crawford	41 (16)	46,618 (13)
Henry Clay	37 (14)	47,136 (13)

MAP 10-2

The Election of 1824   The presidential vote of 1824 was clearly sectional. John Quincy Adams carried his native New England and little else, Henry Clay carried only his own state of Kentucky and two adjoining states, and Crawford's appeal was limited to Virginia and Georgia. Only Andrew Jackson moved beyond the regional support of the Old Southwest to wider appeal and the greatest number of electoral votes. Because no candidate had a majority, however, the election was thrown into the House of Representatives, which chose Adams.

WHAT ROLE DID political parties play in the election of 1824?

10–2
A "Corrupt Bargain" or Politics as Usual? (1824)

MAP EXPLORATION

To explore an interactive version of this map, go to
http://www.prenhall.com/faraghertlc/map10.3

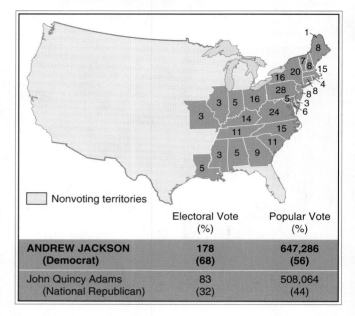

	Electoral Vote (%)	Popular Vote (%)
ANDREW JACKSON (Democrat)	**178 (68)**	**647,286 (56)**
John Quincy Adams (National Republican)	83 (32)	508,064 (44)

MAP 10-3

The Election of 1828   Andrew Jackson's victory in 1828 was the first success of the new national party system. The coalition of state parties that elected him was national, not regional. Although his support was strongest in the South and West, his ability to carry Pennsylvania and parts of New York demonstrated his national appeal.

TO WHAT extent was Andrew Jackson a "popular" president?

in politics grew along with the increasing pace of political activity. At the same time, however, as "manhood" rather than property became the qualification for voting, men began to ignore women's customary political activity and to regard their participation as inappropriate, an attitude that politically active women increasingly resented.

Thus, in a period famous for democratization and "the rise of the common man," the exclusion of important groups—African American men and women of all races—marked the limits of liberalization. It is also true that nowhere else in the world was the right to vote so widespread as it was in the United States. The extension of suffrage to propertyless farm workers and members of the laboring poor in the nation's cities left European observers wondering: Could "mob rule" possibly succeed? The election of 1824 provided the first outline of the answer.

THE ELECTION OF 1824

The 1824 election marked a dramatic end to the political truce that James Monroe had established in 1817. Five candidates, all of them members of the Republican Party, ran for president: William H. Crawford of Georgia, John Quincy Adams of Massachusetts, Henry Clay of Kentucky, Andrew Jackson of Tennessee, and John C. Calhoun of South Carolina, who withdrew before the election to run for vice president.

Because no candidate had an electoral majority, the election was thrown into the House of Representatives, as in the election of 1800. After some political dealing, Henry Clay threw his support to Adams and the House elected Adams president. This was customary and proper: the Constitution gave the House the power to decide, and Clay had every right to advise his followers how to vote. But when Adams named Clay his secretary of state, the traditional stepping-stone to the highest office, Jackson's supporters promptly accused them of a "corrupt bargain." Popular opinion, the new element in politics, supported Jackson. John Quincy Adams served four miserable years as president, knowing that Jackson would challenge him, and win, in 1828.

THE NEW POPULAR DEMOCRATIC CULTURE

As the election of 1824 showed, the spread of universal manhood suffrage meant a change in popular attitudes that spelled the end of personal, elitist politics. Politicians in other states shared Van Buren's vision of tightly organized, broad-based political groups. In Virginia a group known as the Richmond Junto had control of state politics by 1816, and in Tennessee the Nashville Junto, masterminded by John Overton, held sway by 1822. In New Hampshire, Isaac Hill's Concord Regency was firmly in control by 1825.

The techniques of mass campaigns—huge political rallies, parades, and candidates with wide name recognition such as military heroes—were quickly adopted by the new political parties. So were less savory techniques such as lavish food and (especially) drink at polling places, which often turned elections into rowdy, brawling occasions.

The spirit that motivated the new mass politics was democratic pride in participation. Political processions were huge affairs, marked by the often spontaneous participation of men carrying badges and party regalia, banners and placards, and portraits of the candidates, accompanied by bands, fireworks, and the shouting and singing of party slogans and songs. The political party provided some of the same satisfactions that popular sports offer today: excitement, entertainment, and a sense of belonging. In effect, political parties functioned as giant national men's clubs. They made politics an immediate and engrossing topic of conversation and argument for men of all walks of life. In this sense, the political party was the political manifestation of a wider social impulse toward community.

THE ELECTION OF 1828

The election of 1828 was the first to demonstrate the power and effectiveness of the new popular democratic culture and party system. With the help of Martin Van Buren, his campaign manager, Andrew Jackson rode the wave of the new democratic politics to the presidency. Voter turnout in 1828 was more than twice that of 1824. Jackson's party, the Democratic Republicans (they soon dropped "Republicans" and became simply the **Democrats**), spoke the language of democracy, and they opposed the special privilege personified for them by President John Quincy Adams and his National Republican (as distinguished from the earlier Jeffersonian Republican) Party.

Jackson won 56 percent of the popular vote (well over 80 percent in much of the South and West) and a decisive electoral majority of 178 votes to Adams's 83. The vote was interpreted as a victory for the common man. But the most important thing about Jackson's victory was the coalition that achieved it. The new democratically based polit-

Politics, abetted by the publication of inexpensive party newspapers, was a great topic of conversation among men in early nineteenth-century America, as Richard Caton Woodville's 1845 painting *Politics in an Oyster House* suggests.

Richard Caton Woodville, *Politics in an Oyster House*, 1848. The Walters Art Museum

QUICK REVIEW

Expansion of the Franchise

- Opposition to land ownership as qualification for voting.
- Demands that all white men be treated equally.
- As political rights for white men expanded, political opportunities shrunk for women and free black people.

Democrats Political party formed in the 1820s under the leadership of Andrew Jackson; favored states' rights and a limited role for the federal government.

ical organizations—the Richmond and Nashville juntos, the Albany and Concord regencies, with help from Calhoun's organization in South Carolina—worked together to elect him. Popular appeal, which Jackson the military hero certainly possessed, was not enough to ensure victory. To be truly national, a party had to create and maintain a coalition of North, South, and West. The Democrats were the first to do this.

THE JACKSON PRESIDENCY

Andrew Jackson's election ushered in a new era in American politics, an era that historians have called the "Age of the Common Man." Jackson himself, however, was no common man: he was a military hero, a rich slave owner, and an imperious and decidedly undemocratic personality. "Old Hickory," as Jackson was affectionately called, was tough and unbending, just like hickory itself, one of the hardest of woods. Yet he had a mass appeal to ordinary people unmatched—and indeed unsought—by earlier presidents. The secret to Jackson's extraordinary appeal lies in the changing nature of American society. Jackson was the first to respond to the ways in which westward expansion and the extension of the suffrage were changing politics at the national as well as the local and state levels.

A POPULAR PRESIDENT

On March 4, 1829, Andrew Jackson was inaugurated as president of the United States. Jackson himself was still in mourning for his beloved wife Rachel, whose recent death he attributed to the slanders of the campaign. But everyone else was celebrating. The small community of Washington was crowded with strangers, many of them Westerners and common people who had come especially for Jackson's inauguration. Jackson's brief inaugural address was almost drowned out by the cheering of the crowd, and after the ceremony the new president was mobbed by well-wishers. The same unrestrained enthusiasm was evident at a White House reception, where the crowd was large and disorderly. People stood on chairs and sofas to catch glimpses of Jackson and shoved and pushed to reach the food and drink, which were finally carried out to the lawn. In the rush to follow, some people exited through windows rather than the doors. This was the exuberance of democracy in action. It marked something new in American politics. Indeed, Jackson's administration was different from all those before it.

WHAT STEPS did Andrew Jackson take to strengthen the executive branch of the federal government?

10–4
The "Commoner" Takes Office
(1828)

Until 1829, presidential inaugurations had been small, polite, and ceremonial occasions. Andrew Jackson's popularity, however, brought a horde of well-wishers to Washington for his inaugural. Conservative critics, dismayed by the disorderly crowd at Jackson's frontier-style open house at the White House, feared "the reign of King Mob" had begun.

All Creation Going to the White House, by Robert Cruickshank. Library of Congress

A STRONG EXECUTIVE

Andrew Jackson dominated his administration. Except for Martin Van Buren, whom he appointed secretary of state, he mostly ignored the heads of government departments who made up his official cabinet. Instead he consulted with an informal group, dubbed the "Kitchen Cabinet," made up of Van Buren and old western friends. The Kitchen Cabinet did not include John C. Calhoun, the vice president, or either of the other two great sectional representatives, Henry Clay and Daniel Webster. Jackson never forgave Clay for his role in the "corrupt bargain" of 1825, and he saw Daniel Webster as a representative of his favorite political target, the privileged elite.

Jackson freely used the tools of his office to strengthen the executive branch of government at the expense of the legislature and judiciary. By using the veto more frequently than all previous presidents combined (twelve vetoes compared with nine by the first six presidents), Jackson forced Congress to constantly consider his opinions. Even more important, Jackson's "negative activism" restricted federal activity, thereby allowing more power to remain in state hands.

In one of his most famous and unexpected actions, the veto of the Maysville Road Bill of 1830, Jackson refused to allow federal funding of a southern spur of the National Road in Kentucky, claiming such funding should be left to the state. Like Presidents James Madison and James Monroe before him, Jackson believed that federal funding for extensive and expensive transportation measures was unconstitutional because it infringed on the "reserved powers" the Constitution left to the states. The veto was unexpected because it disappointed Jackson's strongest supporters, Westerners who wanted better transportation. But by addressing his veto message to a popular audience, not just to Congress, and by dramatically portraying federal funding as a threat to the popular political principle of states' rights (and by making it clear that he was not opposed to federal funding of all internal improvements), Jackson actually gained political support. He also had the satisfaction of defeating a measure central to the American System proposed by his western rival, Henry Clay. (See Chapter 9).

QUICK REVIEW

Jackson's Inauguration

◆ Westerners and common people crowded into Washington for the inauguration.

◆ Jackson's brief address drowned out by cheering.

◆ The crowd at the White House was large and disorderly.

INTERNAL IMPROVEMENTS: BUILDING AN INFRASTRUCTURE

Despite the ongoing constitutional debate over who should fund internal improvements, no one argued that they should not be funded at all. On the contrary, ordinary people and politicians of all persuasions agreed that both federal and state governments had an important role in encouraging economic growth and in fostering the development of a national market. And that role included subsidizing the costs of the basic infrastructure—the canals and railroads—that would tie the national market together.

WHAT LED to the transportation revolution?

THE TRANSPORTATION REVOLUTION

Between 1800 and 1840 the United States experienced truly revolutionary improvements in transportation. More than any other development, these improvements encouraged Americans to look beyond their local communities to broader ones and to foster the enterprising commercial spirit for which they became so widely known.

The federal government demonstrated its commitment to the improvement of interregional transportation by funding the National Road in 1808, at the time the greatest single federal transportation expense (its eventual cost was $7 million).

Governor DeWitt Clinton is shown pouring a keg of Lake Erie water into New York Harbor at the *Marriage of the Waters* ceremony on November 4, 1825, marking the official opening of his pet project, the Erie Canal. Initially derided as "Clinton's Ditch," the completion of the 364-mile canal opened America's heartland to settlement and international commerce.

C. Y. Turner, *The Marriage of the Waters*. Mural in DeWitt Clinton High School, New York City. Courtesy of Margaret Yardley Voelker and *American Heritage Magazine*

Built of gravel on a stone foundation, it crossed the Appalachian Mountains at Cumberland, Maryland, thereby opening up the West. Built in stages—to Wheeling, Virginia (now West Virginia), by 1818, to Columbus, Ohio, by 1833, to Vandalia, Illinois, almost at the Mississippi River, by 1850—the National Road tied the East and the West together, providing strong evidence of the nation's commitment to both expansion and cohesion and helping to foster a national community.

CANALS AND STEAMBOATS

However much they helped the movement of people, the National Road and other roads were unsatisfactory in a commercial sense. Shipments of bulky goods like grain were too slow and expensive by road. Waterborne transportation was much cheaper and still the major commercial link among the Atlantic seaboard states and in the Mississippi–Ohio river system. But before the 1820s most water routes were north–south or coastal (Boston to Charleston, for example); east–west links were urgently needed. Canals turned out to be the answer.

The Erie Canal—the most famous canal of the era—was the brainchild of New York governor DeWitt Clinton, who envisioned a link between New York City and the Great Lakes through the Hudson River and a 364-mile-long canal stretching from Albany to Buffalo. When Clinton proposed the canal in 1817 it was derisively called "Clinton's Ditch"; the longest then existing American canal was only 27 miles long and had taken nine years to build. Nevertheless, Clinton convinced the New York legislature to approve a bond issue for the canal, and investors (New York and British merchants) subscribed to the tune of $7 million, an immense sum for the day.

Building the canal—40 feet wide, 4 feet deep, 364 miles long, with 83 locks, and more than 300 bridges along the way—was a vast engineering and construction challenge. In the early stages nearby farmers worked for $8 a month, but when malaria hit the workforce in the summer of 1819, many went home. They were replaced by 3,000 Irish contract laborers, who were much more expensive—50 cents a day plus room and board—but more reliable (if they survived). Local peo-

9–3
The Case for the Erie Canal

ple regarded the Irish workers as different and frightening, but the importation of foreign contract labor for this job was a portent of the future. Much of the heavy construction work on later canals and railroads was performed by immigrant labor.

DeWitt Clinton had promised, to general disbelief, that the Erie Canal would be completed in less than ten years, and he made good on his promise. The canal was the wonder of the age. On October 26, 1825, Clinton declared it open in Buffalo and sent the first boat, the *Seneca Chief,* on its way to New York at the incredible speed of four miles an hour. (Ironically, the Seneca Indians, for whom the boat was named, had been removed from the path of the canal and confined to a small reservation.) The Erie Canal provided easy passage to and from the interior, both for people and for goods. It drew settlers like a magnet from the East and, increasingly, from overseas: by 1830, some 50,000 people a year were moving west on the canal to the rich farmland of Indiana, Illinois, and territory farther west. Earlier settlers now had a national, indeed an international, market for their produce. Moreover, farm families themselves became consumers.

Towns along the canal—Utica, Rochester, Buffalo—became instant cities, each an important commercial center in its own right. Perhaps the greatest beneficiary was New York City, which quickly established a commercial and financial supremacy no other American city could match. The Erie Canal decisively turned New York's merchants away from Europe and toward America's own heartland, building both interstate commerce and a feeling of community.

The phenomenal success of the Erie Canal prompted other states to construct similar waterways to tap the rich interior market. Between 1820 and 1840, $200 million was invested in canal building. No other waterway achieved the success of the Erie, which collected $8.5 million in tolls in its first nine years. Nevertheless, the spurt of canal building ended the geographical isolation of much of the country.

An even more important improvement in water transportation, especially in the American interior, was the steamboat. Robert Fulton first demonstrated the commercial feasibility of steamboats in 1807, and they were soon operating in the East. Redesigned with more efficient engines and shallower, broader hulls, steamboats transformed commerce on the country's great inland river system: the Ohio, the Mississippi, the Missouri, and their tributaries. Steamboats were extremely dangerous, however; boiler explosions, fires, and sinkings were common, leading to one of the first public demands for regulation of private enterprise in 1838.

Dangerous as they were, steamboats greatly stimulated trade in the nation's interior. There had long been downstream trade on flatboats along the Mississippi River system, but it was limited by the return trip overland on the arduous and dangerous Natchez Trace. For a time, steamboats actually increased the down-river flatboat trade, because boatmen could now make more round trips in the same amount of time, traveling home by steamboat in speed and comfort. The increased river- and canal-borne trade, like the New England shipping boom of a generation earlier, stimulated urban growth and all kinds of commerce.

RAILROADS

Remarkable as all these transportation changes were, the most remarkable was still to come. Railroads, new in 1830 (when the Baltimore and Ohio Railroad opened with 13 miles of track), grew to an astounding 31,000 miles by 1860. By that date, New England and the Old Northwest had laid a dense network of rails, and several lines had reached west beyond the Mississippi. The South, the least industrialized section of the nation, had fewer railroads. "Railroad mania" surpassed even canal mania as investors—as many as one-quarter of them British— rushed to profit from the new invention.

QUICK REVIEW

The Erie Canal

◆ Link between New York City and the Great Lakes

◆ Built first by local farmers then Irish and imigrant labor

◆ Completed in 10 years

QUICK REVIEW

Railroads

◆ 1830: 13 miles of track in the United States.

◆ 1860: 31,000 miles of track in the United States.

◆ Early railroads had to overcome technological and supply problems.

Early railroads, like the steamboat, had to overcome many technological and supply problems. For some years after the introduction of the railroad, canal boats and coastal steamers carried more freight and at lower cost. It was not until the 1850s that consolidation of local railroads into larger systems began in earnest. But already it was clear that this youngest transportation innovation would have far-reaching social consequences.

COMMERCIAL AGRICULTURE IN THE OLD NORTHWEST

Every advance in transportation—better roads, canals, steamboats, railroads—made it easier for farmers to get their produce to market. Improvements in agricultural machinery increased the amount of acreage a farmer could cultivate. These two developments, added to the availability of rich, inexpensive land in the heartland, moved American farmers permanently away from subsistence agriculture and into production for sale.

The impact of the transportation revolution on the Old Northwest was particularly marked. Settlement of the region, ongoing since the 1790s, accelerated. In the 1830s, after the opening of the Erie Canal, migrants from New England streamed into northern Ohio, Illinois, Indiana, southern Wisconsin, and Michigan and began to reach into Iowa.

Government policy strongly encouraged western settlement. The easy terms of federal land sales were an important inducement: terms eased from an initial rate of $2.00 per acre for a minimum of 320 acres in 1800, to $1.25 an acre for 80 acres in 1820. Still, this was too much for most settlers to pay all at once. Some people simply squatted, taking their chances that they could make enough money to buy the land before someone else bought it. Less daring settlers relied on credit, which was extended by banks, storekeepers, speculators, promoters, and, somewhat later, railroads, which received large grants of federal lands.

The very need for cash to purchase land involved western settlers in commercial agriculture from the beginning. Farmers, and the towns and cities that grew up to supply them, needed access to markets for their crops. Canals, steamboats, and railroads ensured that access, immediately tying the individual farm into national and international commercial networks. The long period of subsistence farming that had characterized colonial New England and the early Ohio Valley frontier was superseded by commercial agriculture stimulated by the transportation revolution.

Commercial agriculture in turn encouraged regional specialization. Ohioans shipped corn and hogs first by flatboat and later by steamboat to New Orleans. Cincinnati, the center of the Ohio trade, earned the nickname "Porkopolis" because of the importance of its slaughterhouses. By 1840, the national center of wheat production had moved west of the Appalachians to Ohio. Wheat flowed from the upper Midwest along the Erie Canal to eastern cities and increasingly to Europe.

At the same time, farmers who grew wheat or any other cash crop found themselves at the mercy of far-off markets, which established crop prices; distant canal or railroad companies, which set transportation rates; and the state of the national economy, which determined the availability of local credit. This direct dependence on economic forces outside the control of the local community was something new. So, too, was the dependence on technology, embodied in expensive new machines that farmers often bought on credit.

New tools made Western farmers unusually productive. John Deere's steel plow (invented in 1837) cut plowing time in half, making cultivation of larger

Cyrus McCormick is shown demonstrating his reaper to skeptical farmers. When they saw that the machine cut four times as much wheat a day as a hand-held scythe, farmers flocked to buy McCormick's invention. Agricultural practices, little changed for centuries, were revolutionized by machines like this.

The Testing of the First Reaping Machine, lithograph, 1831. Courtesy of the Chicago Historical Society

acreages possible. Seed drills were another important advance. But the most remarkable innovation was Cyrus McCormick's reaper, patented in 1834. Earlier, harvesting had depended on manpower alone. A man could cut two or three acres of wheat a day with a cradle scythe, but with the horse-drawn reaper he could cut twelve acres.

EFFECTS OF THE TRANSPORTATION REVOLUTION

Every east–west road, canal, and railroad helped to reorient Americans away from the Atlantic and toward the heartland. This new focus was decisive in the creation of national pride and identity. Transportation improvements such as the Erie Canal and the National Road linked Americans in larger communities of interest beyond the local community in which they lived. Other results were less positive. The technological triumphs of canal building and rail laying fostered a brash spirit of conquest over nature that was to become part of the American myth of the frontier. Furthermore, although every new transportation or communication link broke down local and regional isolation and helped to build a spirit of pride in the nation, it also refocused attention on questions of national politics. The new transportation system caused a subtle political shift, for it strengthened the influence of the North by improving the North's ties with the West more than its ties with the South. In this way, the new modes of communication and transportation served to heat up the politics of the era.

MAP EXPLORATION

To explore an interactive version of this map, go to **http://www.prenhall.com/faragherlc/map10.4**

MAP 10-4

Commercial Links: Rivers, Canals, Roads, 1830, and Rail Lines, 1850 By 1830, the United States was tied together by a network of roads, canals, and rivers. This "transportation revolution" fostered a great burst of commercial activity and economic growth. Transportation improvements accelerated the commercialization of agriculture by getting farmers' products to wider, nonlocal markets. Access to wider markets likewise encouraged new textile and other manufacturers to increase their scale of production. By 1850, another revolutionary mode of transportation, the railroad, had emerged as a vital link to the transportation infrastructure.

HOW DID the transportation revolution of the mid-nineteenth century fuel the American economy?

JACKSON AND HIS OPPONENTS: THE RISE OF THE WHIGS

As transportation improvements increased commercialization and the new democratic politics drew the people of the United States out of localism into larger networks, fundamental questions about national unity arose. What was the correct balance between local interests—the rights of the states—and the powers of the central government? The men who wrote the federal Constitution in Philadelphia in 1787 had not been able to reach agreement on this question. Because the Constitution deliberately left the federal structure ambiguous, all sectional disagreements automatically became constitutional issues that carried a threat to national unity. The great issues of Jackson's presidency expressed this continuing tension between nationalism and sectionalism. Jackson's responses to them created such controversy that a permanent opposition—another political party, known as the **Whigs**—was born.

THE NULLIFICATION CRISIS

The political issue that came to symbolize the divergent sectional interests of North and South, pitting the rights of individual states against the claims of a federal majority, was the protective tariff. As a group, wealthy Southern planters were opposed to tariffs, both because duties raised the cost of the luxury goods they imported from Europe and because they believed in the principle of free trade, fearing that American tariffs would cause other countries to retaliate with tariffs against Southern cotton. Most Southern congressmen, assured that the 1816 tariff was a temporary postwar recovery measure, voted for it. But it was not temporary. As the North industrialized and new industries demanded protection, tariff bills in 1824 and 1828, nicknamed the Tariff of Abominations, raised rates still higher and protected more items. Southerners protested, but they were outvoted in Congress by Northern and Western representatives.

Southerners in Congress lacked the votes to block the tariff and faced the bleak prospect that their economic interests would always be ignored by the majority. Southern opponents of the tariff insisted that it was not a truly national measure but a sectional one that helped only some groups while harming others. Thus, they claimed, it was unconstitutional because it violated the rights of some of the states.

South Carolina reacted to the Tariff of 1828 with the doctrine of nullification, which upheld the right of a state to declare a federal law null and void and to refuse to enforce it within the state. This was not a new argument. Thomas Jefferson and James Madison had used it in the Kentucky and Virginia Resolves of 1798, which they had written in opposing the Alien and Sedition Acts (see Chapter 8). The Hartford Convention of 1814–1815, at which Federalists protested grievances related to the War of 1812, had adopted the same position (see Chapter 9). At issue in each case was the power of the state against that of the federal government.

South Carolina had an important supporter of nullification in the person of John C. Calhoun, who wrote a widely circulated defense of the doctrine, the *Exposition and Protest*, in 1828. Because Calhoun was soon to serve as Andrew Jackson's vice president, he wrote the *Exposition* anonymously. He hoped to use his influence with Jackson to gain support for nullification, but he was disappointed.

Jackson saw nullification as a threat to national unity. As he said at a famous exchange of toasts at the annual Jefferson Day dinner in 1830, "Our Federal Union, it must be preserved." In response to Jackson, Calhoun offered his own toast: "The Union—next to our liberty most dear. May we always remember that it can only

WHO WERE Andrew Jackson's most important opponents and what did they support?

10–8
President Andrew Jackson's Proclamation Regarding Nullification (1832)

Whigs   The name used by advocates of colonial resistance to British measures during the 1760s and 1770s.

Nullification Crisis   Sectional crisis in the early 1830s in which a states' rights party in South Carolina attempted to nullify federal law.

be preserved by distributing equally the benefits and burdens of the Union." The president and the vice president were, thus, in open disagreement on a matter of crucial national importance. The outcome was inevitable: Calhoun lost all influence with Jackson, and two years later he took the unusual step of resigning the vice presidency. Martin Van Buren was elected to the office for Jackson's second term. Calhoun, his presidential aspirations in ruins, became a senator from South Carolina, and in that capacity participated in the last act of the nullification drama.

In 1832 the nullification controversy became a full-blown crisis. In passing the Tariff of 1832, Congress (in spite of Jackson's disapproval) retained high taxes on woolens, iron, and hemp, although it reduced duties on other items. South Carolina responded with a special convention and an Ordinance of Nullification, in which it rejected the tariff and refused to collect the taxes it required. The state further issued a call for a volunteer militia and threatened to secede from the Union if Jackson used force against it. Jackson responded vehemently, denouncing the nullifiers— "Disunion by armed force is treason"—and obtaining from Congress a Force Bill authorizing the federal government to collect the tariff in South Carolina at gunpoint if necessary. Intimidated, the other Southern states refused to follow South Carolina's lead. More quietly, Jackson also asked Congress to revise the tariff. Henry Clay, the Great Pacificator, swung into action and soon, with Calhoun's support, had crafted the Tariff Act of 1833. This measure appeared to meet Southern demands by pledging a return to the tariff rate of 1816 (an average of 20 percent) by 1842. The South Carolina legislature, unwilling to act without the support of other Southern states, quickly accepted this face-saving compromise and repealed its nullification of the tariff of 1832. In a final burst of bravado, the legislature nullified the Force Bill, but Jackson defused the crisis by ignoring this second nullification.

The nullification crisis was the most serious threat to national unity that the United States had ever experienced. South Carolinians, by threatening to secede, had forced concessions on a matter they believed of vital economic importance. They—and a number of other Southerners—believed that the resolution of the crisis illustrated the success of their uncompromising tactics. Most of the rest of the nation simply breathed a sigh of relief, echoing Daniel Webster's sentiment, spoken in the heat of the debate over nullification, "Liberty and Union, now and forever, one and inseparable!"

INDIAN REMOVAL

The official policy of the United States government from the time of Jefferson's administration was to promote the assimilation of Indian peoples by encouraging them to adopt white ways. To Indian groups who resisted "civilization" or who needed more time to adapt, Jefferson offered the alternative of removal from settled areas in the East to the new Indian Territory west of the Mississippi River. Following this logic, at the end of the War of 1812, the federal government signed removal treaties with a number of Indian nations of the Old Northwest, thereby opening up large tracts of land for white settlement (see Chapter 9). In the Southwest, however, the Five Civilized Tribes—the Cherokees, Chickasaws, Choctaws, Creeks, and Seminoles—remained. By the 1830s, under constant pressure from settlers, each of the five tribes had ceded most of its lands, but sizable self-governing groups lived in Georgia, Alabama, Mississippi, and Florida. All of these (except the Seminoles) had moved far in the direction of coexistence with whites, and they resisted suggestions that they should voluntarily remove themselves.

Despite the evidence of successful adaptation to the dominant white culture, in the 1820s the legislatures of Georgia, Alabama, and Mississippi, responding to pressures from land-hungry whites, voted to invalidate federal treaties

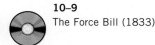
10–9
The Force Bill (1833)

This figurehead of Andrew Jackson, carved in 1834 for the navy frigate *Constitution*, captures the unmovable resolve that made Jackson so popular early in his presidency and so reviled during the Bank War.

Museum of the City of New York (M52.11)

MAP EXPLORATION

To explore an interactive version of this map, go to **http://www.prenhall.com/faraghertlc/map10.5**

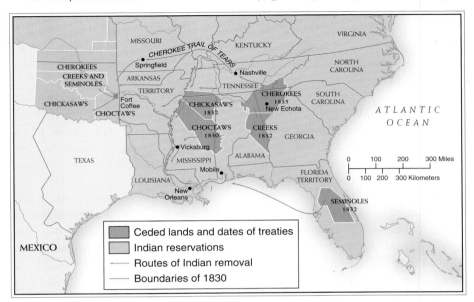

MAP 10-5

Southern Indian Cessions and Removals, 1830s   Pressure on the five major southern Indian peoples—the Cherokees, Chickasaws, Choctaws, Creeks, and Seminoles—that began during the War of 1812 culminated with their removal in the 1830s. Some groups from every tribe ceded their southern homelands peacefully and moved to the newly established Indian Territory west of Arkansas and Missouri. Some, like the Seminoles, resisted by force. Others, like the Cherokees, resisted in the courts but finally lost when President Andrew Jackson refused to enforce a Supreme Court decision in their favor. The Cherokees, the last to move, were forcibly removed by the U.S. Army along the "Trail of Tears" in 1838.

WHAT GROUPS supported the Indian Removal Act?

---

granting special self-governing status to Indian lands. Because the federal government, not the states, bore responsibility for Indian policy, these state actions constituted a challenge to federal authority. In this instance, however, unlike the Nullification Crisis, the resisting states had presidential support.

In 1830, at President Jackson's urging, the U.S. Congress passed the hotly debated **Indian Removal Act**, which appropriated funds for relocation, by force if necessary. When Jackson increased the pressure by sending federal officials to negotiate removal treaties with the southern tribes, most reluctantly signed and prepared to move. The Cherokees, however, fought their removal by using the white man's weapon—the law. At first they seemed to have won: in *Cherokee Nation* v. *Georgia* (1831) and *Worcester* v. *Georgia* (1832) Chief Justice John Marshall ruled that the Cherokees, though not a state or a foreign nation, were a "domestic dependent nation" that could not be forced by the state of Georgia to give up its land against its will. Ignoring the decision, Jackson continued his support for removal.

Faced by the Cherokees' de facto defeat, most of the Choctaws moved west in 1830; the last of the Creeks were forcibly moved by the military in 1836, and the Chickasaws a year later. And in 1838, in the last and most infamous removal, resisting Cherokees were driven west to Oklahoma along what came to be known as the **"Trail of Tears."** A 7,000-man army escorting them watched thousands (perhaps

10–4
Andrew Jackson, First Annual
Message to Congress (1829)

Indian Removal Act   President Andrew Jackson's measure that allowed state officials to override federal protection of Native Americans.

Trail of Tears   The forced march in 1838 of the Cherokee Indians from their homelands in Georgia to the Indian Territory in the West.

QUICK REVIEW

Georgia and the Cherokees

◆ Georgia stole land of Creek Indians in 1825.

◆ Georgia moved against Cherokees in 1828, stripping them of all legal rights.

◆ Stage was set for Indian Removal Act.

10–6
"Memorial of the Cherokee Nation" (1830)

10–10
Black Hawk, "Life of Black Hawk" (1833)

Black Hawk   1832 war in which federal troops and Illinois militia units defeated the Sauk and Fox Indians led by Black Hawk.

a quarter of the 16,000 Cherokees) die along the way. Another futile effort to resist removal, the Black Hawk "war," occurred in the Old Northwest. In 1832, Sac and Fox Indians, led by **Black Hawk**, attempted to move back to their old tribal grounds in Illinois following removal, but settlers saw the move as an invasion and demanded military protection. Federal troops chased the Black Hawk band to Wisconsin, where more than 300 Indians died in a final battle, and Black Hawk himself was taken prisoner. As in the South, the last of the remaining Indians east of the Mississippi were removed by the end of the 1830s.

THE BANK WAR

In 1816 Congress had granted a twenty-year charter to the Second Bank of the United States. The Bank played a powerful role in the expanding American economy, encouraging the growth of strong and stable financial interests and curbing less stable and irresponsible ones.

The Bank was not a government agency but a private institution, the majority of whose directors were appointed by the government. Its stockholders were some of the nation's richest men (New York's John Jacob Astor and Philadelphia's Stephen Girard among them). The Bank was directed by the erudite and aristocratic Nicholas Biddle of Philadelphia. Biddle, a friend of Thomas Jefferson and an avid amateur scientist, was the editor of the journals of Lewis and Clark.

The Bank, which with thirty branches was the nation's largest, performed a variety of functions: it held the government's money (about $10 million), sold government bonds, and made commercial loans. But its most important function was the control it exercised over state banks. At the time, America lacked a national currency. The money in circulation was a mixture of paper money (U.S. notes and the notes of state banks) and gold and silver coins (specie, or hard currency), many of them of foreign origin. Because state banks tended to issue more paper money than they could back with hard currency, the Bank always demanded repayment of its loans to them in coin. This policy forced state banks to maintain adequate reserves, curbed inflationary pressures (overprinting of their banknotes), and restricted speculative activities such as risky loans. In times of recession, the Bank eased the pressure on state banks, demanding only partial payment in coin. Thus, the Bank acted as a currency stabilizer by helping to control the money supply. It brought a semblance of order to what we today would consider a chaotic money system—coins of various weights and a multitude of state banknotes, many of which were discounted (not accepted at full face value) in other states.

The concept of a strong national bank was supported by the majority of the nation's merchants and businessmen and was a key element in Henry Clay's American System. Nevertheless, the Bank had many opponents. Western land speculators, and many Western farmers, chafed at the Bank's tight control over the currency reserves of state banks, claiming it was harmful to western development. Both Western farmers and urban workers had bitter memories of the Panic of 1819, which the Bank had caused (at least in part) by sharply cutting back on available credit. Many ordinary people were uneasy not only about the Bank but about banks of all kinds. They believed that a system based on paper currency would be manipulated by bankers in unpredictable and dangerous ways. Among those who held that opinion was Andrew Jackson, who had hated and feared banks ever since the 1790s, when he had lost a great deal of money in a speculative venture.

Nicholas Biddle, urged on by Henry Clay and Daniel Webster, precipitated the conflict by making early application for rechartering the Bank. Congress approved the application in July 1832. Clay and Webster, though well aware of Jackson's antibank feelings, believed the president would not risk a veto in an election year. They were wrong. Jackson immediately decided on a stinging veto, announcing to Van Buren, "The bank . . . is trying to kill me, but I will kill it!"

And kill it he did that same July, with one of the strongest veto messages in American history. Denouncing the Bank as unconstitutional, harmful to states' rights, and "dangerous to the liberties of the people," Jackson presented himself as the spokesman for the majority of ordinary people and the enemy of special privilege. Asserting that the Bank's "exclusive privileges" were benefiting only the rich, Jackson claimed to speak for the "humble members of society—the farmers, mechanics and laborers"—and to oppose injustice and inequality. In short, the veto spoke directly to many of the hopes and fears of exceptionally rapid economic and social change that Americans felt at this time.

QUICK REVIEW

Jackson and the Bank of the United States

◆ Jackson, and most Westerners, distrusted banks.

◆ Jackson talked about not rechartering the Bank of the United States.

◆ Struggle over future of Bank ended with victory for Jackson.

JACKSON'S REELECTION IN 1832

Jackson's veto message was a great popular success, and it set the terms for the presidential election of 1832. Henry Clay, the nominee of the anti-Jackson forces, lost the battle for popular opinion. Democrats successfully painted Clay as the defender of the Bank and of privilege. His defeat was decisive: he drew only 49 electoral votes, to Jackson's 219.

Although the election was a triumph for Jackson, the **Bank War** continued. The Bank charter did not expire until 1836, but Jackson, declaring that "the hydra of corruption is only scotched, not dead," decided to kill the Bank by transferring its $10 million in government deposits to favored state banks ("pet banks," critics called them). Cabinet members objected, as did the Senate, but Jackson responded that the election had given him a popular mandate to act against the Bank. The president was the direct representative of the people, he claimed, and could act upon the popular will, regardless of the opinion of Congress or even the cabinet. Short of impeachment, there was nothing Congress could do to prevent Jackson from acting on his expansive—and novel—interpretation of presidential powers.

WHIGS, VAN BUREN, AND THE ELECTION OF 1836

But there was someone outside Congress with power to respond: the Bank's director, Nicholas Biddle. "This worthy President thinks that because he has scalped Indians . . . he is to have his way with the Bank," Biddle commented. "He is mistaken." As the government withdrew its deposits, Biddle abruptly called in the Bank's commercial loans, thereby causing a sharp panic and recession in the winter of 1833–1834. Merchants, businessmen, and Southern planters were all furious—at Jackson. His opponents, only a loose coalition up to this time, coalesced into a formal opposition party that called itself the Whigs. Evoking the memory of the Patriots who had resisted King George III in the American Revolution, the new party called on everyone to resist tyrannical "King Andrew." Just as Jackson's own calls for popular democracy had appealed to voters in all regions, so his opponents overcame their sectional differences to unite in opposition to his economic policies and arbitrary methods.

Vice President Martin Van Buren, Jackson's designated successor, won the presidential election of 1836 because the Whigs, unable to agree on a common presidential candidate, ran four sectional candidates. The Whig defeat drove home the weakness of the traditional sectional politics, but the closeness of the popular vote showed that the basis for a united national opposition did exist. In 1840, the Whigs would prove that they had learned this lesson.

10–7
Andrew Jackson, Veto of the Bank Bill (1832)

Bank War   The political struggle between President Andrew Jackson and the supporters of the Second Bank of the United States.

Specie Circular Proclamation issued by President Andrew Jackson in 1836 stipulating that only gold or silver could be used as payment for public land.

This contemporary cartoon bitterly depicts the terrible effects of the Panic of 1837 on ordinary people—bank failures, unemployment, drunkenness, and destitution—which the artist links to the insistence of the rich on payment in specie (as Jackson had required in the Species Circular of 1836). Over the scene waves the American flag, accompanied by the ironic message, "61st Anniversary of our Independence."

Panic of 1837 cartoon, *The Times*. Courtesy of the Library of Congress

THE PANIC OF 1837

Meanwhile, the consequences of the Bank War continued. The recession of 1833–1834 was followed by a wild speculative boom, caused as much by foreign investors as by the expiration of the Bank. Many new state banks were chartered that were eager to give loans, the price of cotton rose rapidly, and speculation in western lands was feverish (in Alabama and Mississippi, the mid-1830s were known as the "Flush Times"). A government surplus of $37 million distributed to the states in 1836 made the inflationary pressures worse. Jackson became alarmed at the widespread use of paper money (which he blamed for the inflation), and in July 1836 he issued the **Specie Circular**, announcing that the government would accept payment for public lands only in hard currency. At the same time, foreign investors, especially British banks, affected by a world recession, called in their American loans. The sharp contraction of credit led to the Panic of 1837 and a six-year recession, the worst the American economy had yet known.

In 1837, some 800 banks suspended business, refusing to pay out any of their $150 million in deposits. The collapse of the banking system led to business closures and outright failures. In the winter of 1837–1838 in New York City alone, one-third of all manual laborers were unemployed and an estimated 10,000 were living in abject poverty. New York laborers took to the streets. Four or five thousand protesters carrying signs reading "Bread, Meat, Rent, Fuel!" gathered at City Hall on February 10, 1838, and then marched to the warehouse of a leading merchant, Eli Hart. Breaking down the door, they took possession of the thousands of barrels of flour Hart had stored there rather than sell at what the mob considered a fair

OVERVIEW

THE SECOND AMERICAN PARTY SYSTEM

Democrats	First organized to elect Andrew Jackson to the presidency in 1828. The Democratic Party spoke for Jeffersonian democracy, expansion, and the freedom of the "common man" from interference from government or from financial monopolies like the Bank of the United States. It found its power base in the rural South and West and among some Northern urban workers. The Democratic Party was the majority party from 1828 to 1860.
Whigs	Organized in opposition to Andrew Jackson in the early 1830s. Heir to Federalism, the Whig Party favored a strong role for the national government in the economy (for example, it promoted Henry Clay's American System) and supported active social reform. Its power base lay in the North and Old Northwest among voters who benefited from increased commercialization and among some Southern planters and urban merchants. The Whigs won the elections of 1840 and 1848.

price. Policemen and state militia who tried to prevent the break-in were beaten by the angry mob. Not until 1843 did the economy show signs of recovery.

In neither 1837 nor 1819 did the federal government take any action to aid victims of economic recession. No banks were bailed out, no bank depositors were saved by federal insurance, no laid-off workers got unemployment payments. Nor did the government undertake any public works projects or pump money into the economy. All of these steps, today seen as essential to prevent economic collapse and to alleviate human suffering, were unheard of in 1819 and 1837. Soup kitchens and charities were mobilized in major cities, but only by private, volunteer groups, not by local or state governments. Panics and depressions were believed to be natural stages in the business cycle, and government intervention was considered unwarranted—although it was perfectly acceptable for government to intervene to promote growth. As a result, workers, farmers, and members of the new business middle class suddenly realized that participation in America's booming economy was very dangerous. The rewards could be great, but so could the penalties.

Martin Van Buren (quickly nicknamed "Van Ruin") spent a dismal four years in the White House presiding over bank failures, bankruptcies, and massive unemployment. Van Buren, who lacked Jackson's compelling personality, could find no remedies to the depression. His misfortune gave the opposition party, the newly formed Whigs, their opportunity.

THE SECOND AMERICAN PARTY SYSTEM

The political struggles of the Jackson era, coupled with the dramatic social changes caused by expansion and economic growth, created the basic pattern of American politics: two major parties, each with at least some appeal among voters of all social classes and in all sections of the country. That pattern, which we call the "Second American Party System," remains to this day.

WHAT WERE the main issues of the campaign of 1840?

WHIGS AND DEMOCRATS

There were genuine differences between the Whigs and the Democrats, but they were not sectional differences. Instead, the two parties reflected just-emerging class and cultural differences. The Democrats, as they themselves were quick to point out, had inherited Thomas Jefferson's belief in the democratic rights of the small, independent yeoman farmer. They had nationwide appeal, especially in the South and West, the most rural regions. Most Democratic voters were opposed to the rapid social and economic changes that accompanied the transportation revolution.

The Whigs were themselves often the initiators and beneficiaries of economic change and were more receptive to it. Heirs of the Federalist belief in the importance of a strong federal role in the national economy (see Chapter 8), they supported the elements of Henry Clay's American System: a strong central government, the Bank of the United States, a protective tariff, and internal improvements. In fact, when it came to improvements, the Whigs wanted to improve people as well as roads. Religion was an important element in political affiliation, and many Whigs were members of evangelical reforming denominations. Reformers believed that everyone, rich and poor, was capable of the self-discipline that would lead to a good life. Thus, Whigs favored government intervention in both economic and social affairs, calling for education and social reforms, such as temperance, that aimed to improve the ordinary citizen. The Whigs' greatest strength was in New England and the northern part of the West (the Old Northwest), the areas most affected by commercial agriculture and factory work.

11–2
Lyman Beecher, Six Sermons on Intemperance (1828)

MAP EXPLORATION

To explore an interactive version of this map, go to
http://www.prenhall.com/faraghertlc/map10.6

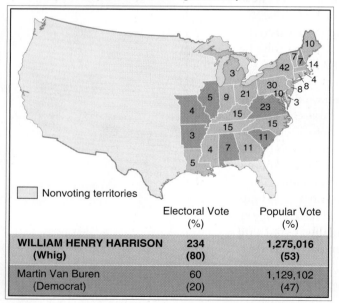

	Electoral Vote (%)	Popular Vote (%)
WILLIAM HENRY HARRISON (Whig)	**234 (80)**	**1,275,016 (53)**
Martin Van Buren (Democrat)	60 (20)	1,129,102 (47)

MAP 10-6

The Election of 1840   The Whigs triumphed in the election of 1840 by beating the Democrats at their own game. Whigs could expect to do well in the commercializing areas of New England and the Old Northwest, but their adopted strategy of popular campaigning worked well in the largely rural South and West as well, contributing to Harrison's victory. The Whigs' choice of John Tyler as vice presidential candidate, another strategy designed to appeal to Southern voters, backfired when Harrison died and Tyler, who did not share Whig principles, became America's first vice president to succeed to the presidency.

WHAT POLICIES did Tyler promote? Which did he reject?

THE CAMPAIGN OF 1840

In 1840, the Whigs set out to beat the Democrats at their own game. Passing over the ever-hopeful Henry Clay, the Whigs nominated a man as much like Andrew Jackson as possible, the aging Indian fighter William Henry Harrison, former governor of the Indiana Territory from 1801 to 1812. In an effort to duplicate Jackson's winning appeal to the South as well as the West, the Whigs balanced the ticket by nominating a Southerner, John Tyler, for vice president. The campaign slogan was "Tippecanoe and Tyler too" (Tippecanoe was the site of Harrison's famous victory over Tecumseh's Indian confederation in 1811). As if this were not enough, Whigs made Harrison out to be a humble man who would be happy to live in a log cabin, although he actually lived in a large and comfortable house. Thus began another long-lived political legend. The Whigs reached out to ordinary people with torchlight parades, barbecues, songs, coonskin caps, bottomless jugs of hard cider, and claims that Martin Van Buren, Harrison's hapless opponent, was a man of privilege and aristocratic tastes. Nothing could be further from the truth: Van Buren was the son of a tavern keeper.

The Whig campaign tactics, added to the popular anger at Van Buren because of the continuing depression, gave Harrison a sweeping electoral victory, 234 votes to 60. Even more remarkable, the campaign achieved the greatest voter turnout up to that time (and rarely equaled since), 80 percent.

THE WHIG VICTORY TURNS TO LOSS: THE TYLER PRESIDENCY

Although the Whig victory of 1840 was a milestone in American politics, the triumph of Whig principles was short-lived. William Henry Harrison, who was sixty-eight, died of pneumonia a month after his inauguration. For the first time in American history the vice president stepped up to the presidency. Not for the last time, important differences between the dead president and his successor reshaped the direction of American politics.

John Tyler of Virginia was a former Democrat who had left the party because he disagreed with Jackson's autocratic style. The Whigs had sought him primarily for his sectional appeal and had not inquired too closely into his political opinions, which turned out to be anti-Whig as well as anti-Jackson. President Tyler vetoed a series of bills embodying all the elements of Henry Clay's American System: tariffs, internal improvements, a new Bank of the United States. In exasperation, congressional Whigs forced Tyler out of the party, and his entire cabinet of Whigs resigned. To replace them, Tyler appointed former Democrats like himself. Thus, the Whig triumph of 1840, one of the clearest victories in American electoral politics, was negated by the stalemate between Tyler and the Whig majority in Congress. The Whigs were to win only one more election, that of 1848.

AMERICAN ARTS AND LETTERS

Jackson's presidency was a defining moment in the development of an American identity. His combination of western belligerency and combative individualism was the strongest statement of American distinctiveness since Thomas Jefferson's agrarianism. Did Jackson speak for all of America? The Whigs did not think so. And the definitions of American identity that were beginning to emerge in popular culture and in intellectual circles were more complex than the message coming from the White House. Throughout the nation, however, there was a widespread interest in information and literature of all kinds. The Age of the Common Man would prove to be the period when American writers and painters found the national themes that allowed them to produce the first distinctively American literature and art.

POPULAR CULTURES AND THE SPREAD OF THE WRITTEN WORD

A print revolution had begun in 1826 when a reform organization, the American Tract Society, installed the country's first steam-powered press. Three years later the new presses had turned out 300,000 Bibles and 6 million religious tracts, or pamphlets. The greatest growth, however, was in newspapers that reached a mass audience. The number of newspapers soared from 376 newspapers in 1810 to 1,200 in 1835. Packed with articles that today would be considered libelous and scandalous, newspapers were entertaining and popular reading, and they rapidly became a key part of democratic popular culture.

Newspapers and pamphlets fostered a variety of popular cultures as well. For Western readers, the Crockett almanacs offered a mix of humorous stories and tall tales attributed to Davy Crockett (the boisterous Tennessee "roarer" who died defending the Alamo in 1836) along with meteorological and climate information. In New York City the immensely popular "penny papers" (so called from their price), the *New York Morning Post* and the *New York Sun*, began appearing in 1833. These papers, with lurid headlines such as "Double Suicide," and "Secret Tryst," fed the same popular appetite for scandal as did other popular publications such as the *Police Gazette* magazine; pamphlets about murder trials, swindlers, and pirates; and temperance dime novels. Throughout the country, religious literature was still most widely read, but a small middle-class audience existed for literary magazines and, among women especially, for sentimental magazines and novels.

QUICK REVIEW

William Henry Harrison of Ohio

◆ Untainted by association with Bank of the United States, Masonic Order, or slaveholding.

◆ Hero of War of 1812.

◆ Selected John Tyler of Virginia as his running mate.

WHAT ROLE did newspapers and pamphlets play in American popular culture in the first half of the nineteenth century?

8–13
Davy Crockett, Advice to Politicians (1833)

Accompanying all these changes in print communication was an invention that outsped them all: the telegraph, so innovative that its inventor spent years fruitlessly seeking private funds to back its application. Finally, with financing from the federal government, Samuel F. B. Morse sent his first message from Washington to Baltimore in 1844. Soon messages in Morse code would be transmitted instantaneously across the continent. The impact of this revolutionary invention, the first to separate the message from the speed at which a human messenger could travel, was immediate. The timeliness of information available to the individual, from important national news to the next train's arrival time, vastly increased. Distant events gained new and exciting immediacy. Everyone's horizon and sense of community was widened.

CREATING A NATIONAL AMERICAN CULTURE

For all the improvements in communication, the United States was a provincial culture, still looking to Britain for values, standards, and literary offerings. In the early years of the nineteenth century, Eastern seaboard cities actively built the cultural foundation that would nurture American art and literature. Philadelphia's American Philosophical Society, founded by Benjamin Franklin in 1743, boasted a distinguished roster of scientists, including Thomas Jefferson—concurrently its president and president of the United States—and Nicholas Biddle, Jackson's opponent in the Bank War. Culturally, Boston ran a close second to Philadelphia, founding the Massachusetts General Hospital (1811) and the Boston Athenaeum (1807), a gentlemen's library and reading room. Southern cities were much less successful in supporting culture. Charleston had a Literary and Philosophical Society (founded in 1814), but the widely dispersed residences of the Southern elite made urban cultural institutions difficult to sustain. Thus, unwittingly, the South ceded cultural leadership to the North.

The cultural picture was much spottier in the West. A few cities, such as Lexington, Kentucky, and Cincinnati, Ohio, had civic cultural institutions, and some transplanted New Englanders maintained connections with New England culture. Most pioneers were at best uninterested and at worst actively hostile to traditional literary culture. This was neither from lack of literacy nor from a failure to read. Newspaper and religious journals both had large readerships in the West: The *Methodist Christian Advocate*, for example, reached 25,000 people yearly (compared with the *North American Review*'s 3,000). The frontier emphasis on the practical was hard to distinguish from antiintellectualism.

Thus, in the early part of the nineteenth century, the gap between the intellectual and cultural horizons of a wealthy Bostonian and a frontier farmer in Michigan widened. Part of the unfinished task of building a national society was the creation of a national culture that could fill this gap. For writers and artists, the challenge was to find distinctively American themes.

Of the Eastern cities, New York produced the first widely recognized American writers. In 1819, Washington Irving published *The Sketch Book*, thus immortalizing Rip Van Winkle and the Headless Horseman. Within a few years James Fenimore Cooper's Leatherstocking novels (of which *The Last of the Mohicans*, published in 1826, is the best known) achieved wide success in both America and Europe. Cooper's novels established the long American experience of westward expansion, of which the conquest of the Indians was a vital part, as a serious and distinctive American literary theme.

It was New England, however, that claimed to be the forge of American cultural independence from Europe. As Ralph Waldo Emerson proclaimed in "The American Scholar," a lecture he delivered in 1837 to the Harvard faculty, "Our

9–10
James F. Cooper, Notions of the Americans (1840)

10–11
A French Traveler Reports on American Society (1835)

day of dependence, our long apprenticeship to the learning of other lands, draws to a close." He went on to encourage American writers to find inspiration in the ordinary details of daily life. His message of cultural self-sufficiency was one that Americans were eager to hear.

ARTISTS AND BUILDERS

Artists were as successful as novelists in finding American themes. Thomas Cole, who came to America from England in 1818, applied the British romantic school of landscape painting to American scenes. He founded the Hudson River school of American painting, a style and subject matter frankly nationalistic in tone.

The Western painters—realists such as Karl Bodmer and George Catlin as well as the romantics who followed them, like Albert Bierstadt and Thomas Moran—drew on the dramatic western landscape and its peoples. Another unusual Western painter, John James Audubon, could at first find no publisher in this country for his striking and sometimes grotesque etchings of American birds. George Caleb Bingham, an accomplished genre painter, produced somewhat tidied-up scenes of real-life American workers, such as flatboatmen on the Missouri River. All these painters

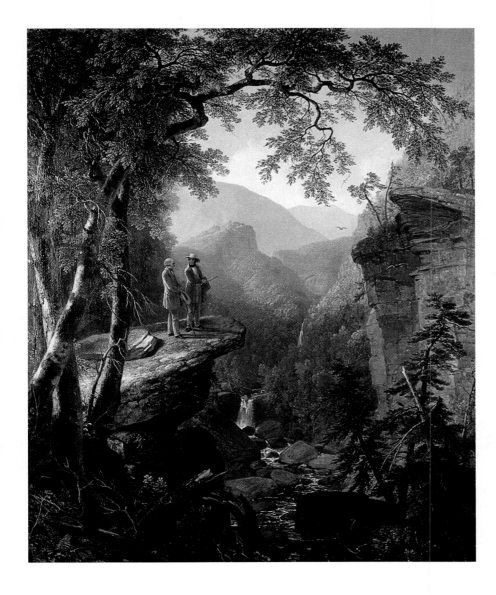

Asher Durand, a member of the Hudson River School of landscape painting, produced this work, *Kindred Spirits*, in 1849 as a tribute to Thomas Cole, the school's leader. Cole is one of the figures depicted standing in a romantic wilderness.

Courtesy of The New York Public Library

found much to record and to celebrate in American life. Ironically, the inspiration for the most prevalent theme, the American wilderness, was profoundly endangered by the rapid western settlement of which the nation was so proud.

The haste and transiency of American life are nowhere so obvious as in the architectural record of this era, which is sparse. The monumental neo-classical style (complete with columns) that Jefferson had recommended for official buildings in Washington continued to be favored for public buildings elsewhere and by private concerns trying to project an imposing image, such as banks. But in general Americans were in too much of a hurry to build for the future, and in balloon-frame construction they found the perfect technique for the present. Balloon-frame structures—which consist of a basic frame of wooden studs fastened with crosspieces top and bottom—could be put up quickly, cheaply, and without the help of a skilled carpenter. Covering the frame with wooden siding was equally simple, and the resultant dwelling was as strong, although not as well insulated, as a house of solid timber or logs. Balloon-frame construction was first used in Chicago in the 1830s, where it created the city almost instantly. The four-room balloon-frame house, affordable to many who could not have paid for a traditionally built dwelling, became standard in that decade. This was indeed housing for the common man and his family.

QUICK REVIEW

The Print Revolution

◆ 1826: American Tract Society installs first steam-powered press in the United States.

◆ Greatest growth was in newspapers.

◆ Newspapers and pamphlets fostered a variety of popular cultures.

CHRONOLOGY

1817	Erie Canal construction begins.
1818	National Road completed to Wheeling, Virginia (now West Virginia).
1821	Martin Van Buren's Bucktails defeat DeWitt Clinton in New York.
	Mexican independence from Spain.
1824	John Quincy Adams elected president by the House of Representatives.
1825	Erie Canal opens.
1826	First American use of the steam-powered printing press.
1828	Congress passes "Tariff of Abominations."
	Andrew Jackson elected president.
	John C. Calhoun publishes *Exposition and Protest* anonymously.
1830	Jackson vetoes Maysville Road Bill.
	Congress passes Indian Removal Act.
	Baltimore and Ohio Railroad opens.
1832	Nullification Crisis begins.
	Jackson vetoes renewal of Bank of the United States charter.

	Jackson reelected president.
1833	National Road completed to Columbus, Ohio.
1834	Cyrus McCormick patents the McCormick reaper.
	Whig party organized.
	British abolish slavery in their Caribbean colonies.
1836	Jackson issues Specie Circular.
	Martin Van Buren elected president.
1837	John Deere invents steel plow.
	Ralph Waldo Emerson first presents "The American Scholar."
	Panic of 1837.
1838	Cherokee removal along the "Trail of Tears."
1840	Whig William Henry Harrison elected president.
	Act of Union merges Upper and Lower Canada.
1841	John Tyler assumes presidency at the death of President Harrison.
1844	Samuel F. B. Morse operates first telegraph.

CONCLUSION

Andrew Jackson's presidency witnessed the building of a strong national party system based on nearly universal white manhood suffrage. At the same time that the nation expanded politically (nine new western states were admitted between 1800 and 1840), construction of new roads, canals, and railroads, and other improvements in transportation and communication, created the infrastructure that united the nation physically. Sectionalism and localism seemed to have been replaced by a more national consciousness that was clearly expressed in the two national political parties, the Whigs and the Democrats. The Second American Party System created new democratic political communities united by common political opinions.

But as the key battles of the Jackson presidency—the Nullification Crisis, Indian removal, the Bank War—showed, the forces of sectionalism resisted the strong nationalizing tendencies of the era. As the next two chapters will show, economic and social forces continued to force the South and the North apart.

SUMMARY

The New Democratic Politics in North America The issue of popular rights arose throughout North America. In the United States, political developments revolved around expansion of suffrage though not universally. The party system also began the process of reorganization.

The Jackson Presidency Andrew Jackson's election ushered in a new era in American politics. An extremely popular leader, Jackson brought to the office a strong vision of what the president should be. Practicing this vision created tensions with other political leaders.

Internal Improvements: Building an Infrastructure Expansion created the need for better movement of goods and people. A transportation revolution resulted that was fueled by hard work and invention. The transportation revolution also influenced the legal and economic development of the nation.

Jackson and His Opponents: The Rise of the Whigs Despite his popularity, Andrew Jackson's stand on several issues provoked strong opposition that helped change the political culture of the nation. The disagreements raised important constitutional issues and solidified political opposition to Jackson.

The Second American Party System The second party system set the pattern for American politics. The national parties developed strategies and techniques designed to appeal to as many people as possible.

American Arts and Letters During the Age of Jackson, a national American culture emerged. American artists and writers discovered national themes to produce the first distinctive American literature and art.

REVIEW QUESTIONS

1. What reasons might a person of the 1820s and 1830s give for opposing universal white manhood suffrage? Suffrage for free African American men? For women of all races?

2. Opponents believed that Andrew Jackson was unsuited in both political experience and temperament to be president of the United States, yet his presidency is considered one of the most influential in American history. Explain the changes in political organization and attitude that made his election possible.

3. Both the Nullification Crisis and Indian removal raised the constitutional issue of the rights of a minority in a nation governed by majority rule. What rights, in your opinion, does a minority have, and what kinds of laws are necessary to defend those rights?

4. Why was the issue of government support for internal improvements so controversial? Who benefited from the transportation revolution? Who lost ground?

5. What were the key differences between Whigs and Democrats? What did each party stand for? Who were their supporters? What were the links between each party's programs and party supporters?

6. What distinctive American themes did the writers, artists, and builders of the 1820s and 1830s express in their works? Are they still considered American themes today?

KEY TERMS

Albany Regency (p. 245)
Bank War (p. 261)
Black Hawk (p. 260)
Democrats (p. 249)
Indian Removal Act (p. 259)

Nullification Crisis (p. 257)
Specie Circular (p. 262)
Trail of Tears (p. 259)
Whigs (p. 257)

RECOMMENDED READING

Donald B. Cole, *The Presidency of Andrew Jackson* (1993). In this recent work, Jackson is seen as just as influential but less commanding and more ambiguous in his political attitudes than in earlier studies.

Ronald P. Formisano, *The Transformation of Political Culture: Massachusetts Parties, 1790s–1840s* (1983). One of many detailed studies that have contributed to our understanding of the development of the second party system.

William W. Freehling, *Prelude to Civil War* (1966). An examination of the Nullification Crisis that stresses the centrality of slavery to the dispute.

Paul W. Gates, *The Farmer's Age: Agriculture, 1815–1860* (1966). The standard source on the growth of commercial agriculture.

Michael Holt, *The Rise and Fall of the American Whig Party* (1999). A massive study that covers its subject in detail.

Reeve Huston, *Land and Freedom: Rural Society, Popular Protest, and Party Politics in Antebellus New York* (2000). How rural ways of life and the Anti-Rent Wars became a part of Jacksonian politics.

John Lauritz Larson, *Internal Improvement: National Public Works and the Promise of Popular Government in the Early United States* (2001). Links internal improvements with political attitudes toward government and examines how they changed.

Jean V. Matthews, *Toward a New Society: American Thought and Culture, 1800–1830* (1991). A valuable survey of American attitudes toward religion, politics, science, nature, and culture in the early nineteenth century.

Simon Newman, *Parades and the Politics of the Street* (1997). Examines how festive culture became an expression of popular political culture.

Robert Remini, *Andrew Jackson and the Source of American Freedom* (1981). An account of Jackson's White House years by his major biographer.

Carol Sheriff, *The Artificial River: The Erie Canal and the Paradox of Progress, 1817–1862* (1996). Shows how the building of the canal changed personal lives and fostered religious beliefs in human perfectability.

Alan Taylor, *William Cooper's Town: Power and Persuasion on the Frontier of the Early American Republic* (1995). The Pulitzer Prize–winning study of the founding and development of Cooperstown, New York, by the father of novelist James Fenimore Cooper. An engrossing study of the effects of the democratization of politics.

George Rogers Taylor, *The Transportation Revolution, 1815–1860* (1951). The indispensable book on all aspects of the American economy during this period.

Harry L. Watson, *Liberty and Power: The Politics of Jacksonian America* (1990). An excellent recent overview of Jacksonian politics.

. . . whatever accidents or misfortunes might attend my flight nothing could be worse than what threatened my stay.
— Hannah Crafts

A slave auction in Virginia. 1861

11

THE SOUTH AND SLAVERY
1790s–1850s

HOW DID attitudes in the South toward slavery change after the invention of the cotton gin?

WHAT WAS life like for the typical slave in the American South?

SLAVE COLLAR
RICHMOND VIRGINIA
SLAVE MARKET

THIS ANTE-BELLUM SLAVE COLLAR HAS AN OLD TAG ATTACHED FROM AN EARLY HISTORICAL SOCIETY COLLECTION. A RARE AND CHOICE RELIC FROM EARLY VIRGINIA.

WHAT ROLE did religion play in African American slave communities?

WHAT WERE the values of yeoman farmers?

WHO MADE the planter elite?

WHAT PROSLAVERY arguments were developed in the first half of the nineteenth century?

AMERICAN COMMUNITIES

Natchez-Under-the-Hill

THE WHARFMASTER HAD JUST OPENED THE PUBLIC AUCTION OF CONFISCATED cargoes in the center of Natchez when a great cry was heard. An angry crowd of flatboatmen, Bowie knives in hand, was storming up the bluffs from the Mississippi shouting, as the local newspaper reported, "threats of violence and death upon all who attempted to sell and buy their property." It was November 1837, and the town council had just enacted a restrictive tax of $10 per flatboat, a measure designed to rid the wharf district known as Natchez-Under-the-Hill of the most impoverished and disreputable of the flatboatmen. The council had made its first confiscation of cargo after nine captains refused to pay this tax. As the boatmen approached, merchants and onlookers shrank back in fear. But the local authorities had called out the militia, and a company of farmers and planters now came marching into the square with their rifles primed and lowered. "The cold and sullen bayonets of the Guards were too hard meat for the Arkansas toothpicks," reported the local press, and "there was no fight." The boatmen sullenly turned and went back down the bluffs. It was the first confrontation in the "Flatboat Wars" that erupted as Mississippi ports tried to bring their troublesome riverfronts under regulation.

The first European to take notice of this "land abundant in subsistence" was a member of Hernando de Soto's expedition in the sixteenth century. The area was "thickly peopled" by the Natchez Indians, he wrote. It was not until the French established the port of Fort Rosalie in the 1720s, however, that Europeans settled in the area. The French destroyed the highly organized society of the Natchez Indians in the 1730s and the port became a major Mississippi River trading center. From Fort Rosalie, French traders bought deerskins, for which there was a large export market, from Choctaw, Chickasaw, and Creek hunters. During the same period, some Africans who had been imported by the French to work as slaves on plantations found roles in the French-Indian trade as boatmen, hunters, soldiers, and interpreters.

When the Spanish took control of the territory in 1763 they laid out the new town of Natchez high on the bluffs, safe from Mississippi flooding. Fort Rosalie, rechristened Natchez-Under-the-Hill, continued to flourish as the produce grown by American farmers in Kentucky and Tennessee moved downriver on flatboats. Thus, Americans became the newest additions to the ethnic diversity of this well-established trading center. When Americans took possession of Mississippi in 1798, the district surrounding the port became the most important center of settlement in the Old Southwest. Once again this abundant land of rich, black soil became thickly peopled, but this time with cotton planters and their African American slaves.

Under-the-Hill gained renown as the last stop for boatmen before New Orleans. There were often as many as 150 boats drawn up at the wharves. The crowds along the riverfront, noted John

James Audubon, who visited in the 1820s, "formed a medley which it is beyond my power to describe." Mingling among American rivermen of all descriptions were trappers and hunters in fur caps, Spanish shopkeepers in bright smocks, French gentlemen from New Orleans in velvet coats, Indians wrapped in their trade blankets, African Americans both free and slave—a pageant of nations and races. Clapboard shacks and flatboats dragged on shore and converted into storefronts served as grog shops, card rooms, dance halls, and hotels. Whorehouses with women of every age and color abounded.

On the bluffs, meanwhile, the town of Natchez had become the winter home to the Southwestern planter elite. They built their mansions with commanding views of the river. A visitor attending a ball at one of these homes was dazzled by the display: "Myriads of wax candles burning in wall sconces, sparkling chandeliers, entrancing music, the scent of jasmine, rose and sweet olive, the sparkle of wine mellowed by age, the flow of wit and brilliant repartee, all were there." Sustaining this American aristocracy was the labor of thousands of enslaved men and women, who lived in the squalid quarters behind the great house and worked the endless fields of cotton. It was they who made possible the greatest accumulations of wealth in early nineteenth-century America.

Natchez ●

The Natchez planters, their wealth and confidence growing with cotton's growing dominance of the local economy, found Under-the-Hill an increasing irritant. The Under-the-Hill elite—gamblers, saloon keepers, and pimps—disturbed the social boundary when they began staying at hotels and even building town houses in Natchez town. And in the wake of the slave revolt led by Nat Turner in Virginia in 1831, in which fifty-five white people were killed, the planters began to feel increasingly threatened by the racial mingling of the riverfront.

In the late 1830s the Natchez elite was jolted by rumors that their slaves were conspiring to murder them during Fourth of July celebrations while Under-the-Hill desperadoes looted their mansions. The rumors reinforced the growing conviction among planters that they could no longer tolerate the polyglot community of the riverfront. The measures that ultimately provoked the flatboatmen's threats in November 1837 soon followed.

In response to these threats, the planters issued an extralegal order giving all the gamblers, pimps, and whores of Under-the-Hill twenty-four hours to evacuate the district. As the Mississippi militia sharpened their bayonets, panic swept the wharves, and that night dozens of flatboats loaded with a motley human cargo headed for the more tolerant community of New Orleans. Other river ports issued similar orders of expulsion. "The towns on the river," one resident remembered, "became purified from a moral pestilence which the law could not cure." Three years later a great tornado hit Under-the-Hill, *leveling the shacks that had served so long as a rendezvous for the rivermen, and gradually the Mississippi reclaimed the old river bottom.*

These two communities—Natchez, home to the rich slave-owning elite, and Natchez-Under-the-Hill, the bustling polyglot trading community—epitomize the paradox of the American South in the early nineteenth century. Enslaved African Americans grew the region's most lucrative crop, cotton. On the resulting profits, aristocratic Southerners built a sumptuous and distinctive lifestyle for themselves. The boatmen and traders of Natchez-Under-the-Hill who *brought the cotton and other products to market were vital to the planters' prosperity. But the polyglot racial and social mixing of Natchez-Under-the-Hill threatened the system of control, built on a rigid distinction between free white people and enslaved black people by which the planters maintained slavery. Because the slave owners could not control the boatmen, they expelled them. This defensive reaction—to seal off the world of slavery from the wider commercial world—exposed the vulnerability of the slave system at the very moment of its greatest commercial success.*

COTTON AND SOUTHERN EXPANSION

Slavery had long dominated Southern life. African American slaves grew the great export crops of the colonial period—tobacco, rice, and indigo—on which slave owners' fortunes were made, and their presence shaped Southern society and culture (see Chapter 4). Briefly, in the early days of American independence, the slave system waned, only to be revived by the immense

HOW DID attitudes in the South towards slavery change after the invention of the cotton gin?

 MAP EXPLORATION
To explore an interactive version of this map, go to
http://www.prenhall.com/faraghertlc/map11.1

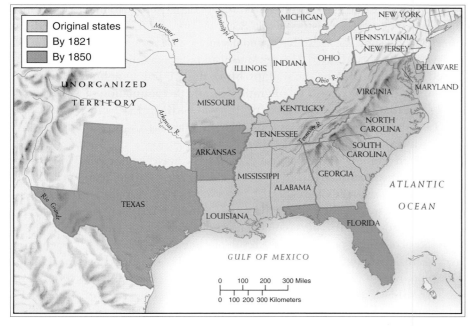

MAP 11-1
The South Expands, 1790–1850   This map shows the dramatic effect cotton production had on southern expansion. From the original six states of 1790, westward expansion, fueled by the search for new cotton lands, added another six states by 1821, and three more by 1850.

WHAT IMPACT did the relationship between cotton production and westward expansion have on the Indian population of the South?

IMAGE KEY
for pages 272–273

a. A chain used to tie gangs of slaves.
b. "The Shadow" plantation of Louisiana.
c. A slave auction in Virginia, 1861.
d. A whip of coiled rope used on slaves.
e. An auction of eight black slaves.
f. Mature cotton bolls on the stem of a plant.
g. Slaves carry sacks of cotton on their heads on a South Carolina plantation field.
h. A slave collar with an attached tag from the slave market in Richmond, Virginia.
i. African American worshippers in a sketch by Joseph Becker.
j. A log cabin in New Braunfels, Texas in a painting by Carl G. von Iwonski.
k. Colonel and Mrs. James A. Whiteside in a James Cameron painting.
l. A proslavery cartoon, 1841.

profitability of cotton in a newly industrializing world. The overwhelming economic success of cotton and the slave system on which it depended created a distinctive regional culture quite different from that developing in the North.

THE COTTON GIN AND EXPANSION INTO THE OLD SOUTHWEST

Short-staple cotton had long been recognized as a crop ideally suited to Southern soils and growing conditions. But it had one major drawback: the seeds were so difficult to remove from the lint that it took an entire day to hand-clean a single pound of cotton. The invention in 1793 that made cotton growing profitable was the result of collaboration between a young Northerner named Eli Whitney, recently graduated from Yale College, and Catherine Greene, a South Carolina plantation owner and widow of Revolutionary War General Nathanael Greene, who had hired Whitney to tutor her children. Whitney built a prototype cotton engine, dubbed "gin" for short, a simple device consisting of a hand-cranked cylinder with teeth that tore the lint away from the seeds. At Greene's suggestion, the teeth were made of wire. With the cotton gin it was possible to clean more than fifty pounds of cotton a day. Soon large and small planters in the inland regions of Georgia and South Carolina had begun to grow cotton. By 1811, this area was producing 60 million pounds of cotton a year, and exporting most of it to England.

Other areas of the South quickly followed South Carolina and Georgia into cotton production. New land was wanted because cotton growing rapidly depleted the soil. The profits to be made from cotton growing drew a rush of Southern farmers into the so-called black belt—an area stretching through western Georgia, Alabama, and Mississippi that was blessed with exceptionally fertile soil. Following the War of 1812, Southerners were seized by "Alabama Fever." In one of the swiftest migrations in American history, white Southerners and their slaves flooded into western Georgia and the areas that would become Alabama and Mississippi (the Old Southwest). On this frontier, African American pioneers (albeit involuntary ones) cleared the forests, drained the swamps, broke the ground, built houses and barns, and planted the first crops. This migration caused the population of Mississippi to double and that of Alabama to grow sixteenfold between 1810 and 1820.

Like the simultaneous expansion into the Old Northwest, settlement of the Old Southwest took place at the expense of the region's Indian population (see Chapter 9). Beginning with the defeat of the Creeks at Horseshoe Bend in 1814 and ending with the Cherokee forced migration along the "Trail of Tears" in 1838, the Five Civilized Tribes—the Cherokees, Chickasaws, Choctaws, Creeks, and Seminoles—were forced to give up their lands and move to Indian Territory (see Chapter 10).

On the southern frontier, as on the northern frontier, the killing, confinement, and removal of Indian peoples was the result of white expansion and settlement motivated by the hunger for land and profit. In the South, however, there was an additional motivation, rooted in slavery, for Indian removal: there was simply no room in the Southern social order for anything other than white and black, master and slave. Literate, slave-owning "redskins" confused this simple picture: they were too "civilized" to be like slaves, but the wrong color to be masters. Thus, Southern Indian removal, like Southern expansion, was dictated by the needs of the slave system.

CHANGING ATTITUDES TOWARD SLAVERY

In the flush of freedom following the American Revolution, all the Northern states abolished slavery or passed laws for gradual emancipation and a number of slave owners in the Upper South freed their slaves (see Chapter 7).

Thomas Jefferson, ever the optimist, claimed that "a total emancipation with the consent of the masters" could not be too far in the future. Nevertheless, Southern legislatures were unwilling to write steps toward emancipation into law, preferring to depend on the charity of individual slave owners. Between 1776 and 1786 all the states except South Carolina and Georgia either banned or heavily taxed the international slave trade. Following the successful slave revolt in Haiti in 1791 all the Southern states banned the importation of foreign slaves, fearing that Caribbean revolutionaries might incite their own slaves to rebellion.

But attitudes rapidly changed in the South following the invention of the cotton gin in 1793 and the realization of the riches to be made from cotton. White Southerners believed that only African slaves could be forced to work day after day, year after year, at the rapid and brutal pace required in the cotton fields of large plantations in the steamy southern summer. As the production of cotton climbed higher every year in response to a seemingly inexhaustible international demand, so too did the demand for slaves and the conviction of Southerners that slavery was an economic necessity.

It was clear, however, that national opinion found the international slave trade abhorrent, and on January 1, 1808, the earliest date permitted by the Constitution, a bill to abolish the importation of slaves became law. Although a small number of slaves continued to be smuggled from Africa, the growth of the slave labor force after 1808 depended primarily on natural increase. And the ban on foreign importations vastly increased the importance of the internal slave trade.

THE INTERNAL SLAVE TRADE

The cotton boom caused a huge increase in the domestic slave trade. Plantation owners in the Upper South (Delaware, Kentucky, Maryland, Virginia, and Tennessee) sold their slaves to meet the demand for labor in the new and expanding cotton-growing regions of the Old Southwest.

Cumulatively, between 1820 and 1860 nearly 50 percent of the slave population of the Upper South took part against their will in Southern expansion. More slaves—an estimated 1 million—were uprooted by this internal slave trade and enforced migration in the early nineteenth century than were brought to North America during the entire time the international slave trade was legal (see Chapter 4).

Purchased by slave traders from owners in the Upper South, slaves were gathered together in notorious "slave pens" in places like Richmond and Charleston and then moved south by train or boat. In the interior, they were carried as cargo on steamboats on the Mississippi River, hence the dreaded phrase "sold down the river." Often slaves moved on foot, chained together in groups of fifty or more known as "coffles." Arriving at a central market in the Lower South like Natchez, New Orleans, or Mobile, the slaves, after being carefully inspected by potential buyers, were sold at auction to the highest bidder.

Although popular stereotype portrayed slave traders as unscrupulous outsiders who persuaded kind and reluctant masters to sell their slaves, the historical truth is much harsher. Traders, far from being shunned by slave-owning society, were often respected community members. Similarly, the sheer scale of the slave trade makes it impossible to believe that slave owners only reluctantly parted with their slaves at times of economic distress. Instead, it is clear that many owners sold slaves and separated slave families not out of necessity but to increase their profits.

6–10
Benjamin Banneker, Letter to Thomas Jefferson (1791)

QUICK REVIEW

The Economics of Slavery

- Worldwide demand for cotton supported slavery.
- Export of cotton a dynamic part of American economy.
- Northern industry directly connected to slavery.

The immense size of the internal slave trade made sights like this commonplace on Southern roads. Groups of slaves, chained together in gangs called coffles, were marched from their homes in the Upper South to cities in the Lower South, where they were auctioned to new owners.

Library of Congress

THE ECONOMICS OF SLAVERY

The insatiable demand for cotton was a result of the technological and social changes that we know today as the **Industrial Revolution**. Beginning early in the eighteenth century, a series of inventions resulted in the mechanized spinning and weaving of cloth in the world's first factories in the north of England. The ability of these factories to produce unprecedented amounts of cotton cloth revolutionized the world economy. The invention of the cotton gin came at just the right time. British textile manufacturers were eager to buy all the cotton that the South could produce.

Indeed, the export of cotton from the South was the dynamic force in the developing American economy in the period 1790–1840. Just as the international slave trade had been the dynamic force in the Atlantic economy of the eighteenth century (see Chapter 4), Southern slavery financed Northern industrial development in the nineteenth century.

The connection between Southern slavery and Northern industry was very direct. Most mercantile services associated with the cotton trade (insurance, for example) were in Northern hands and, significantly, so was shipping. This economic structure was not new. In colonial times, New England ships dominated the African slave trade. Some New England families invested some of their profits in the new technology of textile manufacturing in the 1790s. Other merchants made their money from cotton shipping and brokerage.

COTTON CULTURE

Cotton cultivation created a different kind of society in the South than in the North. At a time when the North was experiencing the greatest spurt of urban growth in the nation's history, Southern cities did not keep pace. Charleston, for example, one of America's five largest cities in 1800, had a population of only 41,000 in 1860, compared with Boston's 177,840 and Baltimore's 212,418. The one exception was New Orleans, the great port at the mouth of the extensive Mississippi River transportation system. In 1860 New Orleans was the nation's fifth largest city, with a population of 169,000. The nine other leading cities were all

Industrial Revolution Revolution in the means and organization of production.

Northern or Western. Most of the South remained rural: less than 3 percent of Mississippi's population lived in cities of more than 2,500 residents, and only 10 percent of Virginia's did. There was no question that concentration on plantation agriculture diverted energy and resources from the South's cities. The agrarian ideal, bolstered by the cotton boom, encouraged the antiurban and anticommercial sentiments of many white Southerners.

The failure of the South to industrialize at the Northern rate was not a matter of ignorance but of choice. Southern capital was tied up in land and slaves, and Southerners, buoyed by the world's insatiable demand for cotton, saw no reason to invest in economically risky railroads, canals, and factories. Nor were they eager to introduce the disruptive factor of free wage labor into the tightly controlled slave system. Cotton was safer.

Thus, the cotton boom created a distinctive regional culture. Although cotton was far from being the only crop (the South actually devoted more acreage to corn than to cotton in 1860), its vast profitability affected all aspects of society.

TO BE A SLAVE

The slave population, estimated at 700,000 in 1790, grew to more than 4 million in 1860. After 1808 (when official American participation in the international slave trade ceased) the growth occurred because of natural increase—that is, through births within the slave population. A distinctive African American slave community, which had first emerged in the eighteenth century (see Chapter 4), matured in the early years of the nineteenth century.

WHAT WAS life like for the typical slave in the American South?

THE MATURING OF THE AMERICAN SLAVE SYSTEM

The explosive growth of cotton plantations changed the nature of Southern slave labor. In 1850, 55 percent of all slaves were engaged in cotton growing. Another 20 percent labored to produce other crops: tobacco (10 percent), rice, sugar, and hemp. About 15 percent of all slaves were domestic servants, and the remaining 10 percent worked in mining, lumbering, industry, and construction.

Cotton growing concentrated slaves on plantations, in contrast to the more dispersed distribution on smaller farms in earlier generations. Although more than half of all slave owners owned five slaves or fewer, 75 percent of all slaves now lived in groups of ten or more. This disproportionate distribution could have a major impact on a slave's life, for it was a very different matter to be the single slave of a small farmer as opposed to being a member of a 100-person black community on a large plantation. The size of cotton plantations fostered the growth of African American slave communities.

On the other hand, the westward expansion of cotton undermined the stability of these communities. As expansion to the Southwest accelerated, so did the demand for slaves in the newly settled regions, thus fueling the internal slave trade. Slaves were increasingly clustered in the Lower South, as Upper South slave owners sold slaves "down the river" or migrated westward with their entire households. An estimated 1 million slaves migrated involuntarily to the Lower South between 1820 and 1860.

Finally, of all the New World slave societies, the one that existed in the American South was the only one that grew by natural increase rather than through the constant importation of captured Africans. This fact alone made the African American community of the South different from the slave societies of Cuba, the Caribbean islands, and Brazil. The first things to understand, then, are the circumstances of survival and growth.

MAP EXPLORATION
To explore an interactive version of this map, go to
http://www.prenhall.com/faragherlc/map11.2

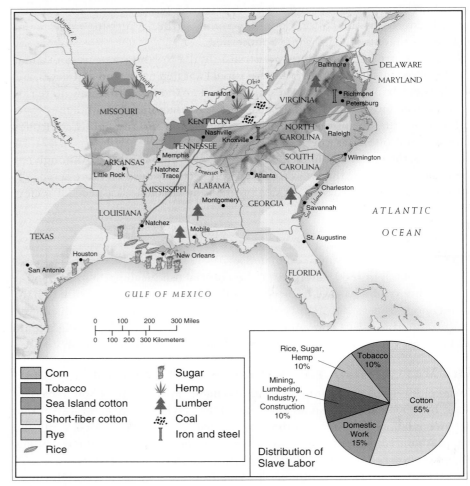

MAP 11-2

Agriculture, Industry, and Slavery, 1850 The distribution of the slave population in the South was determined by agricultural and industrial patterns. In 1850, 55 percent of all slaves worked in cotton, 10 percent in tobacco, and another 10 percent in rice, sugar, and hemp. Ten percent worked in mining, lumbering, industry, and construction, and 15 percent worked as domestic servants. Slaves were not generally used to grow corn, the staple crop of the yeoman farmer.

WHY WAS slave labor more prevalent in certain types of agriculture and industries, and not in others?

QUICK REVIEW

Life and Death

◆ Mortality rate of slave children under five was twice that of white counterparts.

◆ Infectious diseases were endemic in the South.

◆ Malnutrition and lack of basic sanitation took a high toll on slaves.

THE CHALLENGE TO SURVIVE

Slave owners thought of the health of their slaves in several ways. First and foremost, they demanded labor from their slaves, and they provided the food, housing, and clothing to keep them healthy enough to work. They also wanted them to be healthy enough to reproduce, for every slave baby increased the wealth of the owner. These sometimes contradictory demands were played out in the lives of slave women.

Mortality rates for slave children under five were twice those for their white counterparts. Historians now say that mortality was high because pregnant black women were inadequately nourished, worked too hard, or were too frequently pregnant, giving birth to six to eight children at year-and-a-half intervals. At the time, owners often accused women of smothering their infants by rolling over them when asleep.

Health remained a lifelong issue for slaves. Malaria and infectious diseases such as yellow fever and cholera were endemic in the South. White people as well as black people died, as the life expectancy figures for 1850 show: 40–43 years for white people and 30–33 years for African Americans. Slaves were more at risk because of the circumstances of slave life: poor housing, poor diet, and constant, usually heavy work. Sickness was chronic: 20 percent or more of the slave labor force on most plantations were sick at any one time. Many owners believed sick slaves were only "malingering." Because of the poor medical knowledge of the time, they failed to realize that adequate diet, warm housing, and basic sanitation might have prevented the pneumonia and dysentery that killed or weakened many slaves and that exacted an especially high toll on very young children.

FROM CRADLE TO GRAVE

9–12
The Trials of a Slave Girl

Slavery was a lifelong labor system, and the constant and inescapable issue between master and slave was how much work the slave would—or could—be forced to do. White Southern slave owners claimed that by housing, feeding, and clothing their slaves from infancy to death they were acting more humanely than Northern industrialists who employed people only during their working years. But in spite of occasional instances of manumission—the freeing of a slave—the child born of a slave was destined to remain a slave.

Children lived with their parents (or with their mother if the father was a slave on another farm or plantation) in housing provided by the owner. Slaves owned by small farmers usually had only a bed or mattress to sleep on in the attic or a back room. Larger slave owners housed slaves in one-room cabins with dirt floors and few furnishings (a table, stools, a cooking pot and a few dishes, a bed, or corn-shuck mattresses).

Masters supplied food to their slaves. One common ration for a week was three pounds of meat, four quarts of corn meal, and some molasses for each person. Often slaves were encouraged to supplement their diet by keeping their own gardens, and by hunting—though not, of course, with guns. The opportunity to garden and to hunt, in other words not to be completely dependent on their masters, was one slaves cherished. Slaves were also provided with clothes, usually of rough homespun cloth: two shirts, two pairs of pants, and a pair of shoes a year for men, and enough cloth for women to make an equal number of smocks for themselves and their children yearly. This clothing was barely adequate, and in severe winters slaves suffered badly.

From birth to about age seven, slave children played with one another and with white children, observing and learning how to survive. They saw the penalties: black adults, perhaps their own parents, whipped for disobedience; black women, perhaps their own sisters, violated by white men. And they might see one or both parents sold away as punishment or for financial gain. They would also see signs of white benevolence: special treats for children at holidays, appeals to loyalty from the master or mistress, perhaps friendship with a white child.

The children would learn slave ways of getting along: apparent acquiescence in white demands; pilfering; malingering, sabotage, and other methods of slowing the relentless work pace. Fanny Kemble, a British actress married to a Georgian, was quick to note the pretense in the "outrageous flattery" she received from her husband's slaves. But many white Southerners genuinely believed that their slaves were both less intelligent and more loyal than they really were.

Most slaves spent their lives as field hands, working in gangs with other slaves under a white overseer, who was usually quick to use his whip to keep up the work pace. But there were other occupations. In the "big house" there were jobs for women as cooks, maids, seamstresses, laundresses, weavers, and nurses. Black men became coachmen, valets, and gardeners, or skilled craftsmen—carpenters, mechanics, and blacksmiths. Some children began learning these occupations at age seven or eight, often in an informal apprentice system. Other children, both boys and girls, were expected to take full care of younger children while the parents were working. Of course, black children had no schooling of any kind: in most of the Southern states, it was against the law to teach a slave to read, although indulgent owners often rewarded their "pet" slaves by teaching them in spite of the law. At age twelve, slaves were considered full grown and put to work in the fields or in their designated occupation.

HOUSE SERVANTS

At first glance, working in the big house might seem to have been preferable to working in the fields. Physically it was much less demanding, and house slaves were often better fed and clothed. They also had much more access to information, for white people, accustomed to servants and generally confident of their loyalty, often forgot their presence and spoke among themselves about matters of interest to the slaves: local gossip, changes in laws or attitudes, policies toward disobedient or rebellious slaves.

For many white people, one of the worst surprises of the Civil War was the eagerness of their house slaves to flee. Considered by their masters the best treated and the most loyal, these slaves were commonly the first to leave or to organize mass desertions. Even the Confederacy's first family, President Jefferson Davis and his wife Varina, were chagrined by the desertion of their house servants in 1864.

8–1
Memoirs of a Monticello Slave, as Dictated to Charles Campbell by Isaac (1847)

From the point of view of the slave, the most unpleasant thing about being a house servant (or the single slave of a small owner) was the constant presence of white people. There was no escape from white supervision. Many slaves who were personal maids and children's nurses were required to live in the big house and rarely saw their own families. Cooks and other house servants were exposed to the tempers and whims of all members of the white family, including the children, who prepared themselves for lives of mastery by practicing giving orders to slaves many times their own age. And house servants, more than any others, were forced to act grateful and ingratiating. The demeaning images of Uncle Tom and the ever-smiling mammy derive from the roles slaves learned as the price of survival. At the same time, genuine intimacy was possible, especially between black nurses and white children. But these were bonds that the white children were ultimately forced to reject as the price of joining the master class.

ARTISANS AND SKILLED WORKERS

A small number of slaves were skilled workers: weavers, seamstresses, carpenters, blacksmiths, mechanics. More slave men than women achieved skilled status (partly because many jobs considered appropriate for women, like cooking, were not thought of as skilled). Solomon Northup, a Northern free African American kidnapped into slavery, explained in his 1853 narrative, *Twelve Years a Slave*, that he had been forced to do a variety of work. He had had three owners and had been hired out repeatedly as a carpenter and as a driver of other slaves in a sugar mill; he had also been hired out to clear land for a new Louisiana plantation and to cut sugar cane. Black people worked as lumberjacks (of the 16,000 lumber workers in the South, almost all were slaves), as miners, as deckhands and stokers on Mississippi riverboats, as stevedores loading cotton on the docks of Charleston, Savannah, and New Orleans, and sometimes as workers in the handful of Southern factories. Because slaves were their masters' property, the wages of the slave belonged to the owner, not the slave.

The extent to which slaves made up the laboring class was most apparent in cities. A British visitor to Natchez in 1835 noted slave "mechanics, draymen, hostelers, labourers, hucksters and washwomen and the heterogeneous multitude of every other occupation." In the North, all these jobs were performed by white workers. In part, because the South failed to attract as much immigrant labor as the North, Southern cities offered both enslaved and free black people opportunities in skilled occupations such as blacksmithing and carpentering that free African Americans in the North were denied.

FIELD WORK AND THE GANG SYSTEM OF LABOR

A full 75 percent of all slaves were field workers, and it was these workers who were most directly affected by the labor system employed on cotton plantations. Cotton was a crop that demanded nearly year-round labor: from planting in April to constant hoeing and cultivation through June to a picking season that began in August and lasted until December. The work was less skilled than on tobacco or sugar plantations, but more constant. Owners divided their slaves into gangs of twenty to twenty-five, a communal labor pattern reminiscent of parts of Africa, but with a crucial difference—these workers were supervised by overseers with whips. Field hands, both men and women, worked from "can see to can't see" (sunup to sundown) summer and winter, and frequently longer at harvest, when eighteen-hour days were common. Work days were shorter in the winter, perhaps only ten hours.

Work was tedious in the hot and humid Southern fields, and the overseer's whip was never far away. Cotton growing was hard work: plowing and planting, chopping weeds with a heavy hoe, and picking the ripe cotton from the stiff and scratchy bolls at the rate of 150 pounds a day. A strong, hardworking slave— a "prime field hand"—was valuable property, worth at least $1,000 to the master. Slaves justifiably took pride in their strength but aged fast. Poor diet, heavy labor, and the constant threat of the whip undermined health. When they were too old to work, they took on other tasks within the black community, such as caring for young children. Honored by the slave community, the elderly were tolerated by white owners, who continued to feed and clothe them until their deaths. Few actions show the hypocrisy of Southern paternalism more clearly than the speed with which white owners evicted their elderly slaves in the 1860s when the end of the slave system was in sight.

SOLD "DOWN THE RIVER"

The experience of slaves who were sold or forced by their owners to migrate to the newly opened cotton lands of the Southwest sheds light on the dynamics and tensions underlying the South's cotton-induced prosperity. Although some owners brought existing slave communities with them, the most common experience was that of the individual slave, forcibly separated from family and kin and sent alone with other strangers to a new life far away. For these individual slaves, migration to the Southwest was a long ordeal.

Upper South slaveowners sold slaves to large trading firms, who collected them during the summer in slave pens in Baltimore, Richmond, Nashville, and other Northern cities. When the weather cooled, slaves were sent south in chains on foot in coffles, by sailing ship, or by steamboat on the Mississippi to be sold in

Gang System The organization and supervision of slave field hands into working teams on Southern plantations.

This painting shows slaves being inspected by potential buyers at a slave market. Slaves were often threatened with punishment if they did not present a good appearance and manner that would fetch a high price.

Taylor, *An American Slave Market*, 1852. Oil on canvas. Chicago Historical Society

New Orleans. There, in the streets outside of large slave pens near the French Quarter, thousands of slaves were displayed and sold each year. Dressed in new clothes provided by the traders and exhorted by the traders to walk, run, and otherwise show their stamina, slaves were presented to buyers. For their part, suspicious buyers, unsure that traders and slaves themselves were truthful, poked, prodded, and frequently stripped male and female slaves to be sure they were as healthy as the traders claimed. Aside from obvious signs of illness, buyers often looked for scars on a slave's back: too many scars were a sign of the frequent whippings that a rebellious or "uppity" slave had provoked.

Once sold, slaves could face a variety of conditions. A number, especially in the early years of settlement in the Old Southwest, found themselves in frontier circumstances. Young male slaves were chosen for the backbreaking work of cutting trees and clearing land for cultivation. Some worked side by side with their owners to clear the land for small farms devoted to raising food for immediate consumption. In these circumstances slaves were often highly self-reliant and expected by owners to hunt and fish to supplement the basic diet. This relatively cooperative and permissive attitude was also evident on larger farms engaged in the variety of tasks required in mixed farming. But uniformity and strict discipline were the rule on cotton plantations. Owners eager to clear land rapidly so as to make quick profits often drove the clearing crews at an unmerciful pace. And they attempted to impose strict discipline and a rapid pace on the work gangs that planted, hoed, and harvested cotton. Slaves from other parts of the South, used to more individual and less intense work, hated the cotton regime and most of all hated the overseers who enforced it. They also fought to retain their rights to supplement the owner-supplied diet with their own garden produce and by hunting.

Thus, the new land in the Old Southwest that appeared to offer so much opportunity for owners bred tensions caused by forcible sale and migration, by the organization and pace of cotton cultivation, and by the owners' efforts to abrogate what slaves saw as traditional rights.

THE AFRICAN AMERICAN COMMUNITY

Surely no group in American history has faced a harder job of community building than the black people of the antebellum South. Living in intimate, daily contact with their oppressors, African Americans nevertheless created an enduring culture of their own, a culture that had far-reaching and lasting influence on all of Southern life and American society as a whole (see Chapter 4). Within their own communities, African American values and attitudes, and especially their own forms of Christianity, played a vital part in shaping a culture of endurance and resistance.

Few African Americans were unfortunate enough to live their lives alone among white people. Over half of all slaves lived on plantations with twenty or more other slaves, and others, on smaller farms, had links with slaves on nearby properties. Urban slaves were able to make and sustain so many secret contacts with other African Americans in cities or towns that slave owners wondered whether slave discipline could be maintained in urban settings. There can be no question that the bonds among African Americans were what sustained them during the years of slavery.

In law, slaves were property, to be bought, sold, rented, worked, and otherwise used (but not abused or killed) as the owner saw fit. But slaves were also human beings, with feelings, needs, and hopes. Even though most white Southerners believed black people to be members of an inferior, childish race, all but the most brutal masters acknowledged the humanity of their slaves. Furthermore, as a practical matter, white owners had long since learned that unhappy or rebellious slaves were poor workers. White masters learned to live with the two key institutions of African American community life: the family and the African American church.

SLAVE FAMILIES

No Southern state recognized slave marriages in law. Most owners, though, not only recognized but also encouraged them, sometimes even performing a kind of wedding ceremony for the couple. Masters sometimes tried to arrange marriages, but slaves usually found their own mates, sometimes on their own plantation, sometimes elsewhere. Masters encouraged marriage among their slaves,

WHAT ROLE did religion play in African-American slave communities?

13–1
State v. *Boon* (1801)

QUICK REVIEW

Slave Families

- Marriage not legally recognized but encouraged among slaves.
- Parents made great efforts to teach and protect their children.
- The internal slave trade made separation a constant danger.

Five generations of one family on a South Carolina plantation are gathered together for this 1862 picture, providing living evidence of the importance of kinship in the building of African American communities.

Library of Congress

QUICK REVIEW

Religion and Slavery

◆ A variety of African religions survived in America.

◆ The Great Awakening introduced many slaves to Christianity.

◆ Most planters favored Christianity among slaves only if they had control.

believing it made the men less rebellious, and for economic reasons they were eager for the slave women to have children.

Whatever marriages meant to the masters, to slaves they were a haven of love and intimacy in a cruel world and the basis of the African American community. Husbands and wives had a chance, in their own cabins, to live their own lives among loved ones. Husband and wife cooperated in loving and sheltering their children and teaching them survival skills. Above all, family meant continuity. Parents made great efforts to teach their children the family history and to surround them with a supportive and protective kinship network.

The strength of these ties is shown by the many husbands, wives, children, and parents who searched for each other after the Civil War when slavery came to an end. As the ads in black newspapers indicate, some family searches went on into the 1870s and 1880s, and many ended in failure.

Given the vast size of the internal slave trade, fear of separation was constant—and real. Separations of slave families were common. One in every five slave marriages was broken, and one in every three children sold away from their families. These figures clearly show that slave owners' support for slave marriages was secondary to their desire for profits.

In the face of constant separation, slave communities attempted to act like larger families. Following practices developed early in slavery, children were taught to respect and learn from all the elders, to call all adults of a certain age "aunt" or "uncle," and to call children of their own age "brother" or "sister" (see Chapter 4). Thus, in the absence of their own family, separated children could quickly find a place and a source of comfort in the slave community to which they had been sold.

The kinship of the entire community, where old people were respected and young ones cared for, represented a conscious rejection of white paternalism. The slaves' ability, in the most difficult of situations, to structure a community that expressed their values, not those of their masters, was extraordinary. Equally remarkable was the way in which African Americans reshaped Christianity to serve their needs.

AFRICAN AMERICAN RELIGION

Slaves brought religions from Africa but were not allowed to practice them, for white people feared religion would create a bond among slaves that might lead to rebellion. African religions managed to survive in the slave community in forms that white people considered as "superstition" or "folk belief," such as the medicinal use of roots by conjurers. Religious ceremonies survived, too, in late-night gatherings deep in the woods where the sound of drumming, singing, and dancing could not reach white ears (see Chapter 4).

Most masters of the eighteenth century made little effort to Christianize their slaves, afraid they might take the promises of universal brotherhood and equality too literally. The Great Awakening, which swept the South after the 1760s, introduced many slaves to Christianity, often in mixed congregations with white people (see Chapter 5). The transformation was completed by the **Second Great Awakening**, which took root among black and white Southerners in the 1790s. The number of African American converts, preachers, and lay teachers grew rapidly, and a distinctive form of Christianity took shape.

The first African American Baptist and Methodist churches were founded in Philadelphia in 1794 by the Reverend Absalom Jones and the Reverend Richard Allen. In 1816, the Reverend Allen joined with African American ministers from other cities to form the African Methodist Episcopal (AME) denomination. By the 1830s, free African American ministers like Andrew Marshall of Savannah and many more enslaved black preachers and lay ministers preached, sometimes secretly, to slaves. Their message was one of faith and love, of deliverance, of the coming of the promised land.

African Americans found in Christianity a powerful vehicle to express their longings for freedom and justice. But why did their white masters allow it? Some white people, themselves converted by the revivals, doubtless believed that they should not deny their slaves the same religious experience. But the evangelical religion of the early nineteenth century was also a powerful form of social control. Southern slave owners, seeking to counteract the appeal of African American religion, expected their Christianity to make their slaves obedient and peaceful. Forbidding their slaves to hold their own religious gatherings, owners insisted that their slaves attend white church services. Slaves were quick to realize the owners' purpose. As a former Texas slave recalled: "We went to church on the place and you ought to heard that preachin'. Obey your massa and missy, don't steal chickens and eggs and meat, but nary a word 'bout havin' a soul to save." But at night, away from white eyes, they held their own prayer meetings.

In churches and in spontaneous religious expressions, the black community made Christianity its own. Fusing Christian texts with African elements of group activity, such as the circle dance, the call-and-response pattern, and, above all, group singing, black people created a unique community religion full of emotion, enthusiasm, and protest. Nowhere is this spirit more compelling than in the famous spirituals: "Go Down Moses," with its mournful refrain "Let my people go"; the rousing "Didn't My Lord Deliver Daniel . . . and why not every man"; the haunting "Steal Away."

Nevertheless, this was not a religion of rebellion, for that was unrealistic for most slaves. Black Christianity was an enabling religion: it helped slaves to survive, not as passive victims of white tyranny but as active opponents of an oppressive system that they daily protested in small but meaningful ways.

FREEDOM AND RESISTANCE

Whatever their dreams, most slaves knew they would never escape. Almost all successful escapes in the nineteenth century (approximately 1,000 a year) were from the Upper South (Delaware, Maryland, Virginia, Kentucky, and Missouri). A slave in the Lower South or the Southwest simply had too far to go to reach freedom. In addition, white Southerners were determined to prevent escapes. Slave patrols were a common sight on Southern roads. Any black person without a pass from his or her master was captured (usually roughly) and returned home to certain punishment. But despite almost certain recapture, slaves continued to flee and to help others do so. Escaped slave Harriet Tubman of Maryland, who made nineteen rescue missions freeing 300 slaves in all, had extraordinary determination and skill.

Second Great Awakening Religious revival among black and white Southerners in the 1790s.

Harriet Tubman escaped in 1849 from slavery in Maryland and returned nineteen times to free almost 300 other slaves. Here Tubman (at left), the most famous "conductor" on the Underground Railroad, is shown with some of those she led to freedom.

Courtesy of Sophia Smith Collection, Smith College

13–3
Nat Turner, Confession (1831)

This drawing shows the moment, almost two months after the failure of his famous and bloody slave revolt, when Nat Turner was accidentally discovered in the woods near his home plantation. Turner's cool murder of his owner and methodical organization of his revolt deeply frightened many white Southerners.

Courtesy of the Library of Congress

Slaves who knew they could not reach freedom still frequently demonstrated their desire for liberty or their discontent over mistreatment by taking unauthorized leave from their plantation. Hidden in nearby forests or swamps, provided with food smuggled by other slaves from the plantation, the runaway might return home after a week or so, often to rather mild punishment. Temporary flight by any slave was a warning sign of discontent that a wise master did not ignore.

SLAVE REVOLTS

The ultimate resistance, however, was the slave revolt. Southern history is dotted with stories of former slave conspiracies and rumors of current plots (see Chapter 4). Every white Southerner knew about the last-minute failure of Gabriel Prosser's insurrection in Richmond in 1800 and the chance discovery of Denmark Vesey's plot in Charleston in 1822. But when in 1831, Nat Turner actually started a rebellion in which a number of white people were killed, Southern fears were greatly magnified.

A literate man, Nat Turner was a lay preacher, but he was also a slave. It was Turner's intelligence and strong religious commitment that made him a leader in the slave community and, interestingly, these very same qualities led his master, Joseph Travis, to treat him with kindness even though Turner had once run away for a month after being mistreated by an overseer. Turner began plotting his revolt after a religious vision in which he saw "white spirits and black spirits engaged in battle"; "the sun was darkened—the thunder rolled in the Heavens, and blood flowed in streams." Turner and five other slaves struck on the night of August 20, 1831, first killing Travis, who, Turner said, "was to me a kind master, and placed the greatest confidence in me; in fact, I had no cause to complain of his treatment of me."

Moving from plantation to plantation and killing a total of fifty-five white people, the rebels numbered sixty by the next morning, when they fled from a group of armed white men. More than forty blacks were executed after the revolt, including Turner, who was captured accidentally after he had hidden for two months in the woods. Thomas R. Gray, a white lawyer to whom Turner dictated a lengthy confession before his death, was impressed by Turner's composure. "I looked on him," Gray said, "and my blood curdled in my veins." If intelligent, well-treated slaves such as Turner could plot revolts, how could white Southerners ever feel safe?

Gabriel's Rebellion, the Denmark Vesey plot, and **Nat Turner's Revolt** were the most prominent examples of organized slave resistance, but they were far from the only ones. Conspiracies and actual or rumored slave resistance began in colonial times (see Chapter 4) and never ceased. These plots exposed the truth white Southerners preferred to ignore: Only force kept Africans and African Americans enslaved, and because no system of control could ever be total, white Southerners could never be completely safe from the possibility of revolt. Nat Turner brought white Southerners' fears to the surface. After 1831, the possibility of slave insurrection was never far from their minds.

One of the ways Charleston attempted to control its African American population was to require all slaves to wear badges showing their occupation. After 1848, free black people also had to wear badges, which were decorated, ironically, with a liberty cap.

Courtesy of the American Numismatic Society of New York

FREE AFRICAN AMERICANS

Another source of white disquiet was the growing number of free African Americans. By 1860, nearly 250,000 free black people lived in the South. For most, freedom dated from before 1800, when antislavery feeling among slave owners in the Upper South was widespread and cotton cultivation had yet to boom.

Most free black people lived in the countryside of the Upper South, where they worked as tenant farmers or farm laborers. Urban African Americans were much more visible. Life was especially difficult for female-headed families because only the most menial work—street peddling and laundry work, for example—was available to free black women. The situation for African American males was somewhat better. Although they were discriminated against in employment and in social life, there were opportunities for skilled black craftsmen in trades such as blacksmithing and carpentry. Cities such as Charleston, Savannah, and Natchez were home to flourishing free African American communities that formed their own churches and fraternal orders.

Throughout the South in the 1830s, state legislatures tightened **black codes**—laws concerning free black people. Free African Americans could not carry firearms, could not purchase slaves (unless they were members of their own family), and were liable to the criminal penalties meted out to slaves (that is, whippings and summary judgments without a jury trial). They could not testify against whites, hold office, vote, or serve in the militia. In other words, except for the right to own property, free blacks had no civil rights.

7–6
An African American Calls for an End to Slavery (1791)

Gabriel's Rebellion   Slave revolt that failed when Gabriel Prosser, a slave preacher and blacksmith, organized a thousand slaves for an attack on Richmond, Virginia, in 1800.

Nat Turner's Revolt   Uprising of slaves in Southampton County, Virginia, in the summer of 1831 led by Nat Turner that resulted in the death of fifty-five white people.

THE WHITE MAJORITY

Two-thirds of all Southerners did not own slaves, yet slave owners dominated the social and political life of the region. Who were the two-thirds of white Southerners who did not own slaves, and how did they live? Throughout the South, slave owners occupied the most productive land: tobacco-producing areas in Virginia and Tennessee, coastal areas of South Carolina and Georgia where rice and cotton grew, sugar lands in Louisiana, and large sections of the cotton-producing black belt, which stretched westward from South Carolina to Texas. Small farmers, usually without slaves, occupied the rest of the rural land and a small middle class lived in the cities of the South.

WHAT WERE the values of yeoman farmers?

THE MIDDLE CLASS

In the predominantly rural South, cities provided a home for a commercial middle class of merchants, bankers, factors (agents), and lawyers on whom the agricultural economy depended to sell its produce to a world market. Urban growth lagged far

Black codes   Laws passed by states and municipalities denying many rights of citizenship to free black people before the Civil War.

behind the North. The cities that grew were major shipping centers for agricultural goods: the river cities of Louisville, St. Louis, Memphis, and New Orleans, and the cotton ports of Mobile and Savannah. Formal educational institutions, libraries, and cultural activities were located in cities, and so were the beginnings of the same kind of entreprenurial and commercial spirit so evident in the North.

The effort of William Gregg of South Carolina to establish the cotton textile industry illustrates some of the problems facing Southern entrepreneurs. Gregg became convinced that textile factories were a good way to diversify the Southern economy and to provide a living for poor whites. He enthusiastically publicized the findings of his tour of Northern textile mills but found a cool reception. His request to the planter-dominated South Carolina legislature for a charter of incorporation for a textile mill passed by only one vote. In 1846 he built a model mill and a company town in Graniteville, South Carolina, that attracted poor white families as employees. Gregg adapted Southern paternalism to industry, providing a school and churches and prohibiting alcohol and dancing, yet paying his workers 20 percent less than Northern wages.

John Letcher, a lawyer and politician in Lexington, Virginia, had typical moderate, urban, middle-class attitudes. A Democrat, he served four terms in the U.S. Congress in the 1850s, where he acquired a reputation as a moderate in favor of limited government, earning the nickname "Honest John Letcher, Watchdog of the Treasury." Elected governor of Virginia in 1860, he led his state out of the Union once the Civil War began and devoted his efforts to unity in pursuit of Confederate war aims. Like some other members of the urban middle class, he owned only enough slaves (a family with children) to do the domestic work for his own family, and at one time, early in his career, he had favored gradual emancipation.

Many Southern planters scorned members of the commercial middle class like Letcher and Gregg because they had to please their suppliers and customers, and thus lacked, in their eyes, true independence. No one cherished his independence more than the **yeoman** farmer.

Yeomen

The word "yeoman," originally a British term for a farmer who works his own land, is often applied to independent farmers of the South, most of whom lived on family-sized farms. Although yeoman farmers sometimes owned a few slaves, in general they and their families worked their land by themselves. Typical of the yeoman-farmer community was northwestern Georgia, once home to the Creeks and Cherokees but now populated by communities of small farmers who grew enough vegetables to feed their families, including corn, which they either ate themselves or fed to hogs. In addition, these farmers raised enough cotton every year (usually no more than one or two bales) to bring in a little cash.

Where yeomen and large slave owners lived side by side, as in the Georgia black belt where cotton was the major crop, slavery again provided a link between the rich and middle class. Large plantation owners often bought food for their slaves from small local farmers, ground the latter's corn in the plantation mill, ginned their cotton, and transported and marketed it as well. But although planters and much smaller yeomen were part of a larger community network, in the black belt the large slave owners were clearly dominant. Only in their own up-country communities did yeomen feel truly independent.

Yeoman   Independent farmers of the South, most of whom lived on family-sized farms.

QUICK REVIEW

Yeoman Farmers

◆ Most independent farmers in the South lived on family farms.

◆ Farmers formed tight networks of friends and family.

◆ Slavery linked large planters and yeoman farmers.

POOR WHITE PEOPLE

Not all small farmers were on an equal footing. One-third of the farmers in the Georgia upcountry were tenant farmers. Some were farmers' sons, striking out on their own while waiting to inherit their fathers' land. But others were poor whites with little hope of improving their condition. From 30 to 50 percent of all Southern white people were landless, a proportion similar to that in the North. But the existence of slavery affected the opportunities for Southern poor white people. Slaves made up the permanent, stable work force in agriculture and in many skilled trades. Many poor white people led highly transient lives in search of work, such as doing farm labor at harvest time, which was only temporary. Others were tenant farmers working under share-tenancy arrangements that kept them in debt to the landowner.

Relationships between poor whites and black slaves were complex. White men and women often worked side by side with black slaves in the fields and were socially and sexually intimate with enslaved and free African Americans. White people engaged in clandestine trade to supply slaves with items like liquor that slave owners prohibited, helped slaves to escape, and even (in an 1835 Mississippi case) were executed for their participation in planning a slave revolt. At the same time, the majority of poor white people insisted, sometimes violently, on their racial superiority over black people. For their part, many African American slaves, better dressed, better nourished, and healthier, dismissed them as "poor white trash." But the fact was that the difficult lives of poor whites, whom one contemporary described as "a third class of white people," served to blur the crucial racial distinction between independent whites and supposedly inferior, dependent black people on which the system of slavery rested.

YEOMAN VALUES

In 1828 and 1832, Southern yeomen and poor white men voted overwhelmingly for Andrew Jackson. They were drawn variously to his outspoken policy of ruthless expansionism, his appeals to the common man, and his rags-to-riches ascent from poor boy to rich slave owner. It was a career many hoped to emulate. The dominance of the large planters was due at least in part to the ambition of many yeomen, especially those with two or three slaves, to expand their holdings and become rich. These farmers, enthusiastic members of the lively democratic politics of the South, supported the leaders they hoped to join.

But for a larger group of yeomen, independence and not wealth was most important. Many Southern yeomen lived apart from large slaveholders, in the up-country regions where plantation agriculture was unsuitable. The very high value Southern yeomen placed on freedom grew directly from their own experience as self-sufficient property-owning farmers in small, family-based communities and from the absolute, patriarchal control they exercised over their own wives and children. This was a way of life that Southern "plain folk" were determined to preserve. It made them resistant to the economic opportunities and challenges that capitalism and industrialization posed for Northern farmers, which Southern yeomen perceived as encroachments on their freedom.

The irony was that the freedom yeomen so prized rested on slavery. White people could count on slaves to perform the hardest and worst labor, and the degradation of slave life was a daily reminder of the freedom they enjoyed in comparison. Slavery meant that all white people, rich and poor, were equal in the sense that they were all free. This assumption of white skin privilege had formed in the eighteenth century as slavery became the answer to the South's labor problem (see Chapter 4). The democratization of politics in the early nineteenth century and the enactment of nearly universal white manhood suffrage perpetuated the belief in white skin privilege, even though the gap between rich and poor white people was widening.

PLANTERS

Remarkably few slave owners fit the popular stereotype of the rich and leisured plantation owner with hundreds of acres of land and hundreds of slaves. Only 36 percent of Southern white people owned slaves in 1830, and only 2.5 percent owned fifty slaves or more. Just as yeomen and poor whites were diverse, so, too, were Southern slave owners.

SMALL SLAVE OWNERS

The largest group of slave owners were small yeomen taking the step from subsistence agriculture to commercial production. To do this in the South's agricultural economy, they had to own slaves. But upward mobility was difficult. Owning one or two slaves increased farm production only slightly, and it was hard to accumulate the capital to buy more. One common pattern was for a slave owner to leave one or two slaves to farm while he worked another job (this arrangement usually meant that his wife had assumed responsibility for their supervision). In other cases, small farmers worked side by side with their slaves in the fields. In still other cases, owners hired out their slaves to larger slave owners.

In every case, the owner was economically vulnerable: a poor crop or a downturn in cotton prices could wipe out his gains and force him to sell his slaves. When times improved, he might buy a new slave or two and try again, but getting a secure footing on the bottom rung of the slave-owner ladder was very difficult. The roller-coaster economy of the early nineteenth century did not help matters, and the Panic of 1837 was a serious setback to many small farmers.

For a smaller group of slave owners, the economic struggle was not so hard. Middle-class professional men—lawyers, doctors, and merchants—frequently managed to become large slave owners because they already had capital (the pay from their professions) to invest in land and slaves. Sometimes they received payment for their services not in money but in slaves. These owners were the most likely to own skilled slaves—carpenters, blacksmiths, and other artisans—and to rent them out for profit. By steady accumulation, the most successful members of this middle class were able to buy their way into the slave-owning elite and to confirm that position by marrying their sons or daughters into the aristocracy.

THE PLANTER ELITE

The slave-owning elite, those 2.5 percent who owned fifty slaves or more, enjoyed the prestige, the political leadership, and the lifestyle to which many white Southerners aspired. Almost all great slave owners inherited their wealth. They were rarely self-made men, although most tried to add to the land and slaves they had inherited. Men of wealth and property had led Southern politics since colonial times, but increasingly after 1820 it was men from the middle classes who were most often elected to political office. As the nation moved toward universal manhood suffrage, planters tried to learn how to appeal to the popular

---

WHO MADE up the planter elite?

Slaveholding and Class Structure in the South, 1830
The great mass of the Southern white population were yeoman farmers. In 1830, slave owners made up only 36 percent of the Southern white population; owners of more than fifty slaves constituted a tiny 2.5 percent. Yet they and the others who were middling planters dominated politics, retaining the support of yeomen who prized their freedom as white men above class-based politics.
U.S. Bureau of the Census.

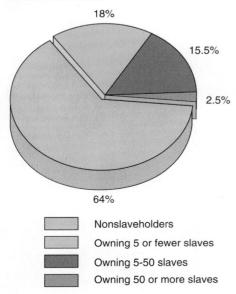

- Nonslaveholders
- Owning 5 or fewer slaves
- Owning 5-50 slaves
- Owning 50 or more slaves

vote, but most never acquired "the common touch." It was the smaller slave owners who formed a clear majority in every Southern state legislature before 1860.

The eastern seaboard had first given rise to a class of rich planters in the colonial period. As Southerners and slave owning spread westward, membership in the elite broadened to include the new wealth of Alabama, Mississippi, Louisiana, and Texas. The rich planters of the Natchez community were popularly called "nabobs" (from a Hindi word for Europeans who had amassed fabulous wealth in India).

The extraordinary concentration of wealth in Natchez—in 1850 it was the richest county in the nation—fostered a self-consciously elite lifestyle that derived not from long tradition, but from suddenly acquired riches.

PLANTATION LIFE

The urban life of the Natchez planters was unusual. Many wealthy planters, especially those on new lands in the Old Southwest, lived in isolation on their plantations with their families and slaves. Through family networks, common boarding school experience, political activity, and frequent visiting, the small new planter elite consciously worked to create and maintain a distinctive lifestyle that was modeled on that of the English aristocracy, as Southerners understood it. This entailed a large estate, a spacious, elegant mansion, and lavish hospitality. For men, the gentlemanly lifestyle meant immersion in masculine activities such as hunting, soldiering, or politics, and a touchy concern with "honor" that could lead to duels and other acts of bravado. Women of the slave-owning elite, in contrast, were expected to be gentle, charming, and always welcoming of relatives, friends, and other guests.

But this gracious image was at odds with the economic reality. Large numbers of black slaves had to be forced to work to produce the wealth of the large plantations. A large plantation was an enterprise that required many hands, many skills, and a lot of management. Large plantation owners might have overseers or black drivers to supervise field work, but frequently they themselves had direct financial control of daily operations.

A paternalistic ideology infused the life of large plantations that permitted the planter elite to rationalize their use of slaves and the submissiveness they demanded of wives. According to this ideology, each plantation was a family composed of both black and white. The master, as head of the plantation, was head of the family, and the mistress was his "helpmate." The master was obligated to provide for all of his family, both black and white, and to treat them with humanity. In return, slaves were to work properly and do as they were told, as children would. Most elite slave owners spoke of their position of privilege as a duty and a burden. (Their wives were even more outspoken about the burdensome aspects of supervising slave labor, which they bore more directly than their husbands.) John C. Calhoun spoke for many slave owners when he described the plantation as "a little community" in which the master directed all operations so that the abilities and needs of every member, black and white, were "perfectly harmonized." Convinced of their own benevolence, slave owners expected not only obedience, but also gratitude from all members of their great "families."

THE PLANTATION MISTRESS

Southern paternalism not only laid special burdens on plantation mistresses but also put restrictions on their lives and activities not experienced by Northern women of the same social rank. The difficulties experienced by these in some

QUICK REVIEW

Plantation Mistresses

♦ Mistresses ran the household staff.

♦ Mistresses were responsible for arrangements for visitors.

♦ Husbands were usually the real authority on the plantation.

ways quite privileged women illustrate the way the slave system affected every aspect of the personal life of slave owners.

Plantation mistresses spent most of their lives tending "family" members—including slaves—in illness and in childbirth and supervising their slaves' performance of such daily tasks as cooking, housecleaning, weaving, and sewing. In addition, the plantation mistress often had to spend hours, even days, of behind-the-scenes preparation for the crowds of guests she was expected to welcome in her role as elegant and gracious hostess.

Despite the reality of the plantation mistress's daily supervision of an often extensive household, she did not rule it: her husband did. The plantation master was the source of authority to whom wife, children, and slaves were expected to look for both rewards and punishments. A wife who challenged her husband or sought more independence from him threatened the entire paternalistic system of control. After all, if she were not dependent and obedient, why should slaves be? In addition, although many Southern women were deeply affected by evangelical religion and exhortations to care for those in need, their response was personal rather than social. Enlisting in reform movements like their Northern counterparts would have been far too threatening to the system of slave control to be tolerated in the South, for it might have led slaves to believe that their lives, too, could be improved.

Many Southern women also suffered deeply from their isolation from friends and kin. Sometimes the isolation of life on rural plantations could be overcome by long visits, but women with many small children and extensive responsibilities found it difficult to leave. Plantation masters, on the other hand, often traveled widely for political and business reasons.

Plantation women in the Old Southwest, many of whom had moved unwillingly and now were far from their families on the eastern seaboard, were particularly lonely. Mary Kendall wrote, "For about three weeks I did not have the pleasure of seeing one white female face, there being no white family except our own upon the plantation." She was surrounded by women, but the gap between the white mistress and her black slaves was generally unbridgeable.

Although on every plantation black women served as nursemaids to young white children and as lifelong maids to white women, usually accompanying them when they moved as brides into their own homes, there are few historical examples of genuine sympathy and understanding of black women by white women of the slave-owning class. Few of the latter seemed to understand the sadness, frustration, and despair often experienced by their lifelong maids, who were forced to leave their own husbands and children to serve in their mistresses' new homes. A number of Southern women did rail against "the curse of slavery," but few meant the inhumanity of the system; most were actually complaining about the extra work entailed by housekeeping with slaves. Years later many former slaves remembered their mistresses as being kinder than their masters, but fully a third of such accounts mention cruel whippings and other punishments by white women.

COERCION AND VIOLENCE

There were generous and benevolent masters, but most large slave owners believed that constant discipline and coercion were necessary to make slaves work hard. Some slave owners used their slaves with great brutality. Owners who killed slaves were occasionally brought to trial (and usually acquitted), but no legal action was taken in the much more frequent cases of excessive punishment, general abuse, and rape. All Southern slave owners, not just those who experienced the special tensions

This Louisiana slave named Gordon was photographed in 1863 after he had escaped to Union lines during the Civil War. He bears the permanent scars of the violence that lay at the heart of the slave system. Few slaves were so brutally marked, but all lived with the threat of beatings if they failed to obey.

National Archives and Records Administration

of new and isolated plantations in the Old Southwest, were engaged in a constant battle of wills with their slaves that owners frequently resolved by violence.

One of the most common violations of the paternalistic code of behavior (and of Southern law) was the sexual abuse of female slaves by their masters. Usually, masters forcibly raped their women slaves at will, and slave women had little hope of defending themselves from these attacks. Sometimes, however, long-term intimate relationships between masters and slaves developed.

It was rare for slave owners to publicly acknowledge fathering slave children or to free these children, and black women and their families were helpless to protest their treatment. Equally silenced was the master's wife, who for reasons of modesty as well as her subordinate position was not supposed to notice either her husband's infidelity or his flagrant crossing of the color lines. As Mary Boykin Chesnut, wife of a South Carolina slave owner, vehemently confided to her diary: "God forgive us, but ours is a monstrous system. . . . Like the patriarchs of old, our men live all in one house with their wives and their concubines, and the mulattoes one sees in every family partly resemble the white children."

THE DEFENSE OF SLAVERY

"Slavery informs all our modes of life, all our habits of thought, lies at the basis of our social existence, and of our political faith," announced South Carolina planter William Henry Trescot in 1850, explaining why the South would secede from the Union before giving up slavery. Slavery bound white and black Southerners together in tortuous ways that eventually led, as Trescot had warned, to the Civil War.

The sheer numbers of African Americans reinforced white people's perpetual fears of black retaliation for the violence exercised by the slave master. Every rumor of slave revolts, real or imagined, kept those fears alive. The basic question was this: What might slaves do if they were not controlled?

DEVELOPING PROSLAVERY ARGUMENTS

Southerners increasingly sought to justify slavery. They found justifications for slavery in the Bible and in the histories of Greece and Rome, both slave-owning societies. The strongest defense was a legal one: the Constitution allowed slavery. Though never specifically mentioned in the final document, slavery had been a major issue between North and South at the Constitutional Convention in 1787. In the end, the delegates agreed that seats in the House of Representatives would be apportioned by counting all of the white population and three-fifths of the black people (Article I, Section 2, Paragraph 3); they included a clause requiring the return of runaway slaves who had crossed state lines (Article IV, Section 2, Paragraph 3); and they agreed that Congress could not abolish the international slave trade for twenty years (Article I, Section 9, Paragraph 1). There was absolutely no question: the Constitution did recognize slavery.

The Missouri Crisis of 1819–1820 alarmed most Southerners, who were shocked by the evidence of widespread antislavery feeling in the North. South Carolinians viewed **Denmark Vesey's conspiracy**, occurring only two years after the Missouri debate, as an example of the harm that irresponsible Northern antislavery talk could cause. After Nat Turner's revolt in 1831, Governor John Floyd of Virginia blamed the uprising on "Yankee peddlers and traders" who supposedly told slaves that "all men were born free and equal." Thus, Northern antislavery opinion and the fear of slave uprisings were firmly linked in Southern minds.

WHAT PROSLAVERY arguments were developed in the first half of the nineteenth century?

Denmark Vesey's conspiracy The most carefully devised slave revolt in which rebels planned to seize control of Charleston in 1822 and escape to freedom in Haiti, a free black republic, but they were betrayed by other slaves, and seventy-five conspirators were executed.

MAP EXPLORATION

To explore an interactive version of this map, go to
http://www.prenhall.com/faraghertlc/map11.3

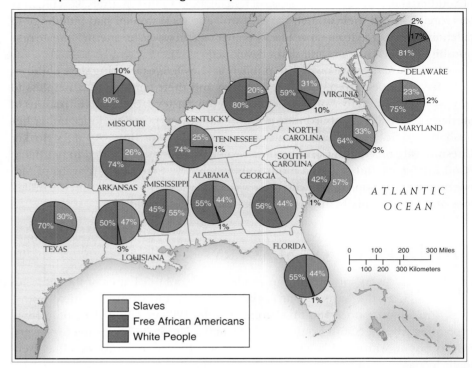

MAP 11-3 Population Patterns in the South, 1850
In South Carolina and Mississippi the enslaved African American population outnumbered the
white population; in four other Lower South states the percentage was above 40 percent. These
ratios frightened many white Southerners. White people also feared the free black population,
though only three states in the Upper South and Louisiana had free black populations of over 3
percent. Six states had free black populations that were so small (less than 1 percent) as to be sta-
tistically insignificant.

WHERE WERE the greatest concentrations of African Americans?
How would you explain the patterns the map reveals?

AFTER NAT TURNER

In 1831 the South began to close ranks in defense of slavery. Several factors contributed to this regional solidarity. Nat Turner's revolt was important, linked as it
was in the minds of many Southerners with antislavery agitation from the North.
Militant abolitionist William Lloyd Garrison began publishing the *Liberator*, the
newspaper that was to become the leading antislavery organ, in 1831. The British
gave notice that they would soon abolish slavery on the sugar plantations of the
West Indies, an action that seemed to many Southerners much too close to home.
Emancipation for West Indian slaves came in 1834. Finally, 1831 was the year
before the Nullification Crisis (see Chapter 10) was resolved. Although the other
Southern states did not support the hotheaded South Carolinians who called for
secession, they did sympathize with the argument that the federal government
had no right to interfere with a state's special interest (namely, slavery).

In 1835, a crowd broke into a Charleston post office, made off with bundles
of antislavery literature, and set an enormous bonfire, to fervent state and

regional acclaim. By 1835, every Southern legislature had tightened its laws concerning control of slaves. For example, they tried to blunt the effect of abolitionist literature by passing laws forbidding slaves to learn how to read. By 1860, it is estimated, only 5 percent of all slaves could read. Slaves were forbidden to gather for dances, religious services, or any kind of organized social activity without a white person present. Other laws made manumission illegal and placed even more restrictions on the lives of free black people.

Attempts were made to stifle all open debate about slavery within the South; dissenters were pressured to remain silent or to leave. A few, such as James G. Birney and Sarah and Angelina Grimké of South Carolina, left for the North to act on their antislavery convictions, but most chose silence. Southern politicians painted melodramatic pictures of a beleaguered white South hemmed in on all sides by "fanatic" antislavery states, while at home Southerners were forced to contemplate what might happen when they had "to let loose among them, freed from the wholesome restraints of patriarchal authority . . . an idle, worthless, profligate set of free negroes" whom they feared would "prowl the . . . streets at night and [haunt] the woods during the day armed with whatever weapons they could lay their hands on."

Finally, Southern apologists moved beyond defensiveness to develop proslavery arguments. One of the first to do this was James Henry Hammond, elected a South Carolina congressman in 1834. In 1836 Hammond delivered a major address to Congress in which he denied that slavery was evil. Rather, he claimed, it had produced "the highest toned, the purest, best organization of society that has ever existed on the face of the earth."

In 1854 another Southern spokesman, George Fitzhugh, asserted that "the negro slaves of the South are the happiest, and, in some sense, the freest people in the world" because all the responsibility for their care was borne by concerned white masters. Fitzhugh contrasted Southern paternalism with the heartless individualism that ruled the lives of Northern "wage slaves."

CHANGES IN THE SOUTH

In spite of these defensive and repressive proslavery measures, which made the South seem monolithic in Northern eyes, there were some surprising indicators of dissent. Most came from up-country nonslaveholders. One protest occurred in the Virginia state legislature in 1832, when nonslaveholding delegates, alarmed by the Nat Turner rebellion, forced a two-week debate on the merits of gradual abolition. In the final vote, abolition was defeated 73 to 58. The subject was never raised again.

But slavery was not a static system. From the 1830s on, financial changes increasingly underlined class differences among Southern whites. It was harder to become a slaveholder: from 1830 to 1860 slave owners declined from 36 to 25 percent of the population.

An even more alarming trend was evident in Southern cities, where the slave system was disintegrating. The number of urban slaves had greatly decreased because plantation owners deeply distrusted the effect of cities on the institution of slavery. Urban slaves led much more informed lives than rural ones and were often in daily contact with free black and urban poor white people. Many slaves were hired out and a number even hired out their own time, making them nearly indistinguishable from Northern "free labor." Other urban slaves worked in commercial and industrial enterprises in jobs that were nearly indistinguishable from those of white workers. Planters viewed all of these changes with suspicion, yet they also had to acknowledge that Southern cities were successful and bustling centers of commerce.

In North Carolina, disputes between slave owners and nonslaveholders erupted in print in 1857, when Hinton Helper published an attack on slavery in

13–2
A Black Abolitionist Speaks Out (1829)

13–4
An Abolitionist Defends the Amistad Mutineers (1839)

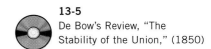

13-5
De Bow's Review, "The Stability of the Union," (1850)

a book entitled *The Impending Crisis*. His protest was an indicator of the growing tensions between the haves and the have-nots in the South. Equally significant, though, Helper's book was published in New York, where he was forced to move once his views became known.

In spite of these signs of tension and dissent, the main lines of the Southern argument were drawn in the 1830s and remained fixed thereafter. The defense of slavery stifled debate within the South, prevented a search for alternative labor systems, and narrowed the possibility of cooperation in national politics. In time, it made compromise impossible.

CONCLUSION

The amazing growth of cotton production after 1793 transformed the South and the nation. Physically, the South expanded explosively westward. Cotton production was based on the labor of African American slaves, who built strong communities under extremely difficult circumstances. The cohesion of African American families and the powerful faith of African American Christianity were the key community elements that bred a spirit of endurance and resistance. White Southerners, two-thirds of whom did not own slaves, denied their real dependence on slave labor by claiming equality in white skin privilege, while slave owners boasted of their own paternalism. In the 1830s, the South defensively closed ranks against real and perceived threats to the slave system. In this sense, the white South was nearly as trapped as the African American slaves they claimed to control. And in defending the slave system, the South was increasingly different from the dynamic capitalist free-labor system that was gaining strength in the North.

CHRONOLOGY

1790s	Second Great Awakening.
	Black Baptist and African Methodist Episcopal churches founded.
1793	Cotton gin invented.
1800	Gabriel Prosser's revolt discovered in Virginia.
1806	Virginia tightens law on manumission of slaves.
1808	Congress prohibits U.S. participation in the international slave trade.
1816–1820	"Alabama Fever": Migration to the Old Southwest.
1819–1820	Missouri Crisis.
1822	Denmark Vesey's conspiracy in Charleston.
1831	Nat Turner's revolt in Virginia.
	William Lloyd Garrison begins publishing antislavery newspaper, the *Liberator*.
1832	Nullification Crisis.
1832–1838	"Flush Times": Second wave of westward expansion.

1832	Virginia legislature debates and defeats a measure for gradual emancipation.
1834	Britain frees slaves throughout the empire, including in its Caribbean colonies.
1835	Charleston crowd burns abolitionist literature.
	Tightening of black codes completed by Southern legislatures.
1836	Congress passes "gag rule" to prevent discussion of antislavery petitions.
	James Henry Hammond announces to Congress that slavery is not evil.
1846	William Gregg opens model textile mill at Graniteville, South Carolina.
1854	George Fitzhugh publishes *Sociology for the South*, a defense of slavery.
1857	Hinton Helper publishes *The Impending Crisis*, an attack on slavery.

SUMMARY

Cotton and Southern Expansion The growing profitability of cotton stimulated western expansion and increased support for slavery. As cotton became the dynamic force in the American economy, plantation-oriented production strongly influenced the development of Southern society and culture along different lines from the North.

To Be a Slave In the age of King Cotton, slavery and the African American community matured. Cotton concentrated slaves on large plantations where they faced harsh conditions and lifelong labor. Distinct divisions emerged among slaves who worked in the house, as skilled labor, or in the fields. But all faced the potential of moving or being sold to plantations in the Southwest.

The African American Community Despite the harshness of slavery, African Americans developed a strong, enduring culture based on family, religion, and resistance to slavery. Families offered a sense of continuity in an uncertain environment, performing essential survival skill functions. African Americans also adapted Christianity to their needs and condition. In addition, they practiced numerous forms of resistance. Free African Americans, meanwhile, lived a precarious existence.

The White Majority Most white Southerners did not own slaves. The white majority lived in cities and in rural areas. A class structure developed based on wealth and land ownership. Rural whites espoused attitudes and values in tune with Andrew Jackson and the ideal of the common man.

Planters The planters were an elite class. They developed a way of life and ideology that combined "benevolent" and harsh treatment of slaves.

The Defense of Slavery Drawing from several sources, Southerners defended slavery. Slave owners became more unified after 1830. Still, changes in the South led to attacks on slavery.

REVIEW QUESTIONS

1. How did cotton production after 1793 transform the social and political history of the South? How did the rest of the nation benefit? In what way was it an "international phenomenon"?

2. What were the two key institutions of the African American slave community? How did they function, and what beliefs did they express?

3. The circumstances of three very different groups—poor whites, educated and property-owning American Indians, and free African Americans—put them outside the dominant Southern equations of white equals free and black equals slave. Analyze the difficulty each group encountered in the slave-owning South.

4. Who were the yeoman farmers? What was their interest in slavery?

5. Southern slaveholders claimed that their paternalism justified their ownership of slaves, but paternalism implied obligations as well as privileges. How well do you think slaveholders lived up to their paternalistic obligations?

6. How did slave owners justify slavery? How did their defense change over time?

KEY TERMS

Black codes(p. 289)

Denmark Vesey's conspiracy(p. 295)

Gabriel's Rebellion(p. 289)

Gang System(p. 283)

Industrial Revolution(p. 278)

Nat Turner's Revolt(p. 289)

Second Great Awakening(p. 287)

Yeoman(p. 290)

RECOMMENDED READING

Ira Berlin, *Slaves without Masters* (1974). A full portrait of the lives of free black people in the South before the Civil War.

Charles C. Bolton, *Poor Whites of the Antebellum South: Tenants and Laborers in Central North and Northeast Mississippi* (1994). A careful consideration of a hitherto "invisible" population.

Orville Vernon Burton, *In My Father's House Are Many Mansions: Family and Community in Edgefield, South Carolina* (1985). A detailed community study that considers the farms, families, and everyday relations of white and black people in the period 1850–1880.

Thomas D. Clark and John D. W. Guice, *Frontiers in Conflict: The Old Southwest, 1795–1830* (1989). Considers the Indian nations and their removal, white settlement, and the economic development of the region.

Catherine Clinton, *The Plantation Mistress: Woman's World in the Old South* (1982). Illustrates how slavery shaped the lives of elite white women. The exclusive focus on white women, however, neglects the black women with whom they lived on a daily basis.

Drew Gilpin Faust, *James Henry Hammond and the Old South* (1982). This outstanding biography uses the complex and interesting story of one man's life and ambitions to tell a larger story about Southern attitudes and politics.

Lacy K. Ford Jr., *Origins of Southern Radicalism: The South Carolina Upcountry, 1800–1860* (1988). One of a growing number of studies of up-country nonslaveholders and their commitment to liberty and equality.

Eugene Genovese, *Roll, Jordan, Roll: The World the Slaves Made* (1974). The landmark book that redirected the attention of historians from slaves as victims to the slave community as an active participant in the paternalism of the Southern slave system.

Steven Hahn, *The Roots of Southern Populism: Yeoman Farmers and the Transformation of the Georgia Upcountry, 1850–1890* (1983). One of the first studies of the changing world of Southern yeomen.

Walter Johnson, *Soul by Soul: Life Inside the Antebellum Slave Market* (1999). A fascinating study of the workings and meanings of the New Orleans slave markets.

Peter Kolchin, *American Slavery 1619–1877* (1993). A well-written, comprehensive survey.

Bruce Levine, *Half Slave and Half Free: The Roots of Civil War* (1992). A useful survey of the different lines of development of the Northern and Southern economies and the political conflicts between the regions.

Stephanie McCurry, *Masters of Small Worlds: Yeoman Households, Gender Relations, and the Political Culture of the Antebellum South Carolina Low Country* (1995). A study of yeomen that links their prized political and economic independence with their strong patriarchal control over their own families.

Donald P. McNeilly, *The Old South Frontier: Cotton Plantations and the Formation of Arkansas Society, 1819–1861* (2000). Traces slavery and society in Arkansas from frontier to cotton plantations.

James Oakes, *The Ruling Race: A History of American Slaveholders* (1982). Oakes disagrees with Genovese's characterization of paternalism and sees slave owners instead as entrepreneurial capitalists. Especially useful for distinguishing the various classes of slave owners.

Brenda Stevenson, *Life in Black and White: Family and Community in the Slave South* (1996). A careful study of families, black and white, in Louden County, Virginia, that illustrates the difficulties both free and enslaved African American families faced.

Michael Tadman, *Speculators and Slaves: Masters, Traders, and Slaves in the Old South* (1989). Examines the extent, organization, and values of the internal slave trade.

Now if rights are founded on the nature of moral being, then the mere circumstance of sex does not give to man higher rights and responsibilities, than to woman. To suppose that it does, would be to deny the self-evident truth, that the physical constitution is the mere instrument of the moral nature.

—Angelina Emily Grimké, October 2, 1837

LOWELL OFFERING

November, 1845.

"Is Saul also among the prophets?"

A REPOSITORY
OF ORIGINAL ARTICLES, WRITTEN BY
"FACTORY GIRL."

LOWELL: MISSES CURTIS & FARLEY.
BOSTON: JORDAN & WILEY, 121
Washington street.
1845.

MERRIMACK MILLS AND BOARDING-
(LOWELL.)

12

INDUSTRY AND THE NORTH
1790s–1840s

HOW WAS work divided along gender lines in preindustrial society?

WHAT WAS millwork like for the typical factory worker?

WHAT ROLE did women play in the new mechanized workplace?

WHAT VALUES were promoted by the new middle class?

AMERICAN COMMUNITIES
Women Factory Workers Form a Community in Lowell, Massachusetts

IN THE 1820S AND 1830S, YOUNG FARM WOMEN FROM ALL OVER New England flocked to Lowell to work a twelve-hour day in one of the first cotton textile factories in America. Living six to eight in a room in nearby boardinghouses, the women of Lowell earned an average of $3 a week. Some also attended inexpensive night-time lectures or classes. Lowell, considered a model factory town, drew worldwide attention. As one admirer of its educated workers said, Lowell was less a factory than a "philanthropic manufacturing college."

The Boston investors who financed Lowell were businessmen, not philanthropists, but they wanted to keep Lowell free of the dirt, poverty, and social disorder that made English factory towns notorious. Built in 1823, Lowell boasted six neat factory buildings grouped around a central clock tower, the area pleasantly landscaped with flowers, shrubs, and trees. Housing was similarly well ordered: a Georgian mansion for the company agent; trim houses for the overseers; row houses for the mechanics and their families; and boardinghouses, each supervised by a responsible matron, for the work force that made Lowell famous—young New England farm women.

The choice of young women as factory workers seemed shockingly unconventional. In the 1820s and 1830s, young unmarried women simply did not live alone; they lived and worked with their parents until they married. In these years of growth and westward expansion, however, America was chronically short of labor, and the Lowell manufacturers were shrewd enough to realize that young farm women were an untapped labor force. For farmers' sons, the lure of acquiring their own farms in the West was much stronger than factory wages, but for their sisters, escaping from rural isolation and earning a little money was an appealing way to spend a few years before marriage. To attract respectable young women, Lowell offered supervision both on the job and at home, with strict rules of conduct, compulsory religious services, cultural opportunities such as concerts and lectures, and cash wages.

When they first arrived in Lowell, the young women were often bewildered by the large numbers of townspeople and embarrassed by their own rural clothing and ways of speech. The air of the mill was hot, humid, and full of cotton lint, and the noise of the machinery—"The buzzing and hissing and whizzing of pulleys and rollers and spindles and flyers"—was constant. Very quickly, however, other women workers—often their own sisters or neighbors who had preceded them to the mill—helped them adjust. It was company policy for senior women to train the newcomers. The work itself was simple, consisting largely of knotting broken threads on spinning machines and power looms. Most women enjoyed the work. They were not bothered by the long hours; farm people were accustomed to long days. One woman wrote home: "The work is not disagreeable. It tried my patience sadly at first, but in general I like it very much. It is easy to do, and does not require very violent exertion, as much of our farm work does."

The most novel aspect of textile mills was a rigid work schedule. Power-driven machinery operated at a sustained, uniform pace throughout every mill; human workers had to learn to do the same. Each mill published elaborate schedules and imposed fines and penalties on latecomers. It was this kind of precise work schedule that represented the single largest change from preindustrial work habits; it was the hardest for workers to adjust to. Moreover, each mill positioned one or two overseers on every floor to make sure the pace was maintained. Men held these positions, and they earned more than the women who made up most of the work force; this arrangement was unquestioned.

Why did young women come to Lowell? Some worked out of need and some to add to their family's income, but most regarded Lowell as an opportunity. It was escape from rural isolation and from parental supervision, a chance to buy the latest fashions and learn "city ways," to attend lectures and concerts, to save for a dowry or to pay for an education. As writer Lucy Larcom, one of the most famous workers, said, the young farm women who came to Lowell sought "an opening into freer life." Working side by side and living in company boardinghouses with six to twelve other women, some of whom might be relatives or friends from home, the Lowell women built a close, supportive community for themselves.

The owners of Lowell made large profits. They also drew praise for their carefully managed community with its intelligent and independent work force. But their success was short-lived. In the 1830s, because of competition and poor economic conditions, the owners imposed wage cuts and work speedups that their model work force did not take lightly. Although the Lowell women had been brought together under a system of paternalistic control, the close bonds they forged in the boardinghouses gave them the courage and solidarity to "turn out" in spontaneous protests, which were, however, unsuccessful in reversing the wage cuts. By 1850 the "philanthropic manufacturing college" was no more. The original Lowell work force of New England farm girls had been replaced by poor Irish immigrants of both sexes, who tended more machines for much less pay than their predecessors. Now Lowell was simply another mill town.

The history of Lowell epitomizes the process by which the North (both the New England and the Middle Atlantic states) began to change from a society composed largely of self-sufficient farm families (Jefferson's "yeoman farmers") to one of urban wage-workers in an industrial economy. Industrialization did not occur overnight. Large factories were not common until the 1880s, but by that decade most workers had already experienced a fundamental change in their working patterns. Once under way, the market revolution changed the very basis of community: how people worked, how they thought, how they lived. In the early years of the nineteenth century, Northern communities led this transformation, fostering attitudes far different from those prevalent in the South.

PREINDUSTRIAL WAYS OF WORKING

The Lowell mill was a dramatic example of the ways factories changed traditional ways of working and living. When Lowell began operation, 97 percent of all Americans still lived on farms, and most work was done in or near the home. There was a community network of barter and mutual obligation. Work was slow, unscheduled, and task oriented. A rural artisan worked when he had orders, responding to demand, not to the clock. "Home" and "work" were not separate locations or activities, but intermixed.

URBAN ARTISANS AND WORKERS

In urban areas, skilled craftsmen had controlled preindustrial production since the early colonial period. Trades were perpetuated through a formal system of apprenticeship in which a boy went to work in the shop of a master, usually at the age of twelve or fourteen. Over the next three to seven years the young apprentice learned all aspects of the craft, gaining increasing responsibility and status as the day approached when he could strike out on his own. During that time, the master not only taught the apprentice his trade but also housed, fed, and clothed him. Usually the apprentice lived with the master craftsman and was treated more like a member of the family than an employee. Thus, the family-learning model used on farms was formalized in the urban apprenticeship system. At the end of the contract period, the apprentice became a journeyman craftsman. Journeymen worked for wages in the shop of a master craftsman until they had enough capital to set up shop for themselves.

Although women as well as men did task-oriented skilled work, the formal apprenticeship system was exclusively for men. Because it was assumed that women would marry, most people thought that all girls needed to learn were domestic skills. Women who needed or wanted work, however, found a small niche of respectable occupations as domestic servants, laundresses, or seamstresses, often in the homes of the wealthy, or as cooks in small restaurants or as food vendors on the street. Some owned and managed boardinghouses. Prostitution, another common female occupation (especially in seaport cities), was not respectable.

PATRIARCHY IN FAMILY, WORK, AND SOCIETY

Like the farm family, an entire urban household was commonly organized around one kind of work. Usually the family lived at the shop or store, and all family members worked with the craftsman at his trade. A printer's wife, for example, would be capable of keeping most of the shop's functions going in the printer's absence and of supervising the work of apprentices and her children. Some artisans, like blacksmiths, needed shops separate from their homes but probably relied on their children to fetch and carry and to help with some of the work. Others, like bakers, who generally had to get up in

HOW WAS work divided along gender lines in preindustrial society?

IMAGE KEY

for pages 302–303

a. A magazine from the Lowell, Massachusetts mills.

b. The Merrimack textile mills with boarding houses, Lowell, Massachusetts.

c. Well-dressed nineteenth-century adults enjoy a formal picnic outdoors.

d. A metal lunch pail of a nineteenth–century factory worker.

e. Nineteenth-century cartoon depicting allegorical figures representing wealth and pride.

f. A one dollar banknote from the Manufacturers Bank of Lowell, Massachusetts.

g. Eight hundred women operatives march through the streets of Lynn, Massachusetts during the 1860 New England shoemaker strike; a wood engraving from *Frank Leslie's Illustrated Newspaper*.

h. A nineteenth-century family portrait.

Every small community had artisans such as blacksmiths and wheelwrights who did such essential work as shoeing horses and mending wagons for local farmers. Artist John Neagle's heroic image of the blacksmith Pat Lyon presents him as the very model of honest industry.

John Neagle, *Pat Lyon at the Forge*. Museum of Fine Arts Boston

QUICK REVIEW

Apprentices

◆ Trades were controlled through a system of apprenticeship.

◆ Apprentices learned their craft over a three-to-seven-year period.

◆ Apprentices usually lived with the master craftsman overseeing their training.

WHAT WAS mill work like for the typical factory worker?

the middle of the night to perform their work, relied on their wives to sell their products during the day.

In both rural and urban settings, working families were organized along strictly patriarchal lines. The man had unquestioned authority to direct the lives and work of family members and apprentices and to decide on occupations for his sons and marriages for his daughters. His wife had many crucial responsibilities—feeding, clothing, child rearing, taking care of apprentices, and all the other domestic affairs of the household—but in all these duties she was subject to the direction of her husband. Men were heads of families and bosses of artisanal shops; although entire families were engaged in the enterprise, the husband and father was the trained craftsman, and assistance by the family was informal and generally unrecognized.

The patriarchal organization of the family was reflected in society as a whole. Legally, men had all the power: neither women nor children had property or legal rights. For example, a married woman's property belonged to her husband, a woman could not testify on her own behalf in court, and in the rare cases of divorce the husband kept the children, for they were considered his property. When a man died, his son or sons inherited his property. The basic principle was that the man, as head of the household, represented the common interests of everyone for whom he was responsible—women, children, servants, apprentices. He thus controlled everything of value, and he alone could vote for political office.

THE SOCIAL ORDER

In this preindustrial society everyone, from the smallest yeoman farmer to the largest urban merchant, had a fixed place in the social order. The social status of artisans was below that of wealthy merchants, but decidedly above that of common laborers. Yeoman farmers, less grand than large landowners, ranked above tenant farmers and farm laborers. Although men of all social ranks mingled in their daily work, they did not mingle as equals, for great importance was placed on rank and status, which were distinguished by dress and manner. Although by the 1790s many artisans who owned property were voters and vocal participants in urban politics, few directly challenged the traditional authority of the rich and powerful to run civic affairs. The rapid spread of universal white manhood suffrage after 1800 democratized politics (see Chapter 10). At the same time, economic changes undermined the preindustrial social order. New York cabinetmaker Duncan Phyfe and sailmaker Stephen Allen amassed fortunes from their operations. Allen when he retired, was elected mayor of New York, customarily a position reserved for gentlemen. These artisans owed much of their success to the ever-expanding effects of the economic upheaval known as the market revolution.

THE MARKET REVOLUTION

The **market revolution**, the most fundamental change American communities ever experienced, was the outcome of three interrelated developments: rapid improvements in transportation (see Chapter 10), commercialization, and industrialization. Improved transportation allowed both people and goods to move with new ease and speed. Commercialization involved the replacement of household self-sufficiency and barter with the production of goods for a cash market. And industrialization involved the use of power-driven machinery to produce goods once made by hand.

THE ACCUMULATION OF CAPITAL

In the Northern states, the business community was composed largely of merchants in the seaboard cities: Boston, Providence, New York, Philadelphia, and Baltimore. Many had made substantial profits in the international shipping boom of the period 1790–1807 (as discussed in Chapter 9). Such extraordinary opportunities attracted enterprising people. John Jacob Astor, who had arrived penniless from Germany in 1784, made his first fortune in the Pacific Northwest fur trade with China and eventually dominated the fur trade in the United States through his American Fur Company. Astor made a second fortune in New York real estate, and when he retired in 1834 with $25 million he was reputed to be the wealthiest man in America. Many similar stories of success, though not as fabulous as Astor's, demonstrated that risk-takers might reap rich rewards in international trade.

When the early years of the nineteenth century posed difficulties for international trade, some of the nation's wealthiest men turned to local investments. In Providence, Rhode Island, Moses Brown and his son-in-law William Almy began to invest some of the profits the Brown family had reaped from a worldwide trade in iron, candles, rum, and African slaves in the new manufacture of cotton textiles. Cincinnati merchants banded together to finance the building of the first steamboats to operate on the Ohio River.

Wealth in Boston, 1687–1848				
Percent of the Population	*Percent of Wealth Held (%)*			
	1687	*1771*	*1833*	*1848*
Top 1 percent	10	16	33	37
Top 10 percent	42	65	75	82
Lowest 80 percent	39	29	14	4

The table tracing the distribution of wealth in Boston reflects the gains made by merchants during the international shipping boom of 1790–1807 and the way in which intermarriage between wealthy families consolidated these gains.

Much of the capital for the new investments came from banks, especially those in seaport cities that had been established for the international trade. But an astonishing amount of capital was raised through family connections. In the late eighteenth century, members of the business communities in the seaboard cities had begun to consolidate their position and property by intermarriage. In Boston, such a strong community developed that when Francis Cabot Lowell needed $300,000 in 1813 to build the world's first automated cotton mill in Waltham, Massachusetts (the prototype of the Lowell mills), he had only to turn to his family network.

Southern cotton provided the capital for continuing development. Because Northerners built the nation's ships, controlled the shipping trade, and provided the nation's banking, insurance, and financial services, the astounding growth in Southern cotton exports enriched Northern merchants almost as much as Southern planters. In 1825, for example, of the 204,000 bales of cotton shipped from New Orleans, about one-third (69,000) were transshipped through the Northern ports of New York, Philadelphia, and Boston. Although imperfectly understood at the

Market revolution The outcome of three interrelated developments: rapid improvements in transportation, commercialization, and industrialization.

Putting-out system   Production of goods in private homes under the supervision of a merchant who "put out" the raw materials, paid a certain sum per finished piece, and sold the completed item to a distant market.

time, the development of Northern industry was paid for by enslaved African American labor. The fact is that the surprising wealth that cotton brought to Southern planters fostered the market revolution.

THE PUTTING-OUT SYSTEM

Initially, the American business community invested not in machinery and factories but in the "putting-out system" of home manufacture, thereby expanding and transforming it. In this significant departure from preindustrial work, people still produced goods at home, but under the direction of a merchant, who "put out" the raw materials to them, paid them a certain sum per finished piece, and sold the completed item to a distant market. A look at the shoe industry in Lynn, Massachusetts, shows how the **putting-out system** transformed American manufacturing.

Long a major center of the shoe industry, Lynn, in 1800, produced 400,000 pairs of shoes—enough for every fifth person in the country. The town's 200 master artisans and their families, including journeymen and apprentices, worked together in hundreds of small home workshops called "ten-footers" (from their size, about ten feet square). The artisans and journeymen cut the leather, the artisans' wives and daughters did the binding of the upper parts of the shoe, the men stitched the shoe together, and children and apprentices helped where needed. In the early days, the artisan commonly bartered his shoes for needed products. Sometimes an artisan sold his shoes to a larger retailer in Boston or Salem. Although production of shoes in Lynn increased yearly from 1780 to 1810 as markets widened, shoes continued to be manufactured in traditional artisanal ways.

The investment of merchant capital in the shoe business changed everything. In Lynn, a small group of Quaker shopkeepers and merchants, connected by family, religious, and business ties, took the lead in reorganizing the trade. Financed by the bank they founded in 1814, Lynn capitalists like Micajah Pratt built large, two-story central workshops to replace the scattered ten-footers. Pratt employed a few skilled craftsmen to cut leather for shoes, but he put out the rest of the shoemaking to less-skilled workers who were no longer connected by family ties. Individual farmwomen and children sewed the uppers, which, when completed, were soled by farm men and boys. Putting-out workers were paid on a piecework basis; the men and boys earned more than the women and children, but much less than a master craftsman or a journeyman. This arrangement allowed the capitalist to employ much more labor for the same investment than with the traditional artisan workshop. Shoe production increased enormously: the largest central shop in 1832 turned out ten times more shoes than the largest shopkeeper had sold in 1789. Gradually the putting-out system and central workshops replaced artisan's shops. Some artisans became wealthy owners of workshops, but most became wage earners, and the apprenticeship system eventually disappeared.

The putting-out system moved the control of production from the individual artisan households to the merchant capitalists, who could now control labor costs, production goals, and shoe styles to fit certain markets. For example, the Lynn trade quickly monopolized the market for cheap boots for Southern slaves and Western farmers, leaving workshops in other cities to produce shoes for wealthier customers. This specialization of the national market—indeed, even thinking in terms of a national market—was new. Additionally, and most important

This carved and painted figure, designed as a whirligig and trade sign, shows a woman at a spinning wheel. Until cotton textile mills industrialized this work, spinning was one of the most time-consuming tasks that women and young girls did at home.

Woman at Spinning Wheel, ca. 1850–1870. Carved and painted wood and iron. Photographed by Ken Burris. Shelburne Museum, Shelburne, Vermont from the capitalist's point of view, the owner of the business controlled the workers and could cut back or expand the labor force as economic and marketplace conditions warranted. The unaccustomed severity of economic slumps like the Panics of 1819 and 1837 made this flexibility especially desirable.

While the central workshop system prevailed in Lynn and in urban centers like New York City, the putting-out system also fostered a more dispersed form of home production. By 1810 there were an estimated 2,500 so-called outwork weavers in New England, operating handlooms in their own homes. Other crafts that rapidly became organized according to the putting-out system were flax and wool spinning, straw braiding, glove making, and the knitting of stockings. For example, the palm-leaf hat industry that supplied farm laborers and slaves in the South and West relied completely on women and children, who braided the straw for the hats at home part-time. Absorbed into families' overall domestic routines, the outwork activity seemed small, but the size of the industry itself was surprising: in 1837, 33,000 Massachusetts women braided palm-leaf hats, whereas only 20,000 worked in the state's cotton textile mills. They were producing for a large national market, made possible by the dramatic improvements in transportation that occurred between 1820 and 1840.

THE SPREAD OF COMMERCIAL MARKETS

Although the putting-out system meant a loss of independence for artisans such as those in Lynn, Massachusetts, New England farm families liked it. From their point of view, the work could easily be combined with domestic work, and the pay was a new source of income that they could use to purchase mass-produced goods rather than spend the time required to make these things themselves. It was in this way that farm families moved away from the local barter system and into a larger market economy.

Commercialization, or the replacement of barter by a cash economy, did not happen immediately or uniformly throughout the nation. Fixed prices for goods produced by the new principles of specialization and division of labor appeared first along established trade routes. Rural areas in established sections of the country that were remote from trade routes continued in the old ways. Strikingly, however, Western farming frontiers were commercial from the very start (see Chapter 10). The existence of a cash market was an important spur to westward expansion.

BRITISH TECHNOLOGY AND AMERICAN INDUSTRIALIZATION

Important as were the transportation revolution and the commercialization made possible by the putting-out system, the third component of the market revolution, industrialization, brought the greatest changes to personal lives. Begun in Britain in the eighteenth century, industrialization was the result of a series of technological changes in the textile trade. In marked contrast to the putting-out system, in which capitalists had dispersed work into many individual households, industrialization required workers to concentrate in factories and pace themselves to the rhythms of power-driven machinery.

The simplest and quickest way for America to industrialize was to copy the British, but the British, well aware of the value of their machinery, enacted laws forbidding its export and even the emigration of skilled workers. Over the years, however, Americans managed to lure a number of British artisans to the United States.

In 1789 Samuel Slater, who had just finished an apprenticeship in the most up-to-date cotton spinning factory in England, disguised himself as a farm laborer and slipped out of England without even telling his mother good-bye. In Providence, Rhode Island, he met Moses Brown and William Almy, who had been trying without

QUICK REVIEW

The Putting-Out System

◆ Production of goods at home under the supervision of a merchant.

◆ Lynn, Massachusetts used putting-out system to become a center of the shoe industry.

◆ System gave control of production to merchant capitalists.

This early nineteenth-century watercolor shows Slater's mill, the first cotton textile mill in the United States, which depended on the waterpower of Pawtucket Falls for its energy. New England was rich in swiftly flowing streams that could provide power to spinning machines and power looms.

"Pawtucket Bridge and Falls." Rhode Island Historical Society

success to duplicate British industrial technology. Having carefully committed the designs to memory before leaving England, Slater promptly built copies of the latest British machinery for Brown and Almy. Slater's mill, as it became known, began operation in 1790. It was the most advanced cotton mill in America.

Following British practice, Slater drew his work force primarily from among young children (ages seven to twelve) and women, whom he paid much less than the handful of skilled male workers he hired to keep the machines working. The yarn spun at Slater's mill was then put out to local home weavers, who turned it into cloth on handlooms. As a result, home weaving flourished in areas near the mill, giving families a new opportunity to make money at a task with which they were already familiar.

Soon many other merchants and mechanics followed Slater's lead, and the rivers of New England were soon dotted with mills wherever waterpower could be tapped.

THE LOWELL MILLS

Another way to deal with British competition was to beat the British at their own game. With the intention of designing better machinery, a young Bostonian, Francis Cabot Lowell, made an apparently casual tour of British textile mills in 1810. Lowell, the founder of the Lowell mills described in the opening of this chapter, made a good impression on his English hosts, who were pleased by his interest and his intelligent questions. They did not know that each night, in his hotel room, Lowell made sketches from memory of the machines he had inspected during the day.

Lowell was more than an industrial spy, however. When he returned to the United States, he went to work with a Boston mechanic, Paul Moody, to improve on the British models. Lowell and Moody not only made the machinery for spinning cotton more efficient, but they also invented a power loom. This was a great advance, for now all aspects of textile manufacture, from the initial cleaning and carding (combing) to the production of finished lengths of cloth, could be gathered together in the same factory. Such a mill required a much larger capital investment than a small spinning mill such as Slater's, but Lowell's family network gave him access to the needed funds. In 1814 he opened the world's first integrated cotton mill in Waltham, near Boston. It was a great success: in 1815, the

This 1850 engraving by the American Banknote company shows women tending looms at Lowell. The contrast between this industrial activity and the picture of a woman spinning at home (p. 308) illustrates one of the most important effects of industrialization: Now machines, not individuals, determined the pace of production.

Print Collection, Miriam and Ira D. Wallach Division of Art, Prints and Photographs, The New York Public Library, Astor, Lenox and Tilden Foundations

Boston Associates (Lowell's partners) made profits of 25 percent, and their efficiency allowed them to survive the intense British competition following the War of 1812 (see Chapter 9). Many smaller New England mills did not survive. The lesson was clear: size mattered.

The Boston Associates took the lesson to heart, and when they moved their enterprise to a new location in 1823, they thought big. They built an entire town at the junction of the Concord and Merrimack rivers where the village of East Chelmsford stood, renaming it Lowell in memory of Francis, who had died, still a young man, in 1817. As the opening of this chapter describes, the new industrial community boasted six mills and company housing for all the workers. In 1826 the town had 2,500 inhabitants; ten years later the population was 17,000.

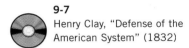

9-7
Henry Clay, "Defense of the American System" (1832)

FAMILY MILLS

Lowell was unique. No other textile mill was ever such a showplace. None was as large, integrated so many tasks, or relied on such a homogeneous work force. Its location in a new town was also unusual. Much more common in the early days of industrialization were small rural spinning mills, on the model of Slater's first mill, built on swiftly running streams near existing farm communities. Because the owners of smaller mills often hired entire families, their operations came to be called family mills. The employment pattern at these mills followed that established by Slater at his first mill in 1790. Children aged eight to twelve, whose customary job was "doffing" (changing) bobbins on the spinning machines, made up 50 percent of the work force. Women and men each made up about 25 percent of the work force, but men had the most skilled and best paid jobs.

Relations between these small rural mill communities and the surrounding farming communities were often difficult, as the history of the towns of Dudley and Oxford, Massachusetts, shows. Samuel Slater, now a millionaire, built three small mill communities near these towns in the early years of the nineteenth century. Each consisted of a small factory, a store, and cottages and a boardinghouse for workers. Slater's mills provided a substantial amount of work for local people, putting out to them both the initial cleaning of the raw cotton and the much more lucrative weaving of the spun yarn. But in spite of this economic link, relations between Slater and his workers on one side and the farmers and shopkeepers of the Dudley and Oxford communities on the other were stormy. They disagreed over the building of mill dams (essential for the mill power supply, these dams sometimes flooded

Building Types
- Factories
- Boarding Houses
- Other company housing
- Hotels
- Churches
- Municipal buildings
- Other buildings (mostly residences)

MAP 12-1 Lowell, Massachusetts, 1832 This town plan of Lowell, Massachusetts, in 1832 illustrates the comprehensive relationship the owners envisaged between the factories and the workforce. The mills are located on the Merrimack River, while nearby are the boardinghouses for the single young female workers, row houses for the male mechanics and their families, and houses for the overseers. Somewhat farther away is the mansion of the company agent.

HOW DID the plan of the town of Lowell affect the people who lived there?

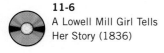

11-6
A Lowell Mill Girl Tells
Her Story (1836)

local fields), over taxes, over the upkeep of local roads, and over schools. The debates were so constant, and so heated, that in 1831 Slater petitioned the Massachusetts General Court to create a separate town, Webster, that would encompass his three mill communities. For their part, the residents of Dudley and Oxford became increasingly hostile to Slater's authoritarian control, which they regarded as undemocratic. Their dislike carried over to the workers as well. Disdaining the mill workers for their poverty and transiency, people in the rural communities began referring to them as "operatives," making them somehow different in their work roles from themselves. Industrial work thus led to new social distinctions.

"THE AMERICAN SYSTEM OF MANUFACTURES"

Not all American industrial technology was copied from British inventions, for there were many home-grown inventors. The concept of interchangeable parts, realized first in gun manufacturing, was so unusual that the British soon dubbed it the **American system**. Standardized production quickly revolutionized the manufacture of items as simple as nails and as complicated as clocks. American businesses mass-produced high-quality goods for ordinary people earlier in America than in Britain or any European country. The availability of these goods was a practical demonstration of American beliefs in democracy and equality.

In 1798 Eli Whitney contracted with the government to make 10,000 rifles in twenty-eight months, an incredibly short period had he been planning to produce each rifle by hand in the traditional way. Whitney's ideas far outran his performance. It took him ten years to fulfill his contract, and even then he had not managed to perfect the production of all the rifle parts. Two other New Englanders, Simeon North and John Hall, created milling machines that could grind parts to the required specifications and brought the concept to fruition, North in 1816 and Hall in 1824. When the system of interchangeable machine-made parts was adopted by the other national armory, at Springfield, Massachusetts, the Springfield rifle got its name.

OTHER FACTORIES

Although cotton textile mills were the first and best known of the early factories, some factories produced other items, among them metal and iron. Like the textile mills, many of these factories were rural because they depended on natural water sources for power or because they needed to be near their raw materials, such as iron ore. And like the early textile mills, these first heavy industries initially coexisted with the traditional artisanal system.

The rapid development of the steamship industry in Cincinnati illustrates both the role of merchant capital and the coexistence of old and new production methods. Cincinnati's first steamboat, financed by local merchant capital, was commissioned in 1816. It proved so successful that by 1819 one-quarter of all western steamboats were being built in Cincinnati. At the same time, much of the detail work on the steamboat was performed by traditional artisans such as cabinetmakers, upholsterers, tinsmiths, and blacksmiths, who did record-breaking amounts of work in their small, independent shops. In this way, new factory methods and industrial techniques were often coupled with old craft techniques.

 # MAP EXPLORATION

To explore an interactive version of this map, go to
http://www.prenhall.com/faraghertlc/map12.2

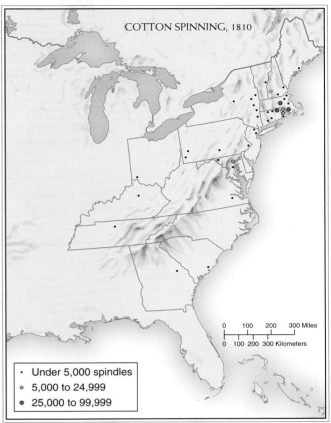

- · Under 5,000 spindles
- ◦ 5,000 to 24,999
- ● 25,000 to 99,999

MAP 12-2 The Growth of Cotton Textile Manufacturing, 1810–1840
Although cotton textile manufacturing spread to other parts of the country after 1810, New England never lost its early lead. By 1839, the extent of industrialization in New England far outstripped that of other regions. Although much of New England was still rural, more and more residents were drawn into the market economy. Nationally, the proportion of wage laborers rose from 12 percent in 1800 to 40 percent in 1860. The majority of them were New Englanders who had made the transition from artisan to worker.

HOW DID the growth of cotton textile manufacturing between 1810 and 1840 transform the way people lived and worked?

FROM ARTISAN TO WORKER

The changes wrought by the market revolution had major and lasting effects on ordinary Americans. The proportion of wage laborers in the nation's labor force rose from 12 percent in 1800 to 40 percent by 1860. Most of these workers were employed in the North, and almost half were women, performing outwork in their homes. The young farm woman who worked at Lowell for a year or two and then returned home; the master craftsman in Lynn who expanded his shop with the aid of merchant capital; the home weaver who prospered on outwork from Slater's mill—all were participating, often unknowingly, in fundamental personal and social changes.

WHAT ROLE did women play in the new mechanized workplace?

American system A technique of production pioneered in the United States that relied on precision manufacturing with the use of interchangeable parts.

9-9
The Harbinger, Female Workers of Lowell (1836)

PERSONAL RELATIONSHIPS

The immense increase in productivity made possible by the principles of division of labor and specialization effectively destroyed artisan production and the apprenticeship system. For example, in New York by the mid-1820s, tailors and shoemakers were teaching apprentices only a few simple operations, in effect using them as helpers. Printers undercut the system by hiring partly trained apprentices as journeymen. In almost every trade, apprentices no longer lived with the master's family, and their parents received cash payment for the child's work. Thus, in effect, the apprenticeship system was replaced by child labor.

The breakdown of the patriarchal relationship between the master craftsman and his workers became an issue in the growing political battle between the North and the South over slavery. Southern defenders of slavery compared their cradle-to-grave responsibility to their slaves with Northern employers' "heartless" treatment of their "wage slaves." Certainly the new Northern employer assumed less responsibility for individual workers than had the traditional artisan. Although the earliest textile manufacturers, like those at Lowell, provided housing for their workers, workers soon became responsible for their own food and housing. Moreover, Northern employers felt no obligation to help or care for old or disabled workers. Southerners were right: this was a heartless system. But Northerners were also right: industrialization was certainly freer than the slave system, freer even than the hierarchical craft system, although it sometimes offered only the freedom to starve.

MECHANIZATION AND WOMEN'S WORK

Industrialization posed a major threat to the status and independence of skilled male workers. In trade after trade, mechanization meant that most tasks could be performed by unskilled labor. In fact, work in the textile mills was so simple that children came to form a large part of the workforce.

Mechanization changed the nature of women's work as well. The industrialization of textiles—first in spinning, then in weaving—relieved women of a time-consuming home occupation. To supplement family income, women now had the choice of following textile work into the factory or finding other kinds of home work.

The 1820s saw the birth of the garment industry. In New York City, employers began hiring women to sew ready-made clothing, at first rough, unfitted clothing for sailors and Southern slaves, but later overalls and shirts for Westerners and finer items, such as men's shirts. Most women performed this work at low piecework rates in their homes. Although by 1860 Brooks Brothers, the famous men's clothing firm, had 70 "inside" workers in a model central workshop, the firm relied primarily on putting out sewing to 3,000 women who worked at home. The gendered division of labor disadvantaged women outworkers. The low pay and seasonal nature of the industry became notorious. Manufacturers in the garment trade made their profits not from efficient production but by obtaining intensive labor for very low wages. The lower the piece rate, the more each woman, sewing at home, had to produce to earn enough to live. The invention of the sewing machine only made matters worse. Manufacturers dropped their piecework rates still lower, and some women found themselves working fifteen to eighteen hours a day, producing more than they ever had but earning the same pay.

Figure 12-1 Occupations of Women Wage Earners in Massachusetts, 1837 This chart shows how important outwork was for women workers. Textile work in factories occupied less than 20 percent of women, while outwork in palm-leaf hats, straw bonnets, and boots and shoes accounted for over half of the total workforce. Teaching was a new occupation for women in 1837. The small percentage of 3.6 would grow in the future.

Based on Thomas Dublin, *Transforming Women's Work* (Ithaca, NY: Cornell University Press, 1991), table 1.1, p. 20.

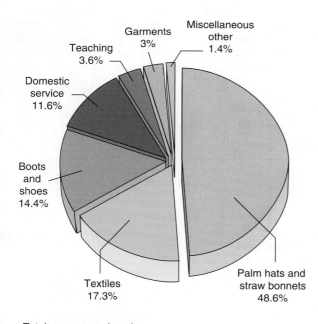

Garments 3%
Miscellaneous other 1.4%
Teaching 3.6%
Domestic service 11.6%
Boots and shoes 14.4%
Textiles 17.3%
Palm hats and straw bonnets 48.6%

Total women employed
105,977

THE CASH ECONOMY

Another effect of the market revolution was the transformation of a largely barter system into a cash economy. For example, a farm woman might pay in butter and eggs for a pair of shoes handmade for her by the local shoemaker. A few years later that same woman, now part of the vast New England outwork industry, might buy ready-made footwear with the cash she had earned from braiding straw for hats. Community economic ties were replaced by distant, sometimes national ones.

The pay envelope became the only direct contact between factory worker and (often absentee) owner. For workers, this change was both unsettling and liberating. On the minus side, workers were no longer part of a settled, orderly, and familiar community. On the plus side, they were now free to labor wherever they could, at whatever wages their skills or their bargaining power could command. That workers took their freedom seriously is evidenced by the very high rate of turnover—50 percent a year—in the New England textile mills.

But if moving on was a sign of increased freedom of opportunity for some workers, for others it was an unwanted consequence of the market revolution. In New England, for example, many quite prosperous artisans and farmers faced disruptive competition from factory goods and Western commercial agriculture. They could remain where they were only if they were willing to become factory workers or commercial farmers. Often the more conservative choice was to move west and try to reestablish one's traditional lifestyle on the frontier.

FREE LABOR

At the heart of the industrializing economy was the notion of free labor. Originally, "free" referred to individual economic choice—that is, to the right of workers to move to another job rather than be held to a position by customary obligation or the formal contract of apprenticeship or journeyman labor. But "free labor" soon came to encompass as well the range of attitudes—hard work, self-discipline, and a striving for economic independence—that were necessary for success in a competitive, industrializing economy. These were profoundly individualistic attitudes, and owners cited them in opposing labor unions and the use of strikes to achieve wage goals.

For their part, many workers were inclined to define freedom more collectively, arguing that their just grievances as free American citizens were not being heard. As a group of New Hampshire female workers rhetorically asked, "Why [is] there . . . so much want, dependence and misery among us, if forsooth, we are freemen and freewomen?"

EARLY STRIKES

Rural women workers led some of the first strikes in American labor history. In 1824, in one of the first of these actions, women workers at a Pawtucket, Rhode Island, textile mill led their co-workers, female and male, out on strike to protest wage cuts and longer hours.

More famous were the strikes that the women at the model mill at Lowell led. The first serious trouble came in 1834, when 800 women participated in a spontaneous turnout to protest a wage cut of 25 percent. The owners were shocked and outraged by the strike, considering it both unfeminine and ungrateful. The workers, however, were bound together by a sense of sisterhood and were protesting not just the attack on their economic independence, but also the blow to their position as "daughters of freemen

QUICK REVIEW

Women in the Workforce

◆ Industrialization threatened skilled male workers.

◆ Mechanization created opportunities for women to work outside the home.

◆ The growing garment industry of the 1820s depended on cheap female labor.

This timetable from the Lowell Mills illustrates the elaborate time schedules that the cotton textile mills expected their employees to meet. For workers, it was difficult to adjust to the regimentation imposed by clock time, in contrast to the approximate times common to preindustrial work.

Baker Library, Graduate School of Business Administration, Harvard University

TIME TABLE OF THE LOWELL MILLS,

To take effect on and after Oct. 21st, 1851.

The Standard time being that of the meridian of Lowell, as shown by the regulator clock of JOSEPH RAYNES, 43 Central Street

	From 1st to 10th inclusive.				From 11th to 20th inclusive.				From 21st to last day of month.			
	1st Bell	2d Bell	3d Bell	Eve.Bell	1st Bell	2d Bell	3d Bell	Eve.Bell	1st Bell	2d Bell	3d Bell	Eve.Bell
January,	5.00	6.00	6.50	*7.30	5.00	6 00	6.50	*7.30	5.00	6.00	6.50	*7.30
February,	4.30	5.30	6.40	*7.30	4.30	5.30	6.25	*7.30	4.30	5.30	6.15	*7.30
March,	5.40	6.00		*7.30	5.20	5.40		*7.30	5.05	5.25		6.35
April,	4.45	5.05		6.45	4.30	4.50		6.55	4.30	4.50		7.00
May,	4 30	4.50		7.00	4.30	4.50		7.00	4.30	4.50		7 00
June,	"	"		"	"	"		"	"	"		"
July,	"	"		"	"	"		"	"	"		"
August,	"	"		"	"	"		"	"	"		"
September,	4.40	5.00		6.45	4.50	5.10		6.30	5.00	5.20		*7.30
October,	5.10	5.30		*7.30	5.20	5.40		*7.30	5.35	5.55		*7.30
November,	4.30	5.30	6.10	*7.30	4.30	5.30	6.20	*7.30	5.00	6.00	6.35	*7.30
December,	5.00	6.00	6.45	*7.30	5.00	6.00	6.50	*7.30	5.00	6.00	6.50	*7.30

* Excepting on Saturdays from Sept. 21st to March 20th inclusive, when it is rung at 20 minutes after sunset.

YARD GATES,

Will be opened at ringing of last morning bell, of meal bells, and of evening bells; and kept open Ten minutes.

MILL GATES.

Commence hoisting Mill Gates, Two minutes before commencing work.

WORK COMMENCES,

At Ten minutes after last morning bell, and at Ten minutes after bell which "rings in" from Meals.

BREAKFAST BELLS.

During March "Ring out" . . . . at . . . . 7.30 a. m. . . . . "Ring in" at 8:05 a. m.
April 1st to Sept. 20th inclusive . . . . . at . . . . 7 00 " " . . . . " " at 7.35 " "
Sept. 21st to Oct. 31st inclusive . . . . . at . . . . 7.30 " " . . . . " " at 8.05 " "
Remainder of year work commences after Breakfast.

DINNER BELLS.

"Ring out" . . . . 12.30 p. m . . . . "Ring in" . . . . 1.05 p. m.

In all cases, the *first* stroke of the bell is considered as marking the time.

still." Nevertheless, the wage cuts were enforced, as were more cuts in 1836, again in the face of a turnout. Many women simply packed their clothes in disgust and returned home to the family farm.

A New Social Order

WHAT VALUES were promoted by the new middle class?

The market revolution reached into every aspect of life, down to the most personal family decisions. It also fundamentally changed the social order, creating a new middle class with distinctive habits and beliefs.

Wealth and Class

There had always been social classes in America. Since the early colonial period planters in the South and merchants in the North had comprised a wealthy elite. Somewhere below the elite, but above the mass of people, were the "middling sort": a small professional group that included lawyers, ministers, schoolteachers, doctors, public officials, some prosperous farmers, prosperous urban shopkeepers and innkeepers, and a few wealthy artisans such as Boston silversmith Paul Revere. "Mechanics and farmers"—artisans and yeoman farmers—made up another large group, and the laboring poor, consisting of ordinary laborers, servants, and marginal farmers were below them. At the very bottom were the paupers—those dependent on public charity—and the enslaved. This was the "natural" social order that fixed most people in the social rank to which they were born.

The market revolution ended this stable and hierarchical social order, creating the dynamic and unstable one we recognize today: upper, middle, and working classes, whose members all share the hope of climbing as far up the social ladder as they can. This social mobility was new.

The major transformation came in the lives of the "middling sort." The market revolution downgraded many independent artisans but elevated others, like Duncan Phyfe and Stephen Allen of New York. Other formerly independent artisans or farmers (or more frequently, their children) joined the rapidly growing ranks of managers and white-collar workers such as accountants, bank tellers, clerks, bookkeepers, and insurance agents. Occupational opportunities shifted dramatically in just one generation. In Utica, New York, for example, 16 percent of the city's young men held white-collar jobs in 1855, compared with only 6 percent of their fathers. At the same time, 15 percent fewer younger men filled artisanal occupations than older men.

These new white-collar workers owed not only their jobs, but also their lifestyles to the new structure and organization of industry. The new economic order demanded certain habits and attitudes of workers: sobriety, responsibility, steadiness, and hard work. Thus, a new middle class with distinctively new attitudes was formed.

Religion and Personal Life

Religion, which had undergone dramatic changes since the 1790s, played a key role in the emergence of the new attitudes. The Second Great Awakening had supplanted the orderly and intellectual Puritan religion of early New England. The new evangelistic religious spirit, which stressed the achievement of salvation through personal faith, was more democratic and more enthusiastic than the earlier faith. The concept of original sin, the cornerstone of Puritan belief, was replaced by the optimistic belief that a willingness to be saved was enough to ensure salvation. Conversion and repentance were now community experiences, often taking place in huge revival meetings in which an entire congregation focused on the sinners about to be saved. The converted bore a heavy personal responsibility to demonstrate their faith in their own daily lives through morally respectable behavior. In this way the new religious feeling fostered individualism and self-discipline.

QUICK REVIEW

Class Consciousness

◆ Social class always existed in America.

◆ Market revolution downgraded some independent artisans and elevated others.

◆ New work patterns helped form distinctive attitudes of new middle class.

In 1825, in Utica, New York, and other towns along the recently opened Erie Canal, evangelist Charles G. Finney began a series of dramatic revival meetings. His spellbinding message reached both rich and poor, converting members of all classes to the new evangelistic religion. In 1830, made famous by these gatherings, Finney was invited by businessmen to preach in Rochester. Prayer meetings were held in schools and businesses, impromptu religious services in people's homes. Middle-class women in particular carried Finney's message by prayer and pleading to the men of their families, who found that evangelism's stress on self-discipline and individual achievement helped them adjust to new business conditions.

THE NEW MIDDLE-CLASS FAMILY

The market revolution and the new evangelism also affected women's family roles. Women took the lead in making certain their families joined them in converting to the new, more emotional approach to religion. And when production moved into the hands of paid factory workers, the husband's direct connection with the household was broken: he became a manager of workers and was no longer the undisputed head of a family unit that combined work and personal life.

Wives, on the other hand, remained at home, where they were still responsible for cooking, cleaning, and other domestic tasks but no longer contributed directly to what had been the family enterprise. Instead, women took on a new responsibility, that of providing a quiet, well-ordered, relaxing refuge from the pressures of the industrial world. Catharine Beecher's *Treatise on Domestic Economy,* first published in 1841, became the standard housekeeping guide for a generation of middle-class American women. In it, Beecher combined innovative ideas for household design (especially in the kitchen, where she introduced principles of organization) with medical information, child-rearing advice, recipes, and numerous discussions of the mother's moral role in the family. The book clearly filled a need: for many pioneer women, it was the only book besides the Bible that they carried west with them.

As the work roles of middle-class men and women diverged, so did social attitudes about appropriate male and female characteristics and behavior. Men were

In a time before ready-made clothing was available, middle-class women used *Godey's Ladies Book* as a pattern book, taking elaborate fashion illustrations such as this one from 1856 to local seamstresses, or remaking older dresses to fit the current trends.

CORBIS © Bettmann/CORBIS.

expected to be steady, industrious, responsible, and painstakingly attentive to their business. They had little choice: in the competitive, uncertain, and rapidly changing business conditions of the early nineteenth century, these qualities were essential for men who hoped to hold their existing positions or to get ahead. In contrast, women were expected to be nurturing, gentle, kind, moral, and selflessly devoted to their families. They were expected to operate within the "woman's sphere"— the home.

The maintenance or achievement of a middle-class lifestyle required the joint efforts of husband and wife. More cooperation between them was called for than in the preindustrial, patriarchal family. The nature of the new, companionate marriage that evolved in response to the market revolution was reflected most clearly in decisions concerning children.

FAMILY LIMITATION

Middle-class couples chose to have fewer children than their predecessors. Children who were being raised to succeed in the middle class placed considerable demands on family resources: They required more care, training, and education than children who could be put to work at traditional tasks at an early age. The dramatic fall in the birthrate during the nineteenth century (from an average of seven children per woman in 1800 to five in 1860) is evidence of conscious decisions about family limitation, first by members of the new middle class and later by working-class families. Few couples used mechanical methods of contraception such as the condom, partly because these were difficult to obtain and partly because most people associated their use with prostitution and the prevention of venereal disease rather than with family planning. Instead, people used birth control methods that relied on mutual consent: coitus interruptus (withdrawal before climax), the rhythm method (intercourse only during the woman's infertile period), and, most often, abstinence or infrequent intercourse.

When mutual efforts at birth control failed, married women often sought a surgical abortion, a new technique that was much more reliable than the folk remedies women had always shared among themselves. Surgical abortions were widely advertised after 1830, and widely used, especially by middle-class married women seeking to limit family size. Some historians estimate that one out of every four pregnancies was aborted in the years 1840–1860 (about the same rate as in 1990). The rising rate of abortion by married women (in other words, its use as birth control) prompted the first legal bans; by 1860, twenty states had outlawed the practice.

Accompanying the interest in family limitation was a redefinition of sexuality. Doctors generally recommended that sexual urges be controlled, but they believed that men would have much more difficulty exercising such control than women, partly because, they also believed, women were uninterested in sex. (Women who were visibly interested ran the risk of being considered immoral or "fallen," and thereupon shunned by the middle class.)

Many women of the late eighteenth century wanted to be free of the medical risks and physical debility that too-frequent childbearing brought, but they had little chance of achieving that goal until men became equally interested in family limitation. The rapid change in attitudes toward family size that occurred in the early nineteenth century has been repeated around the world as other societies undergo the dramatic experience of industrialization. It is a striking example of the ways economic changes affect our most private and personal decisions.

CHRONOLOGY

1790	Samuel Slater's first mill opens in Rhode Island.		**1816**	First protective tariff.
1793	Cotton gin invented.		**1820s**	Large-scale outwork networks develop in New England.
1798	Eli Whitney contracts with the federal government for 10,000 rifles, which he undertakes to produce with interchangeable parts.		**1823**	Lowell mills open.
			1824	John Hall successfully achieves interchangeable parts at Harpers Ferry armory.
1807	Embargo Act excludes British manufactures.			Women lead strike at Pawtucket textile mill.
1810	Francis Cabot Lowell tours British textile factories. First steamboat on the Ohio River.		**1825**	Erie Canal opens.
1812	Micajah Pratt begins his own shoe business in Lynn, Massachusetts.		**1830**	Charles G. Finney's Rochester revivals.
			1834	First strike at Lowell mills.
1813	Francis Cabot Lowell raises $300,000 to build his first cotton textile factory at Waltham, Massachusetts.		**1841**	Catharine Beecher's *Treatise on Domestic Economy* published.
1815	War of 1812 ends; British competition in manufactures resumes.		**1845**	New England Female Labor Reform Association formed.

MIDDLE-CLASS CHILDREN

Child rearing had been shared in the preindustrial household, boys learning farming or craft skills from their fathers while girls learned domestic skills from their mothers. The children of the new middle class, however, needed a new kind of upbringing, one that involved a long period of nurturing in the beliefs and personal habits necessary for success. Mothers assumed primary responsibility for this training, in part because fathers were too busy, and also because people believed that women's superior qualities of gentleness, morality, and loving watchfulness were essential to the task.

Fathers retained a strong role in major decisions concerning children, but mothers commonly turned to other women for advice on daily matters. Through their churches, women formed maternal associations for help in raising their children to be religious and responsible.

Middle-class families sacrificed to keep their sons in school or in training for their chosen professions, and they often housed and fed their sons until the young men had "established" themselves financially and could marry. Mothers took the lead in an important informal activity: making sure their children had friends and contacts that would be useful when they were old enough to consider careers and marriage. Matters such as these, rarely considered by earlier generations living in small communities, now became important in the new middle-class communities of America's towns and cities.

11-3
"Early Habits of Industry,"
The Mother's Magazine (1834)

Contrary to the growing myth of the self-made man, middle-class success was not a matter of individual achievement. Instead it was usually based on a family strategy in which fathers provided the money and mothers the nurturance. The reorganization of the family described in this section was successful: from its shelter and support emerged generations of ambitious, responsible, and individualistic middle-class men. But although boys were trained for success, this was not an acceptable goal for their sisters. Women were trained to be the nurturing, silent "support system" that undergirded male success. And women were also expected to ease the tensions of the transition to new middle-class behavior by acting as models and monitors of traditional values.

CONCLUSION

The market revolution involved three transformations: improvements in transportation, commercialization, and industrialization. Each began at different times. The transportation revolution (discussed in Chapter 10), usually dated from 1825 (the year of the opening of the Erie Canal), accelerated with the building of railroads in the 1830s and 1840s. Commercialization began earlier, around 1805, as a consequence of the reorganization of manufacturing through the putting-out system by Northern entrepreneurs. After 1805, the cash purchase of items manufactured elsewhere slowly eroded local barter arrangements. American industrialization began with Samuel Slater's small cotton spinning mill in Rhode Island in 1790, but the most famous early example was the mill town of Lowell, Massachusetts, whose factories opened in 1823. These three transformations, taken together, constituted the market revolution that, by changing the ways people worked, changed how they thought.

SUMMARY

Preindustrial Ways of Working Preindustrial society followed patterns of work and living that showed signs of change by the 1790s. In rural areas, the transformation from traditional to commercial agriculture had begun. Among urban artisans and workers, changes in traditional modes of work and living were also evident.

The Market Revolution The market revolution was the most fundamental change American communities ever experienced. A variety of innovations and inventions helped place the production and distribution of goods on an industrial, commercial footing. In the process, methods of manufacturing changed drastically.

From Artisan to Worker Industrialization transformed the nature and status of work, destroying or weakening traditional methods and systems of production. At the same time, the market revolution dramatically altered the way people bought, traded, and sold goods. The ongoing changes led to collective action by workers.

A New Social Order The market revolution transformed the social order creating the social classes we have today. During the late eighteenth and early nineteenth centuries, evangelical religion spread rapidly. Family roles were also substantially altered, as were child-rearing methods.

REVIEW QUESTIONS

1. What changes in preindustrial life and work were caused by the market revolution?

2. This chapter argues that when people begin doing new kinds of work, their beliefs and attitudes change. Give three examples of such changes described in the chapter. Can you think of other examples?

3. Discuss the opinion offered by historian David Potter that mass production has been an important democratizing force in American politics. Do you agree? Why or why not?

4. Consider the portrait of the nineteenth-century middle-class family offered in this chapter and imagine yourself as a member of such a family. What new aspects of family relations would you welcome? Which would be difficult? Why?

KEY TERMS

American system (p. 313)   **Putting-out system** (p. 308)
Market revolution (p. 306)

RECOMMENDED READING

Christopher Clark, *The Roots of Rural Capitalism: Western Massachusetts, 1780–1860* (1990). The most thorough examination to date of how the commercial spirit changed rural life.

Alan Dawley, *Class and Community: The Industrial Revolution in Lynn* (1976). A pathbreaking study of the shift from artisanal to wage labor.

Thomas Dublin, *Women at Work: The Transformation of Work and Community in Lowell, Massachusetts, 1826–1860* (1979). A careful look at the female workers of Lowell and their changing conditions.

Thomas Dublin, *Transforming Women's Work: New England Lives in the Industrial Revolution* (1994). A thoughtful study of the effects of women's outwork.

Karen Halttunen, *Confidence Men and Painted Women: A Study of Middle-Class Culture in America* (1982). Shows the importance of sentimentalism to the new middle class.

David Houndshell, *From the American System to Mass Production, 1800–1932* (1984). How an entire network of New England "mechanics" contributed to the invention of interchangeable parts.

Shawn Johansen, *Family Men: Middle-Class Fatherhood in Early Industrializing America* (2001). New research on the domestic involvement of fathers.

Paul Johnson, *A Shopkeeper's Millennium: Society and Revivals in Rochester, New York, 1815–1837* (1978). A study of the changing relationship between masters and workers in Rochester.

Bruce Laurie, *Artisans into Workers: Labor in Nineteenth-Century America* (1989). Using many specific examples, this book traces the changes in labor described in this chapter.

Jonathan Prude, *The Coming of Industrial Order: Town and Factory Life in Rural Massachusetts, 1810–1860* (1983). A major source of information on family mills.

Steven J. Ross, *Workers on the Edge: Work, Leisure and Politics in Industrializing Cincinnati, 1788–1890* (1985). Studies the growth of wage labor in a major western city.

Mary Ryan, *The Making of the Middle Class* (1981). A study of Utica, New York, demonstrating the role of women in the family strategies of the new middle class.

Charles Sellers, *The Market Revolution: Jacksonian America, 1815–1846* (1991). A synthesis of the political, religious, and economic change of the period.

Christine Stansell, *City of Women: Sex and Class in New York, 1789–1860* (1983). Explores women's work and the social dynamics of rapidly growing New York City.

Our duties originate, not from difference of sex, but from the diversity of the relations of life, the various gifts and talents committed to our care, and the different eras in which we live.

—Angelina Emily Grimké, October 2, 1837

An abolitionist freeing a slave from his shackles: A colored woodcut, c. 1840, from an American antislavery almanac.

PICTORIAL PRIMER.

9 and 9 make 18

10 and 10 make 20

STEAMBOAT.

Here is a Steamboat full of passengers, how swift it glides along, and makes the water foam. Steamboats were invented by Robert Fulton, and the first one was built in New-York.

PICTORIAL PRIMER.

Boy Flying a Kite.

Here is a boy just coming from school, he has learned his lesson well, and his teacher has rewarded him with a kite. He will raise it very high in the air, it will not fall down while the wind blow... are made...

13

COMING TO TERMS WITH THE NEW AGE
1820S–1850S

WHO MIGRATED to America
in the first half of the nineteenth century?

WHO WERE the major
proponents of the labor movement?

WHAT ROLE did women play
in the development of American education?

WHO WERE the abolitionists
and what were their racial attitudes?

WHAT CONNECTIONS were there between
the women's rights movement and previous movements
for social reform?

Seneca Falls: Women Reformers Respond to the Market Revolution

IN THE SUMMER OF 1848, A SMALL ADVERTISEMENT APPEARED IN an upstate New York newspaper announcing a "convention to discuss the social, civil, and religious condition and rights of woman," to be held at Seneca Falls on July 19 and 20.

Charlotte Woodward, a nineteen-year-old glove maker who did outwork in her rural home, saw the advertisement and persuaded six friends to join her in the forty-mile journey to the convention. "At first we travelled quite alone," she recalled. "But before we had gone many miles we came on other wagon-loads of women, bound in the same direction. As we reached different crossroads we saw wagons coming from every part of the country, and long before we reached Seneca Falls we were a procession."

To the surprise of the convention organizers, almost 300 men and women attended the two-day meeting. The focus of their discussions was the **Declaration of Sentiments**, a petition for women's rights modeled on the Declaration of Independence. "We hold these truths to be self-evident," it announced: "That all men and women are created equal." Men had deprived women of legal rights, of the right to own their own property, of custody of their children in cases of divorce, of the right to higher education (at that time only Oberlin College and Mount Holyoke Female Seminary admitted women), of full participation in religious worship and activity, and of the right to vote. After discussion, the attendees approved all the resolutions, and all but the last of them, which a minority found too radical, unanimously. Buoyed by the success of this first women's rights convention, they promptly planned another one three weeks later in New York's largest upstate city, Rochester, to reach new supporters and to develop strategies to implement their resolutions.

The fight for women's rights was only one of many reform movements that emerged in the United States in the wake of the economic and social disruptions of the market revolution. The Seneca Falls region was itself deeply affected by that revolution. A farming frontier in 1800, it had been drawn into national commerce in 1828 when it was reached by an offshoot of the Erie Canal. It was drawn even further into the modern age when the railroad arrived in 1841. A village of 200 in 1824, Seneca Falls had grown to a town of over 4,000 by 1842. It was now a center for flour milling (in 1845, the nine mills in the town produced a total of 2,000 barrels of flour a day) and manufacturing, and a hub of the outwork network of which Charlotte Woodward was a part. Swamped by newcomers (among them a growing number of poor Irish Catholics), the inhabitants of Seneca Falls struggled to maintain a sense of community. They formed volunteer organizations of all kinds—religious, civic,

social, educational, recreational. And they became active participants in reform movements seeking to counteract the effects of industrialization, rapid growth, and the influx of newcomers.

Many reformers belonged to liberal religious groups with wide social perspectives. Perhaps a third of those attending the women's rights convention, for example, were members of the Wesleyan Methodist Society of Seneca Falls, which had broken with the national Methodist organization because it would not take a strong stand against slavery. Another quarter were Progressive Quakers of the nearby town of Waterloo, who had broken with their national organization for the same reason. Many attendees at the Women's Rights convention were also active in the temperance movement, a more limited but extremely popular reform cause dedicated to promoting abstinence from alcohol.

The idea for the Women's Rights convention emerged during a meeting in early July 1848, between Lucretia Mott—a Philadelphia Quaker and the nation's best-known woman reformer—and Elizabeth Cady Stanton of Seneca Falls, wife of a well-known antislavery orator and niece of a leading reform philanthropist. It was in the context of friendship and shared concern for reform that the two began planning the convention that was held two weeks later.

The women's rights movement that took shape from this convention proved exceptionally long-lasting. Stanton, soon to form a working partnership with former temperance worker Susan B. Anthony, devoted the rest of her life to women's rights.

But what of Charlotte Woodward, a local farm girl, unaware of the national reform community? Why was she there? In this age of hopefulness and change she wanted a better life for herself. She was motivated, she said, by "all the hours that I sat and sewed gloves for a miserable pittance, which, after it was earned, could never be mine." By law and custom her father, as head of the household, was entitled to her wages. "I wanted to work," she explained, "but I wanted to choose my task and I wanted to collect my wages." The reforming women of Seneca Falls, grouped together on behalf of social improvement, had found in the first women's rights convention a way to speak for the needs of working women such as Charlotte Woodward as well as for themselves.

All over the North, in communities like Seneca Falls as well as in cities like New York, Americans gathered together in reform organizations to try to solve the problems that the market revolution posed for work, family life, personal and social values, and urban growth. Through these organizations local women and men became participants in wider communities of concern.

URBAN AMERICA

lthough the market revolution affected all aspects of American life, nowhere was its impact so noticeable as in the cities.

THE GROWTH OF CITIES

The market revolution dramatically increased the size of America's cities, with the great seaports leading the way. The proportion of America's population living in cities increased from only 7 percent in 1820 to almost 20 percent in 1860, a rate of growth greater than at any other time in the country's history. The nation's five largest cities in 1850 were the same as in 1800, with one exception. New York, Philadelphia, Baltimore, and Boston still topped the list, but New Orleans had edged out Charleston (see Chapters 9 and 11). The rate of urban growth was extraordinary. All four Atlantic seaports grew at least 25 percent each decade between 1800 and 1860, and often much more. New York, which grew from 60,000 in 1800 to 202,600 in 1830 and to more than 1 million in 1860, emerged as the nation's most populous city, its largest port, and its financial center.

Philadelphia, which had been the nation's largest city in 1800, was half the size of New York in 1850. Nevertheless, its growth was substantial—from 70,000 in 1800 to 389,000 in 1850 and to 565,529 in 1860. Philadelphia became as much an industrial as a commercial city.

Baltimore, with 212,418 residents in 1860, was about half the size of Philadelphia. The city's merchants, hoping to counter the threat posed by the Erie Canal to their trade links with the trans-Appalachian West, financed the nation's first important railroad, the Baltimore and Ohio, which began operation in 1830. Although Baltimore remained the east coast center of the tobacco trade with Europe, by 1850 its major partner in foreign trade was Brazil, to which it shipped flour and from which it imported coffee.

Boston, in colonial times, had dominated the triangular trade linking Britain and the West Indies. By 1860, with a population of 177,840, the city had emerged as the center of a new triangular trade: the ships of Boston merchants carried New England cotton cloth, shoes, and other manufactured goods to the South, delivered Southern cotton to British and European ports, and returned to Boston with European manufactured goods. Boston still dominated the China trade as well.

New Orleans, fed by the expansion of cotton throughout the South and commercial agriculture in the Mississippi Valley, had a population of 168,675 in 1860, and this population, as had been true in 1800, was the most racially diverse of any large city. In the 1850s, New Orleans handled about half the nation's cotton exports and by 1860, its exports—$5 million in 1815—had risen to $107 million.

The market revolution oriented the attention of each of these major seaports away from the oceans and toward trade with the nation's interior. Prosperous merchants in these cities now depended on American exports rather than European imports for their profits.

Another result of the market revolution was the appearance of "instant" cities at critical points on the new transportation network. Utica, New York, once a frontier trading post, was transformed by the opening of the Erie Canal into a commercial and manufacturing center. Chicago, on the shores of Lake Michigan, was transformed by the coming of the railroad into a major junction for water and rail transport. The city, which emerged as a fur trading center around Fort

WHO MIGRATED to America in the first half of the nineteenth century?

 11–10 Declaration of Sentiments and Resolutions, Woman's Rights Convention, Seneca Falls, New York (1848)

IMAGE KEY
for pages 322–323

a. A map of western New York State in 1811 including the proposed Erie Canal route, the Finger Lakes, Lake Ontario, and Lake Erie.
b. An abolitionist freeing a slave from his shackles: colored woodcut, c. 1840, from an American antislavery almanac.
c. Pages from an *American Pictorial Primer*, c. 1845.
d. A Cotton gin used to separate cotton from its seeds, stems, etc.
e. New York's most notorious slum, Five Points, is illustrated in this 1859 lithograph.
f. The seal of the General Society of Mechanics and Tradesman.
g. Dorothea Dix, a crusader for mental health reforms.
h. Frederick Douglass (1817?–1895), a portrait attributed to E. Hammond.

Declaration of Sentiments   The resolutions passed at the Seneca Falls Convention in 1848 calling for full female equality, including the right to vote.

QUICK REVIEW

"Instant" Cities

◆ Utica, New York transformed by opening of Erie Canal.

◆ Railroad made growth of Chicago possible.

◆ Chicago's population reached 100,000 in 1860.

Dearborn, an army post built in 1803, had become, by the 1850s, a hub of trade boasting grain storage facilities, slaughterhouses, and warehouses of all kinds. Farm implement manufacturers such as Cyrus McCormick built manufacturing plants there to serve the needs of Midwest farmers. By 1860 Chicago had a population of 100,000, making it the nation's eighth largest city (after Cincinnati and St. Louis).

PATTERNS OF IMMIGRATION

One of the key aspects of urban growth was a surge in immigration to the United States that began in the 1820s and accelerated dramatically after 1830. From an annual figure of about 20,000 in 1831, immigration ballooned to a record 430,000 in 1854 before declining in the years prior to the Civil War. The proportion of immigrants in the population jumped from 1.6 percent in the 1820s to 11.2 percent in 1860. In the nation's cities, the proportion was vastly larger: by 1860, nearly half of New York's population (48 percent) was foreign-born.

Most of the immigrants to the United States during this period came from Ireland and Germany. Political unrest and poor economic conditions in Germany and the catastrophic Potato Famine of 1845–1850 in Ireland were responsible for an enormous surge in immigration from those countries between 1845 and 1854. The starving, desperate "Famine Irish" who crowded into Eastern seaports were America's first large refugee group. Between them, the Germans and the Irish represented the largest influx of non-English immigrants the country had known (many Americans found the Irish dialect as strange as a foreign language). They were also the poorest: most of the Irish arrived destitute. In addition, most of the Irish and half of the Germans were Catholics, an unwelcome novelty to many Protestant Americans.

The influx of mostly poor, mostly Catholic foreigners provoked nativist hostility among many Protestant, native-born Americans, including many leaders of the major reform movements (see Chapter 15). It would be a mistake, however, to think that immigration was unwelcome to everyone. Industries needed willing workers, and Western states were eager for settlers. In 1852 Wisconsin appointed a commissioner of emigration with responsibility for attracting Europeans to the state.

Immigrant labor fueled the nation's expanding economy and helped turn wilderness into farmland. Many of the changes in industry and transportation that accompanied the market revolution would have been impossible without immigrants. Irish contract workers, for example, were essential to the completion of the Erie Canal in 1825.

Few immigrants found life in the United States pleasant or easy. In addition to the psychological difficulties of leaving a home and familiar ways behind, most immigrants endured harsh living and working conditions. America's cities were unprepared for the social problems posed by large numbers of immigrants. Until the 1880s, the task of receiving immigrants fell completely on cities and states, not the federal government. New York City, by far the largest port of entry, did not even establish an official reception center until 1855, when Castle Garden, at the bottom of Manhattan Island (near present-day Battery Park), was so designated.

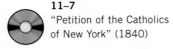

11–7
"Petition of the Catholics of New York" (1840)

IRISH IMMIGRATION

The first major immigrant wave to test American cities was caused by the catastrophic Irish Potato Famine of 1845–1849. Irish emigration to the United States dated from colonial times; young people who knew they could not hope to own

Wright's Grove, shown here in an 1868 illustration, was the popular picnic grounds and beer garden for the large German community on Chicago's North Side. Establishments such as this horrified American temperance advocates, who warned about the dangerous foreign notion of mixing alcohol with family fun.

Chicago Historical Society

land in Ireland had long looked to America for better opportunities. Indeed, from 1818 to 1845, at least 10,000 Irish emigrated yearly. But in the latter year Ireland's green fields of potato plants turned black with blight. The Irish had two choices: starve or leave. One million people died, and another 1.5 million emigrated, the majority to the United States. Starving, diseased (thousands died of typhus during the voyage), and destitute, hundreds of thousands (250,000 in 1851 alone) disembarked in the east coast ports of New York, Philadelphia, Boston, and Baltimore. Lacking the money to go inland and begin farming, they remained in the cities. Crowded together in miserable housing, desperate for work at any wages, foreign in their religion and pastimes (drinking and fighting, their critics said), tenaciously nationalistic and bitterly anti-British, they created ethnic enclaves of a kind new to American cities.

The largest numbers of Irish came to New York, which managed to absorb them. But Boston, a much smaller and more homogeneous city, was overwhelmed by the Irish influx. By 1850, a quarter of Boston's population was Irish, most of them recent immigrants. Boston, the home of Puritanism and the center of American intellectualism, did not welcome illiterate Irish Catholic peasants. All over the city in places of business and in homes normally eager for domestic servants the signs went up: "No Irish Need Apply."

GERMAN IMMIGRATION

Germans, like the Irish, had a long history of emigration to America. The nineteenth-century immigration of Germans began somewhat later and more slowly than that of the Irish, but by 1854 it had surpassed the Irish influx. Some German peasants, like the Irish, were driven from their homeland by potato blight in the mid-1840s. But the typical German immigrant was a small farmer or artisan dislodged by the same market forces at work in America: the industrialization of production and consolidation and the commercialization of farming. There was also a small group of middle-class liberal intellectuals who left the German states

QUICK REVIEW

Immigration at Mid-Century

◆ Surge of immigrants fueled growth of cities after the 1830s.

◆ Economic and political upheaval spurred mass migration from Europe.

◆ Famine drove large numbers of Irish to America.

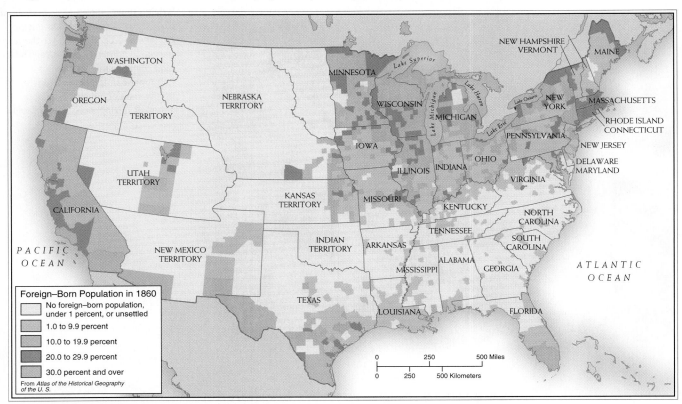

MAP 13-1 Distribution of Foreign-Born Residents of the United States in 1860   The ethnic composition of the American population was increased by Irish and German immigration in the 1840s and 1850s, Chinese attraction to the California gold rush, Mormon recruitment of Scottish and English followers to Utah, and the reclassification of Mexicans after the Mexican-American War as foreigners in what had been their own lands.

HOW DID events in Europe affect the flow of immigrants to the United States in the 1840s and 1850s?

(Germany was not yet a unified nation) after 1848 when attempts at revolution had failed. On the whole, German migrants were not as poor as the Irish, and they could afford to move out of the east coast seaports to other locations.

The first two major ports of embarkation for the Germans were Bremen (in northern Germany) and Le Havre (in northern France), which were also the main ports for the importation of American tobacco and cotton. The tobacco boats bore the Bremen passengers to Baltimore, and the cotton ships took them to New Orleans, a major entry point for European immigrants until the Civil War. From these ports, many Germans made their way up the Mississippi and Ohio valleys, where they settled in Pittsburgh, Cincinnati, and St. Louis and on farms in Ohio, Indiana, Missouri, and Texas.

German agricultural communities took a distinctive form that fostered cultural continuity. Immigrants formed predominantly German towns by clustering, or taking up adjoining land. A small cluster could support German churches, German-language schools, and German customs and thereby attract other Germans, some directly from Europe and some from other parts of the United States. Such communities reinforced the traditional values of German farmers, such as persistence, hard work, and thrift.

Another area attracting immigrants in the early nineteenth century was Gold Rush California, which drew, among others, numbers of Chinese (see Chapter 14). The Chinese who came to California worked in the mines, most as independent prospectors. Other miners disliked their industriousness and their clannishness. By the mid-1860s, Chinese workers made up 90 percent of the laborers building the Central Pacific Railroad, replacing more expensive white laborers and sowing the seeds of the long-lasting hostility of American workers toward Chinese. In the years to come, as hostility against the Chinese broke into violence, Chinatowns in San Francisco and elsewhere served a vital function as safe refuges for the Chinese who remained in the United States.

CLASS STRUCTURE AND LIVING PATTERNS IN THE CITIES

Although per capita income in America is estimated to have doubled between 1800 and 1850, the gap between rich and poor increased and became glaringly apparent in the nation's cities. The benefits of the market revolution were unequally distributed. In the cities there was a very small group of wealthy people with a net worth of more than $5,000 (about 3 percent of the population), a very large group of poor people with a net worth of $100 or less (nearly 70 percent), and a middle class with incomes in between (25–30 percent).

Differences in income affected every aspect of urban life. Very poor families, including almost all new immigrants, performed unskilled labor in jobs where the future was uncertain at best, lived in cheap rented housing, moved frequently, and depended on more than one income to survive. Artisans and skilled workers with incomes of $500 or more could live adequately, though often in cramped quarters that also served as their shops. A middle-class family with an income of more than $1,000 a year could live comfortably in a house of four to six rooms complete with carpeting, wallpaper, and good furniture. The very rich built mansions and large town houses and staffed them with many servants. In the summer they left the cities for country estates or homes at seaside resorts such as Newport, Rhode Island, which attracted wealthy families from all over the country.

Early nineteenth-century cities lacked municipal water supplies, sewers, and garbage collection. People drank water from wells, used outdoor privies that often contaminated the water supply, and threw garbage and slop out the door to be foraged by roaming herds of pigs. Clearly, this was a recipe for disease, and every American city suffered epidemics of sanitation-related diseases such as yellow fever, cholera, and typhus. Philadelphia's yellow fever epidemic of 1793 caused 4,000 deaths and stopped all business with the outside world for more than a month.

Yet the cities were slow to take action. In part this was due to poor medical understanding of disease but at least equally to expense. In response to the yellow fever epidemic, Philadelphia completed a city water system in 1801, but users had to pay a fee, and only the richest subscribed in the early days. Neither New York nor Boston had a public water system until the 1840s. Garbage collection remained a private service, and cities charged property owners for the costs of sewers, water mains, and street paving. Poorer areas of the cities could not afford the costs.

Provision of municipal services forced residential segregation. Richer people clustered in neighborhoods that had the new amenities. Increasingly, the poor clustered in bad neighborhoods that became known as slums. The worst New York slum in the nineteenth century was Five Points, a stone's throw from city hall. There, immigrants, free black people, and criminals were crammed into rundown buildings known in the slang of the time as "rookeries." Notorious gangs of thieves and pickpockets with names such as the Plug Uglies and the Shirt Tails dominated the district. Starvation and murder were commonplace.

MAP EXPLORATION

To explore an interactive version of this map, go to **http://www.prenhall.com/faraghertlc/map13.2**

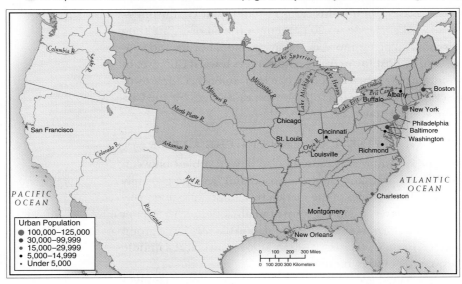

MAP 13-2A
American Cities, 1820

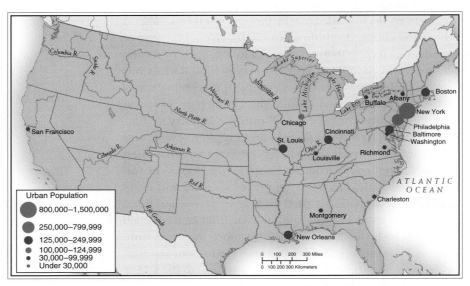

MAP 13-2B

American Cities, 1860   The cities of North America grew more rapidly between 1820 and 1860 than at any other time in the nation's history. Eastern seaport cities remained the largest, but New York grew to twice the size of the second largest city, Philadelphia. New York's growth, due in large part to the increase in trade following the opening of the Erie Canal, illustrates the importance of trade between port cities and the nation's interior. Inland river cities like Cincinnati and St. Louis and the great Mississippi seaport of New Orleans grew rapidly. San Francisco, Louisville, and Buffalo— still villages in 1820—grew also, but Chicago, which rapidly emerged as a hub for both water and rail transport, surpassed them all.

Statistical Abstract of the United States.

WHAT WERE the most important factors underlying the growth of American cities in the mid-nineteenth century?

After 1830, when urban growth was augmented by increasing immigration from Europe, middle-class Americans increasingly saw slums as the home of strange and foreign people, who deserved less than American-born citizens. In this way, residential patterns came to embody larger issues of class and citizenship.

ETHNIC NEIGHBORHOODS

To poverty-stricken Irish immigrants, these same slums represented not only family ties and familiar ways, but also community support as they learned how to survive in new surroundings. Isolated partly by their own beliefs (for Catholics fully reciprocated the hatred and fear that Protestants had shown them), Irish immigrants created their own communities in Boston and New York, their major destinations. They raised the money to erect Catholic churches with Irish priests. They established parochial schools with Irish nuns as teachers and sent their children to them in preference to the openly anti-Catholic public schools. They formed mutual aid societies based on kinship or town of origin in Ireland. Men and women formed religious and social clubs, lodges, and brotherhoods and their female auxiliaries. Irishmen manned fire and militia companies as well. This dense network of associations served the same purpose that social welfare organizations do today: providing help in time of need and offering companionship in a hostile environment.

Germans who settled in urban areas also built their own ethnic enclaves—"Little Germanies"—in which they sought to duplicate the rich cultural life of German cities. Like the Irish, the Germans formed church societies, mutual benefit societies, and fire and militia companies to provide mutual support. The Germans also formed networks of leisure organizations: singing societies, debating and political clubs, concert halls like New York's Beethoven Hall, theaters, turnvereins (gymnastics associations), and beer gardens. They published German-language newspapers as well.

Ethnic clustering, then, allowed new immigrants to hold onto aspects of their culture that they valued and to transplant them to American soil. Many native-born Americans, however, viewed ethnic neighborhoods with deep suspicion.

URBAN POPULAR CULTURE

The size, diversity, and changing working conditions in American cities bred a new, rougher, urban popular culture. Taverns that served as neighborhood centers of drink and sociability were also frequent centers of brawls and riots. Community groups such as fire engine companies that had once included men of all social classes now attracted rough young laborers who formed their own youth gangs and defended "their" turf against other gangs. Some trades, such as that of butcher, became notorious for starting fights in taverns and grog shops.

Theaters, which had been frequented by men of all social classes, provided another setting for violence. By the 1830s, middle-class and upper-class men withdrew to more respectable theaters to which they could bring their wives and daughters. Workers found new amusements in theaters such as the Lafayette Circus, which featured dancing girls and horseback riders as well as theatrical acts. Another popular urban working-class amusement was the blackface minstrel show. White actors (often Irish) blacked their faces and entertained audiences with songs (including the famous "Dixie," written by an Irishman as a blackface song), dances, theatrical skits, and antiblack political jokes.

Another challenge to middle-class respectability came from the immensely popular "penny papers," which began publication in 1833, and the rapidly growing number of political papers (see Chapter 10). This exuberant urban popular culture was unquestionably a part of the same new democratic political spirit that led to the great upsurge in political participation discussed in Chapter 10. And it was the inspiration for some of America's most innovative writers, foremost among them urban journalist, Democratic Party activist, and poet Walt Whitman, who distilled his passionate love for the variety and commonness of the American people in *Leaves of Grass*, a book of free-verse poems published in 1855. Regarded at the time as scandalous because of its frank language, Whitman's poetry nevertheless captured the driving energy and democratic spirit of the new urban popular culture. In a rather more sinister way, so did the writings of Edgar Allan Poe, who found the inspiration for his gothic horror stories such as "The Murders in the Rue Morgue" (1841) and "The Mystery of Marie Roget" (1842) not in Europe (as his titles might suggest), but in contemporary American crimes.

URBAN LIFE OF FREE AFRICAN AMERICANS

By 1860, there were nearly half a million free African Americans in the United States, constituting about 11 percent of the country's total black population. More than half of all free African Americans lived in the North, mostly in cities. Philadelphia and New York had the largest black communities: 22,000 African Americans in Philadelphia and 12,500 in New York (another 4,313 lived just across the East River in Brooklyn). There were much smaller but still significant black communities in the New England cities of Boston, Providence, and New Haven and in Ohio cities like Cincinnati.

Free African Americans in Northern cities faced residential segregation (except for the domestic servants who lived in with white families), pervasive job discrimination, segregated public schools, and severe limitations on their civil rights. In addition to these legal restrictions there were matters of custom: African Americans of all economic classes endured daily affronts, such as exclusion from public concerts, lectures, and libraries, and segregation or exclusion from public transportation.

In common with Irish and German immigrants, African Americans created defenses against the larger hostile society by building their own community structures. They formed associations for aiding the poorest members of the community, for self-improvement, and for socializing. Tired of being insulted by the white press, African American communities supported their own newspapers. The major community organization was the black Baptist or African Methodist Episcopal (AME) church, which served, as one historian put it, as "a place of worship, a social and cultural center, a political meetingplace, a hiding place for fugitives, a training ground for potential community leaders, and one of the few places where blacks could express their true feelings."

Employment prospects for black men deteriorated from 1820 to 1850. Those who had held jobs as skilled artisans were forced from their positions, and their sons denied apprenticeships, by white mechanics and craftsmen who were themselves suffering from the effects of the market revolution. Limited to day labor, African Americans found themselves in direct competition with the new immigrants, especially the Irish, for jobs. On the waterfront, black men lost their jobs as carters and longshoremen to the Irish. One of the few occupations to remain open to them was that of seaman. More than 20 percent of all American sailors in 1850 were black, and over the years their ranks included an increasing number of runaway slaves. The pay was poor and the conditions miserable, but many black men found more equality aboard ship than they did ashore. Mothers, wives, and daughters were left ashore to work as domestic servants (in competition with Irishwomen), washerwomen, and seamstresses.

Free African Americans suffered many forms of discrimination, but as this 1850 daguerreotype of an unknown woman shows, they sought to achieve the same levels of education and economic comfort as other Americans.

Zelsa P. Mackay Collection. Courtesy George Eastman House

THE LABOR MOVEMENT AND URBAN POLITICS

Universal white manhood suffrage and the development of mass politics (see Chapter 10), coupled with the rapid growth of cities, changed urban politics. The traditional leadership role of the wealthy elite waned. In their place were professional politicians whose job it was to make party politics work. In New York and in other large cities, this change in politics was spurred by working-class activism.

THE TRADITION OF ARTISANAL POLITICS

Protests by urban workers had been an integral part of the older social order controlled by the wealthy elite. In the eighteenth century, when only men of property could vote, such demonstrations usually indicated widespread discontent or economic difficulty among workers. They served as a warning signal that the political elite rarely ignored.

By the 1830s the status of artisans and independent craftsmen in the nation's cities had changed. Workers' associations came to include defensive and angry workers who were acutely conscious of their declining status in the economic and social order. Tentatively at first, but then with growing conviction, they became active defenders of working-class interests.

What was new was the open antagonism between workers and employers. The community of interest between masters and workers in preindustrial times broke down. Workers realized they had to depend on other workers, not employers, for support. In turn, employers and members of the middle class began to take urban disorders much more seriously than their grandfathers might have done.

THE UNION MOVEMENT

Urban worker protest against changing conditions quickly took the form of party politics. The Workingmen's Party was founded in Philadelphia in 1827, and chapters quickly formed in New York and Boston as well. Using the language of class warfare—"two distinct classes . . . those that live by their own labor and they that live upon the labor of others"—the "Workies" campaigned for the ten-hour day and the preservation of the small artisanal shop. They also called for the end of government-chartered monopolies—banks were high on the list. And they were in favor of a public school system and cheap land in the West. Although the Workies themselves did not survive as a party, Jacksonian Democrats were quick to pick up on some of their themes. The Democrats attracted many Workingmen's votes in 1832.

Both major parties competed for the votes of urban workers. Nevertheless, neither major political party really spoke to the primary need of workers—for well-paid, stable jobs that assured them independence and respect. Unsatisfied with the response of political parties, workers turned to labor organization to achieve their goals.

Between 1833 and 1837 a wave of strikes in New York City cut the remaining ties between master craftsmen and the journeymen who worked for them. In 1833, journeymen carpenters struck for higher wages. Workers in fifteen other trades came to their support, and within a month the strike was won. The lesson was obvious: if skilled workers banded together across craft lines, they could improve their conditions. The same year, representatives from nine different craft groups formed the General Trades Union (GTU) of New York. By 1834 similar groups had sprung up in over a dozen cities. In 1834 representatives of several local GTUs met in Baltimore and organized the National Trades Union (NTU). In its founding statement the NTU criticized the "unjustifiable distribution of the wealth of society in the hands of a few individuals," which had created for working people "a humiliating, servile dependency, incompatible with . . . natural equality."

WHO WERE the major proponents of the labor movement?

QUICK REVIEW

Unions
- In the late 1830s and early 1840s unions won important victories.
- Unions concentrated on artisanal rights and virtues.
- American-born artisans increasingly saw immigrants as a threat to job security.

Tammany Society A fraternal organization of artisans begun in the 1780s that evolved into a key organization of the new mass politics in New York City.

Convinced that unions were dangerous, New York employers took striking journeymen tailors to court in 1836. Judge Ogden Edwards pronounced the strikers guilty of conspiracy and declared unions un-American. The GTU responded with a mass rally at which Judge Edwards was burned in effigy. A year later, stunned by the effects of the Panic of 1837, the GTU collapsed. The founding of these general unions, a visible sign of a class-based community of interest among workers, is generally considered to mark the beginning of the American labor movement. However, these early unions included only white men in skilled trades who made up only a small percentage of all workers. The majority of workers—men in unskilled occupations, all free African Americans, and all women—were excluded.

BIG-CITY MACHINES

As America's cities experienced unprecedented growth, the electorate mushroomed. In New York, for example, the number of voters grew from 20,000 in 1825 to 88,900 in 1855. Furthermore, by 1855 half of the voters were foreign-born. At the time, America was the only country in the world where propertyless white men had the vote. The job of serving this largely working-class electorate and making the new mass political party work at the urban level fell to a new kind of career politician—the boss—and a new kind of political organization—the machine.

In New York City, the **Tammany Society**, begun in the 1780s as a fraternal organization of artisans, slowly evolved into the key organization of the new mass politics. Tammany, which was affiliated with the national Democratic Party, reached

By 1855, half the voters in New York City were foreign-born. This 1858 engraving of an Irish bar in the Five Points area appeared in the influential *Harper's Weekly*. It expressed the dislike of temperance reformers for immigrants and their drinking habits and the dismay of political reformers that immigrant saloons and taverns were such effective organizing centers for urban political machines.

Frank and Marie-Therese Wood Print Collections, The Picture Bank voters by using many of the techniques of mass appeal made popular earlier by craft organizations—parades, rallies, current songs, and party newspapers.

Along with these new techniques of mass appeal went new methods of organization: a tight system of political control beginning at the neighborhood level with ward committees and topped by a chairman of a citywide general committee. At the citywide level, ward leaders—bosses—bartered the loyalty and votes of their followers for positions on the city payroll for party members and community services for their neighborhood. This was machine politics. Through it workers, although they lacked the political or organizational strength to challenge the harmful effects of the market revolution, could use their numbers to ameliorate some of its effects at the local level. Machine politics served to mediate increasing class divisions and ethnic diversity as well. The machines themselves offered personal ties and loyalties—community feeling—to recent arrivals in the big cities (increasingly, immigrants from Europe) and help in hard times to workers who cast their votes correctly.

SOCIAL REFORM MOVEMENTS

As the opening of this chapter describes, the earliest response to the dislocations caused by the market revolution was community based and voluntary. The reform message was vastly amplified by inventions such as the steam printing press, which made it possible to publish reform literature in great volume. Soon there were national networks of reform groups.

Alexis de Tocqueville commented on the vast extent of American voluntary associations and their many purposes. "In no country in the world," he noted, "has the principle of association been more successfully used, or more unsparingly applied to a multitude of different objects, than in America."

EVANGELISM, REFORM, AND SOCIAL CONTROL

Evangelical religion was fundamental to social reform. Men and women who had been converted to the enthusiastic new faith assumed personal responsibility for making changes in their own lives. Members of evangelistic religions expected to convert the world and create the perfect moral and religious community on earth. Much of America was swept by the fervor of moralistic reform, and it was the new middle class, by applying new notions of morality to the movement, who set the agenda for reform.

Reform efforts arose from the recognition that the traditional methods of small-scale local relief were no longer adequate. Reformers realized that large cities had to make large-scale provisions for social misfits and that institutional rather than private efforts were needed. This thinking was especially true of the institutional reform movements that began in the 1830s, such as the push for insane asylums. At this time, of course, the federal government provided no such relief.

A second characteristic of the reform movements was a belief in the basic goodness of human nature. All reformers believed that the condition of the unfortunate—the poor, the insane, the criminal—would improve in a wholesome environment. Thus, insane asylums were built in rural areas, away from the noise and stress of the cities, and orphanages had strict rules that were meant to encourage discipline and self-reliance. Prison reform carried this sentiment to the extreme. On the theory that bad social influences were largely responsible for crime, some "model" prisons completely isolated prisoners from one another, making them eat, sleep, work, and do required Bible reading in their own cells. The failure of these prisons to achieve dramatic changes for the better in their inmates (a number of

WHAT ROLE did women play in the development of American education?

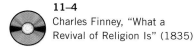

11–4
Charles Finney, "What a Revival of Religion Is" (1835)

isolated prisoners went mad, and some committed suicide) or to reduce crime was one of the first indications that reform was not a simple task.

A third characteristic of the reform movements was their moralistic dogmatism. Reformers were certain they knew what was right and were determined to see their improvements enacted. It was a short step from developing individual self-discipline to imposing discipline on others. The reforms that were proposed thus took the form of social controls. Lazy, sinful, intemperate, or unfit members of society were to be reformed for their own good, whether they wanted to be or not. This attitude was bound to cause controversy; by no means did all Americans share the reformers' beliefs, nor did those for whom it was intended always take kindly to being the targets of the reformers' concern.

Indeed, some aspects of the social reform movements were harmful. The evangelical Protestantism of the reformers promoted a dangerous hostility to Catholic immigrants from Ireland and Germany that repeatedly led to urban riots. The temperance movement, in particular, targeted immigrants for their free drinking habits. Seeking uniformity of behavior rather than tolerance, the reformers thus helped to promote the virulent nativism that infected American politics between 1840 and 1860 (see Chapter 15).

Regional and national reform organizations quickly grew from local projects to deal with social problems such as drinking, prostitution, mental illness, and crime. In 1828, for example, Congregationalist minister Lyman Beecher joined other ministers in forming a General Union for Promoting the Observance of the Christian Sabbath; the aim was to prevent business on Sundays. The Sabbath reformers engaged in political action but remained aloof from direct electoral politics, stressing their religious mission. In any case, **sabbatarianism** was controversial. Workingmen (who usually worked six days a week) were angered when the General Union forced the Sunday closure of their favorite taverns and were quick to vote against the Whigs, the party perceived to be most sympathetic to reform thinking.

EDUCATION AND WOMEN TEACHERS

Women became deeply involved in reform movements through their churches. Nearly every church had a maternal association, where mothers gathered to discuss ways to raise their children as true Christians. These associations reflected a new and more positive definition of childhood. The Puritans had believed that children were born sinful and that their wills had to be broken before they could become godly. Educational reformers, however, tended to believe that children were born innocent and needed gentle nurturing and encouragement if they were to flourish. At home, mothers began to play the central role in child rearing. Outside the home, women helped spread the new public education pioneered by Horace Mann, secretary of the Massachusetts State Board of Education.

Although literacy had long been valued, especially in New England, schooling since colonial times had been a private enterprise and a personal expense. Town grammar schools, required in Massachusetts since 1647, had been supported primarily by parents' payments, with some help from local property taxes. In 1827, Massachusetts pioneered compulsory education by legislating that public schools be supported by public taxes. Soon schooling for white children between the ages of five and nineteen was common, although, especially in rural schools, the term might be only a month or so long. Uniformity in curriculum and teacher training, and the grading of classes by ability—measures pioneered by Horace Mann in the 1830s—quickly caught on in other states. In the North and West (the South lagged far behind), more and more children went to school, and more and more teachers, usually young single women, were hired to teach them.

QUICK REVIEW

Women and Reform

◆ Women often became involved in reform through their churches.

◆ Maternal associations focused on raising of children as true Christians.

◆ Women helped spread public education of children.

Sabbatarianism   Reform movement that aimed to prevent business on Sundays.

The spread of public education created the first real career opportunity for women. The great champion of teacher training for women was Catharine Beecher, daughter of Lyman, who clearly saw her efforts as part of the larger work of establishing "the moral government of God." By 1850 women were dominant in primary school teaching, which had come to be regarded as an acceptable occupation for educated young women during the few years between their own schooling and marriage. For some women, teaching was a great adventure; they enthusiastically volunteered to be "schoolmarms" on the distant western frontiers of Wisconsin and Iowa or to be missionary teachers in distant lands. For others, a few years of teaching was quite enough. Low pay (half of what male schoolteachers earned) and community supervision (women teachers had to board with families in the community) were probably sufficient to make almost any marriage proposal look appealing.

TEMPERANCE

The largest reform organization of the period, the **American Society for the Promotion of Temperance**, founded in 1826, boasted more than 200,000 members by the mid-1830s. Dominated by evangelicals, local chapters used revival methods—lurid **temperance** tracts detailing the evils of alcohol, large prayer and song meetings, and heavy group pressure—to encourage young men to stand up, confess their bad habits, and "take the pledge" not to drink. Here again, women played an important role.

Traditionally, drinking had been a basic part of men's working lives. It concluded occasions as formal as the signing of a contract and accompanied such informal activities as card games. Drink was a staple offering at political speeches, rallies, and elections. Much of the drinking was well within the bounds of sociability, but the widespread use (more than seven gallons of hard liquor per capita in 1830—more than twice as much as today's rate) must have encouraged drunkenness.

There were many reasons to support temperance. Men drank hard cider and liquor—whiskey, rum—in abundance. Heavy-drinking men hurt their families economically by spending their wages on drink. Excessive drinking also led to violence and crime, both within the family and in the larger society. But there were other reasons for the temperance movement. The new middle class, preoccupied with respectability, morality, and efficiency, found the old easygoing drinking ways unacceptable. As work patterns changed, employers banned alcohol at work and increasingly considered drinking men not only unreliable, but also immoral. Temperance became a social and political issue. Whigs, who embraced the new morality, favored it; Democrats, who in Northern cities consisted increasingly of immigrant workers, were opposed.

The Panic of 1837 affected the temperance movement. Whereas most temperance crusaders in the 1820s had been members of the middle class, the long depression of 1837–1843 prompted artisans and skilled workers to give up or at least cut down substantially on drinking. Forming associations known as Washington Temperance Societies, these workers spread the word that temperance was the workingman's best chance to survive economically and to maintain his independence. Their wives, gathered together in Martha Washington Societies, were frequently even more committed to temperance than their husbands.

By the mid-1840s alcohol consumption had been more than halved, to less than two gallons per capita, about the level of today. Concern over drinking would remain constant throughout the nineteenth century and into the twentieth.

Catharine E. Beecher, author of the women's *A Treatise on Domestic Economy for the Use of Young Ladies at Home, and at School* (1841).

The Schlesinger Library, Radcliffe Institute, Harvard University

11–11
Horace Mann on Education and National Welfare

11–5
Temperance and the Washingtonians (1836)

11–2
Lyman Beecher, Six Sermons on Intemperance (1828)

American Society for the Promotion of Temperance Largest reform organization of its time dedicated to ending the sale and consumption of alcoholic beverages.

Temperance Reform movement originating in the 1820s that sought to eliminate the consumption of alcohol.

Evangelist Dorothea Dix's efforts to publicize the horrific conditions suffered by insane women in asylums led to the establishment of public institutions for the insane.

Library of Congress

11–12
John Humphrey Noyes and Bible Communism (1845–1849)

10–1
Joseph Smith and the Beginnings of Mormonism (1823)

Female Moral Reform Society
Antiprostitution group founded by evangelical women in New York in 1834.

Seneca Falls convention The first convention for women's equality in legal rights, held in upstate New York in 1848.

Shakers The followers of Mother Ann Lee, who preached a religion of strict celibacy and communal living.

MORAL REFORM, ASYLUMS, AND PRISONS

Alcohol was not the only "social evil" that reform groups attacked. Another was prostitution, which was common in the nation's port cities. The customary approach of evangelical reformers was to "rescue" prostitutes, offering them the salvation of religion, prayer, and temporary shelter. The success rate was not very high. As an alternative to prostitution, reformers usually offered domestic work, a low-paying and restrictive occupation that many women scorned. Nevertheless, campaigns against prostitution, generally organized by women, continued throughout the nineteenth century. One of the earliest and most effective antiprostitution groups was the **Female Moral Reform Society**. Founded by evangelical women in New York in 1834 (the first president was Lydia Finney), it boasted 555 affiliates throughout the country by 1840.

Another dramatic example of reform was the asylum movement, spearheaded by the woman evangelist Dorothea Dix. In 1843, Dix horrified the Massachusetts state legislature with the results of her several years of study into the conditions to which insane women were subjected. Dix's efforts led to the establishment of a state asylum for the insane in Massachusetts and to similar institutions in other states. Between 1843 and 1854 Dix traveled more than 30,000 miles to publicize the movement for humane treatment of the insane. By 1860 twenty-eight states had public institutions for the insane.

Other reformers were active in related causes, such as prison reform and the establishment of orphanages, homes of refuge, and hospitals. Model penitentiaries were built in Auburn and Ossining (known as "Sing Sing"), New York, and in Philadelphia and Pittsburgh. Characterized by strict order and discipline, these prisons were supposed to reform rather than simply incarcerate their inmates, but their regimes of silence and isolation caused despair more often than rehabilitation.

UTOPIANISM AND MORMONISM

Amid all the political activism and reform fervor of the 1830s, a few people chose escape into utopian communities and new religions. The upstate New York area along the Erie Canal was the seedbed for this movement, just as it was for evangelical revivals and reform movements like the **Seneca Falls convention**. The area was so notable for its reform enthusiasms that it has been termed "the Burned-Over District," a reference to the waves of reform that swept through like forest fires.

Apocalyptic religions tend to spring up in places experiencing rapid social change. The Erie Canal region, which experienced the full impact of the market revolution in the early nineteenth century, was such a place. A second catalyst is hard times, and the prolonged depression that began with the Panic of 1837 led some people to embrace a belief in imminent catastrophe. The Millerites (named for their founder, William Miller) believed that the Second Coming of Christ would occur on October 22, 1843. In anticipation, members of the church sold their belongings and bought white robes for their ascension to heaven. When the Day of Judgment did not take place as expected, most of Miller's followers drifted away. But a small group persisted. Revising their expectations, they formed the core of the Seventh-Day Adventist faith, which is still active today.

The **Shakers**, founded by "Mother" Ann Lee in 1774, were the oldest utopian group. An offshoot of the Quakers, the Shakers espoused a radical social philosophy that called for the abolition of the traditional family in favor of a family of brothers and sisters joined in equal fellowship. Despite its insistence on celibacy, the Shaker movement grew between 1820 and 1830, eventually reaching twenty settlements in eight states with a total membership of 6,000. The Shaker's simple and highly structured lifestyle, their isolation from the changing world, and their belief in equality drew new followers, especially among women.

The most successful of the nineteenth-century communitarian movements was also a product of the Burned-Over District. In 1830, a young man named Joseph Smith founded the Church of Jesus Christ of Latter-Day Saints, based on the teachings of the Book of Mormon, which he claimed to have received from an angel in a vision.

Initially, Mormonism, as the new religion became known, seemed little different from the many other new religious groups and utopian communities of the time. But under the benevolent but absolute authority of its patriarch, Joseph Smith, it rapidly gained distinction for its extraordinary communitarianism. Close cooperation and hard work made the Mormon community successful, attracting both new followers and the animosity of neighbors, who resented Mormon exclusiveness and economic success. The Mormons were harassed in New York and driven west to Ohio and then Missouri. Finally they seemed to find an ideal home in Nauvoo, Illinois, where in 1839 they built a model community, achieving almost complete self-government and isolation from non-Mormon neighbors. But in 1844, dissension within the community over Joseph Smith's new doctrine of polygamy (marriage between one man and more than one woman, simultaneously) gave outsiders a chance to intervene. Smith and his brother were arrested peacefully but were killed by a mob from which their jailers failed to protect them.

The beleaguered Mormon community decided to move beyond reach of harm. Led by Brigham Young, the Mormons migrated in 1846 to the Great Salt Lake in present-day Utah. After several lean years (once a grasshopper plague was stopped by the providential arrival of sea gulls, who ate the insects), the Mormon method of communal settlement proved successful. Their hopes of isolation were dashed, however, by the California Gold Rush of 1849.

MAP EXPLORATION
To explore an interactive version of this map, go to
http://www.prenhall.com/faraghertlc/map13.3

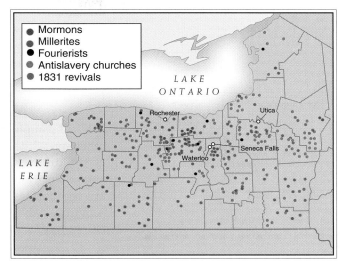

MAP 13-3
Reform Movements in the Burned-Over District
The so-called Burned-Over District, the region of New York State most changed by the opening of the Erie Canal, was a seedbed of religious and reform movements. The Mormon Church originated there and Utopian groups and sects like the Millerites and the Fourierists thrived. Charles G. Finney held some of his most successful evangelical revivals in the district. Antislavery feeling was common in the region, and the women's rights movement began at Seneca Falls.
Whitney Cross, *The Burned-Over District* (1950; reprint, New York: Hippocrene Books, 1981).

WHY WERE the many religious revivals and reform movements in the Burned-Over District in the 1830s and 1840s strongest in this region of the country?

ANTISLAVERY AND ABOLITIONISM

The antislavery feeling that was to play such an important role in the politics of the 1840s and 1850s also had its roots in the religious reform movements that began in the 1820s and 1830s. Three groups—free African Americans, Quakers, and militant white reformers—worked to bring an end to slavery, but each in different ways.

WHO WERE the abolitionists and what were their racial attitudes?

THE AMERICAN COLONIZATION SOCIETY

The first official attempt to "solve" the problem of slavery was a plan for gradual emancipation of slaves (with compensation to their owners) and their resettlement in Africa. This plan was the work of the **American Colonization Society**, formed in 1817 by Northern religious reformers and a number of Southern slave owners. The Society was ineffective; by 1830, it had managed to send only 1,400 black people to a colony in Liberia, West Africa.

American Colonization Society
Organization, founded in 1817 by antislavery reformers, that called for gradual emancipation and the removal of freed blacks to Africa.

AFRICAN AMERICANS' FIGHT AGAINST SLAVERY

For free African Americans the freedom of other black people had always been a major goal. Most rejected colonization, insisting instead on a commitment to the immediate end of slavery and the equal treatment of black people in America. By 1830 there were at least fifty black abolitionist societies in the North. These organizations held yearly national conventions, where famous African American abolitionists like Frederick Douglass, Harriet Tubman, and Sojourner Truth spoke. The first African American newspaper, founded in 1827 by John Russwurm and Samuel Cornish, announced its antislavery position in its title, *Freedom's Journal.*

In 1829 David Walker, a free African American in Boston, wrote a widely distributed pamphlet, ***Appeal to the Colored Citizens of the World***, that encouraged slave rebellion. White Southerners blamed pamphlets such as these and the militant articles of African American journalists for stirring up trouble among Southern slaves, and in particular for Nat Turner's revolt in 1831. The vehemence of white Southern reaction testifies to the courage of that handful of determined free African Americans who persisted in speaking for their enslaved brothers and sisters long before most white Northerners even noticed.

ABOLITIONISTS

The third and best-known group of antislavery reformers was headed by William Lloyd Garrison. In 1831 Garrison broke with the gradualist persuaders of the American Colonization Society and began publishing his own paper, the *Liberator*. Garrison, the embodiment of moral indignation, was totally incapable of compromise. His approach was to mount a sweeping crusade condemning slavery as sinful and demanding its immediate abolishment. He took the radical step of demanding full social equality for African Americans, referring to them individually as "a man and a brother" and "a woman and a sister." Garrison's determination electrified the antislavery movement, but his inability to compromise limited his effectiveness as a leader.

Moral horror over slavery engaged many Northerners deeply in the abolitionist movement. They flocked to hear firsthand accounts of slavery by Frederick Douglass and Sojourner Truth, and by the white sisters from South Carolina, Angelina and Sarah Grimké. Northerners eagerly read slave narratives and books such as Theodore Weld's 1839 treatise *American Slavery As It Is* (based in part on the recollections of Angelina Grimké, whom Weld had married) that provided graphic details of abuse under slavery. Lyman Beecher's daughter, Harriet Beecher Stowe, was to draw on the Grimké-Weld book for her immensely popular antislavery novel *Uncle Tom's Cabin*, published in 1852.

The style of abolitionist writings and speeches was similar to the oratorical style of the religious revivalists. The abolitionists were confrontational, denunciatory, and personal in their message, much like the evangelical preachers.

They also adopted another tactic of revivalists and temperance workers when, to enhance their powers of persuasion, they began to publish great numbers of antislavery tracts. In 1835 alone they mailed more than a million pieces of antislavery literature to Southern states. This tactic drew a backlash: Southern legislatures banned abolitionist literature, encouraged the harassment and abuse of anyone distributing it, and looked the other way when proslavery mobs seized and burned it. Most serious, the majority of Southern states reacted by toughening laws concerning emancipation, freedom of movement, and all aspects of slave behavior. Ironically, then, the immediate impact of abolitionism in the South was to stifle dissent and make the lives of slaves harder (see Chapter 11).

Even in the North, controversy over abolitionism was common. A tactic that abolitionists borrowed from revivalists—holding large and emotional meetings—opened

QUICK REVIEW

The American Colonization Society

◆ Formed in 1817 with the goal of resettling slaves in Africa.

◆ Members included Northern religious reformers and some Southern slave owners.

◆ By 1830, the Society had only managed to send 1,400 people to Liberia, West Africa.

Appeal to the Colored Citizens of the World Written by David Walker, a published insistence that "America is more our country, than it is the whites'—we have enriched it with our blood and tears."

the door to mob action. Crowds of people often disrupted such meetings, especially those addressed by Theodore Weld, whose oratorical style earned him the title of "the Most Mobbed Man in the United States." William Lloyd Garrison was stoned, dragged through the streets, and on one occasion almost hanged by a Boston mob.

ABOLITIONISM AND POLITICS

Abolitionism began as a social movement but soon intersected with sectional interests and became a national political issue. In the 1830s, massive abolitionist petition drives gathered a total of nearly 700,000 petitions requesting the abolition of slavery and the slave trade in the District of Columbia but were rebuffed by Congress. At Southern insistence and with President Andrew Jackson's approval, Congress passed a "gag rule" in 1836 that prohibited discussion of antislavery petitions.

Many Northerners viewed the gag rule and censorship of the mails, which Southerners saw as necessary defenses against abolitionist frenzy, as alarming threats to free speech. First among them was Massachusetts representative John Quincy Adams, the only former president ever to serve in Congress after leaving the executive branch. Adams so publicly and persistently denounced the gag rule as a violation of the constitutional right to petition that it was repealed in 1844.

John Quincy Adams was also a key figure in the abolitionists' one undoubted victory, the fight to free the fifty-three slaves on the Spanish ship *Amistad* and return them to Africa. Although the Africans successfully mutinied against the *Amistad's* crew in 1839, when the ship was found in American waters a legal battle over their "ownership" ensued, during which the Africans themselves were held in jail. Prominent abolitionists, most notably Lewis Tappan, financed the legal fight that went all the way to the Supreme Court, where Adams won the case for the *Amistad* defendants against the American government, which supported the Spanish claim.

Although abolitionist groups raised the nation's emotional temperature, they failed to achieve the moral unity they had hoped for, and they began to splinter. Frederick Douglass and William Lloyd Garrison parted ways when Douglass, refusing to be limited to a simple recital of his life as a slave, began to make specific suggestions for improvements in the lives of free African Americans. When Douglass chose the path of political action, Garrison denounced him as "ungrateful." Douglass and other free African Americans worked under persistent discrimination, even from antislavery whites; some of the latter refused to hire black people or to meet with them as equals. While many white reformers eagerly pressed for civil equality for African Americans, they did not accept the idea of social equality. On the other hand, black and white "stations" worked closely in the risky enterprise of passing fugitive slaves north over the famous Underground Railroad, as the various routes by which slaves made their way to freedom were called. Contrary to abolitionist legend, however, it was free African Americans, rather than white people, who played the major part in helping the fugitives.

In 1840 the abolitionist movement formally split. The majority moved toward party politics (which Garrison abhorred), founding the **Liberty Party** and choosing James G. Birney (whom Theodore Weld had converted to abolitionism) as their presidential candidate. Thus, the abolitionist movement, which began as an effort at moral reform, took its first major step into politics, and this step in turn led to the formation of the Republican Party in the 1850s and to the Civil War.

"Am I not a Woman and a Sister?"

The engraving of a chained female slave was made by Patrick Reason, a black artist, in 1835. The accompanying message, "Am I Not a Woman and a Sister?" spoke particularly to white female abolitionists in the North, who were just becoming active in antislavery movements in the 1830s.

Library of Congress

Liberty Party   The first antislavery political party, formed in 1840.

THE WOMEN'S RIGHTS MOVEMENT

WHAT CONNECTIONS

were there between the women's
rights movement and previous
movements for social reform?

Americanwomen, without the vote or a role in party politics, found a field of activity in social reform movements. There was scarcely a reform movement in which women were not actively involved. Often men were the official leaders of such movements, and some women—especially those in the temperance, moral reform, and abolitionist movements—formed all-female chapters to define and implement their own policies and programs.

The majority of women did not participate in these activities, for they were fully occupied with housekeeping and child rearing (families with five children were the average). A few women—mostly members of the new middle class, who could afford servants—had the time and energy to look beyond their immediate tasks. Led thereby to challenge social restrictions, some, like the Grimké sisters, found that their commitment carried them beyond the limits of what was considered acceptable activity for women.

THE GRIMKÉ SISTERS

Sarah and Angelina Grimké, members of a prominent South Carolina slaveholding family, rejected slavery out of religious conviction and moved north to join a Quaker community near Philadelphia. In the 1830s, these two sisters found themselves drawn into the growing antislavery agitation in the North. Because they knew about slavery firsthand, they were in great demand as speakers. At first they spoke to "parlor meetings" of women only, as was considered proper, but as the meetings got larger and larger, the sisters realized that they had become the first female public speakers in America. In 1837 Angelina Grimké became the first woman to address a meeting of the Massachusetts state legislature.

Whereas male antislavery orators were criticized by the press and by conservative ministers for their abolitionist position, the Grimké sisters were criticized for speaking out simply because they were women. A letter from a group of ministers cited the Bible in reprimanding the sisters for stepping out of "woman's proper sphere" of silence and subordination. Sarah Grimké answered the ministers in her 1838 *Letters on the Equality of the Sexes and the Condition of Women*, claiming that "men and women were CREATED EQUAL. . . . Whatever is right for a man to do, is right for woman."

Women in the antislavery movement found it a constant struggle to be heard. Some solved the problem of male dominance by forming their own groups, like the Philadelphia Female Anti-Slavery Society. In the antislavery movement and other reform groups as well, men accorded women a secondary role, even when—as was frequently the case—women constituted a majority of the members.

WOMEN'S RIGHTS

The Seneca Falls Convention of 1848, the first women's rights convention in American history, was an outgrowth of almost twenty years of female activity in social reform. Every year after 1848 women gathered to hold women's rights conventions and to work for political, legal, and social equality. Over the years, in response to persistent lobbying, states passed property laws more favorable to women and altered divorce laws to allow women to retain custody of children. Teaching

Women's gatherings, like the first women's rights convention in Seneca Falls in 1848 and this meeting of strikers in Lynn in 1860, were indicators of widespread female activism.

Lynn Museum

ND STITCHERS HELD AT LYNN, FEB. 28, FOR ADOPTING A LIST OF PRICES; MRS. E. HALL, PRESIDING.—(See page 284.)

positions in higher education opened up to women, as did jobs in some other occupations, and women gained the vote in some states, beginning with Wyoming Territory in 1869. In 1920, seventy-two years after universal woman suffrage was first proposed at Seneca Falls, a woman's right to vote was at last guaranteed in the Nineteenth Amendment to the Constitution.

Women played a vital role in all the social movements of the day. In doing so they implicitly challenged the popular notion of separate spheres for men and women—the public world for him, home and family for her. The separate spheres argument, although it heaped praise on women for their allegedly superior moral qualities, was meant to exclude them from political life. The reforms discussed in this chapter show clearly that women reformers believed they had a right and a duty to propose solutions for the moral and social problems of the day. Empowered by their own religious beliefs and activism, the Seneca Falls reformers spoke for all American women when they demanded an end to the unfair restrictions they suffered as women.

QUICK REVIEW

Seneca Falls Convention

◆ 1848: First women's rights convention in American history.

◆ Every year after 1848 conventions gathered to work for equality.

◆ Efforts resulted in political and legal advances.

CONCLUSION

Beginning in the 1820s, the market revolution changed the size and social order of America's preindustrial cities and towns. Immigration, dramatically rapid population growth, and changes in working life and class structure created a host of new urban problems. Older, face-to-face methods of social control no longer worked. To fill the gap, new kinds of associations—the political party, the religious crusade, the reform cause, the union movement—sprang up. These associations were new manifestations of the deep human desire for social

11–13
Sojourner Truth, Address to the Woman's Rights Convention, Akron, Ohio (1851)

CHRONOLOGY

1817	American Colonization Society founded.
1820s	Shaker colonies grow.
1826	American Society for the Promotion of Temperance founded.
1827	Workingmen's Party founded in Philadelphia.
	Freedom's Journal begins publication.
	Public school movement begins in Massachusetts.
1829	David Walker's *Appeal to the Colored Citizens of the World* is published.
1830	Joseph Smith founds Church of Jesus Christ of Latter-Day Saints (Mormon Church).
	Charles G. Finney's revivals in Rochester.
1831	William Lloyd Garrison begins publishing antislavery newspaper, the *Liberator*.
1832	Immigration begins to increase.
1833	American Anti-Slavery Society founded by William Lloyd Garrison and Theodore Weld.
1834	First Female Moral Reform Society founded in New York.
	National Trades Union formed.

1836	Congress passes "gag rule" to prevent discussion of antislavery petitions.
1837	Angelina Grimké addresses Massachusetts legislature.
	Sarah Grimké, *Letters on the Equality of the Sexes and the Condition of Women*.
	Panic begins seven-year depression.
1839	Theodore Weld publishes *American Slavery As It Is*.
1840s	New York and Boston complete public water systems.
1840	Liberty Party founded.
1843	Millerites await the end of the world.
	Dorothea Dix spearheads asylum reform movement.
1844	Mormon leader Joseph Smith killed by mob.
1845	New York creates city police force.
	Beginning of Irish Potato Famine and mass Irish immigration into the United States.
1846	Mormons begin migration to the Great Salt Lake.
1848	Women's Rights Convention at Seneca Falls.

connection, for continuity, and—especially in the growing cities—for social order. A striking aspect of these associations was the uncompromising nature of the attitudes and beliefs on which they were based. Most groups were formed of like-minded people who wanted to impose their will on others. Such intolerance boded ill for the future. If political parties, religious bodies, and reform groups were to splinter along sectional lines (as happened in the 1850s), political compromise would be very difficult. In the meantime, however, Americans came to terms with the market revolution by engaging in a passion for improvement. As a perceptive foreign observer, Francis Grund, noted, "Americans love their country not as it is but as it will be."

SUMMARY

Urban America The market revolution radically altered the American city. Substantial growth stimulated by immigration changed patterns of living and culture. These changes also created the need for social order.

The Labor Movement and Urban Politics Changes in work led to the erosion of traditional labor organization and politics. Related to individual conditions and immigration, new forms arose.

Social Reform Movements Evangelical religion stimulated the rise of a broad social reform movement launched largely by the middle class, especially women. It affected such diverse areas of society as education, prisons, and moral reform. This era also witnessed the emergence of utopianism and new religious sects.

Antislavery and Abolitionism The antislavery movement gave rise to a strong abolitionist campaign involving white and black people. In time, abolition of slavery became a national political issue.

The Women's Rights Movement Involvement in social reform movements led women to found organizations to pursue their rights.

REVIEW QUESTIONS

1. What impact did the new immigration of the 1840s and 1850s have on American cities?

2. Why did urbanization produce so many problems?

3. What motivated the social reformers of the period? Were they benevolent helpers or dictatorial social controllers? Study several reform causes and discuss similarities and differences among them.

4. Abolitionism differed little from other reforms in its tactics, but the effects of antislavery activism were politically explosive. Why was this so?

KEY TERMS

American Colonization Society(p. 342)

American Society for the Promotion of Temperance(p. 339)

Appeal to the Colored Citizens of the World(p. 342)

Declaration of Sentiments(p. 326)

Female Moral Reform Society(p. 340)

Liberty Party(p. 344)

Sabbatarianism(p. 338)

Seneca Falls convention(p. 340)

Shakers(p. 341)

Tammany Society(p. 336)

Temperance(p. 339)

RECOMMENDED READING

Tyler Anbinder, *Five Points* (2001). A social history of New York's most notorious slum.

Arthur Bestor, *Backwoods Utopias* (1950). The standard work on utopian communities.

Paul Boyer, *Urban Masses and Moral Order in America, 1820–1920* (1978). Interprets reform as an effort to reestablish the moral order of the preindustrial community.

Amy Bridges, *A City in the Republic: Antebellum New York and the Origins of Machine Politics* (1984). An innovative look at the transition from elite political control to machine politics.

David Grimsted, *American Mobbing, 1828–1865: Toward Civil War* (1998). A national perspective on mob violence, North and South, including political violence.

Oscar Handlin, *Boston's Immigrants: A Study in Acculturation*, rev. ed. (1959). A pathbreaking exploration of conflict and adaptation among Boston's Irish community.

James Oliver Horton and Lois E. Horton, *In Hope of Liberty: Culture, Community and Protest Among Northern Free Blacks, 1700–1860* (1997). A fine portrait that adds the perspective of change over time to earlier studies.

Eric Lott, *Love and Theft: Blackface Minstrelsy and the American Working Class* (1993). Explores the complicated relationships between working-class amusements and racial attitudes.

Steven Mintz, *Moralists and Modernizers: America's Pre-Civil War Reformers* (1995). A brief, but inclusive study of reforms and reformers.

David Roediger, *The Wages of Whiteness* (1991). Explores the links among artisanal republicanism, labor organization, and white racism.

David Rothman, *The Discovery of the Asylum: Social Order and Disorder in the New Republic* (1971). Explores institutional reforms.

Mary Ryan, *Civic Wars: Democracy and Public Life in the American City During the Nineteenth Century* (1997). A study of New York, New Orleans, and San Francisco that argues that urban popular culture was "meeting-place democracy" in action.

Kathryn Sklar, *Catharine Beecher: A Study in American Domesticity* (1973). An absorbing "life and times" that explores the possibilities and limits of women's roles in the early nineteenth century.

Sean Wilentz, *Chants Democratic: New York City and the Rise of the American Working Class, 1788–1850* (1983). An important book, rooted in social history, that reveals how workers acted upon their understanding of republicanism in confronting the changes wrought by the market revolution.

They immigrate constantly, hardly no one
to prevent them, and take possession of
the location that best suits them without either
asking leave or going through any formality
other than that of building their homes.
—José Maria Sánchez

Albert Bierstadt (1830–1902), "The Oregon Trail" (oil on canvas).
Private Collection/Bridgeman Art Library International Ltd., New York

14

THE TERRITORIAL EXPANSION OF THE UNITED STATES

1830s–1850s

WHAT ROLE did the federal government play in the exploration of the West?

WHAT SPARKED the Texas revolt?

WHAT WERE the most important consequences of the Mexican-American War?

WHAT KINDS of people participated in the California Gold Rush?

WHAT KEY factors explain the outcome of the election of 1848?

AMERICAN COMMUNITIES

Texans and Tejanos "Remember the Alamo!"

FOR THIRTEEN DAYS IN FEBRUARY AND MARCH 1836, A FORCE OF 187 Texans held the mission fortress known as the Alamo against a siege by 5,000 Mexican troops under General Antonio López de Santa Anna, president of Mexico. Santa Anna had come north to subdue rebellious Texas, the northernmost part of the Mexican province of Coahuila y Tejas and to place it under central authority. On March 6 he ordered a final assault, and in brutal fighting that claimed over 1,500 Mexican lives, his army took the mission. All the defenders were killed, including Commander William Travis and the well-known frontiersmen Jim Bowie and Davy Crockett. It was a crushing defeat for the Texans, but the cry "Remember the Alamo!" rallied their remaining forces, which, less than two months later, routed the Mexican army and forced Santa Anna to grant Texas independence from Mexico. Today the Alamo, in San Antonio, is one of the most cherished historic shrines in the United States.

But memory is selective: some things tend to be forgotten. Within a generation of the uprising few remembered that many Tejanos, Spanish-speaking people born in Texas, had joined with American settlers fighting for Texas independence. The Americans were concentrated in the central and eastern portions of the huge Texas territory, where during the 1820s the Mexican government had authorized several colonies managed by empresarios (land agents) like Stephen F. Austin. These settler communities consisted mostly of farmers from the Mississippi Valley, who introduced slavery and cotton growing to the rich lands of coastal and upland Texas.

The Tejano community, descended from eighteenth-century Spanish and Mexican settlers, included wealthy rancheros who raised cattle on the shortgrass prairies of south Texas, as well as the cowboys known as vaqueros and the peónes, or poor tenant farmers. Although there was relatively little contact between the Americans and Tejanos, their leaders interacted in San Antonio, the center of regional government. The Tejano elite welcomed the American immigrants and were enthusiastic about their plans for the economic development of Texas. Many Americans married into elite Tejano families, who hoped that by thus assimilating and sharing power with the Americans they could not only maintain but also strengthen their community.

The Mexican state, however, was politically and socially unstable during these first years after its successful revolt against Spain in 1821. Liberals favored a loose federal union, conservatives a strong central state. As a northern frontier province, Texas did not have the benefits of statehood; as a result most Tejanos found themselves taking the liberal side in the struggle, opting for more local control over government activities. When, in 1828, the conservative centralists came to power in Mexico

City and decided the Americans had too much influence in Texas, many Tejanos rose up with the Americans in opposition. In 1832, the Tejano elite of San Antonio and many prominent rancheros went on record in favor of provincial autonomy and a strong role for the Americans.

One of the leaders of the San Antonio community was the wealthy ranchero Juan Nepomuceno Seguín. As Santa Anna's army approached from the south, Seguín recruited a company of Tejano volunteers and joined the American force inside the walls of the Alamo. During the siege, Commander Travis sent Seguín and some of his men for reinforcements. Stopped by Mexican troops on his way across the lines, Seguín called out, "¡Somos paisanos!" (We are countrymen!), confusing the guards just long enough for Seguín and his men to make their escape despite the hail of gunfire that quickly ensued. Seguín returned from his unsuccessful mission to find the burned bodies of the Alamo defenders, including seven San Antonio Tejanos. "Texas será libre!" (Texas shall be free!) Seguín called out as he directed the burial of the Alamo defenders.

In April, Seguín led a regiment of Tejanos in the decisive battle of San Jacinto that won independence for Texas.

At first Tejanos were pleased with independence and played an important political role in the new Republic of Texas. The liberal Lorenzo de Zavala was chosen vice president, and Seguín became the mayor of San Antonio. But soon things began to change, illustrating a recurring pattern in the American occupation of new lands—a striking shift in the relations between different cultures in frontier areas. Most commonly, in the initial stage newcomers blended with native peoples, creating a "frontier of inclusion." The first hunters, trappers, and traders on every American frontier—west of the Appalachians, in the Southwest, and in the Far West—married into the local community and tried to learn native ways. Outnumbered Americans adapted to local societies as a matter of simple survival.

A second, unstable stage occurred when the number of Americans increased and they began occupying more and more land or, as in California, "rushing" in great numbers to mine gold, overrunning native communities. The usual result was warfare and the rapid growth of hostility and racial prejudice—all of which was largely absent in earlier days.

A third stage—that of stable settlement—occurred when the native community had been completely "removed" or isolated. In this "frontier of exclusion," racial mixing was rare. Generally, when Europeans pushed American Indians onto reservations they cut themselves off from sources of human history that could have helped them more fully understand the country into which

San Antonio

they had moved. And in Texas, American settlers—initially invited in by Mexicans and Tejanos—developed an anti-Mexican passion, regarding all Spanish-speakers as their Mexican enemies rather than their Tejano allies.

Unscrupulous Americans exploited these prejudices to acquire Tejano property. If the rancheros were "sufficiently scared," one wrote, they would "make an advantageous sale of their lands," and if "two or three hundred of our troops should be stationed here, I have no doubt but a man could make some good speculations." Tejanos were attacked and forced from their homes; some of their villages were burned to the ground. "On the pretext that they were Mexicans," Seguín wrote, Americans treated Tejanos "worse than brutes . . . My countrymen ran to me for protection against the assaults or exactions of these adventurers."

But even in his capacity as mayor Seguín could do little, and in 1842 he and his family, like hundreds of other Tejano families, fled south to Mexico in fear for their lives.

Thus, the Tejanos became symbols of a romanticized past rather than full participants in the building of Western communities. Spanish-speaking communities in Texas, and later in New Mexico and California, like the communities of Indians throughout the West, became conquered peoples. "White folks and Mexicans were never made to live together," a Texas woman told a traveler a few years after the revolution. "The Mexicans had no business here," she said, and the Americans might "just have to get together and drive them all out of the country." The descendants of the first European settlers of the American Southwest had become foreigners in the land their people had lived in for two centuries.

EXPLORING THE WEST

There seemed to be no stopping the expansion of the American people. By 1840 they had occupied all of the land east of the Mississippi River and had organized all of it (except for Florida and Wisconsin) into states. Of the ten states admitted to the Union between 1800 and 1840, all but one were west of the Appalachian Mountains. Less than sixty years after the United States gained its independence, the majority of its population lived west of the original thirteen states. This rapid expansion was caused by the market revolution and, especially, the extraordinary expansion of transportation and commerce (see Chapter 12).

Many Americans looked eagerly westward to the vast unsettled reaches of the Louisiana Purchase: to Texas, Santa Fé, and trade with Mexico, and even to the Far West, where New England sea captains had been trading for furs since the 1790s. By 1848 the United States had gained all of these coveted Western lands. This chapter examines the way the United States became a continental nation, forming many frontier communities in the process. Exploring the vast continent of North America and gaining an understanding of its geography took several centuries and the efforts of many people.

THE FUR TRADE

The fur trade, which flourished from the 1670s to the 1840s, was an important spur to exploration on the North American continent. In the 1670s, the British Hudson's Bay Company and its French Canadian rival, Montreal's North West Company, began exploring beyond the Great Lakes in the Canadian West in search of beaver pelts. Traders and trappers for both companies depended on the goodwill and cooperation of the native peoples of the region.

Not until the 1820s were American companies able to challenge British dominance of the trans-Mississippi fur trade. In 1824, William Henry Ashley of the Rocky Mountain Fur Company instituted the "rendezvous" system. This yearly trade fair, was a boisterous, polyglot, many-day affair at which trappers of many nationalities—Americans and Indian peoples, French Canadians, and métis, as well as Mexicans from Santa Fé and Taos—gathered to trade, drink, and gamble.

WHAT ROLE did the federal government play in the exploration of the West?

IMAGE KEY
for pages 346–347

a. A tanned buffalo skin.
b. A long wooden pipe of the Mandan tribe.
c. Albert Bierstadt (1830–1902), "The Oregon Trail."
d. Cactus with a large pink flower.
e. A model of a Plains Indian tepee.
f. John Gast's "American Progress," c. 1872, depicting America heading westward.
g. "The Interior of Fort Laramie," 1858–1860, by Alfred Jacob Miller.
h. "General Winfield Scott at the Siege of Vera Cruz, March 1847" by Nathaniel Currier.
i. A drawing of an 1855 San Francisco gambling saloon.

The artist Alfred Jacob Miller, a careful observer of the Western fur trade, shows us a mountain man and his Indian wife in his 1837 *Bourgeois Walker & His Wife.* Both Walker and his wife worked together to trap and prepare beaver pelts for market.

The Walters Art Museum, Baltimore (37.1940.78).

Santa Fé Trail   The 900-mile trail opened by American merchants for trading purposes following Mexico's liberalization of the formerly restrictive trading policies of Spain.

Like the British and French before them, most American trappers sought accommodation and friendship with Indian peoples: nearly half of them contracted long-lasting marriages with Indian women, who not only helped in the trapping and curing of furs but also acted as vital diplomatic links between the white and Indian worlds.

For all its adventure, the American fur trade was short-lived. By the 1840s, the population of beaver in Western streams was virtually destroyed, and the day of the mountain man was over.

GOVERNMENT-SPONSORED EXPLORATION

The federal government played a major role in the exploration and development of the West. The exploratory and scientific aspects of the Lewis and Clark expedition in 1804–1806 set a precedent for many government-financed quasi-military expeditions. In 1806 and 1807, Lieutenant Zebulon Pike led an expedition to the Rocky Mountains in Colorado. Major Stephen Long's exploration and mapping of the Great Plains in the years 1819–1820 was part of a show of force meant to frighten British fur trappers out of the West. Then, in 1843 and 1844, another military explorer, John C. Frémont, mapped the overland trails to Oregon and California.

Beginning with Long's expedition, the results of these surveys were published by the government, complete with maps, illustrations, and, after the Civil War, photographs. These publications fed a strong popular appetite for pictures of the breathtaking scenery of the Far West and information about its inhabitants. These images of the American West made a powerful contribution to the emerging American self-image. American pride in the land—the biggest of this, the longest of that, the most spectacular of something else—was founded on the images brought home by government surveyors and explorers.

EXPANSION AND INDIAN POLICY

While American artists like Alfred Jacob Miller and George Catlin were painting the way of life of western Indian peoples, eastern Indian tribes were being removed from their homelands to Indian Territory (present-day Oklahoma, Kansas, and Nebraska), a region west of Arkansas, Missouri, and Iowa on the eastern edge of the Great Plains, widely regarded as unfarmable and popularly known as the Great American Desert. The justification for this western removal, as Thomas Jefferson had explained early in the century, was the creation of a space where Indian people could live undisturbed by white people while they slowly adjusted to "civilized" ways. But the government officials who negotiated the removals failed to predict the tremendous speed at which white people would settle the West.

As a result, encroachment on Indian Territory was not long in coming. The territory was crossed by the **Santa Fé Trail**, established in 1821; in the 1840s the northern part was crossed by the heavily traveled Overland Trails to California, Oregon, and the Mormon community in Utah. In 1854, the government abolished the northern half of Indian Territory, establishing the Kansas and Nebraska Territories in its place and opening them to immediate white settlement. The tribes of the area—the Potawatomis, Wyandots, Kickapoos, Sauks, Foxes, Delawares, Shawnees, Kaskaskias, Peorias, Piankashaws, Weas, Miamis, Omahas, Otos, and Missouris—signed treaties accepting either vastly reduced reservations or allotments. Those who accepted allotments—sections of private land—often sold them, under pressure, to white people. Thus many of the Indian people who had hoped for independence and escape from white pressures in Indian Territory lost both their autonomy and their tribal identity.

The people in the southern part of Indian Territory, in what is now Oklahoma, fared somewhat better. Those members of the southern tribes—the Cherokees,

MAP EXPLORATION

To explore an interactive version of this map, go to **http://www.prenhall.com/faraghertlc/map14.1**

MAP 14-1

Exploration of the Continent, 1804–1830   Lewis and Clark's "voyage of discovery" of 1804–1806 was the first of many government-sponsored western military expeditions. Crossing the Great Plains in 1806, Lieutenant Zebulon Pike was captured by the Spanish in their territory and taken to Mexico but returned in 1807 via Texas. Major Stephen Long, who crossed the Plains in 1819–1820, found them "arid and forbidding." Meanwhile fur trappers, among them the much-traveled Jedediah Smith, became well acquainted with the West as they hunted beaver for their pelts.

WHAT ROLE did the routes taken by major expeditions westward between 1804 and 1830 play in shaping United States policy in the West?

QUICK REVIEW

Indian Policy

◆ Eastern tribes removed from their homelands to Indian Territory.

◆ Settlement of the West led to encroachment on Indian Territory.

◆ Indians increasingly concentrated in reduced reservations or allotments.

WHAT SPARKED

the Texas revolt?

Chickasaws, Choctaws, Creeks, and Seminoles—who had survived the trauma of forcible removal from the Southeast in the 1830s quickly created impressive new communities. The five tribes divided up the territory and established self-governing nations with their own schools and churches. The societies they created were not so different from the American societies from which they had been expelled. The five tribes even carried slavery west with them: an elite economic group established plantations and shipped their cotton to New Orleans like other Southerners. Until after the Civil War, these southern tribes were able to withstand outside pressures and remain the self-governing communities that treaties had assured them they would be.

THE POLITICS OF EXPANSION

America's rapid expansion had many consequences, but perhaps the most significant was that it reinforced Americans' sense of themselves as pioneering people. In the 1890s Frederick Jackson Turner, America's most famous historian, observed that the repeated experience of settling new frontiers across the continent had shaped Americans into a uniquely adventurous, optimistic, and democratic people. Other historians have disagreed with Turner, but there is no question that his view of the frontier long ago won the battle for popular opinion. Ever since the time of Daniel Boone, venturing into the wilderness has held a special place in the American imagination, seen almost as an American right.

MANIFEST DESTINY, AN EXPANSIONIST IDEOLOGY

How did Americans justify their restless expansionism? In 1845 newspaperman John O'Sullivan coined the phrase by which expansionism became famous. It was, he wrote, "our **manifest destiny** to overspread the continent allotted by Providence for the free development of our yearly multiplying millions." Sullivan argued that Americans had a God-given right to bring the benefits of American democracy to other, more backward peoples—meaning Mexicans and Indians—by force, if necessary. The notion of manifest destiny summed up the powerful combination of pride in what America had achieved and missionary zeal and racist attitudes toward other peoples that lay behind the thinking of many expansionists.

Behind the bravado was some new international thinking about the economic future of the United States. After the devastating Panic of 1837 (see Chapter 10), many politicians became convinced that the nation's prosperity depended on vastly expanded trade with Asia. Senator Thomas Hart Benton of Missouri had been advocating trade with India by way of the Missouri and Columbia rivers since the 1820s (not the easiest of routes, as Lewis and Clark had shown). Soon Benton and others were pointing out how much Pacific trade would increase if the United States held the magnificent harbors of the west coast, among them Puget Sound in the Oregon Country, held jointly with Britain, and the bays of San Francisco and San Diego, both in Mexican-held California.

Expansionism was deeply tied to national politics. O'Sullivan, whose "manifest destiny" became the expansionist watchword, was not a neutral observer: he was the editor of the *Democratic Review,* a party newspaper. Most Democrats were wholehearted supporters of expansion, whereas many Whigs (especially in the North) opposed it. Whigs welcomed most of the changes wrought by industrialization but advocated strong government policies that would guide growth and development within the country's existing boundaries; they feared (correctly) that expansion would raise the contentious issue of the extension of slavery to new territories.

On the other hand, many Democrats feared the industrialization that the Whigs welcomed. Where the Whigs saw economic progress, Democrats saw economic depres-

Manifest Destiny   Doctrine, first expressed in 1845, that the expansion of white Americans across the continent was inevitable and ordained by God.

sion (the Panic of 1837 was the worst the nation had experienced), uncontrolled urban growth, and growing social unrest. For many Democrats, the answer to the nation's social ills was to continue to follow Thomas Jefferson's vision of establishing agriculture in the new territories in order to counterbalance industrialization (see Chapter 9). Another factor in the political struggle over expansion in the 1840s was that many Democrats were Southerners, for whom the continual expansion of cotton-growing lands was a matter of social faith as well as economic necessity.

These were politicians' reasons. The average farmer moved west for many other reasons: land hunger, national pride, plain and simple curiosity, and a sense of adventure.

QUICK REVIEW

Manifest Destiny

◆ Manifest Destiny distinguished by its explicitly racial component.

◆ Doctrine operated as a self-serving justification for territorial aggrandizement.

◆ Manifest Destiny associated with Democratic party.

THE OVERLAND TRAILS

The 2,000-mile trip on the Overland Trails from the banks of the Missouri River to Oregon and California usually took seven months, sometimes more. Travel was slow, dangerous, tedious, and exhausting. Forced to lighten their loads as animals died and winter weather threatened, pioneers often arrived at their destination with little food and few belongings. Uprooted from family and familiar surroundings, pioneers faced the prospect of being, in the poignant and much-used biblical phrase, "strangers in a strange land." Yet despite the risks, settlers streamed west: 5,000 to Oregon by 1845 and about 3,000 to California by 1848 (before the discovery of gold).

Pioneers had many motives for making the trip. Glowing reports from Oregon's Willamette Valley, for example, seemed to promise economic opportunity and healthy surroundings, an alluring combination to farmers in the malaria-prone Midwest who had been hard hit by the Panic of 1837. But rational motives do not tell the whole story. Many men were motivated by a sense of adventure, by a desire to experience the unknown, or, as they put it, to "see the elephant." Women were more likely to think of the trip as *A Pioneer's Search for an Ideal Home*, the title that Phoebe Judson chose for her account of her family's 1852 trip to Oregon.

Few pioneers traveled alone, partly because they feared Indian attack (which was rare), but largely because they needed help fording rivers or crossing mountains with heavy wagons. Most Oregon pioneers traveled with their families but usually also joined a larger group, forming a "train." In the earliest years, when the route was still uncertain, trains hired a "pilot," generally a former fur trapper. Often the men of the wagon train drew up semimilitary constitutions, electing a leader. Democratic as this process appeared, not everyone was willing to obey the leader, and many trains experienced dissension and breakups along the trail. But in essence all pioneers—men, women, and children—were part of a new, westward-moving community in which they had to accept both the advantages and disadvantages of community membership.

Wagon trains started westward as soon as the prairies were green (thus ensuring feed for the livestock). The daily routine was soon established. Men took care of the moving equipment and the animals, while the women cooked and kept track of the children. Slowly, at a rate of about fifteen miles a day, the wagon trains moved west along the Platte River, crossing the Continental Divide at South Pass in present-day Wyoming. West of the Rockies the climate was much drier. The long, dusty stretch along the Snake River in present-day southern Idaho finally gave way to Oregon's steep and difficult Blue Mountains and to the dangerous rafting down the Columbia River, in which many drowned and all were drenched by the cold winter rains of the Pacific Northwest. California-bound migrants faced even worse hazards: the complete lack of water in the Humbolt Sink region of northern Nevada and the looming Sierra

12-4
John L. O'Sullivan, "The Great Nation of Futurity" (1845)

17-2
Lydia Allen Rudd, Diary of Westward Travel (1852)

MAP EXPLORATION

To explore an interactive version of this map, go to
http://www.prenhall.com/faraghertlc/map14.2

MAP 14-2

The Overland Trails, 1840 All the great trails west started at the Missouri River. The Oregon, California, and Mormon Trails followed the Platte River into Wyoming, crossed South Pass, and divided in western Wyoming. The much harsher Santa Fé Trail stretched 900 miles southwest across the Great Plains. All of the trails crossed Indian Territory and, to greater or lesser extent, Mexican possessions as well.

WHAT DANGERS did settlers face as they followed the overland trails?

Oregon Trail Overland trail of more than two thousand miles that carried American settlers from the Midwest to new settlements in Oregon, California, and Utah.

Nevadas, which had to be crossed before the winter snows came. (Members of the ill-fated Donner party, snowbound on the Nevada side of that range in 1846–1847, resorted to cannibalism before they were rescued.)

In addition to the ever-present tedium and exhaustion, wagon trains were beset by such trail hazards as illness and accident. Danger from Indian attack, which all pioneers feared, was actually very small. It appears that unprovoked white attacks on Indians were more common than the reverse.

In contrast, cholera killed at least a thousand people a year in 1849 and in the early 1850s when it was common along sections of the trail along the Platte River. Spread by contaminated water, cholera caused vomiting and diarrhea, which in turn led to extreme dehydration and death, often in one night. In the afflicted regions, trailside graves were a frequent and grim sight. Drownings were not uncommon, nor were accidental ax wounds or shootings, and children sometimes fell out of wagons and were run over.

By 1860 almost 300,000 people had traveled the Overland Trails to Oregon or California. Ruts from the wagon wheels can be seen in a number of places along the route even today. In 1869, the completion of the transcontinental railroad marked the end of the wagon train era.

OREGON

The American settlement of Oregon provides a capsule example of the stages of frontier development. The first contacts between the region's Indian peoples and Europeans were commercial. Spanish, British, Russian, and American ships traded for sea otter skins from the 1780s to about 1810. Subsequently land-based groups scoured the region for beaver skins as well. In this first "frontier of inclusion" there were frequent sexual contacts between Indians and Europeans.

Both Great Britain and the United States claimed the Oregon Country by right of discovery, but in the Convention of 1818 the two nations agreed to occupy it jointly, postponing a final decision on its disposition. In reality, the British clearly dominated the region. In 1824 the Hudson's Bay Company consolidated Britain's position by establishing a major fur trading post at Fort Vancouver, on the banks of the Columbia River. Like all other fur-trading ventures, the post exemplified the racial mixing of a "frontier of inclusion." Fort Vancouver housed a polyglot population of eastern Indians (Delawares and Iroquois), local Chinook Indians, French and métis from Canada, British traders, and Hawaiians.

The first permanent European settlers in Oregon were retired fur trappers and their Indian wives and families. They favored a spot in the lush and temperate Willamette Valley that became known as French Prairie, although the inhabitants were a mixed group of Americans, British, French Canadians, Indian peoples, and métis. The next to arrive were Protestant and Catholic missionaries. None of these missionaries was very successful. Epidemics had taken the lives of many of the region's peoples, and those who were left were disinclined to give up their nomadic life and settle down as the missionaries wanted them to do.

Finally, in the 1840s, came the Midwest farmers who would make up the majority of Oregon's permanent settlers, carried on the wave of enthusiasm known as "Oregon fever" and lured by free land and patriotism. By 1845 Oregon boasted 5,000 American settlers, most of them living in the Willamette Valley.

For these early settlers, life was at first very difficult. Most arrived in late autumn, exhausted from the strenuous overland journey. They could not begin to farm until the spring, and so they depended on the earlier settlers for their survival over the winter. In the earliest years American settlers got vital help from the Hudson's Bay Company, even though its director, John McLoughlin, had been ordered by the British government not to encourage American settlement.

Joint occupancy of Oregon by the Americans and the British continued until 1846. Initially, a peaceful outcome seemed doubtful. President James K. Polk coined the belligerent slogan "Fifty-four Forty or Fight," suggesting that the United States would go to war if it didn't get control of all the territory south of 54°40′ north latitude, the border between Russian Alaska and British Canada. In office, however, Polk was willing to compromise. In June 1846, Britain and the United States concluded a treaty establishing the 49th parallel as the U.S.–Canada border but leaving the island of Vancouver in British hands. In 1849 the Hudson's Bay Company closed Fort Vancouver and moved its operations to Victoria, thus ending the Pacific Northwest's largely successful experience with joint occupancy. Oregon's Donation Land Claim Act of 1850 codified the practice of giving 320 acres to each white male age eighteen or over and 640 acres to each married couple to settle in the territory (African Americans, Hawaiians, and American Indians were excluded).

The white settlers realized that they had to forge strong community bonds if they hoped to survive on their distant frontier. Cooperation and mutual aid were the rule. Until well into the 1850s, residents organized yearly parties that traveled back along the last stretches of the **Oregon Trail** to help straggling parties making their way to the territory. Kinship networks were strong and vital: many pioneers came to join family who had migrated before them.

Relations with the small and unthreatening disease-thinned local Indian tribes were generally peaceful until 1847, when Cayuse Indians killed the missionaries Marcus and Narcissa Whitman. Their deaths triggered a series of "wars" against the remaining native people. A "frontier of exclusion" had been achieved. Nonetheless, the process by which Oregon became part of the United States (it was admitted as a state in 1859) was relatively peaceful, especially when compared with American expansion into the Spanish provinces of New Mexico and Texas.

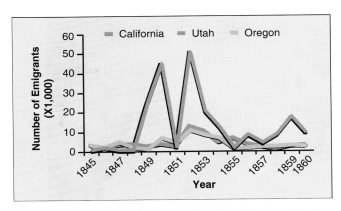

Overland Emigration to Oregon, California, and Utah, 1840–1860

Before 1849 the westward migration consisted primarily of family groups going to Oregon or Utah. The discovery of gold in California dramatically changed the migration: through 1854 most migrants were single men "rushing" to California, which remained the favored destination up until 1860. Over the twenty-year period from 1840 to 1860 the Overland Trails were transformed from difficult and dangerous routes to well-marked and well-served thoroughfares.

John Unruh Jr., *The Plains Across* (Champaign-Urbana: University of Illinois Press, 1979), pp. 119–20.

This watercolor of tiny Oregon City in 1846 suggests how small the American population of the Oregon Territory was when its status was being decided in America's favor. With just 953 inhabitants in 1850, Oregon City was the largest city in the territory.

Henry James Warre, *American Settlement of Oregon City, 1846*. Watercolor. Courtesy American Antiquarian Society (#33).

Alfred Jacob Miller painted the busy life of Fort Laramie, a multiracial trading fort, in 1837. Bent's Fort, another multiracial trading center, would have looked much like this.

The Interior of Fort Laramie, 1858–1860. The Walters Art Museum, Baltimore (37.1940.1).

12-3
Across the Plains with Catherine Sager Pringle in 1844

Tejanos Persons of Spanish or Mexican descent born in Texas.

Painted by George Catlin about 1834, this scene, *Comanche Village Life,* shows how the everyday life of the Comanches was tied to buffalo. The women in the foreground are scraping buffalo hide, and buffalo meat can be seen drying on racks. The men and boys may be planning their next buffalo hunt.

Art Resource, N.Y.

THE SANTA FÉ TRADE

Commerce with Santa Fé, first settled by colonists from Mexico in 1609 and the center of the Spanish frontier province of New Mexico, had long been desired by American traders, but Spain had forcefully resisted American penetration. For example, Lieutenant Zebulon Pike's Great Plains and Rocky Mountain exploration of 1806–1807 ended ignominiously with his capture by Spanish soldiers.

When Mexico gained its independence from Spain in 1821, this exclusionary policy changed. American traders were now welcome in Santa Fé, but the trip over the legendary Santa Fé Trail from Independence, Missouri, was a forbidding 900 miles of arid plains, deserts, and mountains. On the Santa Fé trail, unlike the Oregon Trail, there was serious danger of Indian attack, for neither the Comanches nor the Apaches of the southern high plains tolerated trespassers. In 1825, at the urging of Senator Benton and others, Congress voted federal protection for the Santa Fé Trail, even though much of it lay in Mexican territory. The number of people venturing west in the trading caravans increased yearly because the profits were so great (the first American trader to reach Santa Fé, William Becknell, realized a thousand percent profit). By the 1840s, a few hundred American trappers and traders (called *extranjeros,* or "foreigners") lived permanently in New Mexico. In Santa Fé, some American merchants married daughters of important local families.

Settlements and trading posts soon grew up along the long Santa Fé Trail. One of the most famous was Bent's Fort, on the Arkansas River in what is now eastern Colorado, which did a brisk trade in beaver skins and buffalo robes. Like most other trading posts, it had a multiethnic population. In the 1840s the occupants included housekeeper Josefa Tafoya of Taos, whose husband was a carpenter from Pennsylvania; an African American cook; a French tailor from New Orleans; Mexican muleteers; and a number of Indian women, including the two Cheyenne women who were the (successive) wives of William Bent, cofounder of the fort. The three small communities of Pueblo, Hardscrabble, and Greenhorn, spinoffs of Bent's Fort, were populated by men of all nationalities and their Mexican and Indian wives. All three communities lived by trapping, hunting, and a little farming. This racially and economically mixed existence was characteristic of all early trading frontiers except for Texas.

MEXICAN TEXAS

In 1821, when Mexico gained its independence from Spain, there were 2,240 Tejano (Spanish-speaking) residents of Texas. Established in 1716 as a buffer against possible French attack on New Spain, the main Texas settlements of Nacogdoches, Goliad, and San Antonio remained small, far-flung frontier outposts (see Chapter 5). As elsewhere in New Spain, society was divided into two classes: the *ricos* (rich), who claimed Spanish descent, and the mixed-blood *pobres* (poor). Tejano town life was traditionally hierarchical, dominated by the ricos, who were connected by blood or marriage with the great ranching families. The most colorful figures on the ranchos were *mestizo* (mixed-blood) *vaqueros,* renowned for their horsemanship; Americanization of their name made "buckaroos" of the American cowboys to whom they later taught their skills. Most **Tejanos** were neither ricos nor vaqueros but small farmers or common laborers who led hardscrabble frontier lives. But all Tejanos, rich and poor, faced the constant threat of raids by Comanche Indians.

Legendary warriors, the Comanches raided the small Texas settlements at will and even struck deep into Mexico itself. The nomadic Comanches followed the immense buffalo herds on which they depended for food and clothing. Their relentless raids on the Texas settlements rose from a determination to hold onto this rich buffalo territory, for the buffalo provided all that they wanted. They had no interest in being converted by mission priests or incorporated into mixed-race trading communities.

AMERICANS IN TEXAS

In 1821, seeking to increase the strength of its buffer zone between the heart of Mexico and the marauding Comanches, the Mexican government granted Moses Austin of Missouri an area of 18,000 square miles within the territory of Texas. Moses died shortly thereafter, and the grant was taken up by his son Stephen F. Austin, who became the first American *empresario* (land agent). From the beginning, the American settlement of Texas differed markedly from that of other frontiers. Elsewhere, Americans frequently settled on land to which Indian peoples still held title, or, as in the case of Oregon, they occupied lands to which other countries also made claim. In contrast, the Texas settlement was fully legal: Austin and other **empresarios** owned their lands as a result of formal contracts with the Mexican government. In exchange, Austin agreed that he and his colonists would become Mexican citizens and would adopt the Catholic religion.

Additionally, in startling contrast with the usual frontier free-for-all, Austin's community was populated with handpicked settlers, Austin insisting that "no frontiersman who has no other occupation than that of hunter will be received— no drunkard, no gambler, no profane swearer, no idler." Austin chose instead prosperous Southern slaveowners eager to expand the lands devoted to cotton. Soon Americans (including African American slaves, to whose presence the Mexican government turned a blind eye) outnumbered Tejanos by nearly two to one: in 1830 there were an estimated 7,000 Americans and 4,000 Tejanos living in Texas.

The Austin settlement of 1821 was followed by others, twenty-six in all, concentrating in the fertile river bottoms of east Texas (along the Sabine River) and south central Texas (the Brazos and the Colorado rivers). These large settlements were highly organized farming enterprises whose principal crop was cotton, grown by African American slave labor and sold in the international market. By the early 1830s, Americans in Texas, ignoring the border between Mexican Texas and the United States, were sending an estimated $500,000 worth of goods (mostly cotton) yearly to New Orleans for export.

Austin's colonists and those who settled later were predominantly Southerners who viewed Texas as a natural extension of the cotton frontier in Mississippi and Louisiana (see Chapter 11). These settlers created "enclaves" (self-contained communities) that had little contact with Tejanos or Indian peoples. In fact, although they lived in Mexican territory, most Americans never bothered to learn Spanish. Nor, in spite of Austin's promises, did they become Mexican citizens or adopt the Catholic religion. Yet because of the nature of agreements made by the empresarios, the Americans could not set up local American-style governments like the one created by settlers in Oregon. Like the immigrants who flooded into east coast cities (see Chapter 13) the Americans in Texas were immigrants to another country—but one they did not intend to adapt to.

Empresarios Agents who received a land grant from the Spanish or Mexican government in return for organizing settlements.

For a brief period Texas was big enough to hold three communities: Comanche, Tejano, and American. The nomadic Comanches rode the high plains of northern and western Texas, raiding settlements, primarily for horses. The Tejanos maintained their ranchos and missions mostly in the South, while American farmers occupied the eastern and South central sections. Each group would fight to hold its land: the Comanches, their rich hunting grounds; the Mexicans, their towns and ranchos; and the newcomers, the Americans, their rich land grants.

THE TEXAS REVOLT

The balance among the three communities in Texas was broken in 1828, when centrists gained control of the government in Mexico City and, in a dramatic shift of policy, decided to exercise firm control over the northern province. As the Mexican government restricted American immigration, outlawed slavery, levied customs, duties and taxes, and planned other measures, Americans seethed and talked of rebellion. Bolstering their cause were as many as 20,000 additional Americans, many of them openly expansionist, who flooded into Texas after 1830. These most recent settlers did not intend to become Mexican citizens. Instead, they planned to take over Texas.

Between 1830 and 1836, in spite of the mediation efforts of Austin (who was imprisoned for eighteen months by the Mexican government for his pains), the mood on both the Mexican and the American-Texan sides became more belligerent. In the fall of 1835 war finally broke out. After the disastrous defeat at the **Alamo**, the Mexican general Antonio López de Santa Anna pursued the remaining army of American and Tejano volunteers commanded by General Sam Houston. On April 21, 1836, at the San Jacinto River in eastern Texas, Santa Anna thought he had Houston trapped at last. Confident of victory against the exhausted Texans, Santa Anna's army rested in the afternoon, failing even to post sentries. Although Houston advised against it, Houston's men voted to attack immediately rather than wait until the next morning. Shouting "Remember the Alamo!" for the first time, the Texans completely surprised their opponents and won an overwhelming victory. On May 14, 1836, Santa Anna signed a treaty fixing the southern boundary of the newly independent Republic of Texas at the Rio Grande. The Mexican Congress, however, repudiated the treaty and refused to recognize Texan independence.

THE REPUBLIC OF TEXAS

In the eyes of the Mexicans, the American insistence on the Rio Grande boundary was little more than a blatant effort to stake a claim to New Mexico, an older and completely separate Spanish settlement. An effort by the Republic of Texas in 1841 to capture Santa Fé was easily repulsed.

The Republic of Texas was unexpectedly rebuffed in another quarter as well. The U.S. Congress refused to grant it statehood when, in 1837, Texas applied for admission to the Union. Petitions opposing the admission of a fourteenth slave state (there were then thirteen free states) poured into Congress. Congressman (and former president) John Quincy Adams of Massachusetts led the opposition to the admission of Texas. Congress debated and ultimately dropped the Texas application. President Jackson did extend diplomatic recognition to the Republic of Texas, on March 3, 1837, less than twenty-four hours before he left office.

The unresolved conflict with Mexico put heavy stress on American–Tejano relations. Following a temporary recapture of San Antonio by Mexican forces in 1842, positions hardened. Many more of the Tejano elite fled to Mexico, and Americans discussed banishing or imprisoning all Tejanos until the border issue was settled. This was, of course, impossible. Culturally, San Antonio remained a Mexican city long after the Americans had declared independence. The Americans in

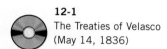

12-1
The Treaties of Velasco
(May 14, 1836)

Alamo   Franciscan mission at San Antonio, Texas that was the site in 1836 of a siege and massacre of Texans by Mexican troops.

MAP EXPLORATION

To explore an interactive version of this map, go to **http://www.prenhall.com/faraghertlc/map14.3**

MAP 14-3A

MAP 14-3B

Texas: From Mexican Province to U.S. State In the space of twenty years, Texas changed shape three times. Initially part of the Mexican province of Coahuila y Tejas, it became the Republic of Texas in 1836, following the Texas Revolt, and was annexed to the United States in that form in 1845. Finally, in the Compromise of 1850 following the Mexican-American War, it took its present shape.

WHO SUPPORTED the formation of the Republic of Texas? What were the forces that resulted in eventual statehood?

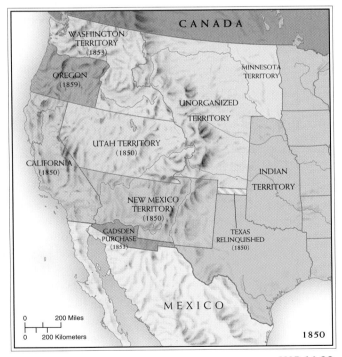

MAP 14-3C

the Republic of Texas were struggling to reconcile American ideals of democracy with the reality of subordinating those with a prior claim, the Tejanos, to the status of a conquered people.

American control over the other Texas residents, the Indians, was also slow in coming. Although the coastal Indian peoples were soon killed or removed, the Comanches still rode the high plains of northern and western Texas. West of the Rio Grande, equally fierce Apache bands were in control. Both groups soon learned to distrust American promises to stay out of their territory, and they did not hesitate to raid settlements and to kill trespassers. Not until after the Civil War and major campaigns by the U.S. Army were these fierce Indian tribes conquered.

TEXAS ANNEXATION AND THE ELECTION OF 1844

Texans continued to press for annexation to the United States, while at the same time seeking recognition and support from Great Britain. The idea of an independent and expansionist republic on its southern border that might gain the support of America's traditional enemy alarmed many Americans. Annexation thus became an urgent matter of national politics. This issue also added to the troubles

359

of the governing Whig Party that was already deeply divided by the policies of John Tyler, who had become president by default when William Harrison died in office (see Chapter 10). Tyler raised the issue of annexation in 1844, hoping thereby to ensure his reelection, but the strategy backfired. Presenting the annexation treaty to Congress, Secretary of State John Calhoun awakened sectional fears by connecting Texas with the urgent need of Southern slave owners to extend slavery.

In a storm of antislavery protest, Whigs rejected the treaty proposed by their own president and ejected Tyler himself from the party. In his place, they chose Henry Clay, the party's longtime standard-bearer, as their presidential candidate. Clay took a noncommittal stance on Texas, favoring annexation, but only if Mexico approved. Since Mexico's emphatic disapproval was well known, Clay's position was widely interpreted as a politician's effort not to alienate voters on either side of the fence.

In contrast, in the Democratic Party wholehearted and outspoken expansionists seized control. Sweeping aside their own senior politician, Van Buren, who like Clay tried to remain uncommitted, the Democrats nominated their first "dark horse" candidate, James K. Polk of Tennessee. They enthusiastically endorsed Polk's platform, which called for "the re-occupation of Oregon and the re-annexation of Texas at the earliest practicable period."

Polk won the 1844 election by the narrow margin of 40,000 popular votes (although he gained 170 electoral votes to Clay's 105). An ominous portent for the Whigs was the showing of James G. Birney of the Liberty Party, who polled 62,000 votes, largely from Northern antislavery Whigs. Birney's third-party campaign was the first political sign of the growing strength of antislavery opinion. Nevertheless, the 1844 election was widely interpreted as a mandate for expansion. Thereupon John Tyler, in one of his last actions as president, pushed through Congress a joint resolution (which did not require the two-thirds approval by the Senate necessary for treaties) for the annexation of Texas.

THE MEXICAN–AMERICAN WAR

James K. Polk lived up to his campaign promises. In 1846 he peacefully added Oregon south of the 49th parallel to the United States; in 1848, following the **Mexican-American War**, he acquired Mexico's northern provinces of California and New Mexico as well. Thus, with the annexation of Texas, the United States, in the short space of three years, had added 1.5 million square miles of territory, an increase of nearly 70 percent. Polk was indeed the "manifest destiny" president.

ORIGINS OF THE WAR

In the spring of 1846, just as the controversy over Oregon was drawing to a peaceful conclusion, tensions with Mexico grew more serious. Because the United States accepted the Texas claim of all land north of the Rio Grande, it found itself embroiled in a border dispute with Mexico. In June 1845, Polk sent General Zachary Taylor to Texas, and by October a force of 3,500 Americans was on the Nueces River with orders to defend Texas in the event of a Mexican invasion.

Polk had something bigger than border protection in mind. He coveted the continent clear to the Pacific Ocean. At the same time that he sent Taylor to Texas, Polk secretly instructed the Pacific naval squadron to seize the California ports if Mexico declared war. He also wrote the American consul in Monterey, Thomas Larkin, that a peaceful takeover of California by its residents—Spanish Mexicans and Americans alike—would not be unwelcome.

WHAT WERE the most important consequences of the Mexican-American War?

12-5
Thomas Corwin, Against the Mexican War (1847)

Mexican-American War War fought between Mexico and the United States between 1846 and 1848 over control of territory in southwest North America.

In November 1845, Polk sent a secret envoy, John Slidell, to Mexico with an offer of $30 million or more for the Rio Grande border in Texas and Mexico's provinces of New Mexico and California. When the Mexican government refused even to receive Slidell, an angry Polk ordered General Taylor and his forces south to the Rio Grande, into the territory that Mexicans considered their soil. In April 1846 a brief skirmish between American and Mexican soldiers broke out in the disputed zone. Polk seized on the event, sending a war message to Congress: "Mexico has passed the boundary of the United States, has invaded our territory and shed American blood upon American soil. . . . War exists, and, notwithstanding all our efforts to avoid it, exists by the act of Mexico herself." This last claim of President Polk's was, of course, contrary to fact. On May 13, 1846, Congress declared war on Mexico.

MAP EXPLORATION

To explore an interactive version of this map, go to **http://www.prenhall.com/faraghertlc/map14.4**

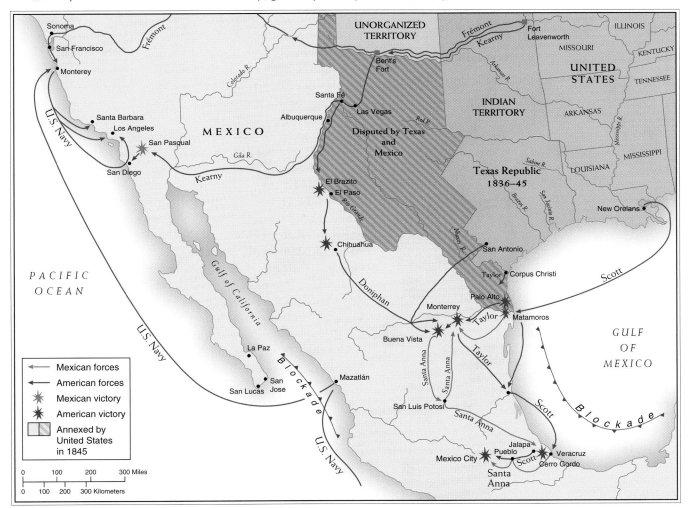

MAP 14-4

The Mexican-American War, 1846–1848   The Mexican-American War began with an advance by U.S. forces into the disputed area between the Nueces River and the Rio Grande in Texas. The war's major battles were fought by General Zachary Taylor in northern Mexico and General Winfield Scott in Vera Cruz and Mexico City. Meanwhile Colonel Stephen Kearny secured New Mexico and, with the help of the U.S. Navy and John C. Frémont's troops, California.

WHY WAS the United States more successful than Mexico in achieving its goals?

QUICK REVIEW

War with Mexico

◆ Polk sought a war that would give United States control of California.

◆ Mexico fought hard but could not match American military.

◆ Treaty of Guadalupe Hidalgo (1848): Mexico gave up claim to Texas north of Rio Grande, Alta California, and New Mexico.

MR. POLK'S WAR

From the beginning, the Mexican-American War was politically divisive. Whig critics in Congress, among them a gawky young congressman from Illinois named Abraham Lincoln, questioned Polk's account of the border incident. They accused the president of misleading Congress and of maneuvering the country into an unnecessary war. It is with these suspicions that the history of congressional concern over the way presidents have exercised their war powers begins. The issue would again be prominent, for example, more than a hundred years later during the Vietnam War and in the Reagan years. As the Mexican-American War dragged on and casualties and costs mounted—13,000 Americans and 50,000 Mexicans died and the United States spent $97 million—opposition increased, especially among Northern antislavery Whigs.

The Northern states witnessed both mass and individual protests against the war. In Massachusetts, the legislature passed a resolution condemning Polk's declaration of war as unconstitutional, and philosopher-writer Henry David Thoreau went to jail rather than pay the taxes he believed would support the war effort. Thoreau's dramatic gesture was undercut by his aunt, who paid his fine after he had spent only one night in jail. Thoreau then returned to his cabin on Walden Pond, where he wrote his classic essay "Civil Disobedience," justifying the individual's moral right to oppose an immoral government.

Whigs termed the war with Mexico "Mr. Polk's War," but the charge was not just a Whig jibe. Although he lacked a military background, Polk assumed the overall planning of the war's strategy.

By the end of 1846 the northern provinces that Polk had coveted were secured, but contrary to his expectations, Mexico refused to negotiate. In February 1847, General Santa Anna of Alamo fame attacked the American troops led by General Taylor at Buena Vista but was repulsed by Taylor's small force. A month later, in March 1847, General Winfield Scott launched an amphibious attack on the coastal city of Veracruz and rapidly captured it. After six months of brutal fighting against stubborn Mexican resistance, American troops reacted bitterly to their high casualty rates by retaliating against Mexican citizens with acts of murder, robbery, and rape. Scott finally took Mexico City in September, and Mexican resistance came to an end.

With the American army went a special envoy, Nicholas Trist, who delivered Polk's terms for peace. In the Treaty of Guadalupe Hidalgo, signed February 2, 1848, Mexico ceded its northern provinces of California and New Mexico (which included present-day Arizona, Utah, Nevada, and part of Colorado) and accepted the Rio Grande as the boundary of Texas. The United States agreed to pay Mexico $15 million and assume about $2 million in individual claims against that nation.

When Trist returned to Washington with the treaty, however, Polk was furious. He had actually recalled Trist after Scott's sweeping victory, intending to send a new envoy with greater demands, but Trist had ignored the recall order. "All

 MAP EXPLORATION

To explore an interactive version of this map, go to
http://www.prenhall.com/faraghertlc/map14.5

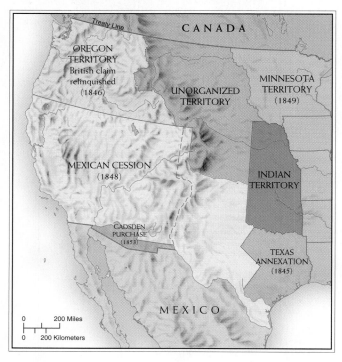

MAP 14-5
Territory Added, 1845–1853 James K. Polk was elected president in 1844 on an expansionist platform. He lived up to most of his campaign rhetoric by gaining the Oregon Country (to the forty-ninth parallel) peacefully from the British, Texas by the presidential action of his predecessor John Tyler, and present-day California, Arizona, Nevada, Utah, New Mexico, and part of Colorado by war with Mexico. In the short space of three years, the size of the United States grew by 70 percent. In 1853, the Gadsden Purchase added another 30,000 square miles.

WHAT CHALLENGES DID the United States face as it absorbed substantial new territories?

Mexico!" had become the phrase widely used by those in favor of further expansion, Polk among them. But two very different groups opposed further expansion. The first group, composed of Northern Whigs, included such notables as Ralph Waldo Emerson, who grimly warned, "The United States will conquer Mexico, but it will be as the man swallows arsenic, which brings him down in turn. Mexico will poison us." The second group was composed of Southerners who realized that Mexicans could not be kept as conquered people but would have to be offered territorial government as Louisiana had been offered in 1804. Senator John C. Calhoun of South Carolina, leading the opposition, warned against admitting "colored and mixed-breed" Mexicans "on an equality with people of the United States." Bowing to these political protests, Polk reluctantly accepted the treaty. A later addition, the $10 million Gadsden Purchase of parts of present-day New Mexico and Arizona, added another 30,000 square miles to the United States in 1853.

The unprecedented immediacy of the news reporting of the Mexican-American War, transmitted for the first time by telegraph, is captured here by Richard Caton Woodville in *War News from Mexico* (1848). By including an African American man and child, the artist is also voicing a political concern about the effect of the war on slavery.

Richard Caton Woodville, *War News from Mexico,* oil on canvas. Manovgian Foundation on loan to the National Gallery of Art, Washington, DC.

THE PRESS AND POPULAR WAR ENTHUSIASM

The Mexican-American War was the first war in which regular, on-the-scene reporting by representatives of the press caught the mass of ordinary citizens up in the war's daily events. Thanks to the recently invented telegraph, newspapers could get the latest news from their reporters, who were among the world's first war correspondents. The "penny press," with more than a decade's experience of reporting urban crime and scandals, was quick to realize that the public's appetite for sensational war news was apparently insatiable. For the first time in American history, accounts by journalists, and not the opinions of politicians, became the major shapers of popular attitudes toward a war.

The reports from the battlefield united Americans in a new way: they became part of a temporary, but highly emotional, community linked by newsprint and buttressed by public gatherings. In the spring of 1846, news of Zachary Taylor's victory at Palo Alto prompted the largest meeting ever held in the cotton textile town of Lowell, Massachusetts. In May 1847, New York City celebrated the twin victories at Veracruz and Buena Vista with fireworks, illuminations, and a "grand procession" estimated at 400,000 people. Generals Taylor and Scott became overnight heroes, and in time both became presidential candidates. Exciting, sobering, and terrible, war news had a deep hold on the popular imagination. It was a lesson newspaper publishers never forgot.

CALIFORNIA AND THE GOLD RUSH

In the early 1840s California was inhabited by many seminomadic Indian tribes whose people numbered approximately 50,000. There were also some 7,000 **Californios**, descendants of the Spanish Mexican pioneers who had begun to settle in 1769.

WHAT KINDS
of people participated
in the California Gold Rush?

RUSSIAN-CALIFORNIO TRADE

The first outsiders to penetrate the isolation of Spanish California were not Americans but Russians. Evading Spanish regulations, Californios traded with the Russian American Company in Sitka, Alaska. A mutually beneficial barter of California food for iron tools and woven cloth from Russia was established in 1806. This arrangement became even brisker after the Russians settled Fort Ross (near present-

Californios   Californians of Spanish descent.

day Mendocino) in 1812. Agricultural productivity declined after 1832, when the Mexican government ordered the secularization of the California missions, and the Russians regretfully turned to the rich farms of the Hudson's Bay Company in the Pacific Northwest for their food supply. In 1841, they sold Fort Ross, and the Russian-Californio connection came to an end.

EARLY AMERICAN SETTLEMENT

It was Johann Augustus Sutter, a Swiss who had settled in California in 1839, becoming a Mexican citizen, who served as a focal point for American settlement in the 1840s. Sutter held a magnificent land grant in the Sacramento Valley. At the center of his holdings was Sutter's Fort, a walled compound that was part living quarters and part supply shop for his vast cattle ranch, which was run largely on forced Indian labor. In the 1840s, Sutter offered valuable support to the handful of American overlanders who chose California over Oregon, the destination preferred by most pioneers. Most of these Americans, keenly aware that they were interlopers in Mexican territory, settled near Sutter in California's Central Valley, away from the Californios clustered along the coast.

The 1840s immigrants made no effort to intermarry with the Californios or to conform to Spanish ways. They were bent on taking over the territory. In June 1846 these Americans banded together at Sonoma in the Bear Flag Revolt (so called because their flag bore a bear emblem), declaring independence from Mexico. The American takeover of California was not confirmed until the Treaty of Guadalupe Hidalgo in 1848. In the meantime, California was regarded by most Americans merely as a remote, sparsely populated frontier, albeit one with splendid potential.

GOLD!

In January 1848 carpenter James Marshall noticed small flakes of gold in the millrace at Sutter's Mill (present-day Coloma). But not until autumn did the east coast hear the first rumors about the discovery of gold in California. The reports were confirmed in mid-November when an army courier arrived in Washington carrying a tea caddy full of gold dust and nuggets. The spirit of excitement and adventure so recently aroused by the Mexican-American War was now directed toward California, the new El Dorado. Thousands left farms and jobs and headed west, by land and by sea, to make their fortune. Later known as "forty-niners" for the year the Gold Rush began in earnest, these people came from all parts of the United States—and, indeed, from all over the world. They transformed what had been a quiet ranching paradise into a teeming and tumultuous community in search of wealth in California's rivers and streams.

Eighty percent of the forty-niners were Americans. They came from every state. The Gold Rush was an eye-opening expansion of their horizons for the many who had known only their hometown folks before. The second largest group of migrants were from nearby Mexico and the west coast of Latin America (13 percent). The remainder came from Europe and Asia.

The presence of Chinese miners surprised many Americans. Several hundred Chinese arrived in California in 1849 and 1850, and in 1852 more than 20,000 landed in San Francisco hoping to share in the wealth of "Gum Sam" (Golden Mountain).

In 1849, as the Gold Rush began in earnest, San Francisco, the major entry port and supply point, sprang to life. From a settlement of 1,000 in 1848 it grew to a city of 35,000 in 1850. This surge suggested that the real money to be made in California was not in panning for gold but from feeding, clothing, housing,

---

QUICK REVIEW

Discovery of Gold

◆ Gold discovered at Sutter's Mill in 1848.

◆ Most forty-niners were Americans.

◆ Gold rush led rapid growth of San Francisco.

provisioning, and entertaining the miners. Among the first to learn that lesson was the German Jewish immigrant Levi Strauss, who sold so many tough work pants to miners that his name became synonymous with his product. The white population of California jumped from an estimated pre–Gold Rush figure of 11,000 to more than 100,000 by 1852. California was admitted into the Union as a state in 1850.

MINING CAMPS

As had occurred in San Francisco, most mining camps boomed almost instantly to life, but unlike San Francisco, they were empty again within a few years. They were generally dirty and dreary places. Most miners lived in tents or hovels, unwilling to take time from mining to build themselves decent quarters. They cooked monotonous meals of beans, bread, and bacon, or, if they had money, bought meals at expensive restaurants and boardinghouses (where the table might be no more than a plank over two flour barrels). They led a cheerless, uncomfortable, and unhealthy existence, especially during the long, rainy winter months, with few distractions apart from the saloon, the gambling hall, and the prostitute's bed.

Most miners were young, unmarried, and unsuccessful. Only a small percentage ever struck it rich in California. Increasingly, those who stayed on in California had to give up the status of independent miners and become wage earners for large mining concerns.

As in San Francisco, a more reliable way to earn money in the camps was to supply the miners. Every mining community had its saloonkeepers, gamblers, prostitutes, merchants, and restaurateurs. Like the miners themselves, these people were transients, always ready to pick up and move at the word of a new gold strike. The majority of women in the early mining camps were prostitutes. Some grew rich or married respectably, but most died young of drugs, venereal disease, or violence. Most of the other women were hardworking wives of miners, and in this predominantly male society they made good money doing domestic work: keeping boardinghouses, cooking, doing laundry.

Partly because few people put any effort into building communities—they were too busy seeking gold—violence was endemic in mining areas, and much of it was racial. Discrimination, especially against Chinese, Mexicans, and African Americans, was common. Frequently miners' claims were "jumped": thieves would rob them of the gold they had accumulated, kill them, or chase them away, and then file their own claim for the victims' strike. Or unscrupulous miners might use the law to their advantage to secure the claims of others without violence—for example, by taking advantage of the prohibitively high mining tax on foreigners.

By the mid-1850s, the immediate effects of the Gold Rush had passed. California had a booming population, a thriving agriculture, and a corporate mining industry. The Gold Rush also left California with a population that was larger, more affluent, and (in urban San Francisco) more culturally sophisticated than that in other newly settled territories. It was also significantly more multicultural than the rest of the nation, for many of the Chinese and Mexicans, as well as immigrants from many European countries, remained in California after the Gold Rush subsided. But the Gold Rush left some permanent scars, and not just on the foothills landscape: the virtual extermination of the California Indian peoples, the dispossession of many Californios who were legally deprived of their land grants, and the growth of racial animosity toward the Chinese in particular.

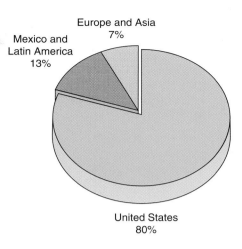

Mexico and Latin America 13%

Europe and Asia 7%

United States 80%

Where the Forty-Niners Came From
Americans drawn to the California Gold Rush of 1849 encountered a more diverse population than most had previously known. Nearly as novel to them as the 20 percent from foreign countries was the regional variety from within the United States itself.

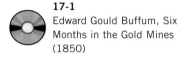

17-1
Edward Gould Buffum, Six Months in the Gold Mines (1850)

Chinese first came to California in 1849 attracted by the Gold Rush. Frequently, however, they were forced off their claims by intolerant whites. Rather than enjoy an equal chance in the gold fields they were often forced to work as servants or in other menial occupations.

Head of Auburn Ravine, 1852, Gold miners with Chinese laborers, California State Library (912).

WHAT KEY factors explain the outcome of the election of 1848?

THE POLITICS OF MANIFEST DESTINY

I n three short years, from 1845 to 1848, the territory of the United States grew an incredible 70 percent, and a continental nation took shape. This expansion, pushed by economic desires and feelings of American cultural superiority, led directly to the emergence of the divisive issue of slavery as the dominant issue in national politics.

THE WILMOT PROVISO

In 1846, almost all the Northern members of the Whig Party opposed Democratic president James Polk's belligerent expansionism on antislavery grounds. Northern Whigs correctly feared that expansion would reopen the issue of slavery in the territories. But the outpouring of popular enthusiasm for the Mexican-American War convinced most Whig congressmen that they needed to vote military appropriations for the war in spite of their misgivings.

Ironically it was not the Whigs but a freshman Democratic congressman from Pennsylvania, David Wilmot, who opened the door to sectional controversy over expansion. In August 1846, only a few short months after the beginning of the Mexican-American War, Wilmot proposed, in an amendment to a military appropriations bill, that slavery be banned in all the territories acquired from Mexico. He was ready, Wilmot said, to "sustain the institutions of the South as they exist," but not to extend them. In the debate and voting that followed, something new and ominous occurred: Southern Whigs joined Southern Democrats to vote against the measure, while Northerners of both parties supported it. Sectional interest had triumphed over party loyalty. **Wilmot's Proviso** triggered the first breakdown of the national party system and reopened the debate about the place of slavery in the future of the nation.

The Wilmot Proviso was so controversial that it was deleted from the necessary military appropriations bills during the Mexican-American War. But in 1848,

Wilmot's Proviso   The amendment offered by Pennsylvania Democrat David Wilmot in 1846 which stipulated that "as an express and fundamental condition to the acquisition of any territory from the Republic of Mexico . . . neither slavery nor involuntary servitude shall ever exist in any part of said territory."

following the Treaty of Guadalupe Hidalgo, the question of the expansion of slavery could no longer be avoided or postponed. Antislavery advocates from the North argued with proslavery Southerners in a debate that was much more prolonged and more bitter than in the Missouri Crisis debate of 1819. Civility quickly wore thin: threats were uttered and fistfights broke out on the floor of the House of Representatives. The Wilmot Proviso posed a fundamental challenge to both parties. Neither the Democrats nor the Whigs could take a strong stand on the amendment because neither party could get its Northern and Southern wings to agree.

THE FREE-SOIL MOVEMENT

Why did David Wilmot propose this controversial measure? Wilmot, a Northern Democrat, was propelled not by ideology but by the pressure of practical politics. The dramatic rise of the Liberty Party, founded in 1840 by abolitionists, threatened to take votes away from both the Whig and the Democratic parties. The Liberty Party won 62,000 votes in the 1844 presidential election, all in the North. This was more than enough to deny victory to the Whig candidate, Henry Clay.

The Liberty Party took an uncompromising stance against slavery. The party proposed to prohibit the admission of slave states to the Union, end slavery in the District of Columbia, and abolish the interstate slave trade that was vital to the expansion of cotton growing into the Old Southwest (see Chapter 11). Liberty Party members also favored denying office to all slaveholders (a proposal that would have robbed all the Southern states of their senators). Liberty Party doctrine was too uncompromising for the mass of Northern voters, who immediately realized that the Southern states would leave the Union before accepting it. Still, as the 1844 vote indicated, many Northerners opposed slavery. From this sentiment the Free-Soil Party was born.

Free-Soilers were willing to allow slavery to continue in the existing slave states because they supported the Union, not because they approved of slavery. They were unwilling, however, to allow the extension of slavery to new and unorganized territory. If the South were successful in extending slavery, they argued, Northern farmers who moved west would find themselves competing at an economic disadvantage with large planters using slave labor. Free-Soilers also insisted that the Northern values of freedom and individualism would be destroyed if the slave-based Southern labor system were allowed to spread.

OVERVIEW

EXPANSION CAUSES THE FIRST SPLITS IN THE SECOND AMERICAN PARTY SYSTEM

1844	Whigs reject President John Tyler's move to annex Texas and expel him from the Whig Party. Southern Democrats choose expansionist James K. Polk as their presidential candidate, passing over Martin Van Buren, who is against expansion.
	Liberty Party runs abolitionist James Birney for president, attracting Northern antislavery Whigs.
1846	The Wilmot Proviso, proposing to ban slavery in the territories that might be gained in the Mexican-American War, splits both parties: Southern Whigs and Democrats oppose the measure; Northern Whigs and Democrats support it.
1848	The new Free-Soil Party runs Northern Democrat Martin Van Buren for president, gaining 10 percent of the vote from abolitionists, antislavery Whigs, and some Northern Democrats. This strong showing by a third party causes Democrat Lewis Cass to lose the electoral votes of New York and Pennsylvania, allowing the Whig Zachary Taylor to win.

In reality many Free-Soilers meant "antiblack" when they said "antislavery." They proposed to ban all African American people from the new territories (a step that four states—Indiana, Illinois, Iowa, and Oregon—took but did not always enforce), thus "solving" the race issue by ignoring it.

THE ELECTION OF 1848

A swirl of emotions—pride, expansionism, sectionalism, abolitionism, free-soil sentiment—surrounded the election of 1848. The Treaty of Guadalupe Hidalgo had been signed earlier in the year, and the vast northern Mexican provinces of New Mexico and California and the former Republic of Texas had been incorporated into the United States. But the issues raised by the Wilmot Proviso remained to be resolved, and every candidate had to have an answer to the question of whether slavery should be admitted in the new territories.

CHRONOLOGY

1609	First Spanish settlement in New Mexico.
1670s	British and French Canadians begin fur trade in western Canada.
1716	First Spanish settlements in Texas.
1769	First Spanish settlement in California.
1780s	New England ships begin sea otter trade in Pacific Northwest.
1790	First American ship visits Hawaii.
1803	Louisiana Purchase.
1804–1806	Lewis and Clark expedition.
1806	Russian-Californio trade begins.
1806–1807	Zebulon Pike's expedition across the Great Plains to the Rocky Mountains.
1819–1820	Stephen Long's expedition across the Great Plains.
1821	Hudson's Bay Company gains dominance of western fur trade.
	Mexico seizes independence from Spain.
	Santa Fé Trail opens, soon protected by U.S. military.
	Stephen F. Austin becomes first American empresario in Texas.
1824	First fur rendezvous sponsored by Rocky Mountain Fur Company.
	Hudson's Bay Company establishes Fort Vancouver in Oregon Country.
1830	Indian Removal Act moves eastern Indians to Indian Territory.

1834	Jason Lee establishes first mission in Oregon Country.
1835	Texas revolts against Mexico.
1836	Battles of the Alamo and San Jacinto.
	Republic of Texas formed.
1843–1844	John C. Frémont maps trails to Oregon and California.
1844	Democrat James K. Polk elected president on an expansionist platform.
1845	Texas annexed to the United States as a slave state.
	John O'Sullivan coins the phrase "manifest destiny."
1846	Oregon question settled peacefully with Britain.
	Mexican-American War begins.
	Bear Flag Revolt in California.
	Wilmot Proviso.
1847	Cayuse Wars begin in Oregon.
	Americans win battles of Buena Vista, Veracruz, and Mexico City.
1848	Treaty of Guadalupe Hidalgo.
	Free-Soil Party captures 10 percent of the popular vote in the North.
	General Zachary Taylor, a Whig, elected president.
1849	California Gold Rush.

Lewis Cass of Michigan, the Democratic nominee for president (Polk, in poor health, declined to run for a second term), proposed to apply the doctrine of **popular sovereignty** to the crucial slave–free issue. This democratic-sounding notion of leaving the decision to the citizens of each territory was based on the Jeffersonian faith in the common man's ability to vote both his own self-interest and the common good. In fact, however, popular sovereignty was an admission of the nation's failure to resolve sectional differences. Moreover, the doctrine of popular sovereignty was deliberately vague about when a territory would choose its status. Would it do so during the territorial stage? at the point of applying for statehood? Clearly, this question was crucial, for no slave owner would invest in new land if the territory could later be declared free, and no abolitionist would move to a territory that was destined to become a slave state. Cass hoped his ambiguity on this point would win him votes in both North and South.

For their part, the Whigs passed over perennial candidate Henry Clay and turned once again to a war hero, General Zachary Taylor. Taylor, a Louisiana slaveholder, refused to take a position on the Wilmot Proviso, allowing both Northern and Southern voters to hope that he agreed with them. Privately, Taylor opposed the expansion of slavery. In public, he evaded the issue by running as a war hero and a national leader who was above sectional politics.

The deliberate vagueness of the two major candidates displeased many Northern voters. An uneasy mixture of disaffected Democrats (among them David Wilmot) and Whigs joined former Liberty Party voters to support the candidate of the Free-Soil Party, former president Martin Van Buren. Van Buren, angry at the Democratic Party for passing him over in 1844 and displeased with the growing Southern dominance of the Democratic Party, ran as a spoiler. He knew he could not win the election, but he could divide the Democrats. In the end, Van Buren garnered 10 percent of the vote (all in the North). The vote for the Free-Soil Party cost Cass the electoral votes of New York and Pennsylvania, and General Zachary Taylor won the election with only 47 percent of the popular vote. This was the second election after 1840 that the Whigs had won by running a war hero who could duck hard questions by claiming to be above politics. Uncannily, history was to repeat itself: Taylor, like William Henry Harrison, died before his term was completed, and the chance he offered to maintain national unity—if ever it existed—was lost.

CONCLUSION

In the decade of the 1840s, westward expansion took many forms, from relatively peaceful settlement in Oregon, to war with Mexico over Texas, to the overwhelming numbers of gold rushers who changed California forever.

The election of 1848, virtually a referendum on manifest destiny, yielded ironic results. James K. Polk, who presided over the unprecedented expansion, did not run for a second term, and thus the Democratic Party gained no electoral victory to match the military one. The electorate that had been so thrilled by the war news voted for a war hero—who led the antiexpansionist Whig Party. The election was decided by Martin Van Buren, the Free-Soil candidate who voiced the sentiments of the abolitionists, a reform group that had been insignificant just a few years before. The amazing expansion achieved by the Mexican-American War—America's manifest destiny—made the United States a continental nation but stirred up the issue that was to tear it apart. Sectional rivalries and fears now

QUICK REVIEW

Slavery and the Election of 1848

◆ Democratic candidate Lewis Cass argued that territorial residents should decide issue of slavery.

◆ Whig nominee Zachary Taylor remained silent on slavery issue.

◆ Taylor's election gave country first president from Lower South.

Popular sovereignty   A solution to the slavery crisis suggested by Michigan senator Lewis Cass by which territorial residents, not Congress, would decide slavery's fate.

dominated every aspect of politics. Expansion, once a force for unity, now divided the nation into Northerners and Southerners, who could not agree on the community they shared—the federal Union.

SUMMARY

Exploring the West Economics and the federal government spurred exploration of the West. Companies competing for the fur trade were one source of exploration. After the Louisiana Purchase, the federal government sponsored several expeditions to map the new territory. Expansion followed exploration raising the "Indian Problem" again.

The Politics of Expansion Fueled by the belief in manifest destiny, American expansion followed several paths. Open lands motivated thousands of Americans to follow overland trails to Oregon and California. The Oregon settlement led to a dispute with Great Britain that was resolved diplomatically. In the Southwest, trade led to settlement and forts along the Santa Fé trail. American also settled in Texas, but they eventually rebelled and founded the Republic of Texas, creating a conflict that affected the election of 1844.

The Mexican-American War Tensions with Mexico, partly fueled by expansionist ideology, led to war. Public opinion was divided on the war, but the United States obtained the present-day Southwest as a result of the war.

California and the Gold Rush The Russians came first to Spanish California but were followed by the Americans. After the United States annexed California, the discovery of gold spurred immigration by Americans, Chinese, and Mexicans, among others. Mining camps proliferated, but most proved temporary settlements.

The Politics of Manifest Destiny Growing pride in democracy raised American confidence, but the addition of land triggered a growing debate over the extension of slavery.

REVIEW QUESTIONS

1. Define and discuss the concept of manifest destiny.

2. Trace the different ways in which the frontiers in Oregon, Texas, and California moved from frontiers of inclusion to frontiers of exclusion.

3. Take different sides (Whig and Democrat) and debate the issues raised by the Mexican-American War.

4. Referring back to Chapter 13, compare the positions of the Liberty Party and the Free-Soil Party. Examine the factors that made the free-soil doctrine politically acceptable to many and abolitionism so controversial.

KEY TERMS

Alamo (p. 364)
Californios (p. 369)
Empresarios (p. 363)
Manifest destiny (p. 356)
Mexican-American War (p. 366)

Oregon Trail (p. 360)
Popular sovereignty (p. 374)
Santa Fé Trail (p. 356)
Tejanos (p. 362)
Wilmot's Proviso (p. 372)

RECOMMENDED READING

Arnoldo De Leon, *The Tejano Community, 1836–1900* (1982). Traces the changing status of Tejanos after Texas came under the control of American Texans.

John Mack Faragher, *Women and Men on the Overland Trail* (1979). One of the first books to consider the experience of women on the journey west.

William Goetzman, *Exploration and Empire: The Explorer and the Scientist in the Winning of the American West* (1966). Considers the many government-sponsored explorations of the West.

Julie Roy Jeffrey, *Converting the West: A Biography of Narcissa Whitman* (1991). Makes a clear connection between the missionary Whitman's evangelical upbringing and her failure to understand the culture of Oregon's Cayuse Indians.

Robert W. Johannsen, *To the Halls of the Montezumas: The Mexican War in the American Imagination* (1985). A lively book that explores the impact of the Mexican-American War on public opinion.

Susan Johnson, *Roaring Camp: The Social World of the California Gold Rush* (2000). A beautifully written study of the varieties of mining camp experience.

Paul D. Lack, *The Texas Revolutionary Experience: A Political and Social History, 1835–1836* (1992). A political and social history that stresses the chaotic and discordant nature of the Texas Revolt.

Janet Lecompte, *Pueblo, Hardscrabble, Greenhorn: The Upper Arkansas, 1832–1856* (1978). A social history that portrays the racial and ethnic diversity of the trading frontier.

Michael Morrison, *Slavery and the American West: The Eclipse of Manifest Destiny and the Coming of the Civil War* (1997). In a study of competing ideas over the future of the West, the author stresses the links between expansion and sectional disagreements.

Malcolm Rohrbough, *Days of Gold: The California Gold Rush and the American Nation* (1997). A lively history that emphasizes the effects of this "great American epic" on the national self-image.

David J. Weber, *The Mexican Frontier, 1821–1846: The American Southwest under Mexico* (1982). A fine study of the history of the Southwest before American conquest. The author is a leading borderlands historian.

Richard White, *"It's Your Misfortune and None of My Own": A History of the American West* (1991). A major reinterpretation that focuses on the history of the region itself rather than on the westward expansion of Americans. Pays much more attention to Spanish Mexicans and Indian peoples than earlier texts.

This horror, this nightmare abomination!
Can it be in my country! It lies like lead on
my heart, it shadows my life with sorrow . . .

— *Harriet Beecher Stowe, December 16, 1852*

The slave Eliza is attacked by vicious dogs while crossing with her baby the ice floes of a frozen river in a poster advertising an 1881 theatrical production of Uncle Tom's Cabin.

15

WHY DID people in the North and the South tend to see the issue of slavery differently?

WHAT WAS the intent of the Compromise of 1850?

WHY DID Stephen Douglas support the Kansas-Nebraska Act?

WHAT WAS the outcome of the *Dred Scott* decision?

WHAT ROLE did the issue of slavery play in the election of 1860?

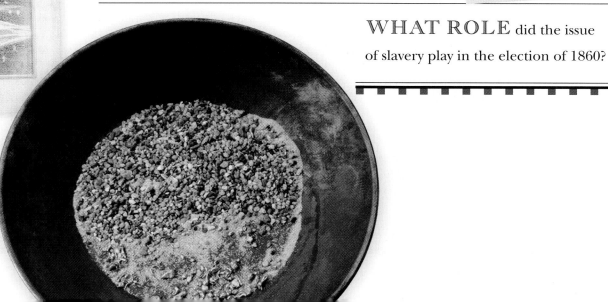

Illinois Communities Debate Slavery

ON SEVEN OCCASIONS THROUGH THE LATE SUMMER AND AUTUMN *of 1858, in each of the seven small Illinois towns of Ottawa, Freeport, Jonesboro, Charleston, Galesburg, Quincy, and Alton, thousands of Illinois farmers and townspeople put aside their daily routines and customary chores; climbed into carriages, farm wagons, carts, and conveyances of all sorts; and converged on their local town green. Entertained by brass bands, pageantry, and vast quantities of food and local gossip, they waited impatiently for the main event, the chance to take part in the debate on the most urgent question of the day—slavery. Two Illinois politicians—Democratic Senator Stephen A. Douglas and his Republican challenger, Springfield lawyer Abraham Lincoln, the principal figures in the debates—presented their views in three hours of closely reasoned argument. But they did not speak alone. Cheers, boos, groans, and shouted questions from active, engaged listeners punctuated all seven of the now famous confrontations between the two men. Although commonly referred to as the* **Lincoln-Douglas debates,** *these were really community events in which Illinois citizens—who, as did Americans everywhere, held varying political beliefs—took part. Some individuals were proslavery, some antislavery, and many were undecided, but all were agreed that democratic politics gave them the means to air their opinions and resolve their differences.*

Democrat Stephen Douglas was the leading Democratic contender for the 1860 presidential nomination, but before he could mount a campaign for national office he had first to win reelection to the Illinois seat he had held in the U.S. Senate for twelve years. His vote against allowing slavery in Kansas had alienated him from the strong Southern wing of his own party and had put him in direct conflict with its top leader, President James Buchanan. Because the crisis of the Union was so severe and Douglas's role so pivotal, his reelection campaign clearly previewed the 1860 presidential election. For the sake of its future, the Republican Party had to field a strong opponent: it found its candidate in Abraham Lincoln.

Lincoln had represented Illinois in the House of Representatives in the 1840s but had lost political support in 1848 because he had opposed the Mexican-American War. Developing a prosperous Springfield law practice, he had been an influential member of the Illinois Republican Party since its founding in 1856. Although he had entered political life as a Whig, Lincoln was radicalized by the issue of the extension of slavery. Even though his wife's family were Kentucky slave owners, Lincoln's commitment to freedom and his resistance to the spread of slavery had now become absolute: for him, freedom and Union were inseparable.

Much less well known than Douglas, Lincoln was the underdog in the 1858 Senate race, and thus it was he who challenged Douglas to debate. Both were eloquent and powerful speakers—and they had to be. The three-hour debates were held without amplification of any kind. Nevertheless, in every town, audiences of 10,000 to 15,000 listened attentively and responded vocally to each speaker's long and thought-packed arguments.

Douglas had many strengths going into the debates. He spoke for the Union, he claimed, pointing out that the Democratic Party was a national party whereas the Republican Party was only sectional. He repeatedly appealed to the racism of much of his audience with declarations such as, "I would not blot out the great inalienable rights of the white men for all the negroes that ever existed!" He repeatedly called his opponent a "Black Republican," implying that Lincoln and his party favored the social equality of whites and blacks, even race mixing.

Lincoln did not believe in the social equality of the races, but he did believe wholeheartedly that slavery was a moral wrong. Pledging the Republican Party to the "ultimate extinction" of slavery, Lincoln continually warned that Douglas's position would lead to the opposite result: the spread of slavery everywhere. Although in this argument Lincoln was addressing the Northern fear of an expansionist "slave power," he strove at the same time to present himself as a moderate. He did not favor the breakup of the Union, but he never wavered from his antislavery stance.

The first of the seven debates, held in Ottawa on Saturday, August 21, 1858, showed not only the seriousness but also the exuberance of the democratic politics of the time. By early morning the town was jammed with people. Then the debate got under way, enthralling an estimated 12,000 people. Ottawa, in Northern Illinois, was pro-Republican, and the audience heckled Douglas unmercifully. At the second debate, a week later in Freeport, Douglas's use of the phrase "Black Republicans" drew angry shouts of "White, white" from the crowd. But as the debates moved south in the state, where Democrats predominated, the tables were turned, and Lincoln sometimes had to plead for a chance to be heard.

Although Douglas won the 1858 senatorial election in Illinois, the acclaim that Lincoln gained in the famous debates helped establish the Republicans' claim to be the only party capable of stopping the spread of slavery and made Lincoln himself a strong contender for the Republican presidential nomination in 1860. The Illinois people who participated in the community debates of 1858 showed the strong faith Americans held in their democratic institutions and the hope—finally shattered in the election of 1860—that a lasting political solution to the problem of slavery could be found.

Illinois

AMERICA IN 1850

In 1850, after half a century of rapid growth and change, America was a very different nation from the republic of 1800. Geographic expansion, population increase, economic development, and the changes wrought by the market revolution had transformed the struggling new nation. Economically, culturally, and politically, Americans had forged a strong sense of national identity.

EXPANSION AND GROWTH

America was now a much larger nation than it had been in 1800. Through war and diplomacy, the country had grown to continental dimensions, more than tripling in size from 890,000 to 3 million square miles. Its population had increased enormously: from 5.3 million in 1800 to more than 23 million, 4 million of whom were African American slaves and 2 million new immigrants, largely from Germany and Ireland. Comprising just sixteen states in 1800, America in 1850 had thirty-one, and more than half of the population lived west of the Appalachians.

America was also much richer: it is estimated that real per capita income doubled between 1800 and 1850. Southern cotton, which had contributed so much to American economic growth, continued to be the nation's principal export, but it was no longer the major influence on the domestic economy. The development of manufacturing in the Northeast and the increased economic importance of the Midwest had serious domestic political implications. As the South's share of responsibility for economic growth waned, so did its political importance—at least in the eyes of many Northerners. Thus, the very success of the United States both in geographic expansion and economic development served to undermine the role of the slave South in national politics and to hasten the day of open conflict between it and the free-labor North and Midwest.

POLITICAL PARTIES AND SLAVERY

The Second American Party System forged in the great controversies of Andrew Jackson's presidency (see Chapter 10) was a national party system. In their need to mobilize great masses of recently enfranchised voters to elect a president every four years, politicians created organized party structures that overrode deeply rooted sectional differences. Politicians from all sections of the country cooperated because they knew their party could not succeed without national appeal. At a time when the ordinary person still had very strong sectional loyalties, the mass political party created a national community of like-minded voters. Yet, by the election of 1848, sectional interests were eroding the political "glue" in both parties. Although each party still appeared united, sectional fissures already ran deep.

Political splits were preceded by divisions in other social institutions. Disagreements about slavery had already split the country's great religious organizations into Northern and Southern groups, the Presbyterians in 1837, the Methodists in 1844, and the Baptists in 1845. (Some of these splits turned out to be permanent. The Southern Baptist Convention, for example, is still a separate body.) The abolitionists had been posing this simple yet uncompromising choice between slavery or freedom since the 1830s. Moreover, they had been insisting on a compelling distinction: as Liberty Party spokesman Salmon P. Chase said, "Freedom is national; slavery only is local and sectional."

WHY DID people in the North and the South tend to see the issue of slavery differently?

14–7
A White Southerner Speaks Out Against Slavery (1857)

IMAGE KEY

for pages 372–373

a. Dred Scott and his family, c. 1857.

b. The slave Eliza is attacked by vicious dogs while crossing ice floes of a river with her baby in a poster advertising a production of *Uncle Tom's Cabin*.

c. A portrait photo of John Brown (1800–1859).

d. An old fashioned black stovepipe hat with a narrow brim like the one worn by Abe Lincoln.

e. A poster of *Uncle Tom's Cabin* with an illustration of a slave woman standing in the doorway of a log cabin. The copy describes various editions of the book for sale.

f. Robert Marshall Root's painting of the Lincoln-Douglas debate.

g. A contemporary colored engraving of the inside of the Armory at Harper's Ferry, Virginia, where John Brown and his men were trapped by the fire of the U.S. Marines under the command of Col. Robert E. Lee, October 18, 1859.

h. Gold ore and gravel in a shallow pan like those used by '49ers.

Lincoln-Douglas debates Series of debates in the 1858 Illinois senatorial campaign during which Douglas and Lincoln staked out their differing opinions on the issue of slavery.

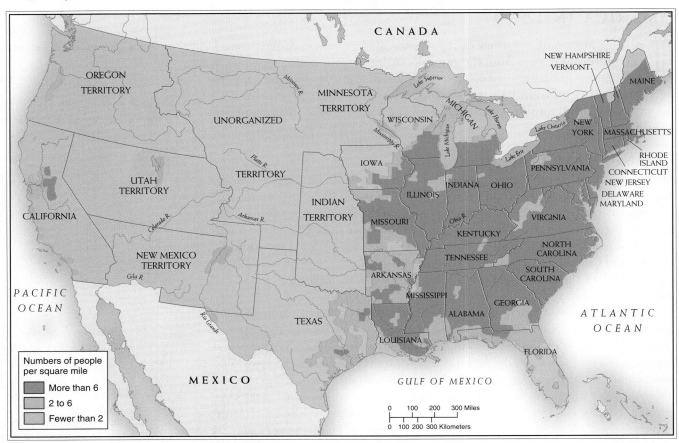

MAP 15-1 U.S. Population and Settlement, 1850 By 1850, the United States was a continental nation. Its people, whom Thomas Jefferson had once thought would not reach the Mississippi River for forty generations, had not only passed the river but leapfrogged to the west coast. In comparison to the America of 1800 the growth was astounding.

WHAT WERE the reasons behind these growth patterns?

STATES' RIGHTS AND SLAVERY

But was freedom national and slavery sectional, or was it the other way around? Southern politicians took the latter view, as their foremost spokesman, South Carolina's John C. Calhoun, made ringingly clear throughout his long career.

In 1828 Calhoun had begun the protracted Nullification Crisis by asserting the constitutional right of states to "nullify" national laws that were harmful to their interests (see Chapter 10). Calhoun argued, as others have since, that the states' rights doctrine protected the legitimate rights of a minority in a democratic system governed by majority rule.

In 1847, Calhoun responded to the 1846 Wilmot Proviso with an elaboration of the states' rights argument. In spite of the apparent precedents of the Northwest Ordinance of 1787 and the Missouri Compromise, Calhoun argued that Congress did not have a constitutional right to prohibit slavery in the territories. The territories, he said, were the common property of all the states, North and South, and Congress could not discriminate against slave owners as they moved West. On the contrary, Calhoun argued, slave owners had a constitutional right to the protection of their property wherever they moved. Of course, Calhoun's legally correct description of African American slaves as property enraged abolitionists. But on behalf of the South, Calhoun was expressing the belief—and the fear—that his interpretation of the Constitution was the only protection for slave owners, whose right to own slaves (a fundamental right in Southern eyes) was being attacked. Calhoun's position on the territories quickly became Southern dogma: anything less than full access to the territories was unconstitutional. Slavery, Calhoun and other Southerners insisted, had to be national.

As Congressman Robert Toombs of Georgia put the case in 1850, there was very little room for compromise:

> I stand upon the great principle that the South has the right to an equal participation in the territories of the United States. . . . She will divide with you if you wish it, but the right to enter all or divide I shall never surrender. . . . Deprive us of this right and appropriate the common property to yourselves, it is then your government, not mine. Then I am its enemy. . . . Give us our just rights, and we are ready . . . to stand by the Union. . . . Refuse [them], and for one, I will strike for independence.

NORTHERN FEARS OF "THE SLAVE POWER"

The words of Southerners like Calhoun and Toombs confirmed for many Northerners the warnings of antislavery leaders that they were endangered by a menacing "slave power." Liberty Party leader James Birney, in a speech in 1844, was the first to add this phrase to the nation's political vocabulary. "The slave power," Birney explained, was a group of aristocratic slave owners who not only dominated the political and social life of the South but also conspired to control the federal government as well, posing a danger to free speech and free institutions throughout the nation.

Birney's warnings about "the slave power" seemed in 1844 merely the overheated rhetoric of an extremist group of abolitionists. But the defensive Southern political strategies of the 1850s were to convince an increasing number of Northern voters that "the slave power" did in fact exist. Thus in Northern eyes the South became a demonic monolith that threatened the national government.

TWO COMMUNITIES, TWO PERSPECTIVES

Ironically, it was a common belief in expansion that made the arguments between Northerners and Southerners so irreconcilable. Southerners had been the strongest supporters of the Mexican-American War, and they still hoped to expand into Cuba, believing that the slave system must grow or wither. On the other hand, although many Northern Whigs had opposed the Mexican-American War, most did so for antislavery reasons, not because they opposed expansion. The strong showing of the Free-Soil Party (which evolved out of the Liberty Party) in the election of 1848 (getting 10 percent of the popular vote) was proof of that. Basically, both North and South believed in manifest destiny, but each on its own terms.

Similarly, both North and South used the language of basic rights and liberties in the debate over expansion. But Free-Soilers were speaking of personal liberty, whereas Southerners meant their right to own a particular kind of property (slaves) and to maintain a way of life based on the possession of that property.

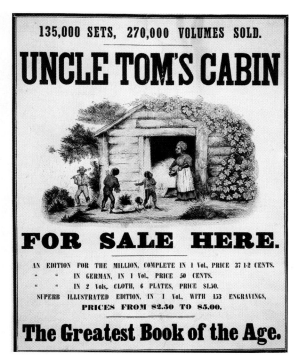

135,000 SETS, 270,000 VOLUMES SOLD.

UNCLE TOM'S CABIN

FOR SALE HERE.

AN EDITION FOR THE MILLION, COMPLETE IN 1 Vol., PRICE 37 1-2 CENTS.
"   "   IN GERMAN, IN 1 Vol., PRICE 50 CENTS.
"   "   IN 2 Vols., CLOTH, 6 PLATES, PRICE $1.50.
SUPERB ILLUSTRATED EDITION, IN 1 Vol., WITH 153 ENGRAVINGS,
PRICES FROM $2.50 TO $5.00.

The Greatest Book of the Age.

This poster advertises *Uncle Tom's Cabin*, the best-selling novel by Harriet Beecher Stowe. This poignant story of long-suffering African American slaves had an immense impact on Northern popular opinion, swaying it decisively against slavery. In that respect, the poster's boast, "the greatest book of the age" was correct.
©Bettmann/CORBIS (BE001033)

13–5
De Bow's Review, "The Stability of the Union," (1850)

QUICK REVIEW

Regional Stereotypes

◆ Northern perspective: South an economic backwater dominated by immoral slave owners.

◆ Southern perspective: North a beneficiary of cotton industry dominated by hypocritical manufacturers.

◆ By 1850s stereotypes were fixed in many people's minds.

In 1850, the three men who had long represented America's three major regions attempted to resolve the political crisis brought on by the applications of California and Utah for statehood. Henry Clay is speaking; John C. Calhoun stands third from right; and Daniel Webster is seated at the left with his head in his hand. Both Clay and Webster were ill, and Calhoun died before the Compromise of 1850 was arranged by a younger group of politicians led by Stephen A. Douglas.

Courtesy of the Library of Congress

WHAT WAS the intent of the Compromise of 1850?

13–7
George Fitzhugh, "The Blessings of Slavery" (1857)

14–4
A Dying Statesman Speaks Out Against the Compromise of 1850

Compromise of 1850 The four-step compromise which admitted California as a free state, allowed the residents of the New Mexico and Utah territories to decide the slavery issue for themselves, ended the slave trade in the District of Columbia, and passed a new fugitive slave law to enforce the constitutional provision stating that a slave escaping into a free state shall be delivered back to the owner.

By 1850, North and South had created fixed stereotypes of the other. To antislavery Northerners, the South was an economic backwater dominated by a small slave-owning aristocracy who lived off the profits of forced labor and deprived poor whites of their democratic rights and the fruits of honest work. The slave system was not only immoral, but also a drag on the entire nation, for, in the words of Senator William Seward of New York, it subverted the "intelligence, vigor and energy" that were essential for national growth. In contrast, the dynamic and enterprising commercial North boasted a free labor ideology that offered economic opportunity to the common man and ensured his democratic rights (see Chapter 12).

Things looked very different through Southern eyes. Far from being economically backward, the South, through its export of cotton, was, according to Southerners, the great engine of national economic growth from which the North benefited. Slavery was not only a blessing to an inferior race but also the cornerstone of democracy, for it ensured the freedom and independence of all white men without entailing the bitter class divisions that marked the North. Slave owners accused Northern manufacturers of hypocrisy for practicing "wage slavery" without the paternal benevolence they claimed to bestow on their slaves.

By the early 1850s, these vastly different visions of the North and the South—the result of many years of political controversy—had become fixed, and the chances of national reconciliation increasingly slim.

THE COMPROMISE OF 1850

By 1850 the issue raised by the Wilmot Proviso—whether slavery should be extended to the new territories—could no longer be ignored. Overnight, the California Gold Rush had turned a remote frontier into a territory with a booming population. In 1849 both California and Utah applied for statehood. Should these territories be admitted as slave or free states? A simmering border war between Texas, a slave state, and New Mexico, which seemed likely to be a free state, had to be settled, as did the issue of the debts Texas had incurred as an independent republic. Closer to home, antislavery forces demanded the end of slavery in the District of Columbia, while slave owners complained that Northerners were refusing to return escaped slaves, as federal law mandated.

DEBATE AND COMPROMISE

The **Compromise of 1850** was the final act in the political careers of the three aging men who in the public mind best represented America's sections: Westerner Henry Clay; Southerner John C. Calhoun; and Daniel Webster, spokesman for the North. It was sadly appropriate to the bitter sectional argument of 1850 that the three men contributed great words to the debate but that the compromise itself was enacted by younger men.

On July 9, 1850, in the midst of the debate, President Zachary Taylor died of acute gastroenteritis. When Vice President Millard Fillmore assumed the presidency, however, he helped adjust the Compromise of 1850 to Southern liking. Fillmore was a moderate Northern Whig and more pro-Southern than the Southern-born Taylor had been. Moreover, although Clay had assembled all the necessary parts of the bargain, it was not he but members of a younger political generation, and in particular the rising young Democrat from Illinois, Stephen Douglas, who drove the Compromise of 1850 through Congress. The final product consisted of five separate bills (it had been impossible to obtain a majority for a comprehensive measure), embodying three separate compromises.

First, California was admitted as a free state, but the status of the remaining former Mexican possessions was left to be decided by **popular sovereignty** (a vote of the territory's inhabitants) when they applied for statehood. (Utah's application for statehood was not accepted until 1896 because of controversy over the Mormon practice of polygamy.) The result was, for the time being, fifteen slave states and sixteen free states. Second, Texas (a slave state) was required to cede land to New Mexico Territory (free or slave status undecided). In return, the federal government assumed $10 million of debts Texas had incurred before it became a state. Finally, the slave trade, but not slavery itself, was ended in the District of Columbia, but a stronger fugitive slave law was enacted.

Jubilation and relief greeted the news that compromise had been achieved. In Washington, where the anxiety and concern had been greatest, drunken crowds

Popular sovereignty   A solution to the slavery crisis suggested by Michigan senator Lewis Cass by which territorial residents, not Congress, would decide slavery's fate.

 # MAP EXPLORATION
To explore an interactive version of this map, go to **http://www.prenhall.com/faraghertlc/map15.2**

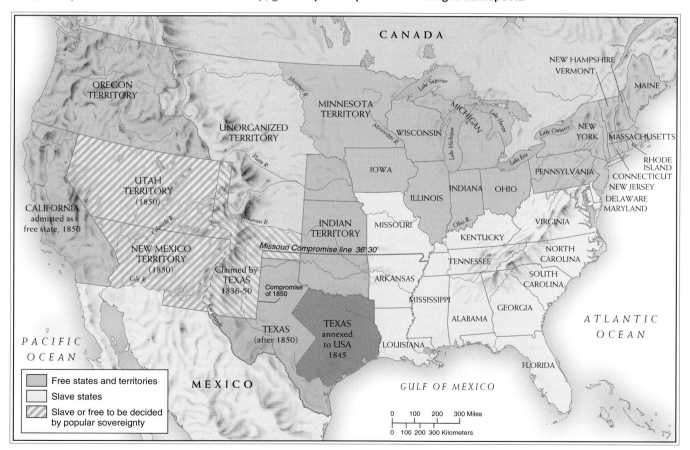

MAP 15-2 The Compromise of 1850   The Compromise of 1850 reflected heightened sectional tensions by being even messier and more awkward than the Missouri Compromise of 1820. California was admitted as a free state, the borders of Texas were settled, and the status of the rest of the former Mexican territory was left to be decided later by popular sovereignty. No consistent majority voted for the five separate bills that made up the compromise.

WHAT GROUPS opposed the Compromise of 1850? Why?

serenaded Congress, shouting, "The Union is saved!" That was certainly true for the moment, but analysis of the votes on the five bills that made up the compromise revealed no consistent majority. The sectional splits within each party that had existed before the compromise remained. In the country as a whole, the feeling was that the problem of slavery in the territories had been solved. Senator Salmon P. Chase of Ohio soberly noted, "The question of slavery in the territories has been avoided. It has not been settled." And many Southerners felt that their only real gain in the contested compromise was the Fugitive Slave Law, which quickly turned out to be an inflammatory measure.

THE FUGITIVE SLAVE ACT

From the early days of their movement, Northern abolitionists had urged slaves to escape, promising assistance and support when they reached the North. Northerners had long been appalled by professional slave catchers, who zealously seized African Americans in the North and took them South into slavery again. Most abhorrent in Northern eyes was that captured black people were at the mercy of slave catchers because they had no legal right to defend themselves. In more than one case, a Northern free African American was captured in his own community and helplessly shipped into slavery.

The **Fugitive Slave Law**, enacted in 1850, dramatically increased the power of slave owners to capture escaped slaves. The full authority of the federal government now supported slave owners, and although fugitives were guaranteed a hearing before a federal commissioner, they were not allowed to testify on their own behalf. Furthermore, the new law imposed federal penalties on citizens who protected or assisted fugitives or who did not cooperate in their return. In Boston, the center of the American abolitionist movement, reaction to the Fugitive Slave Law was fierce. When an escaped slave named Shadrach Minkins was seized in February 1851, a group of African American men broke into the courtroom, overwhelmed the federal marshals, seized Minkins, and sent him safely to Canada. Although the action had community support—a Massachusetts jury defiantly refused to convict the perpetrators—many people, including Daniel Webster and President Fillmore, condemned it as "mob rule."

The federal government responded with overwhelming force. In April 1851, 300 armed soldiers were mobilized to prevent the rescue of Thomas Sims, who was being shipped back into slavery. In the most famous case in Boston, a biracial group

---

QUICK REVIEW

The Fugitive Slave Act

◆ Enacted in 1850.

◆ Increased the power of slave owners to recapture slaves.

◆ Federal government backed rights of slave owners.

13–6
Benjamin Drew, Narratives of Escaped Slaves (1855)

Fugitive Slave Law Part of the Compromise of 1850 that required the authorities in the North to assist Southern slave catchers and return runaway slaves to their owners.

OVERVIEW

THE GREAT SECTIONAL COMPROMISES

Missouri Compromise	1820	Admits Missouri to the Union as a slave state and Maine as a free state; prohibits slavery in the rest of the Louisiana Purchase Territory north of 36°30'. Territory Covered: The entire territory of the Louisiana Purchase, exclusive of the state of Louisiana, which had been admitted to the Union in 1812.
Compromise of 1850	1850	Admits California to the Union as a free state, settles the borders of Texas (a slave state); sets no conditions concerning slavery for the rest of the territory acquired from Mexico. Territory Covered: The territory that had been part of Mexico before the end of the Mexican-American War and the Treaty of Guadalupe Hidalgo (1848): part of Texas, California, Utah Territory (now Utah, Nevada, and part of Colorado), and New Mexico Territory (now New Mexico and Arizona).

of armed abolitionists led by Unitarian clergyman Thomas Wentworth Higginson stormed the federal courthouse in 1854 in an attempt to save escaped slave Anthony Burns. The rescue effort failed, and a federal deputy marshal was killed. President Pierce sent marines, cavalry, and artillery to Boston to reinforce the guard over Burns and ordered a federal ship to be ready to deliver the fugitive back into slavery. When the effort by defense lawyers to argue for Burns's freedom failed, Bostonians raised money to buy his freedom. But the U.S. attorney, ordered by the president to enforce the Fugitive Slave Law in all circumstances, blocked the purchase. The case was lost, and Burns was marched to the docks through streets lined with sorrowing abolitionists. Buildings were shrouded in black and draped with American flags hanging upside down, while bells tolled as if for a funeral.

The Burns case radicalized many Northerners. Conservative Whig George Hilliard wrote to a friend, "When it was all over, and I was left alone in my office, I put my face in my hands and wept. I could do nothing less." During the 1850s, 322 black fugitives were sent back into slavery; only 11 were declared free. Northern popular sentiment and the Fugitive Slave Law, rigorously enforced by the federal government, were increasingly at odds.

In this volatile atmosphere, escaped African Americans wrote and lectured bravely on behalf of freedom. Frederick Douglass, the most famous and eloquent of the fugitive slaves, spoke out fearlessly in support of armed resistance. Openly active in the underground network that helped slaves reach safety in Canada, Douglass himself had been constantly in danger of capture until his friends bought his freedom in 1847. Harriet Jacobs, who escaped to the North after seven years in hiding in the South, wrote bitterly in her *Incidents in the Life of a Slave Girl* (1861) that the Fugitive Slave Law made her feel that "I was, in fact, a slave in New York, as subject to slave laws as I had been in a slave state. . . . I had been chased during half my life, and it seemed as if the chase was never to end."

The Fugitive Slave Law made slavery national and forced Northern communities to confront what that meant. Although most people were still unwilling to grant social equality to the free African Americans who lived in the Northern states, more and more had come to believe that the institution of slavery was wrong. Northern protests against the Fugitive Slave Law bred suspicion in the South and encouraged secessionist thinking. These new currents of public opinion were reflected in the election of 1852.

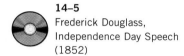

14–5
Frederick Douglass,
Independence Day Speech
(1852)

THE ELECTION OF 1852

The first sign of the weakening of the national party system in 1852 was the difficulty both parties experienced at their nominating conventions. After fifty-two ballots, the Whigs nominated General Winfield Scott (a military hero like the party's previous two candidates) rather than sitting President Fillmore. Many Southern Whigs were angered and alienated by the choice and either abstained during the voting, like Georgia's Alexander Stephens, or, like Robert Toombs, cast a protest vote for the Democratic candidate. Although Southern Whigs were still elected to Congress, their loyalty to the national party was strained to the breaking point. The Whigs never again fielded a presidential candidate.

The Democrats had a wider variety of candidates: Lewis Cass of popular sovereignty fame; Stephen Douglas, architect of the Compromise of 1850; and James Buchanan, described as a "Northern man with Southern principles." Cass, Douglas, and Buchanan competed for forty-nine ballots, each strong enough to block the others, but not strong enough to win. Finally the party turned to a handsome, affable nonentity, Franklin Pierce of New Hampshire, who was thought to have Southern sympathies. Uniting on a platform pledging "faithful execution" of all parts of the Compromise of 1850, including the Fugitive Slave Law, Democrats polled well in the South and in the North. Most Democrats who had voted for the Free-Soil Party in 1848 voted for Pierce. So, in record numbers, did immigrant Irish and German voters, who were eligible for citizenship after three years' residence. The strong immigrant vote for Pierce was a sign of the strength of the Democratic machines in Northern cities (see Chapter 13). Pierce easily won the 1852 election, 254 electoral votes to 42.

"YOUNG AMERICA": THE POLITICS OF EXPANSION

Pierce entered the White House in 1853 on a wave of good feeling. Massachusetts Whig Amos Lawrence reported, "Never since Washington has an administration commenced with the hearty [good] will of so large a portion of the country." This goodwill was soon strained by Pierce's support for the expansionist adventures of the "Young America" movement.

The "Young America" movement began as a group of writers and politicans in the New York Democratic Party who believed in the democratic and nationalistic promise of "manifest destiny" (a term coined by one of their members, John Sullivan). By the 1850s, however, their lofty goals had shrunk to a desire to conquer Central America and Cuba. When in 1858 the perennial conflict between centrists and liberals in Mexico broke into civil war, the fighting served to convince some Southerners that Mexico was ripe for conquest, but ironically, before they could act, America's own Civil War intervened.

During the Pierce administration, several private "filibusters" (from the Spanish *filibustero*, meaning an "adventurer" or "pirate") invaded Caribbean and Central American countries, usually with the declared intention of extending slave territory.

The Pierce administration, not directly involved in the filibustering, *was* deeply involved in an effort to obtain Cuba. In part, the effort was prompted by abortive slave revolts in Cuba in 1843–1844, which led some Cuban slave owners to want annexation to the United States so that slavery could continue. In 1854, Pierce authorized his minister to Spain, Pierre Soulé, to try to force the unwilling Spanish to sell Cuba for $130 million. Soulé met in Ostend, Belgium, with the American ministers to France and England, John Mason and James Buchanan, to compose the offer. At first appealing to Spain to recognize the deep affinities between the Cubans and American Southerners that made them "one people with one destiny," the document went on to threaten to "wrest" Cuba from Spain if necessary. This amazing document, which became known as the Ostend Manifesto, was soon leaked to the press. Deeply embarrassed, the Pierce administration was forced to repudiate it.

The complicity between the Pierce administration and proslavery expansionists was foolhardy and lost it the Northern goodwill with which it had begun. The sectional crisis that preceded the Compromise of 1850 had made obvious the danger of reopening the territorial issue. Ironically, it was not the Young America expansionists but the prime mover of the Compromise of 1850, Stephen A. Douglas, who reignited the sectional struggle over slavery expansion.

THE CRISIS OF THE NATIONAL PARTY SYSTEM

WHY DID Stephen Douglas support the Kansas-Nebraska Act?

In 1854, Douglas introduced the **Kansas-Nebraska Act** and thereby reopened the question of slavery in the territories. Douglas knew he was taking a political risk, but he believed he could satisfy both his expansionist aims and his presidential ambitions. He was wrong. Instead, he pushed the national party system into crisis, first killing the Whigs and then destroying the Democrats.

THE KANSAS-NEBRASKA ACT

Douglas introduced the Kansas-Nebraska Act opening the territory to white settlement because he was an ardent advocate of a transcontinental railroad that he believed would foster American democracy and commerce. He wanted the rail line to terminate in Chicago (in his own state of Illinois) rather than in St. Louis (a rival city), and to achieve that aim, the land west of Iowa and Missouri had to be organized into territories (the first step toward statehood). To get Congress to agree to the organization of the territories, however, he needed the votes of Southern Democrats, who were unwilling to support him unless the new territory was open to slavery.

Douglas thought he was solving his problem by proposing that the status of slavery in the new territories be governed by the principle of popular sovereignty. Douglas thought Southerners would support his bill because of its popular sovereignty provision and Northerners because it favored a Northern route for the transcontinental railroad. Douglas chose to downplay the price he had to pay for

Kansas-Nebraska Act   Law passed in 1854 creating the Kansas and Nebraska Territories but leaving the question of slavery open to residents, thereby repealing the Missouri Compromise.

 MAP EXPLORATION

To explore an interactive version of this map, go to **http://www.prenhall.com/faraghertlc/map15.3**

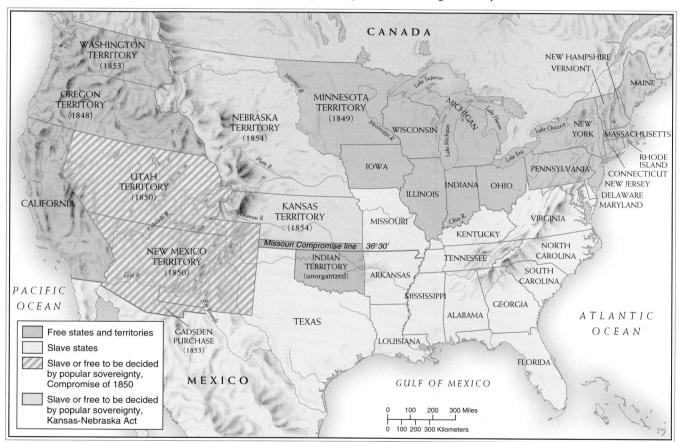

MAP 15-3

The Kansas-Nebraska Act, 1854   The Kansas-Nebraska Act, proposed by Steven A. Douglas in 1854, opened the central and northern Great Plains to settlement. The act had two major faults: it robbed Indian peoples of half the territory guaranteed to them by treaty, and, because it repealed the Missouri Compromise Line, it opened up the lands to warring proslavery and antislavery factions.

WHY DID the act provoke such a passionate response from antislavery activists?

QUICK REVIEW

The Kansas-Nebraska Act

◆ Passed in 1854.

◆ Made the status of slavery in new territories subject to the principal of popular sovereignty.

◆ Act aroused storm of protest in the North.

Southern support—by allowing the possibility of slavery in the new territories his bill in effect repealed the Missouri Compromise of 1820, which barred slavery north of latitude 36°30'.

The Kansas-Nebraska bill passed, but it badly strained the major political parties. Southern Whigs voted with Southern Democrats in favor of the measure, Northern Whigs rejected it absolutely, creating an irreconcilable split that left Whigs unable to field a presidential candidate in 1856. The damage to the Democratic Party was almost as great. In the congressional elections of 1854, Northern Democrats lost two-thirds of their seats (a drop from ninety-one to twenty-five), giving the Southern Democrats (who were solidly in favor of slavery extension) the dominant voice both in Congress and within the party.

Douglas had committed one of the greatest miscalculations in American political history. A storm of protest arose throughout the North. More than 300 large anti-Nebraska rallies occurred during congressional consideration of the bill, and the anger did not subside. Douglas, who confidently believed that "the people of the North will sustain the measure when they come to understand it," found himself shouted down more than once at public rallies when he tried to explain the bill.

The Kansas-Nebraska bill shifted a crucial sector of Northern opinion: the wealthy merchants, bankers, and manufacturers, called the "Cotton Whigs," who had economic ties with Southern slave owners and had always disapproved of abolitionist activity. Convinced that the bill would encourage antislavery feeling in the North, Cotton Whigs urged Southern politicians to vote against it, only to be ignored. Passage of the Kansas-Nebraska Act convinced many Northern Whigs that compromise with the South was impossible.

In Kansas in 1854, hasty treaties were concluded with the Indian tribes who owned the land. Some, such as the Kickapoos, Shawnees, Sauks, and Foxes, agreed to relocate to small reservations. Others, like the Delawares, Weas, and Iowas, agreed to sell their lands to whites. Still others, such as the Cheyennes and Sioux, kept the western part of Kansas Territory (now Colorado)—until gold was discovered there in 1859. Once the treaties were signed, both proslavery and antislavery white settlers began to pour in, and the battle was on.

Kansas soon became a bloody battleground as the two factions struggled to secure the mandate of "popular sovereignty." Free-soilers in Lawrence received shipments of heavy crates, innocuously marked "BOOKS" but actually containing Sharps repeating rifles, sent by Eastern supporters. For their part, proslavery "border ruffians" from Missouri—already heavily armed, with Bowie knives in their boots, revolvers at their waists, rifles slung from their shoulders, and swords at their sides—called for reinforcements. David Atchison exhorted Alabamans: "Let your young men come forth to Missouri and Kansas! Let them come well armed!"

In the summer of 1856, these lethal preparations exploded into open warfare. First, proslavery forces burned and looted the town of Lawrence. The Free State Hotel, among other buildings, was burned to the ground. In retaliation, a grim old man named John Brown led his sons in a raid on the proslavery settlers of Pottawatomie Creek, killing five unarmed people. A wave of violence ensued. Armed bands roamed the countryside, and burnings and killings became commonplace. John Brown and his followers were

This engraving shows "Border Ruffians" from Missouri lining up to vote for slavery in the Kickapoo, Kansas Territory election of 1855. The widespread practice of illegal voting and of open violence earned Kansas the dreadful nickname of "Bleeding Kansas."

The Granger Collection

VOTING IN KICKAPOO.

just one of many bands of marauding murderers who were never arrested, never brought to trial, and never stopped from committing further violence. Peaceful residents of large sections of rural Kansas were repeatedly forced to flee to the safety of military forts when rumors of one or another armed band reached them.

THE POLITICS OF NATIVISM

Meanwhile, sectional pressures continued to reshape national politics. The breakup of the Whig Party left a political vacuum that was filled with one of the strongest bursts of nativism, or antiimmigrant feeling, in American history and by the rapid growth of the new American Party, which formed in 1850 to give political expression to nativism. The new party was in part a reaction to the Democratic Party's success in capturing the support of the rapidly growing population of mostly Catholic foreign-born voters. Irish immigrants in particular voted Democratic, both in reaction to Whig hostility (as in Boston) and because of their own antiblack prejudices. Frequently in competition with free African Americans for low-paying jobs, Irish immigrants were more likely to share the attitudes of Southerners than those of abolitionists.

The reformist and individualistic attitudes of many Whigs inclined them toward nativism. Many Whigs disapproved of the new immigrants because they

This 1855 cartoon by Nathaniel Currier illustrates the Know Nothings' fear of an antidemocratic Catholic "invasion" of America. As the shamrock caught by the boathook is meant to indicate, Irish Catholics were a special target of Know Nothing suspicion.

Courtesy of the Library of Congress

OVERVIEW
POLITICAL PARTIES SPLIT AND REALIGN

Whig Party	Ran its last presidential candidate in 1852. The candidate, General Winfield Scott, alienated many Southern Whigs, and the party was so split it could not field a candidate in 1856.
Democratic Party	Remained a national party through 1856, but Buchanan's actions as president made Southern domination of the party so clear that many Northern Democrats were alienated. Stephen Douglas, running as a Northern Democrat in 1860, won 29 percent of the popular vote; John Breckinridge, running as a Southern Democrat, won 18 percent.
Liberty Party	Antislavery party; ran James G. Birney for president in 1844. He won 62,000 votes, largely from Northern antislavery Whigs.
Free-Soil Party	Ran Martin Van Buren, former Democratic president, in 1848. Gained 10 percent of the popular vote, largely from Whigs but also from some Northern Democrats.
American (Know-Nothing) Party	Nativist party made striking gains in 1854 congressional elections, attracting both Northern and and Southern Whigs. In 1856, its presidential candidate Millard Fillmore won 21 percent of the popular vote.
Republican Party	Founded in 1854. Attracted many Northern Whigs and Northern Democrats. Presidential candidate John C. Frémont won 33 percent of the popular vote in 1856; in 1860 Abraham Lincoln won 40 percent and was elected in a four-way race.

Know-Nothings Name given to the antiimmigrant party formed from the wreckage of the Whig Party and some disaffected Northern Democrats in 1854.

Republican Party Party that emerged in the 1850s in the aftermath of the bitter controversy over the Kansas-Nebraska Act, consisting of former Whigs, some Northern Democrats, and many Know-Nothings.

were poor, Catholic, and often disdainful of the temperance movement. The Catholic Church's opposition to the liberal European revolutions of 1848 also fueled anti-Catholic fears. If America's new Catholic immigrants opposed the revolutions in which other Americans took such pride (believing them to be modeled on the American example), how could the future of America's own democracy be ensured? Finally, nativist Whigs held immigration to be solely responsible for the increases in crime and the rising cost of relief for the poor that accompanied the astoundingly rapid urban growth of the 1830s and 1840s (see Chapter 13).

Nativism drew former Whigs, especially young men in white-collar and skilled blue-collar occupations, to the new American Party. At the core of the party were several secret fraternal societies open only to native-born Protestants who pledged never to vote for a Catholic, on the grounds that all Catholics took their orders straight from the pope in Rome. When questioned about their beliefs, party members maintained secrecy by answering, "I know nothing"—hence the popular name for American Party members, the **Know-Nothings**.

Know-Nothings scored startling victories in Northern state elections in 1854, winning control of the legislature in Massachusetts and polling 40 percent of the vote in Pennsylvania. But in the 1850s, no party could ignore slavery, and in 1855 the American Party split into Northern (antislavery) and Southern (proslavery) wings. Soon after this split, many people who had voted for the Know-Nothings shifted their support to another new party, one that combined many characteristics of the Whigs with a westward-looking, expansionist, free-soil policy. This was the **Republican Party**, founded in 1854.

THE REPUBLICAN PARTY AND THE ELECTION OF 1856

Many constituencies found room in the new Republican Party. Its supporters included many former Northern Whigs who opposed slavery absolutely, many Free-Soil Party supporters who opposed the expansion of slavery but were willing to tolerate it in the South, and many Northern reformers concerned about temperance and Catholicism. The Republicans also attracted the economic core of the old Whig Party—the merchants and industrialists who wanted a strong national government to promote economic growth by supporting a protective tariff, transportation improvements, and cheap land for Western farmers. In quieter times it would have taken this party a while to sort out all its differences and become a true political community. But because of the sectional crisis, the fledgling party nearly won its very first presidential election.

The immediate question facing the nation in 1856 was which new party, the Know-Nothings or the Republicans, would emerge the stronger. But the more important question was whether the Democratic Party could hold together. The two strongest contenders for the Democratic nomination were President Pierce and Stephen A. Douglas. Douglas had proposed the Kansas-Nebraska Act and Pierce had actively supported it. Both men, therefore, had the support of the Southern wing of the party. But it was precisely their support of this act that made Northerners oppose both of them. The Kansas-Nebraska Act's divisive effect on the Democratic Party

MAP EXPLORATION

To explore an interactive version of this map, go to
http://www.prenhall.com/faraghertlc/map15.4

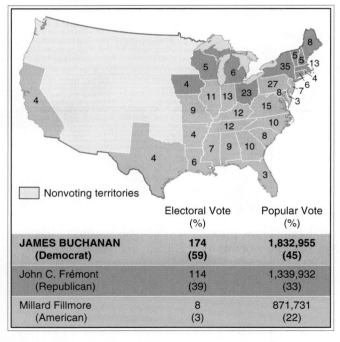

	Electoral Vote (%)	Popular Vote (%)
JAMES BUCHANAN (Democrat)	**174 (59)**	**1,832,955 (45)**
John C. Frémont (Republican)	114 (39)	1,339,932 (33)
Millard Fillmore (American)	8 (3)	871,731 (22)

MAP 15-4
The Election of 1856 Because three parties contested the 1856 election, Democrat James Buchanan was a minority president. Although Buchanan alone had national support, Republican John Frémont won most of the free states, and Millard Fillmore of the American Party gained 40 percent of the vote in most of the slave states.

WHAT GROUPS constituted Buchanan's political base?

THE COMING CRISIS THE 1850s

now became clear: no one who had voted on the bill, either for or against, could satisfy both wings of the party. A compromise candidate was found in James Buchanan of Pennsylvania, the "Northern man with Southern principles." Luckily for him, he had been ambassador to Great Britain at the time of the Kansas-Nebraska Act and, thus, had not had to commit himself.

The election of 1856 appeared to be a three-way contest that pitted Buchanan against explorer John C. Frémont of the Republican Party and the American (Know-Nothing) Party's candidate, former president Millard Fillmore. In fact, the election was two separate contests, one in the North and one in the South. The Southern race was between Buchanan and Fillmore, the Northern race between Buchanan and Frémont. Buchanan won the election with only 45 percent of the popular vote because he was the only national candidate. But the Republicans, after studying the election returns, claimed "victorious defeat," for they realized that in 1860 the addition of just two more Northern states to their total would mean victory. Furthermore, the Republican Party had clearly defeated the American Party in the battle to win designation as a major party. These were grounds for great optimism—and for great concern, for the Republican Party was a sectional rather than a national party; it drew almost all its support from the North. Southerners viewed its very existence as an attack on their vital interests. Thus, the rapid rise of the Republicans posed a growing threat to national unity.

THE DIFFERENCES DEEPEN

In one dreadful week in 1856 the people of the United States heard, in quick succession, about the looting and burning of Lawrence, Kansas, about John Brown's retaliatory massacre at Pottawatomie, and about unprecedented violence on the Senate floor. In the last of these incidents, Senator Charles Sumner of Massachusetts suffered permanent injury in a vicious attack by Congressman Preston Brooks of South Carolina. Trapped at his desk, Sumner was helpless as Brooks beat him so hard with his cane that it broke. A few days earlier, Sumner had given an insulting antislavery speech. Using the abusive, accusatory style favored by abolitionists, he had singled out for ridicule Senator Andrew Butler of South Carolina, Preston Brooks's uncle. In Brooks's mind, he was simply avenging an intolerable affront to his uncle's honor. So far had the behavioral codes of North and South diverged that each man found his own action perfectly justifiable and the action of the other outrageous.

THE *DRED SCOTT* DECISION

Although James Buchanan firmly believed that he alone could hold together the nation so riven by hatred and violence, his self-confidence outran his abilities. He was so deeply indebted to the strong Southern wing of the Democratic Party that he could not take the impartial actions necessary to heal "**Bleeding Kansas**." And his support for a momentous pro-Southern decision by the Supreme Court further aggravated sectional differences.

In *Dred Scott* v. *Sandford*, decided on March 6, 1857, two days after James Buchanan was sworn in, a Southern-dominated Supreme Court attempted—and failed—to solve the political controversy over slavery. Dred Scott had been a slave all his life. His owner, army surgeon John Emerson, had taken Scott on his military assignments during the 1830s to Illinois (a free state) and Wisconsin Territory (a free territory, north of the Missouri Compromise line). During that time Scott married another slave, Harriet, and their daughter Eliza was born in free territory.

WHAT WAS the outcome of the *Dred Scott* decision?

14–6
Kansas Begins to Bleed (1856)

14–8
Dred Scott v. Sandford (1857)

Bleeding Kansas   Violence between pro- and antislavery forces in Kansas Territory after the passage of the Kansas-Nebraska Act in 1854.

This political cartoon shows the devastating impact of the Supreme Court's 1857 *Dred Scott* decision on politics and the election of 1860. Dred Scott, shown with a fiddle in the middle, plays for (clockwise from upper right) Republican Abraham Lincoln and an African American woman; John Bell with an Indian; Northern Democrat Stephen A. Douglas with an Irishman; and Southern Democrat John Breckinridge with President James Buchanan, the "Northern Democrat with Southern sympathies."

Courtesy of the Library of Congress

QUICK REVIEW

The *Dred Scott* Decision

- 1857 attempt by Supreme Court to solve the political controversy over slavery.
- Court ruled that slaves were property and government could not restrain free movement of property.
- Decision invalidated the Missouri Compromise.

Dred Scott **decision** Supreme Court ruling, in a lawsuit brought by Dred Scott, a slave demanding his freedom based on his residence in a free state, that slaves could not be U.S. citizens and that Congress had no jurisdiction over slavery in the territories.

Emerson and the Scotts then returned to Missouri (a slave state) and there, in 1846, Dred Scott sued for his freedom and that of his wife and his daughter born in Wisconsin Territory (who as women had no legal standing of their own) on the grounds that residence in free lands had made them free.

In his decision, Chief Justice Roger B. Taney of Maryland declared the Missouri Compromise unconstitutional. Taney asserted that the federal government had no right to interfere with the free movement of property throughout the territories. Taney was in effect making John C. Calhoun's states' rights position, always considered an extremist Southern position, the law of the land. He then dismissed the *Dred Scott* case on the grounds that only citizens could bring suits before federal courts and that black people—slave or free—were not citizens. With this bold judicial intervention into the most heated issue of the day, Taney intended to settle the controversy over the expansion of slavery once and for all. Instead, he enflamed the conflict.

The five Southern members of the Supreme Court concurred in Taney's decision, as did one Northerner, Robert C. Grier. Historians have found that President-elect Buchanan had pressured Grier, a fellow Pennsylvanian, to support the majority. Two of the three other Northerners vigorously dissented, and the last voiced other objections. This was clearly a sectional decision, and the response to it was sectional. Southerners expressed great satisfaction and strong support for the Court. Many Northerners disagreed so strongly with the *Dred Scott* decision that for the first time they found themselves seriously questioning the power of the Supreme Court to establish the "law of the land."

For the Republican Party, the ***Dred Scott* decision** represented a formidable challenge. By invalidating the Missouri Compromise, the decision swept away the free-soil foundation of the party. But to directly challenge a Supreme Court decision was a weighty matter. The most sensational Republican counterattack—made by both Abraham Lincoln and William Seward—was the accusation that President Buchanan had conspired with the Southern Supreme Court justices to subvert the American political system by withholding the decision until after the presidential election. Lincoln also raised the frightening possibility that "the next *Dred*

Scott decision" would legalize slavery even in free states that abhorred it. President Buchanan's response to events in Kansas, including the drafting of a proslavery constitution, also stoked political antagonisms.

THE LECOMPTON CONSTITUTION

In Kansas the doctrine of popular sovereignty led to continuing civil strife and the political travesty of two territorial governments. The first election of officers to a territorial government in 1855 produced a lopsided proslavery outcome that was clearly the result of illegal voting by Missouri border ruffians. Free-Soilers protested by forming their own government, giving Kansas both a proslavery territorial legislature in Lecompton and a Free-Soil government in Topeka. Because Free-Soil voters boycotted a June 1857 election for a convention to write a constitution for the territory once it reached statehood, the convention had a proslavery majority that wrote the proslavery **Lecompton constitution** and then applied to Congress for admission to the Union under its terms. In the meantime, in October Free-Soil voters had participated in relatively honest elections for the territorial legislature, elections that returned a clear Free-Soil majority. Nevertheless, Buchanan, in the single most disastrous mistake of his administration, endorsed the proslavery constitution because he feared the loss of the support of Southern Democrats. It seemed that Kansas would enter the Union as a sixteenth slave state, making the number of slave and free states equal.

Unexpected congressional opposition came from none other than Stephen Douglas, author of the legislation that had begun the Kansas troubles in 1854. Now, in 1857, in what was surely the bravest step of his political career, Douglas opposed the Lecompton constitution on the grounds that it violated the principle of popular sovereignty. He insisted that the Lecompton constitution must be voted upon by Kansas voters in honest elections (as indeed Buchanan had initially promised). Defying James Buchanan, his own president, Douglas voted with the majority in Congress in April 1858 to refuse admission to Kansas under the Lecompton constitution. In a new referendum, the people of Kansas also rejected the Lecompton constitution, 11,300 to 1,788. Kansas was finally admitted as a free state in January 1861.

The defeat of the Lecompton constitution did not come easily. There was more bloodshed in Kansas, more violence in Congress, and conflict on still another level—the Democratic Party was breaking apart. Douglas had intended to preserve the Democrats as a national party, but instead he lost the support of the Southern wing. Summing up these events, Congressman Alexander Stephens of Georgia wrote glumly to his brother: "All things here are tending my mind to the conclusion that the Union cannot and will not last long."

THE PANIC OF 1857

Adding to the growing political tensions was the short but sharp depression of 1857 and 1858. Technology played a part. In August 1857, the failure of an Ohio investment house—the kind of event that had formerly taken weeks to be widely known—was the subject of a news story flashed immediately over telegraph wires to Wall Street and other financial markets. A wave of panic selling ensued, leading to business failures and slowdowns that threw thousands out of work. The major cause of the panic was a sharp but temporary downturn in agricultural exports to Britain, and recovery was well under way by early 1859.

Because it affected cotton exports less than Northern exports, the **Panic of 1857** was less harmful to the South than to the North. Southerners took this as

Lecompton constitution   Proslavery draft written in 1857 by Kansas territorial delegates elected under questionable circumstances; it was rejected by two governors, supported by President Buchanan, and decisively defeated by Congress.

Panic of 1857   Banking crisis that caused a credit crunch in the North; it was less severe in the South, where high cotton prices spurred a quick recovery.

This painting by Charles G. Rosenberg and James H. Cafferty shows a worried crowd exchanging the latest news on Wall Street during the Panic of 1857. This was the first economic depression in which the telegraph played a part by carrying bad financial news in the West to New York much more rapidly than in the past.

Photograph by J. Cafferty and C. Rosenberg. Courtesy of the Museum of the City of New York (40.54)

proof of the superiority of their economic system to the free-labor system of the North. It seemed that all matters of political discussion were being drawn into the sectional dispute. The next step toward disunion was an act of violence perpetrated by the grim abolitionist from Kansas, John Brown.

JOHN BROWN'S RAID

In the heated political mood of the late 1850s, some improbable people became heroes. None was more improbable than John Brown, the self-appointed avenger who had slaughtered unarmed proslavery men in Kansas in 1856. In 1859, Brown proposed a wild scheme to raid the South and start a general slave uprising. He believed, as did most Northern abolitionists, that discontent among Southern slaves was so great that such an uprising needed only a spark to get going. Significantly, free African Americans—among them Frederick Douglas—did not support Brown, thinking his plan to raid the federal arsenal at Harpers Ferry, Virginia, was doomed to failure. They were right. On October 16, 1859, Brown led a group of twenty-two white and African American men against the arsenal. However, he had made no provision for escape. Even more incredible, he had not notified the Virginia slaves whose uprising it was supposed to initiate. In less than a day the raid was over. Eight of Brown's men (including two of his sons) were dead, no slaves had joined the fight, and Brown himself was captured. Moving quickly to prevent a lynching by local mobs, the state of Virginia tried and convicted Brown (while he was still weak from the wounds of battle) of treason, murder, and fomenting insurrection.

Ludicrous in life, possibly insane, Brown was nevertheless a noble martyr. In his closing speech prior to sentencing, Brown was magnificently eloquent: "Now, if it is deemed necessary that I should forfeit my life for the furtherance of the end of justice, and mingle my blood further with the blood of my children and with the blood of millions in this slave country whose rights are disregarded by wicked, cruel, and unjust enactments, I say, let it be done."

Brown's death by hanging on December 2, 1859, was marked throughout Northern communities with public rites of mourning not seen since the death of George Washington. Church bells tolled, buildings were draped in black, ministers preached sermons, prayer meetings were held, abolitionists issued eulogies. Ralph Waldo Emerson said that Brown would "make the gallows as glorious as the cross," and Henry David Thoreau called him "an angel of light." Not all Northerners supported Brown's action, but many people did support the antislavery cause that he represented.

Brown's raid shocked the South because it aroused the greatest fear—that of slave rebellion. Southerners believed that Northern abolitionists were provoking slave revolts, a suspicion apparently confirmed when documents captured at Harper's Ferry revealed that Brown had the financial support of half a dozen members of the Northern elite. These "Secret Six"—Gerrit Smith, George Stearns, Franklin Sanborn, Thomas Wentworth Higginson, Theodore Parker, and Samuel Gridley Howe—had been willing to finance armed attacks on the slave system.

Even more shocking to Southerners than the raid itself was the extent of Northern mourning for Brown's death. Although the Republican Party disavowed Brown's actions, Southerners simply did not believe the party's statements. Senator Robert Toombs of Georgia warned that the South would "never permit this Federal government to pass into the traitorous hands of the Black Republican party." Talk of secession as the only possible response became common throughout the South.

In a contemporary engraving, John Brown and his followers are shown trapped inside the armory at Harper's Ferry in October 1859. Captured, tried, and executed, Brown was regarded as a martyr in the North and a terrorist in the South.

The Granger/Collection (4E95014)

THE SOUTH SECEDES

By 1860, sectional differences had caused one national party, the Whigs, to collapse. The second national party, the Democrats, stood on the brink of dissolution. Not only the politicians but also ordinary people in both the North and the South were coming to believe there was no way to avoid what in 1858 William Seward (once a Whig, now a Republican) had called an "irrepressible conflict."

THE ELECTION OF 1860

The split of the Democratic Party into Northern and Southern wings that had occurred during President Buchanan's tenure became official at the Democratic nominating conventions in 1860. The party convened first in Charleston, South Carolina, the center of secessionist agitation. It was the worst possible location in which to attempt to reach unity. Although Stephen Douglas had the support of the plurality of delegates, he did not have the two-thirds majority necessary for

WHAT ROLE

did the issue of slavery play in the election of 1860?

MAP EXPLORATION

To explore an interactive version of this map, go to
http://www.prenhall.com/faraghertlc/map15.5

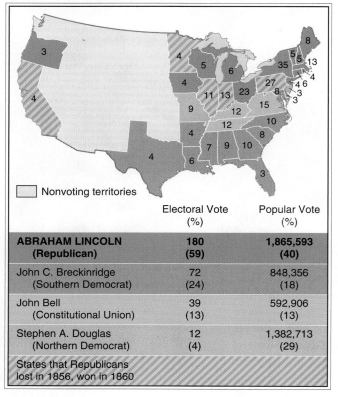

☐ Nonvoting territories

	Electoral Vote (%)	Popular Vote (%)
ABRAHAM LINCOLN (Republican)	**180 (59)**	**1,865,593 (40)**
John C. Breckinridge (Southern Democrat)	72 (24)	848,356 (18)
John Bell (Constitutional Union)	39 (13)	592,906 (13)
Stephen A. Douglas (Northern Democrat)	12 (4)	1,382,713 (29)
States that Republicans lost in 1856, won in 1860		

MAP 15-5

The Election of 1860 The election of 1860 was a sectional election. Lincoln won no votes in the South, Breckinridge none in the North. The contest in the North was between Lincoln and Douglas, and although Lincoln swept the electoral vote, Douglas's popular vote was uncomfortably close. The large number of Northern Democratic voters opposed to Lincoln was a source of political trouble for him during the Civil War.

WHAT DO the results of the election of 1860 tell us about support for Lincoln in the North on the eve of the Civil War?

Constitutional Union Party National party formed in 1860, mainly by former Whigs, that emphasized allegiance to the Union and strict enforcement of all national legislation.

John Brown's raid New England abolitionist John Brown's ill-fated attempt to free Virginia's slaves with a raid on the federal arsenal at Harper's Ferry, Virginia, in 1859.

nomination. As the price of their support, Southerners insisted that Douglas support a federal slave code—a guarantee that slavery would be protected in the territories. Douglas could not agree without violating his own belief in popular sovereignty and losing his Northern support. After ten days, fifty-nine ballots, and two Southern walkouts, the convention ended where it had begun: deadlocked.

In June, the Democrats met again in Baltimore. The Douglasites, recognizing the need for a united party, were eager to compromise wherever they could, but most Southern Democrats were not. More than a third of the delegates bolted. Later, holding a convention of their own, they nominated Buchanan's vice president, John C. Breckinridge of Kentucky. The remaining two-thirds of the Democrats nominated Douglas, but everyone knew that a Republican victory was inevitable. To make matters worse, some Southern Whigs joined with some border-state nativists to form the **Constitutional Union Party**, which nominated John Bell of Tennessee.

Republican strategy was built on the lessons of the 1856 "victorious defeat." The Republicans planned to carry all the states Frémont had won, plus Pennsylvania, Illinois, and Indiana. The two leading Republican contenders were Senator William H. Seward of New York and Abraham Lincoln of Illinois. Seward, the party's best-known figure, had enemies among party moderates, who thought he was too radical, and among nativists with whom he had clashed in the New York Whig Party. Lincoln, on the other hand, appeared new, impressive, more moderate than Seward, and certain to carry Illinois. Lincoln won the nomination on the third ballot.

The election of 1860 presented voters with one of the clearest choices in American history. On the key issue of slavery, Breckinridge supported its extension to the territories; Lincoln stood firmly for its exclusion. Douglas attempted to hold the middle ground with his principle of popular sovereignty; Bell vaguely favored compromise as well. The Republicans offered other platform planks designed to appeal to Northern voters: support for a homestead act (free western lands), for a transcontinental railroad, for other internal improvements, and for a higher tariff. Although they spoke clearly against the extension of slavery, Republicans sought to dispel their radical abolitionist image. The Republican platform condemned **John Brown's raid** as "the gravest of crimes," repeatedly denied that Republicans favored the social equality of black people, and strenuously affirmed that they sought to preserve the Union. In reality, Republicans simply did not believe the South would secede if Lincoln won. In this the Republicans were not alone; few Northerners believed Southern threats—Southerners had threatened too many times before.

The only candidate who spoke urgently and openly about the impending threat of secession was Douglas. Breaking with convention, Douglas campaigned personally, in both the North and, bravely, in the hostile South, warning of the danger of dissolution and presenting himself as the only truly national candidate. Realizing his own chances for election were slight, he told his private secretary, "Mr. Lincoln is the next President. We must try to save the Union. I will go South."

In accordance with tradition, Lincoln did not campaign for himself, but many other Republicans spoke for him. The Republicans did not campaign in the South; Breckinridge did not campaign in the North. Each side was, therefore, free to believe the worst about the other. All parties, North and South, campaigned with oratory, parades and rallies, free food and drink. Even in the face of looming crisis, this presidential campaign was the best entertainment of the day.

The mood in the Deep South was close to mass hysteria. Rumors of slave revolts—in Texas, Alabama, and South Carolina—swept the region, and vigilance committees sprang up to counter the supposed threat. In the South Carolina upcountry, the question of secession dominated races for the state legislature. Candidates who advocated "patriotic forbearance" if Lincoln won were soundly defeated. The very passion and excitement of the election campaign moved Southerners toward extremism. Even the weather—the worst drought and heat wave the South had known for years—contributed to the tension.

The election of 1860 produced the second highest voter turnout in U.S. history (81.2 percent, topped only by 81.8 percent in 1876). The election turned out to be two regional contests: Breckinridge versus Bell in the South, Lincoln versus Douglas in the North. Breckinridge carried eleven slave states with 18 percent of the popular vote; Bell carried Virginia, Tennessee, and Kentucky with 13 percent of the popular vote. Lincoln won all eighteen of the free states (he split New Jersey with Douglas) and almost 40 percent of the popular vote. Douglas carried only Missouri, but gained nearly 30 percent of the popular vote. Lincoln's electoral vote total was overwhelming: 180 to a combined 123 for the other three candidates. But although Lincoln had won 54 percent of the vote in the Northern states, his name had not even appeared on the ballot in ten Southern states. The true winner of the 1860 election was sectionalism.

THE SOUTH LEAVES THE UNION

The results of the election shocked Southerners. They were humiliated and frightened by the prospect of becoming a permanent minority in a political system dominated by a party pledged to the elimination of slavery. In Southern eyes the Republican triumph meant they would become unequal partners in the federal enterprise, their way of life (the slave system) existing on borrowed time.

The governors of South Carolina, Alabama, and Mississippi, each of whom had committed his state to secession if Lincoln were elected, immediately issued calls for special state conventions. At the same time, calls went out to Southern communities to form vigilance committees and volunteer militia companies. Cooperationists (the term used for those opposed to immediate secession) were either intimidated into silence or simply left behind by the speed of events.

On December 20, 1860, a state convention in South Carolina, accompanied by all the hoopla and excitement of bands, fireworks displays, and huge rallies, voted unanimously to secede from the Union. In the weeks that followed, conventions in six other Southern states (Mississippi, Florida, Alabama, Georgia, Louisiana, and Texas) followed suit, with the support, on average, of 80 percent of their delegates. Although there was genuine division of opinion in the South, especially in Georgia and Alabama, along customary up-country–low-country lines, none of the Deep South states held anywhere near the number of Unionists that Republicans had hoped. Throughout the South, secession occurred because Southerners no longer believed they had a choice.

In every state that seceded, the joyous scenes of South Carolina were repeated as the decisiveness of action replaced the long years of anxiety and tension. People danced in the streets, most believing the North had no choice but to accept secession

QUICK REVIEW

Northern Response to Secession

♦ Buchanan did nothing in response to secession.

♦ Lincoln refused calls to compromise on the question of slavery.

♦ Lincoln also rejected proposals to let the seven seceding states leave the Union.

14–9
Abraham Lincoln, "A House Divided" (1858)

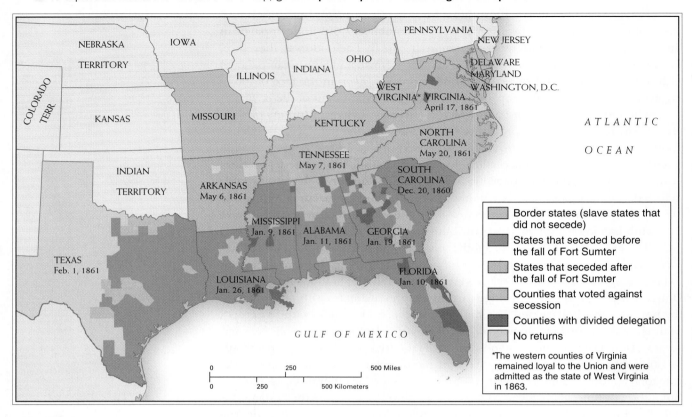

MAP 15-6

The South Secedes The Southern states that would constitute the Confederacy seceded in two stages. The states of the Lower South seceded before Lincoln took office. Arkansas and three states of the Upper South—Virginia, North Carolina, and Tennessee—waited until after the South fired on Fort Sumter. And four border slave states—Delaware, Maryland, Kentucky and Missouri—chose not to secede. Every Southern state (except South Carolina) was divided on the issue of secession, generally along up-country– low-country lines. In Virginia, this division was so extreme that West Virginia split off to become a separate nonslave state and was admitted to the Union in 1863.

WHY WERE some states quicker to secede than others?

peacefully. They ignored the fact that eight other slave states—Delaware, Maryland, Kentucky, Missouri, Virginia, North Carolina, Tennessee, and Arkansas—had not acted—though the latter four states would secede after war broke out. Just as Republicans had miscalculated in thinking Southern threats a mere bluff, so secessionists now miscalculated in believing they would be able to leave the Union in peace.

THE NORTH'S POLITICAL OPTIONS

What should the North do? Buchanan, indecisive as always, did nothing. The decision, thus, rested with Abraham Lincoln, even before he officially became president. One possibility was compromise, and many proposals were suggested, ranging from full adoption of the Breckinridge campaign platform to reinstatement of the Missouri Compromise line. Lincoln cautiously refused them all, making it clear that he would not compromise on the extension of slavery, which was the South's key demand. He hoped, by appearing firm but moderate, to discourage additional Southern states from seceding while giving pro-Union Southerners time to organize. He succeeded in his first aim but not in the second. Lincoln and most of the Republican Party had seriously overestimated the strength of pro-Union sentiment in the South.

A second possibility, suggested by Horace Greeley of the *New York Tribune*, was to let the seven seceding states "go in peace." This is what many secessionists expected, but too many Northerners—including Lincoln himself—believed in the Union for this to happen. As Lincoln said, what was at stake was "the necessity of proving that popular government is not an absurdity. We must settle this question now, whether in a free government the minority have the right to break up the government whenever they choose." The third possibility was force, and this was the crux of the dilemma. Although he believed their action was wrong, Lincoln was loath to go to war to force the seceding states back into the Union. On the other hand, he refused to give up federal powers over military forts and customs posts in the South. These were precisely the powers the seceding states had to command if they were to function as an independent nation. A confrontation was bound to come.

OVERVIEW

THE IRREPRESSIBLE CONFLICT

Declaration of Independence	1776	Thomas Jefferson's denunciation of slavery deleted from the final version.
Northwest Ordinance	1787	Slavery prohibited in the Northwest Territory (north of the Ohio River).
Constitution	1787	Slavery unmentioned but acknowledged in Article I, Section 2, counting three-fifths of all African Americans, slave and free, in a state's population; and in Article I, Section 9, which barred Congress from prohibiting the international slave trade for twenty years.
Louisiana Purchase	1803	Louisiana admitted as a slave state in 1812; no decision about the rest of Louisiana Purchase.
Missouri Compromise	1820	Missouri admitted as a slave state, but slavery prohibited in Louisiana Purchase north of 36°30'.
Wilmot Proviso	1846	Proposal to prohibit slavery in territory that might be gained in Mexican-American War causes splits in national parties.
Compromise of 1850	1850	California admitted as free state; Texas (already admitted in 1845) is a slave state; the rest of Mexican Cession to be decided by popular sovereignty. Ends the slave trade in the District of Columbia, but a stronger Fugitive Slave Law, leading to a number of violent recaptures, arouses Northern antislavery opinion.
Kansas-Nebraska Act	1854	At the urging of Stephen A. Douglas, Congress opens Kansas and Nebraska Territories for settlement under popular sovereignty. Open warfare between proslavery and antislavery factions breaks out in Kansas.
Lecompton Constitution	1857	President James Buchanan's decision to admit Kansas to the Union with a proslavery constitution is defeated in Congress.
***Dred Scott* Decision**	1857	The Supreme Court's denial of Dred Scott's case for freedom is welcomed in the South, condemned in the North.
John Brown's Raid and Execution	1859	Northern support for John Brown shocks the South.
Democratic Party Nominating Conventions	1860	The Democrats are unable to agree on a candidate; two candidates, one Northern (Stephen A. Douglas) and one Southern (John C. Breckinridge) split the party and the vote, thus allowing Republican Abraham Lincoln to win.

ESTABLISHMENT OF THE CONFEDERACY

In February, delegates from the seven seceding states met in Montgomery, Alabama, and created the **Confederate States of America**. They wrote a constitution that was identical to the Constitution of the United States, with a few crucial exceptions: it strongly supported states' rights and made the abolition of slavery practically impossible. These two clauses did much to define the Confederate enterprise.

The Montgomery convention passed over the fire-eaters—the men who had been the first to urge secession—and chose Jefferson Davis of Mississippi as president and Alexander Stephens of Georgia as vice president of the new nation. Both men were known as moderates. The choice of moderates was deliberate, for the strategy of the new Confederate state was to argue that secession was a normal, responsible, and expectable course of action, and nothing for the North to get upset about. This was the theme that President Jefferson Davis of the Confederate States of America struck in his Inaugural Address, delivered to a crowd of 10,000 from the steps of the State Capitol at Montgomery, Alabama, on February 18, 1861. "We have changed the constituent parts," Davis said, "but not the system of our Government." Secession was a legal and peaceful step that, Davis said, quoting from the Declaration of Independence, "illustrates the American idea that governments rest on the consent of the governed . . . and that it is the right of the people to alter or abolish them at will whenever they become destructive of the ends for which they were established."

LINCOLN'S INAUGURATION

The country as a whole waited to see what Abraham Lincoln would do, which at first appeared to be very little. In Springfield, Lincoln refused to issue public statements before his inaugural (although he sent many private messages to Congress and to key military officers), for fear of making a delicate situation worse. Similarly, during a twelve-day whistle-stopping railroad trip east from Springfield, he was careful to say nothing controversial. Eastern intellectuals, already suspicious of a mere "prairie lawyer," were not impressed. Finally, hard evidence of an assassination plot forced Lincoln to abandon his whistle-stops at Harrisburg and, protected by Pinkerton detectives, he traveled incognito into Washington, "like a thief in the night," as he complained. These signs of moderation and caution did not appeal to an American public with a penchant for electing military heroes. Americans wanted leadership and action.

Lincoln continued, however, to offer nonbelligerent firmness and moderation. And at the end of his Inaugural Address on March 4, 1861, as he stood ringed by federal troops called out in case of a Confederate attack, the new president offered unexpected eloquence:

> I am loath to close. We are not enemies, but friends. We must not be enemies. Though passion may have strained, it must not break our bonds of affection. The mystic chords of memory, stretching from every battlefield, and patriot grave, to every living heart and hearthstone, all over this broad land, will yet swell the chorus of the Union, when again touched, as surely they will be, by the better angels of our nature.

Confederate States of America
Nation proclaimed in Montgomery, Alabama, in February 1861, after the seven states of the Lower South seceded from the United States.

CONCLUSION

Americans had much to boast about in 1850. Their nation was vastly larger, richer, and more powerful than it had been in 1800. But the issue of slavery was slowly dividing the North and the South, two communities with

CHRONOLOGY

1820	Missouri Compromise.		Treaties with Indians in Northern part of Indian Territory renegotiated.
1828–1832	Nullification Crisis.		Republican Party formed as Whig Party dissolves.
1846	Wilmot Proviso.		
1848	Treaty of Guadalupe Hidalgo ends Mexican-American War.	**1856**	Burning and looting of Lawrence, Kansas.
			John Brown leads Pottawatomie massacre.
	Zachary Taylor elected president.		Attack on Senator Charles Sumner.
	Free-Soil Party formed.		James Buchanan elected president.
1849	California and Utah seek admission to the Union as free states.	**1857**	*Dred Scott* decision.
			President Buchanan accepts proslavery Lecompton constitution in Kansas.
1850	Compromise of 1850.		Panic of 1857.
	California admitted as a free state.	**1858**	Congress rejects Lecompton constitution.
	American (Know-Nothing) Party formed.		Lincoln-Douglas debates.
	Zachary Taylor dies, Millard Fillmore becomes president.	**1859**	John Brown's raid on Harpers Ferry.
1851	North reacts to Fugitive Slave Law.	**1860**	Four parties run presidential candidates.
	Harriet Beecher Stowe's *Uncle Tom's Cabin* published.		Abraham Lincoln elected president.
			South Carolina secedes from Union.
1852	Franklin Pierce elected president.	**1861**	Six other Deep South states secede.
1854	Ostend Manifesto.		Confederate States of America formed.
	Kansas-Nebraska Act.		Lincoln takes office.

similar origins and many common bonds. The following decade was marked by frantic efforts at political compromise, but politics had failed: the issue of slavery was irreconcilable. The only remaining recourse was war. But although Americans were divided, they were still one people. That made the war, when it came, all the more terrible.

SUMMARY

America in 1850 By 1850, the United States had experienced tremendos growth and change. But growth and change. But growth and change also raised serious social issues and renewed the debate over slavery. The North and South divided over slavery creating two opposing sections with very different viewpoints on the future of the United States.

The Compromise of 1850 The issue of the extension of slavery reached a boilong point in 1850. The Compromise of 1850 addressed several major points of tension. But the election of 1852 showed the political party system was weakening while expansionist movements indicated a troubled future.

The Crisis of the National Party System The Kansas-Nebraska Act triggered a violent confrontation between anti-slave and pro-slave forces. At the same time, nativism emerged as a growing political force. The political party system underwent major changes as the Whigs disappeared and the Repubblican Party rose in the North. The lection of 1856 was won by the Democrats but the strong Republican showing indicated future problems.

The Differences Deepen The Dred Scott decision and the struggle over Kansas's cositution exacerbated the tension and conflict between North and South. The economic panic of 1857 further enflamed the dispute. The increasing violence of the slavery issue was shown by John Brown's raid in Virginia.

The South Secedes The election of 1860 laid bare the differences over slaveryand indicated that few were willing to compromise. Lincoln's elections prompted southern states to secede from the Union. As northen leaders grappled with what to do about the secession, the South formed the Confederacy. Lincoln's Inaugural Address indicated he had no desire for war.

REVIEW QUESTIONS

1. What aspects of the remarkable economic development of the United States in the first half of the nineteenth century contributed to the sectional crisis of the 1850s?

2. How might the violent efforts by abolitionists to free escaped slaves who had been recaptured and the federal armed enforcement of the Fugitive Slave Act have been viewed differently by Northern merchants (the so-called Cotton Whigs), Irish immigrants, and abolitionists?

3. Consider the course of events in "Bloody Kansas" from Douglas's Kansas-Nebraska Act to the congressional rejection of the Lecompton constitution. Were these events the inevitable result of the political impasse in Washington, or could other decisions have been taken that would have changed the outcome?

4. The nativism of the 1850s that surfaced so strongly in the Know-Nothing Party was eclipsed by the crisis over slavery. But nativist sentiment has been a recurring theme in American politics. Discuss why it was strong in the 1850s and why it has emerged periodically since then.

5. Evaluate the character and actions of John Brown. Was he the hero proclaimed by Northern supporters or the terrorist condemned by the South?

6. Imagine that you lived in Illinois, home state to both Douglas and Lincoln, in 1860. How would you have voted in the presidential election, and why?

KEY TERMS

Bleeding Kansas (p. 387)

Compromise of 1850 (p. 378)

Confederate States of America (p. 396)

Constitutional Union Party (p. 392)

Dred Scott **Decision** (p. 388)

Fugitive Slave Law (p. 380)

John Brown's Raid (p. 392)

Kansas-Nebraska Act (p. 383)

Know-Nothings (p. 386)

Lecompton Constitution (p. 389)

Lincoln-Douglas Debates (p. 375)

Panic of 1857 (p. 389)

Popular Sovereignty (p. 379)

Republican Party (p. 386)

RECOMMENDED READING

William L. Barney, *The Secessionist Impulse: Alabama and Mississippi in 1860* (1974). Covers the election of 1860 and the subsequent conventions that led to secession.

Don E. Fehrenbacher, *The Dred Scott Case: Its Significance in American Law and Politics* (1978). A major study by the leading historian on this controversial decision.

Eric Foner, *Free Soil, Free Labor, Free Men: The Ideology of the Republican Party before the Civil War* (1970). A landmark effort that was among the first studies to focus on the free labor ideology of the North and its importance in the political disputes of the 1850s.

Lacey K. Ford Jr., *Origins of Southern Radicalism: The South Carolina Upcountry, 1800–1860* (1988). One of a number of recent studies of the attitudes of up-country farmers in South Carolina who supported secession whole-heartedly.

Homan Hamilton, *Prologue to Conflict: The Crisis and Compromise of 1850* (1964). The standard source on the Compromise of 1850.

Bruce Levine, *Half Slave and Half Free: The Roots of the Civil War* (1992). Good survey of the contrasting attitudes of North and South.

Alice Nichols, *Bleeding Kansas* (1954). The standard source on the battles over Kansas.

David M. Potter, *The Impending Crisis, 1848–1861* (1976). A comprehensive account of the politics leading up to the Civil War.

Anne C. Rose, *Voices of the Marketplace: American Thought and Culture, 1830–1860* (1995). A new study that considers the effects of the concepts of Christianity, democracy, and capitalism on American cultural life.

Kenneth M. Stampp, *America in 1857: A Nation on the Brink* (1990). A study of the "crucial" year by a leading Southern historian.

Albert J. Von Frank, *The Trials of Anthony Burns: Freedom and Slavery in Emerson's Boston* (1998). An eloquent study of the trial and the links between transcendentalist and abolitionist opinion.

Edward L. Widmer, *Young America: The Flowering of Democracy in New York City* (1999). Recovers the idealism of the early years of this literary/political movement and traces its decline.

If it is necessary that I should fall on the battle-field for my Country I am ready.
—Sullivan Ballou

Awaiting combat, 1861: Union Soldiers from New York relax at camp awaiting orders to move to the front. The young men show great confidence and determination for their coming engagements, though one fellow to the left of the tent, perhaps a teenager far from home, seems to long for something as he stares beyond the camera. Note also the young African American with a broom sitting apart from the soldiers.

16

THE CIVIL WAR
1861–1865

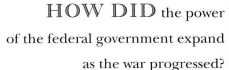

WHAT ADVANTAGES did the North possess at the outset of the Civil War?

HOW DID the power of the federal government expand as the war progressed?

WHAT SUCCESSES did the South enjoy in the early years of the war and how were they achieved?

WHAT IMPACT did the war have on Northern political, economic, and social life?

WHAT SPARKED the New York City draft riots of 1863?

HOW DID Grant and Sherman turn the tide of the war?

AMERICAN COMMUNITIES

Mother Bickerdyke Connects Northern Communities to Their Boys at War

IN MAY 1861 THE REVEREND EDWARD BEECHER INTERRUPTED HIS customary Sunday service at Brick Congregational Church in Galesburg, Illinois, to read a disturbing letter to the congregation. Two months earlier, Galesburg had proudly sent 500 of its young men off to join the Union army. They had not yet been in battle. Yet, the letter reported, an alarming number were dying of diseases caused by inadequate food, medical care, and sanitation at the crowded military camp in Cairo, Illinois. Most army doctors were surgeons, trained to operate and amputate on the battlefield. They were not prepared to treat soldiers sick with dysentery, pneumonia, typhoid, measles—all serious, frequently fatal diseases that could often be cured with careful nursing. The letter writer, appalled by the squalor and misery he saw around him, complained of abuses by the army. The Union army, however, was overwhelmed with the task of readying recruits for battle and had made few provisions for their health when they were not in combat.

The shocked and grieving members of Beecher's congregation quickly decided to send not only supplies, but also one of their number to inspect the conditions at the Cairo camp and to take action. In spite of warnings from a veteran of the War of 1812 that army regulations excluded women from encampments, the congregation voted to send their most qualified member, Mary Ann Bickerdyke, a middle-aged widow who made her living as a "botanic physician." This simple gesture of community concern launched the remarkable Civil War career of "the Cyclone in Calico," who defied medical officers and generals alike in her unceasing efforts on behalf of ill, wounded, and convalescent Union soldiers.

"Mother" Bickerdyke, as she was called, let nothing stand in the way of helping her "boys." When she arrived in Cairo, she immediately set to work cleaning the hospital tents and the soldiers themselves and finding and cooking nourishing food for them. Ordered to leave by the hospital director, who resented her interference, she blandly continued her work. When he reported her to the commanding officer, General Benjamin Prentiss, she quickly convinced the general to let her stay. "I talked sense to him," she later said.

From a peacetime point of view, what Mother Bickerdyke was doing was not unusual. Every civilian hospital had a matron who made sure patients were supplied with clean bed linen and bandages and were fed the proper convalescent diet. But in the context of the war—the sheer number of soldiers, the constant need to set up new field hospitals and commandeer scarce food for an army on the move—it was unusual indeed and required an unusual person. A plain spoken, hardworking woman, totally unfazed by rank or tender masculine egos,

Mother Bickerdyke single-mindedly devoted herself to what she called "the Lord's work." The ordinary soldiers loved her; wise generals supported her. Once, when an indignant officer's wife complained about Bickerdyke's rudeness, General William Tecumseh Sherman joked, "You've picked the one person around here who outranks me. If you want to lodge a complaint against her, you'll have to take it to President Lincoln."

By their actions, Mother Bickerdyke and others like her exposed the War Department's inability to meet the needs of the nation's first mass army. And like the Galesburg congregation, other communities all over the North rallied to make up for the department's shortcomings with supplies and assistance. The efforts of women on the local level—for example, to make clothing for men from their communities who had gone off to the war—quickly took on national dimensions. The Women's Central Association of Relief (WCAR), whose organizers were mostly reformers experienced in the abolitionist, temperance, and education movements, eventually had 7,000 chapters throughout the North. Its volunteers raised funds, made and collected a variety of items—food, clothes, medicine, bandages, and more than 250,000 quilts and comforters—and sent them to army camps and hospitals. Volunteers also provided meals, housing, and transportation to soldiers on furlough. All told, association chapters supplied an estimated $15 million worth of goods to the Union troops.

In June 1861, responding to requests by officials of the WCAR for formal recognition of the organization, President Abraham Lincoln created the United States Sanitary Commission and gave it the power to investigate and advise the Medical Bureau. Henry Bellows, a Unitarian clergyman, became president of the organization, and Frederick Law Olmsted, the author of influential books about the slaveholding South and later the designer of New York's Central Park, was named its executive secretary. The commission's more than 500 "sanitary inspectors" (usually men) instructed soldiers in such matters as water supply, placement of latrines, and safe cooking.

Although at first she worked independently and remained suspicious of all organizations (and even of many other relief workers), in 1862 Mother Bickerdyke was persuaded to become an official agent of "the Sanitary," as it was known. The advantage to her was access to the commission's warehouses and the ability to order from them precisely what she needed. The advantage to the Sanitary was that Mother Bickerdyke was an unequaled fundraiser. In speaking tours throughout Illinois, she touched her female listeners with moving stories of wounded boys whom she had cared for as if they were her own sons. Her words

Memphis

to men were more forceful. It was a man's business to fight, she said. If he was too old or ill to fight with a gun, he should fight with his dollars. With the help of Bickerdyke's blunt appeals, the Sanitary raised $50 million for the Union war effort.

As the Civil War continued, Mother Bickerdyke became a key figure in the medical support for General Ulysses S. Grant's campaigns along the Mississippi River. She was with the army at Shiloh, and as Grant slowly fought his way to Vicksburg, she set up convalescent hospitals in Memphis. Grant authorized her to commandeer any army wagons she needed to transport supplies. Between fifty and seventy "contrabands" (escaped former slaves) worked on her laundry crew. On the civilian side, the Sanitary

Commission authorized her to draw on its supply depots in Memphis, Cairo, Chicago, and elsewhere. She was, thus, in a practical sense a vital "middlewoman" between the home front and the battlefield—and in a symbolic and emotional sense too, as a stand-in for all mothers who had sent their sons to war.

The Civil War was a community tragedy, ripping apart the nation's political fabric and producing more casualties than any other war in the nation's history. Yet in another sense, it was a community triumph. Local communities directly supported and sustained their soldiers on a massive scale in unprecedented ways. As national unity failed, the strength of local communities, symbolized by Mother Bickerdyke, endured.

COMMUNITIES MOBILIZE FOR WAR

A neutral observer in March 1861 might have seen ominous similarities. Two nations—the United States of America (shorn of seven states in the Deep South) and the Confederate States of America—each blamed the other for the breakup of the Union. Two new presidents—Abraham Lincoln and Jefferson Davis—each faced the challenging task of building and maintaining national unity. Two regions—North and South—scorned each other and boasted of their own superiority. But the most basic similarity was not yet apparent: both sides were unprepared for the ordeal that lay ahead.

FORT SUMTER: THE WAR BEGINS

In their Inaugural Addresses, both Abraham Lincoln and Jefferson Davis prayed for peace but positioned themselves for war. Careful listeners to both addresses realized that the two men were on a collision course.

Fort Sumter, a major federal military installation, sat on a granite island at the entrance to Charleston harbor. As long as it remained in Union hands, Charleston, the center of secessionist sentiment, would be immobilized. Thus, it was hardly surprising that Fort Sumter would provide President Lincoln with his first crisis.

On April 6, Lincoln notified the governor of South Carolina that he was sending a relief force to the fort carrying only food and no military supplies. On April 10 Davis ordered General P.G.T. Beauregard to demand the surrender of Fort Sumter and to attack it if the garrison did not comply. On April 12, as Lincoln's relief force neared Charleston harbor, Beauregard opened fire. Two days later, the defenders surrendered and the Confederate Stars and Bars rose over Fort Sumter.

THE CALL TO ARMS

Even before the attack on Fort Sumter, the Confederate Congress had authorized a volunteer army of 100,000 men to serve for twelve months. There was no difficulty finding volunteers. Men flocked to enlist, and their communities sent them off in ceremonies featuring bands, bonfires, and belligerent oratory. For these early recruits, war was a patriotic adventure.

The "thunderclap of Sumter" startled the North into an angry response. The apathy and uncertainty that had prevailed since Lincoln's election disappeared,

WHAT ADVANTAGES

did the North possess at the outset of the Civil War?

15-1
Jefferson Davis, Address to the Provisional Congress of the Confederate States of American (1861)

15-2
The "Cornerstone Speech" (1861)

This Currier and Ives lithograph shows the opening moment of the Civil War. On April 12, 1861, Confederate General P. G. T. Beauregard ordered the shelling of Fort Sumter in Charleston harbor. Two days later, Union Major Robert Anderson surrendered and mobilization began for what turned out to be the most devastating war in American history.

The Granger Collection, New York (0011697/4GCR303)

IMAGE KEY

for pages 400–401

a. A federal flag that flew over Fort Sumter.

b. A photo of engineers of the 8th New York State Militia in front of a tent, 1861.

c. The battle flag of the Second Battalion Hilliard's Alabama Legion. This flag was pierced 83 times during the charge up Snod Grass Hill at Chickamauga, Georgia.

d. The gray cap of a Confederate soldier from the American Civil War.

e. A blue Union soldier's hat with a bugle emblem embroidered on the front.

f. The opening moment of the Civil War, April 12, 1861, at Fort Sumter in Charleston harbor.

g. A painting by William C. Washington, *Jackson Entering the City of Winchester*, shows General "Stonewall" Jackson saving the Virginia town from Union capture in 1862.

h. Robert E. Lee (1807–1870), commander-in-chief of the Confederate armies during the Civil War.

i. American President Abraham Lincoln presents the Emancipation Proclamation to grateful black slaves and white peasants in a political cartoon about education, freedom, and equality.

j. Nurse Ann Bell tending to wounded soldier in a Union hospital.

to be replaced by strong feelings of patriotism. On April 15, Lincoln issued a proclamation calling for 75,000 state militiamen to serve in the federal army for ninety days. Enlistment offices were swamped with so many enthusiastic volunteers that many men were sent home. Free African Americans, among the most eager to serve, were turned away.

The mobilization in Chester, Pennsylvania, was typical of the Northern response to the outbreak of war. A patriotic rally was held at which a company of volunteers (the first of many from the region) calling themselves the "Union Blues" were mustered into the Ninth Regiment of Pennsylvania Volunteers amid cheers and band music. As they marched off to Washington (the gathering place for the Union army), companies of home guards were organized by the men who remained behind. Within a month, the women of Chester had organized a countywide system of war relief that sent a stream of clothing, blankets, bandages, and other supplies to the local troops and provided assistance to their families at home. Such relief organizations, some formally organized, some informal, emerged in every community, North and South, that sent soldiers off to the Civil War. These organizations not only played a vital role in supplying the troops but also maintained the human, local link on which so many soldiers depended. In this sense, every American community accompanied its young men to war.

THE BORDER STATES

The first secession, between December 20, 1860, and February 1, 1861, had taken seven Deep South states out of the Union. Now, in April, the firing on Fort Sumter and Lincoln's call for state militias forced the other Southern states to take sides. Courted—and pressured—by both North and South, four states of the Upper South (Virginia, Arkansas, Tennessee, and North Carolina) joined the original seven in April and May 1861. Virginia's secession tipped the other three toward the Confederacy. The capital of the Confederacy was now moved to Richmond. This meant that the two capitals—Richmond and Washington—were less than 100 miles apart.

Still undecided was the loyalty of the northernmost tier of slave-owning states: Missouri, Kentucky, Maryland, and Delaware. Each controlled vital strategic assets.

Missouri not only bordered the Mississippi River but also controlled the routes to the West. Kentucky controlled the Ohio River. The main railroad link with the West ran through Maryland and the hill region of western Virginia (which split from Virginia to become the free state of West Virginia in 1863). Delaware controlled access to Philadelphia. Finally, were Maryland to secede, the nation's capital would be completely surrounded by Confederate territory.

Delaware was loyal to the Union (less than 2 percent of its population were slaves), but Maryland's loyalty was divided. Lincoln took swift and stern measures to secure Maryland's loyalty. He stationed Union troops along Maryland's crucial railroads, declared martial law in Baltimore, and arrested the suspected ringleaders of the pro-Confederate mob and held them without trial. In July, he ordered the detention of thirty-two secessionist legislators and many sympathizers. Thus was Maryland's loyalty to the Union ensured.

This was the first of a number of violations of basic civil rights during the war, all of which the president justified on the basis of national security.

An even bloodier division occurred in Missouri, where old foes from "Bleeding Kansas" faced off. The proslavery governor and most of the legislature fled to Arkansas, where they declared a Confederate state government in exile. Unionists remained in St. Louis and declared a provisional government that lasted until 1865. Although Missouri had been saved for the Union, the federal military was unable to stop the guerrilla warfare that raged there.

Finally, Lincoln kept Kentucky in the Union by accepting its declaration of neutrality at face value and looking the other way as it became the center of a huge illegal trade with the Confederacy through neighboring Tennessee. By the summer of 1861, Unionists controlled most of the state.

That Delaware, Maryland, Missouri, and Kentucky chose to stay in the Union was a severe blow to the Confederacy. Among them, the four states could have added 45 percent to the white population and military manpower of the Confederacy and 80 percent to its manufacturing capacity. Almost as damaging, the decision of four slave states to stay in the Union punched a huge hole in the Confederate argument that the Southern states were forced to secede to protect the right to own slaves.

THE BATTLE OF BULL RUN

Once sides had been chosen and the initial flush of enthusiasm had passed, the nature of the war, and the mistaken notions about it, soon became clear. The event that shattered the illusions was the First Battle of Bull Run, at Manassas Creek in Virginia in July 1861. Confident of a quick victory, a Union army of 35,000 men marched south, crying "On to Richmond!" So lighthearted and unprepared was the Washington community that the troops were accompanied not only by journalists but also by a crowd of politicians and sightseers. At first the Union troops held their ground against the 25,000 Confederate troops commanded by General P. G. T. Beauregard (of Fort Sumter fame). But when 2,300 fresh Confederate troops arrived as reinforcements, the untrained Northern troops broke ranks in an uncontrolled retreat that swept up the frightened sightseers as well. Soldiers and civilians alike retreated in disarray to Washington.

Bull Run was sobering—and prophetic. The Civil War was the most lethal military conflict in American history, leaving a legacy of devastation on the battlefield and desolation at home. It claimed the lives of nearly 620,000 soldiers, more than the First and Second World Wars combined. One out of every four soldiers who fought in the war never returned home.

15-4
Why They Fought (1861)

15-3
Mary Boykin Chesnut, A Confederate Lady's Diary (1861)

QUICK REVIEW

The First Battle of Bull Run

- July 1861: Beauregard (Confederacy) and McDowell (Union) meet at Manassas.
- Confederate troops repulse a strong Union attack.
- Battle foreshadowed war to come.

15-5
A Confederate General
Assesses First Bull Run (1861)

QUICK REVIEW

Northern Advantages

◆ Two and a half times the South's population.

◆ North controlled much of nation's industrial capacity.

◆ Could field a much larger army.

HOW DID the power of the federal government expand as the war progressed?

THE RELATIVE STRENGTHS OF NORTH AND SOUTH

Over all, in terms of both population and productive capacity, the Union seemed to have a commanding edge over the Confederacy. The North had two and a half times the South's population (22 million to 9 million, of whom 3.5 million were slaves) and enjoyed an even greater advantage in industrial capacity (nine times that of the South). The North produced almost all of the nation's firearms (97 percent), had 71 percent of its railroad mileage, and produced 94 percent of its cloth and 90 percent of its footwear. The North seemed able to feed, clothe, arm, and transport all the soldiers it chose. These advantages were ultimately to prove decisive. But in the short term the South had important assets to counter the advantage of the North.

The first was the nature of the struggle. The most basic principle of the defense of home and community united almost all white Southerners, regardless of their views about slavery. The North would have to invade the South and then control it against guerrilla opposition in order to win.

Second, the military disparity was less extreme than it appeared. Although the North had manpower, its troops were mostly untrained. Moreover, the South, because of its tradition of honor and belligerence (see Chapter 11), appeared to have an advantage in military leaders, the most notable of whom was Robert E. Lee.

Finally, it was widely believed that slavery would work to the South's advantage, for slaves could continue to do the vital plantation work while their masters went off to war. Because of the crucial role of Southern cotton in industrialization, Southerners were confident that the British and French need for Southern cotton would soon bring those countries to recognize the Confederacy as a separate nation.

GOVERNMENTS ORGANIZE FOR WAR

The Civil War forced the federal government to assume powers unimaginable just a few years before. Abraham Lincoln took as his primary task to lead and unify the nation in his responsibility as commander-in-chief. He found the challenge almost insurmountable. Jefferson Davis's challenge was even greater. He had to create a Confederate nation out of a loose grouping of eleven states, each believing strongly in states' rights. Yet in the Confederacy, as in the Union, the conduct of the war required central direction.

LINCOLN AS WAR PRESIDENT

Lincoln's first task as president was to assert control over his own cabinet. Because he had few national contacts outside the Republican Party, Lincoln chose to staff his cabinet with other Republicans, including two who had been his rivals for the presidential nomination: Treasury Secretary Salmon P. Chase, a staunch abolitionist, and Secretary of State William Seward. That the Republican Party was a not-quite-jelled mix of former Whigs, abolitionists, moderate Free-Soilers, and even some prowar Democrats made Lincoln's task as party leader much more difficult than it might otherwise have been.

After the fall of Fort Sumter, military necessity prompted Lincoln to call up the state militias, order a naval blockade of the South, and vastly expand the military budget.

Although James K. Polk had assumed responsibility for overall American military strategy during the Mexican-American War (see Chapter 14), Lincoln was the first president to act as commander-in-chief in both a practical and a symbolic way. His involvement in military strategy sprang from his realization that a civil war presented problems different from those of a foreign war of conquest. Lincoln wanted above all to persuade the South to rejoin the Union, and his every military move was dictated by the hope of eventual reconciliation—hence, his cautiousness, and his acute sense of the role of public opinion.

EXPANDING THE POWER OF THE FEDERAL GOVERNMENT

The greatest expansion in government power during the war was in the War Department, which by early 1862 was faced with the unprecedented challenge of feeding, clothing, and arming 700,000 Union soldiers. Initially the government relied on the individual states to equip and supply their vastly expanded militias. States often contracted directly with textile mills and shoe factories to clothe their troops. In many Northern cities, volunteer groups sprang up to recruit regiments, buy them weapons, and send them to Washington. Other such community groups, like the one in Chester, Pennsylvania, focused on clothing and providing medical care to soldiers. By January 1862 the War Department, under the able direction of Edwin M. Stanton, a former Democrat from Ohio, was able to perform many basic functions of procurement and supply without too much delay or corruption. But the size of the Union army and the complexity of fully supplying it demanded constant efforts at all levels—government, state, and community—throughout the war. Thus, in the matter of procurement and supply, as in mobilization, the battlefront was related to the home front on a scale that Americans had not previously experienced.

The need for money for the vast war effort was pressing. Treasury Secretary Chase worked closely with Congress to develop ways to finance the war. They naturally turned to the nation's economic experts—private bankers, merchants, and managers of large businesses. With the help of Philadelphia financier Jay Cooke, the Treasury used patriotic appeals to sell war bonds to ordinary people in amounts as small as $50. This was the first example in American history of the mass financing of war. Additional sources of revenue were sales taxes and the first federal income tax, (which affected only the affluent).

Most radical of all was Chase's decision—which was authorized only after a bitter congressional fight—to print and distribute Treasury notes (paper money). Until then, the money in circulation had been a mixture of coins and state bank notes issued by 1,500 different state banks. The **Legal Tender Act** of February 1862 created a national currency. Because of its color, the paper bank notes were popularly known as "greenbacks." In 1863, Congress passed the **National Bank Act**, which prohibited state banks from issuing their own notes and forced them to apply for federal charters.

The national currency was widely recognized as a major step toward centralization of economic power in the hands of the federal government. Such a measure would have been unthinkable if Southern Democrats had still been part of the national government. The absence of Southern Democrats also made possible passage of a number of Republican economic measures not directly related to the war.

Although the outbreak of war overshadowed everything else, the Republican Party in Congress was determined to fulfill its campaign pledge of a comprehensive program of economic development. Republicans quickly passed the **Morrill Tariff Act** (1861); by 1864, this and subsequent measures had raised tariffs to more than double their prewar rate. In 1862 and 1864, Congress created two federally chartered corporations to build a transcontinental railroad—the Union Pacific Railroad Company, to lay track westward from Omaha, and the Central Pacific, to lay track eastward from California. Two other measures, both passed in 1862, had long been sought by Westerners. The **Homestead Act** gave 160 acres of public land to any citizen who agreed to live on the land for five years, improve it

Legal Tender Act   Act creating a national currency in February 1862.

National Bank Act   Act prohibiting state banks from issuing their own notes and forcing them to apply for federal charters.

Morrill Tariff Act   Act that raised tariffs to more than double their prewar rate.

Homestead Act   Law passed by Congress in May 1862 providing homesteads with 160 acres of free land in exchange for improving the land within five years of the grant.

by building a house and cultivating some of the land, and pay a small fee. The **Morrill Land Grant Act** gave states public land that would allow them to finance land-grant colleges offering education to ordinary citizens in practical skills such as agriculture, engineering, and military science. Coupled with this act, the establishment of a federal Department of Agriculture in 1862 gave American farmers a big push toward modern commercial agriculture.

These were powerful nationalizing forces. They connected ordinary people to the federal government in new ways. Although many of the executive war powers lapsed when the battles ended, the accumulation of strength by the federal government was never reversed.

DIPLOMATIC OBJECTIVES

To Secretary of State William Seward fell the job of making sure that Britain and France did not extend diplomatic recognition to the Confederacy. Although Southerners had been certain that the need for cotton would gain them European support, they were wrong. British public opinion would not countenance the recognition of a new nation based on slavery. British cotton manufacturers found economic alternatives, first using up their backlog of Southern cotton and then turning to Egypt and India for new supplies.

In 1861, a bankrupt Mexico suffered the ignominy of a joint invasion by British, Spanish, and French troops determined to collect the substantial debts owed by Mexico to their nations. This was a serious violation of Mexican independence, just the kind of European intervention that the Monroe Doctrine had been formulated to prevent (see Chapter 9). When it became clear that France was bent on conquest, Britain and Spain withdrew, and Mexican forces repelled the French troops on May 5, 1862. Ever since, Mexico has celebrated *El Cinco de Mayo*. France eventually prevailed and installed the Austrian archduke Maximilian as emperor. In normal times, the French conquest could have led to war with the United States, but fearing that France might recognize the Confederacy or invade Texas, Seward had to content himself with refusing to recognize the new Mexican government.

JEFFERSON DAVIS AS CONFEDERATE PRESIDENT

Although Jefferson Davis had held national cabinet rank (as secretary of war under President Franklin Pierce), had experience as an administrator, and was a former military man (none of which was true of Abraham Lincoln), he was unable to hold the Confederacy together. Perhaps no one could have.

Davis's first cabinet of six men, appointed in February 1861, included a representative from each of the states of the first secession except Mississippi, which was represented by Davis himself. This careful attention to the equality of the states pointed to the fundamental problem that Davis was unable to overcome. Although he saw the need for unity, he was unable to impose it. Soon his autonomous style of leadership—he wanted to decide every detail himself—angered his generals, alienated cabinet members, and gave Southern governors reason to resist his orders. After the first flush of patriotism had passed, the Confederacy never lived up to its hope of becoming a unified nation.

CONFEDERATE DISAPPOINTMENTS IN DIPLOMACY AND THE ECONOMY

The failure of "cotton diplomacy" was a crushing blow. White Southerners were stunned that Britain and France would not recognize their claim to independence. Well into 1863, the South hoped that a decisive battlefield victory would

---

QUICK REVIEW

Jefferson Davis and the Southern Cause

◆ Davis had experience as an administrator and former military man.

◆ Davis not a leader by personality.

◆ Failed to unify Confederacy.

Morrill Land Grant Act Law passed by Congress in July 1862 awarding proceeds from the sale of public lands to the states for the establishment of agricultural and mechanical colleges.

change the minds of cautious Europeans. In the meantime, plantations continued to grow cotton, but the Confederacy withheld it from market, hoping that lack of raw material for their textile mills would lead the British and French to recognize the Confederacy. The British reacted indignantly, claiming that the withholding of cotton was economic blackmail, and found new sources of cotton. In 1862, when the Confederacy ended the embargo and began to ship its great surplus, the world price of cotton plunged. Then too, the Union naval blockade, weak at first, began to take effect. Cotton turned out to be not so powerful a diplomatic weapon after all.

Perhaps the greatest Southern failure was in the area of finances. At first the Confederate government tried to raise money from the states, but governors refused to impose new taxes. By the time uniform taxes were levied in 1863, it was too late. Heavy borrowing and the printing of great sums of paper money produced runaway inflation (a ruinous rate of 9,000 percent per annum by 1865, compared with 80 percent in the North). Inflation, in turn, caused incalculable damage to morale and prospects for unity.

After the initial surge of volunteers, enlistment in the military fell off, as it did in the North also. In April 1862, the Confederate Congress passed the first draft law in American history, and the Union Congress followed suit in March 1863. The Southern law declared that all able-bodied men between eighteen and thirty-five were eligible for three years of military service. Purchase of substitutes was allowed, as in the North, but in the South the price was uncontrolled, rising eventually to $10,000 in Confederate money. The most disliked part of the draft law was a provision exempting one white man on each plantation with twenty or more slaves. This provision not only seemed to disprove the earlier claim that slavery freed white men to fight, but it aroused class resentments. A bitter phrase of the time complained, "It's a rich man's war but a poor man's fight."

CONTRADICTIONS OF SOUTHERN NATIONALISM

In the early days of the war, Jefferson Davis successfully mobilized feelings of regional identity and patriotism. Many Southerners felt part of a beleaguered region that had been forced to resist Northern tyranny. But most Southerners felt loyalty to their own state and local communities, not to a Confederate nation. The strong belief in states' rights and aristocratic privilege undermined the Confederate cause. Some Southern governors resisted potentially unifying actions such as moving militias outside their home states. Broader measures, such as general taxation, were widely evaded by rich and poor alike. The inequitable draft was only one of many things that convinced the ordinary people of the South that this was a war for privileged slave owners, not for them. With its leaders and citizens fearing (perhaps correctly) that centralization would destroy what was distinctively Southern, the Confederacy was unable to mobilize the resources—financial, human, and otherwise—that might have prevented its destruction by Northern armies.

The contrast between the hope and valor of these young Southern volunteer soldiers, photographed shortly before the first battle of Bull Run, and the later advertisements for substitutes is marked. Southern exemptions for slave owners and lavish payment for substitutes increasingly bred resentment among the ordinary people of the South.

(a) First Virginia Regiment, Cook Collection. Valentine Museum Library/Richmond History Center; (b) Richmond Dispatch, Courtesy of the Library of Congress

THE FIGHTING THROUGH 1862

Just as political decisions were often driven by military necessity, the basic Northern and Southern military strategies were affected by political considerations as much as by military ones. The initial policy of limited war, thought to be the best route to ultimate reconciliation, ran into difficulties because of the public's impatience for victories. But victories, as the mounting slaughter made clear, were not easy to achieve.

MAP EXPLORATION

To explore an interactive version of this map, go to **http://www.prenhall.com/faraghertlc/map16.1**

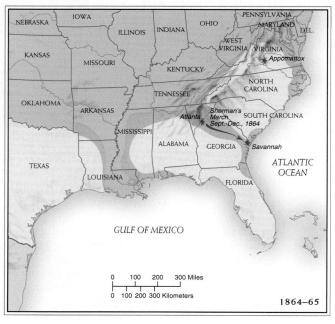

MAP 16-1

Overall Strategy of the Civil War The initial Northern strategy for subduing the South, the so-called Anaconda Plan, entailed strangling it by a blockade at sea and obtaining control of the Mississippi River. But in the end of 1862 it was clear that the South's defensive strategy could only be broken by the invasion of Southern territory. In 1864, Sherman's "March to the Sea" and Grant's hammering tactics in northern Virginia brought the war home to the South. Lee's surrender to Grant at Appomattox Courthouse on April 9, 1865, ended the bloodiest war in the nation's history.

HOW DID the military strategies of the North and the South reflect each side's larger goals?

THE WAR IN NORTHERN VIRGINIA

The initial Northern strategy, dubbed by critics the Anaconda Plan (after the constrictor snake), envisaged slowly squeezing the South with a blockade at sea and on the Mississippi River. Lincoln accepted the basics of the plan, but public clamor for a fight pushed him to agree to the disastrous Battle of Bull Run and then to a major buildup of Union troops in northern Virginia under General George B. McClellan.

Dashing in appearance, McClellan was extremely cautious in battle. In March 1862, after almost a year spent drilling the raw Union recruits and after repeated exhortations by an impatient Lincoln, McClellan committed 120,000 troops to what became known as the **Peninsular campaign**. The objective was to capture Richmond, the Confederate capital. McClellan had his troops and their supplies ferried in 400 ships from Washington to Fortress Monroe, near the mouth of the James River, an effort that took three weeks. Inching up the James Peninsula, by June McClellan's troops were close enough to Richmond to hear the church bells ringing—but not close enough for victory. In a series of battles known as the Seven Days, Robert E. Lee boldly counterattacked, repeatedly catching McClellan off guard. In August, Lincoln, disappointed by McClellan's inaction, ordered him to abandon the campaign and return to the capital.

Jefferson Davis, like Abraham Lincoln, was an active commander-in-chief. After the Seven Days victories, Davis supported a Confederate attack on Maryland. But in the brutal battle of Antietam on September 17, 1862, which claimed more than 5,000 dead and 19,000 wounded, McClellan's army checked Lee's advance. Lee retreated to Virginia, inflicting terrible losses on Northern troops at Fredricksburg when they again made a thrust toward Richmond in December 1862. The war in northern Virginia was stalemated: neither side was strong enough to win, but each was too strong to be defeated.

SHILOH AND THE WAR FOR THE MISSISSIPPI

Although most public attention was focused on the fighting in Virginia, battles in Tennessee and along the Mississippi River proved to be the key to eventual Union victory. The rising military figure in the West was Ulysses S. Grant, who had once resigned from the service because of a drinking problem. In February 1862, Grant captured Fort Henry and Fort Donelson, on the Tennessee and Cumberland rivers, establishing Union control of much of Tennessee.

Moving south with 28,000 men, Grant met a 40,000-man Confederate force commanded by General Albert Sidney Johnston at Shiloh Church in April 1862. After two days of bitter and bloody fighting in the rain, the Confederates withdrew. The losses on both sides were enormous: the North lost 13,000 men, the South 11,000, including General Johnston, who bled to death. Grant kept moving, capturing Memphis in June and beginning a campaign to eventually capture Vicksburg, Mississippi, in November. Earlier that year, naval forces under Admiral

Peninsular campaign Union offensive led by McClellan with the objective of capturing Richmond.

 15-6
Charles Harvey Brewster, Three Letters from the Civil War Front (1862)

MAP EXPLORATION

To explore an interactive version of this map, go to
http://www.prenhall.com/faraghertic/map16.2

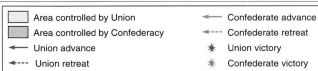

MAP 16-2
Major Battles in the East, 1861–1862 Northern Virginia was the most crucial and the most constant theater of battle. The prizes were the two opposing capitals, Washington and Richmond, only 70 miles apart. By the summer of 1862, George B. McClellan, famously cautious, had achieved only stalemate in the Peninsular campaign. He did, however, turn back Robert E. Lee at Antietam in September.

WHAT WAS the Anaconda Plan? Why did it fail?

MAP EXPLORATION

To explore an interactive version of this map, go to
http://www.prenhall.com/faraghertlc/map16.3

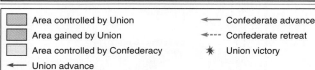

▨ Area controlled by Union	◄— Confederate advance
▨ Area gained by Union	◄---- Confederate retreat
▨ Area controlled by Confederacy	✳ Union victory
◄— Union advance	

MAP 16-3

Major Battles in the West, 1862–1863 Ulysses S. Grant waged a mobile war, winning at Fort Henry and Fort Donelson in Tennessee in February 1862 and at Shiloh in April and capturing Memphis in June. He then laid siege to Vicksburg, as Admiral David Farragut captured New Orleans and began to advance up the Mississippi River.

WHAT ROLE did Indians Play in the Fighting in the West?

David Farragut had captured New Orleans and then continued up the Mississippi River. By the end of 1862 it was clearly only a matter of time before the entire river would be in Union hands.

THE WAR IN THE TRANS-MISSISSIPPI WEST

Although only one Western state, Texas, seceded from the Union, the Civil War was fought in small ways in many parts of the West. Southern hopes for the extension of slavery into the Southwest were reignited by the war, and the just-announced discovery of gold in Colorado impelled the Confederacy to attempt to capture it. Texans mounted an attack on New Mexico, which they had long coveted, and kept their eyes on the larger prizes of Arizona and California. A Confederate force led by General Henry H. Sibley occupied Santa Fé and Albuquerque early in 1862 without resistance, thus posing a serious Confederate threat to the entire Southwest. Confederate hopes were dashed, however, by a ragtag group of 950 miners and adventurers organized into the first Colorado Volunteer Infantry Regiment. After an epic march of 400 miles from Denver, which was completed in thirteen days despite snow and high winds, the Colorado militia stopped the unsuspecting Confederate troops in the Battle of Glorieta Pass on March 26–28, 1862. This dashing action, coupled with the efforts of California militias to safeguard Arizona and Utah from seizure by Confederate sympathizers, secured the Far West for the Union.

Other military action in the West was less decisive. The chronic fighting along the Kansas-Missouri border set a record for brutality when Confederate William Quantrill's Raiders made a predawn attack on Lawrence, Kansas, in August 1863, massacring 150 inhabitants and burning the town. Another civil war took place in Indian Territory, south of Kansas. The southern Indian tribes who had been removed there from the Old Southwest in the 1830s included many who were still bitter over the horrors of their removal by federal troops, and they sympathized with the Confederacy. Union victories at Pea Ridge (in northwestern Arkansas) in 1862 and near Fort Gibson (in Indian Territory) in 1863 secured the area for the Union but did little to stop dissension among the Indian groups themselves. After the Civil War the victorious federal government used the tribes' wartime support for the Confederacy as a justification for demanding further land cessions.

The hostilities in the West showed that no part of the country, and none of its inhabitants, could remain untouched by the Civil War.

THE NAVAL WAR

The Union's naval blockade of the South, intended to cut off commerce between the Confederacy and the rest of the world, was initially unsuccessful. The U.S. Navy had only thirty-three ships with which to blockade 189 ports along 3,500 miles of coastline. Southern blockade runners evaded Union ships with ease: only an estimated one-eighth of all Confederate shipping was stopped in 1862. Moreover, the Confederacy licensed British-made privateers to strike at Northern shipping. In a two-year period one such Confederate raider, the *Alabama,* destroyed sixty-nine Union ships with cargoes valued at $6 million. Beginning in 1863, however, as the Union navy became larger, the blockade began to take effect. In 1864 a third of the blockade runners were captured, and in 1865 half of them. As a result, fewer and fewer supplies reached the South.

For the Union, the most successful naval operation in the first two years of the war was not the blockade but the seizing of exposed coastal areas. The Sea Islands of South Carolina were taken, as were some of the North Carolina islands and Fort Pulaski, which commanded the harbor of Savannah, Georgia. Most damaging to the South was the capture of New Orleans.

THE BLACK RESPONSE

The capture of Port Royal in the South Carolina Sea Islands in 1861 was important for another reason. Whites fled at the Union advance, but 10,000 slaves greeted the troops with jubilation and shouts of gratitude. Union troops had unwittingly freed these slaves in advance of any official Union policy on the status of slaves in captured territory.

Early in the war, an irate Southerner who saw three of his slaves disappear behind Union lines at Fortress Monroe, Virginia, demanded the return of his property, citing the Fugitive Slave Law. The Union commander, Benjamin Butler, replied that the Fugitive Slave Law no longer applied and that the escaped slaves were "contraband of war." News of Butler's decision spread rapidly among the slaves in the region of Fortress Monroe. Two days later, eight runaway slaves appeared; the next day, fifty-nine black men and women arrived at the fort. Union commanders had found an effective way to rob the South of its basic work force. The "contrabands," as they were known, were put to work building fortifications and doing other useful work in Northern camps.

As Union troops drove deeper into the South, the black response grew. When Union General William Tecumseh Sherman marched his army through Georgia in 1864, 18,000 slaves—entire families, people of all ages—flocked to the Union lines. By the war's end, nearly a million black people, fully a quarter of all the slaves in the South, had "voted with their feet" for the Union.

THE DEATH OF SLAVERY

The overwhelming response of black slaves to the Union advance changed the nature of the war. As increasing numbers of slaves flocked to Union lines, the conclusion was unmistakable: the Southern war to defend the slave system did not have the support of slaves themselves. Any Northern policy that ignored the issue of slavery and the wishes of the slaves was unrealistic.

THE POLITICS OF EMANCIPATION

In 1862, as the issue of slavery loomed ever larger, Abraham Lincoln, acutely aware of divided Northern opinion, inched his way toward a declaration of emancipation. Lincoln was correct to be worried about the unity of opinion in the North. Before the war, within the Republican Party, only a small group of abolitionists had favored freeing the slaves. Most Republicans were more concerned about the expansion of slavery than they were about the lives of slaves themselves. They did not favor the social equality of black people, whom they considered inferior. The free-soil movement, for example, was as often antiblack as it was antislave. For their part, most northern

QUICK REVIEW

The War at Sea

♦ Union naval blockade strengthened over time.

♦ Confederate ships had limited success running the blockade.

♦ Restriction of trade hurt the Southern cause.

WHAT impact did the war have on Northern political, economic, and social life.

Democrats were openly antiblack. Irish workers in Northern cities had rioted against free African Americans, with whom they often competed for jobs. There was also the question of what would become of slaves who were freed. Even the most fervent abolitionists had refused to face up to this issue. Northern Democrats effectively played on racial fears in the 1862 congressional elections, warning that freed slaves would pour into Northern cities and take jobs from white laborers.

Nevertheless, the necessities of war edged Lincoln toward a new position. Following the Union victory at Antietam in September 1862, Lincoln issued a preliminary decree: unless the rebellious states returned to the Union by January 1, 1863, he would declare their slaves "forever free." Although Lincoln did not expect the Confederate states to surrender because of his proclamation, the decree increased the pressure on the South by directly linking the slave system to the war effort. Thus the freedom of black people became part of the struggle. Frederick Douglass, the voice of black America, wrote, "We shout for joy that we live to record this righteous decree."

On January 1, 1863, Lincoln duly issued the final **Emancipation Proclamation**, which turned out to be just as tortuous as his earlier responses to public opinion. The proclamation freed the slaves in the areas of rebellion—the areas the Union did not control—but specifically exempted slaves in the border states and in former Confederate areas conquered by the Union. Lincoln's purpose was to meet the abolitionist demand for a war against slavery while not losing the support of conservatives, especially in the border states. But the proclamation was so equivocal that Lincoln's own secretary of state, William Seward, remarked sarcastically, "We show our sympathy with slavery by emancipating slaves where we cannot reach them and holding them in bondage where we can set them free."

One group greeted the Emancipation Proclamation with open celebration. On New Year's Day, hundreds of African Americans gathered outside the White House and cheered the president. Realizing the symbolic importance of the proclamation, free African Americans predicted that the news would encourage Southern slaves either to flee to Union lines or refuse to work for their masters. Both of these things were already happening as African Americans seized on wartime changes to reshape white–black relations in the South. In one sense, then, the Emancipation Proclamation simply gave a name to a process already in motion.

Abolitionists set about moving Lincoln beyond his careful stance in the Emancipation Proclamation. Reformers such as Elizabeth Cady Stanton and Susan B. Anthony lobbied and petitioned for a constitutional amendment outlawing slavery. Congress, at Lincoln's urging, approved and sent to the states a statement banning slavery throughout the United States. Quickly ratified by the Union states in 1865, the statement became the **Thirteenth Amendment** to the Constitution.

BLACK FIGHTING MEN

As part of the Emancipation Proclamation, Lincoln gave his support for the first time to the recruitment of black soldiers. Early in the war, eager black volunteers had been bitterly disappointed at being turned away. Many, like Robert Fitzgerald, a free African American from Pennsylvania, found other ways to serve the Union cause. Fitzgerald first drove a wagon and mule for the Quartermaster Corps, and later, in spite of persistent seasickness, he served in the Union navy. After the Emancipation Proclamation, however, Fitzgerald was able to do what he had wanted to do all along: be a soldier. He enlisted in the Fifth Massachusetts Cavalry, a regiment that, like all the units in which black soldiers served, was 100 percent African American but commanded by white officers.

In Fitzgerald's company of eighty-three men, half came from slave states and had run away to enlist; the other half came mostly from the North but also from

QUICK REVIEW

African American Soldiers

♦ Lincoln supported recruitment of black soldiers as part of the Emancipation Proclamation.

♦ Nearly 200,000 African Americans served in the Union army.

♦ 37,000 African Americans died defending their freedom and the Union.

Emancipation Proclamation Decree announced by President Abraham Lincoln in September 1862 and formally issued on January 1, 1863, freeing slaves in all Confederate states still in rebellion.

Thirteenth Amendment Constitutional amendment ratified in 1865 that freed all slaves throughout the United States.

This painting, *The Storming of Fort Wagner,* shows the attack on the fort near Charleston, South Carolina, by the 54th Massachusetts African American Regiment on July 18, 1863. The attack failed, and more than half the members of this first Union all-black regiment and their white commanding officer, Robert Gould Shaw, were killed.

Kurtz and Allison. Courtesy of the Library of Congress

Canada, the West Indies, and France. Other regiments had volunteers from Africa. The proportion of volunteers from the loyal border states (where slavery was still legal) was upwards of 25 percent—a lethal blow to the slave system in those states.

After a scant two months of training, Fitzgerald's company was sent on to Washington and thence to battle in Northern Virginia. Uncertain of the reception they would receive in Northern cities with their history of antiblack riots, Fitzgerald and his comrades were pleasantly surprised. "We are cheered in every town we pass through," he wrote in his diary. "I was surprised to see a great many white people weeping as the train moved South." White people had reason to cheer: black volunteers, eager and willing to fight, made up 10 percent of the Union army. Nearly 200,000 African Americans (one out of every five black males in the nation) served in the Union army or navy. A fifth of them—37,000—died defending their own freedom and the Union.

Military service was something no black man could take lightly. African American soldiers faced prejudice within the army and had to prove themselves in battle.

Furthermore, the Confederates hated and feared African American troops and threatened to treat any captured black soldier as an escaped slave subject to execution. On at least one occasion, the threats were carried out. In 1864 Confederate soldiers massacred 262 black soldiers at Fort Pillow, Tennessee, after they had surrendered. Although large-scale episodes such as this were rare (especially after President Lincoln threatened retaliation), smaller ones were not. On duty near Petersburg, Virginia, Robert Fitzgerald's company lost a picket to Confederate hatred: wounded in the leg, he was unable to escape from Confederate soldiers, who smashed his skull with their musket butts.

Another extraordinary part of the story of the African American soldiers was their reception by black people in the South, who were overjoyed at the sight of armed black men, many of them former slaves themselves, wearing the uniform of the Union army. As his regiment entered Wilmington, North Carolina, one soldier wrote, "Men and women, old and young, were running throughout the streets, shouting and praising God. We could then truly see what we have been fighting for."

African American soldiers were not treated equally by the Union army. They were segregated in camp, given the worst jobs, and paid less than white soldiers ($10 a

15-8
James Henry Gooding, Letter to President Lincoln (1863)

15-12
Susie King Taylor,
Reminiscences of an Army
Laundress (1902)

WHAT SPARKED the
New York City draft riots of 1863?

month rather than $13). Although they might not be able to do much about the other kinds of discrimination, the men of the Fifty-fourth Massachusetts found an unusual way to protest their unequal pay: they refused to accept it, preferring to serve the army for free until it decided to treat them as free men. The protest was effective; in June 1864 the War Department equalized the wages of black and white soldiers.

THE FRONT LINES AND THE HOME FRONT

Civil War soldiers wrote millions of letters home, more proportionately than in any other American war. Their letters are a testament to the patriotism of both Union and Confederate troops, for the story they tell is frequently one of slaughter and horror.

THE TOLL OF WAR

In spite of early hopes for what one might call a "brotherly" war, one that avoided excessive brutality, Civil War battles were appallingly deadly. One reason was technology: improved weapons, particularly modern rifles, had much greater range and accuracy than the muskets they replaced. Another was that almost all Union and Confederate generals remained committed to the conventional military doctrine of massed infantry offensives—the "Jomini doctrine"—that they had learned in their military classes at West Point. Part of this strategy had been to "soften up" a defensive line with artillery before an infantry assault, but now the range of the new rifles made artillery itself vulnerable to attack. As a result, generals relied less on "softening up" than on immense numbers of infantrymen, hoping that enough of them would survive the withering rifle fire to overwhelm the enemy line. Enormous casualties were a consequence of this basic strategy.

Medical ignorance was another factor in the casualty rate. Because the use of antiseptic procedures was in its infancy, men often died because minor wounds became infected. Gangrene was a common cause of death. Disease was an even more frequent killer, taking twice as many men as were lost in battle. The overcrowded and unsanitary conditions of many camps were breeding grounds for smallpox, dysentery, typhoid, pneumonia, and, in the summer, malaria.

Yet another factor was that both North and South were completely unprepared to handle the supply and health needs of their large armies. Twenty-four hours after the battle of Shiloh, most of the wounded still lay on the field in the rain. Many died of exposure; some, unable to help themselves, drowned.

ARMY NURSES

Many medical supplies that the armies were unable to provide were donated by the United States Sanitary Commission in the North, as described in the opening of this chapter, and by women's volunteer groups in the South. But in addition to supplies, there was also an urgent need for skilled nurses. Under the pressure of wartime necessity, and over the objections of most army doctors, women became army nurses. Hospital nursing, previously considered a job only disreputable women would undertake, now became a suitable vocation for middle-class women. Under the leadership of veteran reformer Dorothea Dix of the asylum movement (see Chapter 13), and in cooperation with the Sanitary Commission (and with the vocal support of Mother Bickerdyke), by the war's end more than 3,000 Northern women had worked as paid army nurses and many more as volunteers.

One of the volunteers was Ellen Ruggles Strong of New York, who, over her husband's objections, insisted on nursing in the Peninsular campaign of 1862. "The

Nurse Ann Bell shown preparing medicine for a wounded soldier. Prompted by the medical crisis of the war, women such as Bell and "Mother" Bickerdyke actively participated in the war effort as nurses.

Union Hospital. Center of Military History, U.S. Army

little woman has come out amazingly strong during these two months," George Templeton Strong wrote in his diary with a mixture of pride and condescension. "Have never given her credit for a tithe of the enterprise, pluck, discretion, and force of character that she has shown. God bless her." Other women organized other volunteer efforts outside the Sanitary Commission umbrella. Perhaps the best known was Clara Barton, who had been a government clerk before the war and consequently knew a number of influential members of Congress. Barton organized nursing and the distribution of medical supplies; she also used her congressional contacts to force reforms in army medical practice, of which she was very critical.

Southern women were also active in nursing and otherwise aiding soldiers, though the South never boasted a single large-scale organization like the Sanitary Commission. The women of Richmond volunteered when they found the war on their doorstep in the summer of 1862. During the Seven Days Battles, thousands of wounded poured into Richmond; many died in the streets because there was no room for them in hospitals. Richmond women first established informal "roadside hospitals" to meet the need, and their activities expanded from there. As in the North, middle-class women at first faced strong resistance from army doctors and even their own families, who believed that a field hospital was "no place for a refined lady." Kate Cumming of Mobile, who nursed in Corinth, Mississippi, after the Battle of Shiloh, faced down such reproofs, though she confided to her diary that nursing wounded men was very difficult: "Nothing that I had ever heard or read had given me the faintest idea of the horrors witnessed here." She and her companion nurses persisted and became an important part of the Confederate medical services. For Southern women, who had been much less active in the public life of their communities than their Northern reforming sisters, this Civil War activity marked an important break with prewar tradition.

Although women had made important advances, most army nurses and medical support staff were men. One volunteer nurse was the poet Walt Whitman, who visited wounded soldiers in the hospital in Washington, D.C. Horrified at the suffering he saw, Whitman also formed a deep admiration for the "incredible

15-7
Clara Barton, Medical Life at the Battfield (1862)

dauntlessness" of the common soldier in the face of slaughter and privation. While never denying the senselessness of the slaughter, Whitman nevertheless found hope in the determined spirit of the common man and woman.

THE LIFE OF THE COMMON SOLDIER

The conditions experienced by the eager young volunteers of the Union and Confederate armies included massive, terrifying, and bloody battles, apparently unending, with no sign of victory in sight. Soldiers suffered from the uncertainty of supply, which left troops, especially in the South, without uniforms, tents, and sometimes even food. They endured long marches over muddy, rutted roads while carrying packs weighing fifty or sixty pounds. Disease was rampant in their dirty, verminous, and unsanitary camps, and hospitals were so dreadful that more men left them dead than alive.

Many soldiers had entered military service with unrealistic, even romantic ideas about warfare. Reality was a rude shock. Desertion was common: an estimated one of every nine Confederate soldiers and one of every seven Union soldiers deserted. Unauthorized absence was another problem. At Antietam, Robert E. Lee estimated that unauthorized absence reduced his strength by a third to a half.

WARTIME POLITICS

In the earliest days of the war, Northerners had joined together in support of the war effort. Democrat Stephen A. Douglas, Lincoln's defeated rival, paid a visit to the White House to offer Lincoln his support. Within a month, Douglas was dead at age forty-eight. The Democrats had lost the leadership of a broad-minded man who might have done much on behalf of Northern unity. By 1862 Democrats had split into two factions: the War Democrats and the Peace Democrats, derogatorily called "**Copperheads**" (from the poisonous snake).

The Democratic Party remained a powerful force in Northern politics. It had received 44 percent of the popular vote in the North in the 1860 election and its united opposition to the emancipation of slaves explains much of Lincoln's equivocal action on this issue. But the Peace Democrats went far beyond opposition to emancipation, denouncing the draft, martial law, and the high-handed actions of "King Abraham."

The leader of the Copperheads, Clement Vallandigham, a former Ohio congressman, advocated an armistice and a negotiated peace that would "look only to the welfare, peace and safety of the white race, without reference to the effect that settlement may have on the African." Western Democrats, he threatened, might form their own union with the South, excluding New England with its radical abolitionists and high-tariff industrialists. Lincoln could not afford to take Vallandigham's threats lightly. Besides, he was convinced that some Peace Democrats were members of secret societies—the Knights of the Golden Circle and the Sons of Liberty—that had been conspiring with the Confederacy. In 1862, Lincoln proclaimed that all people who discouraged enlistments in the army or otherwise engaged in disloyal practices would be subject to martial law. In all, 13,000 people were arrested and imprisoned, including Vallandigham, who was exiled to the Confederacy. Lincoln rejected all protests, claiming that his arbitrary actions were necessary for national security.

Lincoln also faced challenges from the radical faction of his own party. As the war continued, the radicals gained strength. The most troublesome was Salmon P. Chase, who in December 1862 caused a cabinet crisis when he encouraged Senate Republicans to complain that Secretary of State William Seward was "lukewarm" in his support for emancipation. This radical challenge was a portent of the party's difficulties after the war, which Lincoln did not live to see—or prevent.

Copperheads   A term Republicans applied to Northern war dissenters and those suspected of aiding the Confederate cause during the Civil War.

ECONOMIC AND SOCIAL STRAINS ON THE NORTH

Wartime needs caused a surge in Northern economic growth, but the gains were unequally distributed. Early in the war, some industries suffered: textile manufacturers could not get cotton, and shoe factories that had made cheap shoes for slaves were without a market. But other industries boomed—boot making, shipbuilding, and the manufacture of woolen goods such as blankets and uniforms, to give just three examples. Coal mining expanded, as did ironmaking, especially the manufacture of iron rails for railroads. Agricultural goods were in great demand, promoting further mechanization of farming. The McCormick brothers grew rich from sales of their reapers. Women, left to tend the family farm while the men went to war, found that with mechanized equipment they could manage the demanding task of harvesting.

Meeting wartime needs enriched some people honestly, but speculators and profiteers also flourished, as they have in every war. By the end of the war, government contracts had exceeded $1 billion. Not all of this business was free from corruption. New wealth was evident in every Northern city.

For most people, the war brought the day-to-day hardship of inflation. During the four years of the war, the North suffered an inflation rate of 80 percent, or nearly 15 percent a year. This annual rate, three times what is generally considered tolerable, did much to inflame social tensions. Wages rose only half as much as prices, and workers responded by joining unions and striking. Manufacturers, bitterly opposed to unions, freely hired strikebreakers (many of whom were African Americans, women, or immigrants) and formed organizations of their own to prevent further unionization and to blacklist union organizers. Thus both capital and labor moved far beyond the small, localized confrontations of the early industrial period. The formation of large-scale organizations, fostered by wartime demand, laid the groundwork for the national battle between workers and manufacturers that would dominate the last part of the nineteenth century.

Another major source of social tension was conscription. The Union introduced a draft in March 1863. Especially unpopular in the 1863 draft law was a provision that allowed the hiring of substitutes or the payment of a commutation fee of $300. Substitution had been accepted in all previous European and American wars, but the Democratic Party made it an inflammatory issue. Pointing out that $300 was almost a year's wages for an unskilled laborer, they denounced the draft law (88 percent of Democratic congressmen had voted against it). They appealed to popular resentment by calling it "aristocratic legislation" and to fear by running headlines such as "Three Hundred Dollars or Your Life."

Conscription was often marred by favoritism and prejudice. Local officials called up many more poor than rich men and selected a higher proportion of immigrants than nonimmigrants. In reality, however, only 7 percent of all men called to serve actually did so. About 25 percent hired a substitute, another 45 percent were exempted for "cause" (usually health reasons), and another 20–25 percent simply failed to report to the community draft office. Nevertheless, by 1863 many Northern urban workers believed that the slogan "a rich man's war but a poor man's fight," though coined in the South, applied to them as well.

THE NEW YORK CITY DRAFT RIOTS

In the spring of 1863 there were protests against the draft throughout the North. Riots and disturbances broke out in many cities, and several federal enrollment officers were killed. The greatest trouble occurred in New York City between July 13 and July 16, 1863, where a wave of working-class looting, fighting, and lynching claimed the lives of 105 people, many of them African American. The rioting, the

QUICK REVIEW

The Draft Riots

- 1863: Congress passed national conscription law.
- New York, July 1863: looting, fighting, and lynching claim lives of 105 people.
- Racial and class antagonisms fueled riot.

A black man is lynched during the New York City Draft Riots in July 1863. Free black people and their institutions were major victims of the worst rioting in American history until then. The riots were less a protest against the draft than an outburst of frustration over urban problems that had been festering for decades.

Culver Pictures, Inc.

15-11
 A Firsthand Account of the New York Draft Riots (1863)

worst up to that time in American history, was quelled only when five units of the U.S. Army were rushed from the battlefield at Gettysburg, where they had been fighting Confederates the week before.

The riots had several causes. Anger at the draft and racial prejudice were what most contemporaries saw. From a historical perspective, however, the riots had less to do with the war than with the urban growth and tensions described in Chapter 13.

Ironically, African American men, a favorite target of the rioters' anger, were a major force in easing the national crisis over the draft. Though they had been barred from service until 1863, in the later stages of the war African American volunteers filled much of the manpower gap that the controversial draft was meant to address.

THE FAILURE OF SOUTHERN NATIONALISM

The war brought even greater changes to the South. As in the North, war needs led to expansion and centralization of government control over the economy. In many cases, Jefferson Davis himself initiated government control (over railroads, shipping, and war production, for example), often in the face of protest or inaction by governors who favored states' rights. The expansion of government brought sudden urbanization, a new experience for the predominantly rural South. The population of Richmond, the Confederate capital, almost tripled, in large part because the Confederate bureaucracy grew to 70,000 people. Because of the need for military manpower, a good part of the Confederate bureaucracy consisted of women, who were referred to as "government girls." All of this—government control, urban growth, women in the paid work force—was new to Southerners, and not all of it was welcomed.

Even more than in the North, the voracious need for soldiers fostered class antagonisms. When small yeoman farmers went off to war, their wives and families struggled to farm on their own, without the help of mechanization, which they could not afford, and without the help of slaves, which they had never owned. But wealthy men could be exempted from the draft if they had more than twenty slaves. Furthermore, many upper-class Southerners—at least 50,000—avoided military service by paying liberally ($5,000 and more) for substitutes. In the face of these inequities, desertions from the Confederate army soared.

Worst of all was the starvation. The North's blockade and the breakdown of the South's transportation system restricted the availability of food in the South, and these problems were vastly magnified by runaway inflation. Prices in the South rose by an unbelievable 9,000 percent. Speculation and hoarding by the rich made matters even worse. In the spring of 1863 food riots broke out in four Georgia cities (Atlanta among them) and in North Carolina. In Richmond, more than a thousand people, mostly women, broke into bakeries and snatched loaves of bread, crying "Bread! Bread! Our children are starving while the rich roll in wealth!" When the bread riot threatened to turn into general looting, Jefferson Davis himself appealed to the crowd to disperse—but found he had to threaten the rioters with gunfire before they would leave. A year later, Richmond stores sold eggs for $6 a dozen and butter for $25 a pound. One woman wept, "My God! How can I pay such prices? I have seven children; what shall I do?"

Increasingly, the ordinary people of the South, preoccupied with staying alive, refused to pay taxes, to provide food, or to serve in the army. Soldiers were drawn home by the desperation of their families as well as the discouraging course of the war. By January 1865 the desertion rate had climbed to 8 percent a month.

At the same time, the life of the Southern ruling class was irrevocably altered by the changing nature of slavery. By the end of the war, one-quarter of all slaves had fled to the Union lines, and those who remained often stood in a different relationship to their owners. As white masters and overseers left to join the army, white women were left behind on the plantation to cope with shortages, grow crops, and manage the labor of slaves. Lacking the patriarchal authority of their husbands, white women found that white–black relationships shifted, sometimes drastically (as when slaves fled) and sometimes more subtly. Slaves increasingly made their own decisions about when and how they would work, and they refused to accept the punishments that would have accompanied this insubordination in prewar years.

Peace movements in the South were motivated by a confused mixture of realism, war weariness, and the animosity of those who supported states' rights and opposed Jefferson Davis. The anti-Davis faction was led by his own vice president, Alexander Stephens, who early in 1864 suggested a negotiated peace. Peace sentiment was especially strong in North Carolina, where more than a hundred public meetings in support of negotiations were held in the summer of 1863. Davis would have none of it. The peace sentiment, which grew throughout 1864, flourished outside the political system in secret societies such as the Heroes of America and the Red Strings. As hopes of Confederate victory slipped away, conflict expanded beyond the battlefield to include the political struggles that Southern civilians were fighting among themselves.

THE TIDE TURNS

As Lincoln's timing of the Emancipation Proclamation showed, by 1863 the nature of the war was changing. The proclamation freeing the slaves struck directly at the Southern home front and the civilian work force. That same year, the nature of the battlefield war changed as well: the Civil War became the first total war.

HOW DID Grant and Sherman turn the tide of the war?

THE TURNING POINT OF 1863

In the summer of 1863 the moment finally arrived when the North could begin to hope for victory. But for the Union army the year opened with stalemate in the East and slow and costly progress in the West. For the South, 1863 represented its highest hopes for military success and for diplomatic recognition by Britain or France.

Attempting to break the stalemate in northern Virginia, General Joseph "Fighting Joe" Hooker and a Union army of 130,000 men attacked a Confederate army half that size at Chancellorsville in May. In response, Robert E. Lee daringly divided his forces, sending General Thomas "Stonewall" Jackson and 30,000 men on a day-long flanking movement that caught the Union troops by surprise. Although Jackson was killed (shot by his own men by mistake), Chancellorsville was a great Confederate victory; there were 17,000 Union losses. However, Confederate losses were also great: 13,000 men, representing more than 20 percent of Lee's army.

422

MAP EXPLORATION

To explore an interactive version of this map, go to
http://www.prenhall.com/faragertlc/map16.4

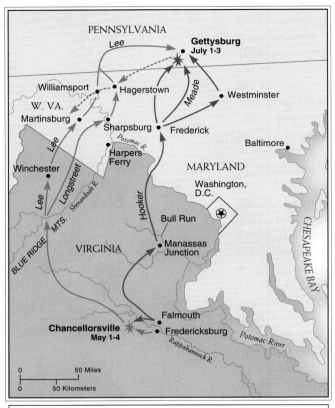

MAP 16-4

The Turning Point: 1863 In June, Lee boldly struck north into Maryland and Pennsylvania, hoping for a victory that would cause Britain and France to demand a negotiated peace on Confederate terms. Instead, he lost the hard-fought battle of Gettysburg, July 1–3. The very next day, Grant's long siege of Vicksburg succeeded. These two great Fourth of July victories turned the tide in favor of the Union. The Confederates never again mounted a major offensive. Total Union control of the Mississippi now exposed the Lower South to attack.

WHAT WAS Lee hoping to achieve with his campaign northward and why was his defeat at Gettysburg the war's turning point?

15-10
John Dooley, Passages from
a Journal (1863)

Though weakened, Lee moved to the attack. In June, in his second and most dangerous single thrust into Union territory, he moved north into Maryland and Pennsylvania. His purpose was as much political as military: he hoped that a great Confederate victory would lead Britain and France to intervene in the war and demand a negotiated peace. The ensuing Battle of Gettysburg, July 1–3, 1863, was another horrible slaughter. The next day a Union officer reported, "I tried to ride over the field but could not, for dead and wounded lay too thick to guide a horse through them."

Lee retreated from the field, leaving more than one-third of his army behind—28,000 men killed, wounded, or missing. His great gamble had failed; he never again mounted a major offensive.

The next day, July 4, 1863, Ulysses S. Grant took Vicksburg, Mississippi, after a costly siege. The combined news of Gettysburg and Vicksburg dissuaded Britain and France from recognizing the Confederacy and checked the Northern peace movement. It also tightened the North's grip on the South, for the Union now controlled the entire Mississippi River. In November, Generals Grant and Sherman broke the Confederate hold on Chattanooga, Tennessee, thereby opening the way to Atlanta.

GRANT AND SHERMAN

In March 1864, President Lincoln called Grant east and appointed him general in chief of all the Union forces. Lincoln's critics were appalled. Grant was an uncouth Westerner (like the president) and (unlike the president) was rumored to have a drinking problem. Lincoln replied that if he knew the general's brand of whiskey, he would send a barrel of it to every commander in the Union army.

Grant devised a plan of strangulation and annihilation. While he took on Lee in northern Virginia, he sent General William Tecumseh Sherman to defeat Confederate general Joe Johnston's Army of Tennessee, which was defending the approach to Atlanta. Both Grant and Sherman exemplified the new kind of warfare. They aimed to inflict maximum damage on the fabric of Southern life, hoping that the South would choose to surrender rather than face total destruction. This decision to broaden the war so that it directly affected civilians was new in American military history and prefigured the total wars of the twentieth century.

In northern Virginia, Grant pursued a policy of destroying civilian supplies. He said he "regarded it as humane to both sides to protect the persons of those found at their homes, but to consume everything that could be used to support or supply armies." One of those supports was slaves. Grant welcomed fleeing slaves to Union lines and encouraged army efforts to put them to work or enlist them as soldiers.

But the most famous example of the new strategy of total war was General Sherman's 1864 march through Georgia.

On September 2, 1864, Sherman captured Atlanta. The battle had been fierce, and the city lay in ruins, but the rest of Georgia now lay open to him. In November, Sherman set out to march the 285 miles to the coastal city of Savannah, living off the land and destroying everything in his path. His military purpose was to tighten the noose around Robert E. Lee's army in northern Virginia by cutting off Mississippi, Alabama, and Georgia from the rest of the Confederacy. But his second purpose, openly stated, was to "make war so terrible" to the people of the South, to "make them so sick of war that generations would pass away before they would again appeal to it." Accordingly, he told his men to seize, burn, or destroy everything in their path (but, significantly, not to harm civilians).

Terrifying to white Southern civilians, Sherman was initially hostile to black Southerners as well. In the interests of speed and efficiency, his army turned away many of the 18,000 slaves who flocked to it in Georgia, causing a number to be recaptured and reenslaved. This callous action caused such a scandal in Washington that Secretary of War Edwin Stanton arranged a special meeting in Georgia with Sherman and twenty African American ministers who spoke for the freed slaves. This meeting in itself was extraordinary: no one had ever before asked slaves what they wanted. Equally extraordinary was Sherman's response in Special Field Order 15, issued in January 1865: he set aside more than 400,000 acres of Confederate land to be given to the freed slaves in forty-acre parcels. This was war of a kind that white Southerners had never imagined.

Far to the North, a much smaller unimaginable event occurred in October, when twenty-six Confederate sympathizers invaded St. Albans Vermont, robbing three banks, setting fires, killing a man—and then escaping over the border into Canada. When a Montreal magistrate released the men on a technicality, American military authorities threatened retaliation if Canadian authorities ever again allowed such an event. Canada was not unprepared for an American attack, but the defenders were British troops: the uncertain diplomatic and naval issues between the Union and Britain had led to the stationing of 14,000 troops to Canada, the largest number of British troops in North America since the War of 1812. The St. Albans incident, minor in itself, caused both the British government and Canadian officials to think seriously about how to defend against the possibility of future American invasions. The answer was obvious: the Canadian provinces, which by 1860 stretched from one coast to the other, would need to be united. In 1867, all of the Canadian provinces joined in confederation and henceforth were known as the Dominion of Canada. In this way, a small Confederate pinprick helped to foster the unity of America's large northern neighbor.

THE 1864 ELECTION

The war complicated the 1864 presidential election. Lincoln was renominated during a low period. Opposed by the radicals, who thought he was too conciliatory toward the South, and by Republican conservatives, who disapproved of the Emancipation Proclamation, Lincoln had little support within his own party.

15-9
Abraham Lincoln, Gettysburg Address (1863)

QUICK REVIEW

Grant's Strategy

◆ Better coordination of Union effort and the application of steady pressure.

◆ The waging of nonstop warfare.

◆ Grant's plan worked in the long run, but at a high cost.

 MAP EXPLORATION
To explore an interactive version of this map, go to
http://www.prenhall.com/faraghertlc/map16.5

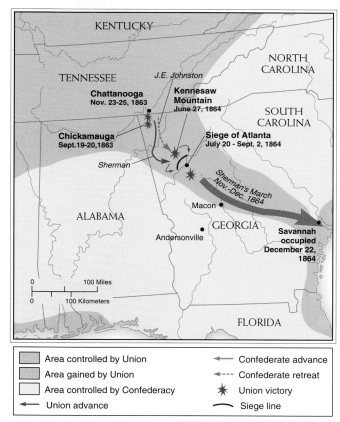

MAP 16-5
Sherman's Campaign in Georgia, 1864   Ulysses S. Grant and William Tecumseh Sherman, two like-minded generals, commanded the Union's armies in the final push to victory. While Grant hammered away at Lee in northern Virginia, Sherman captured Atlanta in September (a victory that may have been vital to Lincoln's reelection) and began his March to the Sea in November 1864.

IN WHAT ways did Sherman's campaign exemplify the new strategy of "total war"?

15-13
General William Tecumseh
Sherman on War (1864)

The Democrats had an appealing candidate: General George McClellan, who proclaimed the war a failure and proposed an armistice to end it. Other Democrats played shamelessly on the racist fears of the urban working class, accusing Republicans of being "negro-lovers" and warning that racial mixing lay ahead.

A deeply depressed Lincoln fully expected to lose the election. "I am going to be beaten," he told an army officer in August 1864, "and unless some great change takes place badly beaten." A great change did take place: Sherman captured Atlanta on September 2. Jubilation swept the North: some cities celebrated with 100-gun salutes. Lincoln won the election with 55 percent of the popular vote. Seventy-eight percent of the soldiers voted for him rather than for their former commander. The vote probably saved the Republican Party from extinction. Furthermore, the election was important evidence of Northern support for Lincoln's policy of unconditional surrender for the South. There would be no negotiated peace; the war would continue.

MAP EXPLORATION

To explore an interactive version of this map, go to
http://www.prenhall.com/faraghertlc/map16.6

Area controlled by Union
Area gained by Union
← Union advance
← Confederate advance
◀--- Confederate retreat
✳ Union victory
✳ Confederate victory
〜 Fortifications

MAP 16-6
The Final Battles in Virginia, 1864–1865   In the war's final phase early in 1865, Sherman closed one arm of a pincers by marching north from Savannah while Grant attacked Lee's last defensive positions in Petersburg and Richmond. Lee retreated from them on April 2 and surrendered at Appomattox Court House on April 9, 1865.

WHAT DESPERATE measures did the South resort to as the war came to an end?

NEARING THE END

As Sherman devastated the lower South, Grant was locked in struggle with Lee in northern Virginia. Grant did not favor subtle strategies. He bluntly said, "The art of war is simple enough. Find out where your enemy is. Get at him as soon as you can. Strike at him as hard as you can, and keep moving on." Following this plan, Grant eventually hammered Lee into submission, but at enormous cost. Lee inflicted heavy losses on the Union army: almost 18,000 at the battle of the Wilderness, more than 8,000 at Spotsylvania, and 12,000 at Cold Harbor. At Cold Harbor, Union troops wrote their names and addresses on scraps of paper and pinned them to their backs, so certain were they of being killed or wounded in battle. Grim and terrible as Grant's strategy was, it proved effective. Rather than pulling back after his failed assaults, he kept moving South, finally settling in for a prolonged siege of Lee's forces at Petersburg. The North's great advantage in population finally began to tell. There were more Union soldiers to replace those lost in battle, but there were no more white Confederates.

In desperation, the South turned to what had hitherto been unthinkable: arming slaves to serve as soldiers in the Confederate army. As Jefferson Davis said in February 1865, "We are reduced to choosing whether the negroes shall fight for or against us." But—and this was the bitter irony—the African American soldiers and their families would have to be promised freedom or they would desert to the Union at the first chance they had. Even though Davis's proposal had the support of General Robert E. Lee, the Confederate Congress balked at first. As one member said, "If slaves make good soldiers our whole theory of slavery is wrong." Finally, on March 13, the Confederate Congress authorized a draft of black soldiers—without mentioning freedom. Although two regiments of African American soldiers were immediately organized in Richmond, it was too late. The South never had to publicly acknowledge the paradox of having to offer slaves freedom so that they would fight to defend slavery.

By the spring of 1865, public support for the war simply disintegrated in the South. Starvation, inflation, dissension, and the prospect of military defeat were too much. In February, Jefferson Davis sent his vice president, Alexander Stephens, to negotiate terms at a peace conference at Hampton Roads. Lincoln would not countenance anything less than full surrender, so the conference failed and Southern resistance faded away.

APPOMATTOX

In the spring of 1865 Lee and his remaining troops, outnumbered two to one, still held Petersburg and Richmond. Starving, short of ammunition, and losing men in battle or to desertion every day, Lee retreated from Petersburg on April 2. The Confederate government fled Richmond, stripping and burning the city. Seven days later, Lee and his 25,000 troops surrendered to Grant at Appomattox Court House. Grant treated Lee with great respect and set a historic precedent by giving the Confederate troops parole. This meant they could not subsequently be prosecuted for treason. Grant then sent the starving army on its way with three days' rations for every man. Jefferson Davis, who had hoped to set up a new government in Texas, was captured in Georgia on May 10. The war was finally over.

DEATH OF A PRESIDENT

Sensing that the war was near its end, Abraham Lincoln visited Grant's troops when Lee withdrew from Petersburg on April 2. Thus it was that Lincoln came to visit Richmond and to sit briefly in Jefferson Davis's presidential office, soon after Davis had left it. As Lincoln walked the streets of the burned and pillaged city, black people poured out to see him and surround him, shouting "Glory to God! Glory! Glory! Glory!" Lincoln in turn said to Admiral David Porter: "Thank God I have lived to see this. It seems to me that I have been dreaming a horrid dream for four years, and now the nightmare is gone." Lincoln had only the briefest time to savor the victory. On the night of April 14, President and Mrs.

This striking photograph by Thomas C. Roche shows a dead Confederate soldier, killed at Petersburg on April 3, 1865, only six days before the surrender at Appomattox. The new medium of photography conveyed the horror of the war with a gruesome reality to the American public.

Courtesy of the Library of Congress

Abraham Lincoln toured Richmond, the Confederate capital, just hours after Jefferson Davis had fled. This photograph, taken April 4, 1865, shows Yankee cavalry horses in the foreground and the smoldering city in the background. It gives a sense of the devastation suffered by the South and the immense task of rebuilding and reconciliation that Lincoln would not live to accomplish.

Courtesy of the Library of Congress

Lincoln went to Ford's Theater in Washington. There Lincoln was shot at point-blank range by John Wilkes Booth, a Confederate sympathizer. He died the next day. For the people of the Union, the joy of victory was muted by mourning for their great leader.

CONCLUSION

In 1865, a divided people had been forcibly reunited by battle. Their nation, the United States of America, had been permanently changed by civil war. Devastating losses among the young men of the country would affect not only their families, but all of postwar society as well. Politically, the deepest irony of the Civil War was that only by fighting it had America become completely a nation. For it was the war that broke down local isolation. Ordinary citizens in local communities, North and South, developed a national perspective as they sent their sons and brothers to be soldiers, their daughters to be nurses and teachers. The question now was whether this strengthened but divided national community, forged in battle, could create a just peace.

CHRONOLOGY

1861 March: Morrill Tariff Act.

April: Fort Sumter falls; war begins.

April: Mobilization begins.

April–May: Virginia, Arkansas, Tennessee, and North Carolina secede.

June: United States Sanitary Commission established.

July: First Battle of Bull Run.

December: French troops arrive in Mexico, followed by British and Spanish forces in January.

1862 February: Legal Tender Act.

February: Battles of Fort Henry and Fort Donelson.

March: Battle of Pea Ridge.

March–August: George B. McClellan's Peninsular campaign.

March: Battle of Glorieta Pass.

April: Battle of Shiloh.

April: Confederate Conscription Act.

April: David Farragut captures New Orleans.

May: *Cinqo de Mayo:* Mexican troops repel French invaders.

May: Homestead Act.

June–July: Seven Days Battles.

July: Pacific Railway Act.

July: Morrill Land Grant Act.

September: Battle of Antietam.

December: Battle of Fredericksburg.

1863 January: Emancipation Proclamation.

February: National Bank Act.

March: Draft introduced in the North.

April: Richmond bread riot.

May: Battle of Chancellorsville.

June: French occupy Mexico City.

July: Battle of Gettysburg.

July: Surrender of Vicksburg.

July: New York City Draft Riots.

November: Battle of Chattanooga.

November: Union troops capture Brownsville, Texas.

1864 March: Ulysses S. Grant becomes general in chief of Union forces.

April: Fort Pillow massacre.

May: Battle of the Wilderness.

May: Battle of Spotsylvania.

June: Battle of Cold Harbor.

June: Maximilian becomes Emperor of Mexico.

September: Atlanta falls.

October: St. Albans incident.

November: Abraham Lincoln reelected president.

November–December: William Tecumseh Sherman's March to the Sea.

1865 April: Richmond falls.

April: Robert E. Lee surrenders at Appomattox.

April: Lincoln assassinated.

December: Thirteenth Amendment to the Constitution becomes law.

SUMMARY

Communities Mobilize for War The attack on Fort Sumter began the Civil War, leading to mobilization by the Union and the Confederacy. The issue of border state loyalties was decided and the first battle was a harbinger of the long, brutal conflict to come. Both sides entered the war with strengths and weaknesses.

Governments Organize for War Both Lincoln and Davis prepared their governments for war. In the North, the federal government expanded its powers greatly and engaged in diplomacy to isolate the Confederacy. Jefferson Davis faced difficulties in mobilizing the Confederate government. The Confederate cause was hurt further by economic and diplomatic disappointments.

The Fighting through 1862 The war was fought on several fronts on land and at sea, including the trans-Mississippi West. Both sides experienced victories and defeats. The Union quickly achieved supremacy of the seas.

The Death of Slavery The response of African Americans North and South profoundly affected the course of the Civil War. The Emancipation Proclamation led to the enlistment of African Americans into the Union army.

The Front Lines and the Home Front Deplorable conditions characterized the front lines. Weaponry, medical treatment, and disease all increased casualties, leading to desertions by soldiers on both sides. On the home front, the North experienced political, economic, and social strains while conditions in the South deteriorated.

The Tide Turns After 1863, the war turned in favor of the North. Military victories with heavy casualties weakened Confederate will and military ability. Lincoln won reelection in 1864 and the war ended the next year but soon after, Lincoln was assassinated.

REVIEW QUESTIONS

1. At the outset of the Civil War, what were the relative advantages of the North and the South, and how did they affect the final outcome?

2. In the absence of the Southern Democrats, in the early 1860s the new Republican Congress was able to pass a number of party measures with little opposition. What do these measures tell you about the historical roots of the Republican Party? More generally, how do you think we should view legislation passed in the absence of the customary opposition, debate, and compromise?

3. The greatest problem facing Jefferson Davis and the Confederacy was the need to develop a true feeling of nationalism. Can the failure of this effort be blamed on Davis's weakness as a leader alone, or are there other causes?

4. In what ways can it be said that the actions of African Americans, both slave and free, came to determine the course of the Civil War?

5. Wars have always unexpected consequences. List some of these consequences both for soldiers and for civilians in the North and in the South.

6. Today Abraham Lincoln is considered one of our greatest presidents, but he did not enjoy such approval at the time. List some of the contemporary criticisms of Lincoln and evaluate them.

KEY TERMS

Emancipation Proclamation (p. 414)
Copperheads (p. 418)
Homestead Act (p. 407)
Legal Tender Act (p. 407)
Morrill Land Grant Act (p. 408)

Morrill Tariff Act (p. 407)
National Bank Act (p. 407)
Peninsular campaign (p. 411)
Thirteenth Amendment (p. 414)

RECOMMENDED READING

Jeanie Attie, *Patriotic Toil: Northern Women and the American Civil War* (1998). A fine study of women's activities in the U.S. Sanitary Commission.

Iver Bernstein, *The New York City Draft Riots* (1990). A social history that places the famous riots in the context of the nineteenth-century's extraordinary urbanization.

David J. Eocher, *The Longest Night* (2001). The most recent and perhaps the longest (990 pages) and most detailed military history of the Civil War.

Paul Escott, *After Secession: Jefferson Davis and the Failure of Confederate Nationalism* (1978). A thoughtful study of Davis's record as president of the Confederacy.

Drew Gilpin Faust, *Mothers of Invention: Women of the Slaveholding South in the American Civil War* (1996). A major study that considers the importance of gender at the white South's "moment of truth."

Alvin Josephy, *The Civil War in the West* (1992). A long-needed study, by a noted Western historian, of the course of the war in the Trans-Mississippi West.

Charles Bryan and Nelson Lankford, eds., *Eye of the Storm: A Civil War Odyssey* (2000). The richly illustrated diary of a Union soldier, including his captivity at Andersonville.

James M. McPherson, *The Negro's Civil War: How American Negroes Felt and Acted during the War for the Union* (1965). One of the earliest documentary collections on African American activity in wartime.

———, *Battle Cry of Freedom: The Civil War Era* (1988). An acclaimed, highly readable synthesis of much scholarship on the war.

———, *The Atlas of the Civil War* (1994). Detailed battle diagrams with clear descriptions.

Pauli Murray, *Proud Shoes: The Story of an American Family* (1956). Murray tells the proud story of her African American family and her grandfather, Robert Fitzgerald.

Phillip Shaw Paludan, *"A People's Contest": The Union at War, 1861–1865* (1988). A highly successful social history of the North during the war.

The Civil War

WHAT DID the photographer include that is missing from the illustrations? What did the illustrators include that is missing from the photograph? What did war look like to the civilian who saw only the illustrations? To the civilian who saw only the photograph? To the civilian who saw both?

Two new media drastically altered the ways in which people on the home front experienced war. One was photography. Mathew B. Brady and other pioneering photographers took thousands of pictures of battlefield scenes, which were then shown in weekly exhibits. For a small fee, the spectator could see photographs of battles fought just days before. The images themselves are of very good quality and quite large. The major drawback was technical. The photographer had to expose his glass plate to the light for a full minute, any movement during that time, created a blur. So, Brady's and other photographic images captured the look of the battlefield after the fighting was over.

The other new medium was the illustrated magazine. *Harper's Illustrated Weekly*, only a few years old at the outbreak of the war, was the biggest with a circulation running into the hundreds of thousands. Its illustrators drew battles as they were happening capturing the charges and the hand-to-hand fighting that the photographer could not. Below is a stereopticon photograph of a *Harper's* artist at Gettysburg, taken for the Brady Company. Viewers looked through a special device which fused the two images. As you examine the images included in this essay, consider these questions.

▼

Courtesy of Library of Congress

"Dead at Gettysburg," a photograph taken for the Brady Company. The dead included ▶ both Union soldiers and a Confederate. For the vast majority of those paying admission to see this and other images, this was the first time they witnessed the carnage of battle.

Courtesy of Library of Congress

◀ "The Battle of Gettysburg—Longstreet's Attack Upon Our Left Center—Blue Ridge In the Distance" appeared in *Harper's Weekly* for July 22, 1863. Note the use of "our" to describe the position of the Union troops. Note too that the viewer is positioned behind the Union lines.

American Antiquary Society

"The Harvest of ▶ Death—Gettysburg, July 4, 1863" appeared in *Harper's Weekly* for July 22, 1863. It shows only Union dead along with dead horses and overturned wagons.

American Antiquary Society

THE HARVEST OF DEATH—GETTYSBURG, July 4, 1863.—[Photographed by A. Gardner, Washington.]

The war passed from words to stones which the white children began to hurl at the colored. Several colored children were hurt and, as they had not resented the rock throwing . . . , the white children became more aggressive and abusive.
— *T. Thomas Fortune, from* Norfolk Journal and Guide, *1866*

Mississippi Freedman School, 1866. Noon at the primary school for Freedmen at Vicksburg, Mississippi.

17

RECONSTRUCTION
1863–1877

WHAT WAS Lincoln's vision of Reconstruction in the South?

WHAT WERE the most important changes in the lives of African Americans in the years immediately following the war?

WHAT MAJOR groups made up the Southern Republicans?

WHAT PRECIPITATED the electoral crisis of 1876?

AMERICAN COMMUNITIES

Hale County, Alabama: From Slavery to Freedom in a Black Belt Community

ON A BRIGHT SATURDAY MORNING IN MAY 1867, 4,000 FORMER slaves eagerly streamed into the town of Greensboro, bustling seat of Hale County in west-central Alabama. They came to hear speeches from two delegates to a recent freedmen's convention in Mobile and to find out about the political status of black people under the Reconstruction Act just passed by Congress. Tensions mounted in the days following this unprecedented gathering as military authorities began supervising voter registration for elections to the upcoming constitutional convention that would rewrite the laws of Alabama. On June 13, John Orrick, a local white, confronted Alex Webb, a politically active freedman, on the streets of Greensboro. Webb had recently been appointed a voter registrar for the district. Orrick swore he would never be registered by a black man and shot Webb dead. Hundreds of armed and angry freedmen formed a posse to search for Orrick but failed to find him. Galvanized by Webb's murder, 500 local freedmen formed a chapter of the Union League, the Republican Party's organizational arm in the South. The chapter functioned as both a militia company and a forum to agitate for political rights.

Violent political encounters between black people and white people were common in Southern communities in the wake of the Civil War. The war had destroyed slavery and the Confederacy but left the political and economic status of newly emancipated African Americans unresolved. Communities throughout the South struggled over the meaning of freedom in ways that reflected their particular circumstances. The 4 million freed people constituted roughly one-third of the total Southern population, but the black–white ratio in individual communities varied enormously. In some places the Union army had been a strong presence during the war, hastening the collapse of the slave system and encouraging experiments in free labor. Other areas had remained relatively untouched by the fighting. In some areas small farms prevailed; in others, including Hale County, large plantations dominated economic and political life.

West-central Alabama had emerged as a fertile center of cotton production just two decades before the Civil War. There, African Americans, as throughout the South's black belt, constituted more than three-quarters of the population. The region was virtually untouched by fighting until the very end of the Civil War. But with the arrival of federal troops in the spring of 1865, African Americans in Hale County, like their counterparts elsewhere, began to challenge the traditional organization of plantation labor.

One owner, Henry Watson, found that his entire work force had deserted him at the end of 1865. "I am in the midst of a large and fertile cotton growing country," Watson wrote to a

Greensboro

partner. "Many plantations are entirely without labor, many plantations have insufficient labor, and upon none are the laborers doing their former accustomed work." Black women refused to work in the fields, preferring to stay home with their children and tend garden plots. Nor would male field hands do any work, such as caring for hogs, that did not directly increase their share of the cotton crop.

Above all, freed people wanted more autonomy. Overseers and owners, thus, grudgingly allowed them to work the land "in families," letting them choose their own supervisors and find their own provisions. The result was a shift from the gang labor characteristic of the antebellum period, in which large groups of slaves worked under the harsh and constant supervision of white overseers, to the sharecropping system, in which African American families worked small plots of land in exchange for a small share of the crop. This shift represented less of a victory for newly freed African Americans than a defeat for plantation owners, who resented even the limited economic independence it forced them to concede to their black work force.

Only a small fraction— perhaps 15 percent—of African American families were fortunate enough to be able to buy land. The majority settled for some version of sharecropping, while others managed to rent land from owners, becoming tenant farmers. Still, planters throughout Hale County had to change the old routines of plantation labor. Local African Americans also organized politically. In 1866 Congress had passed the Civil Rights Act and sent the Fourteenth Amendment to the Constitution to the states for ratification; both promised full citizenship rights to former slaves. Hale County freedmen joined the Republican Party and local Union League chapters. They used their new political power to press for better labor contracts, demand greater autonomy for the black work force, and agitate for the more radical goal of land confiscation and redistribution. "The colored people are very anxious to get land of their own to live upon independently; and they want money to buy stock to make crops," reported one black Union League organizer. "The only way to get these necessaries is to give our votes to the [Republican] party . . . making every effort possible to bring these blessings about by reconstructing the State." Two Hale County former slaves, Brister Reese and James K. Green, won election to the Alabama state legislature in 1869.

It was not long before these economic and political gains prompted a white counterattack. In the spring of 1868, the Ku Klux Klan—a secret organization devoted to terrorizing and intimidating African Americans and their white Republican allies—came to Hale

County. *Disguised in white sheets, armed with guns and whips, and making nighttime raids on horseback, Klansmen flogged, beat, and murdered freed people. They intimidated voters and silenced political activists. Planters used Klan terror to dissuade former slaves from leaving plantations or organizing for higher wages.*

With the passage of the Ku Klux Klan Act in 1871, the federal government cracked down on the Klan, breaking its power temporarily in parts of the former Confederacy. But no serious effort was made to stop Klan terror in the west Alabama black belt, and planters there succeeded in reestablishing much of their social and political control.

The events in Hale County illustrate the struggles that beset communities throughout the South during the Reconstruction era after the Civil War. The destruction of slavery and the Confederacy forced African Americans and white people to renegotiate their old economic and political roles. These community battles both shaped and were shaped by the victorious and newly expansive federal government in Washington. In the end, Reconstruction was only partially successful. Not until the "Second Reconstruction" of the twentieth-century civil rights movement would the descendants of Hale County's African Americans begin to enjoy the full fruits of freedom—and even then not without challenge.

THE POLITICS OF RECONSTRUCTION

When General Robert E. Lee's men stacked their guns at Appomattox, the bloodiest war in American history ended. Although President Abraham Lincoln insisted early on that the purpose of the war was to preserve the Union, by 1863 it had evolved as well into a struggle for African American liberation. Indeed, the political, economic, and moral issues posed by slavery were the root cause of the Civil War, and the war ultimately destroyed slavery, although not racism, once and for all.

The Civil War also settled the Constitutional crisis provoked by the secession of the Confederacy and its justification in appeals to states' rights. The name "United States" would from now on be understood as a singular rather than a plural noun, signaling an important change in the meaning of American nationality. The old notion of the United States as a voluntary union of sovereign states gave way to the new reality of a single nation in which the federal government took precedence over the individual states.

WHAT WAS Lincoln's vision of Reconstruction in the South?

THE DEFEATED SOUTH

The white South paid an extremely high price for secession, war, and defeat. In addition to the battlefield casualties, the Confederate states sustained deep material and psychological wounds. Much of the best agricultural land lay waste. Many towns and cities—including Richmond, Atlanta, and Columbia, South Carolina—were in ruins. By 1865, the South's most precious commodities, cotton and African American slaves, were no longer measures of wealth and prestige. Retreating Confederates destroyed most of the South's cotton to prevent its capture by federal troops. What remained was confiscated by Union agents as contraband of war. The former slaves, many of whom had fled to Union lines during the latter stages of the war, were determined to chart their own course in the reconstructed South as free men and women.

It would take the South's economy a generation to overcome the severe blows dealt by the war. In 1860 the South held roughly 25 percent of the nation's wealth; a decade later it controlled only 12 percent.

Many white Southerners resented their conquered status, and white notions of race, class, and "honor" died hard. A white North Carolinian, for example, who had lost almost everything dear to him in the war—his sons, home, and slaves—recalled in 1865 that in spite of all his tragedy he still retained one thing. "They've

16–2
Carl Schurz, Report on the Condition of the South (1865)

IMAGE KEY
for pages 432–433

a. A young African American boy with new clothes and a book provided by the Freedmen's Bureau.

b. Rocks and stones like those used to hurl at slaves.

c. A colored engraving (1866) depicting noon at the primary school for Freedmen at Vicksburg, Mississippi.

d. Two members of the Ku Klux Klan holding guns and wearing hoods and long robes, pictured in *Harper's Weekly*.

e. Pages 44 and 45 from the New England primer show the religious content of the work.

f. The dead at Gettysburg were strewn across the battlefield.

g. Freedmen (freed black slaves) vote in 1867 while standing in line. The Stars and Stripes hang overhead.

h. Three white men decry the Reconstruction Acts of Congress as "usurpations and unconstitutional, revolutionary, and void" while clasping hands above the fallen body of a black man.

i. The "tramp" became a symbol of the misery caused by industrial depression as seen in this *Harper's Weekly* illustration, "The Tramp," September 2, 1876.

16–9
The Nation, "The State of the South" (1872)

"Decorating the Graves of Rebel Soldiers," *Harper's Weekly*, August 17, 1867. After the Civil War, both Southerners and Northerners created public mourning ceremonies honoring fallen soldiers. Women led the memorial movement in the South which, by establishing cemeteries and erecting monuments, offered the first cultural expression of the Confederate tradition. This engraving depicts citizens of Richmond, Virginia, decorating thousands of Confederate graves with flowers at the Hollywood Memorial Cemetery on the James River. A local women's group raised enough funds to transfer over 16,000 Confederate dead from Northern cemeteries for reburial in Richmond.
The Granger Collection (4E1090.99)

left me one inestimable privilege—to hate 'em. I git up at half-past four in the morning, and sit up till twelve at night, to hate 'em."

Emancipation proved the most bitter pill for white Southerners to swallow, especially the planter elite. Conquered and degraded, and in their view robbed of their slave property, white people responded by regarding African Americans more than ever as inferior to themselves. Emancipation, however, forced white people to redefine their world. The specter of political power and social equality for African Americans made racial order the consuming passion of most white Southerners during the Reconstruction years. In fact, racism can be seen as one of the major forces driving Reconstruction and, ultimately, undermining it.

ABRAHAM LINCOLN'S PLAN

By late 1863, Union military victories had convinced President Lincoln of the need to fashion a plan for the reconstruction of the South (see Chapter 16). Lincoln based his reconstruction program on bringing the seceded states back into the Union as quickly as possible. His Proclamation of Amnesty and Reconstruction of December 1863 offered "full pardon" and the restoration of property, not including slaves, to white Southerners willing to swear an oath of allegiance to the United States and its laws, including the Emancipation Proclamation. Prominent Confederate military and civil leaders were excluded from Lincoln's offer, though he indicated that he would freely pardon them.

The president also proposed that when the number of any Confederate state's voters who took the oath of allegiance reached 10 percent of the number who had voted in the election of 1860, this group could establish a state government that Lincoln would recognize as legitimate. Fundamental to this Ten Percent Plan was acceptance by the reconstructed governments of the abolition of slavery. Lincoln's plan was designed less as a blueprint for reconstruction than as a way to shorten the war and gain white people's support for emancipation.

Lincoln's amnesty proclamation angered those Republicans—known as **Radical Republicans**—who advocated not only equal rights for the freedmen, but also a tougher stance toward the white South. In July 1864, Senator Benjamin F. Wade of Ohio and Congressman Henry W. Davis of Maryland, both Radicals, proposed a harsher alternative to the Ten Percent Plan. The Wade-Davis bill required 50 percent of a seceding state's white male citizens to take a loyalty oath before elections could be held for a convention to rewrite the state's constitution. The Radical Republicans saw reconstruction as a chance to effect a fundamental transformation of Southern society. They thus wanted to delay the process until war's end and to limit participation to a small number of Southern Unionists. Lincoln viewed Reconstruction as part of the larger effort to win the war and abolish slavery. He wanted to weaken the Confederacy by creating new state governments that could win broad support from Southern white people. The Wade-Davis bill threatened his efforts to build political consensus within the Southern states, and Lincoln, therefore, pocket-vetoed it, by refusing to sign it within ten days of the adjournment of Congress.

As Union armies occupied parts of the South, commanders had improvised a variety of arrangements involving confiscated plantations and the African American labor force. For example, in 1862 General Benjamin F. Butler began a policy of transforming slaves on Louisiana sugar plantations into wage laborers under the close supervision of occupying federal troops. Butler's policy required slaves to remain on the estates of loyal planters, where they would receive wages according to a fixed schedule, as well as food and medical care for the aged and sick. Abandoned plantations would be leased to Northern investors.

In January 1865, General William T. Sherman issued Special **Field Order 15**, setting aside the Sea Islands off the Georgia coast and a portion of the South Carolina low-country rice fields for the exclusive settlement of freed people. Each family would receive forty acres of land and the loan of mules from the army—the origin, perhaps, of the famous call for "forty acres and a mule" that would soon capture the imagination of African Americans throughout the South. Sherman's intent was not to revolutionize Southern society but to relieve the demands placed on his army by the thousands of impoverished African Americans who followed his march to the sea. By the summer of 1865 some 40,000 freed people, eager to take advantage of the general's order, had been settled on 400,000 acres of "Sherman land."

Conflicts within the Republican Party prevented the development of a systematic land distribution program. Still, Lincoln and the Republican Congress supported other measures to aid the emancipated slaves. In March 1865 Congress established the **Freedmen's Bureau**. Along with providing food, clothing, and fuel to destitute former slaves, the bureau was charged with supervising and managing "all the abandoned lands in the South and the control of all subjects relating to refugees and freedmen." The act that established the bureau also stated that forty acres of abandoned or confiscated land could be leased to freed slaves or white Unionists, who would have an option to purchase after three years and "such title thereto as the United States can convey."

Radical Republicans A shifting group of Republican congressmen, usually a substantial minority, who favored the abolition of slavery from the beginning of the Civil War and later advocated harsh treatment of the defeated South.

Field Order 15 Order by General William T. Sherman in January 1865 to set aside abandoned land along the southern Atlantic coast for forty-acre grants to freedmen; rescinded by President Andrew Johnson later that year.

Freedmen's Bureau Agency established by Congress in March 1865 to provide social, educational, and economic services, advice, and protection to former slaves and destitute whites; lasted seven years.

On April 14, 1865, while attending the theater in Washington, President Lincoln was shot by John Wilkes Booth. At the time of his assassination, Lincoln's reconstruction policy remained unsettled and incomplete. In its broad outlines the president's plans had seemed to favor a speedy restoration of the Southern states to the Union and a minimum of federal intervention in their affairs. But with his death the specifics of postwar Reconstruction had to be hammered out by a new president, Andrew Johnson of Tennessee, a man whose personality, political background, and racist leanings put him at odds with the Republican-controlled Congress.

ANDREW JOHNSON AND PRESIDENTIAL RECONSTRUCTION

Andrew Johnson, a Democrat and former slaveholder, was a most unlikely successor to the martyred Lincoln. By trade a tailor, educated by his wife, Johnson overcame his impoverished background and served as state legislator, governor, and U.S. senator. Throughout his career Johnson had championed yeoman farmers and viewed the South's plantation aristocrats with contempt.

In 1864 the Republicans, in an appeal to Northern and border state "War Democrats," nominated Johnson for vice president. But despite Johnson's success in Tennessee and in the 1864 campaign, many Radical Republicans distrusted him. In the immediate aftermath of Lincoln's murder, however, Johnson appeared to side with those Radical Republicans who sought to treat the South as a conquered province. But support for Johnson quickly faded as the new president's policies unfolded. Johnson defined Reconstruction as the province of the executive, not the legislative branch, and he planned to restore the Union as quickly as possible. He blamed individual Southerners—the planter elite—rather than entire states for leading the South down the disastrous road to secession.

In the spring of 1865 Johnson granted amnesty and pardon, including restoration of property rights except slaves, to all Confederates who pledged loyalty to the Union and support for emancipation. Fourteen classes of Southerners, mostly major Confederate officials and wealthy landowners, were excluded. But these men could apply individually for presidential pardons. During his tenure Johnson pardoned roughly 90 percent of those who applied. Significantly, he instituted this plan while Congress was not in session. Johnson also appointed provisional governors for seven of the former Confederate states and set highly favorable terms for readmission in the Union. By the fall of 1865 ten of the eleven Confederate states claimed to have met Johnson's requirements to reenter the Union.

Andrew Johnson used the term "restoration" rather than "reconstruction." A lifelong Democrat with ambitions to be elected president on his own in 1868, Johnson hoped to build a new political coalition composed of Northern Democrats, conservative Republicans, and Southern Unionists. Firmly committed to white supremacy, he opposed political rights for the freedmen. Johnson's open sympathy for his fellow white Southerners, his antiblack bias, and his determination to control the course of Reconstruction placed him on a collision course with the powerful Radical wing of the Republican Party.

THE RADICAL REPUBLICAN VISION

Most Radicals were men whose careers had been shaped by the slavery controversy. At the core of their thinking lay a deep belief in equal political rights and equal economic opportunity, both guaranteed by a powerful national government.

QUICK REVIEW

Johnson's Reconstruction Plan

- Johnson extended pardons to Southerners who swore an oath of allegiance.
- He restored property rights to Southerners who swore an oath of allegiance.
- His plan had nothing to say about the voting and civil rights of former slaves.

"The Fifteenth Amendment," 1870. The Fifteenth Amendment, ratified in 1870, stipulated that the right to vote could not be denied "on account of race, color, or previous condition of servitude." This illustration expressed the optimism and hopes of African Americans generated by this Constitutional landmark aimed at protecting black political rights. Note the various political figures (Abraham Lincoln, John Brown, Frederick Douglass) and movements (abolitionism, black education) invoked here, providing a sense of how the amendment culminated a long historical struggle.

Courtesy of the Library of Congress

They argued that once free labor, universal education, and equal rights were implanted in the South, that region would be able to share in the North's material wealth, progress, and fluid social mobility.

In the Radicals' view, the power of the federal government would be central to the remaking of Southern society, especially in guaranteeing civil rights and suffrage for freedmen. In the most far-reaching proposal, Representative Thaddeus Stevens of Pennsylvania called for the confiscation of 400 million acres belonging to the wealthiest 10 percent of Southerners to be redistributed to black and white yeomen and Northern land buyers. "The whole fabric of Southern society must be changed," Stevens told Pennsylvania Republicans in September 1865, "and never can it be done if this opportunity is lost. How can republican institutions, free schools, free churches, free social intercourse exist in a mingled community of nabobs and serfs? If the South is ever to be made a safe republic let her lands be cultivated by the toil of the owners."

Northern Republicans were especially outraged by the stringent "**black codes**" passed by South Carolina, Mississippi, Louisiana, and other states. These were designed to restrict the freedom of the black labor force and keep freed people as close to slave status as possible. Laborers who left their jobs before contracts expired would forfeit wages already earned and be subject to arrest by any white citizen. Vagrancy, very broadly defined, was punishable by fines and involuntary plantation labor. Apprenticeship clauses obliged black children to work without pay for employers. Some states attempted to bar African Americans from land ownership. Other laws specifically denied African Americans equality with white people in civil rights, excluding them from juries and prohibiting interracial marriages.

The black codes underscored the unwillingness of white Southerners to accept the full meaning of freedom for African Americans. The Radicals, although not a majority of their party, were joined by moderate Republicans as growing numbers of Northerners grew suspicious of white Southern intransigence

16–4
Mississippi Black Code (1865)

16–3
Clinton B. Fisk, Plain Counsels for Freedmen (1865)

Black codes   Laws passed by states and municipalities denying many rights of citizenship to free black people before the Civil War.

and the denial of political rights to freedmen. When the Thirty-ninth Congress convened in December 1865, the large Republican majority prevented the seating of the white Southerners elected to Congress under President Johnson's provisional state governments. Republicans also established the Joint Committee on Reconstruction. After hearing extensive testimony from a broad range of witnesses, it concluded that not only were old Confederates back in power in the South, but also that black codes and racial violence required increased protection for African Americans.

As a result, in the spring of 1866, Congress passed two important bills designed to aid African Americans. The landmark Civil Rights bill, which bestowed full citizenship on African Americans, overturned the 1857 *Dred Scott* decision and the black codes. It defined all persons born in the United States (except Indian peoples) as national citizens, and it enumerated various rights, including the rights to make and enforce contracts, to sue, to give evidence, and to buy and sell property. Under this bill, African Americans acquired "full and equal benefit of all laws and proceedings for the security of person and property as is enjoyed by white citizens."

Congress also voted to enlarge the scope of the Freedmen's Bureau, empowering it to build schools and pay teachers, and also to establish courts to prosecute those charged with depriving African Americans of their civil rights. The bureau achieved important, if limited, success in aiding African Americans. Bureau-run schools helped lay the foundation for Southern public education. The bureau's network of courts allowed freed people to bring suits against white people in disputes involving violence, nonpayment of wages, or unfair division of crops. The very existence of courts hearing public testimony by African Americans provided an important psychological challenge to traditional notions of white racial domination.

An angry President Johnson vetoed both of these bills. But his intemperate attacks on the Radicals—he damned them as traitors unwilling to restore the Union—united moderate and Radical Republicans and they succeeded in overriding the vetoes. Congressional Republicans, led by the Radical faction, were now unified in challenging the president's power to direct Reconstruction and in using national authority to define and protect the rights of citizens.

In June 1866, fearful that the **Civil Rights Act** might be declared unconstitutional and eager to settle the basis for the seating of Southern representatives, Congress passed the Fourteenth Amendment. The amendment defined national citizenship to include former slaves ("all persons born or naturalized in the United States") and prohibited the states from violating the privileges of citizens without due process of law. It also empowered Congress to reduce the representation of any state that denied the suffrage to males over twenty-one. Republicans adopted the Fourteenth Amendment as their platform for the 1866 congressional elections and suggested that Southern states would have to ratify it as a condition of readmission. President Johnson, meanwhile, took to the stump in August to support conservative Democratic and Republican candidates. His unrestrained speeches often degenerated into harangues, alienating many voters and aiding the Republican cause.

For their part, the Republicans began an effective campaign tradition known as "waving the bloody shirt"—reminding Northern voters of the hundreds of thousands of Yankee soldiers left dead or maimed by the war. In the November 1866 elections, the Republicans increased their majority in both the House and the Senate and gained control of all the Northern states. The stage was now set for a battle between the president and Congress. Was it to be Johnson's "restoration" or **Congressional Reconstruction**?

QUICK REVIEW

The Tenure of Office Act and Johnson's Impeachment

- Act prohibited the president from removing certain officeholders without the Senate's approval of a successor.

- Johnson deliberately violated the act in February 1868.

- Johnson escaped impeachment by one vote.

16–7
The Fourteenth Amendment (1868)

Civil Rights Act   1866 act that gave full citizenship to African Americans.

Congressional Reconstruction   Name given to the period 1867–1870 when the Republican-dominated Congress controlled Reconstruction-era policy.

CONGRESSIONAL RECONSTRUCTION AND THE IMPEACHMENT CRISIS

United against Johnson, Radical and moderate Republicans took control of Reconstruction early in 1867. In March, Congress passed the first **Reconstruction Act** over Johnson's veto. This act divided the South into five military districts subject to martial law. To achieve restoration, Southern states were first required to call new constitutional conventions, elected by universal manhood suffrage. Once these states had drafted new constitutions, guaranteed African American voting rights, and ratified the Fourteenth Amendment, they were eligible for readmission to the Union.

Congress also passed several laws aimed at limiting Johnson's power. One of these, the **Tenure of Office Act**, stipulated that any officeholder appointed by the president with the Senate's advice and consent could not be removed until the Senate had approved a successor. In this way, congressional leaders could protect Republicans, such as Secretary of War Edwin M. Stanton, entrusted with implementing Congressional Reconstruction. In August 1867, with Congress adjourned, Johnson suspended Stanton and appointed General Ulysses S. Grant interim secretary of war. This move enabled the president to remove generals in the field that he judged to be too radical and replace them with men who were sympathetic to his own views. It also served as a challenge to the Tenure of Office Act. In January 1868, when the Senate overruled Stanton's suspension, Grant broke openly with Johnson and vacated the office. Stanton resumed his position and barricaded himself in his office when Johnson attempted to remove him once again.

Outraged by Johnson's relentless obstructionism, and seizing upon his violation of the Tenure of Office Act as a pretext, radical and moderate Republicans in the House of Representatives again joined forces and voted to impeach the president by a vote of 126 to 47 on February 24, 1868, charging him with eleven counts of high crimes and misdemeanors. To ensure the support of moderate Republicans, the articles of impeachment focused on violations of the Tenure of Office Act, leaving unstated the Republicans' real reasons for wanting the president removed: Johnson's political views and his opposition to the Reconstruction Acts.

An influential group of moderate Senate Republicans feared the damage a conviction might do to the constitutional separation of powers. They also worried about the political and economic policies that might be pursued by Benjamin Wade, the president pro tem of the Senate and a leader of the Radical Republicans, who, because there was no vice president, would succeed to the presidency if Johnson were removed from office. Behind the scenes during his Senate trial, Johnson agreed to abide by the Reconstruction Acts. In May, the Senate voted 35 for conviction, 19 for acquittal—one vote shy of the two-thirds necessary for removal from office. Johnson's narrow acquittal established the precedent that only criminal actions by a president—not political disagreements—warranted removal from office.

MAP EXPLORATION

To explore an interactive version of this map, go to
http://www.prenhall.com/faraghertlc/map17.1

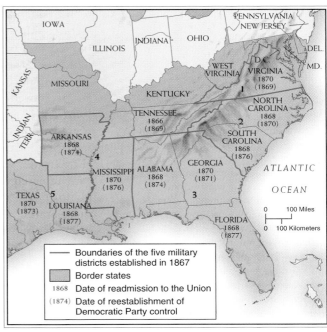

MAP 17-1

Reconstruction of the South, 1866–1877   Dates for the readmission of former Confederate states to the Union and the return of Democrats to power varied according to the specific political situations in those states.

WHAT WERE the competing plans for reconstructing the Southern states?

16–1

"Address from the Colored Citizens of Norfolk, Virginia, to the People of the United States" (1865)

Reconstruction Act   1877 act that divided the South into five military districts subject to martial law.

Tenure of Office Act   Act stipulating that any officeholder appointed by the president with the Senate's advice and consent could not be removed until the Senate had approved a successor.

16–8
Albion W. Tourgee, Letter on
Ku Klux Klan Activities (1870)

Susan B. Anthony (1820–1906) and
Elizabeth Cady Stanton (1815–1902),
the two most influential leaders of the
woman suffrage movement, ca. 1892.
Anthony and Stanton broke with their
longtime abolitionist allies after the Civil
War when they opposed the Fifteenth
Amendment. They argued that the doctrine of universal manhood suffrage it
embodied would give constitutional
authority to the claim that men were the
social and political superiors of women.
As founders of the militant National
Woman Suffrage Association, Stanton and
Anthony established an independent
woman suffrage movement with a broader
spectrum of goals for women's rights and
drew millions of women into public life
during the late nineteenth century.

The Susan B. Anthony House, Rochester, NY

THE ELECTION OF 1868

By the summer of 1868, seven former Confederate states (Alabama, Arkansas,
Florida, Louisiana, North Carolina, South Carolina, and Tennessee) had ratified
the revised constitutions, elected Republican governments, and ratified the Fourteenth Amendment. They had thereby earned readmission to the Union. Though
Georgia, Mississippi, Texas, and Virginia still awaited readmission, the presidential election of 1868 offered some hope that the Civil War's legacy of sectional
hate and racial tension might finally ease.

Republicans nominated Ulysses S. Grant, the North's foremost military hero.
Grant enjoyed tremendous popularity after the war, especially when he broke with
Johnson. Totally lacking in political experience, Grant admitted after receiving the
nomination that he had been forced into it in spite of himself.

Significantly, at the very moment that the South was being forced to enfran-
chise former slaves as a prerequisite for readmission to the Union, the Republicans rejected a campaign plank endorsing black suffrage in the North. Their
platform left "the question of suffrage in all the loyal States . . . to the people of
those States." State referendums calling for black suffrage failed in eight Northern states between 1865 and 1868, succeeding only in Iowa and Minnesota. The
Democrats, determined to reverse Congressional Reconstruction, nominated Horatio Seymour, former governor of New York and a longtime foe of emancipation
and supporter of states' rights.

The **Ku Klux Klan**, founded as a Tennessee social club in 1866, threatened,
whipped, and murdered black and white Republicans to prevent them from voting.
This terrorism enabled the Democrats to carry Georgia and Louisiana,
but it ultimately cost the Democrats votes in the North. In the final tally,
Grant carried twenty-six of the thirty-four states for an electoral college
victory of 214 to 80. But he received a popular majority of less than 53
percent, beating Seymour by only 306,000 votes. Significantly, more than
500,000 African American voters cast their ballots for Grant, demonstrating their overwhelming support for the Republican Party. The Republicans also retained large majorities in both houses of Congress.

In February 1869, Congress passed the **Fifteenth Amendment**,
providing that "the right of citizens of the United States to vote shall not
be denied or abridged . . . on account of race, color, or previous condition of servitude." To enhance the chances of ratification, Congress
required the three remaining unreconstructed states—Mississippi, Texas,
and Virginia—to ratify both the Fourteenth and Fifteenth Amendments
before readmission. They did so and rejoined the Union in early 1870.
The Fifteenth Amendment was ratified in February 1870. In the narrow
sense of simply readmitting the former Confederate states to the Union,
Reconstruction was complete.

WOMAN SUFFRAGE AND RECONSTRUCTION

Many women's rights advocates had long been active in the abolitionist movement. The Fourteenth and Fifteenth Amendments, which
granted citizenship and the vote to freedmen, both inspired and frustrated these activists. For example, Elizabeth Cady Stanton and Susan
B. Anthony, two leaders with long involvement in both the antislavery
and feminist movements, objected to the inclusion of the word "male"
in the Fourteenth Amendment. "If that word 'male' be inserted," Stanton predicted in 1866, "it will take us a century at least to get it out."

OVERVIEW

RECONSTRUCTION AMENDMENTS TO THE CONSTITUTION, 1865–1870

Amendment and Date Passed by Congress	Main Provisions	Ratification Process (3/4 of all states including ex-Confederate states required)
13 (January 1865)	■ Prohibited slavery in the United States	December 1865 (27 states, including 8 Southern states)
14 (June 1866)	■ Conferred national citizenship on all persons born or naturalized in the United States ■ Reduced state representation in Congress proportionally for any state disfranchising male citizens ■ Denied former Confederates the right to hold state or national office ■ Repudiated Confederate debt	July 1868 (after Congress makes ratification a prerequisite for readmission of ex-Confederate states to the Union)
15 (February 1869)	■ Prohibited denial of suffrage because of race, color, or previous condition of servitude	March 1870 (ratification required for readmission of Virginia, Texas, Mississippi, and Georgia)

Insisting that the causes of the African American vote and the women's vote were linked, Stanton, Anthony, and Lucy Stone founded the American Equal Rights Association in 1866. The group launched a series of lobbying and petition campaigns to remove racial and sexual restrictions on voting from state constitutions. Throughout the nation, the old abolitionist organizations and the Republican Party emphasized passage of the Fourteenth and Fifteenth Amendments and withdrew funds and support from the cause of woman suffrage. Disagreements over these amendments divided suffragists for decades.

The radical wing, led by Stanton and Anthony, opposed the Fifteenth Amendment, arguing that ratification would establish an "aristocracy of sex," enfranchising all men while leaving women without political privileges. They argued for a Sixteenth Amendment that would secure the vote for women. Other women's rights activists, including Lucy Stone and Frederick Douglass, asserted that "this hour belongs to the Negro." They feared a debate over woman suffrage at the national level would jeopardize passage of the two amendments.

By 1869 woman suffragists had split into two competing organizations: the moderate American Woman Suffrage Association (AWSA), which sought the support of men, and the more radical all-female National Woman Suffrage Association (NWSA). For the NWSA, the vote represented only one part of a broad spectrum of goals inherited from the Declaration of Sentiments manifesto adopted at the first women's rights convention held in 1848 at Seneca Falls, New York (see Chapter 13).

Although women did not win the vote in this period, they did establish an independent suffrage movement that eventually drew millions of women into political life. The NWSA in particular demonstrated that self-government and

16–10
Susan B. Anthony and the "New Departure" for Women (1873)

Ku Klux Klan   Perhaps the most prominent of the vigilante groups that terrorized black people in the South during Reconstruction era, founded by the Confederate veterans in 1866.

Fifteenth Amendment   Passed by Congress in 1869, guaranteed the right of American men to vote, regardless of race.

democratic participation in the public sphere were crucial for women's emancipation. The failure of woman suffrage after the Civil War was less a result of factional fighting than of the larger defeat of Radical Reconstruction and the ideal of expanded citizenship.

THE MEANING OF FREEDOM

The deep desire for independence from white control formed the underlying aspiration of newly freed slaves. For their part, most Southern white people sought to restrict the boundaries of that independence. As individuals and as members of communities transformed by emancipation, former slaves struggled to establish economic, political, and cultural autonomy. They built on the twin pillars of slave culture—the family and the church—to consolidate and expand African American institutions and thereby laid the foundation for the modern African American community.

Emancipation greatly expanded the choices available to African Americans. It helped build confidence in their ability to effect change without deferring to white people. Freedom also meant greater uncertainty and risk. But the vast majority of African Americans were more than willing to take their chances.

MOVING ABOUT

The first impulse of many emancipated slaves was to test their freedom. The simplest, most obvious way to do this involved leaving home. By walking off a plantation, coming and going without restraint or fear of punishment, African Americans could savor freedom. Throughout the summer and fall of 1865, observers in the South noted enormous numbers of freed people on the move.

Yet many who left their old neighborhoods returned soon afterward to seek work in the general vicinity, or even on the plantation they had left. Many wanted to separate themselves from former owners but not from familial ties and friendships. Others moved away altogether, seeking jobs in nearby towns and cities. Many former slaves left predominantly white counties, where they felt more vulnerable and isolated, for new lives in the relative comfort of predominantly black communities. Many African Americans, attracted by schools, churches, and fraternal societies as well as the army, preferred the city. Between 1865 and 1870, the African American population of the South's ten largest cities doubled, while the white population increased by only 10 percent.

Disgruntled planters had difficulty accepting African American independence. During slavery, they had expected obedience, submission, and loyalty from African Americans. Now many could not understand why so many former slaves wanted to leave despite urgent pleas to continue working at the old place. Many freed people went out of their way to reject the old subservience. Moving about freely was one way of doing this, as was refusing to tip one's hat to white people, ignoring former masters or mistresses in the streets, and refusing to step aside on sidewalks. After encountering an African American who would not step aside, Eliza Andrews, a Georgia plantation mistress, complained, "It is the first time in my life that I have ever had to give up the sidewalk to a man, much less to negroes!" When freed people staged parades, dances, and picnics to celebrate their new freedom, as they did, for example, when commemorating the Emancipation Proclamation, white people invariably condemned them angrily for "insolence," "outrageous spectacles," or "putting on airs."

WHAT WERE the most important changes in the lives of African Americans in the years immediately following the war?

The African American Family

Emancipation allowed freed people to strengthen family ties. For many former slaves, freedom meant the opportunity to reunite with long-lost family members. To track down relatives, freed people trekked to faraway places, put ads in newspapers, sought the help of Freedmen's Bureau agents, and questioned anyone who might have information about loved ones. Many thousands of family reunions, each with its own story, took place after the war.

Thousands of African American couples who had lived together under slavery streamed to military and civilian authorities and demanded to be legally married. By 1870, the two-parent household was the norm for a large majority of African Americans.

Emancipation brought changes to gender roles within the African American family as well. Black men could now serve on juries, vote, and hold office; black women, like their white counterparts, could not. Freedmen's Bureau agents designated the husband as household head and established lower wage scales for women laborers. African American editors, preachers, and politicians regularly quoted the biblical injunction that wives submit to their husbands.

African American men asserted their male authority, denied under slavery, by insisting their wives work at home instead of in the fields. Yet African American women continued to work outside the home, engaging in seasonal field labor for wages or working a family's rented plot. Most rural black families barely eked out a living and, thus, the labor of every family member was essential to survival. The key difference from slave times was that African American families themselves, not white masters and overseers, decided when and where women and children worked.

African American Churches and Schools

The creation of separate African American churches proved the most lasting and important element of the energetic institution building that went on in postemancipation years. Before the Civil War, Southern Protestant churches had relegated slaves and free African Americans to second-class membership. Black worshipers

An overflow congregation crowds into Richmond's First African Baptist Church in 1874. Despite their poverty, freed people struggled to save, buy land, and erect new buildings as they organized hundreds of new black churches during Reconstruction. As the most important African American institution outside the family, the black church, in addition to tending to spiritual needs, played a key role in the educational and political life of the community.

Wood engraving. The Granger Collection (4E1090.98)

were required to sit in the back during services, they were denied any role in church governance, and they were excluded from Sunday schools. Even in larger cities, where all-black congregations sometimes built their own churches, the law required white pastors. In rural areas, slaves preferred their own preachers to the sermons of local white ministers who quoted Scripture to justify slavery and white supremacy.

In communities around the South, African Americans now pooled their resources to buy land and build their own churches. Before these structures were completed, they might hold services in a railroad boxcar, where Atlanta's First Baptist Church began, or in an outdoor arbor, the original site of the First Baptist Church of Memphis. By late 1866 Charleston's African American community could boast of eleven churches in the city—five Methodist, two Presbyterian, two Episcopalian, one Baptist, and one Congregational. In rural areas, different denominations frequently shared the same church building. Churches became the center not only for religious life but for many other activities that defined the African American community: schools, picnics, festivals, and political meetings. They also helped spawn a host of organizations devoted to benevolence and mutual aid, such as burial societies, Masonic lodges, temperance clubs, and trade associations.

The church became the first social institution fully controlled by African Americans. In nearly every community ministers, respected for their speaking and organizational skills, were among the most influential leaders. By 1877 the great majority of black Southerners had withdrawn from white-dominated churches and belonged to black Baptist or Methodist churches.

African American communities received important educational aid from outside organizations. By 1869 the Freedmen's Bureau was supervising nearly 3,000 schools serving over 150,000 students throughout the South. Over half the roughly 3,300 teachers in these schools were African Americans, many of whom had been free before the Civil War. Other teachers included dedicated Northern white women volunteers. Throughout the South in 1865 and 1866, African Americans raised money to build schoolhouses, buy supplies, and pay teachers. Black artisans donated labor for construction, and black families offered room and board to teachers.

LAND AND LABOR AFTER SLAVERY

Most newly emancipated African Americans aspired to quit the plantations and to make new lives for themselves. Leaving the plantation was not as simple as walking off. Some freed people did find jobs in railroad building, mining, ranching, or construction work. Others raised subsistence crops and tended vegetable gardens as squatters. The majority hoped to become self-sufficient farmers. Many former slaves believed they were entitled to the land they had worked throughout their lives. General Oliver O. Howard, chief commissioner of the Freedmen's Bureau, observed that many "supposed that the Government [would] divide among them the lands of the conquered owners, and furnish them with all that might be necessary to begin life as an independent farmer." This perception was not merely a wishful fantasy. Frequent reference in the Congress and the press to the question of land distribution made the idea of "forty acres and a mule" not just a pipe dream but a matter of serious public debate.

Above all, African Americans sought economic autonomy, and ownership of land promised the most independence. "Give us our own land and we take care of ourselves," was how one former slave saw it. "But widout land, de ole massas can hire us or starve us, as dey please." At the Colored Convention in Montgomery, Alabama, in May 1867, delegates argued that the property now owned by planters had been "nearly all earned by the sweat of our brows, not theirs. It has been forfeited to the government by the treason of its owners, and is liable to be confiscated

---

QUICK REVIEW

Black Churches

◆ Many African Americans found inspiration and courage in their religious faith.

◆ Most black churches split from white-dominated congregations after the war.

◆ Black churches created a variety of organizations that served the black community.

whenever the Republican Party demands it." But by 1866 the federal government had already pulled back from the various wartime experiments involving the breaking up of large plantations and the leasing of small plots to individual families.

16–5
James C. Beecher, Report on Land Reform in the South Carolina Islands (1865, 1866)

 MAP EXPLORATION

To explore an interactive version of this map, go to **http://www.prenhall.com/faraghertlc/map17.2**

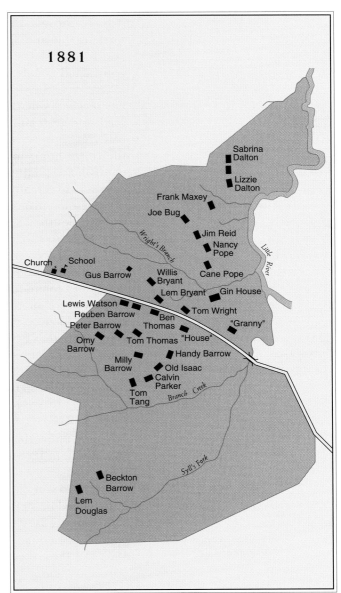

MAP 17-2

The Barrow Plantation, Oglethorpe County, Georgia, 1860 and 1881 (approx. 2,000 acres) These two maps, based on drawings from *Scribner's Monthly*, April 1881, show some of the changes brought by emancipation. In 1860 the plantation's entire black population lived in the communal slave quarters, right next to the white master's house. In 1881 black sharecropper and tenant families lived on individual plots, spread out across the land. The former slaves had also built their own school and church.

WHAT CHANGES in the lives of Black Southerners are reflected in the two maps of the Barrow Plantation?

President Johnson directed General Howard of the Freedmen's Bureau to evict tens of thousands of freed people settled on confiscated and abandoned land in southeastern Virginia, Southern Louisiana, and the Georgia and South Carolina low country. These evictions created a deep sense of betrayal among African Americans. A former Mississippi slave, Merrimon Howard, bitterly noted that African Americans had been left with "no land, no house, not so much as a place to lay our head. . . . We were friends on the march, brothers on the battlefield, but in the peaceful pursuits of life it seems that we are strangers."

By the late 1860s, **sharecropping** had emerged as the dominant form of working the land. Sharecropping represented a compromise between planters and former slaves. Under sharecropping arrangements, individual families contracted with landowners to be responsible for a specific plot. Large plantations were thus broken into family-sized farms. Generally, sharecropper families received one-third of the year's crop if the owner furnished implements, seed, and draft animals, or one-half if they provided their own supplies. African Americans preferred sharecropping to gang labor, as it allowed families to set their own hours and tasks and offered freedom from white supervision and control. For planters, the system stabilized the work force by requiring sharecroppers to remain until the harvest and to employ all family members. It also offered a way around the chronic shortage of cash and credit that plagued the postwar South.

By 1880 about 80 percent of the land in the black belt states—Mississippi, Alabama, and Georgia—had been divided into family-sized farms. Nearly three-quarters of black Southerners were sharecroppers. Through much of the black belt, family and community were one. Often several families worked adjoining parcels of land in common, pooling their labor in order to get by. Men usually oversaw crop production. Women went to the fields seasonally during planting or harvesting, but they mainly tended to household chores and child care. In addition, women frequently held jobs that might bring in cash, such as raising chickens or taking in laundry. The cotton harvest engaged all members of the community, from the oldest to the youngest.

THE ORIGINS OF AFRICAN AMERICAN POLITICS

Inclusion rather than separation was the objective of early African American political activity. In 1865 and 1866, African Americans throughout the South organized scores of mass meetings, parades, and petitions that demanded civil equality and the right to vote. In the cities, the growing web of churches and fraternal societies helped bolster early efforts at political organization.

Hundreds of African American delegates, selected by local meetings or churches, attended statewide political conventions held throughout the South in 1865 and 1866. Previously free African Americans, as well as black ministers, artisans, and veterans of the Union army, tended to dominate these proceedings, setting a pattern that would hold throughout Reconstruction. Convention debates sometimes reflected the tensions within African American communities, such as friction between poorer former slaves and better-off free black people, or between lighter- and darker-skinned African Americans. But most of these state gatherings concentrated on passing resolutions on issues that united all African Americans. The central concerns were suffrage and equality before the law.

The passage of the first Reconstruction Act in 1867 encouraged even more political activity among African Americans. The military started registering the South's electorate, ultimately enrolling approximately 735,000 black and 635,000

16–12
A Sharecrop Contract (1882)

16–11
James T. Rapier, Testimony Before U.S. Senate Regarding the Agricultural Labor Force in the South (1880)

QUICK REVIEW

Southern Republicans

- African American voters.
- White Northerners called "carpetbaggers" by white Southerners.
- Native whites pejoratively termed "scalawags."

Sharecropping Labor system that evolved during and after Reconstruction whereby landowners furnished laborers with a house, farm animals, and tools and advanced credit in exchange for a share of the laborers' crop.

white voters in the ten unreconstructed states. Five states—Alabama, Florida, Louisiana, Mississippi, and South Carolina—had black electoral majorities. Fewer than half the registered white voters participated in the elections for state constitutional conventions in 1867 and 1868. In contrast, four-fifths of the registered black voters cast ballots in these elections. Much of this new African American political activism was channeled through local **Union League** chapters throughout the South.

Begun during the war as a Northern, largely white middle-class patriotic club, the Union League now became the political voice of the former slaves. Union League chapters brought together local African Americans, soldiers, and Freedmen's Bureau agents to demand the vote and an end to legal discrimination against African Americans. It brought out African American voters, instructed freedmen in the rights and duties of citizenship, and promoted Republican candidates.

In 1867 and 1868, the promise of Radical Reconstruction enlarged the scope of African American political participation and brought new leaders to the fore. Many were teachers, preachers, or others with useful skills, such as literacy. For most ordinary African Americans, politics was inseparable from economic issues, especially the land question. Grass-roots political organizations frequently intervened in local disputes with planters over the terms of labor contracts. African American political groups closely followed the congressional debates over Reconstruction policy and agitated for land confiscation and distribution. Perhaps most important, politics was the only arena where black and white Southerners might engage each other on an equal basis.

W. L. Sheppard, "Electioneering at the South," *Harper's Weekly,* July 25, 1868. Throughout the Reconstruction-era South, newly freed slaves took a keen interest in both local and national political affairs. The presence of women and children at these campaign gatherings illustrates the importance of contemporary political issues to the entire African American community.

Courtesy of the Library of Congress

SOUTHERN POLITICS AND SOCIETY

By the summer of 1868, when the South had returned to the Union, the majority of Republicans believed the task of Reconstruction to be finished. Ultimately, they put their faith in a political solution to the problems facing the vanquished South. That meant nurturing a viable two-party system in the Southern states, where no Republican Party had ever existed. If that could be accomplished, Republicans and Democrats would compete for votes, offices, and influence, just as they did in Northern states.

Yet over the next decade the political structure created in the Southern states proved too restricted and fragile to sustain itself. Federal troops were needed to protect Republican governments and their supporters from violent opposition. Congressional action to monitor Southern elections and protect black voting rights became routine. Despite initial successes, Southern Republicanism proved an unstable coalition of often conflicting elements, unable to sustain effective power for very long. By 1877, Democrats had regained political control of all the former Confederate states.

WHAT MAJOR groups made up the Southern Republicans?

SOUTHERN REPUBLICANS

Three major groups composed the fledgling Republican coalition in the postwar South. The first group, African American voters, made up a large majority of Southern Republicans throughout the Reconstruction era.

Union League   Republican party organizations in Northern cities that became an important organizing device among freedmen in Southern cities after 1865.

The second group consisted of white Northerners, derisively called "**carpetbaggers**" by native white Southerners. Most carpetbaggers combined a desire for personal gain with a commitment to reform the "unprogressive" South by developing its material resources and introducing Yankee institutions such as free labor and free public schools. Most were veterans of the Union army who stayed in the South after the war. Others included Freedmen's Bureau agents and businessmen who had invested capital in cotton plantations and other enterprises. Although they made up a tiny percentage of the population, carpetbaggers played a disproportionately large role in Southern politics. They won a large share of Reconstruction offices, particularly in Florida, South Carolina, and Louisiana and in areas with large African American constituencies.

The third major group of Southern Republicans were the native white residents pejoratively termed "**scalawags**." They had even more diverse backgrounds and motives than the Northern-born Republicans. Loyalists during the war and traditional enemies of the planter elite (most were small farmers), these white Southerners looked to the Republican Party for help in settling old scores and relief from debt and wartime devastation.

Deep contradictions strained the alliance of these three groups. Southern Republicans touted themselves as the "party of progress and civilization" and promised a new era of material progress for the region. Republican state conventions in 1867 and 1868 voiced support for internal improvements, public schools, debt relief, and railroad building. Yet few white Southerners identified with the political and economic aspirations of African Americans. Moderate elements more concerned with maintaining white control of the party and encouraging economic investment in the region, outnumbered and defeated "confiscation radicals" who focused on obtaining land for African Americans.

RECONSTRUCTING THE STATES: A MIXED RECORD

With the old Confederate leaders barred from political participation, and with carpetbaggers and newly enfranchised African Americans representing many of the plantation districts, Republicans managed to dominate the ten Southern constitutional conventions of 1867–1869. Most of these conventions produced constitutions that expanded democracy and the public role of the state. The new documents guaranteed the political and civil rights of African Americans, and they abolished property qualifications for officeholding and jury service, as well as imprisonment for debt. They created the first state-funded systems of education in the South, to be administered by state commissioners. The new constitutions also mandated establishment of orphanages, penitentiaries, and homes for the insane. In 1868, only three years after the end of the war, Republicans came to power in most of the Southern states. By 1869, new constitutions had been ratified in all the old Confederate states. "These constitutions and governments," one South Carolina Democrat newspaper vowed bitterly, "will last just as long as the bayonets which ushered them into being, shall keep them in existence, and not one day longer."

Republican governments in the South faced a continual crisis of legitimacy that limited their ability to legislate change. They had to balance reform against the need to gain acceptance, especially by white Southerners. Their achievements were thus mixed. In the realm of race relations there was a clear thrust toward equal rights and against discrimination. Republican legislatures followed up the

Carpetbaggers Northern transplants to the South, many of whom were Union soldiers who stayed in the South after the war.

Scalawags Southern whites, mainly small landowning farmers and well-off merchants and planters, who supported the Southern Republican party during Reconstruction.

The Ku Klux Klan emerged as a potent political and social force during Reconstruction, terrorizing freed people and their white allies. An 1868 Klan warning threatens Louisiana governor Henry C. Warmoth with death. Warmoth, an Illinois-born "carpetbagger," was the state's first Republican governor. Two Alabama Klansmen, photographed in 1868, wear white hoods to hide their identities.

(a) University of North Carolina Southern Historical Collection; (b) Rutherford B. Hayes Presidential Center

federal Civil Rights Act of 1866 with various antidiscrimination clauses in new constitutions and laws prescribing harsh penalties for civil rights violations. African Americans could now be employed in police forces and fire departments, serve on juries, school boards, and city councils, and they could hold public office at all levels of government.

Segregation, though, became the norm in public school systems. African American leaders often accepted segregation because they feared that insistence on integrated education would jeopardize funding for the new school systems. African Americans opposed constitutional language requiring racial segregation in schools; most African Americans were less interested in the abstract ideal of integrated education than in ensuring educational opportunities for their children and employment for African American teachers.

Segregation in railroad cars and other public places was more objectionable to African Americans. By the early 1870s, as black influence and assertiveness grew, laws guaranteeing equal access to transportation and public accommodation were passed in many states. By and large, though, such civil rights laws were difficult to enforce in local communities.

In economic matters, Republican governments failed to fulfill African Americans' hopes of obtaining land. Few former slaves possessed the cash to buy land in the open market, and they looked to the state for help. Republicans tried to weaken the plantation system and promote black ownership by raising taxes on land. Yet even when state governments seized land for nonpayment of taxes, the property was never used to help create black homesteads.

Republican leaders envisioned promoting Northern-style capitalist development—factories, large towns, and diversified agriculture—through state aid. Much Republican state lawmaking was devoted to encouraging railroad construction. Between 1868 and 1872 the Southern railroad system was rebuilt and over 3,000 new miles of track added, an increase of almost 40 percent. But in spite of all the new laws, it proved impossible to attract significant amounts of Northern and European investment capital. The obsession with railroads withdrew resources from education and other programs. As in the North, it also opened the doors to widespread corruption and bribery of public officials. Railroad failures eroded public confidence in the Republicans' ability to govern. The "gospel of prosperity" ultimately failed to modernize the economy or solidify the Republican Party in the South.

WHITE RESISTANCE AND "REDEMPTION"

The emergence of a Republican Party in the reconstructed South brought two parties but not a two-party system to the region. The opponents of Reconstruction, the Democrats, refused to acknowledge Republicans' right to participate in Southern political life. In their view, the Republican Party, supported primarily by the votes of former slaves, was the partisan instrument of the Northern Congress. Since Republicans controlled state governments, this denial of legitimacy meant, in effect, a rejection of state authority itself.

From 1870 to 1872 the Ku Klux Klan fought an ongoing terrorist campaign against Reconstruction governments and local leaders. Although not centrally organized, the Klan was a powerful presence in nearly every Southern state. It acted as a kind of guerrilla military force in the service of the Democratic Party, the planter class, and all those who sought the restoration of white supremacy. In October 1870, after Republicans carried Laurens County in South Carolina, bands of white people drove 150 African Americans from their homes and murdered 13 black and white Republican activists. In March 1871, three African Americans were arrested in Meridian, Mississippi, for giving "incendiary" speeches. At their court hearing, Klansmen killed two of the defendants and the Republican judge, and thirty more African Americans were murdered in a day of rioting. The single bloodiest episode of Reconstruction era violence took place in Colfax, Louisiana, on Easter Sunday 1873. Nearly 100 African Americans were murdered after they failed to hold a besieged courthouse during a contested election.

Southern Republicans looked to Washington for help. In 1870 and 1871 Congress passed three Enforcement Acts designed to counter racial terrorism. These declared that interference with voting was a federal offense. The acts provided for federal supervision of voting, and authorized the president to send the army and to suspend the writ of habeas corpus in districts declared to be in a state of insurrection. The most sweeping measure was the Ku Klux Klan Act of April 1871, which made the violent infringement of civil and political rights a federal crime punishable by the national government. Attorney General Amos T. Akerman prosecuted hundreds of Klansmen in North Carolina and Mississippi. In October 1871 President Grant sent federal troops to occupy nine South Carolina counties and rounded up thousands of Klan members. By the election of 1872, the federal government's intervention had helped break the Klan and restore a semblance of law and order.

The Civil Rights Act of 1875 outlawed racial discrimination in theaters, hotels, railroads, and other public places, but the law proved more an assertion of principle than a direct federal intervention in Southern affairs. Enforcement required African Americans to take their cases to the federal courts, a costly and time-consuming procedure.

As wartime idealism faded, Northern Republicans became less inclined toward direct intervention in Southern affairs. They had enough trouble retaining political control in the North. In 1874 the Democrats gained a majority in the House of Representatives for the first time since 1856. Key Northern states also began to fall to the Democrats. Northern Republicans slowly abandoned the freedmen and their white allies in the South.

Gradually, conservative Democrats "redeemed" one state after another. Virginia and Tennessee led the way in 1869, North Carolina in 1870, Georgia in 1871, Texas in 1873, and Alabama and Arkansas in 1874. In Mississippi, white conservatives employed violence and intimidation to wrest control in 1875 and "redeemed" the state the following year. Republican infighting in Louisiana in 1873 and 1874 led to a series of contested election results, including bloody clashes between black militia and armed whites, and finally to "redemption" by the Democrats in 1877. Once these states returned to Democratic rule, African Americans faced obstacles to voting, more stringent controls on plantation labor, and deep cuts in social services.

Several Supreme Court rulings involving the Fourteenth and Fifteenth Amendments effectively constrained federal protection of African American civil rights. In the so-called **Slaughterhouse cases** of 1873, the Court issued its first ruling on the Fourteenth Amendment. The cases involved a Louisiana charter that gave a New Orleans meat-packing company a monopoly over the city's butchering business on the grounds of protecting public health. A rival group of butchers had sued, claiming the law violated the Fourteenth Amendment, which prohibited states from depriving any person of life, liberty, or property without due process of law. The Court held that the Fourteenth Amendment protected only the former slaves, not butchers, and that it protected only national citizenship rights, not the regulatory powers of states. The ruling in effect denied the original intent of the Fourteenth Amendment—to protect against state infringement of national citizenship rights as spelled out in the Bill of Rights.

Three other decisions curtailed federal protection of black civil rights. In *United States* v. *Reese* (1876) and *United States* v. *Cruikshank* (1876), the Court restricted congressional power to enforce the Ku Klux Klan Act. Future prosecution would depend on the states rather than on federal authorities. In these rulings the Court held that the Fourteenth Amendment extended the federal power to protect civil rights only in cases involving discrimination by states; discrimination by individuals or groups was not covered. The Court also ruled that the Fifteenth Amendment did not guarantee a citizen's right to vote; it only barred certain specific grounds for denying suffrage—"race, color, or previous condition of servitude." This interpretation opened the door for Southern states to disfranchise African Americans for allegedly nonracial reasons. States back under Democratic control began to limit African American voting by passing laws restricting voter eligibility through poll taxes and property requirements.

Slaughterhouse cases Group of cases resulting in one sweeping decision by the U.S. Supreme Court in 1873 that contradicted the intent of the Fourteenth Amendment by decreeing that most citizenship rights remained under state, not federal, control.

Finally, in the 1883 *Civil Rights Cases* decision, the Court declared the Civil Rights Act of 1875 unconstitutional, holding that the Fourteenth Amendment gave Congress the power to outlaw discrimination by states, but not by private individuals. The majority opinion held that black people must no longer "be the special favorite of the laws." Together, these Supreme Court decisions marked the end of federal attempts to protect African American rights until well into the next century.

WHITE YEOMEN, WHITE MERCHANTS, AND "KING COTTON"

The Republicans' vision of a "New South" remade along the lines of the Northern economy failed to materialize. Instead, the South declined into the country's poorest agricultural region. Cotton growing had defined the economic life of large plantations in the coastal regions and black belt communities of the antebellum South. In the post–Civil War years "King Cotton" expanded its realm, as greater numbers of small white farmers found themselves forced to switch from subsistence crops to growing cotton for the market.

 MAP EXPLORATION

To explore an interactive version of this map, go to **http://www.prenhall.com/faraghertlc/map17.3**

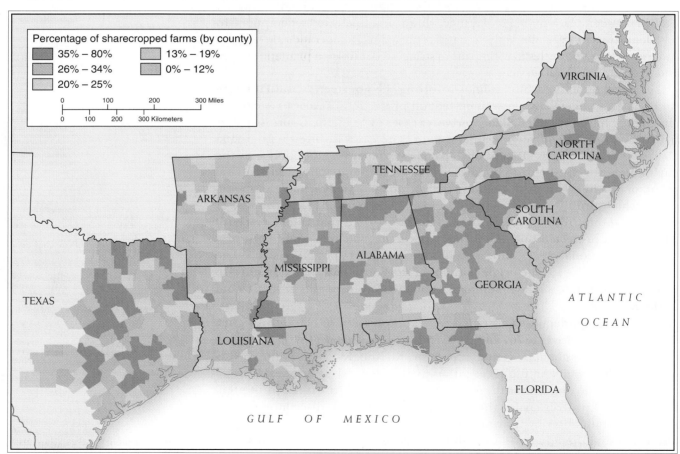

MAP 17-3

Southern Sharecropping and the Cotton Belt, 1880 The economic depression of the 1870s forced increasing numbers of Southern farmers, both white and black, into sharecropping arrangements. Sharecropping was most pervasive in the cotton belt regions of South Carolina, Georgia, Alabama, Mississippi, and east Texas.

HOW DID this new form of labor affect the lives of former slaves?

The spread of the "crop lien" system as the South's main form of agricultural credit forced more and more farmers into cotton growing.

A chronic shortage of capital and banking institutions made local merchants and planters the sole source of credit. They advanced loans to sharecroppers and tenant farmers only in exchange for a lien, or claim, on the year's cotton crop, and they often charged usurious interest rates on advances, while marking up the prices of the goods they sold in their stores. Thus, at the end of the year, sharecroppers and tenants found themselves deep in debt to stores (many owned by Northerners) for seed, supplies, and clothing.

The near total dominance of "King Cotton" inhibited economic growth across the region. Unlike Midwestern and Western farm towns burgeoning from trade in wheat, corn, and livestock, Southern communities found themselves almost entirely dependent on the price of one commodity as more and more farmers turned to cotton growing as the only way to obtain credit. Expanding production depressed prices. Competition from new cotton centers in the world market, such as Egypt and India, accelerated the downward spiral. As cotton prices declined alarmingly, from roughly 11 ¢ per pound in 1875 to 5 ¢ in 1894, per capita wealth in the South fell steadily; by the 1890s it equaled only one-third that of the East, Midwest, or West. Cotton dependency also prevented planters from acquiring the capital to purchase the farm equipment needed to profitably cultivate wheat or corn.

By 1880 about one-third of white farmers and nearly three-quarters of African American farmers in the cotton states were sharecroppers or tenants. Many former slaves and poor white people had tried subsistence farming in the undeveloped backcountry. Yet to obtain precious credit, most found themselves forced to produce cotton for market and, thus, became enmeshed in the debt-ridden crop lien system. In the upcountry and newer areas of cultivation, cotton-dominated commercial agriculture, with landless tenants and sharecroppers as the main work force, had replaced the more diversified subsistence economy of the antebellum era.

With their power based on control of credit and marketing, merchants emerged as a new economic elite unconnected to the antebellum planters whose power had rested on the ownership of land and slaves. But within both the new towns and the old planter elite, white families increasingly defined their social position by celebrating a certain type of ideal household. Women found meaning in their role as upholders of domestic virtue by creating a comfortable home environment and tending to the needs of children and husbands. Men were to be of strong moral fiber and to provide material support for the family. These elite ideals, articulated in magazines, schools, sermons, and other public discourse, rested on a belief that one's ability to reach the standards of womanhood and manhood rested solely upon moral character and individual choice.

RECONSTRUCTING THE NORTH

Abraham Lincoln liked to cite his own rise as proof of the superiority of the Northern system of "free labor" over slavery. But the triumph of the North brought with it fundamental changes in the economy, labor relations, and politics that brought Lincoln's ideal vision into question. The spread of the factory system, the growth of large and powerful corporations, and the rapid expansion of capitalist enterprise all hastened the development of a large unskilled

WHAT PRECIPITATED
the electoral crisis of 1876?

and routinized work force. Rather than becoming independent producers, more and more workers found themselves consigned permanently to wage labor.

The old Republican ideal of a society bound by a harmony of interests had become overshadowed by a grimmer reality of class conflict. A violent national railroad strike in 1877 was broken only with the direct intervention of federal troops. Northern society, like the society of the South, appeared more hierarchical than equal. That same year the last federal troops withdrew from their Southern posts, marking the end of the Reconstruction era. By then, the North had undergone its own "reconstruction" as well.

THE AGE OF CAPITAL

In the decade following Appomattox, the North's economy continued the industrial boom begun during the Civil War. By 1873, America's industrial production had grown 75 percent over the 1865 level. By that time, too, the number of nonagricultural workers in the North had surpassed the number of farmers. Between 1860 and 1880 the number of wage earners in manufacturing and construction more than doubled, from 2 million to over 4 million.

The railroad business both symbolized and advanced the new industrial order. Shortly before the Civil War, enthusiasm mounted for a transcontinental line. Private companies took on the huge and expensive job of construction, but the federal government funded the project, providing the largest subsidy in American history. An 1864 act bestowed a subsidy of $15,000 per mile of track laid over smooth plains country and varying larger amounts up to $48,000 per mile in the foothills and mountains of the Far West. The Union Pacific employed gangs of Irish American and African American workers to lay track heading west from Omaha, while the Central Pacific brought in more than 10,000 men from China to handle the difficult work in the Sierra Nevada mountain region. On May 10, 1869, Leland Stanford, the former governor of California and president of the Central Pacific Railroad, traveled to Promontory Point in Utah Territory to hammer a ceremonial golden spike, marking the finish of the first transcontinental line.

Completion of the transcontinental railroad, May 10, 1869, as building crews for the Union Pacific and Central Pacific meet at Promontory Point, Utah. The two locomotive engineers salute each other, while the chief engineers for the two railroads shake hands. Construction had begun simultaneously from Omaha and Sacramento in 1863, with the help of generous subsidies from Congress. Work crews, consisting of thousands of ex-soldiers, Irish immigrants, and imported Chinese laborers, laid nearly 1,800 miles of new track.

The Granger Collection, New York (4E377.23)

Railroads paved the way for the rapid settlement of the West, and both rural and urban areas grew dramatically over the next several decades. The combined population of Minnesota, the Dakotas, Nebraska, and Kansas, for example, jumped from 300,000 in 1860 to over 2 million in 1880. In the fifty years after 1870, the nation's railroad system expanded to more than a quarter million miles—more than all the rest of the world's railroad track combined.

Railroad corporations became America's first big businesses. Railroads required huge outlays of investment capital, and their growth increased the economic power of banks and investment houses centered on Wall Street. Bankers often gained seats on the boards of directors of these railroad companies, and their access to capital sometimes gave them the real control of railways. A new breed of aggressive entrepreneur sought to ease cutthroat competition by absorbing smaller companies and forming "pools" that set rates and divided the market. A small group of railroad executives, including Cornelius Vanderbilt, Jay Gould, Collis P. Huntington, and James J. Hill, amassed unheard-of fortunes. When he died in 1877, Vanderbilt left his son $100 million. By comparison, a decent annual wage for working a six-day week was around $350.

Railroad promoters, lawyers, and lobbyists became ubiquitous figures in Washington and state capitals, wielding enormous influence among lawmakers. Railroads benefited enormously from government subsidies. Between 1862 and 1872, Congress alone awarded more than 100 million acres of public lands to railroad companies and provided them over $64 million in loans and tax incentives.

Some of the nation's most prominent politicians routinely accepted railroad largesse. The worst scandal of the Grant administration grew out of corruption involving railroad promotion. As a way of diverting funds for the building of the Union Pacific Railroad, an inner circle of Union Pacific stockholders created the dummy Crédit Mobilier construction company. In return for political favors, a group of prominent Republicans received stock in the company. When the scandal broke in 1872, it politically ruined Vice President Schuyler Colfax and led to the censure of two congressmen.

Other industries also boomed in this period, especially those engaged in extracting minerals and processing natural resources. Railroad growth stimulated expansion in the production of coal, iron, stone, and lumber, and these also received significant government aid. For example, under the National Mineral Act of 1866, mining companies received millions of acres of free public land. Oil refining enjoyed a huge expansion in the 1860s and 1870s. As with railroads, an early period of fierce competition soon gave way to concentration. By the late 1870s, John D. Rockefeller's Standard Oil Company controlled almost 90 percent of the nation's oil-refining capacity.

LIBERAL REPUBLICANS AND THE ELECTION OF 1872

With the rapid growth of large-scale, capital-intensive enterprises, Republicans increasingly identified with the interests of business rather than the rights of freedmen or the antebellum ideology of "free labor." The old Civil War–era Radical Republicans had declined in influence. State Republican parties now organized themselves around the spoils of federal patronage rather than grand causes such as preserving the Union or ending slavery. Despite the Crédit Mobilier affair, Republicans had no monopoly on political scandal. In 1871 New York City newspapers reported the shocking story

QUICK REVIEW

The Depression of 1873

◆ End of postwar boom brought depression.

◆ Collapse resulted from commercial overexpansion.

◆ Longest economic contraction in the nation's history until then.

Liberal Republicans   Disaffected Republicans that emphasized the doctrines of classical economics.

MAP EXPLORATION

To explore an interactive version of this map, go to
http://www.prenhall.com/faraghertlc/map17.4

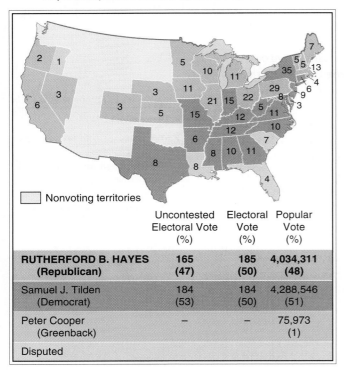

Nonvoting territories

	Uncontested Electoral Vote (%)	Electoral Vote (%)	Popular Vote (%)
RUTHERFORD B. HAYES (Republican)	**165** **(47)**	**185** **(50)**	**4,034,311** **(48)**
Samuel J. Tilden (Democrat)	184 (53)	184 (50)	4,288,546 (51)
Peter Cooper (Greenback)	–	–	75,973 (1)
Disputed			

MAP 17-4
The Election of 1876 The presidential election of 1876 left the nation without a clear-cut winner.

WHAT LED to the electoral crisis of 1876?

of how Democratic Party boss William M. Tweed and his friends had systematically stolen tens of millions from the city treasury. The "Tweed Ring" had received enormous bribes and kickbacks from city contractors and businessmen. But to many, the scandal represented only the most extreme case of the routine corruption that now plagued American political life.

By the end of President Grant's first term, a large number of disaffected Republicans sought an alternative. The **Liberal Republicans**, as they called themselves, emphasized the doctrines of classical economics, stressing the law of supply and demand, free trade, defense of property rights, and individualism. They called for a return to limited government, arguing that bribery, scandal, and high taxes all flowed from excessive state interference in the economy.

Liberal Republicans were also suspicious of expanding democracy. They believed that politics ought to be the province of "the best men"—educated and well-to-do men like themselves, devoted to the "science of government." They proposed civil service reform as the best way to break the hold of party machines on patronage.

Although most Liberal Republicans had enthusiastically supported abolition, the Union cause, and equal rights for freedmen, they now opposed continued federal intervention in the South. The national government had done all it could for the former slaves; they must now take care of themselves. "Root, Hog, or Die" was the harsh advice offered by Horace Greeley, editor of the *New York Tribune*. In the spring of 1872 a diverse collection of Liberal Republicans nominated Greeley to run for president. A longtime foe of the Democratic Party, Greeley nonetheless won that party's presidential nomination as well. He made a new policy for the South the center of his campaign against Grant. All Americans, Greeley urged, must put the Civil War behind them and "clasp hands across the bloody chasm."

Grant easily defeated Greeley, carrying every state in the North and winning 56 percent of the popular vote. Most Republicans were not willing to abandon the regular party organization, and "waving the bloody shirt" was still a potent vote-getter. But the 1872 election accelerated the trend toward federal abandonment of African American citizenship rights. The Liberal Republicans quickly faded as an organized political force. But their ideas helped define a growing conservative consciousness among the Northern public. Their agenda included retreat from the ideal of racial justice, hostility toward trade unions, suspicion of working-class and immigrant political power, celebration of competitive individualism, and opposition to government intervention in economic affairs.

THE DEPRESSION OF 1873

In the fall of 1873 the postwar boom came to an abrupt halt as a severe financial panic triggered a deep economic depression. The collapse resulted from commercial overexpansion, especially speculative investing in the nation's railroad system. By 1876 half the nation's railroads had defaulted on their bonds. Over the next two years more than 100 banks folded and 18,000 businesses shut their doors. The depression that began in 1873 lasted sixty-five months—the longest economic contraction in the nation's history until then.

The human toll of the depression was enormous. As factories began to close across the nation, the unemployment rate soared to about 15 percent. In many cities the jobless rate was much higher; roughly one-quarter of New York City workers were unemployed in 1874. Many thousands of men took to the road in search of work, and the "tramp" emerged as a new and menacing figure on the social landscape. The Pennsylvania Bureau of Labor Statistics noted that never before had "so many of the working classes, skilled and unskilled . . . been moving from place to place seeking employment that was not to be had." Farmers were also hard hit by the depression. Agricultural output continued to grow, but prices and land values fell sharply. As prices for their crops fell, farmers had a more difficult time repaying their fixed loan obligations; many sank deeper into debt.

Mass meetings of workers in New York and other cities issued calls to government officials to create jobs through public works. But these appeals were rejected. Indeed, many business leaders and political figures denounced even meager efforts at charity. They saw the depression as a natural, if painful, part of the business cycle, one that would allow only the strongest enterprises (and workers) to survive.

The depression of the 1870s prompted workers and farmers to question the old free-labor ideology that celebrated a harmony of interests in Northern society. More people voiced anger at and distrust of large corporations that exercised great economic power from outside their communities.

THE ELECTORAL CRISIS OF 1876

With the economy mired in depression, Democrats looked forward to capturing the White House in 1876. New scandals plaguing the Grant administration also weakened the Republican Party. In 1875, a conspiracy surfaced between distillers and U.S. revenue agents to cheat the government out of millions in tax revenues. The government secured indictments against more than 200 members of this "Whiskey Ring," including Orville E. Babcock, Grant's private secretary. Though acquitted, thanks to Grant's intervention, Babcock resigned in disgrace. In 1876, Secretary of War William W. Belknap was impeached for receiving bribes for the sale of trading posts in Indian Territory, and he resigned to avoid conviction.

Democrats nominated Governor Samuel J. Tilden of New York, who brought impeccable reform credentials to his candidacy. In 1871 he had helped expose and prosecute the "Tweed Ring" in New York City. As governor he had toppled the "Canal Ring," a graft-ridden scheme involving inflated contracts for repairs on the Erie Canal. In their platform, the Democrats linked the issue of corruption to an attack on Reconstruction policies. They blamed the Republicans for instituting "a corrupt centralism."

Republican nominee Rutherford B. Hayes, governor of Ohio, also sought the high ground. As a lawyer in Cincinnati he had defended runaway slaves. Later he had distinguished himself as a general in the Union army. Hayes promised, if elected, to support an efficient civil service system, to vigorously prosecute officials who betrayed the public trust, and to introduce a system of free universal education.

On an election day marred by widespread vote fraud and violent intimidation, Tilden received 250,000 more popular votes than Hayes. But Republicans refused to concede victory, challenging the vote totals in the electoral college. Tilden garnered 184 uncontested electoral votes, one shy of the majority required to win, while Hayes received 165. The problem centered in 20 disputed votes from Florida, Louisiana, South Carolina, and Oregon. In each of the three Southern states two sets of electoral votes were returned. In Oregon, which Hayes had unquestionably carried, the Democratic governor nevertheless replaced a disputed Republican elector with a Democrat.

The crisis was unprecedented. In January 1877 Congress moved to settle the deadlock, establishing an Electoral Commission composed of five senators, five representatives, and five Supreme Court justices; eight were Republicans and seven were Democrats. The commission voted along strict partisan lines to award all the contested electoral votes to Hayes. Outraged by this decision, Democratic congressmen threatened a filibuster to block Hayes's inauguration. Violence and stalemate were avoided when Democrats and Republicans struck a compromise in February. In return for Hayes's ascendance to the presidency, the Republicans promised to appropriate more money for Southern internal improvements, to appoint a Southerner to Hayes's cabinet, and to pursue a policy of noninterference ("home rule") in Southern affairs.

Shortly after assuming office, Hayes ordered removal of the remaining federal troops in Louisiana and South Carolina. Without this military presence to sustain them, the Republican governors of those two states quickly lost power to Democrats. "Home rule" meant Republican abandonment of freed people, Radicals, carpetbaggers, and scalawags. It also effectively nullified the Fourteenth and Fifteenth Amendments and the Civil Rights Act of 1866. The **Compromise of 1877** completed repudiation of the idea, born during the Civil War and pursued during Congressional Reconstruction, of a powerful federal government protecting the rights of all American citizens.

Conclusion

Reconstruction succeeded in the limited political sense of reuniting a nation torn apart by the Civil War. The Radical Republican vision, emphasizing racial justice, equal civil and political rights guaranteed by the Fourteenth and Fifteenth Amendments, and a new Southern economy organized around independent small farmers, never enjoyed the support of the majority of its party or the Northern public. The federal government's failure to pursue land reform left former slaves without the economic independence needed for full emancipation. Yet the newly autonomous black family, along with black-controlled churches, schools, and other social institutions, provided the foundations for the modern African American community.

Even as the federal government retreated from the defense of equal rights for black people, it took a more aggressive stance as the protector of business interests. The Hayes administration responded decisively to one of the worst outbreaks of class violence in American history by dispatching federal troops to several Northern cities to break the Great Railroad Strike of 1877. In the aftermath of Reconstruction, the struggle between capital and labor had clearly replaced "the Southern question" as the number one political issue of the day. "The overwhelming labor question has dwarfed all other questions into nothing," wrote an Ohio Republican. "We have home questions enough to occupy attention now."

Compromise of 1877 The Congressional settling of the 1876 election which installed Republican Rutherford B. Hayes in the White House and gave Democrats control of all state governments in the South.

CHRONOLOGY

1865	Freedmen's Bureau established.
	Abraham Lincoln assassinated.
	Andrew Johnson begins presidential Reconstruction.
	Black codes begin to be enacted in Southern states.
	Thirteenth Amendment ratified.
1866	Civil Rights Act passed.
	Congress approves Fourteenth Amendment.
	Ku Klux Klan founded.
1867	Reconstruction Acts, passed over President Johnson's veto, begin congressional Reconstruction.
	Tenure of Office Act.
	Southern states call constitutional conventions.
1868	President Johnson impeached by the House but acquitted in Senate trial.
	Fourteenth Amendment ratified.
	Most Southern states readmitted to Union.
	Ulysses S. Grant elected president.
1869	Congress approves Fifteenth Amendment.
	Union Pacific and Central Pacific tracks meet at Promontory Point in Utah Territory.

	Suffragists split into National Woman.
	Suffrage Association and American Woman Suffrage Association.
1870	Fifteenth Amendment ratified.
1871	Ku Klux Klan Act passed.
	"Tweed Ring" in New York City exposed.
1872	Liberal Republicans break with Grant and Radicals, nominate Horace Greeley for president.
	Crédit Mobilier scandal.
	Grant reelected president.
1873	Financial panic and beginning of economic depression.
	Slaughterhouse cases.
1874	Democrats gain control of House for first time since 1856.
1875	Civil Rights Act.
1876	Disputed election between Samuel Tilden and Rutherford B. Hayes.
1877	Electoral Commission elects Hayes president.
	President Hayes dispatches federal troops to break Great Railroad Strike and withdraws last remaining federal troops from the South.

SUMMARY

The Politics of Reconstruction The end of the Civil War answered some questions about the nation's future but raised serious issues about dealing with the South and the four million ex-slaves. Disagreement arose between the plans of Presidents Lincoln and Johnson versus those of Congress. The Radical Republicans succeeded in implementing their program, including constitutional amendments to guarantee the rights of African Americans.

The Meaning of Freedom The end of slavery created new opportunities and new challenges for African Americans. The first impulse was to move freely about the country. It soon gave way to attempts to build new communities, to accommodate their new status and conditions. Family, churches, and schools served as cornerstones of the new communities, but economic realities of the postwar South severely limited job options. The first attempts to build political power bases also occurred.

Southern Politics and Society Republicans constituted a minority in the South and faced great challenges in developing the party. Issues also arose over attempts to reconstruct the South and also stimulated a strong conservative Democratic resistance that eventually redeemed state governments from Republican rule. A variety of factors plagued attempts to build a "New South" following Northern economic trends.

Reconstructing the North Following the Civil War, the Northern economy followed its path of the expansion of industrialization and the growth of large corporations. The spearhead of development was railroad construction. Economic growth influenced Republicans to ally with businesses, neglecting Radical Republican causes. The depression of 1873 caused great distress and increased tension between labor and capital. Scandals and corruption hurt Republicans in the 1876 election where a stalemate was avoided by a compromise that ended Reconstruction.

REVIEW QUESTIONS

1. How did various visions of a "reconstructed" South differ? How did these visions reflect the old political and social divisions that had led to the Civil War?

2. What key changes did emancipation make in the political and economic status of African Americans? Discuss the expansion of citizenship rights in the post–Civil War years. To what extent did women share in the gains made by African Americans?

3. What role did such institutions as the family, the church, the schools, and the political parties play in the African American transition to freedom?

4. How did white Southerners attempt to limit the freedom of former slaves? How did these efforts succeed, and how did they fail?

5. Evaluate the achievements and failures of Reconstruction governments in the Southern states.

6. What were the crucial economic changes occurring in the North and South during the Reconstruction era?

KEY TERMS

Black Codes (p. 439)

Carpetbaggers (p. 450)

Civil Rights Act (p. 440)

Congressional Reconstruction (p. 440)

Compromise of 1877 (p. 460)

Field Order 15 (p. 437)

Fifteenth Amendment (p. 443)

Freedmen's Bureau (p. 437)

Ku Klux Klan (p. 443)

Liberal Republicans (p. 457)

Radical Republicans (p. 437)

Reconstruction Act (p. 441)

Scalawags (p. 450)

Sharecropping (p. 448)

Slaughterhouse cases (p. 453)

Tenure of Office Act (p. 441)

Union League (p. 449)

RECOMMENDED READING

Paul A. Cimbala and Randall M. Miller, eds., *The Freedmen's Bureau and Reconstruction* (1999). A wide-ranging collection of the latest scholarship, with special attention to recapturing the historical voices of freed people.

Jane Dailey, *Before Jim Crow: The Politics of Race in Post Emancipation Virginia* (2000). A fine study that focuses on the tension between the drive to establish white supremacy and the struggle for biracial coalitions in post–Civil War Virginia politics.

Laura F. Edwards, *Gendered Strife and Confusion: The Political Culture of Reconstruction* (1997). An ambitious analysis of how gender ideologies played a key role in shaping the party politics and social relations of the Reconstruction-era South.

Michael W. Fitzgerald, *The Union League Movement in the Deep South* (1989). Uses the Union League as a lens through which to examine race relations and the close connections between politics and economic change in the post–Civil War South.

Eric Foner, *Reconstruction: America's Unfinished Revolution, 1863–1877* (1988). The most comprehensive and thoroughly researched overview of the Reconstruction era.

William Gillette, *Retreat from Reconstruction: A Political History, 1867–1878* (1979). Covers the national political scene, with special attention to the abandonment of the ideal of racial equality.

Jacqueline Jones, *Labor of Love, Labor of Sorrow* (1985). Includes excellent material on the work and family lives of African American women in slavery and freedom.

Leon Litwack, *Been in the Storm So Long: The Aftermath of Slavery* (1979). A richly detailed analysis of the transition from slavery to freedom; excellent use of African American sources.

Scott Reynolds Nelson, *Iron Confederacies: Southern Railways, Klan Violence, and Reconstruction* (1999). Pathbreaking analysis of how conservative Southern and Northern business interests rebuilt the South's railroad system and also achieved enormous political power within individual states.

Edward Royce, *The Origins of Southern Sharecropping* (1993). A sophisticated, tightly argued work of historical sociology that explains how sharecropping emerged as the dominant form of agricultural labor in the post–Civil War South.

APPENDIX

THE DECLARATION OF INDEPENDENCE

When in the course of human events it becomes necessary for one people to dissolve the political bands which have connected them with another and to assume, among the powers of the earth, the separate and equal station to which the laws of nature and of nature's God entitle them, a decent respect to the opinions of mankind requires that they should declare the causes which impel them to the separation.

We hold these truths to be self-evident, that all men are created equal; that they are endowed by their Creator with certain unalienable rights; that among these are life, liberty, and the pursuit of happiness. That, to secure these rights, governments are instituted among men, deriving their just powers from the consent of the governed; that, whenever any form of government becomes destructive of these ends, it is the right of the people to alter or to abolish it, and to institute a new government, laying its foundation on such principles, and organizing its powers in such form, as to them shall seem most likely to effect their safety and happiness. Prudence, indeed, will dictate that governments long established should not be changed for light and transient causes; and, accordingly, all experience hath shown that mankind are more disposed to suffer, while evils are sufferable, than to right themselves by abolishing the forms to which they are accustomed. But when a long train of abuses and usurpations, pursuing invariably the same object, evinces a design to reduce them under absolute despotism, it is their right, it is their duty, to throw off such government and to provide new guards for their future security. Such has been the patient sufferance of these colonies, and such is now the necessity which constrains them to alter their former systems of government. The history of the present King of Great Britain is a history of repeated injuries and usurpations, all having, in direct object, the establishment of an absolute tyranny over these States. To prove this, let facts be submitted to a candid world:

He has refused his assent to laws the most wholesome and necessary for the public good.

He has forbidden his governors to pass laws of immediate and pressing importance, unless suspended in their operation till his assent should be obtained; and, when so suspended, he has utterly neglected to attend to them.

He has refused to pass other laws for the accommodation of large districts of people, unless those people would relinquish the right of representation in the legislature, a right inestimable to them and formidable to tyrants only.

He has called together legislative bodies at places unusual, uncomfortable, and distant from the depository of their public records, for the sole purpose of fatiguing them into compliance with his measures.

He has dissolved representative houses, repeatedly for opposing, with manly firmness, his invasions on the rights of the people.

He has refused, for a long time after such dissolutions, to cause others to be elected; whereby the legislative powers, incapable of annihilation, have returned to the people at large for their exercise; the state remaining, in the meantime, exposed to all the danger of invasion from without and convulsions within.

He has endeavored to prevent the population of these States; for that purpose, obstructing the laws for naturalization of foreigners, refusing to pass others to encourage their migration hither, and raising the conditions of new appropriations of lands.

He has obstructed the administration of justice by refusing his assent to laws for establishing judiciary powers.

He has made judges dependent on his will alone for the tenure of their offices and the amount and payment of their salaries.

He has erected a multitude of new offices and sent hither swarms of officers to harass our people and eat out their substance.

He has kept among us, in time of peace, standing armies, without the consent of our legislatures.

He has affected to render the military independent of, and superior to, the civil power.

He has combined with others to subject us to a jurisdiction foreign to our Constitution and unacknowledged by our laws, giving his assent to their acts of pretended legislation—

For quartering large bodies of armed troops among us;

For protecting them by mock trial, from punishment for any murders which they should commit on the inhabitants of these States;

For cutting off our trade with all parts of the world;

For imposing taxes on us without our consent;

For depriving us, in many cases, of the benefit of trial by jury;

For transporting us beyond seas to be tried for pretended offences;

For abolishing the free system of English laws in a neighboring province, establishing therein an arbitrary government, and enlarging its boundaries, so as to render it at once an example and fit instrument for introducing the same absolute rule into these colonies;

For taking away our charters, abolishing our most valuable laws, and altering, fundamentally, the powers of our governments.

For suspending our own legislatures and declaring themselves invested with power to legislate for us in all cases whatsoever.

He has abdicated government here by declaring us out of his protection and waging war against us.

He has plundered our seas, ravaged our coasts, burnt our towns, and destroyed the lives of our people.

He is, at this time, transporting large armies of foreign mercenaries to complete the works of death, desolation, and tyranny already begun with circumstances of cruelty and perfidy scarcely paralleled in the most barbarous ages, and totally unworthy the head of a civilized nation.

He has constrained our fellow citizens, taken captive on the high seas, to bear arms against their country, to become the executioners of their friends and brethren, or to fall themselves by their hands.

He has excited domestic insurrections amongst us and has endeavored to bring on the inhabitants of our frontiers, the merciless Indian savages, whose known rule of warfare is an undistinguished destruction of all ages, sexes, and conditions.

In every stage of these oppressions, we have petitioned for redress in the most humble terms; our repeated petitions have been answered only by repeated injury. A prince whose character is thus marked by every act which may define a tyrant is unfit to be the ruler of a free people.

Nor have we been wanting in attention to our British brethren. We have warned them, from time to time, of attempts made by their legislature to extend an unwarrantable jurisdiction over us. We have reminded them of the circumstances of our emigration and settlement here. We have appealed to their native justice and magnanimity, and

we have conjured them, by the ties of our common kindred, to disavow these usurpations, which would inevitably interrupt our connections and correspondence. They, too, have been deaf to the voice of justice and consanguinity. We must, therefore, acquiesce in the necessity which denounces our separation, and hold them, as we hold the rest of mankind, enemies in war, in peace, friends.

We, therefore, the representatives of the United States of America, in general Congress assembled, appealing to the Supreme Judge of the world for the rectitude of our intentions, do, in the name and by the authority of the good people of these colonies, solemnly publish and declare, that these united colonies are, and of right ought to be, free and independent states: that they are absolved from all allegiance to the British Crown, and that all political connection between them and the state of Great Britain is, and ought to be, totally dissolved; and that, as free and independent states, they have full power to levy war, conclude peace, contract alliances, establish commerce, and to do all other acts and things which independent states may of right do. And, for the support of this declaration, with a firm reliance on the protection of Divine Providence, we mutually pledge to each other our lives, our fortunes, and our sacred honor.

THE CONSTITUTION OF THE UNITED STATES OF AMERICA

We the people of the United States, in order to form a more perfect union, establish justice, insure domestic tranquillity, provide for the common defense, promote the general welfare, and secure the blessings of liberty to ourselves and our posterity, do ordain and establish this Constitution for the United States of America.

ARTICLE I

SECTION 1.   All legislative powers herein granted shall be vested in a Congress of the United States, which shall consist of a Senate and House of Representatives.

SECTION 2.   1. The House of Representatives shall be composed of members chosen every second year by the people of the several States, and the electors in each State shall have the qualifications requisite for electors of the most numerous branch of the State legislature.

2. No person shall be a representative who shall not have attained to the age of twenty-five years, and been seven years a citizen of the United States, and who shall not, when elected, be an inhabitant of that State in which he shall be chosen.

3. Representatives and direct taxes[1] shall be apportioned among the several States which may be included within this Union, according to their respective numbers, which shall be determined by adding to the whole number of free persons, including those bound to service for a term of years, and excluding Indians not taxed, three fifths of all other persons.[2] The actual enumeration shall be made within three years after the first meeting of the Congress of the United States, and within every subsequent term of ten years, in such manner as

they shall by law direct. The number of representatives shall not exceed one for every thirty thousand, but each State shall have at least one representative; and until such enumeration shall be made, the State of New Hampshire shall be entitled to choose three, Massachusetts eight, Rhode Island and Providence Plantations one, Connecticut five, New York six, New Jersey four, Pennsylvania eight, Delaware one, Maryland six, Virginia ten, North Carolina five, South Carolina five, and Georgia three.

4. When vacancies happen in the representation from any State, the executive authority thereof shall issue writs of election to fill such vacancies.

5. The House of Representatives shall choose their speaker and other officers; and shall have the sole power of impeachment.

SECTION 3.   1. The Senate of the United States shall be composed of two senators from each State, chosen by the legislature thereof,[3] for six years; and each senator shall have one vote.

2. Immediately after they shall be assembled in consequence of the first election, they shall be divided as equally as may be into three classes. The seats of the senators of the first class shall be vacated at the expiration of the second year, of the second class at the expiration of the fourth year, and of the third class at the expiration of the sixth year, so that one third may be chosen every second year; and if vacancies happen by resignation, or otherwise, during the recess of the legislature of any State, the executive thereof may make temporary appointments until the next meeting of the legislature, which shall then fill such vacancies.[4]

---

[1]See the Sixteenth Amendment.
[2]See the Fourteenth Amendment.

[3]See the Seventeenth Amendment.
[4]See the Seventeenth Amendment.

3. No person shall be a senator who shall not have attained to the age of thirty years, and been nine years a citizen of the United States, and who shall not, when elected, be an inhabitant of that State for which he shall be chosen.

4. The Vice President of the United States shall be President of the Senate, but shall have no vote, unless they be equally divided.

5. The Senate shall choose their other officers, and also a president pro tempore, in the absence of the Vice President, or when he shall exercise the office of the President of the United States.

6. The Senate shall have the sole power to try all impeachments. When sitting for that purpose, they shall be on oath or affirmation. When the President of the United States is tried, the chief justice shall preside: and no person shall be convicted without the concurrence of two thirds of the members present.

7. Judgment in cases of impeachment shall not extend further than to removal from office, and disqualification to hold and enjoy any office of honor, trust or profit under the United States: but the party convicted shall nevertheless be liable and subject to indictment, trial, judgment and punishment, according to law.

SECTION 4. 1. The times, places, and manner of holding elections for senators and representatives, shall be prescribed in each State by the legislature thereof; but the Congress may at any time by law make or alter such regulations, except as to the places of choosing senators.

2. The Congress shall assemble at least once in every year, and such meeting shall be on the first Monday in December, unless they shall by law appoint a different day.

SECTION 5. 1. Each House shall be the judge of the elections, returns and qualifications of its own members, and a majority of each shall constitute a quorum to do business; but a smaller number may adjourn from day to day, and may be authorized to compel the attendance of absent members, in such manner, and under such penalties as each House may provide.

2. Each House may determine the rules of its proceedings, punish its members for disorderly behavior, and, with the concurrence of two thirds, expel a member.

3. Each House shall keep a journal of its proceedings, and from time to time publish the same, excepting such parts as may in their judgment require secrecy; and the yeas and nays of the members of either House on any question shall, at the desire of one fifth of those present, be entered on the journal.

4. Neither House, during the session of Congress, shall, without the consent of the other, adjourn for more than three days, nor to any other place than that in which the two Houses shall be sitting.

SECTION 6. 1. The senators and representatives shall receive a compensation for their services, to be ascertained by law, and paid out of the Treasury of the United States. They shall in all cases, except treason, felony, and breach of the peace, be privileged from arrest during their attendance at the session of their respective Houses, and in going to and returning from the same; and for any speech or debate in either House, they shall not be questioned in any other place.

2. No senator or representative shall, during the time for which he was elected, be appointed to any civil office under the authority of the United States, which shall have been created, or the emoluments whereof shall have been increased, during such time; and no person holding any office under the United States shall be a member of either House during his continuance in office.

SECTION 7. 1. All bills for raising revenue shall originate in the House of Representatives; but the Senate may propose or concur with amendments as on other bills.

2. Every bill which shall have passed the House of Representatives and the Senate, shall, before it become a law, be presented to the President of the United States; If he approves he shall sign it, but if not he shall return it, with his objections, to that House in which it shall have originated, who shall enter the objections at large on their journal, and proceed to reconsider it. If after such reconsideration two thirds of that House shall agree to pass the bill, it shall be sent, together with the objections, to the other House, by which it shall likewise be reconsidered, and if approved by two thirds of that House, it shall become a law. But in all such cases the votes of both Houses shall be determined by yeas and nays, and the names of the persons voting for and against the bill shall be entered on the journal of each House respectively. If any bill shall not be returned by the President within ten days (Sundays excepted) after it shall have been presented to him, the same shall be a law, in like manner as if he had signed it, unless the Congress by their adjournment prevent its return, in which case it shall not be a law.

3. Every order, resolution, or vote to which the concurrence of the Senate and the House of Representatives may be necessary (except on a question of adjournment) shall be presented to the President of the United States; and before the same shall take effect, shall be approved by him, or being disapproved by him, shall be repassed by two thirds of the Senate and House of Representatives, according to the rules and limitations prescribed in the case of a bill.

SECTION 8. 1. The Congress shall have the power

1. To lay and collect taxes, duties, imposts, and excises, to pay the debts and provide for the common defense and general welfare of the United States; but all duties, imposts, and excises shall be uniform throughout the United States.

2. To borrow money on the credit of the United States;

3. To regulate commerce with foreign nations, and among the several States, and with the Indian tribes;

4. To establish a uniform rule of naturalization, and uniform laws on the subject of bankruptcies throughout the United States;

5. To coin money, regulate the value thereof, and of foreign coin, and fix the standard of weights and measures;

6. To provide for the punishment of counterfeiting the securities and current coin of the United States;

7. To establish post offices and post roads;

8. To promote the progress of science and useful arts, by securing for limited times to authors and inventors the exclusive right to their respective writings and discoveries;

9. To constitute tribunals inferior to the Supreme Court;

10. To define and punish piracies and felonies committed on the high seas, and offenses against the law of nations;

11. To declare war, grant letters of marque and reprisal, and make rules concerning captures on land and water;

12. To raise and support armies, but no appropriation of money to that use shall be for a longer term than two years;

13. To provide and maintain a navy;

14. To make rules for the government and regulation of the land and naval forces;

15. To provide for calling forth the militia to execute the laws of the Union, suppress insurrections and repel invasions;

16. To provide for organizing, arming, and disciplining the militia, and for governing such part of them as may be employed in the service of the United States, reserving to the States respectively, the appointment of the officers, and the authority of training the militia according to the discipline prescribed by Congress;

17. To exercise exclusive legislation in all cases whatsoever, over such district (not exceeding ten miles square) as may, by cession of particular States, and the acceptance of Congress, become the seat of the government of the United States, and to exercise like authority over all places purchased by the consent of the legislature of the State in which the same shall be, for the erection of forts, magazines, arsenals, dockyards, and other needful buildings; and

18. To make all laws which shall be necessary and proper for carrying into execution the foregoing powers, and all other powers vested by this Constitution in the government of the United States, or any department or officer thereof.

SECTION 9. 1. The migration or importation of such persons as any of the States now existing shall think proper to admit, shall not be prohibited by the Congress prior to the year one thousand eight hundred and eight, but a tax or duty may be imposed on such importation, not exceeding ten dollars for each person.

2. The privilege of the writ of habeas corpus shall not be suspended, unless when in cases of rebellion or invasion the public safety may require it.

3. No bill of attainder or ex post facto law shall be passed.

4. No capitation, or other direct, tax shall be laid, unless in proportion to the census or enumeration hereinbefore directed to be taken.[5]

5. No tax or duty shall be laid on articles exported from any State.

6. No preference shall be given by any regulation of commerce or revenue to the ports of one State over those of another: nor shall vessels bound to, or from, one State be obliged to enter, clear, or pay duties in another.

7. No money shall be drawn from the treasury, but in consequence of appropriations made by law; and a regular statement and account of the receipts and expenditures of all public money shall be published from time to time.

8. No title of nobility shall be granted by the United States: and no person holding any office of profit or trust under them, shall, without the consent of the Congress, accept of any present, emolument, office, or title, of any kind whatever, from any king, prince, or foreign State.

SECTION 10. 1 No State shall enter into any treaty, alliance, or confederation; grant letters of marque and reprisal; coin money; emit bills of credit; make any thing but gold and silver coin a tender in payment of debts; pass any bill of attainder, ex post facto law, or law impairing the obligation of contracts, or grant, any title of nobility.

2. No State shall, without the consent of the Congress, lay any imposts or duties on imports or exports, except what may be absolutely necessary for executing its inspection laws: and the net produce of all duties and imposts laid by any State on imports or exports, shall be for the use of the treasury of the United States; and all such laws shall be subject to the revision and control of the Congress.

3. No State shall, without the consent of the Congress, lay any duty of tonnage, keep troops, or ships of war in time of peace, enter into any agreement or compact with another State, or with a foreign power, or engage in war, unless actually invaded, or in such imminent danger as will not admit of delay.

ARTICLE II

SECTION 1. 1. The executive power shall be vested in a President of the United States of America. He shall hold his office during the term of four years, and, together with the Vice President, chosen for the same term, be elected, as follows:

2. Each State shall appoint, in such manner as the legislature thereof may direct, a number of electors, equal to the whole number of senators and representatives to which the State may be entitled in the Congress: but no senator or representative, or person holding any office of trust or profit under the United States, shall be appointed an elector.

The electors shall meet in their respective States, and vote by ballot for two persons, of whom one at least shall not be an inhabitant of the same State with themselves. And they shall make a list of all the persons voted for, and of the number of votes for each; which list they shall sign and certify, and transmit sealed to the seat of the government of the United States, directed to the president of the Senate. The president of the Senate shall, in the presence of the Senate and House of Representatives, open all the certificates, and the votes shall then be counted. The person having the greatest number of votes shall be the President, if such number be a majority of the whole number of electors appointed; and if there be more than one who have such majority, and have an equal number of votes, then the House of Representatives shall immediately choose by ballot one of them for President; and if no person have a majority, then from the five highest on the list the said House shall in like manner choose the President. But in choosing the President, the votes shall be taken by States, the representation from each State having one vote; a quorum for this purpose shall consist of a member or members from two thirds of the States, and a majority of all the States shall be necessary to a choice. In every case after the choice of the President, the person having the greatest number of votes of the electors shall be the Vice President. But if there should remain two or more who have equal votes, the Senate shall choose from them by ballot the Vice President.[6]

3. The Congress may determine the time of choosing the electors, and the day on which they shall give their votes; which day shall be the same throughout the United States.

4. No person except a natural born citizen, or a citizen of the United States, at the time of the adoption of this Constitution,

---

[5]See the Sixteenth Amendment.

[6]Superseded by the Twelfth Amendment.

shall be eligible to the office of President; neither shall any person be eligible to the office who shall not have attained to the age of thirty-five years, and been fourteen years a resident within the United States.

5. In case of the removal of the President from office, or of his death, resignation, or inability to discharge the powers and duties of the said office, the same shall devolve on the Vice President, and the congress may by law provide for the case of removal, death, resignation or inability, both of the President and Vice President, declaring what officer shall then act as President, and such officer shall act accordingly until the disability be removed, or a President shall be elected.

6. The President shall, at stated times, receive for his services a compensation which shall neither be increased nor diminished during the period for which he shall have been elected, and he shall not receive within that period any other emolument from the United States, or any of them.

7. Before he enter on the execution of his office, he shall take the following oath or affirmation:—"I do solemnly swear (or affirm) that I will faithfully execute the office of President of the United States, and will to the best of my ability, preserve, protect and defend the Constitution of the United States."

SECTION 2.   1. The President shall be commander in chief of the army and navy of the United States, and of the militia of the several States, when called into the actual service of the United States; he may require the opinion in writing, of the principal officer in each of the executive departments, upon any subject relating to the duties of their respective offices, and he shall have power to grant reprieves and pardons for offenses against the United States, except in cases of impeachment.

2. He shall have power, by and with the advice and consent of the Senate, to make treaties, provided two thirds of the senators present concur; and he shall nominate, and by and with the advice and consent of the Senate, shall appoint ambassadors, other public ministers and consuls, judges of the Supreme Court, and all other officers of the United States, whose appointments are not herein otherwise provided for, and which shall be established by law; but the Congress may by law vest the appointment of such inferior officers, as they think proper, in the President alone, in the courts of laws, or in the heads of departments.

3. The President shall have power to fill up all vacancies that may happen during the recess of the Senate, by granting commissions which shall expire at the end of their next session.

SECTION 3.   He shall from time to time give to the Congress information of the state of the Union, and recommend to their consideration such measures as he shall judge necessary and expedient; he may, on extraordinary occasions, convene both Houses, or either of them, and in case of disagreement between them with respect to the time of adjournment, he may adjourn them to such time as he shall think proper; he shall receive ambassadors and other public ministers; he shall take care that the laws be faithfully executed, and shall commission all the officers of the United States.

SECTION 4.   The President, Vice President, and all civil officers of the United States, shall be removed from office on impeachment for, and conviction of, treason, bribery, or other high crimes and misdemeanors.

ARTICLE III

SECTION 1. The judicial power of the United States shall be vested in one Supreme Court, and in such inferior courts as the Congress may from time to time ordain and establish. The judges, both of the Supreme and inferior courts, shall hold their offices during good behavior, and shall, at stated times, receive for their services, a compensation, which shall not be diminished during their continuance in office.

SECTION 2.   1. The judicial power shall extend to all cases, in law and equity, arising under this Constitution, the laws of the United States, and treaties made, or which shall be made, under their authority;—to all cases of admiralty and maritime jurisdiction;—to controversies to which the United States shall be a party;[7]—to controversies between two or more States;—between a State and citizens of another State;—between citizens of different States;—between citizens of the same State claiming lands under grants of different States, and between a State, or the citizens thereof, and foreign States, citizens or subjects.

2. In all cases affecting ambassadors, other public ministers and consuls, and those in which a State shall be party, the Supreme Court shall have original jurisdiction. In all the other cases before mentioned, the Supreme Court shall have appellate jurisdiction, both as to law and fact, with such exceptions, and under such regulations as the Congress shall make.

3. The trial of all crimes, except in cases of impeachment, shall be by jury; and such trial shall be held in the State where the said crimes shall have been committed; but when not committed within any State, the trial shall be such place or places as the congress may by law have directed.

SECTION 3.   1. Treason against the United States shall consist only in levying war against them, or in adhering to their enemies, giving them aid and comfort. No person shall be convicted of treason unless on the testimony of two witnesses to the same overt act, or on confession in open court.

2. The Congress shall have power to declare the punishment of treason, but no attainder of treason shall work corruption of blood, or forfeiture except during the life of the person attained.

ARTICLE IV

SECTION 1. Full faith and credit shall be given in each State to the public acts, records, and judicial proceedings of every other State. And the Congress may by general laws prescribe the manner in which such acts, records and proceedings shall be proved, and the effect thereof.

SECTION 2.   1. The citizens of each State shall be entitled to all privileges and immunities of citizens in the several States.[8]

2. A person charged in any State with treason, felony, or other crime, who shall flee from justice, and be found in another State, shall on demand of the executive authority of the State from which he fled, be delivered up to be removed to the State having jurisdiction of the crime.

---

[7]See the Eleventh Amendment.
[8]See the Fourteenth Amendment, Sec. 1.

3. No person held to service or labor in one State under the laws thereof, escaping into another, shall, in consequence of any law or regulation therein, be discharged from such service or labor, but shall be delivered up on claim of the party to whom such service or labor may be due.[9]

SECTION 3.   1. New States may be admitted by the Congress into this Union; but no new State shall be formed or erected within the jurisdiction of any other State, nor any State be formed by the junction of two or more States, or parts of States, without the consent of the legislatures of the States concerned as well as of the Congress.

2. The Congress shall have power to dispose of and make all needful rules and regulations respecting the territory or other property belonging to the United States; and nothing in this Constitution shall be so construed as to prejudice any claims of the United States, or of any particular State.

SECTION 4.   The United States shall guarantee to every State in this Union a republican form of government, and shall protect each of them against invasion; and on application of the legislature, or of the executive (when the legislature cannot be convened) against domestic violence.

ARTICLE V

The Congress, whenever two thirds of both Houses shall deem it necessary, shall propose amendments to this Constitution, or, on the application of the legislatures of two thirds of the several States, shall call a convention for proposing amendments, which in either case shall be valid to all intents and purposes, as part of this Constitution, when ratified by the legislatures of three fourths of the several States, or by conventions in three fourths thereof, as the one or the other mode of ratification may be proposed by the Congress; Provided that no amendment which may be made prior to the year one thousand eight hundred and eight shall in any manner affect the first and fourth clauses in the ninth section of the first article; and that no State, without its consent, shall be deprived of its equal suffrage in the Senate.

ARTICLE VI

1. All debts contracted and engagements entered into, before the adoption of this Constitution, shall be as valid against the United States under this Constitution, as under the Confederation.[10]

2. This Constitution, and the laws of the United States which shall be made in pursuance thereof; and all treaties made, or which shall be made, under the authority of the United States, shall be the supreme law of the land; and the judges in every State shall be bound thereby, any thing in the Constitution or laws of any State to the contrary notwithstanding.

3. The senators and representatives before mentioned, and the members of the several State legislatures, and all executive and judicial officers, both of the United States and of the several States, shall be bound by oath or affirmation to support this Constitution; but no religious test shall ever be required as a qualification to any office or public trust under the United States.

---

[9]See the Thirteenth Amendment.
[10]See the Fourteenth Amendment, Sec. 4.

ARTICLE VII

The ratification of the conventions of nine States shall be sufficient for the establishment of this Constitution between the States so ratifying the same.

Done in Convention by the unanimous consent of the States present the seventeenth day of September in the year of our Lord one thousand seven hundred and eighty-seven, and of the independence of the United States of America the twelfth. In witness whereof we have hereunto subscribed our names.

[Signatories' names omitted]

Articles in addition to, and amendment of, the Constitution of the United States of America, proposed by Congress, and ratified by the legislatures of the several States, pursuant to the fifth article of the original Constitution.

Amendment I
[First ten amendments ratified December 15, 1791]

Congress shall make no law respecting an establishment of religion, or prohibiting the free exercise thereof; or abridging the freedom of speech, or of the press; or the right of the people peaceably to assemble, and to petition the government for a redress of grievances.

Amendment II

A well regulated militia, being necessary to the security of a free State, the right of the people to keep and bear arms, shall not be infringed.

Amendment III

No soldier shall, in time of peace be quartered in any house, without the consent of the owner, nor in time of war, but in a manner to be prescribed by law.

Amendment IV

The right of the people to be secure in their persons, houses, papers, and effects, against unreasonable searches and seizures, shall not be violated, and no warrants shall issue, but upon probable cause, supported by oath or affirmation, and particularly describing the place to be searched, and the persons or things to be seized.

Amendment V

No person shall be held to answer for a capital or otherwise infamous crime, unless on a presentment or indictment of a grand jury, except in cases arising in the land or naval forces, or in the militia, when in actual service in time of war or public danger; nor shall any person be subject for the same offense to be twice put in jeopardy of life or limb; nor shall be compelled in any criminal case to be a witness against himself, nor be deprived of life, liberty, or property, without due process of law; nor shall private property be taken for public use, without just compensation.

Amendment VI

In all criminal prosecutions, the accused shall enjoy the right to a speedy and public trial, by an impartial jury of the State and district wherein the crime shall have been committed, which district shall have been previously ascertained by law, and to be informed of the nature and cause of the accusation; to be confronted with the witnesses against him; to have compulsory process for obtaining witnesses in his favor, and to have the assistance of counsel for his defense.

Amendment VII

In suits at common law, where the value in controversy shall exceed twenty dollars, the right of trial by jury shall be preserved, and no fact tried by a jury shall be otherwise reexamined in any court of the United States, than according to the rules of the common law.

Amendment VIII

Excessive bail shall not be required, nor excessive fines imposed, nor cruel and unusual punishments inflicted.

Amendment IX

The enumeration in the Constitution of certain rights shall not be construed to deny or disparage others retained by the people.

Amendment X

The powers not delegated to the United States by the Constitution, nor prohibited by it to the States, are reserved to the States respectively, or to the people.

Amendment XI [January 8, 1798]

The judicial power of the United States shall not be construed to extend to any suit in law or equity, commended or prosecuted against one of the United States by citizens of another State, or by citizens or subjects of any foreign State.

Amendment XII [September 25, 1804]

The electors shall meet in their respective States, and vote by ballot for President and Vice President, one of whom, at least, shall not be an inhabitant of the same State with themselves; they shall name in their ballots the person voted for as President, and in distinct ballots the person voted for as Vice President, and they shall make distinct lists of all persons voted for as President and of all persons voted for as Vice President, and of the number of votes for each, which lists they shall sign and certify, and transmit sealed to the seat of the government of the United States, directed to the President of the Senate;—The President of the Senate shall, in the presence of the Senate and House of Representatives, open all the certificates and the votes shall then be counted;—The person having the greatest number of votes for President, shall be the President, if such number be a majority of the whole number of electors appointed; and if no person have such majority, then from the persons having the highest numbers not exceeding three on the list of those voted for as President, the House of Representatives shall choose immediately, by ballot, the President. But in choosing the President, the votes shall be taken by States, the representation from each State having one vote; a quorum for this purpose shall consist of a member or members from two thirds of the States, and a majority of all the States shall be necessary to a choice. And if the House of Representatives shall not choose a President whenever the right of choice shall devolve upon them, before the fourth day of March next following, then the Vice President shall act as President,

as in the case of the death or other constitutional disability of the President. The person having the greatest number of votes as Vice President shall be the Vice President, if such number be a majority of the whole number of electors appointed, and if no person have a majority, then from the two highest numbers on the list, the Senate shall choose the Vice President; a quorum for the purpose shall consist of two thirds of the whole number of Senators, and a majority of the whole number shall be necessary to a choice. But no person constitutionally ineligible to the office of President shall be eligible to that of Vice President of the United States.

Amendment XIII [December 18, 1865]

SECTION 1. Neither slavery nor involuntary servitude, except as a punishment for crime whereof the party shall have been duly convicted, shall exist within the United States, or any place subject to their jurisdiction.

SECTION 2. Congress shall have power to enforce this article by appropriate legislation.

Amendment XIV [July 28, 1868]

SECTION 1. All persons born or naturalized in the United States, and subject to the jurisdiction thereof, are citizens of the United States and of the State wherein they reside. No State shall make or enforce any law which shall abridge the privileges or immunities of citizens of the United States; nor shall any State deprive any person of life, liberty, or property, without due process of law; nor deny to any person within its jurisdiction the equal protection of the laws.

SECTION 2. Representatives shall be apportioned among the several States according to their respective numbers, counting the whole number of persons in each State, excluding Indians not taxed. But when the right to vote at any election for the choice of electors for President and Vice President of the United States, representatives in Congress, the executive and judicial officers of a State, or the members of the legislature thereof, is denied to any of the male inhabitants of such State, being twenty-one years of age, and citizens of the United States, or in any way abridged, except for participating in rebellion, or other crime, the basis of representation there shall be reduced in the proportion which the number of such male citizens shall bear to the whole number of male citizens twenty-one years of age in such State.

SECTION 3. No person shall be a senator or representative in Congress, or elector of President and Vice President, or hold any office, civil or military, under the United States, or under any State, who having previously taken an oath, as a member of Congress, or as an officer of the United States, or as a member of any State legislature, or as an executive or judicial officer of any State, to support the Constitution of the United States, shall have engaged in insurrection or rebellion against the same, or given aid or comfort to the enemies thereof. But Congress may by a vote of two thirds of each House, remove such disability.

SECTION 4. The validity of the public debt of the United States, authorized by law, including debts incurred for payment of pensions and bounties for services in suppressing insurrection or rebellion; shall not be questioned. But neither the United States nor any State shall assume or pay any debt or obligation incurred in aid of insurrection or rebellion against the United States, or any claim for the loss or emancipation of any slave; but all such debts, obligations, and claims shall be held illegal and void.

SECTION 5.   The Congress shall have the power to enforce, by appropriate legislation, the provisions of this article.

Amendment XV [March 30, 1870]

SECTION 1. The right of citizens of the United States to vote shall not be denied or abridged by the United States or by any State on account of race, color, or previous condition of servitude.

SECTION 2. The Congress shall have power to enforce this article by appropriate legislation.

Amendment XVI [February 25, 1913]

The Congress shall have power to lay and collect taxes on incomes, from whatever source derived, without apportionment among the several States, and without regard to any census or enumeration.

Amendment XVII [May 31, 1913]

The Senate of the United States shall be composed of two senators from each State, elected by the people thereof, for six years; and each senator shall have one vote. The electors in each State shall have the qualifications requisite for electors of the most numerous branch of the State legislature.

When vacancies happen in the representation of any State in the Senate, the executive authority of such State shall issue writs of election to fill such vacancies: Provided, That the legislature of any State may empower the executive thereof to make temporary appointments until the people fill the vacancies by election as the legislature may direct.

This amendment shall not be so construed as to affect the election or term of any senator chosen before it becomes valid as part of the Constitution.

Amendment XVIII[11] [January 29, 1919]

After one year from the ratification of this article, the manufacture, sale, or transportation of intoxicating liquors within, the importation thereof into, or the exportation thereof from the United States and all territory subject to the jurisdiction thereof for beverage purposes is thereby prohibited.

The Congress and the several States shall have concurrent power to enforce this article by appropriate legislation.

This article shall be inoperative unless it shall have been ratified as an amendment to the Constitution by the legislatures of the several States, as provided in the constitution, within seven years from the date of the submission hereof to the States by Congress.

Amendment XIX [August 26, 1920]

The right of citizens of the United States to vote shall not be denied or abridged by the United States or by any State on account of sex.

Congress shall have the power to enforce this article by appropriate legislation.

---

[11]Repealed by the Twenty-first Amendment.

Amendment XX [January 23, 1933]

SECTION 1.   The terms of the President and Vice President shall end at noon on the 20th day of January and the terms of Senators and Representatives at noon on the 3d day of January, of the years in which such terms would have ended if this article had not been ratified; and the terms of their successors shall then begin.

SECTION 2.   The Congress shall assemble at least once in every year, and such meeting shall begin at noon on the 3d day of January, unless they shall by law appoint a different day.

SECTION 3.   If, at the time fixed for the beginning of the term of President, the President-elect shall have died, the Vice President-elect shall become President. If a President shall not have been chosen before the time fixed for the beginning of his term, or if the President-elect shall have failed to qualify, then the Vice President-elect shall act as President until a President shall have qualified; and the Congress may by law provide for the case wherein neither a President-elect nor a Vice President-elect shall have qualified, declaring who shall then act as President, or the manner in which one who is to act shall be selected, and such person shall act accordingly until a President or Vice President shall have qualified.

SECTION 4. The Congress may by law provide for the case of the death of any of the persons from whom, the House of Representatives may choose a President whenever the right of choice shall have devolved upon them, and for the case of the death of any of the persons from whom the Senate may choose a Vice President whenever the right of choice shall have devolved upon them.

SECTION 5.   Sections 1 and 2 shall take effect on the 15th day of October following the ratification of this article.

SECTION 6.   This article shall be inoperative unless it shall have been ratified as an amendment to the Constitution by the legislatures of three-fourths of the several States within seven years from the date of its submission.

Amendment XXI [December 5, 1933]

SECTION 1.   The Eighteenth Article of amendment to the Constitution of the United States is hereby repealed.

SECTION 2.   The transportation or importation into any State, Territory, or possession of the United States for delivery or use therein of intoxicating liquors in violation of the laws thereof, is hereby prohibited.

SECTION 3.   This article shall be inoperative unless it shall have been ratified as an amendment to the Constitution by conventions in the several States, as provided in the Constitution, within seven years from the date of the submission thereof to the States by the Congress.

Amendment XXII [March 1, 1951]

No person shall be elected to the office of the President more than twice, and no person who has held the office of President, or acted as President, for more than two years of a term to which some other person was elected President shall be elected to the office of the President more than once.

But this article shall not apply to any person holding the office of President when this article was proposed by the Congress, and shall not prevent any person who may be holding the office of President, or acting as President, during the term within which this article becomes operative from holding the office of President or acting as President during the remainder of such term.

This article shall be inoperative unless it shall have been ratified as an amendment to the Constitution by the legislatures of three-fourths of the several States within seven years from the date of its submission to the States by the Congress.

Amendment XXIII [March 29, 1961]

SECTION 1. The District constituting the seat of Government of the United States shall appoint in such manner as the Congress may direct.

A number of electors of President and Vice President equal to the whole number of Senators and Representatives in Congress to which the District would be entitled if it were a State, but in no event more than the least populous State; they shall be in addition to those appointed by the States, but they shall be considered, for the purposes of the election of President and Vice President, to be electors appointed by a State; and they shall meet in the District and perform such duties as provided by the twelfth article of amendment.

SECTION 2. The Congress shall have power to enforce this article by appropriate legislation.

Amendment XXIV [January 23, 1964]

SECTION 1. The right of citizens of the United States to vote in any primary or other election for President or Vice President, for electors for President or Vice President, or for Senator or Representative in Congress, shall not be denied or abridged by the United States or any State by reason of failure to pay any poll tax or other tax.

SECTION 2. The Congress shall have power to enforce this article by appropriate legislation.

Amendment XXV [February 10, 1967]

SECTION 1. In case of the removal of the President from office or of his death or resignation, the Vice President shall become President.

SECTION 2. Whenever there is a vacancy in the office of Vice President, the President shall nominate a Vice President who shall take office upon confirmation by a majority of both Houses of Congress.

SECTION 3. Whenever the President transmits to the President pro tempore of the Senate and the Speaker of the House of Representatives his written declaration that he is unable to discharge the powers and duties of his office, and until he transmits to them a written declaration to the contrary, such powers and duties shall be discharged by the Vice President as Acting President.

SECTION 4. Whenever the Vice President and a majority of either the principal officers of the executive departments or of such other body as Congress may by law provide, transmit to the President pro tempore of the Senate and the Speaker of the House of Representatives their written declaration that the President is unable to discharge the powers and duties of his office, the Vice President shall immediately assume the powers and duties of the office as Acting President.

Thereafter, when the President transmits to the President pro tempore of the Senate and the Speaker of the House of Representatives his written declaration that no inability exists, he shall resume the powers and duties of his office unless the Vice President and a majority of either the principal officers of the executive departments or of such other body as Congress may by law provide, transmit within four days to the President pro tempore of the Senate and the Speaker of the House of Representatives their written declaration that the President is unable to discharge the powers and duties of his office. Thereupon Congress shall decide the issue, assembling within forty-eight hours for that purpose if not in session. If the Congress, within twenty-one days after receipt of the latter written declaration, or, if Congress is not in session, within twenty-one days after Congress is required to assemble, determines by two-thirds vote of both Houses that the President is unable to discharge the powers and duties of his office, the Vice President shall continue to discharge the same as Acting President; otherwise, the President shall resume the powers and duties of his office.

Amendment XXVI [June 30, 1971]

SECTION 1. The right of citizens of the United States who are eighteen years of age or older to vote shall not be denied or abridged by the United States or by any State on account of age.

SECTION 2. The Congress shall have power to enforce this article by appropriate legislation.

Amendment XXVII[12] [May 7, 1992]

No law, varying the compensation for services of the Senators and Representatives, shall take effect until an election of Representatives shall have intervened.

---

[12]James Madison proposed this amendment in 1789 together with the ten amendments that were adopted as the Bill of Rights, but it failed to win ratification at the time. Congress, however, had set no deadline for its ratification, and over the years—particularly in the 1980s and 1990s—many states voted to add it to the Constitution. With the ratification of Michigan in 1992 it passed the threshold of 3/4ths of the states required for adoption, but because the process took more than 200 years, its validity remains in doubt.

PRESIDENT AND VICE PRESIDENT

1. George Washington (1789)
   John Adams (1789)

2. John Adams (1797)
   Thomas Jefferson (1797)

3. Thomas Jefferson (1801)
   Aaron Burr (1801)
   George Clinton (1805)

4. James Madison (1809)
   George Clinton (1809)
   Elbridge Gerry (1813)

5. James Monroe (1817)
   Daniel D. Thompkins (1817)

6. John Quincy Adams (1825)
   John C. Calhoun (1825)

7. Andrew Jackson (1829)
   John C. Calhoun (1829)
   Martin Van Buren (1833)

8. Martin Van Buren (1837)
   Richard M. Johnson (1837)

9. William H. Harrison (1841)
   John Tyler (1841)

10 John Tyler (1841)

11 James K. Polk (1845)
   George M. Dallas (1845)

12 Zachary Taylor (1849)
   Millard Fillmore (1849)

13 Millard Fillmore (1850)

14 Franklin Pierce (1853)
   William R. King (1853)

15 James Buchanan (1857)
   John C. Breckinridge (1857)

16 Abraham Lincoln (1861)
   Hannibal Hamlin (1861)
   Andrew Johnson (1865)

17 Andrew Johnson (1865)

18 Ulysses S. Grant (1869)
   Schuyler Colfax (1869)
   Henry Wilson (1873)

19 Rutherford B. Hayes (1877)
   William A. Wheeler (1877)

20 James A. Garfield (1881)
   Chester A. Arthur (1881)

21. Chester A. Arthur (1881)

22. Grover Cleveland (1885)
   T. A. Hendricks (1885)

23. Benjamin Harrison (1889)
   Levi P. Morgan (1889)

24. Grover Cleveland (1893)
   Adlai E. Stevenson (1893)

25. William McKinley (1897)
   Garret A. Hobart (1897)
   Theodore Roosevelt (1901)

26. Theodore Roosevelt (1901)
   Charles Fairbanks (1905)

27. William H. Taft (1909)
   James S. Sherman (1909)

28. Woodrow Wilson (1913)
   Thomas R. Marshall (1913)

29. Warren G. Harding (1921)
   Calvin Coolidge (1921)

30. Calvin Coolidge (1923)
   Charles G. Dawes (1925)

31. Herbert C. Hoover (1929)
   Charles Curtis (1929)

32. Franklin D. Roosevelt (1933)
   John Nance Garner (1933)
   Henry A. Wallace (1941)
   Harry S. Truman (1945)

33. Harry S. Truman (1945)
   Alben W. Barkley (1949)

34. Dwight D. Eisenhower (1953)
   Richard M. Nixon (1953)

35. John F. Kennedy (1961)
   Lyndon B. Johnson (1961)

36. Lyndon B. Johnson (1963)
   Hubert H. Humphrey (1965)

37. Richard M. Nixon (1969)
   Spiro T. Agnew (1969)
   Gerald R. Ford (1973)

38. Gerald R. Ford (1974)
   Nelson A. Rockefeller (1974)

39. James E. Carter Jr. (1977)
   Walter F. Mondale (1977)

40. Ronald W. Reagan (1981)
   George H. Bush (1981)

41. George H. Bush (1989)
   James D. Quayle III (1989)

42. William J. Clinton (1993)
   Albert Gore (1993)

43. George W. Bush (2001)
   Richard Cheney (2001)

PRESIDENTIAL ELECTIONS (CONTINUED)

Year	Number of States	Candidates	Party	Popular Vote*	Electoral Vote†	Percentage of Popular Vote
1789	11	GEORGE WASHINGTON	No party designations		69	
		John Adams			34	
		Other Candidates			35	
1792	15	GEORGE WASHINGTON	No party designations		132	
		John Adams			77	
		George Clinton			50	
		Other Candidates			5	
1796	16	JOHN ADAMS	Federalist		71	
		Thomas Jefferson	Democratic-Republican		68	
		Thomas Pinckney	Federalist		59	
		Aaron Burr	Democratic-Republican		30	
		Other Candidates			48	
1800	16	THOMAS JEFFERSON	Democratic-Republican		73	
		Aaron Burr	Democratic-Republican		73	
		John Adams	Federalist		65	
		Charles C. Pinckney	Federalist		64	
		John Jay	Federalist		1	
1804	17	THOMAS JEFFERSON	Democratic-Republican		162	
		Charles C. Pinckney	Federalist		14	
1808	17	JAMES MADISON	Democratic-Republican		122	
		Charles C. Pinckney	Federalist		47	
		George Clinton	Democratic-Republican		6	
1812	18	JAMES MADISON	Democratic-Republican		128	
		DeWitt Clinton	Federalist		89	
1816	19	JAMES MONROE	Democratic-Republican		183	
		Rufus King	Federalist		34	
1820	24	JAMES MONROE	Democratic-Republican		231	
		John Quincy Adams	Independent-Republican		1	
1824	24	JOHN QUINCY ADAMS	Democratic-Republican	108,740	84	30.5
		Andrew Jackson	Democratic-Republican	153,544	99	43.1
		William H. Crawford	Democratic-Republican	46,618	41	13.1
		Henry Clay	Democratic-Republican	47,136	37	13.2
1828	24	ANDREW JACKSON	Democrat	647,286	178	56.0
		John Quincy Adams	National Republican	508,064	83	44.0
1832	24	ANDREW JACKSON	Democrat	687,502	219	55.0
		Henry Clay	National Republican	530,189	49	42.4
		William Wirt	Anti-Masonic	33,108	7	2.6
		John Floyd	National Republican		11	

* Percentage of popular vote given for any election year may not total 100 percent because candidates receiving less than 1 percent of the popular vote have been omitted.

† Prior to the passage of the Twelfth Amendment in 1904, the electoral college voted for two presidential candidates; the runner-up became Vice-President. Data from Historical Statistics of the United States, Colonial Times to 1957 (1961), pp. 682–683, and The World Almanac.

PRESIDENTIAL ELECTIONS (CONTINUED)

Year	Number of States	Candidates	Party	Popular Vote	Electoral Vote	Percentage of Popular Vote
1836	26	MARTIN VAN BUREN	Democrat	765,483	170	50.9
		William H. Harrison	Whig		73	
		Hugh L. White	Whig		26	
		Daniel Webster	Whig	739,795	14	49.1
		W. P. Mangum	Whig		11	
1840	26	WILLIAM H. HARRISON	Whig	1,274,624	234	53.1
		Martin Van Buren	Democrat	1,127,781	60	46.9
1844	26	JAMES K. POLK	Democrat	1,338,464	170	49.6
		Henry Clay	Whig	1,300,097	105	48.1
		James G. Birney	Liberty	62,300		2.3
1848	30	ZACHARY TAYLOR	Whig	1,360,967	163	47.4
		Lewis Cass	Democrat	1,222,342	127	42.5
		Martin Van Buren	Free Soil	291,263		10.1
1852	31	FRANKLIN PIERCE	Democrat	1,601,117	254	50.9
		Winfield Scott	Whig	1,385,453	42	44.1
		John P. Hale	Free Soil	155,825		5.0
1856	31	JAMES BUCHANAN	Democrat	1,832,955	174	45.3
		John C. Frémont	Republican	1,339,932	114	33.1
		Millard Fillmore	American ("Know Nothing")	871,731	8	21.6
1860	33	ABRAHAM LINCOLN	Republican	1,865,593	180	39.8
		Stephen A. Douglas	Democrat	1,382,713	12	29.5
		John C. Breckinridge	Democrat	848,356	72	18.1
		John Bell	Constitutional Union	592,906	39	12.6
1864	36	ABRAHAM LINCOLN	Republican	2,206,938	212	55.0
		George B. McClellan	Democrat	1,803,787	21	45.0
1868	37	ULYSSES S. GRANT	Republican	3,013,421	214	52.7
		Horatio Seymour	Democrat	2,706,829	80	47.3
1872	37	ULYSSES S. GRANT	Republican	3,596,745	286	55.6
		Horace Greeley	Democrat	2,843,446	*	43.9
1876	38	RUTHERFORD B. HAYES	Republican	4,036,572	185	48.0
		Samuel J. Tilden	Democrat	4,284,020	184	51.0
1880	38	JAMES A. GARFIELD	Republican	4,453,295	214	48.5
		Winfield S. Hancock	Democrat	4,414,082	155	48.1
		James B. Weaver	Greenback-Labor	308,578		3.4
1884	38	GROVER CLEVELAND	Democrat	4,879,507	219	48.5
		James G. Blaine	Republican	4,850,293	182	48.2
		Benjamin F. Butler	Greenback-Labor	175,370		1.8
		John P. St. John	Prohibition	150,369		1.5
1888	38	BENJAMIN HARRISON	Republican	5,447,129	233	47.9
		Grover Cleveland	Democrat	5,537,857	168	48.6
		Clinton B. Fisk	Prohibition	249,506		2.2
		Anson J. Streeter	Union Labor	146,935		1.3

* Because of the death of Greeley, Democratic electors scattered their votes.

PRESIDENTIAL ELECTIONS   (CONTINUED)

Year	Number of States	Candidates	Party	Popular Vote	Electoral Vote	Percentage of Popular Vote
1892	44	GROVER CLEVELAND	Democrat	5,555,426	277	46.1
		Benjamin Harrison	Republican	5,182,690	145	43.0
		James B. Weaver	People's	1,029,846	22	8.5
		John Bidwell	Prohibition	264,133		2.2
1896	45	WILLIAM MCKINLEY	Republican	7,102,246	271	51.1
		William J. Bryan	Democrat	6,492,559	176	47.7
1900	45	WILLIAM MCKINLEY	Republican	7,218,491	292	51.7
		William J. Bryan	Democrat; Populist	6,356,734	155	45.5
		John C. Woolley	Prohibition	208,914		1.5
1904	45	THEODORE ROOSEVELT	Republican	7,628,461	336	57.4
		Alton B. Parker	Democrat	5,084,223	140	37.6
		Eugene V. Debs	Socialist	402,283		3.0
		Silas C. Swallow	Prohibition	258,536		1.9
1908	46	WILLIAM H. TAFT	Republican	7,675,320	321	51.6
		William J. Bryan	Democrat	6,412,294	162	43.1
		Eugene V. Debs	Socialist	420,793		2.8
		Eugene W. Chafin	Prohibition	253,840		1.7
1912	48	WOODROW WILSON	Democrat	6,296,547	435	41.9
		Theodore Roosevelt	Progressive	4,118,571	88	27.4
		William H. Taft	Republican	3,486,720	8	23.2
		Eugene V. Debs	Socialist	900,672		6.0
		Eugene W. Chafin	Prohibition	206,275		1.4
1916	48	WOODROW WILSON	Democrat	9,127,695	277	49.4
		Charles E. Hughes	Republican	8,533,507	254	46.2
		A. L. Benson	Socialist	585,113		3.2
		J. Frank Hanly	Prohibition	220,506		1.2
1920	48	WARREN G. HARDING	Republican	16,143,407	404	60.4
		James M. Cox	Democrat	9,130,328	127	34.2
		Eugene V. Debs	Socialist	919,799		3.4
		P. P. Christensen	Farmer-Labor	265,411		1.0
1924	48	CALVIN COOLIDGE	Republican	15,718,211	382	54.0
		John W. Davis	Democrat	8,385,283	136	28.8
		Robert M. La Follette	Progressive	4,831,289	13	16.6
1928	48	HERBERT C. HOOVER	Republican	21,391,993	444	58.2
		Alfred E. Smith	Democrat	15,016,169	87	40.9
1932	48	FRANKLIN D. ROOSEVELT	Democrat	22,809,638	472	57.4
		Herbert C. Hoover	Republican	15,758,901	59	39.7
		Norman Thomas	Socialist	881,951		2.2
1936	48	FRANKLIN D. ROOSEVELT	Democrat	27,752,869	523	60.8
		Alfred M. Landon	Republican	16,674,665	8	36.5
		William Lemke	Union	882,479		1.9
1940	48	FRANKLIN D. ROOSEVELT	Democrat	27,307,819	449	54.8
		Wendell L. Willkie	Republican	22,321,018	82	44.8

PRESIDENTIAL ELECTIONS   (CONTINUED)

Year	Number of States	Candidates	Party	Popular Vote	Electoral Vote	Percent- age of Popular Vote
1944	48	FRANKLIN D. ROOSEVELT	Democrat	25,606,585	432	53.5
		Thomas E. Dewey	Republican	22,014,745	99	46.0
1948	48	HARRY S. TRUMAN	Democrat	24,105,812	303	49.5
		Thomas E. Dewey	Republican	21,970,065	189	45.1
		J. Strom Thurmond	States' Rights	1,169,063	39	2.4
		Henry A. Wallace	Progressive	1,157,172		2.4
1952	48	DWIGHT D. EISENHOWER	Republican	33,936,234	442	55.1
		Adlai E. Stevenson	Democrat	27,314,992	89	44.4
1956	48	DWIGHT D. EISENHOWER	Republican	35,590,472	457*	57.6
		Adlai E. Stevenson	Democrat	26,022,752	73	42.1
1960	50	JOHN F. KENNEDY	Democrat	34,227,096	303†	49.9
		Richard M. Nixon	Republican	34,108,546	219	49.6
1964	50	LYNDON B. JOHNSON	Democrat	42,676,220	486	61.3
		Barry M. Goldwater	Republican	26,860,314	52	38.5
1968	50	RICHARD M. NIXON	Republican	31,785,480	301	43.4
		Hubert H. Humphrey	Democrat	31,275,165	191	42.7
		George C. Wallace	American Independent	9,906,473	46	13.5
1972	50	RICHARD M. NIXON‡	Republican	47,165,234	520	60.6
		George S. McGovern	Democrat	29,168,110	17	37.5
1976	50	JIMMY CARTER	Democrat	40,828,929	297	50.1
		Gerald R. Ford	Republican	39,148,940	240	47.9
		Eugene McCarthy	Independent	739,256		
1980	50	RONALD REAGAN	Republican	43,201,220	489	50.9
		Jimmy Carter	Democrat	34,913,332	49	41.2
		John B. Anderson	Independent	5,581,379		
1984	50	RONALD REAGAN	Republican	53,428,357	525	59.0
		Walter F. Mondale	Democrat	36,930,923	13	41.0
1988	50	GEORGE BUSH	Republican	48,901,046	426	53.4
		Michael Dukakis	Democrat	41,809,030	111	45.6
1992	50	BILL CLINTON	Democrat	43,728,275	370	43.2
		George Bush	Republican	38,167,416	168	37.7
		H. Ross Perot	United We Stand, America	19,237,247		19.0
1996	50	BILL CLINTON	Democrat	45,590,703	379	49.0
		Robert Dole	Republican	37,816,307	159	41.0
		H. Ross Perot	Reform	7,866,284		8.0
2000	50	GEORGE W. BUSH	Republican	50,459,624	271	47.9
		Albert Gore, Jr.	Democrat	51,003,328	266	49.4
		Ralph Nader	Green	2,882,985	0	2.7
2004	50	GEORGE W. BUSH	Republican	59,117,523	286	51.1
		John Kerry	Democrat	55,557,584	252	48.0
		Ralph Nader	Green	405,623	0	0.3

* *Walter B. Jones received 1 electoral vote.*

† *Harry F. Byrd received 15 electoral votes.*

‡ *Resigned August 9, 1974: Vice President Gerald R. Ford became President.*

ADMISSION OF STATES INTO THE UNION

State	Date of Admission	State	Date of Admission
1. Delaware	December 7, 1787	26. Michigan	January 26, 1837
2. Pennsylvania	December 12, 1787	27. Florida	March 3, 1845
3. New Jersey	December 18, 1787	28. Texas	December 29, 1845
4. Georgia	January 2, 1788	29. Iowa	December 28, 1846
5. Connecticut	January 9, 1788	30. Wisconsin	May 29, 1848
6. Massachusetts	February 6, 1788	31. California	September 9, 1850
7. Maryland	April 28, 1788	32. Minnesota	May 11, 1858
8. South Carolina	May 23, 1788	33. Oregon	February 14, 1859
9. New Hampshire	June 21, 1788	34. Kansas	January 29, 1861
10. Virginia	June 25, 1788	35. West Virginia	June 20, 1863
11. New York	July 26, 1788	36. Nevada	October 31, 1864
12. North Carolina	November 21, 1789	37. Nebraska	March 1, 1867
13. Rhode Island	May 29, 1790	38. Colorado	August 1, 1876
14. Vermont	March 4, 1791	39. North Dakota	November 2, 1889
15. Kentucky	June 1, 1792	40. South Dakota	November 2, 1889
16. Tennessee	June 1, 1796	41. Montana	November 8, 1889
17. Ohio	March 1, 1803	42. Washington	November 11, 1889
18. Louisiana	April 30, 1812	43. Idaho	July 3, 1890
19. Indiana	December 11, 1816	44. Wyoming	July 10, 1890
20. Mississippi	December 10, 1817	45. Utah	January 4, 1896
21. Illinois	December 3, 1818	46. Oklahoma	November 16, 1907
22. Alabama	December 14, 1819	47. New Mexico	January 6, 1912
23. Maine	March 15, 1820	48. Arizona	February 14, 1912
24. Missouri	August 10, 1821	49. Alaska	January 3, 1959
25. Arkansas	June 15, 1836	50. Hawaii	August 21, 1959

DEMOGRAPHICS OF THE UNITED STATES

POPULATION GROWTH

Year	Population	Percent Increase
1630	4,600	
1640	26,600	478.3
1650	50,400	90.8
1660	75,100	49.0
1670	111,900	49.0
1680	151,500	35.4
1690	210,400	38.9
1700	250,900	19.2
1710	331,700	32.2
1720	466,200	40.5
1730	629,400	35.0
1740	905,600	43.9
1750	1,170,800	29.3
1760	1,593,600	36.1
1770	2,148,100	34.8
1780	2,780,400	29.4
1790	3,929,214	41.3
1800	5,308,483	35.1
1810	7,239,881	36.4
1820	9,638,453	33.1
1830	12,866,020	33.5
1840	17,069,453	32.7
1850	23,191,876	35.9
1860	31,443,321	35.6
1870	39,818,449	26.6
1880	50,155,783	26.0
1890	62,947,714	25.5
1900	75,994,575	20.7
1910	91,972,266	21.0
1920	105,710,620	14.9
1930	122,775,046	16.1
1940	131,669,275	7.2
1950	151,325,798	14.5
1960	179,323,175	18.5
1970	203,302,031	13.4
1980	226,542,199	11.4
1990	248,718,301	9.8
2000	281,421,906	13.1

Source: *Historical Statistics of the United States* (1975); *Statistical Abstract by the United States* (2001).
Note: Figures for 1630–1780 include British colonies within limits of present United States only; Native American population included only in 1930 and thereafter.

WORK FORCE

Year	Total Number Workers (1000s)	Farmers as % of Total	Women as % of Total	% Workers in Unions
1810	2,330	84	(NA)	(NA)
1840	5,660	75	(NA)	(NA)
1860	11,110	53	(NA)	(NA)
1870	12,506	53	15	(NA)
1880	17,392	52	15	(NA)
1890	23,318	43	17	(NA)
1900	29,073	40	18	3
1910	38,167	31	21	6
1920	41,614	26	21	12
1930	48,830	22	22	7
1940	53,011	17	24	27
1950	59,643	12	28	25
1960	69,877	8	32	26
1970	82,049	4	37	25
1980	106,940	3	43	23
1990	125,840	3	45	16
2000	140,863	2	47	12

Source: *Historical Statistics of the United States* (1975); *Statistical Abstract of the United States* (2001).

VITAL STATISTICS (IN THOUSANDS)

Year	Births	Deaths	Marriages	Divorces
1800	55	(NA)	(NA)	(NA)
1810	54.3	(NA)	(NA)	(NA)
1820	55.2	(NA)	(NA)	(NA)
1830	51.4	(NA)	(NA)	(NA)
1840	51.8	(NA)	(NA)	(NA)
1850	43.3	(NA)	(NA)	(NA)
1860	44.3	(NA)	(NA)	(NA)
1870	38.3	(NA)	9.6 (1867)	0.3 (1867)
1880	39.8	(NA)	9.1 (1875)	0.3 (1875)
1890	31.5	(NA)	9.0	0.5
1900	32.3	17.2	9.3	0.7
1910	30.1	14.7	10.3	0.9
1920	27.7	13.0	12.0	1.6
1930	21.3	11.3	9.2	1.6
1940	19.4	10.8	12.1	2.0
1950	24.1	9.6	11.1	2.6
1960	23.7	9.5	8.5	2.2
1970	18.4	9.5	10.6	3.5
1980	15.9	8.8	10.6	5.2
1990	16.7	8.6	9.8	4.7
1997	14.6	8.6	8.9	4.3

Source: *Historical Statistics of the United States* (1975); *Statistical Abstract of the United States* (1999).

RACIAL COMPOSITION OF THE POPULATION

(IN THOUSANDS)

Year	White	Black	Indian	Hispanic	Asian/Pacific Islander
1790	3,172	757	(NA)	(NA)	(NA)
1800	4,306	1,002	(NA)	(NA)	(NA)
1820	7,867	1,772	(NA)	(NA)	(NA)
1840	14,196	2,874	(NA)	(NA)	(NA)
1860	26,923	4,442	(NA)	(NA)	(NA)
1880	43,403	6,581	(NA)	(NA)	(NA)
1900	66,809	8,834	(NA)	(NA)	(NA)
1910	81,732	9,828	(NA)	(NA)	(NA)
1920	94,821	10,463	(NA)	(NA)	(NA)
1930	110,287	11,891	(NA)	(NA)	(NA)
1940	118,215	12,866	(NA)	(NA)	(NA)
1950	134,942	15,042	(NA)	(NA)	(NA)
1960	158,832	18,872	(NA)	(NA)	(NA)
1970	178,098	22,581	(NA)	(NA)	(NA)
1980	194,713	26,683	1,420	14,609	3,729
1990	208,727	30,511	2,065	22,372	2,462
2000	211,461	34,658	2,476	35,306	10,642

Source: U.S. Bureau of the Census, U.S. *Census of Population: 1940*, vol. II, part 1, and vol. IV, part 1; *1950*, vol. II, part 1; *1960*, vol. I, part 1; *1970*, vol. I, part B; and *Current Population Reports*, P25-1095 and P25-1104; *Statistical Abstract of the United States* (2001).

IMMIGRATION BY THE ORIGIN

(IN THOUSANDS)

Period	Europe	Americas	Asia
1820–30	106	12	—
1831–40	496	33	—
1841–50	1,597	62	—
1851–60	2,453	75	42
1861–70	2,065	167	65
1871–80	2,272	404	70
1881–90	4,735	427	70
1891–1900	3,555	39	75
1901–10	8,065	362	324
1911–20	4,322	1,144	247
1921–30	2,463	1,517	112
1931–40	348	160	16
1941–50	621	355	32
1951–60	1,326	997	150
1961–70	1,123	1,716	590
1971–80	800	1,983	1,588
1981–90	762	3,616	2,738
1991–2000	1,100	3,800	2,200

Source: Historical Statistics of the United States (1975); *Statistical Abstract of the United States* (1991); Population Estimates Program, Population Division, U.S. Census Bureau, April 2001.

GLOSSARY

1938 Fair Labor Standards Act Act that established the first federal minimum wage (25 ¢ an hour) and set a maximum work week of forty-four hours for all employees engaged in interstate commerce.

Acquired immune deficiency syndrome (AIDS) A complex of deadly pathologies resulting from infection with the human immunodeficiency virus (HIV).

Actual representation The practice whereby elected representatives normally reside in their districts and are directly responsive to local interests.

Affirmative action A set of policies to open opportunities in business and education for members of minority groups and women by allowing race and sex to be factors included in decisions to hire, award contracts, or admit students to higher education programs.

Alamo Franciscan mission at San Antonio, Texas that was the site in 1836 of a siege and massacre of Texans by Mexican troops.

Albany Regency The tightly disciplined state political machine built by Martin Van Buren in New York.

Alien and Sedition Acts Collective name given to four acts passed by Congress in 1798 that curtailed freedom of speech and the liberty of foreign residents in the United States.

Alliance for Progress Program of economic aid to Latin America during the Kennedy administration.

Allies In World War I, Britain, France, Russia, and other belligerent nations fighting against the Central Powers but not including the United States.

Almanac A combination calendar, astrological guide, and sourcebook of medical advice and farming tips.

American Colonization Society Organization, founded in 1817 by antislavery reformers, that called for gradual emancipation and the removal of freed blacks to Africa.

American Federation of Labor (AFL) Union formed in 1886 that organized skilled workers along craft lines and emphasized a few workplace issues rather than a broad social program.

American Indian Movement (AIM) Group of Native-American political activists who used confrontations with the federal government to publicize their case for Indian rights.

American Society for the Promotion of Temperance Largest reform organization of its time dedicated to ending the sale and consumption of alcoholic beverages.

American system A technique of production pioneered in the United States that relied on precision manufacturing with the use of interchangeable parts.

American System The program of government subsidies favored by Henry Clay and his followers to promote American economic growth and protect domestic manufacturers from foreign competition.

Annapolis Convention Conference of state delegates at Annapolis, Maryland, that issued a call in September 1786 for a convention to meet at Philadelphia to consider fundamental changes.

Anti-Federalists Opponents of the Constitution in the debate over its ratification.

Appeal to the Colored Citizens of the World Written by David Walker, a published insistence that "America is more our country, than it is the whites'—we have enriched it with our blood and tears."

Archaic period The period roughly 10,000 to 2,500 years ago marked by the retreat of glaciers.

Articles of Confederation Written document setting up the loose confederation of states that comprised the first national government of the United States.

Athapascan A people that began to settle the forests in the northwestern area of North America around 5000 B.C.E.

Atlantic Charter Statement of common principles and war aims developed by President Franklin Roosevelt and British Prime Minister Winston Churchill at a meeting in August 1941.

Axis powers The opponents of the United States and its allies in World War II.

Aztecs A warrior people who dominated the Valley of Mexico from 1100–1521.

Bacon's Rebellion Violent conflict in Virginia (1675–1676), beginning with settler attacks on Indians but culminating in a rebellion led by Nathaniel Bacon against Virginia's government.

Bank War The political struggle between President Andrew Jackson and the supporters of the Second Bank of the United States.

Battle of New Orleans Decisive American War of 1812 victory over British troops in January 1815 that ended any British hopes of gaining control of the lower Mississippi River Valley.

Battle of the Bulge German offensive in December, 1944 that penetrated deep into Belgium (creating a "bulge"). Allied forces, while outnumbered, attacked from the north and south. By January, 1945, the German forces were destroyed or routed, but not without some 77,000 Allied casualities.

Bay of Pigs Site in Cuba of an unsuccessful landing by fourteen hundred anti-Castro Cuban refugees in April 1961.

Beaver Wars Series of bloody conflicts, occurring between 1640s and 1680s, during which the Iroquois fought the French for control of the fur trade in the east and the Great Lakes region.

Benjamin Franklin's Plan of Union Plan put forward in 1754 calling for an intercolonial union to manage defense and Indian affairs. The plan was rejected by participants at the Albany Congress.

Beringia A subcontinent bridging Asia and North America, named after the Bering Straits.

Berlin blockade Three-hundred-day Soviet blockade of land access to United States, British, and French occupation zones in Berlin, 1948–1949.

Bill for Establishing Religious Freedom A bill authored by Thomas Jefferson establishing religious freedom in Virginia.

Bill of Rights A written summary of inalienable rights and liberties.

Black codes Laws passed by states and municipalities denying many rights of citizenship to free black people before the Civil War.

Black Hawk 1832 war in which federal troops and Illinois militia units defeated the Sauk and Fox Indians led by Black Hawk.

Black Panther Political and social movement among black Americans, founded in Oakland, California, in 1966 that emphasized black economic and political power.

Black Power Philosophy emerging after 1965 that real economic and political gains for African Americans could come only through self-help, self-determination, and organizing for direct political influence.

Bleeding Kansas Violence between pro– and antislavery forces in Kansas Territory after the passage of the Kansas-Nebraska Act in 1854.

Blitzkrieg German war tactic in World War II ("lightning war") involving the concentration of air and armored firepower to punch and exploit holes in opposing defensive lines.

Bolsheviks Member of the Communist movement in Russia that established the Soviet government after the 1917 Russian Revolution.

Bonus Army Unemployed veterans of World War I gathering in Washington in 1932 demanding payment of service bonuses not due until 1945.

Bosnia A nation in southeast Europe that split off from Yugoslavia and became the site of bitter civil and religious war, requiring NATO and U.S. intervention in the 1990s.

Boston Massacre After months of increasing friction between townspeople and the British troops stationed in the city, on March 5, 1770, British troops fired on American civilians in Boston.

Boston Tea Party Incident that occurred on December 16, 1773, in which Bostonians, disguised as Indians, destroyed £9,000 worth of tea belonging to the British East India Company in order to prevent payment of the duty on it.

Brown v. Board of Education Supreme Court decision in 1954 that declared that "separate but equal" schools for children of different races violated the Constitution.

Cahokia One of the largest urban centers created by Mississippian peoples, containing 30,000 residents in 1250.

Californios Californians of Spanish descent.

Calvinist theology of predestination Belief that God has predestined certain individuals to be saved and others to be damned.

Caminetti Act 1893 act giving the state the power to regulate the mines.

Camp David Accords Agreement signed by Israel in Egypt in 1978 that set the formal terms for peace in the Middle East.

Carpetbaggers Northern transplants to the South, many of whom were Union soldiers who stayed in the South after the war.

Central Intelligence Agency (CIA) Agency established in 1947 that coordinates the gathering and evaluation of military and economic information on other nations.

Central Powers Germany and its World War I allies in Austria, Italy, Turkey, and Bulgaria.

Chinese Exclusion Act Act which suspended Chinese immigration, limited the civil rights of resident Chinese, and forbade their naturalization.

Civil Rights Act 1866 Act that gave full citizenship to African Americans.

Civil Rights Act of 1964 Federal legislation that outlawed discrimination in public accommodations and employment on the basis of race, skin color, sex, religion, or national origin.

Clans Groups of allied families.

Clayton Antitrust Act of 1914 Replaced the old Sherman Act of 1890 as the nation's basic antitrust law. It exempted unions from being construed as illegal combinations in restraint of trade, and it forbade federal courts from issuing injunctions against strikers.

Clovis tradition A powerful new and sophisticated style of tool making, unlike anything found in the Old World.

Coercive Acts Legislation passed by Parliament in 1774; included the Boston Port Act, the Massachusetts Government Act, the Administration of Justice Act, and the Quartering Act of 1774.

Cold war The political and economic confrontation between the Soviet Union and the United States that dominated world affairs from 1946 to 1989.

Committee of Safety Any of the extralegal committees that directed the revolutionary movement and carried on the functions of government at the local level in the period between the breakdown of royal authority and the establishment of regular governments.

Committee on Public Information (CPI) Government agency during World War I that sought to shape public opinion in support of the war effort through newspapers, pamphlets, speeches, films, and other media.

Committees of Correspondence Committees formed in Massachusetts and other colonies in the pre-Revolutionary period to keep Americans informed about British measures that would affect the colonies.

Compromise of 1850 The four-step compromise which admitted California as a free state, allowed the residents of the New Mexico and Utah territories to decide the slavery issue for themselves, ended the slave trade in the District of Columbia, and passed a new fugitive slave law to enforce the constitutional provision stating that a slave escaping into a free state shall be delivered back to the owner.

Compromise of 1877 The Congressional settling of the 1876 election which installed Republican Rutherford B. Hayes in the White House and gave Democrats control of all state governments in the South.

Confederate States of America Nation proclaimed in Montgomery, Alabama, in February 1861, after the seven states of the Lower South seceded from the United States.

Congregationalists Members of Puritan churches governed by congregations.

Congress of Industrial Organizations An alliance of industrial unions that spurred the 1930s organizational drive among the mass-production industries.

Congress of Racial Equality (CORE) Civil rights group formed in 1942 and committed to nonviolent civil disobedience.

Congressional Reconstruction Name given to the period 1867–1870 when the Republican-dominated Congress controlled Reconstruction-era policy.

Conspicuous consumption Highly visible displays of wealth and consumption.

Constitutional Convention Convention that met in Philadelphia in 1787 and drafted the Constitution of the United States.

Constitutional Union Party National party formed in 1860, mainly by former Whigs, that emphasized allegiance to the Union and strict enforcement of all national legislation.

Continental Army The regular or professional army authorized by the Second Continental Congress and commanded by General George Washington during the Revolutionary War.

Continental Congress Convention of delegates from the colonies that first met to organize resistance to the Intolerable Acts.

Contract with America Platform proposing a sweeping reduction in the role and activities of the federal government on which many Republican candidates ran for Congress in 1994.

Contras Nicaraguan exiles armed and organized by the CIA to fight the Sandinista government of Nicaragua.

Copperheads A term Republicans applied to Northern war dissenters and those suspected of aiding the Confederate cause during the Civil War.

Council of Economic Advisors Board of three professional economists established in 1946 to advise the president on economic policy.

Counterculture Various alternatives to mainstream values and behaviors that became popular in the 1960s, including experimentation with psychedelic drugs, communal living, a return to the land, Asian religions, and experimental art.

Coureurs de bois French for "woods runner," an independent fur trader in New France.

Covenant Chain An alliance between the Iroquois Confederacy and the colony of New York which sought to establish Iroquois dominance over all other tribes and thus put New York in an economically and politically dominant position among the other colonies.

Coxey's Army A protest march of unemployed workers, led by Populist businessman Jacob Coxey, demanding inflation and a public works program during the depression of the 1890s.

Cuban missile crisis Crisis between the Soviet Union and the United States over the placement of Soviet nuclear missiles in Cuba.

Culpeper's Rebellion The overthrow of the established government in the Albermarle region of North Carolina by backcountry men in 1677.

Dawes Severalty Act An 1887 law terminating tribal ownership of land and allotting some parcels of land to individual Indians with the remainder opened for white settlement.

D-Day June 6, 1944, the day of the first paratroop drops and amphibious landings on the coast of Normandy, France, in the first stage of Operation Overlord during World War II.

Declaration of Independence The document by which the Second Continental Congress announced and justified its decision to renounce the colonies' allegiance to the British government.

Declaration of Sentiments The resolutions passed at the Seneca Falls Convention in 1848 calling for full female equality, including the right to vote.

Declaratory Act Law passed in 1776 to accompany repeal of the Stamp Act that stated that Parliament had the authority to legislate for the colonies "in all cases whatsoever."

Defense of Marriage Act Act which specified that gay couples would be ineligible for spousal benefits provided by federal law.

Democrats Political party formed in the 1820s under the leadership of Andrew Jackson; favored states' rights and a limited role for the federal government.

Denmark Vesey's conspiracy The most carefully devised slave revolt in which rebels planned to seize control of Charleston in 1822 and escape to freedom in Haiti, a free black republic, but they were betrayed by other slaves, and seventy-five conspirators were executed.

Deregulation Reduction or removal of government regulations and encouragement of direct competition in many important industries and economic sectors.

Détente (French for "easing of tension.") Used to describe the new U.S. relations with China and the Soviet Union in 1972.

Dingley Tariff of 1897 Act which raised import duties to an all-time high.

Dixiecrat States' Rights Democrats.

Dred Scott decision Supreme Court ruling, in a lawsuit brought by Dred Scott, a slave demanding his freedom based on his residence in a free state, that slaves could not be U.S. citizens and that Congress had no jurisdiction over slavery in the territories.

Eastern Front The area of military operations in World War II located east of Germany in eastern Europe and the Soviet Union.

Economic Recovery Tax Act of 1981 A major revision of the federal income tax system.

Edmunds Act 1882 act that effectively disfranchised those who believed in or practiced polygamy and threatened them with fines and imprisonment.

Edmunds-Tucker Act 1887 act which destroyed the temporal power of the Mormon Church by confiscating all assets over $50,000 and establishing a federal commission to oversee all elections in the Utah territory.

Emancipation Proclamation Decree announced by President Abraham Lincoln in September 1862 and formally issued on January 1, 1863, freeing slaves in all Confederate states still in rebellion.

Embargo Act Act passed by Congress in 1807 prohibiting American ships from leaving for any foreign port.

Emergency Banking Act 1933 act which gave the president broad discretionary powers over all banking transactions and foreign exchange.

Empresarios Agents who received a land grant from the Spanish or Mexican government in return for organizing settlements.

Encomienda In the Spanish colonies, the grant to a Spanish settler of a certain number of Indian subjects, who would pay him tribute in goods and labor.

Engagés Catholic immigrants to New France.

Enlightenment Intellectual movement stressing the importance of reason and the existence of discoverable natural laws.

Enumerated goods Items produced in the colonies and enumerated in acts of Parliament that could be legally shipped from the colony of origin only to specified locations.

Environmental Protection Agency Federal agency created in 1970 to oversee environmental monitoring and cleanup programs.

Equal Pay Act of 1963 Act that made it illegal for employers to pay men and women different wages for the same job.

Era of Good Feelings The period from 1817 to 1823 in which the disappearance of the Federalists enabled the Republicans to govern in a spirit of seemingly nonpartisan harmony.

Espionage Act Law whose vague prohibition against obstructing the nation's war effort was used to crush dissent and criticism during World War I.

Farmers' Alliance A broad mass movement in the rural South and West during the late nineteenth century, encompassing several organizations and demanding economic and political reforms.

Federal Highway Act of 1956 Measure that provided federal funding to build a nationwide system of interstate and defense highways.

Federal Reserve Act The 1913 law that revised banking and currency by extending limited government regulation through the creation of the Federal Reserve System.

Federal Trade Commission (FTC) Government agency established in 1914 to provide regulatory oversight of business activity.

Federalism The sharing of powers between the national government and the states.

Federalists Supporters of the Constitution who favored its ratification.

Female Moral Reform Society Antiprostitution group founded by evangelical women in New York in 1834.

Feudalism A medieval European social system in which land was divided into hundreds of small holdings.

Field Order 15 Order by General William T. Sherman in January 1865 to set aside abandoned land along the Southern Atlantic coast for forty-acre grants to freedmen; rescinded by President Andrew Johnson later that year.

Fifteenth Amendment Passed by Congress in 1869, guaranteed the right of American men to vote, regardless of race.

Fireside chat Speeches broadcast nationally over the radio in which President Franklin D. Roosevelt explained complex issues and programs in plain language, as though his listeners were gathered around the fireside with him.

First Continental Congress Meeting of delegates from most of the colonies held in 1774 in response to the Coercive Acts.

The Congress endorsed the Suffolk Resolves, adopted the Declaration of Rights and Grievances, and agreed to establish the Continental Association.

Food and Drug Act Act that established the Food and Drug Administration (FDA), which tested and approved drugs before they went on the market.

Forest Management Act 1897 act which, along with the National Reclamation Act, set the federal government on the path of large-scale regulatory activities.

Frame of Government William Penn's constitution for Pennsylvania which included a provision allowing for religious freedom.

Free silver Philosophy that the government should expand the money supply by purchasing and coining all the silver offered to it.

Free speech movement Student movement at the University of California, Berkeley, formed in 1964 to protest limitations on political activities on campus.

Freedmen's Bureau Agency established by Congress in March 1865 to provide social, educational, and economic services, advice, and protection to former slaves and destitute whites; lasted seven years.

Freedom Summer Voter registration effort in rural Mississippi organized by black and white civil rights workers in 1964.

French and Indian War The last of the Anglo-French colonial wars (1754–1763) and the first in which fighting began in North America. The war ended with France's defeat.

Fugitive Slave Law Part of the Compromise of 1850 that required the authorities in the North to assist Southern slave catchers and return runaway slaves to their owners.

Gabriel's Rebellion Slave revolt that failed when Gabriel Prosser, a slave preacher and blacksmith, organized a thousand slaves for an attack on Richmond, Virginia, in 1800.

Gang System The organization and supervision of slave field hands into working teams on Southern plantations.

General Land Revision Act of 1891 Act which gave the president the power to establish forest reserves to protect watersheds against the threats posed by lumbering, overgrazing, and forest fires.

Geneva Accord Accord that called for reunification and national elections in Vietnam in 1956.

GI Bill Legislation in June 1944 that eased the return of veterans into American society by providing educational and employment benefits.

Gilded Age Term applied to late nineteenth-century America that refers to the shallow display and worship of wealth characteristic of that period.

Glasnost Russian for "openness" applied to Mikhail Gorbachev's encouragement of new ideas and easing of political repression in the Soviet Union.

Gospel of wealth Thesis that hard work and perseverance lead to wealth, implying that poverty is a character flaw.

Gramm-Rudman Law that mandated automatic spending cuts if the government failed to meet fixed deficit reduction goals leading to a balanced budget by 1991.

Grandfather clauses Rules that required potential voters to demonstrate that their grandfathers had been eligible to vote; used in some Southern states after 1890 to limit the black electorate.

Grange The National Grange of the Patrons of Husbandry, a national organization of farm owners formed after the Civil War.

Granger laws State laws enacted in the Midwest in the 1870s that regulated rates charged by railroads, grain elevator operators, and other middlemen.

Great Awakening North American religious revival in the middle of the eighteenth century.

Great Awakening Tremendous religious revival in colonial America striking first in the Middle Colonies and New England in the 1740s and then spreading to the Southern colonies.

Great Compromise Plan proposed at the 1787 Constitutional Convention for creating a national bicameral legislature in which all states would be equally represented in the Senate and proportionally represented in the House.

Great Depression The nation's worst economic crisis, extending through the 1930s, producing unprecedented bank failures, unemployment, and industrial and agricultural collapse.

Great Migration Puritan emigration to North America between 1629 and 1643.

Great Migration The mass movement of African Americans from the rural South to the urban North, spurred especially by new job opportunities during World War I and the 1920s.

Great Society Theme of Lyndon Johnson's administration, focusing on poverty, education, and civil rights.

Great Uprising Unsuccessful railroad strike of 1877 to protest wage cuts and the use of federal troops against strikers; the first nationwide work stoppage in American history.

Half-Way Covenant Plan adopted in 1662 by New England clergy to deal with the problem of declining church membership, allowing children of baptized parents to be baptized whether or not their parents had experienced conversion.

Harlem Renaissance A new African American cultural awareness that flourished in literature, art, and music in the 1920s.

Hepburn Act Act that strengthened the Interstate Commerce Commission (ICC) by authorizing it to set maximum railroad rates and inspect financial records.

Hispanic-American Alliance Organization formed to protect and fight for the rights of Spanish Americans.

Holocaust The systematic murder of millions of European Jews and others deemed undesirable by Nazi Germany.

Homestead Act Law passed by Congress in May 1862 providing homesteads with 160 acres of free land in exchange for improving the land within five years of the grant.

Homestead Act of 1862 1862 act which granted a quarter section (160 acres) of the public domain free to any settler who lived on the land for at least five years and improved it.

Horizontal combination The merger of competitors in the same industry.

House of Burgesses The legislature of colonial Virginia. First organized in 1619, it was the first institution of representative government in the English colonies.

House Un-American Activities Committee (HUAC) Originally intended to ferret out pro-Fascists, it later investigated "un-American propaganda" that attacked constitutional government.

Immigration Act 1921 act setting a maximum of 357,000 new immigrants each year.

Imperialism The policy and practice of exploiting nations and peoples for the benefit of an imperial power either directly through military occupation and colonial rule or indirectly through economic domination of resources and markets.

Indentured Servants Individuals who contracted to serve a master for a period of four to seven years in return for payment of the servant's passage to America.

Indian Removal Act President Andrew Jackson's measure that allowed state officials to override federal protection of Native Americans.

Industrial Revolution Revolution in the means and organization of production.

Initiative Procedure by which citizens can introduce a subject for legislation, usually through a petition signed by a specific number of voters.

Intercourse Act Basic law passed by Congress in 1790 which stated that the United States would regulate trade and interaction with Indian tribes.

International Bank for Reconstruction and Development (World Bank) Designed to revive postwar international trade, it drew on the resources of member nations to make economic development loans to governments for such projects as new dams or agricultural modernization.

International Monetary Fund (IMF) International organization established in 1945 to assist nations in maintaining stable currencies.

Internet The system of interconnected computers and servers that allows the exchange of email, posting of Web sites, and other means of instant communication.

Interstate Commerce Commission (ICC) The 1887 law that expanded federal power over business by prohibiting pooling and discriminatory rates by railroads and establishing the first federal regulatory agency, the Interstate Commerce Commission.

Intolerable Acts American term for the Coercive Acts and the Quebec Act.

Irreconcilables Group of U.S. senators adamantly opposed to ratification of the Treaty of Versailles after World War I.

Island hopping The Pacific campaigns of 1944 that were the American naval versions of the Blitzkrieg.

Issei The first generation of Japanese to come to America starting in the late1800s.

Jay's Treaty Treaty with Britain negotiated in 1794 in which the United States made major concessions to avert a war over the British seizure of American ships.

Jim Crow laws Segregation laws that became widespread in the South during the 1890s.

John Brown's raid New England abolitionist John Brown's ill-fated attempt to free Virginia's slaves with a raid on the federal arsenal at Harper's Ferry, Virginia, in 1859.

Judicial review A power implied in the Constitution that gives federal courts the right to review and determine the constitutionality of acts passed by Congress and state legislatures.

Judiciary Act of 1789 Act of Congress that implemented the judiciary clause of the Constitution by establishing the Supreme Court and a system of lower federal courts.

Kachinas Impersonations of the ancestral spirits by Southwest Indians.

Kansas-Nebraska Act Law passed in 1854 creating the Kansas and Nebraska Territories but leaving the question of slavery open to residents, thereby repealing the Missouri Compromise.

King George's War The third Anglo-French war in North America (1744–1748), part of the European conflict known as the War of the Austrian Succession.

King Philip's War Conflict in New England (1675–1676) between Wampanoags, Narragansetts, and other Indian peoples against English settlers; sparked by English encroachments on native lands.

King William's War The first Anglo-French conflict in North America (1689–1697), the American phase of Europe's War of the League of Augsburg.

King William's War The first of a series of colonial struggles between England and France; these conflicts occurred principally on the frontiers of northern New England and New York between 1689 and 1697.

Knights of Labor Labor union founded in 1869 that included skilled and unskilled workers irrespective of race or gender.

Know-Nothings Name given to the antiimmigrant party formed from the wreckage of the Whig Party and some disaffected Northern Democrats in 1854.

Korean War Pacific war started on June 25, 1950, when North Korea, helped by Soviet equipment and Chinese training, attacked South Korea.

Kosovo Province of Yugoslavia where the United States and NATO intervened militarily in 1999 to protect ethnic Albanians from expulsion.

Ku Klux Klan Perhaps the most prominent of the vigilante groups that terrorized black people in the South during Reconstruction era, founded by the Confederate veterans in 1866.

Land Ordinance of 1785 Act passed by Congress under the Articles of Confederation that created the grid system of surveys by which all subsequent public land was made available for sale.

Landrum-Griffin Act 1959 act that widened government control over union affairs and further restricted union use of picketing and secondary boycotts during strikes.

League of Nations International organization created by the Versailles Treaty after World War I to ensure world stability.

League of Women Voters League formed in 1920 advocating for women's rights, among them the right for women to serve on juries and equal pay laws.

Lecompton constitution Proslavery draft written in 1857 by Kansas territorial delegates elected under questionable circumstances; it was rejected by two governors, supported by President Buchanan, and decisively defeated by Congress.

Legal Tender Act Act creating a national currency in February 1862.

Lend-Lease Act An arrangement for the transfer of war supplies, including food, machinery, and services to nations whose defense was considered vital to the defense of the United States in Word War II.

Liberal Republicans Disaffected Republicans that emphasized the doctrines of classical economics.

Liberty Bonds Interest-bearing certificates sold by the U.S. government to finance the American World War I effort.

Liberty Party The first antislavery political party, formed in 1840.

Limited Nuclear Test-Ban Treaty Treaty, signed by the United States, Britain, and the Soviet Union, outlawing nuclear testing in the atmosphere, in outer space, and under water.

Lincoln-Douglas debates Series of debates in the 1858 Illinois senatorial campaign during which Douglas and Lincoln staked out their differing opinions on the issue of slavery.

Loyalists British colonists who opposed independence from Britain.

Lynching Execution, usually by a mob, without trial.

Manifest destiny Doctrine, first expressed in 1845, that the expansion of white Americans across the continent was inevitable and ordained by God.

Manumissions Grant of freedom to slaves by individual masters.

Marbury v. Madison Supreme Court decision of 1803 that created the precedent of judicial review by ruling as unconstitutional part of the Judiciary Act of 1789.

Market revolution The outcome of three interrelated developments: rapid improvements in transportation, commercialization, and industrialization.

Marshall Plan Secretary of State George C. Marshall's European Recovery Plan of June 5, 1947, committing the United States to help in the rebuilding of post–World War II Europe.

Massachusetts Bay Company A group of wealthy Puritans who were granted a royal charter in 1629 to settle in Massachusetts Bay.

Mayflower Compact The first document of self-government in North America.

McCarthyism Anti-Communist attitudes and actions associated with Senator Joe McCarthy in the early 1950s, including smear tactics and innuendo.

Medicare Basic medical insurance for the elderly, financed through the federal government; program created in 1965.

Mercantilism Economic system whereby the government intervenes in the economy for the purpose of increasing national wealth.

Mesoamerica The region stretching from central Mexico to Central America.

Mexican-American War War fought between Mexico and the United States between 1846 and 1848 over control of territory in southwest North America.

Middle Passage The voyage between West Africa and the New World slave colonies.

Militarism The tendency to see military might as the most important and best tool for the expansion of a nation's power and prestige.

Minutemen Special companies of militia formed in Massachusetts and elsewhere beginning in late 1744.

Missouri Compromise Sectional compromise in Congress in 1820 that admitted Missouri to the Union as a slave state and Maine as a free state and prohibited slavery in the northern Louisiana Purchase territory.

Monroe Doctrine Declaration by President James Monroe in 1823 that the Western Hemisphere was to be closed off to further European colonization and that the United States would not interfere in the internal affairs of European nations.

Monroe Doctrine In December 1823, Monroe declared to Congress that Americans "are henceforth not to be considered as subjects for future colonization by any European power."

Morrill Act of 1862 Act by which "land-grant" colleges acquired space for campuses in return for promising to institute agricultural programs.

Morrill Land Grant Act Law passed by Congress in July 1862 awarding proceeds from the sale of public lands to the states for the establishment of agricultural and mechanical colleges.

Morrill Tariff Act Act that raised tariffs to more than double their prewar rate.

Muckraking Journalism exposing economic, social, and political evils, so named by Theodore Roosevelt for its "raking the muck" of American society.

Multiculturalism Movement that emphasized the unique attributes and achievements of formerly marginal groups and recent immigrants.

My Lai Massacre Killing of twenty-two Vietnamese civilians by U.S. forces during a 1968 search-and-destroy mission.

Nat Turner's Revolt Uprising of slaves in Southampton County, Virginia, in the summer of 1831 led by Nat Turner that resulted in the death of fifty-five white people.

Nation of Islam (NOI) Religious movement among black Americans that emphasizes self-sufficiency, self-help, and separation from white society.

National Aeronautics and Space Administration (NASA) Federal agency created in 1958 to manage American space flights and exploration.

National American Woman Suffrage Association (NAWSA) The organization, formed in 1890, that coordinated the ultimately successful campaign to achieve women's right to vote.

National Association for the Advancement of Colored People Interracial organization co-founded by W. E. B. DuBois in 1910 dedicated to restoring African-American political and social rights.

National Bank Act Act prohibiting state banks from issuing their own notes and forcing them to apply for federal charters.

National Defense Education Act (NDEA) 1958 act that allocated $280 million in grants for state universities to upgrade their science facilities, created $300 million in low-interest loans for college students, and provided fellowship support for graduate students planning to go into college and university teaching.

National Industrial Recovery Act 1933 act which was meant to be a systematic plan for economic recovery.

National Labor Relations Act Act establishing Federal guarantee of right to organize trade unions and collective bargaining.

National Reclamation Act 1902 act which added 1 million acres of irrigated land to the United States.

National Security Council (NSC) The formal policymaking body for national defense and foreign relations, created in 1947 and consisting of the president, the secretary of defense, the secretary of state, and others appointed by the president.

National Security Council Paper 68 (NSC-68) Policy statement that committed the United States to a military approach to the Cold War.

Nationalists Group of leaders in the 1780s who spearheaded the drive to replace the Articles of Confederation with a stronger central government.

Nativism Favoring the interests and culture of native-born inhabitants over those of immigrants.

Neutrality Act of 1939 Permitted the sale of arms to Britain, France, and China.

New Deal coalition Coalition that included traditional-minded white Southern Democrats, big-city political machines, industrial workers of all races, trade unionists, and many Depression-hit farmers.

New deal The economic and political policies of the Roosevelt administration in the 1930s.

New Freedom Woodrow Wilson's 1912 program for limited government intervention in the economy to restore competition by curtailing the restrictive influences of trusts and protective tariffs, thereby providing opportunities for individual achievement.

New Frontier John F. Kennedy's domestic and foreign policy initiatives, designed to reinvigorate sense of national purpose and energy.

New Jersey Plan Proposal of the New Jersey delegation for a strengthened national government in which all states would have an equal representation in a unicameral legislature.

New Lights People who experienced conversion during the revivals of the Great Awakening.

Niagara movement African American group organized in 1905 to promote racial integration, civil and political rights, and equal access to economic opportunity.

Nisei U.S. citizens born of immigrant Japanese parents.

Nonimportation movement A tactical means of putting economic pressure on Britain by refusing to buy its exports to the colonies.

North American Free Trade Agreement (NAFTA) Agreement reached in 1993 by Canada, Mexico, and the United States to substantially reduce barriers to trade.

North Atlantic Treaty Organization (NATO) Organization of ten European countries, Canada, and the United States who together formed a mutual defense pact in April 1949.

Northwest Ordinance of 1787 Legislation that prohibited slavery in the Northwest Territories and provided the model for the incorporation of future territories into the union as co-equal states.

Nullification A constitutional doctrine holding that a state has a legal right to declare a national law null and void within its borders.

Nullification Crisis Sectional crisis in the early 1830s in which a states' rights party in South Carolina attempted to nullify federal law.

Office of Economic Opportunity (OEO) Federal agency that coordinated many programs of the war on poverty between 1964 and 1975.

Old Lights Religious faction that condemned emotional enthusiasm as part of the heresy of believing in a personal and direct relationship with God outside the order of the church.

Omaha Act of 1882 Act which allowed the establishment of individual title to tribal lands.

Open Door American policy of seeking equal trade and investment opportunities in foreign nations or regions.

Open shop Factory of business employing workers whether or not they are union members; in practice, such a business usually refuses to hire union members and follows antiunion policies.

Operation Desert Storm U.S. military campaign to force Iraqi forces out of Kuwait.

Operation Overlord United States and British invasion of France in June 1944 during World War II.

Operation Torch The Allied invasion fo Axis-held North Africa in 1942.

Oregon Trail Overland trail of more than two thousand miles that carried American settlers from the Midwest to new settlements in Oregon, California, and Utah.

Organization of Petroleum Exporting Countries (OPEC) Cartel of oil-producing nations in Asia, Africa, and Latin America that gained substantial power over the world economy in the mid- to late 1970s by controlling the production and price of oil.

Panic of 1857 Banking crisis that caused a credit crunch in the North; it was less severe in the South, where high cotton prices spurred a quick recovery.

Pan-Indian military resistance movement Movement calling for the political and cultural unification of Indian tribes in the late eighteenth and early nineteenth centuries.

Patriots British colonists who favored independence from Britain.

Pendleton Civil Service Reform Act A law of 1883 that reformed the spoils system by prohibiting government workers from making political contributions and creating the Civil Service Commission to oversee their appointment on the basis of merit rather than politics.

Peninsular Campaign Union offensive led by McClellan with the objective of capturing Richmond.

Pentagon Papers Classified Defense Department documents on the history of the United States's involvement in Vietnam, prepared in 1968 and leaked to the press in 1971.

Pequot War Conflict between English settlers and Pequot Indians over control of land and trade in eastern Connecticut.

Perestroika Russian for "restructuring," applied to Mikhail Gorbachev's efforts to make the Soviet economic and political systems more modern, flexible, and innovative.

Persian Gulf War War initiated by President Bush in reponse to Iraq's invasion of Kuwait.

Pilgrims Settlers of Plymouth Colony, who viewed themselves as spiritual wanderers.

Pleistocene Overkill Intensified hunting efforts brought on in response to lowered reproduction and survival rates of large animals.

Plessy v. Ferguson Supreme Court decision holding that Louisiana's railroad segregation law did not violate the Constitution as long as the railroads or the state provided equal accommodations.

Poll taxes Taxes imposed on voters as a requirement for voting.

Popular sovereignty A solution to the slavery crisis suggested by Michigan senator Lewis Cass by which territorial residents, not Congress, would decide slavery's fate.

Populist movement A major third party of the 1890s formed on the basis of the Southern Farmer's Alliance and other reform organizations.

Predestination The belief that God decided at the moment of Creation which humans would achieve salvation.

Preparedness Military buildup in preparation for possible U.S. participation in World War I.

Progressive era An era in the United States (roughly between 1900 and 1917) in which important movements challenged traditional relationships and attitudes.

Prohibition A ban on the production, sale, and consumption of liquor, achieved temporarily through state laws and the Eighteenth Amendment.

Proposition 187 California legislation adopted by popular vote in California in 1994, which cuts off state-funded health and education benefits to undocumented or illegal immigrants.

Proprietary colony A colony created when the English monarch granted a huge tract of land to an individual or group of individuals, who became "lords proprietor."

Protective association Organizations formed by mine owners in response to the formation of labor unions.

Protestant Reformation Martin Luther's challenge to the Catholic Church, initiated in 1517, calling for a return to what he understood to be the purer practices and beliefs of the early church.

Protestants All European supporters of religious reform under Charles V's Holy Roman Empire.

Puritans Individuals who believed that Queen Elizabeth's reforms of the Church of England had not gone far enough in improving the church. Puritans led the settlement of Massachusetts Bay Colony.

Putting-out system Production of goods in private homes under the supervision of a merchant who "put out" the raw materials, paid a certain sum per finished piece, and sold the completed item to a distant market.

Quakers Members of the Society of Friends, a radical religious group that arose in the mid-seventeenth century. Quakers rejected formal theology, focusing instead on the Holy Spirit that dwelt within them.

Quartering Act Acts of Parliament requiring colonial legislatures to provide supplies and quarters for the troops starioned in America.

Quasi-War Undeclared naval war of 1797 to 1800 between the United States and France.

Quebec Act Law passed by Parliament in 1774 that provided an appointed government for Canada, enlarged the boundaries of Quebec, and confirmed the privileges of the Catholic Church.

Queen Anne's War American phase (1702–1713) of Europe's War of the Spanish Succession.

Radical Republicans A shifting group of Republican congressmen, usually a substantial minority, who favored the abolition of slavery from the beginning of the Civil War and later advocated harsh treatment of the defeated South.

Rancherias Dispersed settlements of Indian farmers in the Southwest.

Recall The process of removing an official from office by popular vote, usually after using petitions to call for such a vote.

Reconquista The long struggle (ending in 1492) during which Spanish Christians reconquered the Iberian peninsula from Muslim occupiers.

Reconstruction Act 1877 act that divided the South into five military districts subject to martial law.

Red Scare Post–World War I public hysteria over Bolshevik influence in the United States directed against labor activism, radical dissenters, and some ethnic groups.

Redemptioner Similar to an indentured servant, except that a redemptioner signed a labor contract in America rather than in Europe.

Referendum Submission of a law, proposed or already in effect, to a direct popular vote for approval or rejection.

Renaissance The intellectual and artistic flowering in Europe during the fourteenth, fifteenth, and sixteenth centuries sparked by a revival of interest in classical antiquity.

Republican Party Party that emerged in the 1850s in the aftermath of the bitter controversy over the Kansas-Nebraska Act, consisting of former Whigs, some Northern Democrats, and many Know-Nothings.

Republicanism A complex, changing body of ideas, values, and assumptions, closely related to country ideology, that influenced American political behavior during the eighteenth and nineteenth centuries.

Republicans Party headed by Thomas Jefferson that formed in opposition to the financial and diplomatic policies of the Federalist party; favored limiting the powers of the national government and placing the interests of farmers over those of financial and commercial groups.

Roe v. Wade U.S. Supreme Court decision (1973) that disallowed state laws prohibiting abortion during the first three months (trimester) of pregnancy and establishing guidelines for abortion in the second and third trimesters.

Roosevelt Corollary President Theodore Roosevelt's policy asserting U.S. authority to intervene in the affairs of Latin American nations; an expansion of the Monroe Doctrine.

Royal Proclamation of 1763 Royal proclamation setting the boundary known as the Proclamation Line.

Rush-Bagot Treaty of 1817 Treaty between the United States and Britain that effectively demilitarized the Great Lakes by sharply limiting the number of ships each power could station on them.

Sabbatarianism Reform movement that aimed to prevent business on Sundays.

Sand Creek Massacre The near annihilation in 1864 of Black Kettle's Cheyenne band by Colorado troops under Colonel John Chivington's orders to "kill and scalp all, big and little."

Santa Fé Trail The 900-mile trail opened by American merchants for trading purposes following Mexico's liberalization of the formerly restrictive trading policies of Spain.

Scalawags Southern whites, mainly small landowning farmers and well-off merchants and planters, who supported the Southern Republican party during Reconstruction.

Second Bank of the United States A national bank chartered by Congress in 1816 with extensive regulatory powers over currency and credit.

Second Great Awakening Religious revival among black and white Southerners in the 1790s.

Sedition Act Broad law restricting criticism of America's involvement in World War I or its government, flag, military, taxes, or officials.

Segregation A system of racial control that separated the races, initially by custom but increasingly by law during and after Reconstruction.

Selective Service Act The law establishing the military draft for World War I.

Self-determination The right of a people or a nation to decide on its own political allegiance or form of government without external influence.

Seneca Falls convention The first convention for women's equality in legal rights, held in upstate New York in 1848.

Separatists Members of an offshoot branch of Puritanism. Separatists believed that the Church of England was too corrupt to be reformed and hence were convinced they must "separate" from it to save their souls.

Seven Years' War War fought in Europe, North America, and India between 1756 and 1763, pitting France and its allies against Great Britain and its allies.

Shakers The followers of Mother Ann Lee, who preached a religion of strict celibacy and communal living.

Sharecropping Labor system that evolved during and after Reconstruction whereby landowners furnished laborers with a house, farm animals, and tools and advanced credit in exchange for a share of the laborers' crop.

Shays's Rebellion An armed movement of debt-ridden farmers in western Massachusetts in the winter of 1786–1787. The rebellion created a crisis atmosphere.

Sheppard-Towner Act The first federal social welfare law, passed in 1921, providing federal funds for infant and maternity care.

Sherman Antitrust Act The first federal antitrust measure, passed in 1890; sought to promote economic competition by prohibiting business combinations in restraint of trade or commerce.

Sherman Silver Purchase Act 1890 act which directed the Treasury to increase the amount of currency coined from silver mined in the West and also permitted the U.S. government to print paper currency backed by the silver.

Silicon Valley The region of California including San Jose and San Francisco that holds the nation's greatest concentration of electronics firms.

Sixteenth Amendment of 1913 Authorized a federal income tax.

Slaughterhouse cases Group of cases resulting in one sweeping decision by the U.S. Supreme Court in 1873 that contradicted the intent of the Fourteenth Amendment by decreeing that most citizenship rights remained under state, not federal, control.

Slave Codes A series of laws passed mainly in the Southern colonies in the late seventeenth and early eighteenth centuries to defend the status of slaves and codify the denial of basic civil rights to them.

Social Darwinism The application of Charles Darwin's theory of biological evolution to society, holding that the fittest and wealthiest survive, the weak and the poor perish, and government action is unable to alter this "natural" process.

Social Security Act of 1935 Act establishing federal old-age pensions and unemployment insurance.

Solid South The one-party (Democratic) political system that dominated the South from the 1890s to the 1950s.

Sons of Liberty Secret organizations in the colonies formed to oppose the Stamp Act.

Southern Christian Leadership Conference (SCLC) Black civil rights organization founded in 1957 by Martin Luther King Jr. and other clergy.

Southern Farmers' Alliance The largest of several organizations that formed in the post-Reconstruction South to advance the interests of beleaguered small farmers.

Southern Manifesto A document signed by 101 members of Congress from Southern states in 1956 that argued that the Supreme Court's decision in *Brown* v. *Board of Education of Topeka* itself contradicted the Constitution.

Specie Circular Proclamation issued by President Andrew Jackson in 1836 stipulating that only gold or silver could be used as payment for public land.

Stamp Act Congress October 1765 meeting of delegates sent by nine colonies, held in New York City, that adopted the Declaration of Rights and Grievances and petitioned against the Stamp Act.

Stamp Act Law passed by Parliament in 1765 to raise revenue in America by requiring taxed, stamped paper for legal documents, publications, and playing cards.

States' rights Favoring the rights of individual states over rights claimed by the national government.

Strategic Arms Limitation Treaty Treaty signed in 1972 by the United States and the Soviet Union to slow the nuclear arms race.

Strategic Defense Initiative (SDI) President Reagan's program, announced in 1983, to defend the United States against nuclear missile attack with untested weapons systems and sophisticated technologies.

Student Nonviolent Coordinating Committee (SNCC) Black civil rights organization founded in 1960 that drew heavily on younger activists and college students.

Students for a Democratic Society (SDS) The leading student organization of the New Left of the early and mid-1960s.

Suffrage The right to vote in a political election.

Sugar Act Law passed in 1764 to raise revenue in the American colonies. It lowered the duty from 6 pence to 3 pence per gallon on foreign molasses imported into the colonies and increased the restrictions on colonial commerce.

Sunbelt The states of the American South and Southwest.

Taft-Hartley Act Federal legislation of 1947 that substantially limited the tools available to labor unions in labor-management disputes.

Tammany Society A fraternal organization of artisans begun in the 1780s that evolved into a key organization of the new mass politics in New York City.

Tariff of 1789 Apart from a few selected industries, this first tariff passed by Congress was intended to raise revenue and not protect American manufacturers from foreign competition.

Tariff of 1789 Apart from a few selected industries, this first tariff passed by Congress was intended to raise revenue and not protect American manufacturers from foreign competition.

Tea Act of 1773 Act of Parliament that permitted the East India Company to sell through agents in America without paying the duty customarily collected in Britain, thus reducing the retail price.

Tejanos Persons of Spanish or Mexican descent born in Texas.

Temperance Reform movement originating in the 1820s that sought to eliminate the consumption of alcohol.

Tenements Four– to six-story residential dwellings, once common in New York, built on tiny lots without regard to providing ventilation or light.

Tennessee Valley Authority (TVA) Federal regional planning agency established to promote conservation, produce electric power, and encourage economic development in seven Southern states.

Tenure of Office Act Act stipulating that any officeholder appointed by the president with the Senate's advice and consent could not be removed until the Senate had approved a successor.

The Albany movement Coalition formed in 1961 in Albany, a small city in southwest Georgia, of activists from SNCC, the NAACP, and other local groups.

The Toleration Act Act passed in 1661 by King Charles II ordering a stop to religious persecution in Massachusetts.

Thirteenth Amendment Constitutional amendment ratified in 1865 that freed all slaves throughout the United States.

Timber Culture Act 1873 act which allotted homesteaders an additional 160 acres of land in return for planting and cultivating 40 acres of trees.

Tonkin Gulf resolution Request to Congress from President Lyndon Johnson in response to North Vietnamese torpedo boat attacks in which he sought authorization for "all necessary measures" to protect American forces and stop further aggression.

Tories A derisive term applied to Loyalists in America who supported the king and Parliament just before and during the American Revolution.

Townshend Revenue Acts Acts of Parliament, passed in 1767, imposing duties on colonial tea, lead, paint, paper, and glass.

Trail of Broken Treaties 1972 event staged by the American Indian Movement (AIM) that culminated in a week-long occupation of the Bureau of Indian Affairs in Washington, D.C.

Trail of Tears The forced march in 1838 of the Cherokee Indians from their homelands in Georgia to the Indian Territory in the West.

Transcontinental Treaty of 1819 Treaty between the United States and Spain in which Spain ceded Florida to the United States, surrendered all claims to the Pacific Northwest, and agreed to a boundary between the Louisiana Purchase territory and the Spanish Southwest.

Transoceanic migrations A population migration across oceans.

Treaty of Fort Laramie The treaty acknowledging U.S. defeat in the Great Sioux War in 1868 and supposedly guaranteeing the Sioux perpetual land and hunting rights in South Dakota, Wyoming, and Montana.

Treaty of Ghent Treaty signed in December 1814 between the United States and Britain that ended the War of 1812.

Treaty of Greenville Treaty of 1795 in which Native Americans in the Old Northwest were forced to cede most of the present state of Ohio to the United States.

Treaty of Paris The formal end to British hostilities against France and Spain in February 1763.

Treaty of Tordesillas Treaty negotiated by the pope in 1494 to resolve the territorial claims of Spain and Portugal.

Truman Doctrine Doctrine pronounced in President Harry Truman's statement in 1947 that the United States should assist other nations that were facing external pressure or internal revolution.

Underwood-Simmons Act of 1913 Reform law that lowered tariff rates and levied the first regular federal income tax.

Union League Republican party organizations in Northern cities that became an important organizing device among freedmen in Southern cities after 1865.

United States Constitution The written document providing for a new central government of the United States.

Valley Forge Area of Pennsylvania approximately twenty miles northwest of Philadelphia where General George Washington's Continental troops were quartered from December 1777 to June 1778 while British forces occupied Philadelphia during the Revolutionary War.

Versailles Treaty The treaty ending World War I and creating the League of Nations.

Vertical integration The consolidation of numerous production functions, from the extraction of the raw materials to the distribution and marketing of the finished products, under the direction of one firm.

Virginia Company A group of London investors who sent ships to Chesapeake Bay in 1607.

Virginia Plan Proposal calling for a national legislature in which the states would be represented according to population.

Virtual representation The notion that parliamentary members represented the interests of the nation as a whole, not those of the particular district that elected them.

Volstead Act The 1920 law defining the liquor forbidden under the Eighteenth Amendment and giving enforcement responsibilities to the Prohibition Bureau of the Department of the Treasury.

Voting Rights Act Legislation in 1965 that overturned a variety of practices by which states systematically denied voter registration to minorities.

War Hawks Members of Congress, predominantly from the South and West, who aggressively pushed for a war against Britain after their election in 1810.

War Industries Board (WIB) The federal agency that reorganized industry for maximum efficiency and productivity during World War I.

War of 1812 War fought between the United States and Britain from June 1812 to January 1815 largely over British restrictions on American shipping.

War on poverty Set of programs introduced by Lyndon Johnson between 1963 and 1966 designed to break the cycle of poverty by providing funds for job training, community development, nutrition, and supplementary education.

War Powers Act Gave the U.S. president the power to reorganize the federal government and create new agencies; to establish programs censoring news, information, and abridging civil liberties; to seize foreign-owned property; and award government contracts without bidding.

Watergate A complex scandal involving attempts to cover up illegal actions taken by administration officials and leading to the resignation of President Richard Nixon in 1974.

Welfare capitalism A paternalistic system of labor relations emphasizing management responsibility for employee well-being.

Whigs The name used by advocates of colonial resistance to British measures during the 1760s and 1770s.

Whiskey Rebellion Armed uprising in 1794 by farmers in western Pennsylvania who attempted to prevent the collection of the excise tax on whiskey.

Whitewater Arkansas real estate development in which Bill and Hillary Clinton were investors; several fraud convictions resulted from investigations into Whitewater, but evidence was not found that the Clintons were involved in wrongdoing.

Wilmot's Proviso The amendment offered by Pennsylvania Democrat David Wilmot in 1846 which stipulated that "as an express and fundamental condition to the acquisition of any territory from the Republic of Mexico . . . neither slavery nor involuntary servitude shall ever exist in any part of said territory."

Wobblies Popular name for the members of the Industrial Workers of the World (IWW).

Woman's Christian Temperance Union (WCTU) Women's organization whose members visited schools to educate children about the evils of alcohol, addressed prisoners, and blanketed men's meetings with literature.

Women's Educational and Industrial Union Boston organization offering classes to wage-earning women.

World Trade Organization (WTO) International organization that sets standards and practices for global trade, and the focus of international protests over world economic policy in the late 1990s.

World Wide Web A part of the Internet designed to allow easier navigation of the network through the use of graphical user interfaces and hypertext links between different addresses.

XYZ Affair Diplomatic incident in 1798 in which Americans were outraged by the demand of the French for a bribe as a condition for negotiating with American diplomats.

Yalta Conference Meeting of U.S. President Franklin Roosevelt, British Prime Minister Winston Churchill, and Soviet Premier Joseph Stalin held in February 1945 to plan the final stages of World War II and postwar arrangements.

Yeoman Independent farmers of the South, most of whom lived on family-sized farms.

TEXT CREDITS

Chapter 4: Text: Reproduced from *The American Colonies: From Settlement to Independence* by R. C. Simmons (Copyright © R. C. Simmons 1976) by permission of PFD on behalf of Professor R. C. Simmons; "British Colonial Trade in the Americas, 1714–1773" from Eric Williams, *Capitalism and Slavery*. Copyright 1994 by The University of North Carolina Press. Reprinted with the permission of the publishers; "Value of Colonial Exports by Region, Annual Average, 1768–1772" from James F. Shepherd and Gary M. Walton, *Shipping Maritime Trade and the Economic Development of Colonial America*. Reprinted with the permission of Cambridge University Press.

Chapter 5: Text: "Distribution of Assessed Taxable Wealth in Eighteenth-Century Chester County, Pennsylvania," Copyright © 1968 by Peter N. Steams. Reprinted with the permission of the publishers; From Jackson Turner Main, *The Social Structure of Revolutionary America*. Copyright © 1965 by Princeton University Press. Reprinted by permission of Princeton University Press; Figure 5: From Mechal Sobel, *The World They Made Together: Black and White Values in Eighteenth-Century Virginia*. Copyright © 1987 by Princeton University Press. Reprinted with the permission of Princeton University Press.

Chapter 7: Text: From John McCusker, "How Much Is That in Real Money?" *Proceedings of the American Antiquarian Society*, NS 102 Copyright © 1992 by the American Antiquarian Society. Courtesy of American Antiquarian Society.

Chapter 9: Text: Figure from *America Moves West*, copyright © 1964 by Holt, Rinehart and Winston, renewed 1992 by Louise Riegel, reproduced by permission of the publisher; From Donald Meinig, *The Shaping of America, Volume II: Continental America* Yale University Press, 1994. Reprinted by permission of Yale University Press.

Chapter 10: Text: Reprinted by permission of the publisher from *American Wool Manufacturer*, Volume I, by Arthur Harrison Cole, Cambridge, Mass.: Harvard University Press, p. 280, Copyright 1926 by the President and Fellows of Harvard College.

Chapter 12: Text: Reprinted from Thomas Dublin: "Women and Rural Work" in *Transforming Women's Work: New England Lives in the Industrial Revolution*. Copyright © 1994 by Thomas Dublin. Used by permission of the publisher, Cornell University Press.

Chapter 13: Text: Reprinted from Whitney R. Cross, *The Burned-Over District: The Social & Intellectual History of Enthusiastic Religion in Western New York, 1800–1850*. Copyright © 1950 by Cornell University. Used by permission of the publisher, Cornell University Press.

Chapter 14: Text: From *The Plains Across: The Overland Emigrants and the Trans-Mississippi West, 1840–60*. Copyright 1979 by Board of Trustees of the University of Illinois. Used with permission of the University of Illinois Press; From Warren A. Beck and Ynez D. Haase, *Historical Atlas of California*, The University of Oklahoma Press, 1974. Reprinted by permission of the publisher.

Chapter 16: Text: From Warren A. Beck and Ynez D. Haase, *Historical Atlas of the American West*, The University of Oklahoma Press, 1974. Reprinted by permission of the publisher.

Chapter 18: Text: From John W. Morris, Charles R. Goins and Edwin C. McReynolds, *Historical Atlas of Oklahoma, 3rd Edition*. Copyright © 1965, 1976, 1986 by the University of Oklahoma Press. Reprinted with the permission of the publishers.

Chapter 19: Text: From Bailyn et. al., *The Great Republic: A History of the American People*, Third Edition, Volume One. Copyright © 1985 by D.C. Heath and Company. Reprinted with permission of Houghton Mifflin Company.

Chapter 20: Text: From Carville Earle, *Geographical Inquiry and American Historical Problems*. Copyright © 1992 by the Board of Trustees of the Leland Stanford Junior University. With the permission of Stanford University Press, www.sup.org.

Chapter 22: Text: From *Atlas of American Women* by Barbara C. Shortridge, Macmillan, Copyright 1987. Reprinted by permission of The Gale Group.

Chapter 27: Text: From Allen Ginsberg, "Howl," from *Collected Poems, 1947–1980*. Copyright © 1955 by Allen Ginsberg. Reprinted by permission of HarperCollins Publishers Inc.

Chapter 29: Text: "The Times They are a-Changin" by Bob Dylan. Copyright © 1963, 1964 by Warner Bros. Inc. Copyright renewed 1991 by Special Rider Music. All rights reserved. International copyright secured. Reprinted by permission.

Chapter 31: Text: From Robert Griffith, *Major Problems in American History Since 1945*. Copyright © 1992 by D.C. Heath and Company. Used by permission of Houghton Mifflin Company.

PHOTO CREDITS

Chapter 1 Image Key: a. © Warren Morgan/CORBIS; b. Service Historique de la Marine, Vincennes, France/Lauros/Giraudon/Bridgeman Art Library; c. The Bridgeman Art Library International Ltd. d. Courtesy of the Denver Museum of Nature and Science; e. Photo by David Hiser; f. Neg. No. 32481, photographed by Rota, engraving by de Bry. Courtesy Department of Library Services, American Museum of Natural History.

Chapter 2 Image Key: a. Corbis/ Bettmann; b. The Granger Collection, New York; c. Robert Frerck, Odyssey Productions, Inc.; d. The Granger Collection, New York; e. The Granger Collection.

Chapter 3 Image Key: a. Dorling Kindersley Media Library; b. The New York Public Library, Rare Book Division/Art Resource; c. Getty Images, Inc.- Photodisc; d. Corbis/Bettmann; e. Courtesy of the Pilgrim Society, Plymouth, Massachusetts; f. Crobis/Bettmann; g. Jonathan Carver, A TREATISE ON THE CULTURE OF THE TOBACCO PLANT (London, 1779), Manuscripts and Rare Book Division, Swem Library, College of William and Mary; h. Courtesy, American Antiquarian Society; i. Courtesy of the Museum of the City of New York; j. John Seller Map of New England, 1675. Courtesy of the John Carter Brown Library at Brown University.

Chapter 4 Image Key: a. John Seller Map of New England, 1675. Courtesy of the John Carter Brown Library at Brown University; b. The Granger Collection, New York; c. Dorling Kindersley Media Library; d. Courtesy of the British Library; e. Courtesy, American Antiquarian Society; f. The Library Company of Philadlephia; g. Abby Aldrich Rockefeller Folk Art Center, Williamsburg, Virginia; h. Samuel Scott, Old Custom House Quay Collection. By courtesy of the Board of Trustees of the Victioria and Albert Museum.

Chapter 5 Image Key: a. A. Liz MacAulay, Dorling Kindersley/Worthing Museum; b. the Granger Collection, NY; c. David Murray, Dorling Kindersley Media Library; d. Frank Greenaway, Dorling Kindersley Media Library; e. © Judith Miller Y Dorling Kindersley. F. Dorling Kindersley Media Library; f. Dorling Kindersley Media Library; g. (c) National Maritime Museum, London; h. Library of Congress; i. North Wind Picture Archives; j. John Wollaston "George Whitefiled" ca. 1770. by courtesy of the National Portrait Gallery, London.

Chapter 6 Image Key: a. Dorling Kindersley Media Library; b. Steve Gorton Dorling Kindersley; c. The Granger Collection, New York; d. Dave King, Dorling Kindersley Media Library; e. © Judith Miller & Dorling Kindersley; f. Colonial Williamsburg Foundation; g. © Christie's Images Inc. 2004; h. Library of Congress; i. Library of Congress.

Chapter 7 Image Key: a. Library of Congress; b. Corbis/Bettmann; c. Yale University Art Gallery; d. Corbis/Bettmann; e. Photograph courtesy of the Concord Museum, Concord, MA and the archives of the Lexington Historical Society. David Bohl, photographer; f. anne S.K. Brown Military Collection, John Hay Library, Brown University; g. Benjamin West, 1783 "American commissioners of Preliminary Negotations"; h. Library of Congress.

Chapter 8 Image Key: a, Harry N. Abrams, Inc.; b. Courtesy of the Historical Soceity of Pennsylvania Collection, Atwater kent Museum of Philadelphia; c. Corbis/Bettmann; d. Gallery of the Republic; e. Francis Kemmelmeyer "General George Washington Reviewing the Western Army at Fort Cumberland the 18th of October 1794," after 1794. Oil on paper backed with linen. Dimensions, 18-1/8 × 23 1/8. Courtesy of Winterthur Museum; g. White House Historical Association; h. The Library Company of Philadelphia.

Chapter 9 Image Key: a. Corbis/ Bettmann; b. from the collection of Mac G. and Janelle C. Morris Collection; c. Getty Images–Hutton Archive Photos; d. Smithsonian Institution photo no. 95-3550; e. Museum of the City of New York/Corbis; f. Library of Congress; g. © Bettmann/Corbis; h. John Wesley Jarvis, Black Hawk and His Son, Whirling Thunder, 1833. Oil on cavas. 23 × 30. Gilcrease Museum, Tulsa, Oklahoma; i. Getty Images Inc.–Hulton Archive Photos.

Chapter 10 Image Key: a. national Numismatic Collection/Smithsonian Institution; b. Corbis/Bettmann; c. Library of Congress; d. Getty Images; e. Thomas Coke Ruckle, Fairview Inn or Three Mile House on Old Frederick Road, c. 1829?, watercolor on paper. Collection of the Maryland Historical Society, Baltimore, MD.; f. The Bridgeman Art Library International Ltd.; g. Crockett Almanac, 1841, Prints and photographs division, Library of Congress.

Chapter 11 Image Key: a. Tina Chambers, Dorling Kindersley Media Library; b. Corbis/Bettmann; c. The Granger Collection, New York; d. Library of Congress; e. Library of Congress; f. Dorling Kindersley Media Library; g. Collection of the New York Historical Society; h. William Gladstone; i. Corbis Bettmann; j. Hunter Museum of Art, Chattanooga, TN; k, Library of Congress.

Chapter 12 Image Key: a. Library of Congress; b. Center for Lowell History; c. The New York Public Library, Research Libraries/Art Resource; d. American Textile History Museum; e. Library of Congress; f. Lowell Historical Society; g. Library of Congress; h. Getty Images, Inc.–Taxi.

Chapter 13 Image Key: a. Courtesy of the New York Historical Society, New York City; b. The Granger Collection; c. The Granger Collection; d. © Bettmann/Corbis; e. The Granger Collection; f. Winterthur Museum; g. Library of Congress; h. the Granger Collection; i. Omni-photo Communications, Inc.

Chapter 14 Image Key: a. Geoff Brightling, Dorling Kindersley Media Library; b. Getty Images Inc.–Hutton Archive Photos; c. Albert Bierstadt, "The Oregon Trail," Private collection/Bridgeman Art Library International Ltd., New York; d. Peter Anderson, Dorling Kindersley Media Library; e. Lynton Gardinier, Dorling Kindersley Media Library; f. © Christie's Images Inc. 2004; g. the Walters Art Museum, Baltimore; h. The Granger Collection; I. Collection of the New York Historical Society, New York City.

Chapter 15 Image Key: a. Corbis NY; b. Courtesy of the Library of Congress; c. Corbis NY; d. Corbis/Bettmann; e. Library of Congress; f. Library of Congress; g. Illinois State Historical Library; h. the Granger Collection; i. Getty Images Inc.–PhotoDisc.

Chapter 16 Image Key: a. Getty Images Inc.–Photodisc; b. National Archives and Records Administration; c. Dorling Kindersley Media Library; d. Dorling Kindersley Media Library; e. Dorling Kindersley Media Library; f. the Granger Collection, New York; g. Valentine Museum Library, Richmond, VA; h. Corbis/Bettmann; i. Getty Images Inc.–Hulton Archive Photos; j. Center of Military History, U.S. Army.

Chapter 17 Image Key: a. William Gladstone; b. no source; c. Corbis/Bettmann; d. Specials Collection, Musselman Library, Gettysburg College, Gettysburg, PA; e. Library of Congress; f. the Granger Collection, New York; g. Library of Congress; h. Library of Congress; i. the Picture Bank, Frank & Marie Therese Wood Print Collection.

Chapter 18 Image Key: a. Lynton Gardiner, Dorling Kindersley Media Library; b. The Granger Collection, New York; c. Dave King © Dorling Kindersley Media Library; d. Dorling Kindersley Media Library; e. Library of Congress; f. Idaho State Historical Society; g. Nebraska State Historical Society, Solomon D. Butcher Collection; h. Library of Congress; i. Library of Congress.

Chapter 19 Image Key: a. Library of Congress; b. Lewis W. Hine, George Eastman House; c. Corbis/Bettmann; d., The Granger Collection, New York; e. Collection of the New York Historical Society, New York City; f. The Granger Collection, New York; g. Ford Motor Company.

Chapter 20 Image Key: a. Picture Research Consultants; b. Library of Congress; c. The Granger Collection; d. the Granger Collection, New York; e. Library of Congress; f. Corbis/Bettmann; g. the Granger Collection; h. Library of Congress; I. Library of Congress; j. Library of Congress; k. Harvard University; Library of Congress.

Chapter 21 Image Key: a. Corbis/Bettmann; b. Corbis/Bettmann; c. the Granger Collection, New York; d. Corbis/Bettmann; e. Indiana Historical Society; f. The original Paterson Pageant Program on which this drawing appeared as part of the collection of the American labor museum/Botto House National Landmark. The poster is a copy of the program cover; g. Corbis/Bettmann; h. the Granger Collection.

Chapter 22 Image Key: a. Corbis/Bettmann; b. Getty Images Inc.–Hulton Archive Photos; c. Corbis/Bettmann; d. Richard Ward, Dorling Kindersley Media Library; e. The Granger Collection; f. Library of Congress; g. The Granger Collection; h. National Archives and Records Administration; i. the Granger Collection, New York.

Chapter 23 Image Key: a. Getty Images Inc.–Hulton Archive Photos; b. Corbis/Bettmann; c. Getty Images–Photodisc; d. C. Squared Studios, Getty Images, Inc. Photodisc; e. Wisconsin Historical Society; f. Campbell Soup Company; g. W.A. Swift Photograph Collection, Archives and Special Collections, Ball State University.

Chapter 24 Image Key: a. Corbis/Bettmann; b. Corbis/Bettmann; c. SuperStock, Inc.; d. Corbis/Bettmann; e. Getty Images, Inc. Photodisc; f. Brown Brothers; g. Corbis/Bettmann; h. The Granger Collection © Estate of Ben Shahn/Licensed by VAGA New York; i. Isaac Soyer, "Employment Agency" Oil on canvas. The Whitney Museum of American Art.

Chapter 25 Image Key: a. Andy Crawford, Dorling Kindersley Media Library; b. Corbis/Bettmann; c. Andy Crawford, Dorling Kindersley Media Library; d. the Granger Collection, New York; e. Getty Images Inc.–Hulton Archive Photos; f. Corbis/Bettmann; g. Reiger Communications, Inc.; h. Library of Congress; i. National Archives And Records Administration; j. The Granger Collection, New York.

Chapter 26 Image Key: a. Corbis/Bettmann; b. Getty Images/Time Life Pictures; c. Corbis/Bettmann; d. Getty Images Inc.–Hulton Archive Photos; e. Getty Images/Time Life Pictures; f. Corbis/Bettmann; g. Corbis/ Bettmann; h. Corbis/Bettmann; i. AP/Wide World Photos; j. Corbis/Bettmann.

Chapter 27 Image Key: a. Corbis/Bettmann; b. Getty Images Inc.–Hulton Archive Photos; c. Dorling Kindersley Media Library; d. Getty Images Inc.–Photodisc; e. Bernard Hoffmann/Life Magazine© 1950 Time Pix; f. Sondak, Getty Images, Inc.–Taxi; g. Retna, Ltd.; h. © Springer/Bettmann/Corbis; i. Library of Congress; j. AP/Wide World Photos.

Chapter 28 Image Key: a. Library of Congress; b. Corbis/Bettmann; c. John F. Kennedy Library; d. Library of Congress; e. Dorling Kindersley Media Library; f. Corbis/Bettmann; g. Corbis/Bettmann; h. Corbis/Bettmann.

Chapter 29 Image Key: a. © Royalty-Free/Corbis; b. © Royalty-Free/Corbis; c. © John Paul Filo/Hulton Archive Photos; d. George Meany Memorial Archives; e. AP/Wide World Photos; f. Corbis/ Bettmann; g. Corbis/Bettmann; h. Bernie Boston; i. AP/Wide World Photos; j. AP/Wide World Photos.

Chapter 30 Image Key: a. Telepress Syndicate Agency, Corbis/Bettmann; b. Ron Edmonds, Corbis/Bettmann; c. Corbis/Bettmann; d. Dorling Kindersley Media Library; e. AP/Wide World Photos; f. Joe Marquette, AP/Wide World Photos; g. Corbis/Bettmann; h. Jose L. Pelaez, Corbis/Stock Market.

Chapter 31 Image Key: a. Doug Katner, SIPA Press; b. Author supplied; c. Dorling Kindersley Media Library; d. Dorling Kindersley Media Library; e. Dorling Kindersley Media Library; f. Dorling Kindersley Media Library; g. Dorling Kindersley Media Library; h. Getty Images, Inc.–Agence France Presse; i. Barbara Gauntt/The Clarion-Ledger; j. Author supplied; k. Stephen Crowley, New York Times Pictures.

INDEX

U.S. HISTORY DOCUMENTS CD-ROM

SINGLE PC LICENSE AGREEMENT AND LIMITED WARRANTY

READ THIS LICENSE CAREFULLY BEFORE OPENING THIS PACKAGE. BY OPENING THIS PACKAGE, YOU ARE AGREEING TO THE TERMS AND CONDITIONS OF THIS LICENSE. IF YOU DO NOT AGREE, DO NOT OPEN THE PACKAGE. PROMPTLY RETURN THE UNOPENED PACKAGE AND ALL ACCOMPANYING ITEMS TO THE PLACE YOU OBTAINED THEM.

1. GRANT OF LICENSE and OWNERSHIP: The enclosed computer programs <<and data>> ("Software") are licensed, not sold, to you by Pearson Education, Inc. publishing as Pearson Prentice Hall ("We" or the "Company") and in consideration of your purchase or adoption of the accompanying Company textbooks and/or other materials, and your agreement to these terms. We reserve any rights not granted to you. You own only the disk(s) but we and/or our licensors own the Software itself. This license allows you to use and display your copy of the Software on a single computer (i.e., with a single CPU) at a single location for academic use only, so long as you comply with the terms of this Agreement. You may make one copy for back up, or transfer your copy to another CPU, provided that the Software is usable on only one computer.

2. RESTRICTIONS: You may not transfer or distribute the Software or documentation to anyone else. Except for backup, you may not copy the documentation or the Software. You may not network the Software or otherwise use it on more than one computer or computer terminal at the same time. You may not reverse engineer, disassemble, decompile, modify, adapt, translate, or create derivative works based on the Software or the Documentation. You may be held legally responsible for any copying or copyright infringement that is caused by your failure to abide by the terms of these restrictions.

3. TERMINATION: This license is effective until terminated. This license will terminate automatically without notice from the Company if you fail to comply with any provisions or limitations of this license. Upon termination, you shall destroy the Documentation and all copies of the Software. All provisions of this Agreement as to limitation and disclaimer of warranties, limitation of liability, remedies or damages, and our ownership rights shall survive termination.

4. LIMITED WARRANTY AND DISCLAIMER OF WARRANTY: Company warrants that for a period of 60 days from the date you purchase this SOFTWARE (or purchase or adopt the accompanying textbook), the Software, when properly installed and used in accordance with the Documentation, will operate in substantial conformity with the description of the Software set forth in the Documentation, and that for a period of 30 days the disk(s) on which the Software is delivered shall be free from defects in materials and workmanship under normal use. The Company does not warrant that the Software will meet your requirements or that the operation of the Software will be uninterrupted or error-free. Your only remedy and the Company's only obligation under these limited warranties is, at the Company's option, return of the disk for a refund of any amounts paid for it by you or replacement of the disk. THIS LIMITED WARRANTY IS THE ONLY WARRANTY PROVIDED BY THE COMPANY AND ITS LICENSORS, AND THE COMPANY AND ITS LICENSORS DISCLAIM ALL OTHER WARRANTIES, EXPRESS OR IMPLIED, INCLUDING WITHOUT LIMITATION, THE IMPLIED WARRANTIES OF MERCHANTABILITY AND FITNESS FOR A PARTICULAR PURPOSE. THE COMPANY DOES NOT WARRANT, GUARANTEE OR MAKE ANY REPRESENTATION REGARDING THE ACCURACY, RELIABILITY, CURRENTNESS, USE, OR RESULTS OF USE, OF THE SOFTWARE.

5. LIMITATION OF REMEDIES AND DAMAGES: IN NO EVENT, SHALL THE COMPANY OR ITS EMPLOYEES, AGENTS, LICENSORS, OR CONTRACTORS BE LIABLE FOR ANY INCIDENTAL, INDIRECT, SPECIAL, OR CONSEQUENTIAL DAMAGES ARISING OUT OF OR IN CONNECTION WITH THIS LICENSE OR THE SOFTWARE, INCLUDING FOR LOSS OF USE, LOSS OF DATA, LOSS OF INCOME OR PROFIT, OR OTHER LOSSES, SUSTAINED AS A RESULT OF INJURY TO ANY PERSON, OR LOSS OF OR DAMAGE TO PROPERTY, OR CLAIMS OF THIRD PARTIES, EVEN IF THE COMPANY OR AN AUTHORIZED REPRESENTATIVE OF THE COMPANY HAS BEEN ADVISED OF THE POSSIBILITY OF SUCH DAMAGES. IN NO EVENT SHALL THE LIABILITY OF THE COMPANY FOR DAMAGES WITH RESPECT TO THE SOFTWARE EXCEED THE AMOUNTS ACTUALLY PAID BY YOU, IF ANY, FOR THE SOFTWARE OR THE ACCOMPANYING TEXTBOOK. BECAUSE SOME JURISDICTIONS DO NOT ALLOW THE LIMITATION OF LIABILITY IN CERTAIN CIRCUMSTANCES, THE ABOVE LIMITATIONS MAY NOT ALWAYS APPLY TO YOU.

6. GENERAL: THIS AGREEMENT SHALL BE CONSTRUED IN ACCORDANCE WITH THE LAWS OF THE UNITED STATES OF AMERICA AND THE STATE OF NEW YORK, APPLICABLE TO CONTRACTS MADE IN NEW YORK, EXCLUDING THE STATE'S LAWS AND POLICIES ON CONFLICTS OF LAW, AND SHALL BENEFIT THE COMPANY, ITS AFFILIATES AND ASSIGNEES. THIS AGREEMENT IS THE COMPLETE AND EXCLUSIVE STATEMENT OF THE AGREEMENT BETWEEN YOU AND THE COMPANY AND SUPERSEDES ALL PROPOSALS OR PRIOR AGREEMENTS, ORAL, OR WRITTEN, AND ANY OTHER COMMUNICATIONS BETWEEN YOU AND THE COMPANY OR ANY REPRESENTATIVE OF THE COMPANY RELATING TO THE SUBJECT MATTER OF THIS AGREEMENT. If you are a U.S. Government user, this Software is licensed with "restricted rights" as set forth in subparagraphs (a)-(d) of the Commercial Computer-Restricted Rights clause at FAR 52.227-19 or in subparagraphs (c)(1)(ii) of the Rights in Technical Data and Computer Software clause at DFARS 252.227-7013, and similar clauses, as applicable.

Should you have any questions concerning this agreement or if you wish to contact the Company for any reason, please contact in writing: Legal Department, Prentice Hall, 1 Lake Street, Upper Saddle River, NJ 07450 or call Pearson Education Product Support at 1-800-677-6337.